ASP.NET
IN A NUTSHELL

A Desktop Quick Reference

Related titles from O'Reilly

ASP.NET
IN A NUTSHELL

A Desktop Quick Reference

G. Andrew Duthie & Matthew MacDonald

O'REILLY®

Beijing • Cambridge • Farnham • Köln • Paris • Sebastopol • Taipei • Tokyo

ASP.NET in a Nutshell

by G. Andrew Duthie and Matthew MacDonald

Published by O'Reilly & Associates, Inc., 1005 Gravenstein Highway North, Sebastopol, CA 95472.

O'Reilly & Associates books may be purchased for educational, business, or sales promotional use. Online editions are also available for most titles (*safari.oreilly.com*). For more information contact our corporate/institutional sales department: 800-998-9938 or *corporate@oreilly.com*.

Editor: Ron Petrusha

Production Editor: Ann Schirmer

Cover Designer: Emma Colby

Interior Designer: David Futato

Printing History:

June 2002:   First Edition.

ISBN: 0-596-00116-9
[M]

Table of Contents

Part II: Intrinsic Class Reference

Part III: Namespace Reference

Preface

ASP.NET is the web development technology of Microsoft's .NET development platform. While it has a lot in common with its predecessor, Active Server Pages, ASP.NET is a quantum leap over classic ASP; it adds such new features as rich server controls, a much more powerful programming model, and built-in support for XML web services.

ASP.NET also allows you to access the full richness of the .NET Framework Class Library, which provides classes for everything from sending mail via SMTP to performing multithreaded operations. ASP.NET also brings object-oriented programming to the Web. Object orientation is at the very heart of the .NET Framework, and ASP.NET takes full advantage of it—particularly in the area of its robust server control model.

ASP.NET has many new features and aspects, but with the help of this reference, you'll be up and running before you know it.

Who Is This Book for?

This book is intended primarily as a reference and learning tool for developers who have experience in web development. Both professional and amateur developers should find this book helpful in making the transition from classic ASP (or other web development technologies) to ASP.NET.

This book is not intended for beginners or those with no experience with web development. While the tutorial section that begins the book is intended to bring you up to speed on ASP.NET quickly, it does not teach basic web development skills. Beginners or those with no experience with classic ASP would do well to find a good introductory web development book and then return to this book once they understand the fundamentals of web development.

How to Use This Book

This book consists of an introductory tutorial section, two reference sections, and an appendix. If you're new to ASP.NET, you may want to read through the entire tutorial section from start to finish. This will give you a good exposure to all of the features of ASP.NET and experience writing ASP.NET code.

Once you've become comfortable with the concepts introduced in the tutorial section, the remaining reference sections will help you work through everyday ASP.NET development tasks.

The first reference section provides detailed information on the classes that replace classic ASP intrinsic objects, on the Page class, and on the elements found in the *web.config* file. Each chapter is divided into the following sections to help you locate the information you're looking for quickly:

Introduction
> This section introduces the class and describes its purpose and common uses.

Summary
> This section lists the most commonly used properties, methods, collections, and events of the class. Members that are inherited from a base class or not typically used may be omitted.

Comments/Troubleshooting
> This section provides information about gotchas to watch out for when using the class, as well as other important things to be aware of.

Properties
> This section describes the properties for the class and provides examples of their use.

Collections
> This section describes the collections for the class and provides examples of their use.

Methods
> This section describes the methods for the class and provides examples of their use.

Events
> This section describes the Events for the class, and provides examples of their use. Note that not all classes expose events, so not every chapter will have an Events section.

How This Book Is Structured

ASP.NET in a Nutshell consists of four parts. Part I, *Introduction to ASP.NET*, provides an introductory tutorial to ASP.NET consisting of the following 11 chapters:

Chapter 1, *Introduction*
> Provides an overview of the .NET Framework and the features of ASP.NET.

Chapter 2, *ASP.NET Applications*
> Describes the types of applications that can be written with ASP.NET and discusses the file types used by ASP.NET and the structure of an ASP.NET application.

Chapter 3, *Web Forms*

Describes the structure of ASP.NET Web Forms, including page directives, coding styles, event handling, and page output caching.

Chapter 4, *Web Services*

Describes the web services architecture provided by ASP.NET and shows how to create and consume web services in ASP.NET. It also shows how to publish and locate web services.

Chapter 5, *ASP.NET Server Controls*

Describes the HTML controls and web controls built into ASP.NET and shows how to use them in your ASP.NET pages.

Chapter 6, *User Controls and Custom Server Controls*

Describes two of the reuse techniques available in ASP.NET, user controls and custom server controls, and shows when and how to take advantage of each to enable code reuse in your applications.

Chapter 7, *Data Access and Data Binding*

Describes ADO.NET, the new technology for data access in the .NET Framework, and shows you how to use ADO.NET and the new data binding framework of ASP.NET to quickly build robust data-driven pages.

Chapter 8, *ASP.NET Configuration*

Describes the new configuration system in ASP.NET and shows you how to configure your application for several common scenarios.

Chapter 9, *ASP.NET Security*

Describes the new authentication and authorization features in ASP.NET and shows you how to take advantage of them in your applications.

Chapter 10, *Error Handling, Debugging, and Tracing*

Describes the new structured exception handling features of the Visual Basic .NET language and the tracing feature of ASP.NET. It also shows you how to use these new features, along with the .NET Framework SDK Debugger and/ or Visual Studio .NET, to troubleshoot and debug your applications.

Chapter 11, *ASP.NET Deployment*

Describes the options available for deploying ASP.NET applications and shows you how to take advantage of them.

Like classic ASP, ASP.NET exposes a number of intrinsic objects to every page. These objects provide information on requests, allow sending of or manipulation of responses, and provide useful utility functions. Part II, *Intrinsic Class Reference*, documents each of the classes that provide the functionality for the Application, Context, Request, Response, Server, and Session intrinsics, as well as for the HttpException class and the Page class, which forms the basis for each ASP.NET page. Part II also includes a reference of the most common elements of the *web. config* configuration file.

Because ASP.NET is considerably broader in the scope of its APIs than classic ASP, Part III, *Namespace Reference*, provides a high-level reference of the namespaces that are most relevant to ASP.NET development. These namespaces include:

System.Web
System.Web.Caching

System.Web.Configuration
System.Web.Hosting
System.Web.Mail
System.Web.Security
System.Web.Services
System.Web.Services.Configuration
System.Web.Services.Description
System.Web.Services.Discovery
System.Web.Services.Protocols
System.Web.SessionState
System.Web.UI
System.Web.UI.Design
System.Web.UI.Design.WebControls
System.Web.UI.HtmlControls
System.Web.UI.WebControls

The chapter covering each namespace describes each of the types contained in the namespace, and lists all members of each type.

Finally, the book includes one appendix, *Type, Method, Property, Event, and Field Index*, which contains an alphabetical listing of the types and members found in Part III. You can use it to determine the namespace to which a particular type or member in which you're interested belongs.

Conventions Used in This Book

Te following font conventions are used in this book:

Italic
> Used for pathnames, filenames, program names, Internet addresses, such as domain names and URLs, and new terms where they are defined.

Constant Width
> Used for command lines and options that should be typed verbatim, and names and keywords in program examples. Also used for parameters, attributes, configuration file elements, expressions, statements, and values.

Constant-Width Italic
> Used for replaceable terms, such as variables or optional elements, within syntax lines.

Constant-Width Bold
> Used for emphasis within program code.

How to Contact Us

Please address comments and questions concerning this book to the publisher:

O'Reilly & Associates, Inc.
1005 Gravenstein Highway North
Sebastopol, CA 95472
(800) 998-9938 (in the United States or Canada)
(707) 829-0515 (international/local)
(707) 829-0104 (fax)

To comment or ask technical questions about this book, send email to:

> bookquestions@oreilly.com

There is a web site for this book, which lists errata, examples, or any additional information. You can access this page at:

> http://www.oreilly.com/catalog/aspdotnetnut

For more information about our books, conferences, resource centers, and the O'Reilly Network, see the O'Reilly web site at::

> http://www.oreilly.com

Acknowledgments

I'd like to start by thanking my editor Ron Petrusha for his patience, skills, and technical savvy. It is a pleasure working with an editor who is not only good with words, but sharp with technology. Thanks also to Val Quercia for helping me to sound good and make sense, and to Daniel Creeron, for making sure the book was technically sound.

Thanks to both Doug Reilly and Raja Mani for their contributions to the book. I truly appreciate your efforts. Thanks also to Matthew MacDonald, for his work on the namespace reference, which will hopefully make my work that much more comprehensible.

A big thank you to the ASP.NET team at Microsoft, without whose efforts we would not have this fabulous new technology, and without whose willingness to explain and answer questions, this book would not be nearly as useful. Rob Howard, Susan Warren, and Erik Olson in particular have provided me with much insight and information into how ASP.NET works. I thank you all.

Thanks to Stacey Giard and all the folks at Microsoft who make sure that authors get both the information and the software necessary to do their jobs. It might be possible without their efforts, but it would sure be a lot harder.

Thanks to my mom, for believing in me, encouraging me, and listening to me kvetch when I'm close to a deadline.

And, saving the best for last, I'd like to thank my wife Jennifer, whose cheerful support and tolerance for late nights and long weekends made it possible to finish this book, and whose love makes it all worthwhile.

PART I

Introduction

This part is an introduction to ASP.NET, Microsoft's next-generation technology for developing server-side web applications and web services that work with Internet Information Server. Part I consists of the following chapters:

Chapter 1, *Introduction*
Chapter 2, *ASP.NET Applications*
Chapter 3, *Web Forms*
Chapter 4, *Web Services*
Chapter 5, *ASP.NET Server Controls*
Chapter 6, *User Controls and Custom Server Controls*
Chapter 7, *Data Access and Data Binding*
Chapter 8, *ASP.NET Configuration*
Chapter 9, *ASP.NET Security*
Chapter 10, *Error Handling, Debugging, and Tracing*
Chapter 11, *ASP.NET Deployment*

CHAPTER 1

Introduction

The predecessor to this book, *ASP in a Nutshell*, began with a brief history of the Web development technologies leading up to Active Server Pages. In this book, we're going to leave history to the historians and focus on the future of web development, ASP.NET. To better understand ASP.NET, it is important to understand some key concepts of the .NET development platform. It is also helpful to grasp object-oriented development; OOD is at the very heart of the .NET Framework, which provides the foundation for ASP.NET development. In this chapter, we'll review these concepts, look at new features in ASP.NET, and discuss choosing a language to suit your needs.

.NET Platform Fundamentals

At the core of Microsoft's .NET platform initiative is a new set of technologies known collectively as the *.NET Framework*, which we'll refer to commonly as the Framework. The Framework provides a platform for simplified rapid development of both web-based and Windows-based applications. The Framework has two primary components, the *Common Language Runtime (CLR)* and the *Framework Class Library (FCL)*.

As with many new technologies, there are a host of new terms and acronyms to understand, so we'll assay over the next several sections to introduce and explain the most important ones in the Framework.

The Common Language Runtime (CLR)

The CLR is an execution environment for code written for the .NET Framework. The CLR manages the execution of .NET code, including memory allocation and garbage collection (which helps avoid memory leaks), security (including applying differing trust levels to code from different sources), thread management, enforcing type-safety, and many other tasks.

3

The CLR works with every language available for the .NET Framework. Thus, instead of having a separate runtime for each language, the CLR works for all. Code developed in a .NET language is compiled by the individual language compiler (such as the Visual Basic.NET compiler) into an intermediate format called (appropriately enough) Intermediate Language (IL). At runtime, this IL code generated by the compiler is just-in-time (JIT) compiled by the CLR into native code for the processor type the CLR is running on. This compilation provides the flexibility of being able to develop with multiple languages and target multiple processor types while still retaining the performance of native code at execution time.

 While there is some up-front cost on first execution to the JIT compilation model, the Framework also offers the ability to pregenerate native code at install time through a utility called *NGen.exe*. This utility eliminates the startup cost of JIT compiling the code, at the expense of some of the optimizations that are available with JIT compiling.

The .NET Framework Class Library (FCL)

The FCL is a set of reusable object-oriented classes that provide basic platform functionality, from the data access classes of ADO.NET, to filesystem utility classes (including file, directory, and stream classes), to networking classes that allow easy implementation of DNS resolution, WHOIS lookups, and other network-related functionality. Developers can use the base classes directly or derive from these classes to provide customized functionality.

The FCL also contains all classes that make up ASP.NET. These include classes that implement all of the functionality of the ASP intrinsic objects, as well as classes that provide additional functionality, from a rich engine for caching output and data to the ASP.NET Server Control model. This functionality brings to ASP.NET the simplicity of control-based development that has long been available to Visual Basic developers.

In addition to classes that support Web development, the FCL provides classes for developing console applications, Windows applications, and Windows NT or Windows 2000 Services.

The Common Type System (CTS)

The CTS describes the set of types that are supported by the CLR. This includes both value types, which include primitive data types such as Byte, Int16, Double, and Boolean, and Reference types, which include arrays, classes, and the Object and String types.

Value types are types that store their values directly in memory and are accessed directly by name, as shown below:

```
'VB.NET
Dim myFloat As Single
myFloat = 3.1415
```

```
// C#
float myFloat;
myFloat = 3.1415;
```

In addition to the built-in data types mentioned above, value types also include user-defined value types (types derived from the System.ValueType class) as well as enumerations.

Reference types are types that store a reference to the location of their values, rather than storing the value directly. Frequently, the value is stored as part of a defined class and is referenced through a class member on an instance of the class, as shown here:

```
'VB.NET
'Define class
Class myFloatClass
    Public myFloat As Single
End Class

'Create class instance and assign value
Dim myInstance As New myFloatClass()
myInstance.myFloat = 3.1415
```

```
// C#
// Define class
class myFloatClass
{
    float myFloat;
}

// Create class instance and assign value
myFloatClass myInstance = new myFloatClass();
myFloatClass.myFloat = 3.1415;
```

Individual language compilers may implement types using their own terminology. For example, while the .NET representation of a 32-bit integer is referred to as *Int32*, in Visual Basic.NET, a 32-bit integer is referred to as *Integer* and in C#, a 32-bit integer is referred to as *int*. Internally, however, both Visual Basic's Integer and C#'s int are implemented as the .NET Int32 type.

Boxing and unboxing

Converting to and from value and reference types is accomplished through a process called boxing and unboxing. *Boxing* refers to the implicit conversion of a value type, such as a C# int, to a reference type (usually *Object*). For this conversion to take place, an instance of type Object is created and the value type's value and type is copied into it—in this case, int. *Unboxing* refers to the explicit conversion of an Object type into a specific value type. The code example shown here demonstrates boxing and unboxing.

```
// C#
int myInt = 123; // declare an int and set its value to 123
object myObj = myInt; // value of myInt is boxed into myObject
int myOtherInt = (int)myObject; // unbox myObject into myOtherInt
```

The Common Language Infrastructure (CLI)

The CLI is a subset of the .NET Framework that has been submitted for standardization through the ECMA standards body. The CLI includes the functionality of the Common Language Runtime, as well as specifications for the Common Type System, type safety rules, Metadata, and Intermediate Language. It also includes a subset of the Framework Class Library that includes a Base Class Library (for built-in types and basic runtime functionality), a Network Library (for simple networking services and access to network ports), a Reflection Library (for examining types and retrieving information about types at runtime), an XML Library (for parsing XML), and Floating Point and Extended Array Libraries.

Microsoft has also committed to providing what they refer to as a "shared-source" implementation of the CLI, which will be available for both the FreeBSD and Windows operating systems.

Information on the ECMA standardization process, including documentation of the proposed standards, is available at *http://msdn.microsoft.com/net/ecma/*.

The Common Language Specification (CLS)

The CLS is a subset of the types supported by the CLR, as well as a set of rules that language and compiler designers must follow. The purpose of the CLS is to provide robust interoperability between .NET languages, including the ability to inherit classes written in one .NET language in any other .NET language and cross-language debugging.

The rules defined by the CLS apply only to publicly exposed features of a class. For example, the internal implementation of a class can use non-CLS compliant types (such as the unsigned integer types), but as long as only CLS-compliant members are exposed publicly, the class can still take full advantage of the interoperability features enabled by the CLS.

Classes

While not a term specific to the .NET platform, the term *class* may be new to many ASP developers. A class is essentially the blueprint for an object. It contains the definition for how a particular object will be instantiated at runtime, such as the properties and methods that will be exposed publicly by the object and any internal storage structures.

Developers work with classes by creating instances of the class at runtime using the new keyword, as shown here:

```
// Instantiate the .NET File class in C#
System.IO.StreamReader sr;
sr = new System.IO.StreamReader("C:\\Test.txt");
string Line;

while(sr.Peek() != -1)
{
    Line = sr.ReadLine();
    Response.Write(Server.HtmlEncode(Line) + "<br/>");
}
```

We preface the name of the class, StreamReader, with its namespace name, System.IO, to prevent naming collisions with other classes in different assemblies that might have the same name and to ensure that we get the StreamReader class we expect. We'll discuss namespaces and assemblies later in this section.

 In C#, the lowercase new keyword is used to instantiate classes. In Visual Basic.NET, the New keyword is uppercase, but since the Visual Basic language is not case-sensitive, this is a standard practice, rather than a requirement enforced by the compiler. C#, on the other hand, is case-sensitive, so keep this in mind when switching between C# and VB.NET.

Namespaces

Namespaces, a key part of the .NET Framework, provide scope to both preinstalled framework classes and custom-developed classes. Namespaces are declared for a given set of classes by enclosing those classes in one of the following declarations:

```
// C#
namespace myNamespace
{
    class myClass
    {
        // class implementation code
    }
}

' VB.NET
Namespace myNamespace
    Class myCls
        ' class implementation code
    End Class
End Namespace
```

Namespaces may also be nested, as shown below:

```
' VB.NET
Namespace myFirstNamespace
    Public Class myCls
        ' class implementation code
    End Class
    Namespace mySecondNamespace
        Public Class myCls
            ' class implementation code
        End Class
        Public Class myCls2
            ' class implementation code
        End Class
    End Namespace
End Namespace
```

The above code is perfectly valid because we've declared the second myCls in the nested namespace mySecondNamespace. If we tried to declare two identically named classes within the same namespace, we would get an error. To use the classes we just declared, we can do something like the following:

```
' VB.NET
Imports System
Imports myFirstNamespace
Imports myFirstNamespace.mySecondNamespace

Module namespaces_client_vb

    Sub Main()
        Dim newClass As New myFirstNamespace.myCls
        Dim newClass2 As New myCls2
        Console.WriteLine("Object creation succeeded!")
    End Sub

End Module
```

We use the Imports keyword in Visual Basic.NET to enable the use of member names from these namespaces without explicitly using the namespace name. However, because we used the class name myCls in both the myFirstNamespace and mySecondNamespace namespaces, we need to use the fully qualified name for this class, while we are able to instantiate myCls2 with only the class name. We can just as easily use these classes from C#, as shown here:

```
using System;
using myFirstNamespace;
using myFirstNamespace.mySecondNamespace;

class namespaces_client
{
    public static void Main()
    {
        myFirstNamespace.myCls newClass = new myFirstNamespace.myCls();
        myCls2 newClass2 = new myCls2();
        Console.WriteLine("Object creation succeeded!");
    }
}
```

C# uses the using keyword for importing namespaces. Notice that in both cases, in addition to importing the namespaces we defined, we've also imported the System namespace. This is what allows us to use the Console class defined in the System namespace to write to a console window without referring explicitly to System.Console.

Classes that are part of the .NET Framework are organized by functionality into namespaces that make them easier to locate and use. All classes that are a part of the .NET Framework begin with either System or Microsoft. Examples include:

System
> Contains all the .NET primitive data types as well as utility classes such as Console and Math that are apt to be widely used in .NET applications.

System.Collections

Contains classes used to implement various kinds of collections in .NET, including `ArrayList`, `Dictionary`, and `Hashtable`.

System.Data

Contains classes used to access and manipulate data, as well as child namespaces such as System.Data.SqlClient, which contain data access classes specific to a particular data provider.

System.Web

Contains classes used to process web requests, as well as child namespaces such as System.Web.UI, which contains such classes as the `Page` class, which is the basis for all ASP.NET pages.

Assemblies

Also known as Managed DLLs, *Assemblies* are the fundamental unit of deployment for the .NET platform. The .NET Framework itself is made up of a number of assemblies, including *mscorlib.dll*, among others. The assembly boundary is also where versioning and security are applied.

An assembly contains Intermediate Language (IL) generated by a specific language compiler, an assembly manifest (containing information about the assembly), type metadata, and resources. We'll discuss IL, manifests, and metadata later in this section.

Assemblies can be either private, residing in the directory of the client application from which they are used (or, in the case of ASP.NET, in the */bin* subdirectory of the Web application), or shared. Shared assemblies are stored in a common location called the *Global Assembly Cache (GAC)*. Assemblies that are to be installed in the GAC must be strongly named. Strong naming can be accomplished either through Visual Studio .NET, or you can use the *sn.exe* tool supplied with the .NET Framework SDK to generate a key pair for signing the assembly, and then use the *al.exe* tool to create the signed assembly based on the generated key. We'll demonstrate creating and sharing strongly named assemblies in Chapter 6.

Assemblies are self-describing, thanks to the manifest contained within them. One advantage of their self-describing nature is that it makes it possible for different versions of the same assembly to be run side by side. Clients can then specify the version of the assembly that they require, and the CLR will make sure that the correct version of the assembly is loaded for that client at runtime.

Intermediate Language (IL)

IL, also known as MSIL, is a processor-independent representation of executable code. IL is similar in some ways to assembly code, but it is not specific to a particular CPU; rather, it is specific to the CLR. IL is generated by each of the language compilers that target the CLR. As mentioned above, .NET assemblies contain IL that is to be executed by the CLR.

At runtime, the CLR just-in-time (JIT) compiles the IL to native code, which is then executed. There is also a tool called *ngen.exe*, which is supplied with the .NET Framework SDK and allows you to precompile assemblies to native code at install time and cache the precompiled code to disk. However, while precompiling an assembly to native code will improve the startup time of an assembly, the JIT process used by the CLR performs optimizations that may allow JITed code to perform better than precompiled code.

Managed Execution

Managed execution refers to code whose execution is managed by the CLR. This execution includes memory management, access security, cross-language integration for debugging and/or exception handling, and many other features. Managed assemblies are required to supply metadata that describes the types and members of the code contained within the assembly. This information allows the CLR to manage the execution of the code.

 Note that not all languages in Visual Studio .NET are managed. While Visual C++ offers what are called the "Managed Extensions for Visual C++," it is still possible to write unmanaged code in Visual C++.

Manifests, Metadata, and Attributes

Metadata and manifests are key pieces of the managed execution world. *Manifests* are the portion of an assembly that contains descriptive information about the types contained in the assembly, the members exposed by the assembly, and the resources required by the assembly. The manifest contains *metadata*, which, simply put, is data that describes the assembly. Some metadata is generated by the language compiler at compile time. The developer may add other metadata at design time through the use of attributes. *Attributes* are declarations added to code that describe some aspect of the code or modify the code's behavior at runtime.

Attributes are stored with an assembly as metadata and are used for many purposes in the .NET Framework—from the <webMethod( )> attribute used to turn a normal method into a web service to attributes used to define how custom controls interact with the Visual Studio .NET environment.

Object Orientation in the .NET Platform

The .NET Framework was built to be object oriented from the ground up. What does this mean? For those of you who are unfamiliar with object-oriented programming, here's a quick review:

We've already discussed classes. Classes are the blueprints or templates from which objects are created. Objects, the heart of object-oriented programming, are usable instances of a class. Objects expose properties, which contain data related to or about the object, and/or methods, which allow actions to be performed on the object.

In object-oriented programming, objects need to support three important qualities: encapsulation, inheritance, and polymorphism.

Encapsulation refers to the ability of an object to hide its internal data from outside view and allow access to only that data through publicly available methods. This helps prevent clients from accidentally or purposefully leaving object data in a corrupt state and make it easier for the developer of the class on which the object is based to change the internal implementation of these data members without breaking its clients.

Inheritance refers to the ability to derive one class from another. This allows developers to create a new class based on an existing class. The new class inherits all methods and properties of the existing class. The developer can then add new methods or properties or override existing methods. Inheritance allows you to develop specialized versions of objects that are customized to meet your precise needs. We'll discuss this type of scenario more in Chapter 6.

 The .NET Framework offers only single inheritance—that is, a class may only derive from a single base class. This is different from languages such as C++, which allow classes to be derived from multiple base classes.

Polymorphism refers to the ability of multiple classes derived from the same base class to expose methods with the same name—all of which clients can call in exactly the same way, regardless of the underlying implementation. Thus, a Car class could expose a Start method and a derived class SportsCar could override that Start method to provide a different implementation. From the client's perspective, however, both methods are used the same way.

This is a very high-level overview of object-oriented programming. While we'll discuss object-oriented techniques in more depth throughout the book, those unfamiliar with the topic may want to pick up a book that specifically addresses object-oriented programming.

Why Is It Important? Rapid Development and Reuse!

What's important about the object-oriented nature of the .NET platform is that it allows much faster development than did previous generations of Windows development technologies and offers much greater opportunities for reuse.

Because the functionality of the .NET Framework is exposed as a set of object-oriented classes rather than a set of obscure and finicky API calls, many operations that were difficult or downright impossible in classic ASP are simple in ASP.NET. For example, about ten lines of code can perform a DNS lookup on a domain name using the classes in the System.Net and System.Net.Sockets namespaces.

What's more, because many classes in the .NET framework can be used as base classes, it is easy to reuse them in your own applications by deriving from a class to provide common functionality and then extending the derived class to add functionality specific to your application. In fact, much of the .NET Framework is built this way. For example, all classes that make up the ASP.NET Server Controls are ultimately derived from the Control class of the System.Web.UI namespace, which provides properties and methods common to all server controls.

OO Is at the Heart of Every ASP.NET Page

One of the coolest things about object orientation in ASP.NET is that you don't have to know a thing about how to use it. Every ASP.NET page implicitly inherits from the Page class of the System.Web.UI namespace, which provides access to all ASP.NET implementations of the ASP intrinsic objects such as Request, Response, Session, and Application., and to a number of new properties and methods. One advantage of this is that each page is compiled into an assembly based on the Page class, providing substantial performance improvements over classic ASP.

Object orientation is also the key to another important new feature of ASP.NET: Code-behind. *Code-behind* allows developers to separate executable code from the HTML markup that makes up the user interface. Executable code is placed in a module called a code-behind file, which is associated with the ASP.NET page via an attribute in the page. The code-behind file contains a class that inherits from the Page class. The ASP.NET page then inherits from the code-behind class, and at runtime, the two are compiled into a single executable assembly. This compilation allows a combination of easy separation of UI and executable code at design time with high performance at runtime.

Choosing a Language

Choosing which language to use when developing ASP.NET applications is both easier and harder than choosing a language for classic ASP development. It is harder because it may be intimidating for some to choose between a substantially revised Visual Basic and a completely new language, C#. It is easier because the choice of language no longer requires giving up substantial amounts of functionality for your preferred language.

As in many other cases, including language choice in classic ASP, a lot of the decision is determined by where you're coming from. If you're:

An experienced ASP developer who has used VBScript
You'll probably prefer Visual Basic.NET.

An experienced ASP developer who's used JScript
You'll want to look at C# or JScript.NET (keeping in mind that finding code examples in C# is easier, since the novelty of the language makes it more interesting for many).

An experienced Visual Basic developer
Visual Basic.NET is the obvious choice, but you may also find it worthwhile to check out C#, which offers a lot of the power of C++ without such a steep learning curve.

An experienced C, C++, or Java developer
You'll probably feel right at home with C#, which, as a C-derived language, shares a lot of syntax with these languages.

New to ASP.NET development, with no prior ASP experience
Visual Basic.NET will probably be easiest to learn, although C# runs a close second.

Because of the level of cross-language interoperability in .NET, your choice needn't be an either/or. You can feel free to create applications and classes in Visual Basic.NET, C#, JScript.NET, or any .NET-enabled language, knowing that they will be able to work together smoothly and easily, thanks to the CLR.

Why and When Would I Use ASP.NET?

New projects starting development should use ASP.NET for the following reasons:

- Reduced development time
- Increased performance
- Increased application stability
- Increased scalability
- New ASP.NET features (see the discussion later in this chapter)

In addition to the above factors, ASP.NET, like ASP, is available for free. The only costs associated with ASP.NET development are the costs of the operating system on which you wish to run your application (Windows 2000, Windows XP, or the upcoming Windows .NET Server) and the cost of any development environment you choose to use. Of course, as with classic ASP, you can use free or inexpensive text editors to create your applications. Given that the .NET Framework is a free add-on to Windows (and will be installed by default in the Windows .NET Server line), it is possible to create ASP.NET applications without spending a penny beyond the cost of the operating system and hardware on which it will run. Integrated Development Environments, such as Microsoft Visual Studio .NET, are also available at higher cost.

Why and When Would I Port an Existing Application to ASP.NET?

A trickier question is, "When will it be worthwhile to make the effort to migrate an existing application from ASP to ASP.NET?" The reality is that while classic ASP and ASP.NET have many common features, for most applications, it will not be a trivial task to migrate an application from one to the other. Changes in languages, as well as some changes in the way that ASP.NET operates compared to classic ASP, mean that depending on how your classic ASP application is structured, migration could require a significant amount of effort.

How do you decide whether a migration is worthwhile? If your application is in production, meets your needs functionally and in terms of performance and scalability, and you do not anticipate further development on the application, it's probably best to simply run it as a classic ASP application. One big plus of the ASP.NET architecture is that it runs side by side with classic ASP, so you don't have to migrate applications. Keep in mind, however, that while classic ASP and ASP.NET applications can run side by side, even in the same directory, they do not share Session and Application context. Thus, you will need to devise your own means of transferring any information you store in the Session or Application collections to and from ASP and ASP.NET, if you want to share that information between classic ASP and ASP.NET pages.

If your application is due for a new development cycle or revision, it's worth examining the types of functionality that your application uses and examining whether ASP.NET would be helpful in meeting the needs of the application. For example, if you have an application that struggles to meet your needs in terms of performance and scalability, the improved performance of the compiled-code model of ASP.NET and its new out-of-process Session State support may enable you to meet these goals easily.

What's important to consider is balancing the cost of migration against the benefits offered by migration. In this book, we will discuss the improvements and benefits offered by ASP.NET. It is left as an exercise for the reader to weigh these improvements against one another and determine whether to migrate a particular application.

New Features in ASP.NET

We'll close our introductory look at the .NET platform with a list of new features in ASP.NET and the chapter in which we'll discuss the new feature.

Web Forms
> A new feature that, in combination with an editor such as Visual Studio .NET, provides the ASP.NET developer the same drag and drop development convenience enjoyed by Visual Basic developers for years. Web Forms improve the speed of development by encapsulating frequently used features into server controls, which are declared using a tag-based syntax similar to HTML and XML. We'll discuss Web Forms in Chapter 3 and Chapter 12.

Web services
> Web services allow developers to expose the functionality of their applications via HTTP and XML so that any client who understands these protocols can call them. Web services can make the task of application integration easier, particularly in situations in which application-to-application integration is made difficult by firewalls and/or differing platforms. We'll discuss web services in Chapter 4.

Server controls
> Server controls, as mentioned previously, are declared using an HTML-like syntax, making them easier to work with for page UI designers. They are executed on the server, returning HTML to the browser. Server controls may be manipulated on the server programmatically and provide power and flexibility for applications that must support a variety of browsers. We'll discuss using server controls in Chapter 5 and custom server control development in Chapter 6.

Validation
> One group of server controls is designed to simplify the task of validating user input. It includes controls to validate required fields, to compare one field to another or to a specific value for validation, and to validate user input using regular expressions, which allow you to specify a format that user input must follow to be valid. Validation controls will be discussed in Chapter 5.

Improved security

ASP.NET offers tighter integration with Windows-based authentication, as well as two new authentication modes: forms-based authentication (which allows users to enter authentication credentials in a standard HTML form, with the credentials validated against your choice of backend credential store) and Passport authentication (which makes use of Microsoft's Passport authentication service). We'll discuss these improvements and new techniques in Chapter 9.

CHAPTER 2

ASP.NET Applications

In the last chapter, we introduced the .NET platform, some of its most important concepts, and new features available in ASP.NET. In this chapter, we'll look at the types of applications you can create with ASP.NET, discuss when you might want to use one type over another, explore the structure of ASP.NET applications, and look at the various file types that make up an ASP.NET application.

Application Types

In classic ASP, there was really only one type of application—one in which a client accessed a page with the *.asp* extension and in which that page, either through embedded VBScript or JScript or through script in combination with components built on Microsoft's COM standard, returned HTML to the browser to form the user interface with which the client would interact. Clients typically interacted with the application only through this user interface and did not have the option of creating their own alternative interface to the functionality exposed by the application.

ASP.NET provides an enhanced version of this type of application, which we'll discuss in the next section. ASP.NET also introduces a new type of application, called a web service, which provides clients the ability to use functionality exposed by an application without being tied into that application's user interface implementation.

ASP.NET Web Applications

The ASP.NET Web Application is the type of application most developers will work with on a regular basis. The terminology comes from the description used in the Visual Studio .NET environment to describe the project type used to create this type of application. You may also hear this type of application described as an ASP.NET Web Forms Application. For reasons we'll explore in the next chapter, we prefer the former term.

An ASP.NET Web Application, in its simplest form, consists of a directory made available via HTTP using the IIS administration tool or through the Web Sharing tab of a folder's Properties dialog (or by creating a web application project in Visual Studio .NET) and at least one ASP.NET page, designated by the *.aspx* file extension. This file (or files), whose structure we'll discuss in detail in the next chapter, typically contains a mix of HTML and server-side code. This HTML and server-side code combine to create the final output of the page, which is typically HTML that is sent to the client browser. A simple ASP.NET page is shown in Example 2-1.

Example 2-1. A simple ASP.NET page

```
<%@ Page Language="VB" %>
<html>
<head>
    <title>Simple ASP.NET Page</title>
    <script runat="server">

    Sub SayHello()

        Response.Write("Hello, World!")

    End Sub

    </script>
</head>
<body>

<% SayHello %>

</body>
</html>
```

The page shown in Example 2-1 simply executes the code appearing in the `<script runat="server">` as well as the code appearing in the `<% %>` render block, and will return any resulting text or HTML to the browser, along with the standard HTML tags that are contained in the file. Figure 2-1 shows the output of the page as viewed in Notepad by using the View Source option in Internet Explorer. In this case, the SayHello method uses the Write method of the Response object (the `HttpResponse` class, which supplies this functionality, is discussed in Chapter 17) to output the text "Hello, World!". Because the SayHello method is called from a render block within the body section of the HTML document, "Hello, World!" will appear here in the output that is sent to the browser.

The key to understanding how ASP.NET Web Applications work is understanding that the code in a `<script runat="server">` block or `<% %>` render block(s) is executed on the server—after the client requests the page, but before the output of the page request is sent to the client browser. This allows developers to decide, based on the code they write and the input received from the user, just what output actually is sent to the browser. It also allows additional functionality, such as server-side state management, to be provided to these applications.

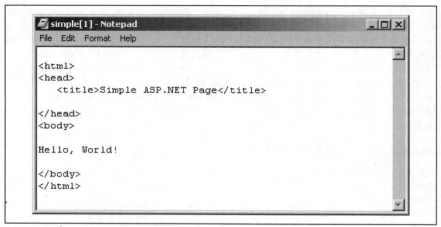

Figure 2-1. Output of a simple ASP.NET page

Besides the containing directory and ASP.NET file(s), an ASP.NET Web Application may also contain configuration files (*Web.Config*), User Control files (*.ascx*), and an application settings file (*Global.asax*), as well as code-behind and class files that provide additional functionality to the application. We'll discuss each of these file types later in this chapter.

ASP.NET Web Services

The other type of application available to ASP.NET developers is the ASP.NET Web Service. Like ASP.NET Web Applications, there are a number of terms floating around for this type of application. (Microsoft refers to web services as "XML Web Services," perhaps in hopes of a positive association between web services and the XML standard.) A *web service* is an application that exposes programmatic functionality to clients over the Internet or an intranet using the underlying plumbing of a developing W3C standard called SOAP. In simple terms, it can be seen as a simple function call across the Internet.

The simplest form of an ASP.NET Web Service consists of a directory made available via HTTP using the IIS administration tool or through the Web Sharing tab of a folder's Properties dialog (or by creating a Web Application project in Visual Studio .NET) and at least one web service file, designated by the *.asmx* file extension. Unlike an ASP.NET page, this file (or files), whose structure we'll discuss in detail in Chapter 4, typically does not contain HTML, but consists solely of server-side code. The methods to be exposed by the web service carry the `WebMethod` attribute (note that the syntax of the `WebMethod` attribute varies depending on the language used). A simple web service is shown in Example 2-2.

What Is SOAP?

The proposed SOAP standard, which at the time of this writing was a W3C Submission (see *http://www.w3.org/Submission/* for information on current submissions) and versioned at 1.1, describes a protocol that may be used within the framework of HTTP (other transport protocols are possible, but the SOAP specification does not define how to use them) to send and receive requests and responses consisting of either specific data or remote procedure calls and responses, or both. The SOAP specification defines the format for messages sent via SOAP, methods for communicating how a message should be processed, and encoding rules for communicating data types across heterogeneous platforms.

Assuming that the proposed SOAP standard is adopted as a W3C Recommendation (*recommendation* is the term used by the W3C to describe stable standards such as HTML 4.01; see *http://www.w3.org* for more information on current recommendations), application developers on a given platform can expose their functionality to others on different platforms in a fashion that makes the differences in platform transparent. As long as both the server and the client follow the SOAP specification, the applications can communicate, regardless of the platform differences.

Since SOAP has not yet been adopted as a recommendation and is still under development, current implementations from Microsoft and other vendors have not yet achieved the level of cross platform interoperability that is promised once SOAP is adopted as a recommendation. As such, you should take the time to test and evaluate the interoperability of your chosen platform(s) before committing substantial resources to web services, if you are planning to use web services to facilitate cross-platform interoperability.

Example 2-2. A simple web service

```
<%@ WebService Language="VB" Class="Hello" %>

Imports System
Imports System.Web.Services

Public Class Hello : Inherits WebService
    <WebMethod()> Public Function SayHello() As String
        Return("Hello, World!")
    End Function
End Class
```

If the *.asmx* file that makes up the above web service is called from a browser, ASP.NET will output a page that documents how the web service should be called, and also provides the ability to test the invocation of the web service. This page is shown in Figure 2-2.

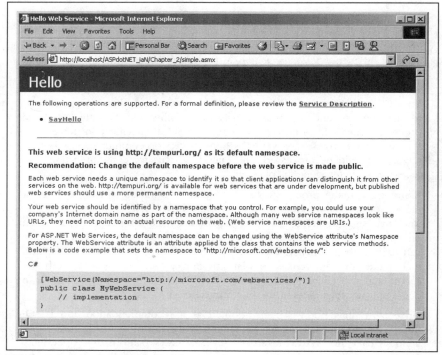

Figure 2-2. Output of a simple web service

When invoked, the web service shown in Example 2-2 will return "Hello, World!" as an XML-formatted response, according to the SOAP 1.1 specification, as shown here:

```
<?xml version="1.0" encoding="utf-8" ?>
<string xmlns="http://tempuri.org/">Hello, World!</string>
```

The documentation page provided by ASP.NET also allows you to review the Web Service Description Language (WSDL) description of your web service. WSDL, which we'll discuss further in Chapter 4, is an XML-based format for describing the functionality exposed by a web service, including the format and data type of input and output parameters, and can be considered a contract for how clients interact with the web service. In this way, WSDL plays a role similar to that of Interface Description Language (IDL) in Microsoft's COM component specification.

 Besides providing a detailed discussion of how to create a web service, Chapter 4 shows you how to consume a web service.

Application Structure and Boundaries

Although it is convenient, for the sake of discussing application types, to divide ASP.NET applications into web applications and web services, the truth is that from a practical standpoint, ASP.NET applications can be comprised of both types; an ASP.NET Web Application may contain *.asmx* files that implement web services, and a web service application may contain *.aspx* files that implement user interfaces for web services or functionality contained in .NET assemblies. Thus, from the standpoint of application structure, ASP.NET Web Applications and ASP.NET Web Services are quite similar.

Application Structure

The structure of an ASP.NET application consists of a site or virtual directory in IIS and at least one ASP.NET page or web service. Optionally, each ASP.NET application may have:

- A single *global.asax* file, located in the root of the application.

- One or more *web.config* files. There can be only one *web.config* file per directory or subdirectory in the application.

- One or more User Control files bearing the *.ascx* extension.

- One or more class files, either for ASP.NET code-behinds or for assemblies used in your application.

- A */bin* directory containing .NET assemblies you wish to use in your application. Assemblies in the */bin* directory are automatically made available to your application.

- ASP.NET Web Applications created in Visual Studio .NET should contain Solution and Project-related files (*.sln*, *.suo*, *.vbproj*, and *.csproj*, for example), a dynamic discovery file for web services (*.vsdisco*), and a default cascading style sheets file (*.css*). These applications may optionally contain resource files (*.resx*), dataset and/or XML schema definitions (*.xsd*), and other file types.

- All ASP.NET applications can contain any type of file (*.htm*, *.asp*, images, etc.) that a classic ASP application could contain. Note, however, that *.asp* pages within an ASP.NET application will not share an Application and Session state with the ASP.NET application.

Figure 2-3 provides a visual explanation of how an ASP.NET application is structured.

Application Boundaries

In ASP.NET, as in classic ASP, the boundary of an application is determined primarily by the site or virtual directory defined for that application in IIS. Requests for ASP.NET pages or web services that reside within that site or virtual directory and its subdirectories are treated as part of the application and have access to application-specific items such as the Application and Session intrinsic objects (provided, respectively, by the HttpApplicationState and HttpSessionState classes). They also share resources with other requests to the application.

Figure 2-3. Structure of an ASP.NET application

Request Lifecycle and Handling

When a request comes in from a client for a file within the purview of IIS (i.e., an HTTP request for a file within one of the sites or virtual directories set up in IIS), IIS checks the file extension of the file being requested and then checks its mapping of file types to handler programs to determine which program should be used to process the request. In the case of a classic ASP application, a request for a file with the *.asp* extension is handled by the *asp.dll* ISAPI application. The App Mappings tab of the Application Configuration dialog for IIS, shown in Figure 2-4, allows you to view and modify the mappings of file extensions to the executables used to handle those extensions, as well as to determine the HTTP verbs (GET, POST, etc.) that qualify the mapping.

Requests for files with the *.aspx* and *.asmx* extensions and for other ASP.NET-related files are handled by the *aspnet_wp.dll* ISAPI application. This application, in turn, hands the requests off to the *aspnet_wp.exe* worker process. Once the request is handed off to the ASP.NET worker process, it handles the rest of the processing:

- If no cached compiled version of the requested resource exists, compiling the code in the page (and in any code-behind page identified with the src attribute).

- Executing the compiled assembly associated with the page or web service, including refreshing any control or page state from a previous request, handling events raised by the request, and rendering the appropriate output to the client.

- Releasing used resources and discarding any transient state information (information not stored in either the Application or Session state collections).

With the exception of the Application state collection, which is available to all clients within a given ASP.NET application, and the Session state collection, which is associated with a specific client by a value either stored in an HTTP cookie on the client or munged into the URL for the application, each individual request to the application is independent from any other, even for that client.

Figure 2-4. The IIS Application Configuration dialog

The practical effect is that each request must contain sufficient information to successfully process the request—whether that information comes from form fields passed from the client, information stored in the Application or Session collections, or even information from cookies or a database.

Application File Types

A number of different file types are associated with an ASP.NET application, and it's important to understand the purpose of each type, even if you aren't using all of them in your current applications. In this section, we'll look at the major file types associated with ASP.NET Web Applications and web services and what each of them does.

web.config

web.config is the file type used for configuration of various settings within an ASP. NET application. Applications may contain more than one *web.config* file (though there may be only one per directory or subdirectory), and the *web.config* files are applied in an hierarchical fashion. What this means is that if you have defined a particular setting (such as the user accounts permitted to access that directory) in the *web.config* file at the root of your application, this setting applies to the application and all of its subdirectories, if it has any. You can override that setting for a particular subdirectory by using a *web.config* file in a subdirectory of the application. The *web.config* files use an XML-based syntax, and both the tag names and their attributes are case-sensitive.

web.config provides configuration settings for:

- Application-specific settings, such as connection string information (since the *web.config* file resides within the web application's file space, it is probably best to avoid storing sensitive information such as passwords in a configuration file).

- Authentication and authorization.

- Browser capabilities (mapping specific functionality to the information retrieved from a User Agent string).

- Compilation settings, including whether an application should be run in debug mode.

- Custom error handling information.

- Globalization settings.

- HttpHandlers and HttpModules associated with the application.

- HttpRuntime settings.

- Application Identity and encryption/decryption key settings.

- ASP.NET Page defaults (for the @ Page directive).

- ASP.NET Process settings, including settings for Web Gardens, and proactive restart of applications based on memory used or number of requests received.

- Code-access security settings, including mappings of trust levels to security policy files, and trust setting for an application.

- Session state settings, including whether to run Session state in process, out of process, or in SQL Server.

- Application Trace settings. Tracing is a useful new feature for debugging and troubleshooting that we'll discuss in Chapter 10.

- Web service settings.

Note that *web.config* is an optional file. Any configuration settings not set in a *web.config* file within the application will be inherited from the server-level configuration file, *machine.config*. A sample *web.config* file is shown in Example 2-3.

Example 2-3. Sample web.config file

```
<?xml version="1.0" encoding="utf-8" ?>
<configuration>

    <system.web>

        <compilation
            defaultLanguage="c#"
            debug="true"/>

        <trace
            enabled="true"
            requestLimit="10"
            pageOutput="false"
            traceMode="SortByTime"
            localOnly="true"/>
```

Example 2-3. Sample web.config file (continued)

```
    <sessionState
        mode="InProc"
        stateConnectionString="tcpip=127.0.0.1:42424"
        sqlConnectionString="data source=127.0.0.1;user id=sa;password="
        cookieless="false"
        timeout="20"/>
    </system.web>

</configuration>
```

We'll discuss how to make changes to *web.config*, and the syntax of the various configuration sections, in Chapter 8.

global.asax

global.asax performs the same function in ASP.NET that *global.asa* performs in classic ASP. That is, it is an optional file that may contain code to respond to Application or Session-level events. Like *global.asa*, there can be only one *global. asax* file per ASP.NET application. Unlike the *global.asa* file in classic ASP, which was parsed, the *global.asax* application file is compiled at runtime into a .NET managed assembly derived from the HttpApplication class. In addition to handling Application and Session-level events, such as Session_OnStart, *global. asax* also allows you to handle events raised by HttpModules associated with your application (in fact, the Session state in ASP.NET is implemented as an Http-Module, so its events are already handled this way).

The *global.asax* file can be constructed one of two ways. The file can contain the event handlers and other code you want associated with your application directly, or it can reference a code-behind class file that contains the event handlers and code to associate with the application. Note that the code-behind used, if any, must inherit from the HttpApplication class in the System.Web namespace. The latter is the way that the *global.asax* files in ASP.NET applications created with Visual Studio .NET are constructed. Example 2-4 shows a typical *global.asax* file that uses code-behind, while Example 2-5 shows the code-behind file it uses.

Example 2-4. global.asax using code-behind

```
<% -- Global.asax file-- %>
<%@ Application Codebehind="Global.asax.vb" Inherits="<namespacename>.Global"
%>
```

Example 2-5. Codebehind file for global.asax in Example 2-4

```
'Global.asax.vb codebehind file

Imports System.Web
Imports System.Web.SessionState

Public Class Global
    Inherits System.Web.HttpApplication
```

Example 2-5. Codebehind file for global.asax in Example 2-4 (continued)

```
Sub Application_BeginRequest(ByVal sender As Object, _
    ByVal e As EventArgs)
    ' Fires at the beginning of each request
End Sub

Sub Application_AuthenticateRequest(ByVal sender As Object, _
    ByVal e As EventArgs)
    ' Fires upon attempting to authenticate the user
End Sub

Sub Application_Error(ByVal sender As Object, ByVal e As EventArgs)
    ' Fires when an error occurs
End Sub

End Class
```

We'll discuss the uses of the *global.asax* file in more detail in Chapters 13 and 19.

.aspx Files

.aspx files, also known as ASP.NET pages or Web Forms, are the meat and potatoes of an ASP.NET Web Application. These files contain the HTML tags, server controls, and code that present a user interface to your users, and process their requests (or call helper functions in business-tier components to do so). Like the *global.asax* file, *.aspx* files may either contain code directly or refer to a codebehind class that contains the code for that page. Note that the code-behind used, if any, must inherit from the Page class in the System.Web.UI namespace. We'll discuss *.aspx* files in detail in Chapter 3.

.asmx Files

.asmx files are the files used to implement ASP.NET Web Services. These files contain the methods, marked with the WebMethod attribute, that will be exposed by your application as web services. Like *global.asax* and *.aspx* files, *.asmx* files may either contain code directly or refer to a code-behind class that implements the methods to be exposed as web services. Note that the code-behind used, if any, must inherit from the WebService class in the System.Web.Services namespace We'll discuss *.asmx* files in detail in Chapter 4.

.ascx Files

.ascx files are used to implement what are known as ASP.NET User Controls. User controls are a technique for code reuse that lies somewhere between the function of the #Include directive in classic ASP (which you can still use in ASP.NET, if you choose) and the function of custom ASP.NET Server Controls. User controls are made up of HTML tags, server controls, and code (or any combination of the above), and can be reused through a simple tag-based syntax. They have the advantages of being simpler to develop than custom Server Controls, as well as offering greater functionality than includes (such as the ability to expose properties and methods). We'll discuss user controls further in Chapters 3 and 6.

Code-Behind and Class Files

In addition to the file types mentioned here, you'll also frequently deal with cod-behind and/or class files. A code-behind file, also known as a code-behind class file, is a file containing .NET managed code (such as VB.NET or C#) that defines a class from which an ASP.NET page file, web service file, or application file, inherits. This inherited relationship is indicated by the codebehind or src attribute, which indicates the file containing the code-behind class, and the inherits attribute, which indicates the namespace name (if any) and the class name of the class to inherit. Example 2-4 shows these attributes in action. At runtime, when the page, the web service, or the application is initialized for the first time, the ASP.NET runtime locates the code-behind file and either executes the compiled assembly associated with it (in the case of the codebehind attribute, which is used when the class will be precompiled) or compiles the class into an assembly dynamically (in the case of the src attribute). We'll discuss the use of code-behind classes and the choice of which attribute to use in greater detail in Chapters 3 and 4.

Class files are simply source code files containing .NET managed code that is organized into namespaces and classes and that has been compiled, using either the Visual Studio .NET environment or the appropriate command-line compiler, into a .NET managed assembly. Class files are typically kept separate from the web application in which their assemblies are used, just as the source code for COM components used in classic ASP applications is typically kept separate from the web tree.

.vb

The *.vb* extension indicates source code files written in Visual Basic .NET. By default, code-behind classes created by the Visual Studio .NET environment use the naming convention `filename.parentfileextension.languageextension`. Thus, a VB .NET code-behind file for an ASP.NET page might have the name *WebForm1.aspx.vb*. This naming convention clearly conveys the relationship between the code-behind file and the page that inherits from it, as well as the language used in the code-behind file, so you can adopt this naming convention or use a similar one, even when not developing in the Visual Studio .NET environment.

.cs

The *.cs* extension indicates source code files written in Microsoft's new C# (pronounced "C Sharp") language. These files, when created by Visual Studio .NET, use the same naming convention as the one just described.

CHAPTER 3

Web Forms

Web Forms are an ASP.NET technology used to create programmable web pages. The main goal of Web Forms is to bring the same productivity to web applications that Visual Basic brought to Windows applications. Web Forms consist of the user interface (UI) and the UI logic written on the server side. The UI and UI logic can reside either in the same file or in separate files.

Web Forms in ASP.NET offer a number of advantages over ASP and other technologies for generating web applications. ASP.NET Web Forms:

- Provide support for any HTML 3.2-compliant browser. Even ASP.NET Server Controls that provide advanced client-side functionality will gracefully degrade for browsers that do not support DHTML or script. These controls will, however, take advantage of such support in browsers such as Internet Explorer 5.0 or later.

- Are built on the Common Language Runtime and provide all the benefits of the runtime, such as managed execution, type safety, and inheritance.

- Can be built with any Common Language Runtime language, including C#, Visual Basic .NET, and JScript .NET.

- Can be created using rapid application development tools such as Visual Studio .NET. You can build a Web Forms page simply by dragging and dropping controls from the VS.NET toolbox onto the page.

- Provide a rich set of server controls that provide almost all the functionality required for a web application. ASP.NET ships with a broad array of built-in server controls.

- Offer a flexible programming model, in which code may be included in the same file as the Web Form, as in the classic ASP model or in separate module files, referred to as code-behind files. Code-behind promotes the separation of code and content, which can improve your code's readability, maintainability, and reusability.

28

- Include state management features that preserve the state of the page and its controls between requests. This facility is explained in detail in the "State Management" section later in this chapter.

- Provide an extensible model that allows you to develop your own controls or purchase third-party controls to add functionality to your application.

Structuring an ASP.NET Page

An ASP.NET page is a declarative text file with the extension .*aspx*. A page consists of structural elements that can perform various operations—ultimately resulting in output of HTML or other MIME-type output that can be handled by the browser. An ASP.NET page can contain any or all of the following elements:

Page directives
Start with the @ symbol, followed by attribute/value pairs, and are used to specify page-level settings, such as the language used in the page or namespaces to be imported. For example, the following code specifies the C# programming language:

```
<%@ Page Language="C#" %>
```

Code declaration blocks
Consist of variable and member declarations within <script>...</script> tags, as follows:

```
<script language="C#" runat="server">
' code goes here
</script>
```

Note that there are limitations on what code you can place in <script> blocks in ASP.NET. In classic ASP, you can write executable code in a <script> block without wrapping that code in a subroutine. In ASP.NET, only variable declarations can be placed outside of a subroutine. Any other executable code not contained in a subroutine will result in an error.

Render code blocks
Used to write inline code and inline expressions within HTML elements. For example:

```
<% int i; %>
<H1><%=Heading%> </H1>
```

There are limitations on what code you can place in render blocks in ASP.NET. In classic ASP, you can define subroutines in render blocks. In ASP.NET, this is not permitted and results in an error.

Server-side comments
As always, comments are used for documentation and testing purposes. You can use them to prevent any code from executing, as in the following example:

```
<%-- Debugging Code To Be Removed --%>
```

Server controls

HTML and web controls declared with the `runat="server"` attribute/value pair. For example, the following code declares an HTML input server control and an ASP TextBox control:

```
<input type="text" id="MyText" runat="server">
<asp:TextBox id="Mytext" runat="server">
```

Server-side object tags

Used to declare and instantiate classic COM components and .NET classes. For example:

```
<object id="MyDataSet" class="System.Data.DataSet">
```

Server-side include directives

Used to include any text file into your page. This is analogous to the code reuse mechanism in classic ASP. For example:

```
<!-- #Include file="TopNavigation.inc" -- >
<!-- #Include virtual="Menus.inc" -- >
```

Literal text

Any text that is not one of the elements listed previously is literal text and appears as it is in the output. This text also includes standard HTML tags. In the following example, "Name" is the literal text:

```
Name: <input type="text" id="txtName">
```

Using @ Directives

ASP.NET provides a number of @ directives—processing instructions that give the runtime and compiler additional information about how you want your code to run. These directives let you enable certain features, specify whether you want your pages to be based on the `System.Web.UI.Page` class (the default) or on a custom class that you name, etc. Under ASP.NET, @ directives can also have attributes that further enhance the configuration ability of the directive.

The list of @ directives in ASP.NET is greatly expanded from classic ASP, which provides only five directives (whose functionality is now provided by attributes of the @ Page directive). The following @ directives are available in ASP.NET:

@ Page

Arguably the most important directive, @ Page is included at the top of each ASP.NET page and allows you to set the page language and enable or disable such features as buffering, session state, and debugging. The @ Page directive has the following attributes:

AspCompat

```
<%@ Page AspCompat="True|False" %>
```

Specifies that the page should be executed in a single-threaded apartment (STA) to provide compatibility with COM components written in Visual Basic 6.0 (or other development tools that create only STA components). This attribute also provides access to unmanaged wrappers of the ASP intrinsic objects (Request, Response, etc.) for components that need access to these objects through ObjectContext or the OnStartPage method. By default, ASP.NET pages run in a multithreaded apartment, so enabling this feature by setting AspCompat to `True` can have a negative impact on the performance of your pages. The default value of this setting is `False`.

AutoEventWireup
```
<%@ Page AutoEventWireup="True|False" %>
```

Specifies that standard events (Page_Load, Page_PreRender, etc.) will be automatically wired to any handlers you provide. The default for this attribute (set in the *machine.config* configuration file) is `True`. Pages created with Visual Studio .NET have this attribute set to `False`, since Visual Studio creates the code to wire up events in a code-behind file for you. As such, turning on `AutoEventWireup` in a page created with Visual Studio .NET results in event handlers firing multiple times.

Buffer
```
<%@ Page Buffer="True|False" %>
```

Specifies whether or not ASP.NET page output should be buffered in memory and sent to the client when the entire page has been rendered, or until the End or Flush method of the `HttpResponse` class is called. (See Chapter 17 for more information on the `HttpResponse` class.) The default value is set to `True`.

ClassName
```
<%@ Page ClassName="classname" %>
```

Specifies the class name to be used for a dynamically compiled page. The default is the filename of the page, with the dot between the filename and the *.aspx* file extension replaced by an underscore (_). This class name appears as the top-level object in the Control Tree when ASP.NET tracing is enabled. See Chapter 10 for more information on tracing in ASP.NET pages and applications.

ClientTarget
```
<%@ Page ClientTarget="UserAgent/Alias" %>
```

Specifies that the page should be rendered using the defined capabilities of one of the browsers defined in the <clientTarget> section of the *web. config* or *machine.config* configuration files. Use of this attribute substitutes the user agent string defined in the <clientTarget> section for the one sent by the actual client browser, causing server controls that query browser capabilities to render for the browser type specified in the `ClientTarget` attribute. Note that setting this attribute to a value other than those defined in the <clientTarget> configuration section results in an exception.

Codebehind
```
<%@ Page Codebehind="path" %>
```

Specifies the code-behind class file that contains code for the page. This attribute is used by the Visual Studio .NET environment when building a project and is ignored by the ASP.NET runtime. Pages using the `Codebehind` attribute must compile their code-behind class manually.

Web Forms

CodePage

```
<%@ Page CodePage="codepage" %>
```

Specifies the code page to be used for the page output.

CompilerOptions

```
<%@ Page CompilerOptions="options" %>
```

Specifies one or more command-line switches to be passed to the compiler for the language specified in the Language attribute. Behavior and availability of this attribute may vary depending on the language used for the page.

ContentType

```
<%@ Page ContentType="MIMEtype" %>
```

Specifies the HTTP content type sent as part of the HTTP headers for the response generated by the page. Can be set to any standard MIME type. This attribute is especially useful when returning types other than text/html—such as when using an ASP.NET page to generate binary image output. In this case, you would set the ContentType attribute to the appropriate MIME type, such as image/jpeg. This attribute performs the same function as the ContentType property of the HttpResponse class. (See Chapter 17 for more information on the HttpResponse class.)

Culture

```
<%@ Page Culture="culturename" %>
```

Specifies the name of the culture to use for formatting numbers, dates, etc. For example, the culture name for United States English is en-US, which is also the default. Setting the Culture attribute to another culture name will result in alternate values, such as the date returned by the Visual Basic *Now* function being formatted for the specified culture.

Debug

```
<%@ Page Debug="True|False" %>
```

Specifies whether the page will be compiled with debug symbols. Enabling debugging allows the use of debuggers to step through code and provides more detailed information in the event of an exception, but also entails a performance penalty. For this reason, the Debug attribute should always be set to False in production applications. Note that the default value, which is False, is set in the <compilation> section of the *machine.config* configuration file.

Description

```
<%@ Page Description="textdescription" %>
```

Specifies a text description of the page. This attribute is ignored by the ASP.NET runtime.

EnableSessionState

```
<%@ Page EnableSessionState="True|False|ReadOnly" %>
```

Specifies whether the page supports session state. This attribute can be used to disable or delay the creation of sessions, which are used for state management. Setting this attribute to False when session state is not utilized can improve the performance of your application. If set to True, code within the page may read or write session values, and if no current session exists for the user, a new Session is created. If set to False, attempts to read or write session values result in an exception, browsing the page will not result in the creation of a new session, and if a session exists for the user, it will be unaffected. If set to ReadOnly, an existing session may be read from, but not written to, and browsing the page will not result in the creation of a new session. The default value, which is set in the <pages> section of the *machine.config* configuration file, is True.

EnableViewState

```
<%@ Page EnableViewState="True|False" %>
```

Specifies whether ViewState is supported for the page. ViewState is a new feature of ASP.NET that allows server control state (as well as developer-specified values) to be persisted across multiple requests to the page. ViewState is stored as a hidden form field containing an encoded text string representing the state of all controls for which ViewState is enabled; thus, any controls for which you want ASP.NET to manage state should be placed inside a server-side <form> tag pair. When ViewState is enabled for a page, individual controls can disable their own ViewState for better performance. Because ViewState is round-tripped between the server and client, you should be cognizant of the size of the ViewState field for the page. Disabling ViewState where it is not necessary (either at the page or control level) may improve performance. The default value, which is set in the <pages> section of the *machine.config* configuration file, is True.

EnableViewStateMac

```
<%@ Page EnableViewStateMAC="True|False" %>
```

Specifies whether ASP.NET should run a machine authentication check (MAC) on the ViewState contents to ensure that the ViewState was not tampered with on the client. This can make your page more secure, but may carry a performance penalty. The default value, which is set in the <pages> section of the *machine.config* configuration file, is False.

ErrorPage

```
<%@ Page ErrorPage="URL" %>
```

Specifies the URL of a page to which the user will be redirected if an unhandled exception occurs. This attribute should be considered a last line of defense in error handling and not a substitute for proper error/exception handling. See Chapter 10 for more information on handling exceptions.

Explicit

```
<%@ Page Explicit="True|False" %>
```

Specifies whether pages written in Visual Basic .NET will be compiled using Option Explicit mode. This mode requires that all variables be explicitly declared before use. The default value, which is set in the <compilation> section of the *machine.config* configuration file, is True. Note that the documentation for the @ Page directive indicates that the default for this attribute is False (while also indicating that the value is set to True in *machine.config*). This may refer to the *vbc.exe* compiler having option explicit turned off by default. Since the explicit attribute in the `<compilation>` element of machine.config is set to `True`, however, the default for ASP.NET pages is effectively `True`.

Inherits

```
<%@ Page Src="path" Inherits="namespace.class" %>
```

Specifies the namespace (optional) and class name of a class from which the page will inherit. This attribute is used with the `Src` or `Codebehind` attribute to specify a code-behind file from which the page should inherit, thus making any properties and/or methods of that class available to the page.

Language

```
<%@ Page Language="languagealias" %>
```

Specifies the language that will be used for server-side `<script>` blocks and render blocks on the page. Typical values are `VB` (for Visual Basic . NET) and `C#`. You can also use the `Language` attribute of a server-side `<script>` tag to specify the desired language for individual `<script>` blocks. Unlike classic ASP, ASP.NET only supports one language per page.

LCID

```
<%@ Page LCID="localeidentifier" %>
```

Specifies the locale identifier (LCID) for the page. The locale identifier is used by functions such as the Visual Basic .NET FormatCurrency function to determine the desired format. For example, setting the `LCID` attribute to 1041 results in FormatCurrency returning values formatted as Japanese yen (¥).

ResponseEncoding

```
<%@ Page ResponseEncoding="encodingname" %>
```

Specifies the encoding to be used for the page response. This attribute can be set to any valid encoding supported by System.Text.Encoding. The default is `Unicode` (`UTF-8`).

Src

```
<%@ Page Src="path" Inherits="namespace.class" %>
```

Specifies the path to a code-behind class to compile dynamically. This attribute is used in conjunction with the `Inherits` attribute to specify a code-behind class for the page that will be compiled when the page is requested (unless a cached version of the compiled assembly for the page already exists). Unlike the `Codebehind` attribute, which is only used by Visual Studio .NET (and is ignored by the ASP.NET runtime), the class file specified by the `Src` attribute is compiled dynamically at runtime.

SmartNavigation

```
<%@ Page SmartNavigation="True|False" %>
```

Specifies whether ASP.NET's SmartNavigation feature is enabled. Smart-Navigation, which is supported only by IE 5.x and later, uses IFrame elements to allow only portions of the page to be refreshed when an ASP. NET page containing a form is posted to the server. This can eliminate the flicker associated with page refresh, and also prevents multiple entries in the browser history from postbacks. The default value, which is set in the `<pages>` section of the *machine.config* configuration file, is `False`.

Strict

```
<%@ Page Strict="True|False" %>
```

Specifies whether pages written in Visual Basic .NET will be compiled using `Option Strict` mode. This mode does not permit any implicit data type conversion that would result in data loss (also known as *narrowing conversions*) and does not allow late binding. `Option Strict` also includes the restrictions of `Option Explicit`, so setting the `Strict` attribute to `True` also requires that all variables be explicitly declared before use. The default value, which is set in the `<compilation>` section of the *machine.config* configuration file, is `False`.

Trace

```
<%@ Page Trace="True|False" %>
```

Specifies whether the ASP.NET tracing feature is enabled for the page. Enabling tracing at the page level results in information about the current request—including request time, HTTP status code, cookie information, page control tree, and HTTP header information—being appended to the page output. Tracing can provide a great deal of information useful for debugging or understanding what is happening with a given page. For performance and security reasons, tracing should not be enabled for production applications. The default value, which is set in the `<trace>` section of the *machine.config* configuration file, is `False`.

TraceMode

```
<%@ Page TraceMode="tracemode" %>
```

Specifies the sort order of entries in the Trace Information section of the page trace. Valid values include `SortByTime`, which sorts entries in the order in which they are processed, and `SortByCategory`, which sorts entries based on the category assigned to the entry. Developers can write custom entries to the trace output using the Trace.Write method and assign categories to these entries. In the `SortByCategory` trace mode, all custom entries using the same category would appear together. The default value, which is set in the `<trace>` section of the *machine.config* configuration file, is `SortByTime`.

Transaction

```
<%@ Page Transaction="transactionmode" %>
```

Specifies the transaction mode of the page. Valid values are `Disabled`, `NotSupported`, `Required`, `RequiresNew`, and `Supported`. Default is `Disabled`.

UICulture

```
<%@ Page UICulture="culturename" %>
```

Specifies the culture that should be used when loading language-specific resources for pages that use resource files.

WarningLevel

```
<%@ Page WarningLevel="warninglevel" %>
```

Specifies the compiler warning level at which ASP.NET should abort compilation of the page and display the warning. The available values for this attribute depend on the language in use. See the documentation for the appropriate compiler for more information.

@ Control

Provides much the same functionality as the @ Page directive, only for ASP. NET user controls. The attributes available for the @ Control directive, which are a subset of those for the @ Page directive, include the following:

```
AutoEventWireup
ClassName
Codebehind (Visual Studio .NET only)
CompilerOptions
Debug
Description
EnableViewState
Explicit
Inherits
Language
Strict
Src
WarningLevel
```

@ Import

Allows access to members of a namespace without using the fully qualified (namespace and member name) name. The @ Import directive has a single attribute, Namespace, which specifies the namespace to import. Multiple @ Import directives must be used to import multiple namespaces, with one @ Import directive for each desired namespace.

@ Implements

Used to specify an interface that the page or control in which the directive appears implements. By implementing an interface, the page developer agrees to provide implementations of all methods and/or properties defined by the interface. Failure to implement any of the members defined by the interface results in a compiler error. The @ Implements directive has a single attribute, Interface, that specifies the .NET interface to be implemented.

@ Register

Allows the instantiation and use of user controls and custom server controls in ASP.NET pages and user controls through an HTML-like tag-based syntax. The @ Register directive is used to specify the tag prefix (similar to the asp: prefix for built-in ASP.NET Server Controls) and the information necessary to locate the user control or custom server control. The @ Register directive supports the following attributes:

TagPrefix

Specifies the prefix to be used to differentiate the tag used to create an instance of the user control or custom server control.

TagName *(user controls only)*

Specifies the tag name (the portion of the tag immediately following the tag prefix, which is separated from the tag name by a colon) used to create an instance of a user control. For custom server controls, the class name of the class that defines the server control is used for the tag name, so this attribute is not necessary.

Namespace *(custom server controls only)*

Specifies the namespace of the custom server control.

Src *(user controls only)*

Specifies the path to the *.ascx* file containing the desired user control.

Assembly *(custom server controls only)*

Specifies the assembly containing the custom server control class.

A complete @ Register directive for a custom server control is:

```
<%@ Register TagPrefix="foo" Namespace="foo" Assembly="bar" %>
```

Assuming a class name of "baz" for the custom server control, the corresponding tag for an instance of the control is shown here:

```
<foo:baz id="myBaz" runat="server"/>
```

See Chapter 6 for additional examples.

@ Assembly

Specifies the name or path to an assembly to be linked in with the current page. This specification makes any classes or interfaces in the assembly available to the page. Note that the following assemblies are linked into pages by default based on the <assemblies> child element of the <compilation> element in the *machine.config* configuration file (see Chapters 8 and 20 for more information on configuration files):

mscorlib
System
System.Data
System.Drawing
System.EnterpriseServices
System.Web
System.Web.Services
System.Xml

Note that the <assemblies> element of *machine.config* also contains a wildcard reference (*) that tells it to link any assemblies residing in the *bin* subdirectory of the application. Any custom assemblies you place in this directory (including custom control assemblies) will be available to your application automatically. Unlike the @ Import directive, this directive does not make it possible to access members of an assembly without using the fully qualified name. The @ Import directive is still required for that. The @ Assembly directive supports two attributes, which are exclusive of one another:

Name

Specifies the name of the assembly to link. This is typically the same as the filename of the assembly, without the file extension (i.e., the assembly name for *System.Web.dll* would be System.Web).

Src

Specifies the path to a class module that is to be dynamically compiled and linked into the current page.

@ OutputCache

Enables and specifies settings for caching the output of ASP.NET pages or user controls. Caching can significantly improve the performance of ASP.NET applications. Output may be cached on the server, on the client, or on intermediate machines, depending on the value of the Location attribute. The @ OutputCache directive supports the following attributes:

Duration

Specifies the time in seconds for the output of the page to be cached. Note that for output cached by the ASP.NET cache engine on the server, cached output may be evicted from the cache before this duration has elapsed if the page is requested infrequently or if there is a shortage of available memory on the web server. This attribute is required.

Location *(pages only)*

Specifies where page output should be cached. Valid values include Any, Client, Downstream, None, or Server. The default is Any. This attribute is supported only for output caching with ASP.NET pages. Attempting to use this attribute for caching user controls results in a parser error.

VaryByCustom

Specifies a custom caching variation scheme. Setting the value to browser varies the cache based on the name and major version number of the client's browser. To use this attribute for any other custom value, you must override the GetVaryByCustomString method of the HttpApplication class in the *global.asax* file.

VaryByHeader *(pages only)*

Specifies a list of one or more HTTP headers, delimited by semicolons, to be used to vary the output cache. Requests with identical values for the specified headers will be served a cached version of the page (if one exists). If no matching page exists in the cache, the page is processed and the resulting output is cached. This attribute is supported only for output caching with ASP.NET pages. Attempting to use this attribute for caching user controls will result in a parser error.

VaryByParam

Specifies a list of one or more HTTP GET or POST parameters, delimited by semicolons, to be used to vary the output cache. Requests with identical values for the specified parameters will receive a cached version of the page (if one exists). If no matching page exists in the cache, the page is processed and the resulting output is cached. This attribute is required. To disable varying the cache by parameter, set the value to none. To vary by all parameters, set the value to the * wildcard.

VaryByControl *(user controls only)*

Specifies a list of one or more properties of a user control, delimited by semicolons, to be used to vary the output cache. Requests with identical values for the specified parameters will receive a cached version of the user control (if one exists). If no matching user control exists in the cache, the user control is processed and the resulting output is cached. This attribute is required unless a VaryByParam attribute has been specified for the user control's @ OutputCache directive.

@ Reference

Specifies the path to an ASP.NET page or user control that will be compiled dynamically and linked into the current page. The @ Reference directive supports the following attributes:

Page

Specifies the path to a page to be dynamically compiled and linked.

Control
Specifies the path to a user control to be dynamically compiled and linked.

Combining User Interface and Code

Although ASP.NET makes it possible to create much more complex, structured web applications, you can continue to use the simple coding style characteristic of ASP in which code and HTML are combined. This is illustrated in Example 3-1, a simple form that displays the message "Hello World" in the browser window.

Example 3-1. A simple Web Form (HelloWorld.aspx)

```
<%@ Page Language="VB" %>
<html>
<head>
<title>My First Web Form</title>
<script runat="server">
    Sub Page_Load(Sender As Object , e As EventArgs )
        Message.Text = "Hello World!"
    End Sub
</script>
</head>
<body>
    <form runat="server">
        <asp:Label id="Message" runat="server" />
    </form>
</body>
</html>
```

This Web Form uses a server control, `<asp:Label>`, to output the text "Hello World". The server control is declared using a tag with the prefix `asp:` followed by the attribute `runat="server"`. The attribute `runat="server"` indicates that the code will run on the server and the output will be sent to the browser. The Label control is used to display static text and can be changed using the control's Text property. The entrypoint into the executable code in Example 3-1 is the event handler for the Page object's Load event, which is called automatically when the page loads.

The tag prefix `asp:` denotes the namespace. Namespaces define the scope of the controls. Namespaces allow the existence of multiple controls with the same name. Using namespaces, the .NET Framework classes are neatly grouped under hierarchies based on their functionality.

When the page is requested from the browser for the first time, it is compiled and cached. The compiled code is then used to generate the content dynamically. You may notice a delay when you request any ASP.NET page for the first time because of the compilation. Subsequent requests will execute much faster.

To understand how an ASP.NET page is rendered on the browser, you should look at the generated HTML content from within the browser, which is accessible by selecting Internet Explorer's View | Source menu option. The generated HTML from Example 3-1 is shown in Example 3-2.

Example 3-2. Generated HTML from an ASP.NET page

```
<html>
<head>
<title>My First Web Form</title>

</head>
<body>
    <form name="_ctl0" method="post" action="HelloWorld.aspx" id="_ctl0">
<input type="hidden" name="__VIEWSTATE"
value="dDw4MDEONzIOMDA7dDw7bDxpPDI+Oz47bDxOPDtsPGk8MT47PjtsPHQ8cDxwPGw8VGV4dD
s+O2w8SGVsbG8gV29ybGQhOz4+Oz470z47Pj47Pj47Pg==" />

        <span id="Message">Hello World!</span>
    </form>
</body>
</html>
```

As you can see by comparing Example 3-1 and Example 3-2, the Label server control has been modified to become the HTML <span> tag. Also notice that a hidden form field stores the state of the Label server control.

Code-Behind Files

ASP.NET promotes the separation of code and content. The use of *code-behind files* is one of the mechanisms that aides the separation of the UI and the UI logic. Developing an ASP.NET page using code-behind files requires two steps:

1. Developing the page's UI using HTML and web controls.
2. Developing the UI logic (code-behind) using any of the .NET languages.

A code-behind file consists of a class inherited from the Page class. It provides an object-oriented way of developing the UI logic of an ASP.NET page. The code-behind file has member variables, event handlers, and helper methods that are called from the event handlers specific to an ASP.NET page. The ASP.NET page and the code-behind file are tightly coupled.

The extension of the code-behind file varies depending upon the .NET programming language you choose to develop the code. Typically, it will be *.cs* for C#, *.vb* for Visual Basic, or *.js* for JScript. You can decide to either precompile the code-behind file or let ASP.NET compile the code-behind file for you.

The Page directive provides the glue between an ASP.NET page and a code-behind file at the beginning of your ASP.NET page. The Inherits attribute of the Page directive specifies the name of the .NET class that encapsulates the UI logic. The Src or Codebehind attribute specifies the path to the filename that contains the .NET class itself. Use the Codebehind attribute if the code-behind file is precompiled; otherwise, use the Src attribute. Note that the Codebehind attribute is used only by Visual Studio .NET; it is ignored by the ASP.NET parser. By contrast, the ASP.NET parser uses the Src attribute to locate and compile the code-behind class.

One of the most commonly used pages in any web application is a sign-in page. Example 3-3 shows the HTML source for a simple ASP.NET sign-in page that uses a code-behind file. Note that this example is not designed to show a secure login procedure, but rather to demonstrate the use of code-behind with a Web Forms page. We'll look at creating a login page in Chapter 9. Also note that this example requires that either the page and code-behind class belong to a Visual Studio .NET project, which Visual Studio would need to build before the page is browsed, or the code-behind class be manually compiled and placed in the application's *bin* subdirectory before the page is browsed.

Example 3-3. ASP.NET page using a code-behind file (CodeBehind.aspx)

```
<%@ Page language="vb" Codebehind="Codebehind.vb"
    Inherits="aspnetian.CodeBehind" %>
<html>
<head></head>
<body>
    <form runat="server">
        <h1>Code-behind demonstration</h1>
        <p>
            <asp:label id="Message" runat="server">
            Enter your name to sign in:
            </asp:label>
        </p>
        <p>
            <table id="SignInTable" cellpadding="5"
                cellspacing="1" bgcolor="Silver" runat="server">
                <tr>
                <td align="right">Name:</td>
                    <td align="left">
                        <asp:textbox id="SignInBox" width="200" runat="server"/>
                    </td>
                </tr>
                <tr>
                    <td colspan="2" align="middle">
                        <asp:button id="SignInButton" runat="server"
                            text="Sign in"/>
                    </td>
                </tr>
            </table>
        </p>
    </form>
</body>
</html>
```

The first line of the page is a Page directive that has the Codebehind and Inherits attributes set to appropriate values. Note that when declaring server controls, we have the option of using both an opening and closing tag (as exemplified by the Message Label control) when the tags contain text to be applied to one of the control's properties (in this case, the Text property), or using a single tag with a closing (/). This follows the standard for XML/XHTML syntax.

The source code for the code-behind file is given in Example 3-4. If you look at the member variables of the code-behind class, they have a one-to-one mapping with the IDs of the controls in the ASP.NET page. This mapping is very important because these member variables are the *programmatic accessors* to the controls in the page. You should also note that they are declared as Protected, which means that they are accessible only within the code-behind class and the Web Form that inherits from the code-behind class.

Example 3-4. Code-behind file (CodeBehind.vb)

```
Imports System
Imports System.Web
Imports System.Web.UI
Imports System.Web.UI.WebControls
Imports System.Web.UI.HtmlControls
Namespace aspnetian

Public Class CodeBehind : Inherits System.Web.UI.Page
    Protected Message As Label
    Protected SignInTable As HtmlTable
    Protected WithEvents SignInButton As Button
    Protected SignInBox As TextBox

    Protected Sub Page_Load(sender As Object, e As EventArgs)
        If Page.IsPostBack Then
            Message.Text = "Time is: " & DateTime.Now() & "<br />" & _
                Message.Text
        End If
    End Sub

    Protected Sub SignInButton_Click(obj As Object, e As EventArgs ) _
        Handles SignInButton.Click
        Message.Text = "Congratulations, " & SignInBox.Text & _
            "!!! You have successfully signed in."
        SignInTable.Visible = false
    End Sub

End Class
End Namespace
```

All code for the page has been removed from the Web Forms page into the code-behind class.

Because the Src attribute is specified in the Page directive, the code-behind file needs to be compiled into a *.dll* file and deployed into the */bin* folder of your application. Since the code-behind file shown in Example 3-4 uses Visual Basic, you will typically invoke the VB compiler with the options shown here:

```
vbc.exe /out:bin\Codebehind.dll /r:System.dll,System.web.dll /t:library
Codebehind.vb
```

For convenience sake, it's usually a good idea to set up a DOS batch file (*.bat* extension) with the compilation instructions. Then you can double-click the batch file in Windows Explorer to recompile the code-behind class. Example 3-5 adds the pause command to allow you to view any warnings or errors returned by the compiler before the command-line window is closed.

Example 3-5. Batch compilation file (MakeCodebehind.bat)

```
vbc.exe /t:library /r:System.dll,System.web.dll /out:bin\Codebehind.dll
Codebehind.vb

pause
```

Because the .NET Framework SDK setup program does not register the path to the command-line compilers, the command in Example 3-5 will work only if you add the path to the compilers to the PATH environment variable. Otherwise, you will need to use the full path to *vbc.exe* in your batch file. To add the path to *vbc.exe* to the PATH environment variable:

1. Right-click the My Computer icon on the desktop and select Properties from the menu.

2. Select the Advanced tab and then click the Environment Variables... button.

3. Under System Variables, scroll to the Path variable, select it, then click Edit...

4. Add a semicolon, followed by the path to *vbc.exe* (typically C:\%windir%\ Microsoft.NET\Framework\%version%\) and click OK.

5. Click OK on the Environment Variables and System Properties dialogs to close them. You may need to reboot for this change to take effect.

In Visual Studio .NET, the compilation of a code-behind class is taken care of automatically when you build the project containing the Web Form that uses it. This is tracked by the Codebehind attribute of the @ Page directive.

Stages of Page Processing

During Web Forms processing, the page goes through distinct stages, which are illustrated in Figure 3-1. The Web Forms processor calls a corresponding page processing event at each stage.

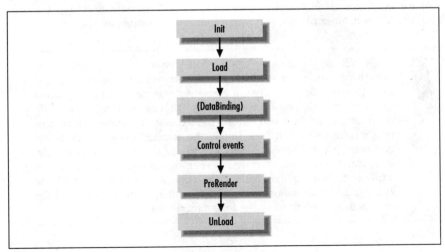

Figure 3-1. The stages of Web Forms page processing

In ASP pages other than *global.asa*, you have to write your program logic sequentially because your code is executed in the order in which it appears (termed *procedural programming*). ASP.NET, on the other hand, features *event-driven programming*, in which the order of execution of a particular code block is not predetermined. You write a block of code called an *event handler* that is executed whenever that event occurs.

If you've developed client-side code or have programmed using Visual Basic, you're already familiar with event-driven programming. ASP.NET takes event-driven programming to the server side, encouraging you to structure your programming logic into event handlers. In ASP.NET, the Page object is the representation of your ASP.NET page, and you can write handlers at the page level. ASP, on the other hand, supports only events at the application and session levels.

The `Page` class inherits all of its important events from the `System.Web.UI.Control` class, which is the ultimate parent of all server controls. This means that all events described below also apply to both built-in and custom server controls because all of these controls ultimately derive from `System.Web.UI.Control`.

We'll examine these events in detail. First, however, we'll examine how an event is associated with a particular event handler in Visual Basic .NET and C#.

Handling Events

There are three main techniques for handling events in ASP.NET, one of which takes advantage of ASP.NET's ability to wire up standard event handlers automatically and two of which rely on wiring up event handlers manually.

Automatic event wiring

When handling events in a page that consists of a single *.aspx* page, it is often simplest to create event handlers in the standard *objectname_eventname* syntax familiar to most Visual Basic programmers. By default, ASP.NET will automatically look for handlers such as Page_Init, Page_Load, Page_PreRender, and Page_UnLoad, and will call them automatically at the appropriate time during page processing.

 While not strictly required, it's a good idea to use the *objectname_ eventname* syntax for event handlers you write for server controls used in your page. By using a consistent standard for naming event handlers, it will be much clearer to anyone reading your code (including yourself, if you haven't looked at it in a while) which procedures are event handlers. Unlike the standard page events inherited from Control, server control events are not wired automatically. You can wire a server control event by adding an *OnEventName* attribute to the tag that defines the control, with the value of the attribute set to the name of the event handler, or by using one of the two methods described in the following sections.

Using AddHandler or += to wire events

One method of wiring up events to event handlers manually is to use the Visual Basic .NET `AddHandler` statement or the C# `+=` operator to hook up an event to a *delegate*. Delegates, which are used to create event handlers, are similar to function pointers, but are type-safe. The following code snippets illustrate hooking up an event handler for the Click event of an ASP.NET Button server control named Button1:

```
// C#
Button1.Click += new System.EventHandler(Button1_Click)

' Visual Basic .NET
AddHandler Button1.Click AddressOf Button1_Click
```

In both cases, the code tells ASP.NET where to find the procedure to execute when the Click event (namely, Button1.Click) is fired. If, for some reason, you want to unwire an event handler, you can use the Visual Basic .NET `RemoveHandler` statement or the C# `-=` operator to accomplish the reverse of AddHandler and +=.

Using the WithEvents and Handles keywords to wire events

Visual Basic .NET developers have a third option for wiring up events: the `WithEvents` and `Handles` keywords. The `WithEvents` keyword precedes the name of a declared control (usually in a code-behind class) and tells ASP.NET that you want to be able to handle the control's events using the `Handles` keyword. The `Handles` keyword is appended to the first line of the event handler procedure and is followed by the object name and the name of the event it handles. The syntax of these keywords is shown in the following code snippet. Note the use of the VB line continuation character, which indicates that both the `Sub` declaration and the `Handles` keyword should be interpreted as a single line of code:

```
Protected WithEvents MyButton As New Button

Private Sub MyButton_Click(sender As Object, e As EventArgs) _
    Handles MyButton.Click
    'Event handling code
End Sub
```

 When using the `AddHandler`, `+=`, or `WithEvents`/`Handles` techniques for wiring up the standard events (Init, Load, etc.) manually, you should add the `AutoEventWireup` attribute to your page's @ Page directive, with the value set to `False`. Otherwise, the event handlers will be called more than once. Fortunately, new pages added to a web project in Visual Studio .NET have this attribute set to `False` by default.

ASP.NET Page and Control Events

Each stage of Web Forms processing shown in Figure 3-1 exposes particular events that can be handled in your code. In this section, we'll examine those events in detail.

Init

The Init event, which is fired with each request, is used to initialize the page. If variables need to be declared and initialized before the majority of page processing begins, the event handler for the Init event is the place to do it. A good example of this is that for C# web projects in Visual Studio .NET, the Page_Init event handler is used to wire up other events handled by a page's code-behind class. The Page_Init handler, in turn, is wired up in the constructor for the code-behind class.

Load

The Load event is fired on every request to the page, immediately after all the controls on the page have been initialized. You can use this event handler for initialization code specific to that page. Since this event is fired every time the page is loaded, and if your page is posted to itself (known as a *postback*), you can use the IsPostBack property of the Page object to write logic that executes only once. For instance, in the code in Example 3-6, you will see the label "Before PostBack" the first time you load the page because, since the page has not been submitted to itself yet, the IsPostBack property is False. When the page is posted back, you will see the label "Posted Back" because the IsPostBack property has become True.

Example 3-6. An ASP.NET page using the Postback property

```
<%@ Page Language="vb" %>
<html>
<head>
<title>IsPostBack Demonstration</title>
<script runat="server" >
    Sub Page_Load(Sender As Object, e As EventArgs)
        If Not IsPostBack Then
            lblMessage.Text = "Before PostBack"
        Else
            lblMessage.Text = "Posted Back"
        End If
    End Sub
</script>
</head>
<body>
    <h1>Demonstration of IsPostBack property</h1>
    <form id="frmPostBack" runat="server">
      <asp:label id="lblMessage" runat="server"/>
      <asp:Button type="Submit" text="Post Back" runat="server"/>
    </form>
</body>
</html>
```

DataBinding

The DataBinding event is fired when the page (or a control) is bound to a data source. This will usually occur when the DataBind method of the Page object is called, generally from the Page_Load event handler. The DataBinding event handler can be used to do any special processing related to the data-binding portion of page processing.

Control events

Server control events are used primarily in an ASP.NET page to write the UI and programming logic of that page. Control events can be categorized broadly as either change events or action events.

The control event handlers are identified by an attribute of the control's tag. For example, in the following tag:

```
<asp:Button id="MyButton" onClick="MyButton_Clicked" runat="server">
```

the attribute/value pair onClick="MyButton_Clicked" connects the control event (the Click event) with its event handler (the MyButton_Clicked procedure).

Change events execute only on the next request to the server. For example, if you have written an event handler for the TextBox_Changed event, only when the page is submitted to the server will the code inside the handler be executed. Server-side change events are not the same as the client-side change events that execute instantly.

The most commonly used Change events and the controls that raise these events are listed in Table 3-1.

Table 3-1. Change events

Event	Description	Controls
OnAdCreated	Raised after creation of the control and immediately before the page is rendered. If an Advertisement file is provided, OnAdCreated is raised after an ad has been selected from the file.	AdRotator
OnDayRender	Raised as each cell is created.	Calendar
OnVisibleMonthChanged	Raised when the user clicks a button for the next or previous month in the Calendar's title.	Calendar
OnSelectionChanged	Raised when the user selects a day, week, or month selector	Calendar, List
OnSelectedIndexChanged	Raised when the user changes the selection.	CheckBoxList, DropDownList, ListBox, RadioButtonList
OnCheckedChanged	Raised when the user clicks the control.	CheckBox, RadioButton
OnPageIndexChanged	Raised when the user clicks a page selection element.	DataGrid

Action events, unlike Change events, are immediately posted back to the server. For example, if you have an event handler for the Command_Click event, the logic inside the handler will be executed the moment you click that command button. Action events exhibit the same behavior whether they are executed on the server or client side.

The most commonly used Action events and the controls that raise them are listed in Table 3-2.

Table 3-2. Action events

Event	Description	Controls
OnClick	Raised when the user clicks the control.	Button, Image-Button, LinkButton
OnCancelCommand	Raised by a control whose Command property is Cancel. Typically, this Button or LinkButton control is declared in the EditItemTemplate.	DataGrid, DataList
OnDeleteCommand	Raised by a control whose Command property is Delete. Typically, this Button or LinkButton control is declared in the ItemTemplate.	DataGrid, DataList
OnEditCommand	Raised by a control whose Command property is Edit. Typically, this Button or LinkButton control is declared in the ItemTemplate.	DataGrid, DataList
OnItemCommand	Raised in the control when an embedded control raises an event that is not already covered by Edit, Cancel, Delete or Update.	DataGrid, DataList
OnUpdateCommand	Raised by a control whose Command property is Update. Typically, this Button or LinkButton control is declared in the EditItemTemplate.	DataGrid, DataList
OnItemCreated	Raised on the server each time a control is created.	DataGrid, DataList
OnSortCommand	Raised when a column is sorted.	DataGrid

PreRender

The PreRender event is fired just before the page (or control) is rendered and sent to the client. The PreRender event is the last chance for page output to be modified before it is sent to the browser. It is also the last event that fires before the ViewState of the controls on the page is saved, so any control changes you wish to have saved to ViewState should be made either before or during this event. ViewState is discussed more fully in the "State Management" section later in this chapter.

Unload

The Page_Unload event is fired after the page is rendered. You can use the Page_Unload event handler to write cleanup code.

For example, in the following snippet, the database connection objConnection is closed:

```
Sub Page_Unload(sender As Object, e As EventArgs )
    ' Close the database connection
    objConnection.Close( )
End Sub
```

State Management

In a typical web page, it is very common for data entry forms to retain their values after the form has been posted and the same page is returned to the client (that is, to retain the values from a posted form in the postback). To implement this feature in classic ASP, you need to determine whether or not the page is requested by a client for the first time. You also need to write code that will display the submitted value in the controls. In contrast, ASP.NET performs state management automatically in postbacks.

ASP.NET uses a simple hidden HTML form field to retain the values automatically during postbacks. There are no ActiveX controls or applets or client-side scripts used to maintain state. Thus, you need not write code to retain values explicitly.

ASP.NET maintains only the state of server controls—i.e., the controls declared with the runat="server" attribute/value pair. State management can be enabled or disabled for individual controls or an entire page by setting the MaintainState property to True (its default value) or False.

Now let's revisit the concept of ViewState, which was introduced earlier in this chapter. ViewState is a collection of information about the properties of an ASP. NET page and its controls (maintained in a hidden form field named _VIEWSTATE.) It exists solely to store the properties of controls that are not transmitted between client and server during postbacks. As the name itself implies, ViewState preserves the state associated with a particular view of a page. It is used by the noninput controls (such as Label and DataGrid) to store their ambient state across requests. Thus, when a page is posted back to the server, and the result of the postback is rendered to the browser, controls such as textboxes and listboxes, will automatically retain their state, unless the control's EnableViewState property has been set to False or the state of the control was modified programmatically on the server.

Only base properties are persisted in the ViewState. Any change in these properties before rendering the page will be persisted.

If your page is not posted back to itself, you can set the property MaintainState to False at the page level to avoid the extra processing and storage space required for maintaining ViewState. You can also disable/enable view state on per control basis.

Caching Page Output

Another new feature of ASP.NET that should not be overlooked is its support for caching—in particular, output caching. Output caching provides the ability to have the rendered output of a page cached for a specified duration simply and easily. By caching the rendered output in memory, subsequent requests for the page can be delivered substantially faster and with considerably less processor utilization than if the page needs to be re-rendered for each request. This can lead to substantial performance increases. The ASP.NET team has reported page delivery two to three times faster when using output caching. Output caching is available for both ASP.NET pages and ASP.NET user controls.

Not every page can be cached in its entirety. Some pages contain too much dynamic information to be cached as a whole, but even these pages may have portions that seldom change. By moving these static portions into user controls (which also provides the possibility of reuse) and then output caching the user controls, at least some performance benefit can be realized—even for very dynamic pages.

The best part about output caching is its simplicity. In its most basic state, caching the output of a page requires a directive like the following (which you should add directly below the @ Page or @ Control directive):

```
<%@ OutputCache Duration="20" VaryByParam="None" %>
```

This directive tells ASP.NET to cache the output of the page for 20 seconds and to return the same cached version of the page for all requests. Example 3-7 demonstrates how to cache the output of a page for 60 seconds and to cache a different version of the page for each different value of the name parameter, when sent as part of the query string of a GET request (for example, *http://localhost/aspnetian/ OutCache.aspx?name=John*). The cache can be varied by form fields in a POST request as well, if desired, by setting the value of the VaryByParam attribute to the name of the form field to vary by.

Example 3-7. Output caching in ASP.NET

```
<%@ Page Language="vb" %>
<%@ OutputCache Duration="60" VaryByParam="name" %>
<html>
<head>
<title>Output Cache Demonstration</title>
<script runat="server" >
    Sub Page_Load(Sender As Object, e As EventArgs)
        lblMessage.Text = "Current time is: " & _
            DateTime.Now()
    End Sub
</script>
</head>
<body>
    <h1>Demonstration of Output Caching</h1>
    <form id="frmPostBack" runat="server">
        <asp:label id="lblMessage" runat="server"/>
    </form>
```

Example 3-7. Output caching in ASP.NET (continued)

```
</body>
</html>
```

As explained in the "Using @ Directives" section earlier in this chapter, you can also have ASP.NET cache multiple versions of a page on the basis of specific HTTP headers by using the `VaryByHeader` attribute, or you can cache multiple versions of a user control on the basis of some of its properties by using the `VaryByControl` attribute. Caching the output of a user control is essentially the same process as that shown in Example 3-7, except that you may not use the `VaryByHeader` attribute in a user control.

Additional Resources

The following sites provide more information on topics discussed in this chapter:

http://www.aspfriends.com/aspfriends/aspngcache.asp
> The home page for the AspFriends.com mailing list (for questions relating to output caching). This page is an excellent resource for caching questions, and members of the ASP.NET team have even been known to answer a question or two here.

http://www.gotdotnet.com/QuickStart/aspplus/
> The ASP.NET QuickStart samples, which can also be installed locally, provide a wide range of examples and sample code and explanations that can be very useful when starting out. The GotDotNet.com site also has sample code available from other users.

CHAPTER 4

Web Services

The primary purpose of ASP.NET web services is to provide access to application functionality through standard web protocols (including HTTP and XML), regardless of the application's location or the platform on which it is built. When your application exposes functionality as a web service, that functionality can be consumed by clients on any platform, presuming the clients understand XML and SOAP and can communicate via the HTTP protocol. More plainly, a web service is a function that is called over the Internet.

An ASP.NET web service can be very simple or it can provide complex functionality. It can return a variety of data types—from simple strings and integer values to complex data types such as classes and datasets. Web services are traditionally thought of as providing only business services (e.g., you call a method, perhaps passing in some parameters, and you receive a return value), but there's no reason why you can't create a web service that returns a chunk of HTML. Doing so would allow you to provide cross-platform access to functionality similar to that provided by ASP.NET Server Controls.

Standards

The ability of web services to fulfill their mission of providing cross-platform interoperability and application integration depends on a number of existing and emerging standards and specifications. The following list describes the most important standards, including their current standardization status. Note that the W3C term for a stable standard is *Recommendation.*

HTTP (Current version 1.1, Recommendation; http://www.w3.org/Protocols)
> HTTP is the standard protocol of the World Wide Web. HTTP is essential to web services because most organizations allow communication over TCP port 80 (the default HTTP port) to traverse their firewalls. This contrasts with protocols such as DCOM, which use ports that are routinely blocked—making them virtually useless for the Internet.

XML (Current version 1.0, Recommendation; http://www.w3.org/XML)

eXtensible Markup Language (XML) provides a standardized way of structuring and communicating data via a tag-based text syntax. Combined with the XML Schema standard, XML allows simple and complex data types to be serialized and deserialized to text for transmission over an HTTP connection.

SOAP (Current version 1.1, Submission; http://www.w3.org/2000/xp)

Simple Object Access Protocol (SOAP) is an emerging standard that specifies how to format RPC-style requests and responses using XML and communicating over HTTP. SOAP is essential to web services. See the sidebar "What is SOAP" in Chapter 2, for more information on the SOAP protocol status and its impact on developing web services.

WSDL (Current version 1.1, Submission; http://www.w3.org/TR/wsdl.html)

Web Services Description Language (WSDL) is a specification for creating XML schemas that describe a web service. This description is analogous to a COM type library in the sense that a WSDL file provides a contract of the publicly exposed members of a web service, just as a type library does for a COM object. By reading the WSDL contract for a web service, clients can learn what methods are exposed by the web service and how to call them.

UDDI (http://www.uddi.org)

Universal Description, Discovery, and Integration (UDDI) is an open platform-neutral framework being developed by Microsoft, IBM, and other vendors to address the need for a way to publish, locate, and integrate web services simply and robustly. Web service developers can register their web services with one of the UDDI directories, and potential clients can search the UDDI directory for web services appropriate to their needs.

SOAP, WSDL, and UDDI are not settled standards. Thus, incompatibilities between different implementations of SOAP and web services are possible if those implementations use different drafts of a given standard. A good example of this possibility is WSDL, which is a successor to an earlier draft specification called SDL. Because of incompatibilities between SDL and WSDL, communicating between a client using SDL and a web service using WSDL (or vice-versa) will probably require some tweaking to achieve interoperability. As specifications such as SOAP and WSDL work their way through the standards process (or in the case of vendor specifications, as they gain acceptance), instances of incompatibility should become rarer.

Web Services Architecture

In ASP.NET, a web service is essentially a listener that monitors a particular URL exposed via HTTP, looking for requests packaged as SOAP messages. When a request arrives, the ASP.NET runtime unpackages the request and calls the method for which the request is intended, passing in any parameters included with the request. If the request has a return value (which is not required), the ASP.NET runtime packages up the return value (based on the XML schema datatype specifications) and sends it to the client as a SOAP message. What this means to developers is that your application doesn't need to know anything about the client that will consume it, other than the fact that it can understand XML and SOAP.

Thus, developers can essentially write methods that will be called as web services just as though they were writing methods that would be called locally.

This functionality is provided by the runtime largely for free. Developers expose their functionality as web services by marking their methods with a specific metadata attribute, the `WebService` attribute. The Common Language Runtime (CLR) takes care of the rest—from packaging and unpackaging SOAP requests to automatically providing HTML documentation of the web service—if it is called from a web browser (rather than by a SOAP request).

Metadata Attributes

Metadata attributes are somewhat similar in concept to attributes on HTML tags or XML elements. Metadata attributes provide additional information about assemblies, classes, and class members to the CLR. Attributes tell the CLR to treat a particular member a certain way or to automatically provide certain functionality (such as the automatic packaging/unpackaging of SOAP requests for web services).

Figure 4-1 illustrates how an ASP.NET web service works.

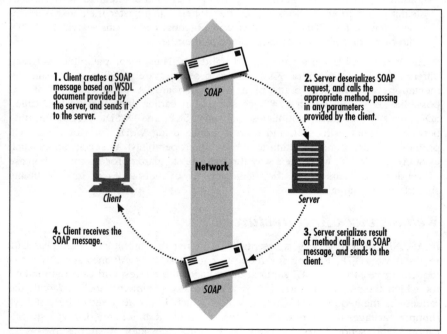

Figure 4-1. Inside an ASP.NET web service

In terms of file structure, web services in ASP.NET are implemented by *.asmx* pages. An *.asmx* page begins with the @ WebService directive, which contains attributes instructing the CLR how to run the web service. The *.asmx* page can either directly contain the code necessary for the web service to operate or can contain a Class attribute in its @ WebService directive that points to a compiled class containing the implementation code. In this latter case, the file containing the source code for the compiled class is called a code-behind file, as introduced in Chapter 3 and illustrated in Figure 4-2.

Figure 4-2. How code-behind works

Creating a Web Service

There are two different coding techniques with which one can construct a web service: inline code and code-behind.

Web Service with Inline Code

Creating a single-file web service is quite simple. All that's required is to create a new file, add an @ WebService directive and a class containing the implementation for the methods you want to expose, and decorate the methods to be exposed with the WebMethod attribute. The @ WebService directive supports the following attributes:

Class

Specifies the name of the class containing the implementation of the web service. This attribute is necessary to allow the ASP.NET runtime to locate the compiled class at runtime.

CodeBehind

Specifies the name of a code-behind file that contains the class that implements the web service. This attribute is used by Visual Studio .NET when building the project containing the code-behind class.

Debug

Specifies whether the web service should be compiled with debug symbols.

Language

Specifies the language used for code written inline in the *.asmx* file.

To demonstrate the creation of a web service, look at Example 4-1, which implements a simple "Quote of the Day" web service.

Example 4-1. Quote of the day application (Qotd.asmx)

```
<%@ WebService Language="VB" Class="Qotd" %>
Imports System
Imports System.Data
Imports System.Web
Imports System.Web.Services

Public Class Qotd

    <WebMethod()> _
    Public Function GetQotd() As String
        Dim QuoteDS As New DataSet()
        Dim Context As HttpContext = HttpContext.Current()
        Dim QuoteXML As String = Context.Server.MapPath("qotd.xml")
        Dim QuoteCount As Integer
        Dim QuoteToReturn As Integer
        Dim Randomizer As New Random()

        QuoteDS.ReadXml(QuoteXML)
        QuoteCount = QuoteDS.Tables(0).Rows.Count
        QuoteToReturn = Randomizer.Next(0, QuoteCount)
        Return QuoteDS.Tables(0).Rows(QuoteToReturn)(0) & _
            "<br /><br />" & QuoteDS.Tables(0).Rows(QuoteToReturn)(1)
    End Function

End Class
```

The WebService directive in Example 4-1 specifies Visual Basic .NET as the language used in the web service and specifies that the web service's implementation is contained in a class named Qotd. The next four lines import several namespaces to save the effort of typing in the namespace name each time a member is used in the code.

Next comes the class definition for the Qotd class. This class contains a single function, GetQotd, which returns a string containing a quote and the name of its author, separated by two HTML line breaks. Note that this definition assumes that the consumer of the web service will display the results as HTML. In a later example, we'll provide a more flexible implementation.

Within the method, you create an ADO.NET dataset (see Chapter 7 for more information on ADO.NET) and use the ReadXml method of the DataSet class to read in the stored quotes from a simple XML file. The contents of this file are shown in Example 4-2. Once the data is loaded into the dataset, you check the Count property to determine how many records exist and then use an instance of the Random

---

class to return a random number from 0 to the record count. This number is then used to retrieve the first and second values (which also happen to be the only values) of the desired row, as shown in the following snippet, and return it to the caller of the method:

```
Return QuoteDS.Tables(0).Rows(QuoteToReturn)(0) & _
    "<br /><br />" & QuoteDS.Tables(0).Rows(QuoteToReturn)(1)
```

Note that since collections in .NET are zero-based, Tables(0) refers to the first table in the Tables collection of the dataset (in this case, the only table). You can access the value of a particular field in a particular row in a specific table by using the following syntax:

```
MyVariable = MyDataset.Tables(tableindex).Rows(rowindex)(fieldindex)
```

Example 4-2. Qotd.xml

```
<Quotes>
  <Quote>
    <QuoteText>Never give in--never, never, never, never, in nothing great
or small, large or petty, never give in except to convictions of honour and
good sense. Never yield to force; never yield to the apparently overwhelming
might of the enemy.</QuoteText>
    <QuoteAuthor>Winston Churchill</QuoteAuthor>
  </Quote>
  <Quote>
    <QuoteText>We shall fight on the beaches. We shall fight on the landing
grounds. We shall fight in the fields, and in the streets, we shall fight in
the hills. We shall never surrender!</QuoteText>
    <QuoteAuthor>Winston Churchill</QuoteAuthor>
  </Quote>
  <Quote>
    <QuoteText>An appeaser is one who feeds a crocodile-hoping it will eat
him last.</QuoteText>
    <QuoteAuthor>Winston Churchill</QuoteAuthor>
  </Quote>
  <Quote>
    <QuoteText>We shape our buildings: thereafter they shape us.</
QuoteText>
    <QuoteAuthor>Winston Churchill</QuoteAuthor>
  </Quote>
  <Quote>
    <QuoteText>Science without religion is lame, religion without science
is blind.</QuoteText>
    <QuoteAuthor>Albert Einstein</QuoteAuthor>
  </Quote>
  <Quote>
    <QuoteText>As far as the laws of mathematics refer to reality, they are
not certain, and as far as they are certain, they do not refer to reality.</
QuoteText>
    <QuoteAuthor>Albert Einstein</QuoteAuthor>
  </Quote>
  <Quote>
    <QuoteText>If A equals success, then the formula is A equals X plus Y
plus Z. X is work. Y is play. Z is keep your mouth shut.</QuoteText>
```

Example 4-2. Qotd.xml (continued)

```
    <QuoteAuthor>Albert Einstein</QuoteAuthor>
  </Quote>
  <Quote>
    <QuoteText>When a man sits with a pretty girl for an hour, it seems
like a minute. But let him sit on a hot stove for a minute-and it's longer
than any hour. That's relativity.</QuoteText>
    <QuoteAuthor>Albert Einstein</QuoteAuthor>
  </Quote>
</Quotes>
```

Once you've added the code in Example 4-1 to a file, saved it with the *.asmx* extension, and created a file called *Qotd.xml* with the text in Example 4-2 in the same virtual directory, you can open the *.asmx* file in a browser to test the implementation. The result should be similar to Figure 4-3.

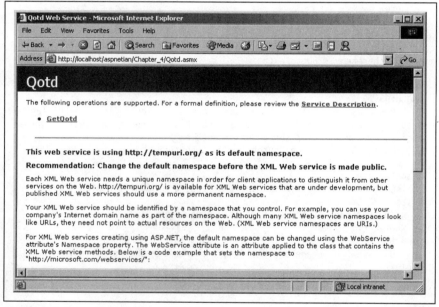

Figure 4-3. Browsing a web service

The main documentation page displayed in Figure 4-3 is generated automatically by the ASP.NET runtime whenever a web service (*.asmx* file) is called from a browser rather than by a SOAP request. You should note three things about the page in Figure 4-3:

- The link to the service description. Accessing this link displays the WSDL contract (see Figure 4-4), which describes the methods exposed by the web service (in much the same way as an IDL file describes a COM object). This contract is also used by .NET clients to generate proxy classes for consuming the web service. This topic is discussed in more detail later in the chapter.

- The link that provides access to a documentation page for the GetQotd method, which is shown in Figure 4-5. If the web service exposed multiple methods, the main documentation page would provide a link for each.

- The main documentation page also displays a recommendation about the default namespace for the web service. This recommendation refers to the XML namespace, which if not specified, defaults to *http://tempuri.org* and should not be confused with the .NET namespaces. A later example demonstrates how to set the default namespace to a unique URL.

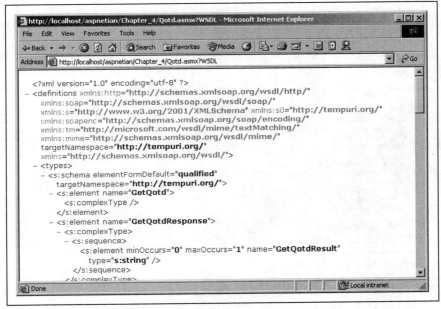

Figure 4-4. Service description for Qotd.asmx

As shown in Figure 4-5, the documentation page for the GetQotd method provides an Invoke button that allows you to test the web service method and that provides documentation on creating SOAP, HTTP GET, and HTTP POST requests for the selected method. In this case, HTTP GET and POST are not shown.

If you click the Invoke button, a new browser window should open, displaying XML text similar to the following snippet. (Note that the quotation and author may vary, since they are selected randomly.)

```
<?xml version="1.0" encoding="utf-8" ?>
<string xmlns="http://tempuri.org/">We shape our buildings: thereafter
    they shape us.<br><br>Winston Churchill</string>
```

Because the GetQotd method returns a string containing HTML formatting (the <br /> tags), it will automatically display the quote and author on separate lines if shown in a browser. But what if a consumer of the web service wants to apply a different format to the quote than the author?

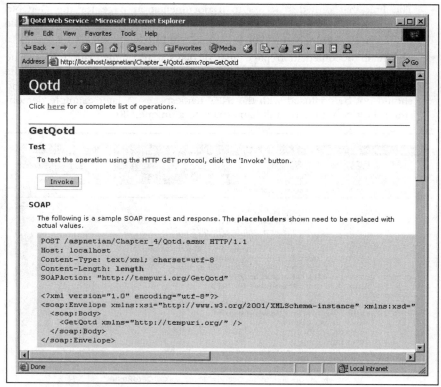

Figure 4-5. GetQotd documentation

With this implementation, they're out of luck, unless they are willing to parse out the two parts and apply the formatting individually that way. To address this issue, look at a modified version of the Qotd web service that uses a code-behind class for its implementation.

Web Service Using Code-Behind

The following snippet is all that's required for the *.asmx* file for our code-behind version of the Qotd web service (*Qotd_cb.asmx*):

```
<%@ WebService Language="VB" Class="aspnetian.Qotd_cb" %>
```

Note that instead of providing the class name, Qotd_cb, we've also added a namespace name, "aspnetian," to reduce the likelihood of naming conflicts. Example 4-3, which contains the code-behind class that implements the web service, defines this namespace.

Example 4-3. Qotd_cb.vb

```
Imports System
Imports System.Data
Imports System.Web
```

O'REILLY BOOK REGISTRATION

Register your book with O'Reilly by completing this card and receive a **FREE** copy of our latest catalog. Or register online at **register.oreilly.com** and, in addition to our catalog, we'll send you email notification of new editions of this book, information about new titles, and special offers available only to registered O'Reilly customers.

Which book(s) are you registering? Please include title and ISBN # (above bar code on back cover)

Title	ISBN #
Title	ISBN #
Title	ISBN #

Name _____ Company/Organization _____

Address _____

City _____ State _____ Zip/Postal Code _____ Country _____

Telephone _____ Email address _____

Have you previously purchased online from O'Reilly? ☐ Yes, my account number is _____ ☐ No

www.oreilly.com

Part #10326

BUSINESS REPLY MAIL

FIRST-CLASS MAIL   PERMIT NO. 80   SEBASTOPOL CA

POSTAGE WILL BE PAID BY ADDRESSEE

O'Reilly & Associates, Inc.
BOOK REGISTRATION
1005 GRAVENSTEIN HIGHWAY NORTH
SEBASTOPOL CA 95472-9910

Example 4-3. Qotd_cb.vb (continued)

```vb
Imports System.Web.Services

Namespace aspnetian

<WebService(Namespace:="http://www.aspnetian.com/webservices/")> _
Public Class Qotd_cb
   Inherits WebService

   <WebMethod()> _
   Public Function GetQotd() As String
      Dim QuoteDS As New DataSet()
      Dim QuoteXML As String = Server.MapPath("qotd.xml")
      Dim QuoteCount As Integer
      Dim QuoteNumber As Integer
      Dim Randomizer As New Random()

      QuoteDS.ReadXml(QuoteXML)
      QuoteCount = QuoteDS.Tables(0).Rows.Count
      QuoteNumber = Randomizer.Next(0, QuoteCount)
      Return QuoteDS.Tables(0).Rows(QuoteNumber)(0) & "<br /><br />" _
         & QuoteDS.Tables(0).Rows(QuoteNumber)(1)
   End Function

   <WebMethod()> _
   Public Function GetQuoteNumber() As Integer
      Dim QuoteDS As New DataSet()
      Dim QuoteXML As String = Server.MapPath("qotd.xml")
      Dim QuoteCount As Integer
      Dim Randomizer As New Random()

      QuoteDS.ReadXml(QuoteXML)
      QuoteCount = QuoteDS.Tables(0).Rows.Count
      Return Randomizer.Next(0, QuoteCount)
   End Function

   <WebMethod()> _
   Public Function GetQuote(QuoteNumber As Integer) As String
      Dim QuoteDS As New DataSet()
      Dim QuoteXML As String = Server.MapPath("qotd.xml")
      Dim QuoteCount As Integer
      Dim QuoteToReturn As String

      QuoteDS.ReadXml(QuoteXML)
      QuoteToReturn = QuoteDS.Tables(0).Rows(QuoteNumber)(0)
      Return QuoteToReturn
   End Function

   <WebMethod()> _
   Public Function GetAuthor(QuoteNumber As Integer) As String
      Dim QuoteDS As New DataSet()
      Dim QuoteXML As String = Server.MapPath("qotd.xml")
      Dim QuoteCount As Integer
```

Web Services

Example 4-3. Qotd_cb.vb (continued)

```
    Dim AuthorToReturn As String

    QuoteDS.ReadXml(QuoteXML)
    AuthorToReturn = QuoteDS.Tables(0).Rows(QuoteNumber)(1)
    Return AuthorToReturn
  End Function

End Class

End Namespace
```

In addition to wrapping the class declaration in a namespace declaration, this example adds a new attribute, WebService, and several new methods. The WebService attribute is added at the class level so we can specify the default namespace (XML namespace) for the web service. This namespace needs to be a value unique to your web service. In the example, the namespace is *http://www. aspnetian.com/webservices/*; for your own web services, you should use your own unique value. You may want to substitute a URL that you control, as doing so will assure you that web services created by others will not use the same value.

The added methods are GetQuoteNumber, GetQuote, and GetAuthor. These methods demonstrate that even though web service requests are sent as XML text, the input and output parameters of web service methods are still strongly typed. These methods address the potential formatting issue discussed previously by allowing clients to retrieve a quote and its author separately in order to accommodate different formatting for each. To ensure that the matching author for the quote is retrieved, the client would first call GetQuoteNumber to retrieve a randomly generated quote number, and then call GetQuote and/or GetAuthor, passing in the received quote number. This provides the client more flexibility, but does not require the web service to keep track of which quote number was sent to a given client.

An important difference between the single-file web service and the code-behind implementation is that for the code-behind version, you must compile the code-behind class into an assembly manually and place it in the *bin* directory before the web service will work. Note that this step is automatic when you build a web service project in Visual Studio .NET. If you're writing code by hand, this step can be accomplished by using a DOS batch file containing the commands shown in the following snippet:

```
vbc /t:library /r:System.Web.dll /r:System.dll /r:System.Web.Services.dll
/r:System.Xml.dll /r:System.Data.dll /out:bin\qotd_cb.dll qotd_cb.vb

pause
```

Note that all command-line options for the *vbc.exe* compiler should be part of a single command. The pause command allows you to see any warnings or errors generated during compilation before the command window is closed.

Inheriting from WebService

In Example 4-1, the Current property of the HttpContext class is used to get a reference to the Context object for the current request. Getting this reference is necessary to access to the Server intrinsic object so that we can call its MapPath method to get the local path to the XML file used to store the quotes. However, as you add more methods that use the XML file, you end up with redundant calls to HttpContext.Current.

For better readability and maintainability, you can eliminate these calls by having the web service class inherit from System.Web.Services.WebService. Inheriting from WebService automatically provides access to the Server, Session, and Application intrinsic objects, as well as to the HttpContext instance for the current request and the User object representing the authenticated user. In the case of Example 4-3, inheriting from WebService eliminates the calls to HttpContext. Current entirely.

Web services that inherit from the WebService class have access to the ASP.NET Session object. However, you should carefully consider whether your application will benefit from storing state information in the Session collection before using it—particularly if your application may need to scale to more than one web server. ASP.NET now provides out-of-process Session state options that can be used in web farm situations. Unfortunately, because these solutions require, at best, an out-of-process call (and at worst, a cross-machine call), using them results in a significant performance penalty. Regardless of your decision, you should always load-test your application to ensure that it will meet your performance and scalability needs.

Figure 4-6 shows the main documentation page for the code-behind version of the Qotd web service. Note that the main documentation page contains links for each new method exposed by the web service. Also note that the page no longer displays the namespace warning/recommendation, since we set the default namespace in this version.

You've written a web service and you tested it by opening the *.asmx* file in a browser and invoking the methods. What's next? Unless your web service will be consumed only by yourself or by someone with whom you have regular communication, you need to publish or advertise your web service in some way. Potential clients also need to locate your web service to use it.

Publishing a web service can be accomplished in either of two ways: through a discovery document or by registering the web service with a UDDI directory.

Discovery Documents

A discovery document is a file with the extension *.disco* that contains references to the WDSL contracts for web services you want to publish, references to documentation for your web services, and/or references to other discovery documents.

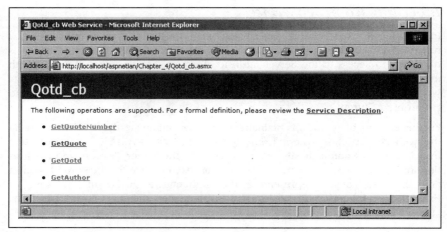

Figure 4-6. Browsing Qotd_cb.asmx

Publishing and Locating Web Services

You can publish a discovery document on your web server and provide clients with a link to or a URL for the discovery document. Clients can then use the *disco.exe* .NET command-line utility to generate WSDL contracts locally for creating proxy classes to communicate with the web service. Example 4-4 shows the format of a discovery document for the Qotd web service.

Example 4-4. Qotd.disco

```
<?xml version="1.0"?>
<discovery xmlns="http://schemas.xmlsoap.org/disco/">
    <contractRef
        ref="http://localhost/aspnetian/Chapter_4/Qotd.asmx?wsdl"
        docRef="http://localhost/aspnetian/Chapter_4/Qotd.asmx"
        xmlns="http://schemas.xmlsoap.org/disco/scl/" />
    <contractRef
        ref="http://localhost/aspnetian/Chapter_4/Qotd_cb.asmx?wsdl"
        docRef="http://localhost/aspnetian/Chapter_4/Qotd_cb.asmx"
        xmlns="http://schemas.xmlsoap.org/disco/scl/" />
</discovery>
```

Once clients know the location of the discovery file, they can use the *disco.exe* command-line utility to create local WSDL files for all of their web services, as shown in the following code snippet:

```
disco http://localhost/aspnetian/Chapter_4/Qotd.disco
```

This line creates local WSDL files for both the Qotd and Qotd_cb web services.

UDDI

The other method used for publishing and locating web services is UDDI. Still in the process of maturing, UDDI works on the principle of providing multiple replicated directories in which public web services are registered. The UDDI web site (*http://www.uddi.com*) contains a list of the participating directory sites from which clients or providers of web services can choose. Providers of web services give relevant information, such as the type of web service, an appropriate category (such as Construction or Financial and Insurance.), and most importantly, the URL for the application's WSDL file. Potential clients can search the UDDI directory for web services that match their needs and then locate and consume them via their WSDL contract.

Consuming a Web Service

In ASP.NET, consuming a web service is nearly as easy as creating one. ASP.NET provides a utility called *wsdl.exe* that can create a proxy class, which is a class that knows all of the necessary details of communicating with the web service via SOAP, as shown in Figure 4-1, and which can be called from a client application the same way as any other managed class, In this way, the proxy class abstracts away the complexities of communication with the web service.

Consuming a web service in ASP.NET requires four steps:

1. Locate the WSDL contract for the desired web service.

2. Create a proxy class by using the *wsdl.exe* command-line utility.

3. Compile the proxy class.

4. Create a new instance of the proxy class in the client application (WinForms, Console, or ASP.NET) and call the desired methods.

In the case of our Qotd_cb web service, you would execute the following command (again, conveniently saved as a DOS batch file) to generate a proxy class based on the web service:

```
wsdl /l:vb /out:Qotd_cb_proxy.vb http://localhost/ASPdotNET_iaN/Chapter_
4/Qotd_cb.asmx?WSDL

pause
```

The /l parameter specifies that the proxy class should be generated in Visual Basic .NET (the default is C#). The /out parameter specifies the name and, optionally, the path of the output file. This is important if you are compiling your proxy class in the same directory as the code-behind class that implements the web service. In this case, if you do not specify the output filename, the file *Qotd_cb.vb* will be overwritten. Once the proxy class has been generated, it should be compiled, and the resulting assembly should be placed in the *bin* directory. This can be accomplished using a command such as the one in the following snippet:

```
vbc /t:library /r:System.Web.dll,System.dll,System.Web.Services.dll,
System.Xml.dll,System.Data.dll /out:bin\qotd_cb_proxy.dll
qotd_cb_proxy.vb

pause
```

Remember that all parameters for the *vbc.exe* compiler should be part of the same command; therefore, there should not be any line breaks if you choose to save the command to a batch file.

Once you've generated and compiled your proxy class, using the web service is exactly like using any other .NET class. You simply create an instance and call the desired methods. Example 4-5 shows the code for a simple ASP.NET page that consumes the Qotd_cb web service.

Example 4-5. Qotd_cb.aspx

```
<%@ Page Language="VB" %>
<%@ Import Namespace="aspnetian" %>
<html>
<head>
<title>Quote of the Day Web service example</title>
<script runat="server">
    Sub Page_Load(Sender As Object , e As EventArgs )
        Dim Quote As New Qotd_cb( )
        Dim QuoteNumber As Integer
        QuoteNumber = Quote.GetQuoteNumber
        Message1.Text = Quote.GetQuote(QuoteNumber)
        Message2.Text = Quote.GetAuthor(QuoteNumber)
    End Sub
</script>
</head>
<body>
    <h1>Demonstration of Quote of the Day Web service</h1>
    <form runat="server">
        <h4><i>"<asp:Literal id="Message1" runat="server" />"</i></h4>
        <h3>--<asp:Literal id="Message2" runat="server" /></h3>
    </form>
</body>
</html>
```

The page imports the aspnetian namespace defined in the Qotd_cb web service class, creates an instance of the proxy class, and then calls the GetQuoteNumber method to retrieve a random quote number. The page then calls the GetQuote and GetAuthor methods, passing in the quote number each time, and returns the result to the Text property of two ASP.NET literal controls. The output of this page is shown in Figure 4-7.

Figure 4-7. Qotd_cb.aspx output

Additional Resources

The following sites provide additional information on the topics discussed in this chapter:

http://www.aspfriends.com/aspfriends/aspngwebservices.asp

The home page for the AspFriends.com mailing list (for questions relating to ASP.NET web services). This home page is an excellent resource for questions on web services, and a wide variety of web services experts answer questions, including well-known authors.

http://www.gotdotnet.com/QuickStart/aspplus/

The ASP.NET QuickStart samples, which can also be installed locally, provide a wide range of examples and sample code and explanations that can be very useful when starting out. The GotDotNet.com site has sample code available from other users and many other features.

http://www.learnXmlws.com/

Run by noted web services expert Yasser Shohoud, this site contains articles, live web services, and code examples intended to teach you how to develop web services of your own.

CHAPTER 5

ASP.NET Server Controls

Controls provide the familiar elements of a graphical user interface (GUI): buttons, drop-down boxes, checkboxes, etc. Server controls are controls that allow server-side processing. They provide a range of functionality—from simple data entry to complex data validation.

ASP.NET ships with a suite of server controls you can use to develop powerful Web Forms pages. A key component of the ASP.NET development model, these server controls abstract significant amounts of programming logic into simple-to-use tags. Server controls make it easy to separate programmatic logic from UI elements using code-behind. In ASP.NET, it's easy for developers to create their own controls from scratch or to build on the functionality of existing controls by creating user controls that combine HTML, server controls and other page elements, or by creating their own custom server controls. We'll discuss both techniques in Chapter 6.

ASP.NET Server Controls are classified as either *HTML controls* or *web controls*. The current chapter summarizes the standard controls and the various methods for creating and modifying them.

HTML Controls

The HTML controls have a one-to-one mapping with HTML tags. You can create HTML controls and change their appearance by modifying their properties. HTML controls have an object model that closely resembles the HTML syntax of the elements, as well as the Dynamic HTML (DHTML) object model.

The attributes of an HTML tag correspond to the properties of the HTML control. The HTML controls are declared by using the standard HTML tags with the attribute runat="server". For example:

```
<input type="text" id="txtName" runat="server">
```

The id attribute is very important for all server controls if you plan to access your control programmatically, since it defines the name by which the object will be referenced in code.

In ASP.NET, the following HTML tags are supported as HTML controls:

```
<a>
<img>
<form>
<table>
<tr>
<th>
<td>
<select>
<textarea>
<button>
All <input> tags
```

You can declare other HTML tags as server-side controls by using the runat="server" attribute/value pair. However, these controls are not supported; instead, unsupported HTML elements are handled by a generic super HTML server control called HtmlGenericControl. The HTML elements you might typically handle in this way include <div>, <span>, <body>, and <font>.

Web Controls

One of the challenges in developing web applications is to provide support for different browsers that have different capabilities, proprietary extensions to HTML, and support for different scripting languages. The only way to render content consistently is to detect the browser type and send the appropriate version of the page to that browser. ASP.NET web controls relieve us of this burden by sniffing the browser type and sending the appropriate content based on the capabilities of the browser. ASP.NET Server Controls use HTML 3.2 for the downlevel clients (older browsers that do not support DHTML and CSS) and can generate Dynamic HTML for the uplevel clients (such as Internet Explorer 5.5 or later). In the current release of ASP.NET, the only controls that make extensive use of DHTML in uplevel browsers are the validation controls (which are discussed in more detail in the "Validation Controls" section later in this chapter). Other controls, such as the Button server control, use client-side JavaScript for initiating postbacks. These postback scripts are designed to work with any Javascript-compatible browser.

Web controls provide an abstract, consistent, and strongly typed object model. They are abstract because their object model does not necessarily reflect HTML syntax. These controls include standard controls like text boxes and radio buttons, as well as rich controls like calendars and data grids. Web controls are always declared with the ASP namespace prefix, sometimes using self-closing tags as follows:

```
<asp:textbox id="txtName" text="Hello, World!" runat="server" />
```

You can alternatively declare a web control by using an opening and closing tag pair. For certain controls, such as the Label and TextBox controls, any text contained between the opening and closing tags will be assigned to the Text property of the control. Thus, the following code fragment is equivalent to the previous one:

```
<asp:textbox id="txtName" runat="server">
    Hello, World!
</asp:textbox>
```

 Like element and attribute names in page declarations, the tag and attribute names used to create server controls declaratively are not case-sensitive. However, because the HTML 4.0 standard specifies that tags and attributes should be in lowercase, it's good coding practice to follow this guideline, even though server control tags are not sent to the browser.

When creating controls programmatically (as discussed later in this chapter), if the language you're using is case-sensitive (such as C#), you'll need to use the correct case when creating controls (e.g., Text-Box versus textbox).

The attributes of web controls declared using the ASP. NET syntax become the properties of the control, and you can access them programmatically. Unlike the HTML controls, the object model of the web controls does not necessarily reflect HTML syntax. The main reason for this behavior is that, depending on the attributes applied to a Web control, it may render one of many HTML elements to the browser. For example, `<asp:textbox>` can render `<input type="text">`, `<input type="password">`, or `<textarea>`, based on the value of the TextBoxMode attribute supplied by the developer at design time.

Using Controls

Server controls have two distinct techniques for using a control in a Web Forms page that can be both useful and confusing: declarative and programmatic techniques. Each has its own purpose, and in some situations (such as when using code-behind), both techniques must be used.

Typically, when you write your pages without code-behind files, you use the declarative technique for using controls in your page. If you need to access those controls programmatically, you would do so by referring to the value of the control's id attribute. For example, if you have an ASP.NET Label control declared as follows:

```
<asp:label id="Message" runat="server"/>
```

you would refer to this control in server-side code as follows:

```
<script runat="server">
    Sub Page_Load()
        Message.Text = "Hello, World!"
    End Sub
</script>
```

If you use code-behind with your pages, or if you wish to create a control dynamically at runtime, you may wish to declare and use a control programmatically, as shown here:

```
Dim Message As New Label()
Message.Text = "Hello, World!"
Page.Controls.Add(Message)
```

Declarative Control Use

Declarative control use is the simpler of the two techniques. Declarative control use utilizes HTML-like tags to declare a server control instance and uses attributes to set control properties. The location of the output of the server control is determined by where in the page the tag is located. This technique also allows HTML visual designers to move tags around, if necessary, without impacting the programmatic logic of the page, which would be contained in either a server-side <script> block or in a code-behind class.

Because this technique is so similar to writing plain vanilla HTML (albeit with different tags), it's frequently used by those familiar with classic ASP programming, once they start using server controls. Example 5-1 shows this technique in action, performing an action that in classic ASP would normally be accomplished using Response.Write. The example uses a Literal control which, unlike using Response.Write from a <script> block, allows more precise control of where the rendered output will appear. Instead of writing output to the browser with Response.Write, the code in the Page_Load event handling procedure sets the Text property of the control to the desired output. When the page is rendered, this output is then sent to the browser.

Example 5-1. SimpleWrite.aspx

```
<%@ Page Language="vb" %>
<html>
<head>
    <title>Declarative Control Example</title>
    <script runat="server">
        Sub Page_Load()
            'Instead of using Response.Write, we set
            '   the Text property of a literal control.
            '   The placement of the literal control
            '   determines where output appears
            Message.Text = "This text set from Page_Load!"
        End Sub
    </script>
</head>
<body>
    <form runat="server">
        <asp:literal id="Message" runat="server"/>
    </form>
</body>
</html>
```

In addition to the precise control of output, another advantage of this technique is better control over the appearance of the rendered output. Developers can use CSS Styles or templates to modify the appearance of the control, as described later in this chapter in the section "Modifying Control Appearance."

Programmatic Control Use

While the declarative technique for control creation is generally simpler and more straightforward, at times you may want or need to create controls dynamically (e.g., in response to some user action). In such cases, developers can create controls programmatically—either in a server-side <script> block within the Web Forms page or in its accompanying code-behind class. You can use either HTML server controls or web controls with this technique.

You define controls programmatically by declaring a variable of the control's type, as shown in the following code snippet (Example 5-2 shows a complete page using this technique):

```
' Visual Basic .NET
Dim myText As New TextBox()

// C#
TextBox myText = new TextBox();
```

The New keyword (new in C#) creates a new instance of the desired control. Note that some controls will accept arguments passed into the constructor for the control. A Literal control, for example, can accept the desired text for the control as an argument passed to the control's constructor, as shown in the following code snippet:

```
Dim Hello As New Literal("Hello, World!")
```

Once the desired control instance has been created, the control must then be added to the Controls collection of either the page itself or of a container control on the page that will be rendered (allowing its child controls to be rendered as well). The following snippet shows adding a control named Hello to the Controls collection exposed by the Page object:

```
Page.Controls.Add(Hello)          ' VB
```

or:

```
Page.Controls.Add(Hello);         // C#
```

It's important to understand that the previous code snippet will add the control named Hello at the end of the Controls collection. This means that the output of the control can actually appear after any static HTML tags because, unless the page contains <% %> render blocks, ASP.NET treats static HTML in the page as Literal controls at runtime. To place a control at a specific point in the page's (or another control's) Controls collection, use the AddAt method instead of Add:

```
Page.Controls.AddAt(3, Hello)
```

The first argument to the AddAt method is the position (starting from 0) at which you'd like to add the control, while the second is a variable representing the control itself.

To better understand how ASP.NET renders static HTML, <% %> render blocks, and server controls, turn on tracing for a page (as discussed in Chapter 10) and look at the control tree generated for pages with various combinations of static HTML, server controls, and render blocks. You will find that for pages containing just static HTML, ASP.NET creates a single LiteralControl to represent this HTML on the server. When you add server controls, any static HTML before, after, or between server controls will be represented on the server as a separate LiteralControl. If you add <% %> render blocks, however, controls will not be created on the server for *any* static HTML. This means that if you wish to manipulate the HTML content of the page on the server, you should avoid using render blocks.

Using the AddAt method, however, may not always allow you to place your control as precisely as you might like. A more precise technique for positioning dynamically created controls on the page is to add a Placeholder control to the page using the declarative technique and then add the dynamically created control(s) to its Controls collection. Because the Placeholder control has no UI of its own, if no controls are added to its Controls collection, nothing is rendered to the browser.

Adding controls dynamically in the middle of a control collection can have unpredictable results when used with pages that post back to the server and maintain their state in ViewState (the default). On postback, the ViewState for controls declared in the Web Forms page is loaded before that of any dynamically created controls. If a control is added to the middle of a control collection, then the page is posted back; you may get errors because the dynamic control for which the ViewState was saved does not exist at the time that ViewState is repopulated.

Example 5-2 shows the use of this technique to create the same output as Example 5-1.

Example 5-2. ProgControl.aspx

```
<%@ Page Language="vb" %>
<html>
<head>
   <title>Programmatic Control Example</title>
   <script runat="server">
      Sub Page_Load()
         'The placement of the Placeholder control
         '   determines where output appears
         Dim Message As New Literal()
         Message.Text = "This text set from Page_Load!"
```

Example 5-2. ProgControl.aspx (continued)

```
            PH.Controls.Add(Message)
        End Sub
    </script>
</head>
<body>
    <form runat="server">
        <asp:placeholder id="PH" runat="server"/>
    </form>
</body>
</html>
```

Finally, if you wish to create controls declaratively in your Web Forms page and manipulate those controls from within a code-behind class, you must programmatically create instances of your controls in the code-behind class with IDs that match those declared in the Web Forms page. Example 5-3 shows a Web Forms page that specifies a code-behind page containing its programmatic logic.

Example 5-3. ProgControl_cb.aspx

```
<%@ Page Language="c#" src="ProgControl_cb.cs" Inherits="aspnetian.
ProgControl" %>
<html>
<head>
    <title>Programmatic Control Example using Code-behind</title>
</head>
<body>
    <form runat="server">
        <asp:placeholder id="PH" runat="server"/>
    </form>
</body>
</html>
```

Example 5-4 shows the code-behind class (written in C#) for the web page in Example 5-3. It creates the control dynamically and adds it to the Controls collection of the PH Placeholder control. Note that the code-behind class declares an instance of the Placeholder class and gives it the same name (ID) as the control declared in the Web Forms page. This allows the code in the code-behind page to manipulate the control at runtime. Also note that this control instance is declared as a protected member, which means that only code within the code-behind class (or classes that inherit from it, including the Web Forms page in Example 5-3) can access it.

Example 5-4. ProgControl_cb.cs

```
using System;
using System.Web;
using System.Web.UI;
using System.Web.UI.WebControls;

namespace aspnetian
{
    public class ProgControl:Page
    {
```

Example 5-4. ProgControl_cb.cs (continued)

```
    protected PlaceHolder PH = new PlaceHolder( );

    void Page_Load( )
    {
        // The placement of the Placeholder control
        //    determines where output appears
        Literal Message = new Literal( );
        Message.Text = "This text set from Page_Load!";
        PH.Controls.Add(Message);
    }
  }
}
```

Types of Web Controls

Web controls fall into five categories: display, input, selection, validation, and special purpose.

Input Controls

Input controls let the user enter data into the application. ASP.NET supports only one input web control: the TextBox. The TextBox behaves like a single-line or multiline edit control, depending on the value of its TextMode property. Its simplified syntax is:

```
<asp:textbox id="SingleText"
    text="Single Line TextBox"
    runat="server" />

<asp:textbox id="PasswordText"
    text="Password"
    textmode="Password"
    runat="server" />

<asp:textbox id="MultiText"
    text="Multiline TextBox"
    textmode="Multiline"
    runat="server" />
```

The TextBox control can then be accessed programmatically with a code fragment like:

```
SingleText.Text = "Hello ASP.NET"
PasswordText.Attributes("Value") = "New Password"
MultiText.Text = "Multiline TextBox can hold many lines of text"
```

Note that the text of a TextBox control using the Password text mode cannot be set directly.

The appearance of input controls when rendered to the browser is shown in Figure 5-1. The code used to generate this figure is shown in Example 5-5.

Figure 5-1. Rendering of input controls

Example 5-5. InputControls.aspx

```
<%@ Page Language="vb" %>
<html>
<head>
    <title>Input Control Example</title>
    <script runat="server">
        Sub Page_Load()
            SingleText.Text = "Hello ASP.NET"
            PasswordText.Attributes("Value") = "New Password"
            MultiText.Text = "Multiline TextBox can hold many lines of text"
        End Sub
    </script>
</head>
<body>
    <h1>Input Control Example</h1>
    <form runat="server">
        <table border="1" cellpadding="5" cellspacing="0">
            <tr>
                <td>
                    Single Line TextBox:
                </td>
                <td>
                    <asp:textbox id="SingleText"
                        text="Single Line TextBox"
                        runat="server" />
                </td>
            </tr>
            <tr>
                <td>
```

Example 5-5. InputControls.aspx (continued)

```
                Password TextBox:
            </td>
            <td>
                <asp:textbox id="PasswordText"
                    text="Password"
                    textmode="Password"
                    runat="server" />
            </td>
        </tr>
        <tr>
            <td>
                Multiline TextBox:
            </td>
            <td>
                <asp:textbox id="MultiText"
                    text="Multiline TextBox"
                    textmode="Multiline"
                    runat="server" />
            </td>
        </tr>
    </table>
  </form>
</body>
</html>
```

Display Controls

Web display controls simply represent static text or images. Table 5-1 lists the display controls ASP.NET supports.

Table 5-1. Display controls

Control	Purpose
Image	Displays the image specified in the control's ImageUrl property.
Label	Displays the text specified in the control's Text property.
Panel	Groups a set of controls (like a Frame control in Windows).
Table	Displays a table of information. This control has two collections: TableRows, which contains the rows; and TableCells, which contains the columns in a row.
TableCell	Represents a cell in a row of a Table control.
TableRow	Represents a row inside a Table control.

The syntax of these web controls is as follows:

```
<asp:label id="MyLabel"
    text="This is a Label Control"
    borderstyle="solid"
    bordercolor="Green"
    runat="Server" />

<asp:image id="MyImage"
    imageurl="aspnet.gif"
    runat="Server" />
```

```
<asp:panel id="MyPanel"
    backcolor="lightblue"
    bordercolor="Green"
    borderwidth="1" >
    <asp:label id="MyLabel2"
        text="Static Text within the Panel"
        runat="Server"/>
    <br>
    <asp:textbox id="PanelTB" text="TextBox inside Panel" runat="Server"/>
</asp:Panel>
```

They can then be accessed programmatically with a code fragment like the following:

```
MyLabel.Text = "New Label"
MyImage.ImageUrl = "NewImage.gif"
MyPanel.BackImageUrl = "NewImage.gif"
```

The appearance of display controls when rendered to the browser is shown in Figure 5-2. The code used to generate this figure is shown in Example 5-6.

Figure 5-2. Rendering of display controls

Example 5-6. DisplayControls.aspx

```
<%@ Page Language="vb" %>
<html>
<head>
    <title>Display Control Example</title>
    <script runat="server">
        Sub Page_Load()
            MyLabel.Text = "New Label"
            MyImage.ImageUrl = "aspnetian.jpg"
        End Sub
    </script>
</head>
<body>
    <h1>Display Control Example</h1>
    <form runat="server">
        <asp:table id="MyTable"
            border="1"
            cellpadding="5"
            cellspacing="0"
            runat="server">
            <asp:tablerow runat="server">
                <asp:tablecell colspan="2" runat="server">
                    Table Control
                </asp:tablecell>
            </asp:tablerow>
            <asp:tablerow runat="server">
                <asp:tablecell runat="server">
                    Label Control:
                </asp:tablecell>
                <asp:tablecell runat="server">
                    <asp:label id="MyLabel"
                        text="This is a Label Control"
                        borderstyle="solid"
                        bordercolor="Green"
                        runat="Server" />
                </asp:tablecell>
            </asp:tablerow>
            <asp:tablerow runat="server">
                <asp:tablecell runat="server">
                    Image Control:
                </asp:tablecell>
                <asp:tablecell runat="server">
                    <asp:image id="MyImage"
                        imageurl="image.jpg"
                        runat="Server" />
                </asp:tablecell>
            </asp:tablerow>
            <asp:tablerow runat="server">
                <asp:tablecell runat="server">
                    Panel Control:
                </asp:tablecell>
                <asp:tablecell runat="server">
                    <asp:panel id="MyPanel"
```

Example 5-6. DisplayControls.aspx (continued)

```
                    backcolor="lightblue"
                    bordercolor="Green"
                    borderwidth="1"
                    runat="server">
                <asp:label id="MyLabel2"
                    text="Static Text within the Panel"
                    runat="Server"/>
                <br>
                <asp:textbox id="PanelTB"
                    text="TextBox inside Panel" runat="Server"/>
            </asp:panel>
        </asp:tablecell>
      </asp:tablerow>
    </asp:table>
  </form>
</body>
</html>
```

Action Controls

Action controls allow users to perform some action on that page, such as navigating to a different URL, submitting a form, resetting a form's values, or executing a client script. Table 5-2 lists the action controls.

Table 5-2. Action controls

Control	Purpose
Button	Displays a command button that posts a form to the server when clicked.
ImageButton	Displays an image that posts a form to the server when clicked.
LinkButton	Displays a hyperlink text that posts a form to the server when clicked.
Hyperlink	Displays a hyperlink text that navigates from one page to another when clicked.

The simplified syntax of these controls is as follows:

```
<asp:button id="MyButton" text="Click Me!!" runat="server"/>

<asp:imagebutton id="MyImageButton"
    imageurl="aspnetian.jpg" runat="Server"/>

<asp:linkbutton id="MyLinkButton" text="Click Me" runat="server"/>

<asp:hyperlink id="MyHyperLink"
    text="Click Me"
    navigateurl="ActionControls.aspx"
    target="_blank"
    runat="server"/>
```

The controls can then be accessed programmatically with code fragments like the following:

```
MyButton.CommandName = "Sort"
MyImageButton.CommandArgument = "Ascending".
```

```
MyLinkButton.CommandName = "Filter"
MyHyperLink.NavigateUrl = "http://dotnet.oreilly.com/"
```

The appearance of action controls when rendered to the browser is shown in Figure 5-3. The code used to generate this figure is shown in Example 5-7.

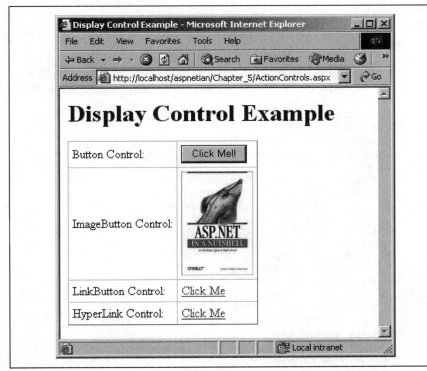

Figure 5-3. Rendering of action controls

Example 5-7. ActionControls.aspx

```
<%@ Page Language="vb" %>
<html>
<head>
    <title>Display Control Example</title>
    <script runat="server">
        Sub Page_Load()
            MyButton.CommandName = "Sort"
            MyImageButton.CommandArgument = "Ascending"
            MyLinkButton.CommandName = "Filter"
            MyHyperLink.NavigateUrl = " http://dotnet.oreilly.com/"
        End Sub
    </script>
</head>
<body>
    <h1>Display Control Example</h1>
    <form runat="server">
```

Example 5-7. ActionControls.aspx (continued)

```
        <asp:table id="MyTable"
          border="1"
          cellpadding="5"
          cellspacing="0"
          runat="server">
          <asp:tablerow runat="server">
            <asp:tablecell runat="server">
              Button Control:
            </asp:tablecell>
            <asp:tablecell runat="server">
              <asp:button id="MyButton" text="Click Me!!" runat="server"/>
            </asp:tablecell>
          </asp:tablerow>
          <asp:tablerow runat="server">
            <asp:tablecell runat="server">
              ImageButton Control:
            </asp:tablecell>
            <asp:tablecell runat="server">
              <asp:imagebutton id="MyImageButton"
                imageurl="aspnetian.jpg" runat="Server"/>
            </asp:tablecell>
          </asp:tablerow>
          <asp:tablerow runat="server">
            <asp:tablecell runat="server">
              LinkButton Control:
            </asp:tablecell>
            <asp:tablecell runat="server">
              <asp:linkbutton id="MyLinkButton"
                text="Click Me" runat="server"/>
            </asp:tablecell>
          </asp:tablerow>
          <asp:tablerow runat="server">
            <asp:tablecell runat="server">
              HyperLink Control:
            </asp:tablecell>
            <asp:tablecell runat="server">
              <asp:hyperlink id="MyHyperLink"
                text="Click Me"
                navigateurl="ActionControls.aspx"
                target="_blank"
                runat="server"/>
            </asp:tablecell>
          </asp:tablerow>
        </asp:table>
      </form>
  </body>
</html>
```

Selection Controls

Selection controls allow the user to select one or more values from a list. They include both the CheckBox and RadioButton controls, which are designed to work in a group. The RadioButton control allows you to select only one option out of the group, whereas the CheckBox control allows you to select zero or more options. Table 5-3 lists the selection controls.

Table 5-3. Selection controls

Control	Purpose
CheckBox	Selects or unselects an option. You can toggle the selection.
RadioButton	Selects only one option out of a group. You can unselect an option only by selecting another RadioButton control in the group.
ListBox	Allows the user to select one or more options from a list represented by ListItem controls. This control always occupies a fixed space in the form.
DropDownList	Allows the user to select only one option out of a list represented by ListItem controls. This control is used where the space in the form is limited.
RadioButtonList	Presents a list of radio buttons represented by ListItem controls and allows selection of only one option.
CheckBoxList	Presents a list of checkboxes represented by ListItem controls and allows you to select zero or more of the options.

The simplified syntax of the selection controls is:

```
<asp:checkbox id="MyCheckBox1"
    text="Vanilla" runat="server"/>

<asp:checkbox id="MyCheckBox2"
    text="Chocolate" runat="server"/>

<asp:radiobutton id="MyRadioButton1" groupname="Group1"
    checked="True" text="Yes" runat="Server"/>

<asp:radiobutton id="MyRadioButton2" groupname="Group1"
    text="No" runat="Server"/>

<asp:listbox id="MyListBox" runat="server">
    <asp:listitem value="Vanilla" selected="true">Vanilla</asp:listitem>
    <asp:listitem value="Chocolate">Chocolate</asp:listitem>
    <asp:listitem value="Strawberry">Strawberry</asp:listitem>
</asp:listbox>

<asp:dropdownlist id="MyDropDownList" runat="server">
    <asp:listitem value="Single" selected="true">Single</asp:listitem>
    <asp:listitem value="Multiline">Multiline</asp:listitem>
    <asp:listitem value="Password">Password</asp:listitem>
</asp:dropdownlist>

<asp:checkboxlist id="MyCheckBoxList"
    repeatdirection="vertical" runat="server">
    <asp:listitem value="Vanilla" text="Vanilla"/>
    <asp:listitem value="Chocolate" text="Chocolate"/>
    <asp:listitem value="Strawberry" text="Strawberry"/>
</asp:checkboxlist>

<asp:radiobuttonlist id="MyRadioButtonList"
    repeatdirection="Horizontal" runat="server">
```

Server
Controls

```
            <asp:listitem value="Female" text="Female" selected="true"/>
            <asp:listitem value="Male" text="Male"/>
        </asp:radiobuttonlist>
```

The controls can then be referenced programmatically with code fragments like the following:

```
MyCheckBox1.Checked = True
MyRadioButton1.Checked = False
MyListBox.SelectionMode = ListSelectionMode.Multiple
MyDropDownList.SelectedIndex = 1
MyCheckBoxList.RepeatDirection = RepeatDirection.Horizontal
MyRadioButtonList.RepeatLayout = RepeatLayout.Table
```

The appearance of the selection controls when rendered to the browser is shown in Figure 5-4. The code used to generate this figure is shown in Example 5-8.

Figure 5-4. Rendering of selection controls

Example 5-8. SelectionControls.aspx

```
<%@ Page Language="vb" %>
<html>
<head>
   <title>Selection Control Example</title>
   <script runat="server">
      Sub Page_Load()
         MyCheckBox1.Checked = True
         MyRadioButton1.Checked = False
         MyListBox.SelectionMode = ListSelectionMode.Multiple
         MyDropDownList.SelectedIndex = 1
         MyCheckBoxList.RepeatDirection = RepeatDirection.Horizontal
         MyRadioButtonList.RepeatLayout = RepeatLayout.Table
      End Sub
   </script>
</head>
<body>
   <h1>Selection Control Example</h1>
   <form runat="server">
      <asp:table id="MyTable"
         border="1"
         cellpadding="5"
         cellspacing="0"
         runat="server">
         <asp:tablerow runat="server">
            <asp:tablecell runat="server">
               CheckBox Control:
            </asp:tablecell>
            <asp:tablecell runat="server">
               <asp:checkbox id="MyCheckBox1"
                  text="Vanilla" runat="server" />
               <asp:checkbox id="MyCheckBox2"
                  text="Chocolate" runat="server" />
            </asp:tablecell>
         </asp:tablerow>
         <asp:tablerow runat="server">
            <asp:tablecell runat="server">
               RadioButton Control:
            </asp:tablecell>
            <asp:tablecell runat="server">
               <asp:radiobutton id="MyRadioButton1" groupname="Group1"
                  checked="True" text="Yes" runat="Server"/>
               <asp:radiobutton id="MyRadioButton2" groupname="Group1"
                  text="No" runat="Server"/>
            </asp:tablecell>
         </asp:tablerow>
         <asp:tablerow runat="server">
            <asp:tablecell runat="server">
               ListBox Control:
            </asp:tablecell>
            <asp:tablecell runat="server">
               <asp:listbox id="MyListBox" runat="server">
                  <asp:listitem value="Vanilla"
```

Example 5-8. SelectionControls.aspx (continued)

```
                  selected="true">Vanilla</asp:listitem>
                <asp:listitem value="Chocolate">Chocolate</asp:listitem>
                <asp:listitem value="Strawberry">Strawberry</asp:listitem>
              </asp:listbox>
            </asp:tablecell>
          </asp:tablerow>
          <asp:tablerow runat="server">
            <asp:tablecell runat="server">
              DropDownList Control:
            </asp:tablecell>
            <asp:tablecell runat="server">
              <asp:dropdownlist id="MyDropDownList" runat="server">
                <asp:listitem value="Single"
                  selected="true">Single</asp:listitem>
                <asp:listitem value="Multiline">Multiline</asp:listitem>
                <asp:listitem value="Password">Password</asp:listitem>
              </asp:dropdownlist>
            </asp:tablecell>
          </asp:tablerow>
          <asp:tablerow runat="server">
            <asp:tablecell runat="server">
              CheckBoxList Control:
            </asp:tablecell>
            <asp:tablecell runat="server">
              <asp:checkboxlist id="MyCheckBoxList"
                repeatdirection="vertical" runat="server">
                <asp:listitem value="Vanilla" text="Vanilla"/>
                <asp:listitem value="Chocolate" text="Chocolate"/>
                <asp:listitem value="Strawberry" text="Strawberry"/>
              </asp:checkboxlist>
            </asp:tablecell>
          </asp:tablerow>
          <asp:tablerow runat="server">
            <asp:tablecell runat="server">
              RadioButtonList Control:
            </asp:tablecell>
            <asp:tablecell runat="server">
              <asp:radiobuttonlist id="MyRadioButtonList"
                repeatdirection="Horizontal" runat="server">
                <asp:listitem value="Female"
                  text="Female" selected="true"/>
                <asp:listitem value="Male" text="Male"/>
              </asp:radiobuttonlist>
            </asp:tablecell>
          </asp:tablerow>
        </asp:table>
      </form>
  </body>
</html>
```

List Controls

List controls render repetitive data and use templates for the customized rendering of data (the so-called *lookless UI*). For example, you can define separate templates for the header, body, and footer of a table of data.

The list controls are also the most common controls used with data binding. We'll discuss data binding in more detail in Chapter 7. Table 5-4 shows the list controls.

Table 5-4. List controls and their purpose

Control	Purpose
DataGrid	In addition to displaying tabular data, this control can function as an Editable Grid that supports selecting, editing, sorting, and paging of data.
DataList	Displays a list of items that the user can select and edit.
Repeater	Displays a repeating list of data items. Their control and layout can be specified using templates.

Remember that DataGrid and DataList controls can be used with or without templates, but Repeater controls must have at least one ItemTemplate. You can also modify the appearance of DataGrids and DataLists by using a series of style properties, each of which ends with Style. These properties include HeaderStyle, ItemStyle, and FooterStyle. For more information on templates and styles, see the section "Modifying Control Appearance" later in this chapter.

The simplified syntax of the list controls is:

```
<asp:datagrid id="MyDataGrid"
    allowpaging="true"
    allowsorting="true"
    alternatingitemstyle-backcolor="LightSkyBlue"
    backcolor="Blue"
    forecolor="White"
    cellpadding="2"
    cellspacing="0"
    headerstyle-backcolor="DarkBlue"
    headerstyle-forecolor="Yellow"
    pagerstyle-mode="NumericPages"
    pagesize="5"
    runat="server"/>

<asp:datalist id="MyDataList"
    alternatingitemstyle-backcolor="LightSkyBlue"
    backcolor="Blue"
    bordercolor="Black"
    cellpadding="2"
    cellspacing="0"
    forecolor="White"
    headerstyle-backcolor="DarkBlue"
    headerstyle-forecolor="Yellow"
    repeatcolumns="1"
    repeatdirection="vertical"
    repeatlayout="table"
```

```
        runat="server">
        <template name="headertemplate">
            Composers
        </template>
        <template name="itemtemplate">
            <%# databinder.eval(container.dataitem, "name") %>
        </template>
    </asp:datalist>

    <asp:repeater id="MyRepeater" runat="server">
        <template name="headertemplate">
            <table cellpadding="5" cellspacing="0">
                <tr>
                    <td>Name<hr/></td>
                    <td>City<hr/></td>
                </tr>
        </template>
        <template name="itemtemplate">
            <tr>
                <td><%# DataBinder.Eval(Container.DataItem, "name") %></td>
                <td><%# DataBinder.Eval(Container.DataItem, "city") %></td>
            </tr>
        </template>
        <template name="footertemplate">
            </table>
        </template>
    </asp:repeater>
```

The controls can then be referenced programmatically with code fragments like the following:

```
MyDataGrid.DataSource = CreateData()
MyDataGrid.DataBind()
MyDataList.DataSource = CreateData()
MyDataList.DataBind()
MyRepeater.DataSource = CreateData()
MyRepeater.DataBind()
```

The appearance of list controls when rendered to the browser is shown in Figure 5-5. The code used to generate this figure is shown in Example 5-9.

Figure 5-5. Rendering of list controls

Example 5-9. ListControls.aspx

```
<%@ Page Language="vb" %>
<%@ Import Namespace="System.Data" %>
<html>
<head>
   <title>List Control Example</title>
   <script runat="server">
      Sub Page_Load()
         MyDataGrid.DataSource = CreateData()
         MyDataGrid.DataBind()
```

Example 5-9. ListControls.aspx (continued)

```
            MyDataList.DataSource = CreateData()
            MyDataList.DataBind()
            MyRepeater.DataSource = CreateData()
            MyRepeater.DataBind()
        End Sub
        Function CreateData() As DataTable
            Dim DT As New DataTable()
            Dim Row1, Row2, Row3, Row4 As DataRow
            DT.Columns.Add(New DataColumn("name", _
                System.Type.GetType("System.String")))
            DT.Columns.Add(New DataColumn("city", _
                System.Type.GetType("System.String")))
            Row1 = DT.NewRow()
            Row1("name") = "W.A. Mozart"
            Row1("city") = "Salzburg"
            DT.Rows.Add(Row1)
            Row2 = DT.NewRow()
            Row2("name") = "Nikolai Rimsky-Korsakov"
            Row2("city") = "Tikhvin"
            DT.Rows.Add(Row2)
            Row3 = DT.NewRow()
            Row3("name") = "George Frideric Handel"
            Row3("city") = "Halle"
            DT.Rows.Add(Row3)
            Row4 = DT.NewRow()
            Row4("name") = "J.S. Bach"
            Row4("city") = "Eisenach"
            DT.Rows.Add(Row4)
            Return DT
        End Function
    </script>
</head>
<body>
    <h1>List Control Example</h1>
    <form runat="server">
        <asp:table id="MyTable"
            border="1"
            cellpadding="5"
            cellspacing="0"
            runat="server">
            <asp:tablerow runat="server">
                <asp:tablecell runat="server">
                    DataGrid Control:
                </asp:tablecell>
                <asp:tablecell runat="server">
                    <asp:datagrid id="MyDataGrid"
                        allowpaging="true"
                        allowsorting="true"
                        alternatingitemstyle-backcolor="LightSkyBlue"
                        backcolor="Blue"
                        forecolor="White"
                        cellpadding="2"
```

Example 5-9. ListControls.aspx (continued)

```
                cellspacing="0"
                headerstyle-backcolor="DarkBlue"
                headerstyle-forecolor="Yellow"
                pagerstyle-mode="NumericPages"
                pagesize="5"
                runat="server"/>
        </asp:tablecell>
    </asp:tablerow>
    <asp:tablerow runat="server">
        <asp:tablecell runat="server">
            DataList Control:
        </asp:tablecell>
        <asp:tablecell runat="server">
            <asp:datalist id="MyDataList"
                alternatingitemstyle-backcolor="LightSkyBlue"
                backcolor="Blue"
                bordercolor="Black"
                cellpadding="2"
                cellspacing="0"
                forecolor="White"
                headerstyle-backcolor="DarkBlue"
                headerstyle-forecolor="Yellow"
                repeatcolumns="1"
                repeatdirection="vertical"
                repeatlayout="table"
                runat="server">
                <headertemplate>
                    Composers
                </headertemplate>
                <itemtemplate>
                    <%# databinder.eval(container.dataitem, "name") %>
                </itemtemplate>
            </asp:datalist>
        </asp:tablecell>
    </asp:tablerow>
    <asp:tablerow runat="server">
        <asp:tablecell runat="server">
            Repeater Control:
        </asp:tablecell>
        <asp:tablecell runat="server">
            <asp:repeater id="MyRepeater" runat="server">
                <headertemplate>
                    <table cellpadding="5" cellspacing="0">
                        <tr>
                            <td>Name<hr/></td>
                            <td>City<hr/></td>
                        </tr>
                </headertemplate>
                <itemtemplate>
                    <tr>
                        <td><%# DataBinder.Eval(Container.DataItem, _
                            "name") %></td>
```

Example 5-9. ListControls.aspx (continued)

```
            <td><%# DataBinder.Eval(Container.DataItem, _
                "city") %></td>
            </tr>
        </itemtemplate>
        <footertemplate>
            </table>
        </footertemplate>
        </asp:repeater>
    </asp:tablecell>
    </asp:tablerow>
    </asp:table>
    </form>
</body>
</html>
```

Rich Controls

These high-level custom controls provide rich user interface and functionality. This release of ASP.NET includes two rich controls: the Calendar control and the AdRotator control. Table 5-5 lists the rich controls.

Table 5-5. Rich controls and their purpose

Control	Purpose
AdRotator	Displays different ad images and, when clicked, will navigate to the URL associated with that image. You can define the rotation schedule in an XML file.
Calendar	Displays a monthly calendar and lets the user select a date.

The simplified syntax of the rich controls is:

```
<asp:adrotator id="MyAdRotator" advertisementfile="ads.xml"
    runat="server" />

<asp:calendar id="MyCalendar"
    showdayheader="true"
    todaydaystyle-backcolor="yellow"
    todaydaystyle-forecolor="blue"
    runat="server"/>
```

These controls can then be referenced programmatically with code fragments like the following:

```
MyAdRotator.KeywordFilter = "Nutshell"
Dim ShortDate As String
ShortDate = MyCalendar.TodaysDate.ToString("D")
MyLabel.Text = "Today is " & ShortDate
```

The appearance of rich controls when rendered to the browser is shown in Figure 5-6. The code used to generate this figure is shown in Example 5-10.

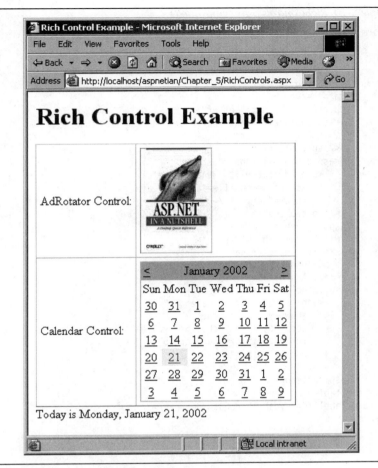

Figure 5-6. Rendering of rich controls

Example 5-10. RichControls.aspx

```
<%@ Page Language="vb" %>
<html>
<head>
   <title>Rich Control Example</title>
   <script runat="server">
      Sub Page_Load()
         MyAdRotator.KeywordFilter = "Nutshell"
         Dim ShortDate As String
         ShortDate = MyCalendar.TodaysDate.ToString("D")
         MyLabel.Text = "Today is " & ShortDate
      End Sub
   </script>
</head>
<body>
   <h1>Rich Control Example</h1>
```

Example 5-10. RichControls.aspx (continued)

```
<form runat="server">
    <asp:table id="MyTable"
        border="1"
        cellpadding="5"
        cellspacing="0"
        runat="server">
        <asp:tablerow runat="server">
            <asp:tablecell runat="server">
                AdRotator Control:
            </asp:tablecell>
            <asp:tablecell runat="server">
                <asp:adrotator id="MyAdRotator"
                    advertisementfile="ads.xml"
                    runat="server" />
            </asp:tablecell>
        </asp:tablerow>
        <asp:tablerow runat="server">
            <asp:tablecell runat="server">
                Calendar Control:
            </asp:tablecell>
            <asp:tablecell runat="server">
                <asp:calendar id="MyCalendar"
                    showdayheader="true"
                    todaydaystyle-backcolor="yellow"
                    todaydaystyle-forecolor="blue"
                    runat="server"/>
            </asp:tablecell>
        </asp:tablerow>
    </asp:table>
    <asp:label id="MyLabel" runat="server"/>
</form>
</body>
</html>
```

Validation Controls

ASP.NET removes the hassle of duplicating validation code, a common problem of performing data validation using ASP, by neatly encapsulating the standard validations into server controls. You can attach the validation control to the control whose value needs to be validated. You can also attach multiple validation controls to a single control. The ASP.NET validation server controls provide server-side validation for all browsers and supply client-side validation via JavaScript for browsers that support Javascript and DHTML. You can also write your own custom client and/or server-side validation functions, as you'll see in the code example for this section.

One feature that most web programmers would like to have is a summary of the validation errors for the values entered into a page's controls. The ValidationSummary control provides this much-desired feature. Table 5-6 lists the validation controls.

Table 5-6. Validation controls

Control	Purpose
CompareValidator	Compares the input in the attached control with a constant value or the property value of another control.
CustomValidator	Invokes custom validation code that you have written.
RangeValidator	Checks if the value is between specified upper and lower limits.
RegularExpressionValidator	Checks if the input matches a pattern defined by a regular expression.
RequiredFieldValidator	Makes sure that the user can't skip the required value.
ValidationSummary	Shows a summary of errors emitted by all validators in that form.

The simplified syntax of the validation controls is:

```
<asp:comparevalidator id="cvCompare"
    controltovalidate="value1"
    controltocompare="value2"
    operator="equal"
    type="integer"
    errormessage="Fields are not equal!"
    display="dynamic"
    runat="server"/>

<asp:customvalidator id="cvDate"
    controltovalidate="year"
    errormessage="Not a valid year!"
    onservervalidate="servervalidation"
    clientvalidationfunction="ClientValidate"
    display="dynamic"
    runat="server"/>

<asp:rangevalidator id="rvCompare"
    controltovalidate="value"
    minimumvalue="0"
    maximumvalue="100"
    type="integer"
    errormessage="Value not in valid range!"
    runat="server"/>

<asp:regularexpressionvalidator id="reZipCode"
    controltovalidate="zipcode"
    validationexpression="^\d{5}$|^\d{5}-\d{4}$"
    errormessage="Not a valid Zip code!"
    display="static"
    runat="server"/>

<asp:requiredfieldvalidator id="rfvLogin"
    controltovalidate="login"
    display="static"
    errormessage="Login cannot be blank!"
    runat="server"/>

<asp:validationsummary id="vsSummary"
    displaymode="bulletlist"
```

```
headertext="Page has the following errors: "
showsummary="true"
showmessagebox="false"
runat="server"/>
```

The controls can then be referenced programmatically with code fragments like this:

```
cvCompare.ControlToCompare = "Value3"
cvDate.ClientValidationFunction="ClientValidateLeapYear"
reZipCode.ValidationExpression="^\d{5}$|^\d{5}$"
rfvLogin.InitialValue = "SomeUser"
vsSummary.DisplayMode = ValidationSummaryDisplayMode.List
```

The appearance of validation controls that have detected invalid input when rendered to the browser is shown in Figure 5-7.

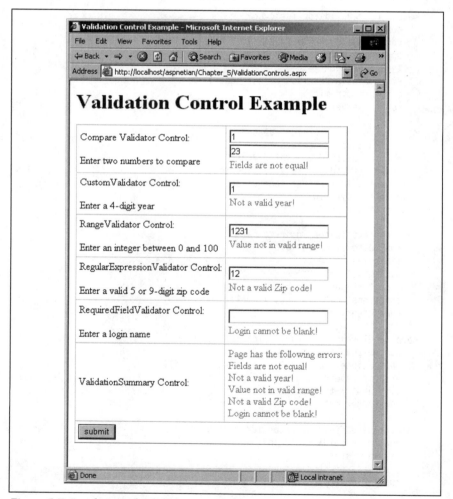

Figure 5-7. Rendering of validation controls

The code used to generate this figure is shown in Example 5-11.

Example 5-11. ValidationControls.aspx

```
<%@ Page Language="vb" %>
<html>
<head>
   <title>Validation Control Example</title>
    <script language="javascript">
    <!--
      function ClientValidate(source, arguments)
      {
          //Declare variables.
          var r, re;
          //Create regular expression object.
          re = new RegExp(/^[1-9][0-9][0-9][0-9]$/);
          //Test for match.
          r = re.test(arguments.Value);
          //Return results.
          arguments.IsValid = r;
      }
    -->
    </script>
    <script runat="server">
       Sub Page_Load()
          vsSummary.DisplayMode = ValidationSummaryDisplayMode.List
       End Sub
       Sub ServerValidation (source As object, args _
          As ServerValidateEventArgs)
          Dim RegExVal As New System.Text.RegularExpressions.Regex("^\d{4}$")
          If RegExVal.IsMatch(args.Value) Then
             args.IsValid = True
          Else
             args.IsValid = False
          End If
       End Sub
    </script>
</head>
<body>
   <h1>Validation Control Example</h1>
   <form runat="server">
      <asp:table id="MyTable"
         border="1"
         cellpadding="5"
         cellspacing="0"
         runat="server">
         <asp:tablerow runat="server">
            <asp:tablecell runat="server">
               Compare Validator Control:
               <br><br>
               Enter two numbers to compare
            </asp:tablecell>
            <asp:tablecell runat="server">
               <asp:textbox id="value1" runat="server"/><br>
               <asp:textbox id="value2" runat="server"/><br>
```

Example 5-11. ValidationControls.aspx (continued)

```
            <asp:comparevalidator id="cvCompare"
                controltovalidate="value1"
                controltocompare="value2"
                operator="equal"
                type="integer"
                errormessage="Fields are not equal!"
                display="dynamic"
                runat="server"/>
        </asp:tablecell>
    </asp:tablerow>
    <asp:tablerow runat="server">
        <asp:tablecell runat="server">
            CustomValidator Control:
            <br><br>
            Enter a 4-digit year
        </asp:tablecell>
        <asp:tablecell runat="server">
            <asp:textbox id="year" runat="server"/><br>
            <asp:customvalidator id="cvDate"
                controltovalidate="year"
                errormessage="Not a valid year!"
                onservervalidate="servervalidation"
                clientvalidationfunction="ClientValidate"
                display="dynamic"
                runat="server"/>
        </asp:tablecell>
    </asp:tablerow>
    <asp:tablerow runat="server">
        <asp:tablecell runat="server">
            RangeValidator Control:
            <br><br>
            Enter an integer between 0 and 100
        </asp:tablecell>
        <asp:tablecell runat="server">
            <asp:textbox id="value" runat="server"/><br>
            <asp:rangevalidator id="rvCompare"
                controltovalidate="value"
                minimumvalue="0"
                maximumvalue="100"
                type="integer"
                errormessage="Value not in valid range!"
                runat="server"/>
        </asp:tablecell>
    </asp:tablerow>
    <asp:tablerow runat="server">
        <asp:tablecell runat="server">
            RegularExpressionValidator Control:
            <br><br>
            Enter a valid 5 or 9-digit zip code
        </asp:tablecell>
        <asp:tablecell runat="server">
            <asp:textbox id="zipcode" runat="server"/><br>
```

Example 5-11. ValidationControls.aspx (continued)

```
            <asp:regularexpressionvalidator id="reZipCode"
                controltovalidate="zipcode"
                validationexpression="^\d{5}$|^\d{5}-\d{4}$"
                errormessage="Not a valid Zip code!"
                display="static"
                runat="server"/>
        </asp:tablecell>
    </asp:tablerow>
    <asp:tablerow runat="server">
        <asp:tablecell runat="server">
            RequiredFieldValidator Control:
            <br><br>
            Enter a login name
        </asp:tablecell>
        <asp:tablecell runat="server">
            <asp:textbox id="login" runat="server"/><br>
            <asp:requiredfieldvalidator id="rfvLogin"
                controltovalidate="login"
                display="static"
                errormessage="Login cannot be blank!"
                runat="server"/>
        </asp:tablecell>
    </asp:tablerow>
    <asp:tablerow runat="server">
        <asp:tablecell runat="server">
            ValidationSummary Control:
        </asp:tablecell>
        <asp:tablecell runat="server">
            <asp:validationsummary id="vsSummary"
                displaymode="bulletlist"
                headertext="Page has the following errors: "
                showsummary="true"
                showmessagebox="false"
                runat="server"/>
        </asp:tablecell>
    </asp:tablerow>
    <asp:tablerow runat="server">
        <asp:tablecell colspan="2" runat="server">
            <asp:button text="submit" runat="server"/>
        </asp:tablecell>
    </asp:tablerow>
</asp:table>
<asp:label id="MyLabel" runat="server"/>
    </form>
</body>
</html>
```

Handling Control Events

One of the most convenient aspects of the new ASP.NET Web Forms model is that it brings event-driven programming, popularized by Visual Basic, to the web world without all the kludginess of the late unlamented Visual Basic WebClasses. As explained in Chapter 3, ASP.NET has a number of built-in events at the page level for which you can write event handlers to execute code.

Moreover, most server controls expose one or more events for which you can write handlers. Table 5-7 shows a list of common events and the controls that support them. These events and controls are in addition to the standard events, such as Init, Load, PreRender, and UnLoad, that are inherited from the base Control class. For example, the Button server control exposes the Click and Command events. These events are both raised when the button is clicked, but while the Click event is usually used simply to handle the event for a single button, the Command event can be used to handle clicking on several buttons (so long as the buttons' CommandName property is set). The CommandName property, along with an optional CommandArgument property, become properties of the CommandEventArgs object, which is passed as a parameter of the Command event handler. You can then examine the CommandName and CommandArgument properties within the event handler code to determine what action(s) to take.

Table 5-7. Control events

Event	Event type	Description	Controls
OnAdCreated	Change	Raised after creation of the control and immediately before the page is rendered. If an Advertisement file is provided, OnAdCreated is raised after an ad has been selected from the file. Passes an AdCreatedEventArgs argument.	AdRotator
OnClick	Action	Raised when the user clicks the control. Passes an EventArgs argument.	Button ImageButton LinkButton
OnCommand	Action	Raised when a button containing OnCommand, CommandName, and CommandArgument attributes is clicked. Passes an CommandEventArgs argument containing the CommandName and CommandArgument attribute values.	Button ImageButton LinkButton
OnSelected-Index-Changed	Change	Raised when the user changes the selection. Passes an EventArgs argument.	CheckBoxList DropDownList ListBox RadioButtonList
OnChecked-Changed	Change	Raised when the user clicks the control. Passes an EventArgs argument.	CheckBox RadioButton
OnPageIn-dexChanged	Change	Raised when the user clicks a page selection element. Passes a Data-GridPageChangedEventArgs argument.	DataGrid

The basic format of an event handler is as follows:

```
' VB.NET
Sub MyButton_Click(Sender As Object, E As EventArgs)
    'Event handling code
End Sub

// C#
void MyButton_Click(object Sender, EventArgs e)
{
```

```
    // Event handling code
}
```

While you can name your event handling procedures whatever you like, it's common to use the *ObjectName_EventName* convention, which makes it very easy to immediately see which procedures are event handlers. All event handlers are passed an Object argument that is a reference to the control from which the event was fired. They are also passed an instance of the EventArgs class or of a class that derives from EventArgs. For example, the OnCommand event of a Button control passes an argument of type CommandEventArgs, which contains information about the command represented by the button:

```
Sub MyButton_Command(Sender As Object, E As CommandEventArgs)
    Message.Text = "Command " & E.CommandName & _
        "was sent."
End Sub
```

As with creating controls, two techniques are available for creating and wiring up event handlers in ASP.NET: declarative and programmatic.

Wiring Up Events in Declarative Tags

The technique typically used to wire up events that are handled in a server-side <script> block, which is probably the simplest way to wire an event handler, is to add the appropriate attribute to the declarative tag used to create the control. The following code snippet sets the OnClick event handler to SubmitBtn_Click:

```
<asp:button id="MyBtn" text="Submit" onclick="MyBtn_Click"
runat="server"/>
```

To handle this event, you would then add the following code to your page in a server-side <script> block:

```
' Visual Basic .NET
Sub MyBtn_Click(sender As Object, e As EventArgs)
    'event handling code
End Sub

//C#
void MyBtn_Click(Object sender, EventArgs e)
{
    // event handling code
}
```

The event handler for the Command event of the Button control is wired up in much the same fashion:

```
<asp:button id="Sort"
    text="Sort"
    commandname="Sort"
    commandargument="Descending"
    oncommand="Button_Command"
    runat="server"/>

<asp:button id="Filter"
    text="Filter"
    commandname="Filter"
```

```
            commandargument="B"
            oncommand="Button_Command"
            runat="server"/>
```

Note that the event handler changes slightly (EventArgs is replaced by the CommandEventArgs subclass, which contains information about the clicked command button):

```
' Visual Basic .NET
Sub Button_Command(sender As Object, ce As CommandEventArgs)
    Select ce.CommandName
        Case "Sort"
            ' Sort logic
        Case "Filter"
            ' Filter logic
    End Select
End Sub
```

```
//C#
void Button_Command(Object sender, CommandEventArgs ce)
{
    switch(cs.CommandName)
    {
        case "Sort":
            // Sort logic
        case "Filter":
            // Filter logic
    }
}
```

It's a good habit to name your event handlers based on the name of the control whose event they handle and the name of the event, separated by an underscore (e.g., MyBtn_Click). However, as you can see from the OnCommand event example, you may want to make an exception sometimes.

Wiring Up Events Programmatically

Programmatic wiring of control events is typically used with code-behind classes; it's a little more complicated than the declarative technique, but still pretty straightforward. Note that programmatic event wiring is language dependent. Two techniques wire up events programmatically in Visual Basic .NET and one wires up events in C#.

The preferred approach for programmatically wiring events in Visual Basic .NET uses the WithEvents and Handles keywords to associate event handlers with events. As the following snippet illustrates, you first declare an instance of the desired control using the WithEvents keyword to indicate that you want event support for the instance.

Then you add the Handles clause to the procedure declaration for the event handler, specifying the object and event that it will handle:

```
Sub Page_Load()
    Protected WithEvents MyButton As New Button()
End Sub
```

```
Sub MyButton_Click(sender As Object, e As EventArgs) _
Handles MyButton.Click
   'Event handling code
End Sub
```

 When declaring control instances in a code-behind class, it's a good idea to use the Protected keyword to ensure that the instance is available only to the class itself and to any class (such as the *.aspx* page) that inherits from it.

An alternate technique in Visual Basic .NET uses the AddHandler statement to specify a control event along with the address of the procedure that should be invoked when that event occurs:

```
Sub Page_Load( )
   Protected MyButton As New Button( )
   AddHandler MyButton.Click, AddressOf MyButton_Click
End Sub

Sub MyButton_Click(sender As Object, e As EventArgs)
   'Event handling code
End Sub
```

A corresponding RemoveHandler statement also allows you to stop handling a particular event. The advantage of this technique is that you can stop and start handling a particular event dynamically. In C#, the += operator is used to assign an event handler to an event:

```
void Page_Load( )
{
   Button MyButton = new Button( );
   MyButton.Click += new EventHandler(this.MyButton_Click);
}

void MyButton_Click(Object sender, EventArgs e)
{
   // Event handling code
}
```

As with Visual Basic's AddHandler keyword, the += operator has a corresponding -= operator that allows you to unwire an event from its handler dynamically.

Modifying Control Appearance

One of the great things about ASP.NET Server Controls is that they are incredibly flexible in allowing developers to define how they should appear on the page. Most server controls expose properties that allow simple formatting, such as fonts and background colors. All server controls also expose properties that allow for setting cascading style sheets (CSS) styles to modify the appearance of a control. Finally, some controls allow the use of templates to further define how the output of the control should appear. Together or individually, these techniques allow ASP.NET developers extensive control over the appearance of their controls.

Properties

Using control properties is the simplest and least powerful technique for modifying the appearance of a control. Example 5-12 shows a page with two Label controls, one of which uses its default settings. The second Label control has one attribute used to set the Font-Name property. Font is a property that is represented by the FontInfo class. Setting the Font-Name attribute sets the value of the FontInfo class' Name member. Note that this second Label control also has the BackColor property set (in this case, to blue) in the Page_Load event handler. The output from Example 5-12 is shown in Figure 5-8.

Example 5-12. ControlProps.aspx

```vb
<%@ Page Language="vb" %>
<html>
<head>
    <title>Control Properties Example</title>
    <script runat="server">
        Sub Page_Load()
            Label2.BackColor = System.Drawing.Color.LightBlue
        End Sub
    </script>
</head>
<body>
    <h1>Control Properties Example</h1>
    <form runat="server">
        <asp:table id="MyTable" border="1" cellpadding="5"
            cellspacing="0" runat="server">
            <asp:tablerow runat="server">
                <asp:tablecell runat="server">
                    Default Label:
                </asp:tablecell>
                <asp:tablecell runat="server">
                    <asp:label id="Label1" runat="server">
                        Hello, World!
                    </asp:label>
                </asp:tablecell>
            </asp:tablerow>
            <asp:tablerow runat="server">
                <asp:tablecell runat="server">
                    Label with Properties:
                </asp:tablecell>
                <asp:tablecell runat="server">
                    <asp:label id="Label2" font-name="arial"
                        runat="server">
                        Hello, World!
                    </asp:label>
                </asp:tablecell>
            </asp:tablerow>
        </asp:table>
    </form>
</body>
</html>
```

Figure 5-8. Control properties

CSS Styles

A more powerful technique for modifying control appearance involves the use of CSS styles. The base HtmlControl class (from which all HTML controls inherit) exposes a Style property, which contains a collection of CSS styles that are rendered at runtime as attributes on the tag generated by the control. The base WebControl class (from which all web controls inherit) also exposes a Style property and adds a CssClass property, which renders the value of the property as a class attribute on the control. This property allows you to set the style of a control using a CSS class defined in a stylesheet, rather than by setting individual styles. Like many other properties of web and HTML controls, the Style and CssClass properties can be set either declaratively (using attributes) or programmatically. Example 5-13 illustrates the use of both properties. Example 5-14 shows the HTML that would be rendered to the browser by Example 5-13. Note that the ViewState hidden field has been removed for clarity.

Example 5-13. ControlStyles.aspx

```
<%@ Page Language="vb" %>
<html>
<head>
   <title>Control Properties Example</title>
   <script runat="server">
      Sub Page_Load()
         Label2.Style("background-color") = "silver"
      End Sub
   </script>
   <style>
      .Hello
      {
          font: 14pt arial;
          color:blue;
      }
```

Example 5-13. ControlStyles.aspx (continued)

```
        </style>
</head>
<body>
    <h1>Control Properties Example</h1>
    <form runat="server">
        <asp:table id="MyTable" border="1" cellpadding="5" cellspacing="0"
            runat="server">
            <asp:tablerow runat="server">
                <asp:tablecell runat="server">
                    HtmlInputText Control:
                </asp:tablecell>
                <asp:tablecell runat="server">
                    <input id="Text1" type="text"
                    style="font: 12pt arial; background-color:silver; color:red;"
                    runat="server"/>
                </asp:tablecell>
            </asp:tablerow>
            <asp:tablerow runat="server">
                <asp:tablecell runat="server">
                    Label with Style:
                </asp:tablecell>
                <asp:tablecell runat="server">
                    <asp:label id="Label2" cssclass="Hello" runat="server">
                        Hello, World!
                    </asp:label>
                </asp:tablecell>
            </asp:tablerow>
        </asp:table>
    </form>
</body>
</html>
```

Example 5-14. Rendered HTML from ControlStyles.aspx

```
<html>
<head>
    <title>Control Properties Example</title>
    <style>
        .Hello
        {
            font: 14pt arial;
            color:blue;
        }
    </style>
</head>
<body>
    <h1>Control Properties Example</h1>
    <form name="_ctl0" method="post" action="ControlStyles.aspx"
        id="_ctl0">
        <table id="MyTable" cellspacing="0" cellpadding="5" border="1"
            border="0" style="border-collapse:collapse;">
            <tr>
            <td>
```

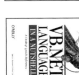
Part # 10452A © 2001 O'Reilly & Associates, Inc. O'Reilly is a registered trademark, and The Internet Runs on O'Reilly Books is a trademark of O'Reilly & Associates, Inc. All other trademarks are property of their respective owners.

The .NET Effect...

A Different Kind

of Animal

O'REILLY®
dotnet.oreilly.com

Example 5-14. Rendered HTML from ControlStyles.aspx (continued)

```
                HtmlInputText Control:
            </td>
            <td>
                <input name="Text1" id="Text1" type="text"
                style="font: 12pt arial; background-color:silver; color:red;"
                />
            </td>
        </tr>
        <tr>
            <td>
                Label with Style:
            </td>
            <td>
                <span id="Label2" class="Hello"
                    style="background-color:silver;">
                    Hello, World!
                </span>
            </td>
        </tr>
    </table>
  </form>
</body>
</html>
```

Templates

Certain controls, most notably the Repeater data-bound control, can also use templates to specify the appearance of the control output. In fact, the Repeater control requires at least one template (the ItemTemplate) to display anything at all.

The Repeater works by rendering anything contained in the HeaderTemplate (if defined) and then rendering the contents of its data source based on the ItemTemplate, AlternatingItemTemplate (if defined), and SeparatorTemplate (if defined).

Once all rows of the data source have been rendered, the Repeater then renders the contents of the FooterTemplate (if defined). Example 5-15 illustrates the use of templates in modifying control output. Figure 5-9 shows the output of *ControlTemplates.aspx.*

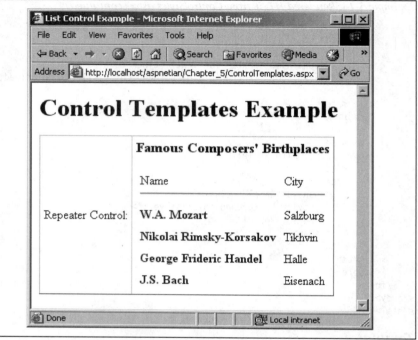

Figure 5-9. Template output

Example 5-15. ControlTemplates.aspx

```
<%@ Page Language="vb" %>
<%@ Import Namespace="System.Data" %>
<html>
<head>
   <title>List Control Example</title>
   <script runat="server">
      Sub Page_Load()
         MyRepeater.DataSource = CreateData()
         MyRepeater.DataBind()
      End Sub
      Function CreateData() As DataTable
         Dim DT As New DataTable()
         Dim Row1, Row2, Row3, Row4 As DataRow
         DT.Columns.Add(New _
            DataColumn("name", System.Type.GetType("System.String")))
         DT.Columns.Add(New _
            DataColumn("city", System.Type.GetType("System.String")))
         Row1 = DT.NewRow()
         Row1("name") = "W.A. Mozart"
         Row1("city") = "Salzburg"
         DT.Rows.Add(Row1)
         Row2 = DT.NewRow()
         Row2("name") = "Nikolai Rimsky-Korsakov"
```

Example 5-15. ControlTemplates.aspx (continued)

```
                Row2("city") = "Tikhvin"
                DT.Rows.Add(Row2)
                Row3 = DT.NewRow()
                Row3("name") = "George Frideric Handel"
                Row3("city") = "Halle"
                DT.Rows.Add(Row3)
                Row4 = DT.NewRow()
                Row4("name") = "J.S. Bach"
                Row4("city") = "Eisenach"
                DT.Rows.Add(Row4)
                Return DT
         End Function
      </script>
</head>
<body>
   <h1>Control Templates Example</h1>
   <form runat="server">
      <asp:table id="MyTable"
         border="1" cellpadding="5" cellspacing="0" runat="server">
         <asp:tablerow runat="server">
            <asp:tablecell runat="server">
               Repeater Control:
            </asp:tablecell>
            <asp:tablecell runat="server">
               <asp:repeater id="MyRepeater" runat="server">
                  <headertemplate>
                     <h3>Famous Composers' Birthplaces</h3>
                     <table cellpadding="5" cellspacing="0">
                        <tr>
                           <td>Name<hr/></td>
                           <td>City<hr/></td>
                        </tr>
                  </headertemplate>
                  <itemtemplate>
                        <tr>
                           <td>
                              <strong>
                        <%# DataBinder.Eval(Container.DataItem, "name") %>
                              <strong>
                           </td>
                           <td>
                        <%# DataBinder.Eval(Container.DataItem, "city") %>
                           </td>
                        </tr>
                  </itemtemplate>
                  <footertemplate>
                     </table>
                  </footertemplate>
               </asp:repeater>
            </asp:tablecell>
         </asp:tablerow>
      </asp:table>
```

Example 5-15. ControlTemplates.aspx (continued)

```
    </form>
</body>
</html>
```

Additional Resources

The following sites provide additional information on the topics discussed in this chapter:

http://www.aspfriends.com/aspfriends/aspngfreeforall.asp

> The home page for the AspFriends.com mailing list (for any questions relating to ASP.NET). This home page is an excellent resource for ASP.NET questions. A number of experts answer questions, including several well-known authors.

http://www.aspfriends.com/aspfriends/aspngdatagridrepeaterdatalist.asp

> The home page for the AspFriends.com mailing list for DataGrid, DataList, and Repeater questions. This is an excellent resource for getting focused answers on working with these controls.

CHAPTER 6

User Controls and
Custom Server Controls

Reuse is a technique that is important to most developers. Reuse allows you to avoid constantly reinventing the wheel by using functionality that has already been built and tested. It increases productivity, by reducing the total amount of code you need to write, and reliability, since by using tested code, you (presumably) already know the code works reliably.

ASP.NET provides a range of options for reuse. The first is the wide variety of built-in server controls that ship with ASP.NET. These server controls alone can eliminate hundreds, or even thousands, of lines of code that needed to be written to achieve the same effect in classic ASP. In addition, the .NET Framework Class Library (FCL) provides hundreds of classes to perform actions (such as sending SMTP email or making network calls) that in classic ASP would have required purchasing a third-party component or making calls into the Win32 API.

Going hand-in-hand with reuse is the concept of *extensibility*, the ability to take the existing functionality provided by the .NET Framework and ASP.NET and extend it to perform actions that are more tailored to your particular applications and problem domains. ASP.NET provides a significant number of avenues for extensibility:

Custom server controls
> Allow you to create entirely new controls for use with ASP.NET or to derive from existing controls and extend or modify their functionality.

Components
> As in classic ASP, components are the primary means for extending an ASP. NET application by encapsulating the application's business logic into an easily reusable form. With the .NET Framework, it's easier than ever to build components, and components are more interoperable across languages than in the COM world. .NET components can also communicate with COM components through an interoperability layer.

HttpHandlers and HttpModules

HttpHandlers are components that are called to perform the processing of specific types of requests made to IIS. HttpModules are components that participate in the processing pipeline of all requests for a given ASP.NET application. These extensibility techniques are beyond the scope of this book, but you can get answers to questions on these topics at *http://www.aspfriends. com/aspfriends/aspnghttphandlers.asp.*

The rest of this chapter discusses employing ASP.NET user controls and custom server controls for reuse and employing custom server controls for extensibility. The chapter also explains how custom server controls can easily be shared across multiple applications, making reuse simpler than ever.

User Controls

The simplest form of reuse in classic ASP is the include file. By adding the following directive:

```
<!-- #include file = "filename.inc" -->
```

ASP developers could place the contents of the specified file inline with the page in which the directive appeared. Unfortunately, this reuse technique is a bit crude and sometimes makes applications harder to debug.

While ASP.NET still supports include files, a better way to provide the same kinds of reuse is through a new feature called *user controls*. User controls consist of HTML, a server-side script, and controls, in a file with the *.ascx* file extension. When added to a Web Forms page, ASP.NET treats user controls as objects; these user controls can expose properties and methods like any other object. The rendered output of user controls can also be cached to improve application performance.

Example 6-1 shows a simple user control that provides navigational links to other examples in this chapter. The user control appears in each example page to demonstrate how the use of a user control can provide a single point for modifying such frequently used elements as headers, footers, and navigation bars.

Example 6-1. Nav.ascx

```
<%@ Control Language="vb" %>
<table cellpadding="0" cellspacing="0">
    <tr>
        <td valign="top">
            <strong>Navigation Bar</strong><br/>
            <hr width='80%'>
            <a href="NavBarClient.aspx"
                onmouseover="img1.src='node_rev.jpg';"
                onmouseout="img1.src='node.jpg';">
                <img border='0' align='absMiddle' alt='NavBar Client'
                    src='node.jpg' id='img1' name='img1'></a>
            <a href="NavBarClient.aspx"
                onmouseover="img1.src='node_rev.jpg';"
                onmouseout="img1.src='node.jpg';">NavBar Client</a>
            <hr width='80%'>
            <a href="UCClient.aspx"
```

Example 6-1. Nav.ascx (continued)

```
                    onmouseover="img2.src='alt_node_rev.jpg';"
                    onmouseout="img2.src='alt_node.jpg';">
                <img border='0' align='absMiddle' alt='User Control Client'
                    src='alt_node.jpg' id='img2' name='img2'></a>
            <a href="UCClient.aspx"
                    onmouseover="img2.src='alt_node_rev.jpg';"
                    onmouseout="img2.src='alt_node.jpg';">User Control Client</a>
            <hr width='80%'>
            <a href="BlogClient.aspx"
                    onmouseover="img3.src='node_rev.jpg';"
                    onmouseout="img3.src='node.jpg';">
                <img border='0' align='absMiddle' alt='Blog Client'
                    src='node.jpg' id='img3' name='img3'></a>
            <a href="BlogClient.aspx"
                    onmouseover="img3.src='node_rev.jpg';"
                    onmouseout="img3.src='node.jpg';">Blog Client</a>
            <hr width='80%'>
            <a href="BlogAdd.aspx"
                    onmouseover="img3.src='alt_node_rev.jpg';"
                    onmouseout="img3.src='alt_node.jpg';">
                <img border='0' align='absMiddle' alt='Add New Blog'
                    src='alt_node.jpg' id='img3' name='img3'></a>
            <a href="BlogAdd.aspx"
                    onmouseover="img3.src='node_rev.jpg';"
                    onmouseout="img3.src='node.jpg';">Add New Blog</a>
            <hr width='80%'>
        </td>
    </tr>
</table>
```

With the exception of the @ Control directive, which is not strictly required, the code in Example 6-1 consists exclusively of HTML and client-side script (for performing a simple mouseover graphics switch). However, the user control could just as easily contain server controls and/or server-side script to perform more complicated tasks.

The @ Control directive performs essentially the same task as the @ Page directive, only for user controls. Chapter 3 lists the attributes of the @ Page and @ Control directives and the purpose of each.

The advantage of using a user control for this type of functionality is that it places all of our navigation logic in a single location. This placement makes it considerably easier to maintain the navigation links for a site. If you used ASP.NET's built-in server controls instead of raw HTML in your navigation user control, you could manipulate those server controls programmatically from the page on which the control is used. For example, you could hide the link to the page that's currently displayed or highlight it in some fashion.

The disadvantage of a user control is that it is not reusable across multiple sites. It's also not usually a good idea to tightly couple user interface elements and data, as this control does, because doing so tends to reduce the reusability of a control. Later in this chapter, you'll see how to improve this user control by turning it into a custom server control.

User controls are made available to a page through the use of either the @ Register directive, which prepares a user control on a page declaratively (i.e., using a tag-based syntax like server controls), or to be included programmatically using the LoadControl method of the TemplateControl class (from which both the Page class and the UserControl class derive).

Example 6-2 shows a page that uses the @ Register directive and a declarative tag to create the user control shown in Example 6-1. The @ Register directive in Example 6-2 tells ASP.NET to look for any <aspnetian:nav> tags with the runat="server" attribute, and when it finds one, create an instance of the user control and place its output where the tag is located. This allows us to place our control very precisely.

Example 6-2. UCClient.aspx

```
<%@ Page Language="vb" %>
<%@ Register TagPrefix="aspnetian" TagName="nav" Src="Nav.ascx" %>
<html>
<head>
</head>
<body>
    <table border="1" width="100%" cellpadding="20" cellspacing="0">
        <tr>
            <td align="center" width="150">
                <img src="aspnetian.jpg"/>
            </td>
            <td align="center">
                <h1>User Control Client Page<h1>
            </td>
        </tr>
        <tr>
            <td width="150">
                <aspnetian:nav runat="server"/>
            </td>
            <td>
                This is where page content might be placed
                <br/><br/><br/><br/><br/><br/><br/><br/><br/>
            </td>
        </tr>
    </table>
</body>
</html>
```

You can instead create the control dynamically using the LoadControl method and add the control to either the Controls collection of the page, or, better yet, to the Controls collection of a PlaceHolder control. The latter allows you to control the location of the user control based on the location of the placeholder. This technique is shown in Example 6-3.

Example 6-3. UCClient_Prog.aspx

```
<%@ Page Language="vb" %>
<html>
```

Example 6-3. UCClient_Prog.aspx (continued)

```
<head>
   <script runat="server">
      Sub Page_Load()
         PH.Controls.Add(LoadControl("Nav.ascx"))
      End Sub
   </script>
</head>
<body>
   <table border="1" width="100%" cellpadding="20" cellspacing="0">
      <tr>
         <td align="center" width="150">
            <img src="aspnetian.jpg"/>
         </td>
         <td align="center">
            <h1>User Control Client Page<h1>
         </td>
      </tr>
      <tr>
         <td width="150">
            <asp:placeholder id="PH" runat="server"/>
         </td>
         <td>
            This is where page content might be placed
            <br/><br/><br/><br/><br/><br/><br/><br/><br/>
         </td>
      </tr>
   </table>
</body>
</html>
```

> If you want to work with the control after loading it using LoadControl, you need to cast the control to the correct type using the *CType* function in Visual Basic .NET or by preceding the control with (*typename*) in C#. Note that this requires that the user control be defined in a class that inherits from UserControl, so this technique would not work with the user control in Example 6-1.

Custom Server Controls

For the reasons cited earlier in the chapter, user controls are not always the ideal choice for reuse. They tend to be very good for quickly reusing existing user interface elements and code, but are not especially useful for developing reusable building blocks for multiple web applications. This is where custom server controls come in.

A custom server control is, in its essence, a class that derives from either the Control or WebControl class of the System.Web.UI namespace, or from one of the classes that derive from these controls. Custom server controls can be used in your

ASP.NET Web Forms pages in very much the same way you use the built-in server controls that come with ASP.NET. There are two primary categories of custom server controls:

Rendered controls

> Rendered controls consist largely of custom rendering of the text, tags, and any other output you desire, which may be combined with the rendered output of any base class your control is derived from. Rendered controls override the Render method of the control they derive from. This method is called automatically by the page containing the control when it's time for the control output to be displayed.

Compositional controls

> Compositional controls get their name from the fact that they are composed of existing controls whose rendered output forms the UI of the custom control. Compositional controls create their constituent controls by overriding the CreateChildControls method of the control they derive from. This method, like the Render method, is automatically called by ASP.NET at the appropriate time.

When designing a new custom server control, you need to consider some issues to decide which type of control to create:

- Does one existing control provide most, but not all, of the functionality you desire? Then a rendered control that derives from that control may be the right choice.

- Could the desired functionality be provided by a group of existing controls? Then a compositional control may be a great way to reuse those controls as a group.

- Do you want to do something that is completely beyond any existing control? Then you may want to derive your control from the Control class and override the Render method to create your custom output.

Note that by default, custom server controls expose all public members of the class from which they are derived. This exposure is important to consider when designing a control for use by other developers if you want to limit the customizations they can make. For instance, you might not want developers to change the font size of your control. In such a case, you should avoid deriving from a control that exposes that property.

Rendered Controls

Perhaps the best way to understand the process of creating a rendered custom server control is to see one. Example 6-4 shows a class written in Visual Basic .NET that implements a custom navigation control with the same functionality as the *Nav. ascx* user control discussed earlier in this chapter. Unlike the user control, which has the linked pages and images hardcoded into the control itself, the custom control in Example 6-4 gets this information from an XML file.

Example 6-4. NavBar.vb

```
Imports Microsoft.VisualBasic
Imports System
```

Example 6-4. NavBar.vb (continued)

```vb
Imports System.Data
Imports System.Drawing
Imports System.IO
Imports System.Text
Imports System.Web
Imports System.Web.UI
Imports System.Web.UI.WebControls


Namespace aspnetian

Public Class NavBar
    Inherits Panel

    Private NavDS As DataSet
    Private _showDividers As Boolean = True

    Public Property ShowDividers() As Boolean
        Get
            Return _showDividers
        End Get
        Set
            _showDividers = value
        End Set
    End Property

    Sub NavBar_Load(sender As Object, e As EventArgs) Handles MyBase.Load

        LoadData()

    End Sub

    Protected Overrides Sub Render(Writer As HtmlTextWriter)

        Dim NavDR As DataRow
        Dim RowNum As Integer = 1
        Dim SB As StringBuilder

        MyBase.RenderBeginTag(Writer)
        MyBase.RenderContents(Writer)

        Writer.Write("<hr width='80%'>" & vbCrLf)

        For Each NavDR In NavDS.Tables(0).Rows

            SB = new StringBuilder()
            SB.Append(vbTab)
            SB.Append("<a href=""")
            SB.Append(NavDR("url"))
            SB.Append(""" onmouseover=""")
            SB.Append("img")
            SB.Append(RowNum.ToString())
            SB.Append(".src='")
```

Controls

Example 6-4. NavBar.vb (continued)

```
SB.Append(NavDR("moimageUrl"))
SB.Append("';""")
SB.Append(" onmouseout="""")
SB.Append("img")
SB.Append(RowNum.ToString())
SB.Append(".src='")
SB.Append(NavDR("imageUrl"))
SB.Append("';""")
SB.Append(" target='")
SB.Append(NavDR("targetFrame"))
SB.Append("'>")
SB.Append(vbCrLf)
SB.Append(vbTab)
SB.Append(vbTab)
SB.Append("<img border='0' align='absMiddle' alt='")
SB.Append(NavDR("text"))
SB.Append("' src='")
SB.Append(NavDR("imageUrl"))
SB.Append("' id='")
SB.Append("img")
SB.Append(RowNum.ToString())
SB.Append("' name='")
SB.Append("img")
SB.Append(RowNum.ToString())
SB.Append("'></a>")
SB.Append(vbTab)
SB.Append("<a href="""")
SB.Append(NavDR("url"))
SB.Append(""" onmouseover="""")
SB.Append("img")
SB.Append(RowNum.ToString())
SB.Append(".src='")
SB.Append(NavDR("moimageUrl"))
SB.Append("';""")
SB.Append(" onmouseout="""")
SB.Append("img")
SB.Append(RowNum.ToString())
SB.Append(".src='")
SB.Append(NavDR("imageUrl"))
SB.Append("';""")
SB.Append(" target='")
SB.Append(NavDR("targetFrame"))
SB.Append("'>")
SB.Append(NavDR("text"))
SB.Append("</a>")
SB.Append(vbCrLf)
If _showDividers = True Then
    SB.Append("<hr width='80%'>")
Else
    SB.Append("<br/><br/>")
End If
SB.Append(vbCrLf)
```

Example 6-4. NavBar.vb (continued)

```
        Writer.Write(SB.ToString())

        RowNum += 1

    Next

    MyBase.RenderEndTag(Writer)

End Sub

Protected Sub LoadData()

    NavDS = New DataSet()

    Try
        NavDS.ReadXml(Page.Server.MapPath("NavBar.xml"))
    Catch fnfEx As FileNotFoundException
        CreateBlankFile()
        Dim Html As String
        Html = "<br>No NavBar.xml file was found, so one was " & _
            "created for you. Follow the directions in the file " & _
            "to populate the required fields and, if desired, " & _
            "the optional fields."
        Me.Controls.Add(New LiteralControl(Html))
    End Try

End Sub

Public Sub CreateBlankFile()
    'Code to create a blank XML file with the fields used by
    '   the control. This code is included as a part of the file
    '   NavBar.vb, included with the sample files for the book.
End Sub

End Class

End Namespace
```

The real meat of the NavBar control begins with the class declaration, which uses the Inherits keyword to declare that the control derives from the Panel control. This gives the control the ability to show a background color, to be hidden or shown as a unit, and to display the contents of its begin and end tags as part of the control.

Next, a couple of local member variables are declared. The location of the declaration is important, since these members need to be accessible to any procedure in the control. A property procedure is then added for the ShowDividers property, which will determine whether the control renders a horizontal line between each node of the control.

In the NavBar_Load method, which handles the Load event for the control (fired automatically by ASP.NET), the LoadData method is called to load the NavBar data from the XML file associated with the control.

Skipping over the Render method temporarily, the LoadData method creates a new instance of the ADO.NET DataSet class and calls its ReadXml method to read the data from the XML file. If no file exists, the LoadData method calls another method (CreateBlankFile) to create a blank XML file with the correct format for use by the developer consuming the control. This technique not only deals gracefully with an error condition; it provides an easier starting point for the developer using the control. Note that the CreateBlankFile method is declared as public, which means it can be called deliberately to create a blank file, if desired.

Last, but certainly not least, the overridden Render method, which is called automatically at runtime when the control is created, iterates through the first (and only) table in the dataset and uses an instance of the StringBuilder class to build the HTML output to render. Once the desired output has been built, the method uses the HtmlTextWriter passed to it by ASP.NET to write the output to the client browser. Note that prior to looping through the rows in the dataset, the render method calls the RenderBeginTag and RenderContents methods of the base Panel control. This renders the opening <div> tag that is the client-side representation of the Panel control, plus anything contained within the opening and closing tags of the NavBar control. Once all the rows have been iterated and their output sent to the browser, the RenderEndTag method is called to send the closing </div> tag to the browser.

You can compile the code in Example 6-4 by using the following single-line command (which can alternatively be placed in a batch file):

```
vbc /t:library /out:bin\NavBar.dll /r:System.dll,System.Data.dll,
System.Drawing.dll,System.Web.dll,System.Xml.dll NavBar.vb
```

The preceding command requires that you create a *bin* subdirectory under the directory from which the command is launched and that you register the path to the Visual Basic compiler in your PATH environment variable. If you have not registered this path, you will need to provide the full path to the Visual Basic .NET compiler (by default, this path is *%windir%\Microsoft.NET\Framework\%version%*).

Example 6-5 shows the XML file used to populate the control, Example 6-6 shows the code necessary to use the NavBar control in a Web Forms page, and Figure 6-1 shows the output of this page.

Example 6-5. NavBar.xml

```
<navBar>
    <!-- node field describes a single node of the control -->
    <node>
        <!-- Required Fields -->
        <!-- url field should contain the absolute or relative
            URL to link to -->
        <url>NavBarClient.aspx</url>
        <!-- text field should contain the descriptive text for
            this node -->
        <text>NavBar Client</text>
        <!-- End Required Fields -->
        <!-- Optional Fields -->
```

Example 6-5. NavBar.xml (continued)

```
    <!-- imageUrl field should contain the absolute or relative
         URL for an image to be displayed in front of the link -->
    <imageUrl>node.jpg</imageUrl>
    <!-- moimageUrl field should contain the absolute or
         relative URL for an image to be displayed in front of
         the link on mouseover -->
    <moImageUrl>node_rev.jpg</moImageUrl>
    <!-- targetFrame field should contain one of the following:
         _blank, _parent, _self, _top  -->
    <targetFrame>_self</targetFrame>
    <!-- End Optional Fields -->
  </node>
  <node>
    <url>UCClient.aspx</url>
    <text>User Control Client</text>
    <imageUrl>alt_node.jpg</imageUrl>
    <moImageUrl>alt_node_rev.jpg</moImageUrl>
    <targetFrame>_self</targetFrame>
  </node>
  <node>
    <url>BlogClient.aspx</url>
    <text>Blog Client</text>
    <imageUrl>node.jpg</imageUrl>
    <moImageUrl>node_rev.jpg</moImageUrl>
    <targetFrame>
    </targetFrame>
  </node>
  <node>
    <url>BlogAdd.aspx</url>
    <text>Add New Blog</text>
    <imageUrl>alt_node.jpg</imageUrl>
    <moImageUrl>alt_node_rev.jpg</moImageUrl>
    <targetFrame>
    </targetFrame>
  </node>
</navBar>
```

Example 6-6. NavBarClient.aspx

```
<%@ Page Language="vb" %>
<%@ Register TagPrefix="aspnetian" Namespace="aspnetian"
   Assembly="NavBar" %>
<html>
<head>
  <script runat="server">
    Sub Page_Load()
      'NB1.CreateBlankFile()
    End Sub
  </script>
</head>
<body>
  <table border="1" width="100%" cellpadding="20" cellspacing="0">
    <tr>
```

Example 6-6. NavBarClient.aspx (continued)

```
            <td align="center" width="150">
              <img src="aspnetian.jpg"/>
            </td>
            <td align="center">
              <h1>NavBar Control Client Page<h1>
            </td>
          </tr>
          <tr>
            <td width="150">
              <form runat="server">
                <aspnetian:NavBar id="NB1"
                    showdividers="False" runat="server">
                  <strong>Navigation Bar</strong>
                  <br/>
                </aspnetian:NavBar>
              </form>
            </td>
            <td>
              This is where page content might be placed
              <br/><br/><br/><br/><br/><br/><br/><br/><br/>
            </td>
          </tr>
        </table>
    </body>
    </html>
```

Compositional Controls

As mentioned earlier in the chapter, compositional controls render their output by combining appropriate controls within the CreateChildControls method, which is overridden in the custom control.

Example 6-7 shows the C# code for a compositional control that provides simple functionality for a *blog* (which is short for web log). The control has two modes: Add and Display. The mode is determined by the internal member _mode, which can be accessed by the public Mode property.

Like the NavBar control created in the previous example, the class definition for the Blog control specifies that the class derives from the Panel control (using C#'s : syntax), and also implements the INamingContainer interface. The INamingContainer interface contains no members, so there's nothing to actually implement. It's simply used to tell the ASP.NET runtime to provide a separate naming scope for controls contained within the custom control. This helps avoid the possibility of naming conflicts at runtime.

Also like the NavBar control, the Blog control uses an XML file to store the individual Blog entries. The example uses the same method of retrieving the data, namely creating a dataset and calling its ReadXml method, passing in the name of the XML file.

Figure 6-1. NavBarClient.aspx output

In addition to declaring the _mode member variable and the BlogDS dataset, the example declares two Textbox controls (which will be used when adding a new blog entry) and two more string member variables (_addRedirect and _email).

The code in Example 6-7 then creates public property accessors for all three string variables. The Mode property determines whether the control displays existing blogs or displays fields for creating a new blog. The AddRedirect property takes the URL for a page to redirect to when a new blog is added. The Email property takes an email address to link to in each new blog field.

Next, the program overrides the OnInit method of the derived control to handle the Init event when it is called by the runtime. In this event handler, you call the Load-Data method, which, like the same method in the NavBar control, loads the data from the XML file or, if no file exists, creates a blank file. It then calls the OnInit method of the base class to ensure that necessary initialization work is taken care of.

Next is the overridden CreateChildControls method. Like the Render method, this method is called automatically by the ASP.NET runtime when the page is instantiated on the server. Unlike the Render method, you don't want to call the CreateChildControls method of the base class, or you'll create a loop in which this method calls itself recursively (and the ASP.NET process will hang). In the Create-ChildControls method, you check the value of the _mode member variable and call either the DisplayBlogs method or the NewBlog method, depending on the value of _mode. Note that this value is set by default to display, so if the property is not set, the control will be in display mode. Also note that the example uses the ToLower method of the String class to ensure that either uppercase or lowercase attribute values work properly.

The DisplayBlogs method iterates through the data returned in the dataset and instantiates controls to display this data. We use an if statement to determine whether more than one entry in a row has the same date. If so, we display only a single date header for the group of entries with the same date. We add an Html-Anchor control to each entry to facilitate the readers' ability to bookmark the URL for a given entry. Then we write out the entry itself and add a contact email address and a link to the specific entry at the end of each entry.

Example 6-7. Blog.cs

```
using System;
using System.Data;
using System.Drawing;
using System.IO;
using System.Web;
using System.Web.UI;
using System.Web.UI.HtmlControls;
using System.Web.UI.WebControls;

namespace aspnetian
{

public class Blog:Panel, INamingContainer
{

    protected DataSet BlogDS;
    protected TextBox TitleTB;
    protected TextBox BlogText;

    private string _addRedirect;
    private string _email;
    private string _mode = "display";

    public string AddRedirect
    {
        get
        {
            return this._addRedirect;
        }
        set
        {
            this._addRedirect = value;
        }
    }

    public string Email
```

Example 6-7. Blog.cs (continued)

```csharp
{
   get
   {
      return this._email;
   }
   set
   {
      this._email = value;
   }
}

public string Mode
{
   get
   {
      return this._mode;
   }
   set
   {
      this._mode = value;
   }
}

protected override void OnInit(EventArgs e)
{
   LoadData();
   base.OnInit(e);
}

protected override void CreateChildControls()
{
   if (this._mode.ToLower() != "add")
   {
      DisplayBlogs();
   }
   else
   {
      NewBlog();
   }
}

protected void LoadData()
{
   BlogDS = new DataSet();

   try
   {
      BlogDS.ReadXml(Page.Server.MapPath("Blog.xml"));
   }
   catch (FileNotFoundException fnfEx)
   {
      CreateBlankFile();
```

Example 6-7. Blog.cs (continued)

```
            LoadData();
        }
    }

    protected void DisplayBlogs()
    {
        DateTime BlogDate;
        DateTime CurrentDate = new DateTime();

        DataRowCollection BlogRows = BlogDS.Tables[0].Rows;
        foreach (DataRow BlogDR in BlogRows)
        {
            string BDate = BlogDR["date"].ToString();
            BlogDate = new DateTime(Convert.ToInt32(BDate.Substring(4, 4)),
                Convert.ToInt32(BDate.Substring(0, 2)),
                Convert.ToInt32(BDate.Substring(2, 2)));

            if (CurrentDate != BlogDate)
            {
                Label Date = new Label();
                Date.Text = BlogDate.ToLongDateString();
                Date.Font.Size = FontUnit.Large;
                Date.Font.Bold = true;
                this.Controls.Add(Date);
                this.Controls.Add(new LiteralControl("<br/><br/>"));
                CurrentDate = BlogDate;
            }

            HtmlAnchor Anchor = new HtmlAnchor();
            Anchor.Name = "#" + BlogDR["anchorID"].ToString();
            this.Controls.Add(Anchor);

            Label Title = new Label();
            Title.Text = BlogDR["title"].ToString();
            Title.Font.Size = FontUnit.Larger;
            Title.Font.Bold = true;
            this.Controls.Add(Title);

            this.Controls.Add(new LiteralControl("<p>"));
            LiteralControl BlogText = new LiteralControl("<div>" +
                BlogDR["text"].ToString() + "</div>");
            this.Controls.Add(BlogText);
            this.Controls.Add(new LiteralControl("</p>"));

            HyperLink Email = new HyperLink();
            Email.NavigateUrl = "mailto:" + BlogDR["email"].ToString();
            Email.Text = "E-mail me";
            this.Controls.Add(Email);

            this.Controls.Add(new LiteralControl(" | "));

            HyperLink AnchorLink = new HyperLink();
            AnchorLink.NavigateUrl = Page.Request.Url.ToString() + "#" +
```

Example 6-7. Blog.cs (continued)

```csharp
            BlogDR["anchorID"].ToString();
        AnchorLink.Text = "Link";
        this.Controls.Add(AnchorLink);

        this.Controls.Add(new LiteralControl("<hr width='100%'/><br/>"));
    }
}

protected void NewBlog()
{
    Label Title = new Label();
    Title.Text = "Create New Blog";
    Title.Font.Size = FontUnit.Larger;
    Title.Font.Bold = true;
    this.Controls.Add(Title);

    this.Controls.Add(new LiteralControl("<br/><br/>"));

    Label TitleLabel = new Label();
    TitleLabel.Text = "Title: ";
    TitleLabel.Font.Bold = true;
    this.Controls.Add(TitleLabel);
    TitleTB = new TextBox();
    this.Controls.Add(TitleTB);

    this.Controls.Add(new LiteralControl("<br/>"));

    Label BlogTextLabel = new Label();
    BlogTextLabel.Text = "Text: ";
    BlogTextLabel.Font.Bold = true;
    this.Controls.Add(BlogTextLabel);
    BlogText = new TextBox();
    BlogText.TextMode = TextBoxMode.MultiLine;
    BlogText.Rows = 10;
    BlogText.Columns = 40;
    this.Controls.Add(BlogText);

    this.Controls.Add(new LiteralControl("<br/>"));

    Button Submit = new Button();
    Submit.Text = "Submit";
    Submit.Click += new EventHandler(this.Submit_Click);
    this.Controls.Add(Submit);
}

protected void Submit_Click(object sender, EventArgs e)
{
    EnsureChildControls();
    AddBlog();
}

protected void AddBlog()
```

Example 6-7. Blog.cs (continued)

```
    {
        DataRow NewBlogDR;
        NewBlogDR = BlogDS.Tables[0].NewRow();
        NewBlogDR["date"] = FormatDate(DateTime.Today);
        NewBlogDR["title"] = TitleTB.Text;
        NewBlogDR["text"] = BlogText.Text;
        NewBlogDR["anchorID"] = Guid.NewGuid().ToString();
        NewBlogDR["email"] = _email;
        BlogDS.Tables[0].Rows.InsertAt(NewBlogDR, 0);
        BlogDS.WriteXml(Page.Server.MapPath("Blog.xml"));
        Page.Response.Redirect(_addRedirect);
    }

    protected string FormatDate(DateTime dt)
    {
        string retString;

        retString = String.Format("{0:D2}", dt.Month);
        retString += String.Format("{0:D2}", dt.Day);
        retString += String.Format("{0:D2}", dt.Year);
        return retString;
    }

    protected void CreateBlankFile()
    {
        // code to create new file...omitted to conserve space
    }

} // closing bracket for class declaration

} // closing bracket for namespace declaration
```

Displaying the blog entries is only half the battle. While it would certainly be possible to edit the XML file directly in order to add a new blog entry, it makes much more sense to make this a feature of the control. This is what the NewBlog method does. In the NewBlog method, we instantiate Label and TextBox controls for data entry and a Button control to submit the new blog entry. When the Button is clicked, the Submit_Click event handler method is called when the control is re-created on the server. The Submit_Click event handler, in turn, calls the AddBlog method to insert a new row into the BlogDS dataset and then writes the contents of the dataset back to the underlying XML file. Before using the control, of course, we'll need to compile it and place it in the application's *bin* directory. The following snippet can be used to compile the control:

```
csc /t:library /out:bin\blog.dll /r:system.dll,system.data.dll,
system.xml.dll,system.web.dll blog.cs
```

Example 6-8 shows the ASP.NET code necessary to instantiate the Blog control programmatically. Note the use of the PlaceHolder control to precisely locate the Blog control output. For this code to work correctly, the compiled assembly containing the Blog control must reside in the application's *bin* subdirectory. Figure 6-2 shows the output of the control when used in the client page shown in Example 6-8.

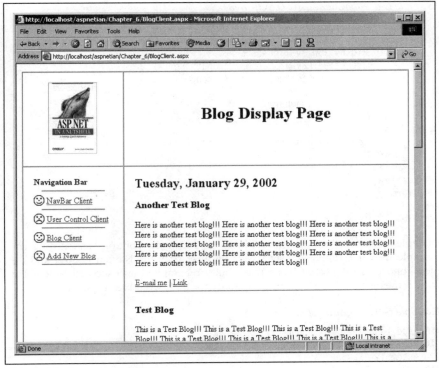

Figure 6-2. Output of BlogClient.aspx

Example 6-8. BlogClient.aspx

```
<%@ Page Language="vb" debug="true" %>
<%@ Register TagPrefix="aspnetian" Namespace="aspnetian"
   Assembly="NavBar" %>
<html>
<head>
    <script runat="server">
        Sub Page_Load()
            Dim Blog1 As New Blog()
            PH.Controls.Add(Blog1)
        End Sub
    </script>
</head>
<body>
    <form runat="server">
    <table border="1" width="100%" cellpadding="20" cellspacing="0">
        <tr>
            <td align="center" width="150">
              <img src="aspnetian.jpg"/>
            </td>
            <td align="center">
              <h1>Blog Display Page<h1>
            </td>
```

Example 6-8. BlogClient.aspx (continued)

```
              </tr>
              <tr>
                  <td width="150" valign="top">
                      <aspnetian:NavBar id="NB1" runat="server">
                          <strong>Navigation Bar</strong>
                          <br/>
                      </aspnetian:NavBar>
                  </td>
                  <td>
                      <asp:placeholder id="PH" runat="server"/>
                  </td>
              </tr>
          </table>
          </form>
      </body>
      </html>
```

Example 6-9 shows the code necessary to instantiate the control declaratively. The
example uses the TagPrefix aspnetian2 because both the NavBar control and the
Blog control use the same namespace, but are compiled into separate assemblies
(which means that using the same TagPrefix for both would result in an error).

Example 6-9. BlogAdd.aspx

```
<%@ Page Language="vb" debug="true" %>
<%@ Register TagPrefix="aspnetian" Namespace="aspnetian"
    Assembly="NavBar" %>
<%@ Register TagPrefix="aspnetian2" Namespace="aspnetian"
    Assembly="Blog" %>
<html>
<head>
    <script runat="server">
        Sub Page_Load()
            'Uncomment the line below to explicitly create a blank
            '   XML file, then comment the line out again to run the control
            'NB1.CreateBlankFile()
        End Sub
    </script>
</head>
<body>
    <form runat="server">
    <table border="1" width="100%" cellpadding="20" cellspacing="0">
        <tr>
            <td align="center" width="150">
                <img src="aspnetian.jpg"/>
            </td>
            <td align="center">
                <h1>Blog Add Page<h1>
            </td>
        </tr>
        <tr>
            <td width="150" valign="top">
```

Example 6-9. BlogAdd.aspx (continued)

```
            <aspnetian:NavBar id="NB1" runat="server">
                <strong>Navigation Bar</strong>
                <br/>
            </aspnetian:NavBar>
        </td>
        <td>
            <aspnetian2:Blog id="Blog1"
                mode="Add"
                addredirect="BlogClient.aspx"
                email="graymad@att.net"
                runat="server"/>
        </td>
    </tr>
    </table>
    </form>
</body>
</html>
```

As you can see, whether the control is used programmatically or declaratively, the amount of code necessary to provide simple blogging functionality is made trivial by the use of a custom server control. Note that you can also have the same page use the Blog control in either Display or Add mode, depending on the user's actions, as explained in the following section.

Adding Design-Time Support

While using the Blog control in a Web Forms page is fairly simple, it's still not 100 percent intuitive. For example, without documentation, there's no way for someone using the Blog control to know what the appropriate values for the Mode property are. Without explicitly telling developers using the control about the Add mode, it would be difficult for them to discover and use this mode on their own.

For developers using Visual Studio .NET (or another IDE that supports IntelliSense), you can solve this problem by adding design-time support to the control. This is done by using a combination of special metadata attributes added to the control and custom XSD schemas to support IntelliSense statement completion for Web Forms pages. IntelliSense support in code-behind modules is automatic and requires no additional coding.

Part of the challenge of providing design-time support for custom server controls is that different editors in the Visual Studio IDE require different techniques to support design-time functionality. Custom controls automatically support IntelliSense statement completion when working with code-behind modules in Visual Basic .NET or C#. Figure 6-3 shows this statement completion in action for the Blog control.

Unfortunately, when editing Web Forms pages, automatic support for statement completion does not extend to the Design or HTML views (nor does Visual Studio provide built-in support for viewing and editing properties in the Property browser without additional work in your control). To complicate things further, one technique is necessary for supporting IntelliSense in the Property browser and Design view of the Web Forms editor, while another is necessary for supporting it in the HTML view of the Web Forms editor.

Controls

Figure 6-3. IntelliSense in code-behind

The technique required for supporting property browsing in Design view uses metadata attributes to inform Visual Studio .NET about how to handle the properties. Supporting statement completion and property browsing in HTML view requires creating a custom XSD schema that describes the types in your control. We'll discuss both techniques in the next sections.

Metadata attributes

Visual Studio .NET provides rich support for designing and modifying controls visually by using drag-and-drop techniques and tools, such as the Property browser, and related designers, such as the color picker. Support for these tools is provided by a series of metadata attributes that you can add to your control. These attributes tell the Visual Studio IDE whether to display any properties that your control exposes in the Properties browser, what type the properties are, and which designer should be used to set the properties' values.

To support editing of the AddRedirect property in the Property browser, we would add the following attributes before the Property procedure, as shown in the following code snippet:

```
[
Browsable(true),
Category("Behavior"),
Description("URL to which the page should redirect after
    successful submission of a new Blog entry."),
Editor(typeof(System.Web.UI.Design.UrlEditor), typeof(UITypeEditor))
]
```

```
public string AddRedirect
{ // property procedure code }
```

These attribute declarations allow the property to be displayed in the Property browser, set the desired category for the property (when properties are sorted by category), provide a description of the property, and tell Visual Studio .NET to use the UrlEditor designer to edit the property's value.

The attribute syntax shown in this section is for C#. In C#, attributes take the form:

```
[AttributeName(AttributeParams)]
```

In Visual Basic .NET, attributes are declared with the following syntax:

```
<AttributeName(AttributeParams)>
```

Visual Basic .NET requires that the attribute declaration appear on the same line as the member it's modifying, so it's usually a good idea to follow the attribute with a VB line continuation character to improve readability:

```
<AttributeName(AttributeParams)> _
Public Membername()
```

In both C# and VB, you can declare multiple attributes within a single set of [ ] or <> brackets by separating multiple attributes with commas.

In addition to setting attributes at the property level, you can set certain attributes at the class and assembly levels. For example, you can use the assembly-level attribute `TagPrefix` to specify the tag prefix to use for any controls contained in the assembly. Visual Studio .NET then inserts this tag prefix automatically when you add an instance of the control to a Web Forms page from the Visual Studio toolbox. The following code snippet shows the syntax for the `TagPrefix` attribute. This attribute should be placed within the class module that defines the control, but outside the class and namespace declarations.

```
[
assembly: TagPrefix("aspnetian", "aspnetian").
]

namespace aspnetian
{ // control classes, etc. }
```

To complete the integration of a control in the Visual Studio .NET environment, add the `ToolBoxData` attribute (which tells Visual Studio .NET your preferred tag name for controls inserted from the toolbox) to the class that implements the control:

```
[
ToolboxData("<{0}:Blog runat=server></{0}:Blog>")
]
public class Blog:Panel, INamingContainer
{ // control implementation }
```

Once compiled, the control will support automatic insertion of the @ Register directive, tag prefix, and tag name for the Blog control. To add the control to the Visual Studio .NET toolbox, follow these simple steps:

1. In Design view, select the Web Forms tab of the Visual Studio .NET toolbox.

2. Right-click anywhere in the tab and select Customize Toolbox.

3. Select the .NET Framework Components tab, and then click Browse.

4. Browse to the location of the compiled control assembly, select it, and click Open.

5. Click OK.

Once the control has been added to the toolbox, you can add it to a Web Forms page by either double-clicking the control or dragging and dropping it from the toolbox onto the Web Forms page. In either case, Visual Studio .NET will automatically insert the correct @ Register directive, including setting the TagPrefix based on the assembly-level attribute, and will also create a set of tags for the control with the tag name specified in the ToolBoxData attribute.

Adding a designer

As written, the Blog control will not have any visible interface in the Design view of the Web Forms editor. This can make it more difficult to select the control on the page, and also may make it more difficult to understand what the control will look like at runtime. To correct this problem, we can add support for a designer that will render HTML at design time that approximates the look of the Blog control at runtime. Note that you can also create designers that completely reproduce the runtime output of a control, but doing so is more involved and beyond the scope of this book

All server control designers derive from the class System.Web.UI.Design. ControlDesigner, which exposes a number of methods you can override to provide design-time rendering for your control. Example 6-10 overrides the GetDesignTimeHtml method to return simple HTML. Note that the example shows the entire designer class for the Blog control, which you can add to the existing *Blog.cs* class file (making sure that the class declaration is within the namespace curly braces).

Example 6-10. BlogDesigner class

```
public class BlogDesigner:ControlDesigner
{
    public override string GetDesignTimeHtml()
    {
        return "<h1>Blog</h1><hr/><hr/>";
    }
}
```

To tie this designer into the Blog class, we use the Designer attribute, as shown in the following snippet. Note that this code also adds a Description attribute that describes what the control does.

```
[
Description("Simple Blog control. Supports display of Web log / news
    items from an XML file."),
Designer(typeof(aspnetian.BlogDesigner)),
ToolboxData("<{0}:Blog runat=server></{0}:Blog>")
]
public class Blog:Panel, INamingContainer
{ // class implementation }
```

As you can see, the BlogDesigner class is extremely simple, but it adds a lot to the control's design-time appearance on a web page, as shown in Figure 6-4.

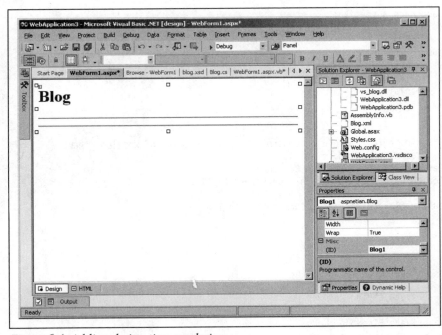

Figure 6-4. Adding design-time rendering

Example 6-11 shows the code for the Blog control, updated with attributes to enable design-time support for the control in Design view and the Property browser. Note that the example adds several using directives to import the namespaces needed to support the attributes and designer classes we've used. The example also adds an enumeration to be used for the value of the Mode property and a new property, SeparatorColor.

Example 6-11. Updated Blog.cs

```
using System;
using System.ComponentModel;
using System.Data;
using System.Drawing;
using System.Drawing.Design;
using System.IO;
```

Example 6-11. Updated Blog.cs (continued)

```
using System.Web;
using System.Web.UI;
using System.Web.UI.Design;
using System.Web.UI.HtmlControls;
using System.Web.UI.WebControls;

[
assembly: TagPrefix("aspnetian", "aspnetian")
]

namespace aspnetian
{

public enum BlogMode
{
    Add,
    Display
}

[
Description(@"Simple Blog control. Supports display of Web log / news
    items from an XML file."),
Designer(typeof(aspnetian.BlogDesigner)),
ToolboxData("<{0}:Blog runat=server></{0}:Blog>")
]
public class Blog:Panel, INamingContainer
{

    protected DataSet BlogDS;
    protected TextBox TitleTB;
    protected TextBox BlogText;

    private string _addRedirect;
    private string _email;
    private BlogMode _mode;
    private Color _separatorColor = Color.Black;

    [
    Browsable(true),
    Category("Behavior"),
    Description("URL to which the page should redirect after
        successful submission of a new Blog entry."),
    Editor(typeof(System.Web.UI.Design.UrlEditor), typeof(UITypeEditor))
    ]
    public string AddRedirect
    {
        get
        {
            return this._addRedirect;
        }
        set
```

Example 6-11. Updated Blog.cs (continued)

```
        {
            this._addRedirect = value;
        }
    }


    [
    Browsable(true),
    Category("Behavior"),
    Description("Email address the control will use for listing in new
        Blog entries.")
    ]
    public string Email
    {
        get
        {
            return this._email;
        }
        set
        {
            this._email = value;
        }
    }


    [
    Browsable(true),
    Category("Behavior"),
    Description("Controls whether existing Blogs are displayed, or
        fields for creating a new Blog entry.")
    ]
    public BlogMode Mode
    {
        get
        {
            return this._mode;
        }
        set
        {
            this._mode = value;
        }
    }


    [
    Browsable(true),
    Category("Appearance"),
    Description("Controls the color of the line that separates Blog
        entries when in display mode.")
    ]
    public Color SeparatorColor
    {
        get
        {
            return this._separatorColor;
        }
```

Example 6-11. Updated Blog.cs (continued)

```
      set
      {
         this._separatorColor = value;
      }
   }

   protected override void OnInit(EventArgs e)
   {
      LoadData();
      base.OnInit(e);
   }

   protected override void CreateChildControls()
   {
      if (this._mode != BlogMode.Add)
      {
         DisplayBlogs();
      }
      else
      {
         NewBlog();
      }
   }

   protected void LoadData()
   {
      BlogDS = new DataSet();

      try
      {
         BlogDS.ReadXml(Page.Server.MapPath("Blog.xml"));
      }
      catch (FileNotFoundException fnfEx)
      {
         CreateBlankFile();
         LoadData();
      }
   }

   protected void DisplayBlogs()
   {
      DateTime BlogDate;
      DateTime CurrentDate = new DateTime();

      DataRowCollection BlogRows = BlogDS.Tables[0].Rows;
      foreach (DataRow BlogDR in BlogRows)
      {
         string BDate = BlogDR["date"].ToString();
         BlogDate = new DateTime(Convert.ToInt32(BDate.Substring(4, 4)),
            Convert.ToInt32(BDate.Substring(0, 2)),
            Convert.ToInt32(BDate.Substring(2, 2)));
```

Example 6-11. Updated Blog.cs (continued)

```
        if (CurrentDate != BlogDate)
        {
            Label Date = new Label();
            Date.Text = BlogDate.ToLongDateString();
            Date.Font.Size = FontUnit.Large;
            Date.Font.Bold = true;
            this.Controls.Add(Date);
            this.Controls.Add(new LiteralControl("<br/><br/>"));
            CurrentDate = BlogDate;
        }

        HtmlAnchor Anchor = new HtmlAnchor();
        Anchor.Name = "#" + BlogDR["anchorID"].ToString();
        this.Controls.Add(Anchor);

        Label Title = new Label();
        Title.Text = BlogDR["title"].ToString();
        Title.Font.Size = FontUnit.Larger;
        Title.Font.Bold = true;
        this.Controls.Add(Title);

        this.Controls.Add(new LiteralControl("<p>"));
        LiteralControl BlogText = new LiteralControl("<div>" +
            BlogDR["text"].ToString() + "</div>");
        this.Controls.Add(BlogText);
        this.Controls.Add(new LiteralControl("</p>"));

        HyperLink Email = new HyperLink();
        Email.NavigateUrl = "mailto:" + BlogDR["email"].ToString();
        Email.Text = "E-mail me";
        this.Controls.Add(Email);

        this.Controls.Add(new LiteralControl(" | "));
        HyperLink AnchorLink = new HyperLink();
        AnchorLink.NavigateUrl = Page.Request.Url.ToString() + "#" +
            BlogDR["anchorID"].ToString();
        AnchorLink.Text = "Link";
        this.Controls.Add(AnchorLink);

        this.Controls.Add(new LiteralControl("<hr color='" +
            _separatorColor.ToKnownColor() + "' width='100%'/><br/>"));
    }
}

protected void NewBlog()
{
    Label Title = new Label();
    Title.Text = "Create New Blog";
    Title.Font.Size = FontUnit.Larger;
    Title.Font.Bold = true;
    this.Controls.Add(Title);
```

Example 6-11. Updated Blog.cs (continued)

```csharp
        this.Controls.Add(new LiteralControl("<br/><br/>"));

        Label TitleLabel = new Label();
        TitleLabel.Text = "Title: ";
        TitleLabel.Font.Bold = true;
        this.Controls.Add(TitleLabel);
        TitleTB = new TextBox();
        this.Controls.Add(TitleTB);

        this.Controls.Add(new LiteralControl("<br/>"));

        Label BlogTextLabel = new Label();
        BlogTextLabel.Text = "Text: ";
        BlogTextLabel.Font.Bold = true;
        this.Controls.Add(BlogTextLabel);
        BlogText = new TextBox();
        BlogText.TextMode = TextBoxMode.MultiLine;
        BlogText.Rows = 10;
        BlogText.Columns = 40;
        this.Controls.Add(BlogText);

        this.Controls.Add(new LiteralControl("<br/>"));

        Button Submit = new Button();
        Submit.Text = "Submit";
        Submit.Click += new EventHandler(this.Submit_Click);
        this.Controls.Add(Submit);
    }

    protected void Submit_Click(object sender, EventArgs e)
    {
        EnsureChildControls();
        AddBlog();
    }

    protected void AddBlog()
    {
        DataRow NewBlogDR;
        NewBlogDR = BlogDS.Tables[0].NewRow();
        NewBlogDR["date"] = FormatDate(DateTime.Today);
        NewBlogDR["title"] = TitleTB.Text;
        NewBlogDR["text"] = BlogText.Text;
        NewBlogDR["anchorID"] = Guid.NewGuid().ToString();
        NewBlogDR["email"] = _email;
        BlogDS.Tables[0].Rows.InsertAt(NewBlogDR, 0);
        BlogDS.WriteXml(Page.Server.MapPath("Blog.xml"));
        Page.Response.Redirect(_addRedirect);
    }

    protected string FormatDate(DateTime dt)
    {
        string retString;
        retString = String.Format("{0:D2}", dt.Month);
```

Example 6-11. Updated Blog.cs (continued)

```
        retString += String.Format("{0:D2}", dt.Day);
        retString += String.Format("{0:D2}", dt.Year);
        return retString;
    }

    public void CreateBlankFile()
    {
        // code to create new file...omitted to conserve space
    }

}

public class BlogDesigner:ControlDesigner
{
    public override string GetDesignTimeHtml()
    {
        return "<h1>Blog</h1><hr/><hr/>";
    }
}

}
```

Custom schemas and Visual Studio annotations

As much as the metadata attributes described in the previous section help provide support for the Blog control at design time, they're missing one important piece: IntelliSense support for adding tags and attributes in the HTML view of the Web Forms editor. For developers who are more comfortable working in HTML than in WYSIWYG style, this oversight is significant.

Since the HTML view of the Web Forms editor uses XSD schemas to determine which elements and attributes to make available in a Web Forms page, to correct the oversight, we need to implement an XSD schema that describes the Blog control and the attributes that it supports. Optionally, we can add annotations to the schema that tell Visual Studio .NET about the various elements and how we'd like them to behave.

Example 6-12 contains the portion of the XSD schema specific to the Blog control. The actual schema file (which is available in the sample code for the book) also contains type definitions for the Panel control from which the Blog control is derived, as well as other necessary attribute and type definitions. These definitions were copied from the *asp.xsd* schema file created for the built-in ASP.NET Server Controls.

 You should never modify the *asp.xsd* schema file directly, but should copy any necessary type or attribute definitions to your custom schema file. While this may seem redundant, if you edit *asp.xsd* directly and a later installation or service pack for the .NET Framework overwrites this file, your custom schema entries would be lost.

Example 6-12. Blog.xsd

```xml
<?xml version="1.0" encoding="utf-8" ?>
<xsd:schema targetNamespace="urn:http://www.aspnetian.com/schemas"
    elementFormDefault="qualified"
    xmlns="urn:http://www.aspnetian.com/schemas"
    xmlns:xsd="http://www.w3.org/2001/XMLSchema"
    xmlns:vs="http://schemas.microsoft.com/Visual-Studio-Intellisense"
    vs:friendlyname="Blog Control Schema"
    vs:ishtmlschema="false"
    vs:iscasesensitive="false"
    vs:requireattributequotes="true" >
    <xsd:annotation>
        <xsd:documentation>
            Blog Control schema.
        </xsd:documentation>
    </xsd:annotation>

    <xsd:element name="Blog" type="BlogDef" />

    <!-- <aspnetian:Blog> -->
    <xsd:complexType name="BlogDef">
        <!-- <aspnetian:Blog>-specific attributes -->
        <xsd:attribute name="AddRedirect" type="xsd:string"
            vs:builder="url"/>
        <xsd:attribute name="Email" type="xsd:string"/>
        <xsd:attribute name="Mode" type="BlogMode"/>
        <xsd:attribute name="SeparatorColor" type="xsd:string"
            vs:builder="color"/>
        <!-- <asp:Panel>-specific attributes -->
        <xsd:attribute name="BackImageUrl" type="xsd:anyURI" />
        <xsd:attribute name="HorizontalAlign" type="HorizontalAlign" />
        <xsd:attribute name="Wrap" type="xsd:boolean" />
        <xsd:attribute name="Enabled" type="xsd:boolean" />
        <xsd:attribute name="BorderWidth" type="ui4" />
        <xsd:attribute name="BorderColor" type="xsd:string"
            vs:builder="color" />
        <xsd:attribute name="BorderStyle" type="BorderStyle" />
        <xsd:attributeGroup ref="WebControlAttributes" />
    </xsd:complexType>

    <!-- DataTypes -->
    <xsd:simpleType name="BlogMode">
        <xsd:restriction base="xsd:string">
            <xsd:enumeration value="Add" />
            <xsd:enumeration value="Display" />
        </xsd:restriction>
    </xsd:simpleType>
</xsd:schema>
```

In Example 6-12, note the targetNamespace and xmlns attributes on the root
schema element, which define the XML namespace for the control's schema. The
value of the targetNamespace and xmlns attributes will also be used as an attribute
in your Web Forms page to "wire up" the schema. The <xsd:element> tag defines

the root Blog element. The `<xsd:complexType>` tag defines the attributes for the Blog element, which includes the web control attributes referenced by the `<xsd:attributeGroup>` tag. Finally, the `<xsd:simpleType>` tag defines the enumeration for the BlogMode type used as one of the attributes for the Blog element.

Note that Example 6-12 uses the vs:builder annotation to tell Visual Studio .NET to use the Url builder for the `AddRedirect` attribute and the Color builder for the `SeparatorColor` attribute. The vs:builder annotation is one of many annotations available to modify schemas. The most commonly used annotations are listed in Table 6-1.

Table 6-1. Common Visual Studio .NET annotations

Annotation	Purpose	Valid values
vs:absolutepositioning	Used at the root `<schema>` element to determine whether Visual Studio may insert style attributes for positioning.	true/false
vs:blockformatted	Indicates whether leading whitespace may be added to the element during automatic formatting.	true/false
vs:builder	Specifies the builder to be used for editing the related property's value.	color, style, or url
vs:deprecated	Allows a related property to be marked as 'deprecated', which prevents it from showing up in the Properties browser and in statement completion.	true/false
vs:empty	Used at the element level to indicate that Visual Studio .NET should use single tag syntax for the related tag (no end tag).	true/false
vs:friendlyname	Used at the root level to provide a display name for the schema.	
vs:iscasesensitive	Used at the root level and specifies whether Visual Studio .NET will treat the related tags in a case-sensitive manner.	true/false
vs:ishtmlschema	Used at the root level and specifies whether the schema is an HTML document schema.	true/false
vs:nonbrowseable	Used at the attribute level and specifies that the attribute should not appear in statement completion.	true/false
vs:readonly	Used at the attribute level and specifies that the attribute may not be modified in the Properties window.	true/false
vs:requireattribute-quotes	Used at the root level and specifies that the attribute values must have quotes.	true/false

Once you've built your XSD schema, save it to the same location as the *asp.xsd* file (which defaults to *C:\ProgramFiles\MicrosoftVisualStudio.NET\Common7\ Packages\schemas\xml*).

To allow Visual Studio .NET to read your custom schema, you'll need to add an `xmlns` attribute to the `<body>` tag of the page in which you wish to use the schema, as shown in the following snippet:

```
<body xmlns:aspnetian="urn:http://www.aspnetian.com/schemas">
```

Notice that this code uses the `aspnetian` prefix with the `xmlns` attribute to specify that the schema is for controls prefixed with the `aspnetian` tag prefix. This recall is set up by the `TagPrefix` attribute (described in the previous section on "Metadata attributes"). The value of the `xmlns` attribute should be the same as the `targetNamespace` attribute defined at the root of the schema.

Once you've wired up your schema via the `xmlns` attribute, you should be able to type an opening < character and have the Blog control appear as one of the options for statement completion, as shown in Figure 6-5.

Figure 6-5. Statement completion in HTML view

Example 6-13 shows the code for a page that uses the Blog control from Visual Studio .NET, including the `xmlns` attribute added to the <body> element.

Example 6-13. BlogClient_VS.aspx

```
<%@ Register TagPrefix="aspnetian" Namespace="aspnetian"
    Assembly="Blog" %>
<%@ Page Language="vb" AutoEventWireup="True" Debug="True"%>
<!DOCTYPE HTML PUBLIC "-//W3C//DTD HTML 4.0 Transitional//EN">
<html>
    <head>
        <title>Blog Client</title>
        <meta content="Microsoft Visual Studio.NET 7.0" name="GENERATOR">
        <meta content="Visual Basic 7.0" name="CODE_LANGUAGE">
        <meta content="JavaScript" name="vs_defaultClientScript">
        <meta content="http://schemas.microsoft.com/intellisense/ie5"
```

Example 6-13. BlogClient_VS.aspx (continued)

```
        name="vs_targetSchema">
    <script runat="server">
        Sub Page_Load()
            If Request.QueryString("mode") = "add" Then
                Blog1.Mode = BlogMode.Add
                Link1.Visible = False
                Link2.Visible = False
            Else
                Blog1.Mode = BlogMode.Display
                Link1.Visible = True
                Link2.Visible = True
            End If
        End Sub
    </script>
</head>
<body xmlns:aspnetian="urn:http://www.aspnetian.com/schemas">
    <form id="Form1" method="post" runat="server">
        <p><asp:hyperlink id="Link1" runat="server"
            navigateurl="WebForm1.aspx?mode=add">
            Add Blog
            </asp:hyperlink></p>
        <p><aspnetian:blog id="Blog1" addredirect="WebForm1.aspx"
            email="andrew@aspnetian.com" runat="server" >
            </aspnetian:blog></p>
        <p><asp:hyperlink id="Link2" runat="server"
            navigateurl="WebForm1.aspx?mode=add">
            Add Blog
            </asp:hyperlink></p>
    </form>
</body>
</html>
```

Notice that Example 6-13 provides support for both displaying and adding blog entries from within the same page; this is done by omitting the Mode property in the tag that defines the control and setting the Mode programmatically (based on whether or not the page request was the result of the user clicking one of the "Add Blog" Hyperlink controls added to the page).

When the page is loaded for the first time, it will be in Display mode. Clicking one of the hyperlinks will request the page with the mode QueryString element set to add, which will cause the page to render in Add mode.

Adding Client Script

Sometimes you may want to use client-side script in your ASP.NET pages, either with controls or independent of them. In classic ASP, it was possible to write client script to the browser using Response.Write. However, this could get very messy— particularly if you needed to write the same set of code for use with more than one form element.

The ASP.NET Page class provides several methods for sending client script to the browser that make this process simpler and more reliable.

These methods include:

RegisterClientScriptBlock
>   Renders a string containing the specified client script to the browser.

RegisterHiddenField
>   Adds an <input> element whose type is set to hidden.

IsClientScriptBlockRegistered
>   Allows you to test whether a given named script block has been already registered by another control to avoid redundancy.

You might use these methods to pop up a message box on the client with the number of Blogs that currently exist in the XML file. To accomplish this, add the following snippet to the DisplayBlogs method of the Blog control:

```
Page.RegisterClientScriptBlock("Blog", "<script>alert('There are now " +
    BlogRows.Count + " Blogs!');</script>");
```

Then, if any other controls need to use the same script, call IsClientScriptBlock-Registered, passing it the name of the script shown above, Blog, to determine whether to call RegisterClientScriptBlock again. In this way, a single client-side script block may be shared among multiple controls.

Sharing Controls Across Applications

The architecture of the .NET Framework makes using a custom server control or other assembly as simple as copying that assembly to the *bin* subdirectory of your application and adding the appropriate directives and tags to your page. However, there may be times when you would like multiple applications on the same machine to be able to use the same control, without having multiple local copies of the control's assembly floating around.

Fortunately, .NET addresses this need with the Global Assembly Cache (GAC), a repository of shared assemblies that are accessible to all .NET applications on a given machine. Adding your own control assemblies to the GAC is a relatively straightforward process that requires four steps:

1. Use the *sn.exe* command-line utility to create a public key pair for use in signing your control:

    ```
    sn.exe -k Blog.snk
    ```

2. Add the AssemblyKeyFileAttribute to the file containing the control code, passing the path to the keyfile created in Step 1 as an argument. (This is an assembly-level attribute, so it should be placed outside of any namespace or class definitions.) When compiled, this attribute will result in a strongly named assembly that can be placed in the GAC:

    ```
    [assembly: AssemblyKeyFileAttribute("Blog.snk")]
    ```

3. Recompile the control.

4. Add the control to the GAC, either by dragging and dropping the assembly in Windows Explorer or by using the *gacutil.exe* utility, as follows:

    ```
    gacutil -i Blog.dll
    ```

Note that as with the *csc.exe* and *vbc.exe* command-line compilers, using the *sn.exe* and *gacutil.exe* utilities without a fully qualified path requires that you have the path to these utilities registered as part of your PATH environment variable. The *sn.exe* and *gacutil.exe* utilities are typically located in the *\FrameworkSDK\bin* directory, which is installed either under *ProgramFiles\Microsoft.NET* or *ProgramFiles\MicrosoftVisualStudio.NET*, depending on whether you've installed just the .NET Framework SDK or Visual Studio .NET.

Once you've added the control assembly to the GAC, you can now use it from any application on the machine. One caveat: to use custom controls that are installed in the GAC, you must supply the version, culture, and public key information for the assembly when adding the @ Register directive for the control, as shown in the following snippet (which should appear on a single line):

```
<%@ Register TagPrefix="aspnetian" Namespace="aspnetian" Assembly="Blog,
    Version=0.0.0.0, Culture=neutral, PublicKeyToken=6bd31f35fc9a113b" %>
```

If you've added your control to the Visual Studio .NET toolbox, when you use the control from the toolbox, the correct @ Register directive will be generated for you automatically.

Additional Resources

The following sites provide additional information on the topics discussed in this chapter:

http://www.aspfriends.com/aspfriends/aspngcontrolscs.asp
> Home page for the AspFriends.com mailing list (for any questions relating to building custom server controls in C#).

http://www.aspfriends.com/aspfriends/aspngcontrolsvb.asp
> Home page for the AspFriends.com mailing list (for any questions relating to building custom server controls in Visual Basic .NET).

http://www.aspfriends.com/aspfriends/aspngreuse.asp
> Home page for the AspFriends.com mailing list (for general reuse questions). Whether you're working on user controls or custom server controls, you can get good answers to your questions on this list.

http://www.aspnextgen.com/
> The DotNetJunkies site, run by Microsoft MVP Award winners Donny Mack and Doug Seven, contains many ASP.NET tutorials, including some on building custom server controls and user controls.

Controls

CHAPTER 7

Data Access and Data Binding

While writing simple applications without ever accessing data from a backend data store is certainly possible, most applications will, at some point, need to do so. Fortunately, the .NET Framework provides a rich set of classes designed to simplify the process of reading and writing data to both SQL Server and other backend data stores. These classes are collectively referred to as ADO.NET.

This chapter provides an overview of ADO.NET and the various tasks it facilitates—from reading data with the SqlDataReader class to updating data with the DataSet and SqlDataAdapter classes. The chapter also discusses reading from and writing to XML files and provides examples of binding retrieved data to ASP.NET Server Controls.

Data Access and Architecture

Almost everyone agrees that in all but the smallest applications, it is important to avoid performing data access directly from the ASP.NET Web Forms themselves. Accessing data directly from within a Web Form inherently ties the user interface code to the database and table schema that currently exist, making it more difficult to reuse data-access code and maintain the user interface code and backend data.

To keep the code as simple and straightforward as possible, the examples in this chapter perform data access directly from the pages. In a production application, this code should generally reside in either data-tier or business-tier components, which should return XML, a dataset, or some other database-independent structure to the presentation tier for data binding. Remember that you should always perform data calculations and modifications on a tier other than the presentation tier.

ADO.NET: An Overview

The combination of ASP.NET and ADO.NET provides great flexibility in terms of data sources. Unlike classic ADO, in which support for XML was bolted on after the basic interfaces were written, ADO.NET was written from the ground up to deal with XML and does so quite handily. For example, the DataSet class provides built-in support for reading from and writing to XML files and streams, and also provides support for reading, writing, and inferring (from the structure of a table retrieved from a DBMS) XSD schemas. This makes working with XML data quite easy, as demonstrated in the custom control examples in Chapter 6.

ADO.NET also provides excellent support for reading data from a DBMS, including a set of classes for fast, efficient access to data in SQL Server databases and another set of classes to support OLE DB data sources. Most importantly, in the DataSet class, ADO.NET provides an abstract, in-memory representation of data. By design, once the DataSet class is populated, it knows nothing about the backend source from which its data was retrieved; it only knows about the structure of the tables and data it contains and the relationships between them. This allows a great deal of flexibility when manipulating data, passing data between application tiers, or translating data between different DBMS systems.

The .NET Framework ships with two .NET Data Providers. These data providers are represented by the System.Data.SqlClient namespace, which contains classes for accessing SQL Server data, and the System.Data.OleDb namespace, which contains classes for accessing data sources using an OLE DB provider. Each provider has a class that derives from the DbDataAdapter base class, which acts as a translator between a data source and the DataSet class, as explained in the next section. For the SqlClient namespace, this class is SqlDataAdapter. For OleDB, it is OleDbDataAdapter.

Reading Data

There are two basic techniques for reading data in ADO.NET: using data readers and datasets. Additionally, data may be read from either a backend DBMS, such as SQL Server, or from a simple (or complex) XML file. In the next several sections, we'll discuss these techniques and data sources.

Reading from a Database

The following sections describe the use of data readers and datasets, provide an example, and discuss why one would use one technique over the other.

Using a data reader

The data reader technique consists of using an instance of either the SqlDataReader or OleDbDataReader class to retrieve the data in a similar fashion to a forward-only, read-only database cursor. Data readers provide lightweight access to data that is recommended when retrieving data for display in a Web Forms page or for other circumstances in which the overhead of a dataset is not desirable.

Authentication and Security

When accessing data from a backend database, one of the decisions you'll need to make is how to authenticate the user or application against the database's login credentials. It is fairly common for applications to pass a user ID and password as part of the connection string when opening a connection to the database. However, this is generally not the most secure method, since it requires storing this information in a place where the application can retrieve it when needed.

An even more serious mistake is to have an application log into the database using a privileged account, such as the SQL Server *sa* account. This mode of access allows all queries to run with *sa* privileges. If a malicious user were able to insert a query, they could delete data, modify security settings, or worse, possibly run the xp_cmdshell stored procedure, which would allow them to do just about anything on the database server.

Application code should *never* be run with a system administrator-level account. In fact, if you're going to run application code using a specific user ID and password to log into the database, you should create separate accounts for each application, including distinct accounts for reading and updating. If a particular part of an application requires only read access to the data, then it should use account credentials that are restricted to read-only access. This can help prevent the database or data from being compromised.

When using SQL Server, however, database access should be performed using a trusted connection wherever possible. All examples in this chapter use trusted connections because they do not require storing sensitive information (user IDs and passwords) where someone might be able to get at them.

Because of the security context in which the ASP.NET worker process is run, using trusted connections requires you to take one of two actions:

- Setting up the desired database to allow access to the ASPNET account used to run the ASP.NET worker process.
- Turning on Windows Authentication and Impersonation and providing the individual user accounts of those who will access the application with required access to the database. See Chapter 9 and Chapter 20 for more information on changing the authentication mode.

About the Examples

For the sake of simplicity and consistency, all examples in this chapter that access data from a DBMS use the Pubs sample database in the NetSDK named instance of the Microsoft Data Engine (MSDE). MSDE is a slimmed-down version of SQL Server that fills a role that is similar to Microsoft Access for desktop applications. The NetSDK instance may be installed along with the .NET Framework SDK samples, after installing either the .NET Framework SDK or Visual Studio .NET.

All examples in this chapter use trusted connections rather than pass a user ID and password as part of the connection string. As explained later in the chapter, this requires either adding the ASPNET account under which ASP. NET is run to the desired database or enabling Windows authentication and impersonation in the *web.config* file for the application. The examples in this chapter use the former technique.

Among the sample files included with the book is a batch file named *Add_ASPNET.bat* that adds the ASPNET account to the NetSDK MSDE instance and assigns it the required permissions in the Pubs sample database. This batch file uses the *Add_ASPNET.sql* file for its commands. Before running *Add_ASPNET.bat*, you will need to open *Add_ASPNET.sql* in a text editor and change all instances of <machine or domain> to the name of the machine or domain containing the ASPNET account. If you modify the *machine.config* file to have the ASP.NET worker process run under a different account than ASPNET, you should modify *Add_ASPNET.sql* to use that account name—including the machine or domain name of the account.

Add_ASPNET.bat itself uses a trusted connection to access MSDE, so you must run this batch file while logged in using an account that has administrative access to the NetSDK instance of MSDE (by default, this will include any members of the Administrators group on the machine on which MSDE is installed). Running *Add_ASPNET.bat* should result in output that looks like that shown in Figure 7-1.

Once you've run *Add_ASPNET.bat*, you're ready to run the samples included with this chapter, which are downloadable from the O'Reilly web site at *http://examples.oreilly.com/aspdotnetnut/*.

Figure 7-1. Output of Add_ASPNET.bat

Example 7-1 shows the implementation of a SqlDataReader object, which retrieves two columns from the Titles table of the Pubs sample database from the NetSDK instance of MSDE. The output from Example 7-1 should look similar to Figure 7-2.

Example 7-1. ReadTitles.aspx

```
<%@ Page Language="VB" %>
<%@ Import Namespace="System.Data.SqlClient" %>
<html>
    <title>SqlDataReader Example</title>
    <head>
        <script runat="server">
            Sub Page_Load()
                Dim ConnStr As String = "Data Source=(local)\NetSDK;" & _
                    "Initial Catalog=Pubs;Trusted_Connection=True;"
                Dim SQL As String = "SELECT title, price FROM titles " & _
                    "WHERE PRICE IS NOT NULL"
                Dim PubsConn As New SqlConnection(ConnStr)
                Dim TitlesCmd As New SqlCommand(SQL, PubsConn)
                Dim Titles As SqlDataReader
                PubsConn.Open()
                Titles = TitlesCmd.ExecuteReader()
                Output.Text = "<table>"
                While Titles.Read()
                    Output.Text &= "<tr>"
                    Output.Text &= "<td>" & Titles.GetString(0) & "</td>"
                    Output.Text &= "<td>$" & _
                        Format(Titles.GetDecimal(1), "##0.00") & "</td>"
                    Output.Text &= "</tr>"
                End While
                Output.Text &= "</table>"
                Titles.Close()
                PubsConn.Close()
            End Sub
        </script>
    </head>
<body>
    <h1>SqlDataReader Example</h1>
    <asp:label id="Output" runat="server"/>
</body>
</html>
```

Example 7-1 begins by adding an @ Import directive to import the System.Data. SqlClient namespace. The example uses an ASP.NET Label control called Output for the display of the retrieved data. To get the data, we create string variables for the connection string and the desired SQL statement and then create a new SqlConnection instance, passing the variable containing the desired connection string to its constructor, which initializes the appropriate properties on the connection. We then create a new SqlCommand instance, passing the SQL string and the new connection object to its constructor. Then we create a SqlDataReader object variable, open the connection to the database, and set the SqlDataReader object variable to the instance returned by the ExecuteReader method of the SqlCommand class.

To display the data, we begin by sending an HTML <table> tag to the Text property of the Label control and then loop through the contents of the data reader, adding a row with two cells for each row in the data reader. The SqlDataReaders' Read method advances the reader to the next available row and returns a Boolean indicating whether there is more data to read. This makes it ideal for looping through data. Note that the example uses the Visual Basic .NET *Format* function to format the price data with trailing zeros.

Finally, once we've read through all the rows in the data reader, we append a closing </table> tag to the Text property of the label and close both the data reader and the connection. It is very important that you close both when using a data reader, since failing to close either object can negatively impact the scalability of your application by interfering with the built-in connection pooling mechanism provided by ADO.NET.

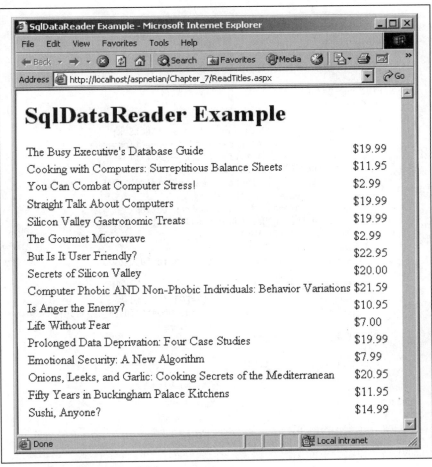

Figure 7-2. Output of ReadTitles.aspx

Dataset and data adapter

For circumstances when simply reading through a set of rows once is not sufficient, or if you plan to modify data that you've retrieved for later updating on the
backend data store, the data reader will not be sufficient to meet your needs. For
these occasions, the DataSet class (part of the System.Data namespace) and the
SqlDataAdapter provide more functionality and flexibility than the SqlDataReader,
albeit at the cost of additional overhead.

Example 7-2 retrieves the same data as Example 7-1, but uses a SqlDataAdapter and
a DataSet instead of the SqlDataReader. This example is written in C#, to demonstrate that the basic syntax of calling the ADO.NET classes is very similar in both VB.
NET and C#, with the major difference being the variable declaration syntax.

Example 7-2. ReadTitles_DataSet.aspx

```
<%@ Page Language="C#" %>
<%@ Import Namespace="System.Data" %>
<%@ Import Namespace="System.Data.SqlClient" %>
<html>
    <title>DataSet Example</title>
    <head>
        <script runat="server">
            void Page_Load()
            {
                String ConnStr = "Data Source=(local)\\NetSDK;"
                    + "Initial Catalog=Pubs;Trusted_Connection=True;";
                String SQL = "SELECT title, price FROM titles "
                    + "WHERE PRICE IS NOT NULL";
                SqlDataAdapter TitlesAdpt = new SqlDataAdapter(SQL, ConnStr);
                DataSet Titles = new DataSet();
                // No need to open or close the connection
                //    since the SqlDataAdapter will do this automatically.
                TitlesAdpt.Fill(Titles);
                Output.Text = "<table>";
                foreach (DataRow Title in Titles.Tables[0].Rows)
                {
                    Output.Text += "<tr>";
                    Output.Text += "<td>" + Title[0] + "</td>";
                    Output.Text += "<td>" + String.Format("{0:c}", Title[1])
                        + "</td>";
                    Output.Text += "</tr>";
                }
                Output.Text += "</table>";
            }
        </script>
    </head>
<body>
    <h1>DataSet Example</h1>
    <asp:label id="Output" runat="server"/>
</body>
</html>
```

In addition to the @ Import statement for the System.Data.SqlClient namespace, we add another @ Import statement to import the System.Data namespace, which allows us to call the DataSet and DataRow classes without fully qualifying their namespace name.

As in Example 7-1, we begin by creating a connection string and a SQL statement, but unlike Example 7-1, we do not need to create instances of the SqlConnection and SqlCommand objects; by passing the SQL statement and connection string to the constructor of the SqlDataAdapter class, the data adapter instance creates the connection and command objects internally.

Now, instead of creating a SqlDataReader, we create a new SqlDataAdapter, passing in the SQL statement and connection string created earlier, and then create a new dataset. We then call the SqlDataAdapter's Fill method to retrieve the data and store it in the dataset. When the Fill method is called, the SqlDataAdapter creates a connection based on the provided connection string, opens it, executes the query, and then closes the connection. This feature results in simpler and cleaner code and reduces the likelihood of forgetting to close a connection.

 If you open a connection associated with a SqlDataAdapter object (or an OleDbDataAdapter object) before calling Fill or Update, the data adapter will not close the connection automatically. If you open the connection explicitly, always be sure to close it, or you may find your scalability suffering.

Once the dataset has been filled, we loop through the rows in the first (and only) table of the dataset by using the C# foreach statement, sending output to the Text property of the Label control, as in Example 7-1. Note that the example actually declares the DataRow instance Title within the foreach statement. In Visual Basic .NET, you would declare the instance outside of the loop and then refer to it by name in the For Each statement.

Also note that in C#, when referring by index to items such as the tables in the DataSet object or the items in a DataRow object, you must use square brackets (rather than the parentheses you would use in Visual Basic .NET). This is consistently one of the biggest gotchas in moving from VB.NET to C# and vice-versa. One final difference in the looping code between Examples 7-1 and 7-2 is that since the VB.NET Format function is not available for formatting the price data, we use the static Format method exposed by the String class instead; it formats the data as currency and includes the appropriate regional currency symbol for the current system.

Another important point to observe about the code in Example 7-2 is that because we're not keeping a database connection open while looping through the data, we can take as much time as we'd like in displaying the data without affecting the ability of others to obtain connections to the database. We can also use the ASP.NET cache engine to cache the entire dataset for later use, if desired, so that we don't have to retrieve the data again. For data that is updated infrequently, this can result in a significant performance improvement, since it is far faster to retrieve a dataset from memory than to requery the data from the database.

The output of Example 7-2 should look much like Figure 7-2 (with the exception of the heading, which will read "DataSet Example").

Reading from XML

One of the neat things about the DataSet class is that it doesn't require a data adapter or a backend DBMS. Instead, you can populate a dataset from an XML file or stream by using the DataSet's ReadXml method. The ReadXml method is overloaded and can read from a Stream, a TextReader, an XmlReader, or from a file by passing the filename as a string. This last technique is illustrated in the custom control examples in Chapter 6, both of which use the ReadXml method to populate a dataset with data from an XML file.

Data Binding

Although Examples 7-1 and 7-2 are written in different languages and use different techniques for retrieving data, they both write out the rendering code for formatting the data manually. In simple examples like these, this does not seem too burdensome. When doing more complex rendering, though, it can become quite involved and produce code that is difficult to maintain.

When working with data in a rich client application, the solution has been to use data-bound controls to display data, allowing the controls to take care of the rendering of each row of data based on control properties set by the developer. Microsoft introduced a similar idea for web development by adding client-side data-binding features to Internet Explorer. However, these features were only useful when you could be certain that all of your clients were using Internet Explorer, and in some cases, their use entailed expensive marshalling of data to the client.

ASP.NET introduces a new server-side data binding feature that addresses these issues. Data binding to server controls in ASP.NET can significantly reduce the amount of code that needs to be written and maintained for displaying data. In addition, since all data binding occurs on the server side and only HTML is returned to the client, server-side data binding provides great cross-browser compatibility.

You can perform data binding against properties for single-value binding or against data sources that contain multiple rows, such as collections, data tables, and data views, allowing rich formatting of data with a minimum of code. Data binding can be performed explicitly by using the <%# %> syntax, or implicitly by setting the data source of a bindable control to an appropriate object (objects to be bound to must implement the IEnumerable interface). In both cases, the data binding occurs when the Databind method of the page or control is called. Note that when Databind is called at the page level, the Page class will, in turn, call Databind on all of its constituent controls. Therefore, if you have a large number of controls on a page, only a few of which are databound, it may be more efficient to call the Databind method of these controls directly.

Binding to Properties

Example 7-3, one of the simplest possible implementations of data binding, binds to a property exposed at the page level. In this example, we create a public member variable called FontColor, and in the Page_Load event handler, we set its value to "Red". In the body of the page, we use the <%# %> syntax to tell ASP.NET to evaluate the contents of these brackets when the DataBind method of the page is called. Back in Page_Load, we call DataBind, which substitutes the value of the FontColor property for the two data binding expressions in the body. The output of Example 7-3 is shown in Figure 7-3. Example 7-4 shows the HTML produced by Example 7-3.

Example 7-3. BindProperty.aspx

```
<%@ Page Language="VB" %>
<html>
<head>
    <title>Simple DataBinding Example</title>
    <script runat="server">
        Dim FontColor As String
        Sub Page_Load( )
            FontColor = "Red"
            DataBind( )
        End Sub
    </script>
</head>
<body>
    <h1>Simple DataBinding Example</h1>
    The value for FontColor is
        <font color="<%# FontColor %>"><%# FontColor %></font>.
</body>
</html>
```

Figure 7-3. Output of BindProperty.aspx

Example 7-4. HTML Output of BindProperty.aspx

```
<html>
<head>
   <title>Simple DataBinding Example</title>
</head>
<body>
   <h1>Simple DataBinding Example</h1>
   The value for FontColor is
      <font color="Red">Red</font>.
</body>
</html>
```

Binding to Collections

While more involved than binding to a property, binding to a collection is still quite simple. Example 7-5 uses an ArrayList to store values that will be bound to an ASP.NET DropDownList control. The DropDownList control and a Label control for output are declared in the body of the page. Setting the autopostback attribute of the DropDownList control to True results in the page being posted back to the server any time the selection in the dropdown is changed. In the Page_Load event handler, if the page request is not the result of a postback, we declare a new ArrayList and add three items to it. Next, we set the DataSource property of the DropDownList control to be the ArrayList, call the page's DataBind method (which calls DataBind on its children), and then set the initial selection of the DropDown-List to the first item.

Whether or not the request is the result of a postback, we then set the output text via the Label's Text property and set the foreground color of the Label control based on the value of the selected item in the dropdown. Note that because the ForeColor property is of type System.Drawing.Color, the example uses the From-Name method exposed by the Color class to translate the string containing the color name to an appropriate instance of the Color class. The output of Example 7-5 is shown in Figure 7-4.

Example 7-5. BindCollection.aspx

```vb
<%@ Page Language="VB" %>
<html>
<head>
    <title>Collection DataBinding Example</title>
    <script runat="server">
        Dim FontColor As String
        Sub Page_Load()
            If Not IsPostBack Then
                Dim Colors As New ArrayList()
                Colors.Add("Red")
                Colors.Add("Green")
                Colors.Add("Blue")
                Color.DataSource = Colors
                DataBind()
                Color.SelectedIndex = 0
            End If
            Output.Text = "The value for FontColor is " & _
                Color.SelectedItem.Value & "."
            Output.ForeColor = _
                System.Drawing.Color.FromName(Color.SelectedItem.Value)
        End Sub
    </script>
</head>
<body>
    <h1>Collection DataBinding Example</h1>
    <form runat="server">
        Choose a color from the list for the font color:
        <asp:dropdownlist id="Color" autopostback="True" runat="server"/>
        <br/>
        <asp:label id="Output" runat="server"/>
    </form>
</body>
</html>
```

Figure 7-4. Output of BindCollection.aspx

Binding to DataViews

Binding to richer data sources, such as DataTables and DataViews, is even more powerful than binding to collections, though still relatively simple. The DataView class provides a representation of the data in a DataTable that can be sorted and filtered, and also implements the necessary interfaces that allow it to be databound. These data sources can be used by:

- Retrieving data in a dataset and binding to the constituent DataTables

- Building DataViews, based on the data in the data table, or retrieving the table's DefaultView property, which returns an unsorted, unfiltered DataView

- Creating DataTables and/or DataViews programmatically

Binding a DataTable or DataView to controls such as DataGrid, DataList, and Repeater provides an extremely powerful technique for displaying and editing data with a minimum of code. It also provides substantial flexibility in how the data is formatted and displayed.

The examples in the sections entitled "Inserting and Updating Data" and "Deleting Data" demonstrate how to bind the default DataView of a table to a DataGrid for display.

Inserting and Updating Data

Reading and binding data is all very well, but for most applications, it's only part of what the application needs to do. Another important feature is the ability to insert new rows and/or update existing rows of data. As with reading data, the DataSet and SqlDataAdapter (or OleDbDataAdapter) classes come in handy. Another class that is extremely useful is the SqlCommandBuilder (or OleDbCommandBuilder) class, which is discussed later in this section.

Example 7-6, while more complicated than previous examples, adds a relatively small amount of code to support adding and updating rows to the Pubs Titles table.

Example 7-6. InsertUpdateTitles.aspx

```
<%@ Page Language="VB" %>
<%@ Import Namespace="System.Data" %>
<%@ Import Namespace="System.Data.SqlClient" %>
<html>
<head>
   <title>Insert/Update Example</title>
   <script runat="server">
      Dim Titles As New DataSet()
      Dim TitlesAdpt As New SqlDataAdapter()

      Sub Page_Load(Sender As Object, e As EventArgs)
         If Not IsPostBack Then
            GetTitleData("")
            BindGrid()
         End If
      End Sub
```

Example 7-6. InsertUpdateTitles.aspx (continued)

```
Sub Add_Click(Sender As Object, e As EventArgs)
    Page.RegisterHiddenField("EditMode", "Add")
    title_id.ReadOnly = False
    Display.Visible = False
    InsertUpdate.Visible = True
End Sub

Sub Cancel_Click(Sender As Object, e As EventArgs)
    Response.Redirect("InsertUpdateTitles.aspx")
End Sub

Sub Edit_Click(sender As Object, e As DataGridCommandEventArgs)
    GetTitleData("WHERE title_id = '" & e.Item.Cells(1).Text & "'")
    title_id.Text = Titles.Tables(0).Rows(0)(0)
    title.Text = Titles.Tables(0).Rows(0)(1)
    type.Text = Titles.Tables(0).Rows(0)(2)
    pub_id.Text = Titles.Tables(0).Rows(0)(3)
    price.Text = String.Format("{0:c}", Titles.Tables(0).Rows(0)(4))
    advance.Text = Titles.Tables(0).Rows(0)(5)
    royalty.Text = Titles.Tables(0).Rows(0)(6)
    ytd_sales.Text = Titles.Tables(0).Rows(0)(7)
    notes.Text = Titles.Tables(0).Rows(0)(8)
    pubdate.Text = Titles.Tables(0).Rows(0)(9)
    Page.RegisterHiddenField("EditMode", "Update")
    Display.Visible = False
    InsertUpdate.Visible = True
End Sub

Sub BindGrid()
    TitleGrid.DataSource = Titles.Tables(0).DefaultView
    TitleGrid.DataBind()
End Sub

Sub GetTitleData(WhereClause As String)
    Dim ConnStr As String = "Data Source=(local)\NetSDK;" & _
        "Initial Catalog=Pubs;Trusted_Connection=True;"
    Dim SQL As String = "SELECT * FROM titles " & WhereClause
    Dim PubsConn As New SqlConnection(ConnStr)
    Dim TitlesCmd As New SqlCommand(SQL, PubsConn)
    TitlesAdpt.SelectCommand = TitlesCmd
    Dim TitlesCB As New SqlCommandBuilder(TitlesAdpt)
    ' No need to open or close connection,
    '   since the SqlDataAdapter will do this automatically.
    TitlesAdpt.Fill(Titles)
End Sub

Sub Submit_Click(Sender As Object, e As EventArgs)
    Select Case Request.Form("EditMode")
        Case "Add"
            GetTitleData("")
            Dim NewRow As DataRow = Titles.Tables(0).NewRow
            NewRow(0) = title_id.Text
```

Example 7-6. InsertUpdateTitles.aspx (continued)

```
                    NewRow(1) = title.Text
                    NewRow(2) = type.Text
                    NewRow(3) = pub_id.Text
                    NewRow(4) = Convert.ToDecimal(price.Text.Replace("$", ""))
                    NewRow(5) = advance.Text
                    NewRow(6) = royalty.Text
                    NewRow(7) = ytd_sales.Text
                    NewRow(8) = notes.Text
                    NewRow(9) = pubdate.Text
                    Titles.Tables(0).Rows.Add(NewRow)
                    TitlesAdpt.Update(Titles)
                Case "Update"
                    GetTitleData("WHERE title_id = '" & title_id.Text & "'")
                    Titles.Tables(0).Rows(0)(0) = title_id.Text
                    Titles.Tables(0).Rows(0)(1) = title.Text
                    Titles.Tables(0).Rows(0)(2) = type.Text
                    Titles.Tables(0).Rows(0)(3) = pub_id.Text
                    Titles.Tables(0).Rows(0)(4) = _
                        Convert.ToDecimal(price.Text.Replace("$", ""))
                    Titles.Tables(0).Rows(0)(5) = advance.Text
                    Titles.Tables(0).Rows(0)(6) = royalty.Text
                    Titles.Tables(0).Rows(0)(7) = ytd_sales.Text
                    Titles.Tables(0).Rows(0)(8) = notes.Text
                    Titles.Tables(0).Rows(0)(9) = pubdate.Text
                    TitlesAdpt.Update(Titles)
            End Select
            Response.Redirect("InsertUpdateTitles.aspx")
        End Sub
    </script>
</head>
<body>
    <h1>Insert/Update Example</h1>
    <form runat="server">
        <asp:panel id="Display" runat="server">
            <asp:datagrid id="TitleGrid"
                oneditcommand="Edit_Click"
                runat="server">
                <columns>
                    <asp:editcommandcolumn
                        buttontype="PushButton" edittext="Edit"/>
                </columns>
            </asp:datagrid>
            <asp:button id="Add"
                text="Add New Title" onclick="Add_Click" runat="server"/>
        </asp:panel>
        <asp:panel id="InsertUpdate" visible="False" runat="server">
            <table border="0">
                <tr>
                    <td>Title ID</td>
                    <td>
                        <asp:textbox id="title_id"
                            readonly="True" runat="server"/>
```

Example 7-6. InsertUpdateTitles.aspx (continued)

```
            </td>
        </tr>
        <tr>
            <td>Title</td>
            <td>
                <asp:textbox id="title" runat="server"/>
            </td>
        </tr>
        <tr>
            <td>Type</td>
            <td>
                <asp:textbox id="type" runat="server"/>
            </td>
        </tr>
        <tr>
            <td>Publisher ID</td>
            <td>
                <asp:textbox id="pub_id" runat="server"/>
            </td>
        </tr>
        <tr>
            <td>Price</td>
            <td>
                <asp:textbox id="price" runat="server"/>
            </td>
        </tr>
        <tr>
            <td>Advance</td>
            <td>
                <asp:textbox id="advance" runat="server"/>
            </td>
        </tr>
        <tr>
            <td>Royalty</td>
            <td>
                <asp:textbox id="royalty" runat="server"/>
            </td>
        </tr>
        <tr>
            <td>Year-to-date Sales</td>
            <td>
                <asp:textbox id="ytd_sales" runat="server"/>
            </td>
        </tr>
        <tr>
            <td>Notes</td>
            <td>
                <asp:textbox id="notes"
                    textmode="MultiLine"
                    rows="5"
                    columns="20"
                    runat="server"/>
```

Example 7-6. InsertUpdateTitles.aspx (continued)

```
                 </td>
             </tr>
             <tr>
                <td>Publishing Date</td>
                <td>
                   <asp:textbox id="pubdate" runat="server"/>
                </td>
             </tr>
             <tr>
                <td>
                   <asp:button id="Submit"
                       text="Submit" onclick="Submit_Click" runat="server"/>
                </td>
                <td>
                   <asp:button id="Cancel"
                       text="Cancel" onclick="Cancel_Click" runat="server"/>
                </td>
             </tr>
          </table>
       </asp:panel>
    </form>
</body>
</html>
```

The discussion of the code begins with the <body> section of the page. This
section contains a server-side <form> element, which provides support for page
postbacks and adds automatic support for such things as control state management. Contained within the form are two Panel controls, which render as <div>
elements on the client. Panel controls are very useful when you want to provide
more than one set of user interface elements on a page, but only want to display
one at a given time.

Inside the first Panel control, which will display items from the Titles table, we
declare a DataGrid control, to which we add a ButtonColumn control to provide
access to the edit mode of the page and a Button control that will allow us to add a
new item. To enable handling of the Edit button in the DataGrid, we set the Data-
Grid's onEditCommand attribute to the name of the event handler for the Edit button.

The second Panel control contains the form fields that will be used to edit or add
a new item, as well as Submit and Cancel buttons. It makes sense for the default
mode for the page to be displayed, so we set the Visible property of the second
panel control to False. Note that we also set the ReadOnly property of the title_id
textbox to True to prevent this field from being edited for existing data, since the
Title ID field is what uniquely identifies a title in the table.

Turning to the code, note that the example declares both the DataSet and
SqlDataAdapter classes at the page level so that they will be available to all
procedures.

In the Page_Load event handler, we check to see if the current request is the result
of a postback. If not, we call the GetTitleData method (passing an empty string).
The GetTitleData method, which allows us to pass a Where clause argument to be

appended to the SQL string, uses the techniques demonstrated previously to retrieve the desired set of rows from the Titles table in the Pubs database.

The main difference between Example 7-5 and the previous examples is that the code in Example 7-5 declares a new SqlCommandBuilder instance, passing it a SqlDataAdapter instance whose SelectCommand property is already set. Here's where ADO.NET magic really happens. The SqlCommandBuilder will automatically generate appropriate Insert, Update, and Delete commands for the Select statement set on the data adapter and populate the InsertCommand, UpdateCommand, and DeleteCommand properties of the SqlDataAdapter with these values. This step saves us the trouble of having to create these statements manually.

If you want to construct Insert, Update, and Delete statements yourself or use stored procedures for these commands, you are free to do so. You can do so by creating separate SqlCommand objects with the desired properties and then setting the InsertCommand, UpdateCommand, or DeleteCommand property of the SqlDataAdapter to the newly created SqlCommand instance.

Once we've filled the dataset with data from the Titles table, we call BindGrid from Page_Load. Calling BindGrid sets the DataSource property of the DataGrid control to the DefaultView property of the first table in the dataset, which returns a DataView containing all the data in the table. At this point, the output of the page should look like Figure 7-5.

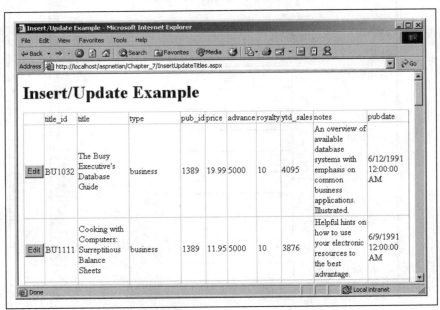

Figure 7-5. Display mode output of InsertUpdateTitles.aspx

The user viewing the page has two options: click the Edit button for one of the rows or scroll down to the bottom of the page and click the Add New Title button (not shown in Figure 7-5).

Clicking the Edit button invokes the Edit_Click event handler, which calls GetTitle-Data, passing a WHERE clause that causes it to retrieve only the selected row. Next, it sets the form fields in the second panel control to the values returned from GetTitleData, and then registers a hidden form field that indicates that we're updating a row (as opposed to adding a new row). This will become important later, when we submit our changes. Finally, we set the Visible property of the first panel to False and the second to True, which displays the form fields for editing.

If the Add New Title button is clicked, we register a hidden form field (indicating that the Add mode is enabled), set the ReadOnly property of the title_id textbox to False (since we'll need a title ID for the new row), and then reverse the visibility properties of the panel controls again to display the blank form fields. At this point, the output of the page should look like Figure 7-6.

Figure 7-6. Add mode output of InsertUpdateTitles.aspx

In Edit or Add mode, if the user clicks the Cancel button, we simply call Response. Redirect and redirect back to the original page, essentially starting the whole process over again.

If the user clicks Submit, we use a Select Case statement to evaluate whether we're adding a new row or updating an existing one. If we're adding a new row, we call GetTitleData, call the NewRow method of the first table object to create a new DataRow instance, and then set the item values of the new row to the values in the form fields. Once all values have been set, we add the row to the Data-Table and (outside of the Select Case statement) call the SqlDataAdapter's Update method, which updates the backend database with the new row.

If we're updating an existing row, we call GetTitleData with a WHERE clause for that specific row, set its items to the values in the form fields, and call Update again to save the changes to the backend database. Once we've called Update, we call Response.Redirect to redirect the user back to the original page, which again clears the decks and starts from scratch (with the new data, of course).

Example 7-5 demonstrates "last-in-wins" data concurrency. Be aware that using this type of concurrency control can result in overwriting changes made by another user between the time data was queried and when it was updated. In a multiuser environment, you should always carefully consider the potential costs and effects of multiple users attempting to update the same data simultaneously and design your applications accordingly. Strategies can include locking data from the time it is read until the update is complete, or using a timestamp before updating to ensure that the data was not modified from its last known state.

Deleting Data

Example 7-7 shows how you can use the DataSet and SqlDataAdapter classes to delete data from the Titles table. This example shows the implementation of an ASP.NET page that displays data from the Titles table and allows users to delete a row from the table by clicking a button.

Unless you don't care about the state of the Pubs sample database, it would probably be a good idea to back up the database before deleting any of the rows in the Titles table (just in case you want to restore the database to its original state later).

As with the previous example, we use a DataGrid control to display the items in the dataset. However, in this case, we set the AutoGenerateColumns property of the DataGrid to False and supply BoundColumn controls for each displayed column. This provides greater flexibility in displaying the data, including the ability to determine which columns are displayed, the header to use for each column, and in the case of the price data, the ability to specify a format string for the data. This example also adds an <alternatingitemstyle> tag to specify that every other row should have a background color of silver. To enable handling of the Delete button, we set the DataGrid's onDeleteCommand method to the name of the event handler for the Delete button.

As with the previous example, Example 7-7 declares both the DataSet and SqlDataAdapter instances at the page level to make them available to all procedures; in the Page_Load event handler, we call GetTitleData and BindGrid, which perform the same operations as in the previous example (although this version of GetTitleData does not allow a WHERE clause).

Once the data is displayed, the user can click the Delete button for a row, which invokes the Delete_Click event handler. In Delete_Click, we call GetTitleData to fill the dataset, and then call the Delete method of the selected row (using the Item. ItemIndex property of the DataGridCommandEventArgs parameter passed to the event handler to determine the correct row to delete). Once the row is deleted from the dataset, we call the Update method of the SqlDataAdapter, passing it the modified dataset, and then call Response.Redirect to redirect the user to the original page.

Example 7-7. DeleteTitles.aspx

```
<%@ Page Language="VB" %>
<%@ Import Namespace="System.Data" %>
<%@ Import Namespace="System.Data.SqlClient" %>
<html>
<head>
    <title>Delete Example</title>
    <script runat="server">
        Dim Titles As New DataSet()
        Dim TitlesAdpt As New SqlDataAdapter()

        Sub Page_Load(Sender As Object, e As EventArgs)
            If Not IsPostBack Then
                GetTitleData()
                BindGrid()
            End If
        End Sub

        Sub BindGrid()
            TitleGrid.DataSource = Titles.Tables(0).DefaultView
            TitleGrid.DataBind()
        End Sub

        Sub GetTitleData()
            Dim ConnStr As String = "Data Source=(local)\NetSDK;" & _
                "Initial Catalog=Pubs;Trusted_Connection=True;"
            Dim SQL As String = "SELECT * FROM titles"
            Dim PubsConn As New SqlConnection(ConnStr)
            Dim TitlesCmd As New SqlCommand(SQL, PubsConn)
            TitlesAdpt.SelectCommand = TitlesCmd
            Dim TitlesCB As New SqlCommandBuilder(TitlesAdpt)
            ' No need to open or close connection,
```

Example 7-7. DeleteTitles.aspx (continued)

```
            '   since the SqlDataAdapter will do this automatically.
            TitlesAdpt.Fill(Titles)
        End Sub

        Sub Delete_Click(Sender As Object, e As DataGridCommandEventArgs)
            GetTitleData()
            Titles.Tables(0).Rows(e.Item.ItemIndex).Delete
            TitlesAdpt.Update(Titles)
            Response.Redirect("DeleteTitles.aspx")
        End Sub
    </script>
</head>
<body>
    <h1>Delete Example</h1>
    <form runat="server">
        <asp:datagrid id="TitleGrid"
            ondeletecommand="Delete_Click"
            cellpadding="3"
            autogeneratecolumns="false"
            runat="server">
            <columns>
                <asp:buttoncolumn buttontype="PushButton"
                    text="Delete" commandname="Delete" />
                <asp:boundcolumn headertext="Title ID"
                    datafield="title_id"/>
                <asp:boundcolumn headertext="Title"
                    datafield="title"/>
                <asp:boundcolumn headertext="Type"
                    datafield="type"/>
                <asp:boundcolumn headertext="Publisher ID"
                    datafield="pub_id"/>
                <asp:boundcolumn headertext="Price"
                    datafield="price" dataformatstring="{0:c}"/>
            </columns>
        </asp:datagrid>
    </form>
</body>
</html>
```

The output of Example 7-7 is shown in Figure 7-7.

Additional Resources

The following sites provide additional information on the topics discussed in this chapter:

http://www.aspfriends.com/aspfriends/aspngdata.asp
Home page for the AspFriends.com mailing list (for questions relating to ASP. NET data access).

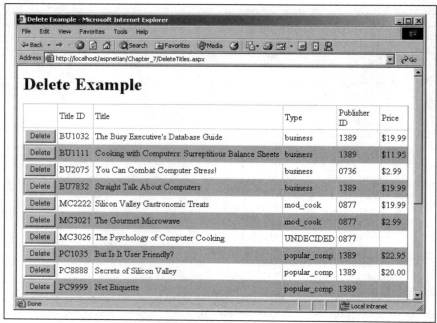

Figure 7-7. Output of DeleteTitles.aspx

http://www.aspfriends.com/aspfriends/aspngdatagridrepeaterdatalist.asp
> Home page for the AspFriends.com mailing list (for questions relating to the use of the data-bound controls, including DataGrid, DataList, and Repeater controls).

http://www.aspnextgen.com/
> The DotNetJunkies site, run by Microsoft MVP Award winners Donny Mack and Doug Seven. This site contains many ASP.NET tutorials, including tutorials on data access and data binding.

CHAPTER 8

ASP.NET Configuration

When working with ASP.NET, you'll be called on to configure an ASP.NET application. One major advantage that ASP.NET has over classic ASP is that most of the important configuration options for ASP.NET applications are stored in configuration files that reside in the web application directory. This makes it considerably easier to migrate an application from one server to another or to replicate an application across a Web Form, since the application's configuration information will be copied along with the Web Forms, code-behind classes, and assemblies that make up the application.

Understanding Configuration Files

In ASP.NET, configuration information is stored in one of two files: *machine.config* or *web.config*. There is only one *machine.config* file per machine; it contains the default configuration information for every web application, as well as other application types, on the machine. This information includes Windows Forms applications, remoting settings, and other network settings. You should use extreme caution when editing *machine.config* to avoid accidentally making changes that break other applications. It's probably a good idea to back up the *machine.config* file before editing it, in case you need to restore the original settings.

web.config is an optional configuration file that is stored with each web application. If an application contains a *web.config* file, the file takes precedence over *machine.config* (i.e., the settings in *web.config* override those in *machine.config*). If a web application does not contain a *web.config* file, it inherits its settings from *machine.config*. An application may have multiple *web.config* files, but each must reside in its own directory or subdirectory.

The *web.config* files in an application are hierarchical. Just as the settings in a *web. config* file in the application root will override the settings in *machine.config*, the settings in a *web.config* file in a subdirectory will override those in a *web.config* file in the parent directory.

ASP.NET provides a facility for locking down configuration settings so they cannot be overridden by child configuration files. If a configuration setting has been locked down in *machine.config*, an exception will be thrown if you attempt to override that setting in *web.config*. In addition, certain settings are limited to machine or application scope, Attempting to override these settings at application or subdirectory scope will also result in an exception being thrown.

The syntax of the *machine.config* and *web.config* files is based on XML. Each configuration section consists of a parent element that may in turn contain attributes or child elements. In the following snippet, the <configuration> and <system.web> elements are standard elements that are required in each web.config file. The <authentication> and <authorization> elements are parent configuration elements, while the <deny> element is a child element of the <authorization> element:

```
<configuration>
    <system.web>
        <authentication mode="Windows"/>
        <authorization>
            <deny users="?"/>
        </authorization>
    </system.web>
<configuration>
```

The configuration of an ASP.NET application depends on which elements you include in your *web.config* file and on the values of their attributes (and any attributes of their child elements). Chapter 20 documents the configuration elements in detail. Most of this chapter looks at practical examples of how to set common configuration settings.

Modifying Configuration Settings

The most important part of configuration for the web developer is, of course, understanding how to modify the configuration files to achieve the desired ends. Unfortunately, in the first release of the .NET Framework and Visual Studio .NET, there aren't any rich GUI tools for editing configuration files (which sounds like a great third-party opportunity). As a result, editing configuration files is not terribly straightforward. The next several examples illustrate the basic techniques for editing *web.config* files.

Remember that ASP.NET configuration files follow XML syntax rules, including case-sensitivity of element and attribute names. Element and attribute names in ASP.NET configuration files typically use camel casing, in which the first letter of the initial word is lowercase and the first letter of each subsequent word is uppercase.

Also note that some (but not all) attribute *values* are case sensitive. While this case sensitivity is specific to the ASP.NET implementation rather than to XML, it's still a good idea to follow the case used in the examples when modifying configuration files.

Related IIS Settings

It is very important to understand that ASP.NET configuration is distinct from IIS configuration. In most cases, configuring an ASP.NET application requires no changes to the configuration of IIS. One exception is that the settings for IIS may still need to be configured to make certain authentication modes, such as Windows authentication, work (although in many cases, the defaults will work fine).

The reason why most configuration settings do not require changes to IIS configuration is that when a request is made for a resource that is handled by ASP.NET, IIS is only involved long enough to hand that request over to the ASP.NET worker process, which is completely separate from IIS. In fact, you can host ASP.NET applications without even using IIS with the classes in the System.Web.Hosting namespace. The operation of the ASP.NET worker process is configured by *machine.config* and *web.config*, while IIS configuration settings remain in the IIS metabase.

Changing the Authentication Mode

Modifying the <authentication> element of *web.config* should give you a good idea how configuration files work. The <authentication> element is included in the *machine.config* file with the following default settings:

```
<!--
    authentication Attributes:
        mode="[Windows|Forms|Passport|None]"
-->
<authentication mode="Windows">

    <!--
        forms Attributes:
            name="[cookie name]" - Name of the cookie used for Forms
                Authentication
            loginUrl="[url]" - Url to redirect client to for Authentication
            protection="[All|None|Encryption|Validation]" - Protection mode
                for data in cookie
            timeout="[seconds]" - Duration of time for cookie to be valid
                (reset on each request)
            path="/" - Sets the path for the cookie
    -->
    <forms name=".ASPXAUTH" loginUrl="login.aspx" protection="All"
        timeout="30" path="/">

        <!--
            credentials Attributes:
                passwordFormat="[Clear|SHA1|MD5]" - format of user password
                    value stored in <user>
        -->
        <credentials passwordFormat="SHA1">
```

```
        <!-- <user name="UserName" password="password"/> -->
      </credentials>

    </forms>

    <!--
        passport Attributes:
          redirectUrl=["url"] - Specifies the page to redirect to, if the
              page requires authentication, and the user has not signed on
              with passport
    -->
    <passport redirectUrl="internal"/>

  </authentication>
```

These configuration settings give the machine-wide defaults for authentication in
ASP.NET applications. Windows authentication is enabled by default. Note that for
Windows authentication to function properly, some form of IIS authentication
other than Anonymous must be enabled. The *machine.config* settings also specify
defaults for the attributes of the <forms> element, which is used in Forms authentication, and for the <passport> element.

Notice that the formatting of the configuration settings denotes the parent/child
relationships of the elements. Both the <forms> and <passport> elements are children of the <authentication> element, while the <credentials> element is the
child of the <forms> element. The <user> element (commented out in the
preceding code) is in turn the child of the <credentials> element.

You would see the <forms> element specified only in *machine.config* when the
mode attribute of the <authentication> element is set to Windows, a setting that
does not require any child elements. The reason for this is that these settings are
used as defaults for various authentication methods. Supplying values for the
attributes of the <forms> element at the machine level provides defaults that are
inherited by any application using Forms authentication automatically, while any
attribute values for the <forms> element contained in *web.config* files for specific
applications override these settings.

Example 8-1 shows an <authentication> element for an application that uses
Windows authentication. The <authorization> element is also shown. In this case,
this element denies access to anonymous users, which forces authentication, if it
has not already occurred.

Example 8-1. Windows authentication settings

```
<configuration>
  <system.web>
    <authentication mode="Windows"/>
    <authorization>
      <deny users="?"/>
    </authorization>
  </system.web>
</configuration>
```

Consider an application in which you want to use Forms authentication (discussed further in Chapter 9) to enable authentication against your own custom credential store. In this case, you would use an authentication element such as that shown in Example 8-2, along with its child <forms> element, and the <authorization> element shown in Example 8-1. Note that the <forms> element is required only if you want to override the settings specified in *machine.config*. Example 8-2 specifies a different login page (*myLogin.aspx*) to which unauthenticated users are redirected.

Example 8-2. Forms authentication settings

```
<configuration>
  <system.web>
    <authentication mode="Forms">
      <forms loginUrl="myLogin.aspx"/>
    </authentication>
    <authorization>
      <deny users="?"/>
    </authorization>
  </system.web>
<configuration>
```

Configuring Out-of-Process Session State

The <sessionState> configuration element in *machine.config* sets the following machine-wide defaults:

```
<!-- sessionState Attributes:
    mode="[Off|InProc|StateServer|SQLServer]"
    stateConnectionString="tcpip=server:port"
    stateNetworkTimeout="timeout for network operations with State Server,
        in seconds"
    sqlConnectionString="valid System.Data.SqlClient.SqlConnection string,
        minus Initial Catalog"
    cookieless="[true|false]"
    timeout="timeout in minutes"
-->
<sessionState mode="InProc"
    stateConnectionString="tcpip=127.0.0.1:42424"
    stateNetworkTimeout="10"
    sqlConnectionString="data source=127.0.0.1;user id=sa;password="
    cookieless="false"
    timeout="20"/>
```

Unlike the <authentication> element, the <sessionState> element has no children, only attributes. Like the <authentication> element, the usage of the <sessionState> element in *machine.config* contains a combination of attributes not normally seen in practice, since the purpose of the attributes is to set machine-wide defaults. For example, the default mode of in-process session state (InProc) requires no additional attributes to function. In fact, if you want to use InProc, you do not need to add a <sessionState> element to your *web.config* file at all. Examples 8-3 and 8-4 show the appropriate settings for the <sessionState> element for out-of-process session state using the ASP.NET state service and SQL Server session state, respectively.

Example 8-3. Out-of-process state with state service

```
<configuration>
  <system.web>
    <sessionState mode="StateServer"
        stateConnectionString="tcpip=StateServerName:42424"
        stateNetworkTimeout="30" />
  </system.web>
<configuration>
```

Example 8-3 sets the mode attribute to `StateServer`, which uses the ASP.NET state NT service installed with ASP.NET to store session state settings for multiple machines. This setting requires the `stateConnectionString` attribute; Since the default setting of 127.0.0.1 (the local machine loopback address) is not terribly useful for sharing state information across multiple machines, you need to replace it with the name of the machine that is responsible for maintaining this information (`StateServerName`, in the example).

In out-of-process session state scenarios, a single machine is designated to maintain session values for multiple ASP.NET servers. Therefore, each server using the shared session information should be configured to point to the same state server. To compensate for potential network latency issues, the example changes the default `stateNetworkTimeout` value of 10 seconds to 30 seconds. Note that inherent in this decision is a tradeoff between avoiding timeouts and potentially poorer application performance.

Inherent in either type of out-of-process session state is a substantial performance hit due to the need to cross process and/or machine boundaries to retrieve session state information. You should use out-of-process session state only when your need for scalability outweighs your need for absolute performance. You should also test the performance of your chosen session state mode with a tool such as the Microsoft Web Stress tool to ensure that it meets your performance and scalability needs.

Example 8-4. Out-of-process state with SQL Server

```
<configuration>
  <system.web>
    <sessionState mode="SQLServer"
        sqlConnectionString="data source=ServerName;user
id=name;password=pwd"
        cookieless="true"/>
  </system.web>
</configuration>
```

Example 8-4 sets the mode attribute to `SQLServer`, which uses an SQL Server database called ASPState to store session state values to be shared across multiple machines. This database is set up using the *InstallSqlState.sql* batch file installed by default in the directory *%windir%\Microsoft.NET\Framework\%version%*, where *%windir%* is the Windows directory and *%version%* is the version number of the installed framework (the version number is prefixed with a v in the actual path).

The SQLServer mode requires the use of the sqlConnectionString attribute. You should always override this attribute, since its default uses the local 127.0.0.1 loopback address and uses the SQL Server sa account to connect to the ASPState database. Neither is a good practice in a production application. In Example 8-4, set the data source portion of the connection string to the name of the designated SQL Server state machine and set the user ID and password to an account set up to read and write state data.

Example 8-4 also sets the cookieless attribute to True, anticipating that some users may have disabled cookies. Setting this attribute to True places the session identifier within the URL of all requests, allowing session use without cookies. Note that applications designed for cookieless sessions should use relative rather than absolute URLs for internal links.

A word on security: As noted previously, the default settings for sqlConnectionString use the SQL Server sa, or system administrator, account to connect to the ASPState database. This is not a good security practice. Instead, you should always set up a separate account that is purpose-specific (in this case, to read and write session state data) and use that account for connecting to the state database. You may even want to consider setting up a separate account for each ASP.NET application for this purpose; this allows you to track and audit access to the ASPState database on a per application basis more easily. These steps can help minimize the possibility of database security being compromised through over-permissive security settings.

Modifying Trace Settings

Tracing is a nifty feature of ASP.NET that allows recording and viewing of a host of valuable information about page requests. Like the other configuration elements considered in this chapter, the <trace> element appears in *machine.config* to set machine-wide default values:

```
<!--
    trace Attributes:
        enabled="[true|false]" - Enable application tracing
        localOnly="[true|false]" - View trace results from localhost only
        pageOutput="[true|false]" - Display trace ouput on individual pages
        requestLimit="[number]" - Number of trace results available in
            trace.axd
        traceMode="[SortByTime|SortByCategory]" - Sorts trace result
            displays based on Time or Category
-->
<trace enabled="false"
    localOnly="true"
```

```
pageOutput="false"
requestLimit="10"
traceMode="SortByTime"/>
```

The settings in *machine.config* turn tracing off by default, which is a good thing. Since tracing carries performance overhead, you should enable it only when you are actually using it—usually during development or troubleshooting of an ASP.NET application. You should rarely enable tracing on a deployed production application, both for performance reasons and also to avoid the possibility of trace information being viewed by site visitors. See Chapter 10 for a more detailed discussion of application tracing. Example 8-5 shows the <trace> element modified to enable tracing for an application, with trace output being displayed on each page.

Example 8-5. Enabling tracing

```
<configuration>
    <system.web>
        <trace enabled="true"
            pageOutput="true"/>
    </system.web>
</configuration>
```

You can enable tracing by setting the enabled attribute to True and direct the trace output to the page by setting the pageOutput attribute to True. The remaining attributes should retain their default values as set in *machine.config*.

Locking Down Configuration Settings

All of the previous examples rely on the ability to override settings in *machine.config* with settings in the *web.config* file for an individual application. As mentioned earlier, you can also use a *web.config* file located in a child folder of an application to override settings in a parent *web.config* file. However, what if the application developer or the server administrator doesn't want certain settings to be overridden? No problem. The configuration system provides a special element, <location>, that serves this purpose handily.

The basic structure of the <location> element consists of the opening element tag with two attributes, path and allowOverride, followed by the elements to be locked down, and the closing element tag. For example:

```
<location path="pathtocontrol" allowOverride="True|False">
    <!-- Settings to lock down -->
</location>
```

The path attribute, which is optional when locking down configuration settings, is used to specify the application or filename to be controlled by the <location> element. If omitted, the <location> element's settings apply to all children of the configuration file in which it appears. Example 8-6 shows a <location> element which, when added to *machine.config*, requires all ASP.NET applications on the machine to use Windows authentication.

Example 8-6. Locking down configuration settings

```
<configuration>
  <system.web>
    <location allowOverride="False">
      <authentication mode="Windows"/>
    </location>
  </system.web>
<configuration>
```

Note that the <location> element can also be used to configure settings for a child application, directory, or file from a parent configuration file. When used in this manner, the path attribute is required and the allowOverride attribute is optional.

Additional Resources

The following sites provide additional information on the topics discussed in this chapter:

http://www.aspfriends.com/aspfriends/aspngconfig.asp
> The home page for the AspFriends.com mailing list (for questions relating to ASP.NET configuration).

http://msdn.microsoft.com/library/default.asp?url=/library/en-us/cpgenref/html/ gngrfaspnetconfigurationsectionschema.asp
> The MSDN online reference for the ASP.NET configuration file schema.

CHAPTER 9

ASP.NET Security

Security is an extremely complicated subject, and ASP.NET security is not much less so. This chapter discusses the approaches you can take to secure your ASP. NET applications. Absent from the discussion are the topics of network, server, and infrastructure security. This should not be interpreted to mean these topics are unimportant. On the contrary, without properly securing any supporting servers and infrastructure, the measures you take to secure your application with the tools made available by the .NET Framework will be for naught. A discussion of these topics, however, is beyond the scope of this book. The security section of the Microsoft TechNet web site, referenced at the end of this chapter, contains a wealth of information on how to properly secure your servers and network, including tools to assist you in this important task.

Securing access to an application or to the resources belonging to an application involves two processes: authentication and authorization. This chapter explains how these processes relate to ASP.NET and how each fits into the overall scheme of allowing or preventing access to ASP.NET application resources. The discussion focuses on the three authentication methods the ASP.NET runtime provides: *Windows*, *Forms*, and *Passport*. The chapter also discusses ACL-based and URL authorization, as well as strategies for obtaining secure access to data and securing web services. The discussion also touches briefly on *code access security*, which underlies the ASP.NET security model.

Authentication Methods

Authentication is the process of positively identifying the person or program making a request. Authentication does not inherently grant access to resources (a function performed by authorization), but provides developers (or the runtime) with a known identity on which to base the decision of whether the request should be granted.

In a classic ASP application, you had essentially two options for authenticating users: rely on IIS to authenticate users based on Windows accounts and later authorize these users based on NT Access Control Lists (ACLs); or roll your own authentication from the ground up to authenticate users against a back-end credentials data store (or potentially against Microsoft Active Directory). Each option had disadvantages. Windows authentication's most secure mode, Integrated Security, required all users to use Internet Explorer (and would not work over many proxy servers), while the roll-your-own option required an extraordinary amount of work to build and test.

ASP.NET provides three built-in options for authentication:

Windows
> Provides similar functionality to IIS authentication in classic ASP, though with some important differences, described in the next section.

Forms
> Provides a rich infrastructure for "roll-your-own" security scenarios. This authentication provider will be used most often in Internet scenarios.

Passport
> Allows ASP.NET developers to take advantage of Microsoft's Passport single sign-in solution.

All authentication options for ASP.NET are configured either at the machine-level using the *machine.config* file or at the application level using the *web.config* file. Appropriately, you configure the authentication settings using the <authentication> element, along with its associated attributes and children.

 Authentication settings cannot be configured below the application level. If you need to set different authentication settings on a child directory of an application, you will need to configure that directory as an application in IIS.

Windows

As mentioned earlier, Windows authentication provides much the same functionality in ASP.NET as IIS authentication did in classic ASP; it authenticates users based on Windows accounts stored either on the local server or on an associated domain controller. The main reason for choosing the Windows authentication provider is that it requires the least code to implement. Of the three modes of built-in authentication in ASP.NET, Windows authentication is the only one that requires you to configure IIS in addition to configuring the authentication settings in *machine.config* or *web.config*.

As with IIS authentication in classic ASP, Windows authentication is primarily useful in situations in which one of the following conditions exists:

- All clients are using Internet Explorer 4.x or higher, and there are no proxy servers for authentication requests to cross. This is most commonly the case in an intranet scenario and is rare for Internet applications.

- The security requirements of the application make it acceptable to use Basic or Digest IIS authentication (which both have limitations that make them somewhat less secure than Integrated authentication).

- The security requirements for the application make it acceptable to allow anonymous users access to the entire application.

Typically, Windows authentication is used in conjunction with impersonation (see the upcoming section "Impersonation" for more information) to allow the ASP.NET process to make requests using the security context of the authenticated user. You can then restrict access to resources using NTFS Access Control Lists (ACLs) or grant database access by setting up the Windows account of the desired user as a login for the database in question. For more information about this technique, see the section "Code Access Security" later in this chapter.

ASP.NET Windows authentication works by obtaining the security context of the user from IIS (see Figure 9-1). The first step in configuring an application to use Windows authentication is to modify the IIS configuration settings to require one of the nonanonymous authentication methods. To do so, follow these directions:

1. Open the Internet Services Manager.

2. In the lefthand pane, drill down to the web site or virtual root of the application you want to configure.

3. Right-click the application's folder and select Properties to display the <application name> Properties dialog.

4. Click the Directory Security tab, and then click the Edit... button in the Anonymous access and authentication control section.

5. Deselect the Anonymous access checkbox and select one or more of the authentication checkboxes (Basic, Digest, or Integrated Windows).

6. Click OK to dismiss the Authentication methods dialog; then click OK again to dismiss the Properties dialog. Now you're ready to configure your ASP.NET application.

While Basic authentication enables the use of Windows accounts for authentication in a wider array of scenarios, remember that Basic authentication sends the username and password in clear text. This can be an unacceptable risk, particularly if the application does not use Secure Sockets Layer (SSL) encryption to protect the communications. Before selecting Basic authentication as an option, make sure you understand the security ramifications of this choice and that you've taken the necessary steps to mitigate risks associated with this approach.

Similarly, Digest authentication requires that passwords be stored in clear text on the domain controller where the accounts exist. If you decide to use Digest authentication, make sure that the domain controller is secured from network attacks and is physically secured to prevent unauthorized parties from accessing the passwords.

As shown in Figure 9-1, once a client making a request is authenticated by IIS, the request, along with the security context of the authenticated user, is handed off to the ASP.NET worker process. From this point on, ASP.NET alone is in control.

Figure 9-1. Windows authentication process

For ASP.NET to use the security context provided by IIS, the ASP.NET application must be configured for Windows authentication. This configuration is done by adding an <authentication> element to the *web.config* file for the application and setting its mode attribute to Windows, as shown in the following code snippet:

```
<?xml version="1.0" encoding="utf-8" ?>
<configuration>
    <system.web>
        <authentication mode="Windows"/>
        <!--
            Other configuration elements
        -->
    </system.web>
</configuration>
```

Note that because the <authentication> element does not require any child elements for Windows mode, you can use a single tag with a closing / character rather than using a full closing tag.

Impersonation

By default, the ASP.NET worker process runs in the context of a special account called ASPNET. This account has very few privileges, so requests made for ACL-protected resources (such as files in the filesystem) will fail unless permissions are explicitly granted to the ASPNET account. This mechanism helps make ASP.NET applications more secure out of the box.

An alternative to granting explicit permissions to the ASPNET account is to run the ASP.NET worker process in the context of the SYSTEM account, a highly privileged account that allows many types of requests to succeed without a need for impersonation. For example, since SQL Server by default allows access to anyone in the local administrators group, running the ASP.NET worker process as SYSTEM makes it possible to connect to a local SQL Server database using a trusted connection without using impersonation.

While this may solve some permissions problems, in practice, running as SYSTEM is not a good idea, since it provides more privileges than are necessary for running most ASP.NET applications. One consequence of this is that any vulnerabilities that occur in IIS or the ASP.NET runtime may then potentially provide system-level access to those who exploit them. Running the ASP.NET worker process using the ASPNET account significantly reduces the risk of such an exploit.

This setting is controlled by the username attribute of the <processModel> element in *machine.config*.

In most Windows authentication situations, you should enable impersonation to allow the ASP.NET worker process to make requests using the security context of the authenticated user. In classic ASP, impersonation is enabled by default. You can enable impersonation in ASP.NET by adding the <identity> element to the *web.config* file for the application, with its impersonate attribute set to True, as shown in the following code snippet:

```
<?xml version="1.0" encoding="utf-8" ?>
<configuration>
   <system.web>
      <authentication mode="Windows"/>
      <identity impersonate="true"/>
      <!--
         Other configuration elements
      -->
   </system.web>
</configuration>
```

Once impersonation is enabled, you can use NTFS ACLs to authorize accounts for access to resources. For more information on this technique, see the section entitled "Authorization" later in this chapter.

Passport

The Passport authentication module enables ASP.NET applications to take advantage of Microsoft's Passport universal sign-in infrastructure to authenticate users. The Passport system allows each user to have a single password and login (the email address associated with their Passport account) for multiple web sites or applications. This can greatly simplify the login process from the user's perspective, as well as reduce the administrative overhead associated with maintaining user accounts (such as having to send forgetful users their password via email).

To enable Passport authentication in ASP.NET, you need to download and install the Passport SDK. See *http://www.passport.com/business* for instructions on where and how to obtain the SDK.

 While you can obtain the Passport SDK and set up a test site for free, you have to pay a license fee to use Passport in a production application. Make sure that you understand all the costs involved before implementing Passport authentication.

Once you've installed the SDK, you need to configure Passport according to the accompanying instructions. Finally, you need to configure the ASP.NET application to use Passport authentication, as shown in the following code snippet:

```
<?xml version="1.0" encoding="utf-8" ?>
<configuration>
    <system.web>
        <authentication mode="Passport">
            <passport redirectUrl="someLocalpage.aspx"/>
        </authentication>
        <!--
            Other configuration elements
        -->
    </system.web>
</configuration>
```

Note that the `<passport>` element and the `redirectUrl` attribute are optional and are used to specify an internal URL to redirect to if the users making the request have not signed in using their Passport account. If the `<passport>` element is omitted, users who have not logged in using their Passport account will be redirected to a login page on a Passport login server.

Forms

Forms authentication is probably the most useful built-in ASP.NET authentication module because it provides a very flexible infrastructure for roll-your-own security scenarios. When an application is configured to use Forms authentication, requests for protected resources are redirected to a specified login page, unless the request is accompanied by an authentication token contained in a cookie. For more information on protecting resources when using Forms authentication, see "Authorization," later in this chapter.

Logging in

In the login page, the site developer writes code to check the credentials entered by the user against a backend credentials store. This store can be a relational database such as SQL Server, an XML file, Microsoft Active Directory, or any other storage location of your choice. If the credentials match those stored in the backend credential store, the developer calls the RedirectFromLoginPage method of the `FormsAuthentication` helper class to send the user back to the page that they originally requested and to set either a session cookie or a persistent cookie containing the authentication token on the user's machine. Once the user is authenticated, he or she can access other resources in the same application without logging in again.

To better illustrate the process by which Forms authentication operates, let's look at an example. In this example, which is based on live code I use to protect downloads on my company site, files in a specific subdirectory of an application are protected using Forms authentication.

The example uses the following files:

web.config
> Configuration file used to enable Forms authentication and to specify the desired access restrictions. See Chapter 8 and Chapter 20 for more information on *web.config*.

Login.aspx
> Login page for the application. Accepts login credentials from the user and, if they are valid, redirects the user to the requested URL.

Register.aspx
> Registration page for the application. Allows unregistered users to select login credentials for accessing the application.

Logout.aspx
> Clears the Forms authentication cookie, effectively logging the user out of the secure portion of the application.

Users.xml
> XML file containing the credentials of registered users. Passwords are stored as SHA1-hashed text strings.

To set up Forms authentication, the application is configured with the *web.config* file shown in Example 9-1, which is placed in the root of the application.

Example 9-1. web.config file for Forms authentication

```
<?xml version="1.0" encoding="utf-8" ?>
<configuration>
    <location path="files">
        <system.web>
            <authorization>
                <deny users="?"/>
            </authorization>
        </system.web>
    </location>
    <system.web>
        <authentication mode="Forms">
            <forms name=".ASPNETIAN"
                loginUrl="Login.aspx"
                protection="All"
                timeout="60" />
        </authentication>
    </system.web>
</configuration>
```

The <authentication> element in Example 9-1 configures the application to use Forms authentication. Its child element, <forms>, provides a number of key security elements: a name for the Forms authentication cookie (.ASPNETIAN); the type of protection (encryption, validation, all, or none) for the authentication cookie; the timeout for the cookie (60 minutes in this case, the default being 30); and a login page to send unauthenticated users to. Note that since the example uses *Login.aspx*, the default, we could omit this attribute.

The <authorization> element, which is tied to the *files* subdirectory through the use of the <location> tag, denies access to any nonauthenticated user. For a more complete discussion of the <authorization> element, see "Authorization," later in this chapter.

With this configuration in place, if a user does not already have an authentication cookie, a request for any files in the *files* subdirectory (presuming the file type is handled by ASP.NET) results in the user being redirected to the login page. What if the file type that you want to protect isn't handled by ASP.NET by default? In that case, you can follow these steps to add that type in the IIS configuration for the application:

1. Open the Internet Services Manager applet and locate the application you want to configure.

2. Right-click the application's icon and select Properties.

3. In the Properties dialog, select the Directory (or Home Directory) tab, and click the Configuration... button.

4. On the App Mappings tab, click the Add button.

5. In the Add/Edit Application Extension Mapping dialog, click the Browse... button and browse to the location of *aspnet_isapi.dll*. Typically, this location will be the directory *%windir%\Microsoft.NET\Framework\%version%*, where *%version%* is the version number of the installed .NET Framework. You may need to change the Files of type: drop-down to *.dll to locate this file. Once you've located it, select it and click Open.

6. Now enter the file extension you want to protect (such as *.zip*) or enter .* to associate all file types with ASP.NET.

7. Click OK to accept changes and close each open dialog.

8. Repeat for additional desired file types.

 Using .* to map all file types to ASP.NET is a quick and easy way to protect all types of files for an application configured to use Forms authentication. You should not, however, use this technique if your application contains files, such as classic ASP pages, that are handled by a different ISAPI application because the .* mapping will take precedence and will prevent these file types from working properly.

Once all desired file types are mapped to the ASP.NET ISAPI handler,* any request made for one of those file types in the *files* subdirectory results in the user being redirected to *Login.aspx* if they do not already have a Forms authentication cookie for this application. The code for *Login.aspx* is shown in Example 9-2.

Example 9-2. Login.aspx

```
<%@ Page Language="VB" %>
<%@ Import Namespace="System.Data" %>
<%@ Import Namespace="System.Web.Security" %>
<html>
<head>
<title>Login Page</title>
<script runat="server">
    Sub Login_Click(Sender As Object, e As EventArgs)
        Dim LoginDS as DataSet
        If Cache("LoginDS") Is Nothing Then
            LoginDS = New DataSet()
            LoginDS.ReadXml(Server.MapPath("Users.xml"))
            Cache.Insert("LoginDS", LoginDS, _
                New CacheDependency(Server.MapPath("Users.xml")))
        Else
            LoginDS = Cache("LoginDS")
        End If
        If LoginDS.Tables(0).Select("Email='" & _
            Email.text & "'").Length > 0 Then
            Dim LoginRow() As DataRow = LoginDS.Tables(0).Select("Email='" _
                & Email.text & "'")
            If LoginRow(0).Item("Password").ToString = _
                FormsAuthentication.HashPasswordForStoringInConfigFile( _
                Password.Text, "SHA1") Then
                FormsAuthentication.RedirectFromLoginPage( _
                Email.Text, Persist.Checked)
            Else
                Message.Text = "Incorrect Password!"
            End If
        Else
            Message.Text = "Email not found. Have you " & _
                "<a href='register.aspx?page=" & _
                Server.UrlEncode(Request.RawUrl) & "'>registered</a>?"
        End If
    End Sub
</script>
</head>
<body>
    <form runat="server">
        <table border="0">
            <tr>
                <td>Email: </td>
                <td><asp:textbox id="Email" runat="server"/></td>
```

---

* The ISAPI hander takes requests from IIS and hands them off to the ASP.NET worker process, which runs as a separate executable.

Example 9-2. Login.aspx (continued)

```
        </tr>
        <tr>
          <td>Password: </td>
          <td><asp:textbox id="Password"
                 textmode="Password" runat="server"/></td>
        </tr>
        <tr>
          <td>Persist Authentication Cookie?</td>
          <td><asp:checkbox id="Persist"
                 checked="False" runat="server"/></td>
        </tr>
        <tr>
          <td><asp:button text="Submit"
                 onclick="Login_Click" runat="server"/></td>
          <td><input type="reset" value="Cancel" runat="server"/></td>
        </tr>
      </table>
      <asp:label id="Message" forecolor="Red" runat="server"/>
    </form>
  </body>
</html>
```

The tag-based section of *Login.aspx* is fairly straightforward and presents the user with textboxes in which to input an email address (used for a login ID) and password. The tag-based section also specifies a checkbox that allows users to persist the authentication cookie (so they won't need to login again from their machine).

To make coding a little easier, the example adds @ Import directives for both the System.Data and System.Web.Security namespaces. Thus, you can access their members without explicitly adding the namespace name.

In the Login_Click event handler, the example declares a local DataSet variable and populates it either from the ASP.NET cache or the *Users.xml* file (see Example 9-5), which contains the credentials of registered users. If the dataset is populated from the XML file, we then insert the dataset into the cache for later retrieval (which eliminates the need to read the file, if it has not changed).

The call to Cache.Insert sets up a file dependency on the *Users.xml* file. If that file changes, the cached dataset will be ejected from the cache and the new data will be loaded from the file on the next login request. This allows us to take advantage of the performance advantages of caching, but still ensure that we're always dealing with fresh data.

Once we have a dataset containing all current users, we ensure that the email entered by the user is contained in the table, using the DataTable's Select method:

```
If LoginDS.Tables(0).Select("Email='" & _
        Email.text & "'").Length > 0 Then
```

If the email exists, we get a DataRow containing the credentials associated with that user. We can then compare this hashed password in the dataset with a hashed version of the password entered by the user, which is returned by the HashPasswordForStoringInConfigFile method of the FormsAuthentication class. If the two versions of the password match, we redirect the user back to the page he or she requested by calling the RedirectFromLoginPage method of the FormsAuthentication class. RedirectFromLoginPage automatically redirects the user to the page specified by the ReturnUrl query string argument. This argument is automatically appended when the user is initially redirected to *Login.aspx*. RedirectFromLoginPage also sets the .ASPNETIAN cookie containing the Forms authentication token. The following code snippet illustrates this process:

```
Dim LoginRow() As DataRow = LoginDS.Tables(0).Select("Email='" _
    & Email.text & "'")
If LoginRow(0).Item("Password").ToString = _
    FormsAuthentication.HashPasswordForStoringInConfigFile( _
    Password.Text, "SHA1") Then
    FormsAuthentication.RedirectFromLoginPage(Email.Text, _
    Persist.Checked)
Else
    Message.Text = "Incorrect Password!"
End If
```

If the email address exists, but the password is incorrect, we set the Text property of the Message Label control to inform the user. If the entered email address does not exist, we set the label text to a message that includes a link to a registration page so that the user can self-register. Note that the link includes a query string argument named page, which *Register.aspx* uses to redirect the user back to *Login. aspx* with the original ReturnUrl query string argument intact. Registration is handled by the *Register.aspx* page, shown in Example 9-3.

Example 9-3. Register.aspx

```
<%@ Page Language="VB" %>
<%@ Import Namespace="System.Data" %>
<%@ Import Namespace="System.Web.Security" %>
<html>
<head>
<title>Registration Page</title>
<script runat="server">
    Sub Register_Click(Sender As Object, e As EventArgs)
        If Page.IsValid Then
            Dim LoginDS as New DataSet()
            LoginDS.ReadXml(Server.MapPath("Users.xml"))
            If LoginDS.Tables(0).Select("Email='" & _
                Email.text & "'").Length = 0 Then
                Dim NewUser As DataRow
                NewUser = LoginDS.Tables(0).NewRow()
                NewUser("Email") = Email.Text
                NewUser("Password") = _
                    FormsAuthentication.HashPasswordForStoringInConfigFile( _
                    Password.Text, "SHA1")
                LoginDS.Tables(0).Rows.Add(NewUser)
                LoginDS.WriteXml(Server.MapPath("Users.xml"))
                Response.Redirect(Request.QueryString("Page"))
            Else
                Message.Text = "User with email: <i>" & Email.Text & _
                    "</i> already exists. Please choose another email address."
```

Example 9-3. Register.aspx (continued)

```
          End If
        End If
    End Sub
</script>
</head>
<body>
    <form runat="server">
        <table border="0" cellspacing="10">
            <tr>
                <td>Email: </td>
                <td><asp:textbox id="Email" runat="server"/></td>
            </tr>
            <tr>
                <td>Desired Password: </td>
                <td><asp:textbox id="Password"
                        textmode="Password" runat="server"/></td>
            </tr>
            <tr>
                <td>Confirm Password: </td>
                <td><asp:textbox id="PasswordConfirm"
                        textmode="Password" runat="server"/></td>
            </tr>
            <tr>
                <td><asp:button text="Submit"
                        onclick="Register_Click" runat="server"/></td>
                <td><input type="reset" value="Cancel" runat="server"/></td>
            </tr>
        </table>
        <asp:comparevalidator id="comparePasswords"
            controltovalidate="Password"
            controltocompare="PasswordConfirm"
            display="dynamic"
            text="Passwords must match!"
            operator="Equal"
            runat="server"/>
        <asp:requiredfieldvalidator id="requireEmail"
            controltovalidate="Email"
            display="dynamic"
            text="Email address required!"
            runat="server"/>
        <asp:requiredfieldvalidator id="requirePassword"
            controltovalidate="Password"
            display="dynamic"
            text="Password required!"
            runat="server"/>
        <asp:label id="Message" runat="server"/>
    </form>
</body>
</html>
```

The tag-based portion of *Register.aspx* is similar to *Login.aspx*, except that the example adds a textbox (for confirmation of the desired password) and the following three validation controls:

- A CompareValidator control to validate that the Password and PasswordConfirm textbox values match.

- A RequiredFieldValidator to ensure that the user enters an email address so we don't have entries in the XML file with null email values.

- A RequiredFieldValidator to ensure that the user enters a password so we don't have entries in the XML file with null password values.

If we want to provide even more validation measures, we could also add a RegularExpressionValidator to ensure that the provided email address is valid (or at least in the correct format for a valid email address). However, the previously mentioned validators are sufficient to at least ensure that the user enters something.

In the Register_Click event handler, we first test to ensure that the page is valid (i.e., that all validation controls on the page report are valid). This test avoids wasting processor time to perform work on invalid data. If the user's browser supports DHTML, the page will not even be submitted until the validation control's requirements have been met, thanks to the ability of these controls to perform client-side validation (in addition to the server-side validation that is always performed).

If the page is valid, we declare a local DataSet variable and populate it from the *Users.xml* file. Then we check to make sure that the email address the user entered does not already exist in the file. If it does, we use the Text property of an ASP. NET Label control to ask the user to choose another email address.

If the email address does not exist in the file, we create a new DataRow, populate it with the user's chosen email address and a hashed version of the password,* add the new row to the dataset, and save the dataset back to the XML file, as shown in the following code snippet. Note that this technique does not control concurrency, so if someone modified the contents of the XML file between the time this code read from the file and when it writes to the file, those changes would be overwritten:

```
Dim NewUser As DataRow
NewUser = LoginDS.Tables(0).NewRow()
NewUser("Email") = Email.Text
NewUser("Password") = _
    FormsAuthentication.HashPasswordForStoringInConfigFile( _
    Password.Text, "SHA1")
LoginDS.Tables(0).Rows.Add(NewUser)
LoginDS.WriteXml(Server.MapPath("Users.xml"))
```

Once we've written the new user's information to *Users.xml*, we redirect the user to the page specified by the page's query string argument, as shown in the following line of code:

```
Response.Redirect(Request.QueryString("Page"))
```

---

* Again, you use the FormsAuthentication.HashPasswordForStoringInConfigFile method to hash the password.

Once the user is registered, they should be able to log in successfully. But what about logging out? Although the need for such a mechanism might not be immediately obvious, it is valuable in some instances.

Logging out

Consider an application that deals with sensitive information or is likely to be used from public computers. In such cases, you might want to provide the user with some way to log out to prevent others from accessing private information or accessing application resources using the user's account. In Forms authentication, this is quite simple. You call the static SignOut method of the FormsAuthentication class, as Example 9-4 illustrates. You would redirect users to *Logout.aspx* to accomplish the logout. You could also create a user control containing a button that, when clicked, calls the SignOut method and add that user control to all secured pages of your application.

Example 9-4. Logout.aspx

```
<%@ Page Language="VB" %>
<%@ Import Namespace="System.Web.Security" %>
<html>
<head>
<title>Logout Page</title>
<script runat="server">
    Sub Page_Load(Sender As Object, e As EventArgs)
        FormsAuthentication.SignOut()
        Message.Text = "You have been logged out."
    End Sub
</script>
</head>
<body>
    <asp:label id="Message" runat="server"/>
</body>
</html>
```

Example 9-5 shows the contents of the *Users.xml* file. This example shows how simple an XML file for this purpose can be.

Example 9-5. Users.xml

```
<?xml version="1.0" standalone="yes"?>
<Users>
  <User>
    <Email>andrew@aspnetian.com</Email>
    <Password>816010E041FA485C6E2383C649343D3A0CAD4D25</Password>
  </User>
</Users>
```

Security

Authorization

Authorization is the process of determining whether the user identified by the authentication process is allowed to access the resource that they're requesting or whether to take the action that they're attempting to take (such as updating data in a database). While authentication asks the question "Who are you?", authorization asks the question "Are you allowed to do that?" The answer to that question determines whether the user's action is allowed.

Authorization in ASP.NET takes three forms, which are all discussed in this section: ACL-based authorization, URL authorization, and programmatic authorization.

ACL-Based Authorization

Access Control Lists (ACLs) are used in Windows NT, Windows 2000, and Windows XP to control access to system resources, such as files and folders in the NTFS filesystem. You can assign Windows user accounts or groups to the ACL for a given resource to allow that user or group access to the resource, or determine what type of access (read, write, change, etc.) is authorized.

ACL-based authorization is useful primarily when using Windows authentication in ASP.NET. ASP.NET can use the authenticated user identity to perform ACL checks and can also make requests for ACL-protected resources by using the user's security context, if impersonation has been enabled.

To protect a file using ACL authorization, right-click the desired file in Windows Explorer and select Properties. Next, click the Security tab to view the current users, groups, and permissions on the file (as shown in Figure 9-2). Use the Add and Remove buttons to add or remove user or group accounts and the checkboxes in the Permissions section to modify permissions for the selected user.

 In Windows XP, the Security tab may not appear in the Properties dialog for a file or folder if Simple File Sharing is enabled. To see if this feature is enabled (and to disable it and make the Security tab available), Select Tools → Folder Options in Windows Explorer. Then select the View tab, and then in the Advanced Settings section, clear the "Use simple file sharing (recommended)" checkbox.

One of the first things you might do in the example above is remove the Everyone group from the folder, since this group (as the name suggests) allows anyone who can access the computer to access this file.

 Use caution when removing special accounts (such as the SYSTEM account) from the ACLs for a given resource. Some operating system files require the SYSTEM account to have access to them for the OS to function, so removing those permissions can cause major problems, up to and including not being able to start the OS.

Figure 9-2. File properties dialog

URL Authorization

URL authorization uses the `<allow>` or `<deny>` elements of the `<authorization>` configuration element to control access to folders and files within the application, as we saw in the example on Forms authentication. Access can be allowed or denied based on username, role, and/or HTTP verb used to request the resource. Thus, to allow user Marcie to access any resource in the application with any HTTP verb, but to prevent user Charles from making POST requests, we'd add the following `<authentication>` section to the *web.config* file at the root of the application:

```
<authorization>
    <allow verb="GET" users="*" />
    <allow verb="POST" users="Marcie" />
    <deny verb="POST" users="Charles" />
    <deny users="?" />
</authorization>
```

As we saw in Example 9-1, you can also use the `<location>` tag with the path attribute to control access to a specific folder or file:

```
<location path="filetoprotect.aspx">
    <system.web>
        <authorization>
            <deny users="?"/>
        </authorization>
    </system.web>
</location>
```

Because the <location> tag in *web.config* requires its own <system.web> tag pair, the <location> tag should always appear inside the <configuration> and </configuration> tags, but outside the <system.web> and </system.web> tags. You can define as many different <location> tags as you like, and each can contain its own URL authorization restrictions.

To specify domain rather than local accounts or groups, use the *domainname\userorgroupname* format when specifying the name in the <allow> or <deny> element. There are two wildcards for users, both of which we've seen already. The asterisk (*) refers to all users, while the question mark (?) refers to anonymous (unauthenticated) users. Finally, multiple users or groups can be specified in the <allow> or <deny> elements by separating the list of users or groups with commas.

Programmatic Authorization

You can also perform programmatic checks at runtime to determine whether a user should be allowed to perform certain actions. The primary means of doing this is the IsInRole method, which is defined by the IPrincipal interface and accessible from the User property of the Page class. As with ACL-based authorization, this method is most useful when you're using Windows authentication and want to check whether the authenticated user belongs to a particular Windows group, such as a managers group. The use of IsInRole is shown in the following code snippet:

```
If Page.User.IsInRole("Managers") Then
    'perform some action restricted to managers
Else
    Message.Text = "You must be a manager to perform this action"
End If
```

Code Access Security

Code access security is a new .NET runtime feature that can dramatically reduce the likelihood of applications performing damaging actions by putting significant restrictions in place on untrusted or partially trusted code. While using code access security programmatically in an application is well beyond the scope of this book, even if you never call a single method related to code access security, your ASP.NET applications still use it through settings configured in the *machine.config* configuration file.

The <trustLevel> element in *machine.config* defines the mapping of named trust levels to policy files that define the code access security policies associated with a given named trust level. The <trust> element in *machine.config* sets the default trust level to Full.

If you want to restrict the actions that a given application can take, you can do so by adding a <location> tag to *machine.config* that specifies the path to that application and contains a <trust> element specifying the desired trust level, as shown in the following code snippet. Setting the allowOverride attribute to False will prevent the trust level from being overridden in the application's *web.config* file:

```
<location path="Application1" allowOverride="False">
    <system.web>
        <trust level="Low"/>
```

```
    </system.web>
  </location>
```

 As with *web.config*, the <location> tag in *machine.config* must be placed outside of the <system.web> tags, but must also appear after the <configSections> section, or an exception will be thrown.

Additional Resources

The following sites provide additional information on the topics discussed in this chapter:

http://www.aspfriends.com/aspfriends/aspngsec.asp
> The home page for the AspFriends.com mailing list (for questions relating to ASP.NET security).

http://www.gotdotnet.com/team/upgrade/v1/aspnet_account_readme.doc
> The GotDotNet reference on changes to the ASP.NET worker process security identity and the effects these changes have had on performing tasks in ASP.NET that require elevated security permissions.

http://msdn.microsoft.com/nhp/Default.asp?contentid=28001369
> The MSDN reference for .NET security.

http://www.microsoft.com/technet/security/
> The Microsoft TechNet Security home page. The TechNet security site contains articles, patches, and tools that can help you properly configure and secure Windows 2000, IIS, and other Microsoft products to ensure that your applications are not compromised through incorrect server configuration or unpatched vulnerabilities.

CHAPTER 10

Error Handling, Debugging, and Tracing

Most code samples in this book don't include code intended to handle errors. It's not that error handling isn't important; but error handling can be complex, and for the most part we've tried to keep the sample code as simple and clear as possible. Since you'll need to deal with errors in the real world of application programming, the first part of this chapter discusses the variety of techniques available in ASP.NET for handling errors, including custom error pages and structured exception handling—a new feature of Visual Basic .NET.

In addition to handling errors in ASP.NET applications, most developers want to figure out what's causing those errors. To that end, the latter part of this chapter discusses debugging using either the .NET Framework SDK debugger or Visual Studio .NET. The chapter also covers use of the ASP.NET trace feature to trouble-shoot application problems.

Error Handling

The goal of error handling (also known as exception handling) is quite simple: to prevent exceptions or errors thrown during the execution of an application request from reaching users. Ideally, users should not know that an exception occurred, or they should at least be provided with an informative message that tells them what they can do to resolve the problem. ASP.NET provides three techniques for achieving this goal:

Custom error pages
    Allow you to assign one or more error pages to be displayed when an exception occurs.

Page_Error and Application_Error events
    Writing event handlers for either or both of these events allows you to catch and handle exceptions at the page or application level.

Structured exception handling
> New to Visual Basic .NET, this type of exception handling allows exceptions to be caught and handled in particular blocks of code.

These three techniques provide broadest (custom error pages, which can handle exceptions from any page in the application) to narrowest (structured exception handling, which handles exceptions for a specific block of code) coverage for handling application exceptions. Figure 10-1 illustrates the relationship of these exception handling techniques to both the exception (shown at the center) and the user, who you're trying to prevent from encountering the exception.

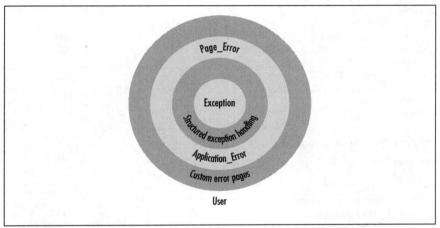

Figure 10-1. Exception handling techniques

The following sections describe these techniques and explain how they fit into an ASP.NET application. Note that you can use all three techniques together, individually, or in whatever combination you like. Using all three techniques in combination would provide broad coverage for most exceptions and more robust specific exceptions handling, but at the cost of maintaining your exception-handling logic in more places.

Custom Error Pages

The most general, but arguably the simplest, technique for handling exceptions in ASP.NET applications is to implement one or more custom error pages. You can do this by creating a web page to display an error message to the user. Then you specify that page as the default error page (or to handle a specific class of error) in *web.config*, using the <customError> configuration element. Example 10-1 shows a *web.config* file that defines a default custom error page called *Error.aspx.* Example 10-2 shows the custom error page itself, which simply displays the path of the page on which the error occurred. Example 10-3 shows the code for a page that will generate a NullReferenceException (which has an HTTP status code of 500).

Example 10-1. Enabling custom errors in web.config

```xml
<?xml version="1.0" encoding="utf-8" ?>
<configuration>
   <system.web>
      <customErrors defaultRedirect="Error.aspx" mode="On" />
   </system.web>
</configuration>
```

Example 10-2. Error.aspx

```
<%@ Page Language="VB" %>
<html>
<head>
   <title>Error page</title>
</head>
<body>
<h1>Error page</h1>
Error originated on: <%=Request.QueryString("aspxerrorpath") %>
</body>
</html>
```

Example 10-3. Throw500.aspx

```
<%@ Page Language="VB" Debug="True" %>
<html>
<head>
   <title>Throw an Error</title>
   <script runat="server">
      Sub Page_Load()
         Dim NullText As String = Nothing
         Message.Text = NullText.ToString()
      End Sub
   </script>
</head>
<body>
   <asp:label id="Message" runat="server"/>
</body>
</html>
```

Instead of the On mode setting for the <customErrors> element, you can set the mode to RemoteOnly or Off (note that these values are case sensitive). Off will cause detailed error messages containing information about an unhandled exception to be returned to the client, regardless of whether the request is local or remote. Since you don't want users to see error messages if you can avoid it, it's best not to use this value in a production application. RemoteOnly (the default) displays detailed error messages for requests originating from the local host, but displays custom errors to remote clients. On displays custom errors to any client, regardless of whether the request is local or remote. This is a good practice for production applications, since it prevents potentially sensitive information or source code from being displayed to clients, while allowing administrators or developers to view the page locally to read this information.

In addition to providing a default error page, the <customErrors> element also supports the use of child <error> elements to specify custom error pages for specific classes of errors, such as authentication (HTTP 403) or Not Found (HTTP 404) errors, as shown in the following code snippet:

```
<customErrors defaultRedirect="Error.aspx" mode="On">
    <error statusCode="403" redirect="ErrorAccessDenied.aspx"/>
    <error statusCode="404" redirect="ErrorNotFound.aspx"/>
</customErrors>
```

Any errors for which there is not a specific <error> element defined are handled by the page specified by the defaultRedirect attribute. Having different error pages for specific errors allows you to provide more informative messages to users, and perhaps offer some instructions on how the errors can be remedied, while still providing a generic handler for errors outside the scope of the specified handlers.

Another important thing you can do in a custom error page, whether specific or generic, is provide logging or notification of the error so that the site developer or administrator knows that there is a problem and can take action to fix it. In ASP. NET, this process is fairly simple and can be accomplished through the use of the MailMessage and SmtpMail classes, which reside in the System.Web.Mail namespace. Example 10-4 shows a custom error page that uses these classes to notify a site administrator of the error and the page on which it occurred.

Example 10-4. Error_SendMail.aspx

```
<%@ Page Language="VB" %>
<%@ Import Namespace="System.Web.Mail" %>
<html>
<head>
    <title>Error page</title>
    <script runat="server">
        Sub Page_Load()
            Dim Mail as New MailMessage()
            'Change the values below to valid email addresses
            Mail.To = "<valid email address>"
            Mail.From = "<valid email address>"
            Mail.Subject = "aspnetian.com error"
            Mail.Body = "An Exception occurred in page " & _
                Request.QueryString("aspxerrorpath")
            'If your SMTP server is not local, change the property below
            '   to a valid server or domain name for the SMTP server
            SmtpMail.SmtpServer = "localhost"
            SmtpMail.Send(Mail)
        End Sub
    </script>
</head>
<body>
<h1>Error page</h1>
Error originated on: <%=Request.QueryString("aspxerrorpath") %>
<br/>
An email has been sent to the administrator of this site notifying them of
the error.
</body>
</html>
```

For the code in Example 10-4 to work, you need to provide valid email addresses for the To and From properties of the MailMessage object instance.

If an unhandled exception occurs in a custom error page, no further redirect will occur, so the user will see a blank page. This situation makes it extremely important for you to ensure that no unhandled exceptions occur in custom error pages. For example, it might be a good idea to wrap the call to *SmtpMail.Send* in Example 10-4 in a Try...Catch block) to handle potential problems with connecting to the specified SMTP server. For more information about using the Try...Catch block, see "Structured Exception Handling," later in this chapter.

The advantage of using custom error pages is that it allows you to handle a lot of errors from a single location (or a small number of locations). The disadvantage is that there's not much you can do to handle the error, other than display a helpful message and notify someone that an error occurred. The reason for this is that you don't have access to the actual exception object in a custom error page, which means you can neither display information about the specific exception nor take steps to handle it.

Page_Error and Application_Error

A technique that overcomes the limitations of custom error pages, while still providing the ability to handle a broad range of application errors, is the use of the Error event defined by the Page and HttpApplication classes. Unless AutoEventWireup has been set to False (the default in Web Forms pages created with Visual Studio .NET), ASP.NET automatically calls page or application-level handlers with the name Page_Error or Application_Error if an unhandled exception occurs at the page or application level, respectively. The handler for Page_Error should be defined at the page level, as shown in Example 10-5, while the handler for Application_Error should be defined in the application's *global.asax* file, as shown in Example 10-6.

Example 10-5. Throw500_Page_Error.aspx

```
<%@ Page Language="VB" %>
<%@ Import Namespace="System.Web.Mail" %>
<html>
<head>
    <title>Throw an Error</title>
    <script runat="server">
        Sub Page_Load()
            Dim NullText As String = Nothing
            Message.Text = NullText.ToString()
        End Sub
        Sub Page_Error(Source As Object, E As EventArgs)
            Dim ex As Exception = Server.GetLastError()
            If Not ex Is Nothing Then
                Dim Mail as New MailMessage()
                'Change the values below to valid email addresses
                Mail.To = "<valid email address>"
                Mail.From = "<valid email address>"
                Mail.Subject = "aspnetian.com error"
```

Example 10-5. Throw500_Page_Error.aspx (continued)

```
            Mail.Body = "An Exception occurred in page " & _
                Request.RawUrl & ":" & vbCrLf
            Mail.Body &= ex.ToString() & vbCrlf & vbCrlf
            Mail.Body &= "was handled from Page_Error."
            'If your SMTP server is not local, change the property below
            '   to a valid server or domain name for the SMTP server
            SmtpMail.SmtpServer = "localhost"
            SmtpMail.Send(Mail)
            Server.ClearError()
        End If
        Response.Write("An error has occurred. " & _
            "The site administrator has been notified.<br/>" & _
            "Please try your request again later.")
    End Sub
  </script>
</head>
<body>
  <asp:label id="Message" runat="server"/>
</body>
</html>
```

Example 10-5 deliberately causes a NullReferenceException exception by calling ToString on an object that is set to Nothing. In Page_Error, we retrieve this exception by calling Server.GetLastError. The example then creates and sends an email that includes the exception details (calling ToString on an exception object returns the error message and the call stack as a string).

Finally, the code clears the exception by calling Server.ClearError. This last step is important because neither the Page_Error nor the Application_Error handler clears the exception by default. If you don't call ClearError, the exception will bubble up to the next level of handling. For example, if you define both a Page_Error handler at the page level and an Application_Error handler in *global.asax,* and you do not call ClearError in Page_Error, the Application_Error handler is invoked in addition to Page_Error. This can be a useful behavior if expected—for example, if you wish to use Page_Error to generate useful messages, while using Application_ Error to log all errors or send notifications. If you're not expecting it, though, this behavior can be confusing, to say the least.

Example 10-6 does essentially the same thing as Example 10-5, but handles errors at the application level, rather than at the page level. You can still access the Server object to get the exception that was thrown. Since Application_Error may handle exceptions for web services as well as for Web Forms pages, Example 10-6 does not attempt to use Response.Write to send a message to the user.

Example 10-6. global.asax

```
<%@ Import Namespace="System.Web.Mail" %>
<script language="VB" runat="server">
    Sub Application_Error(sender As Object, e As EventArgs)
        Dim ex As Exception = Server.GetLastError()
        If Not ex Is Nothing Then
            Dim Mail as New MailMessage()
            'Change the values below to valid email addresses
```

Example 10-6. global.asax (continued)

```
        Mail.To = <valid email address>
        Mail.From = <valid email address>
        Mail.Subject = "aspnetian.com error"
        Mail.Body = "An Exception occurred in page " & _
            Request.RawUrl & ":" & vbCrLf
        Mail.Body &= ex.ToString() & vbCrlf & vbCrlf
        Mail.Body &= "was handled from Application_Error."
        'If your SMTP server is not local, change the property below
        '   to a valid server or domain name for the SMTP server
        SmtpMail.SmtpServer = "localhost"
        SmtpMail.Send(Mail)
        Server.ClearError()
    End If
  End Sub
</script>
```

Structured Exception Handling

The most specific technique for exception handling, and the most useful in terms of gracefully recovering from the exception, is structured exception handling. Structured exception handling should be familiar to developers of Java and C++, for which it is standard practice, but it is new to the Visual Basic .NET language. Microsoft's new language, C#, also provides built-in support for structured exception handling.

In structured exception handling, you wrap code that may throw an exception in a Try...Catch block, as shown in the following code snippet:

```
'VB.NET
Try
    ' Code that may cause an exception
Catch ex As Exception
    ' Exception handling code
Finally
    ' Code executes whether or not an exception occurs
End Try

//C#
try
{
    // Code that may cause an exception
}
catch (Exception ex)
{
    // Exception handling code
}
finally
{
    // Code executes whether or not an exception occurs
```

The Try statement (lowercase try in C#) warns the runtime that the code contained within the Try block may cause an exception; the Catch statement (catch in C#) provides code to handle the exception. You can provide more than one `Catch` statement, with each handling a specific exception, as shown in the following code snippet. Note that each exception to be handled must be of a type derived from the base `Exception` class:

```
'VB.NET
Try
    ' Code that may cause an exception
Catch nullRefEx As NullReferenceException
    ' Code to handle null reference exception
Catch ex As Exception
    ' Generic exception handling code
End Try

//C#
try
{
    // Code that may cause an exception
}
catch (NullReferenceException nullRefEx)
{
    // Code to handle null reference exception
}
catch (Exception ex)
{
    // Generic exception handling code
}
```

 When using multiple `Catch` blocks, the blocks for specific exceptions should always appear before any `Catch` block for generic exceptions, or the specific exceptions will be caught by the generic exception handler.

The `Finally` statement (`finally` in C#) is also useful in structured exception handling. When used in conjunction with a `Try...Catch` block, the `Finally` statement allows you to specify code that will always be run regardless of whether an exception is thrown. This can be especially useful if you need to run clean-up code that might not otherwise run if an exception occurred, such as code that closes a database connection. Example 10-7 shows a page that attempts to connect to the Pubs SQL Server database and execute a command that returns a SqlDataReader. If either the connection attempt or the command results in an exception, the code in the `Catch` block will be executed. The code in the `Finally` block tests to see if the data reader and/or connection are open. If they are, it closes them.

Example 10-7. ReadTitles.aspx

```
<%@ Page Language="VB" %>
<%@ Import Namespace="System.Data" %>
<%@ Import Namespace="System.Data.SqlClient" %>
<html>
    <title>Try-Catch-Finally Example</title>
```

Example 10-7. ReadTitles.aspx (continued)

```
<head>
    <script runat="server">
        Sub Page_Load()
            Dim ConnStr As String = "Data Source=(local)\NetSDK;" & _
                "Initial Catalog=Pubs;Trusted_Connection=True;"
            Dim SQL As String = "SELECT title, price FROM title " & _
                "WHERE PRICE IS NOT NULL"
            Dim PubsConn As New SqlConnection(ConnStr)
            Dim TitlesCmd As New SqlCommand(SQL, PubsConn)
            Dim Titles As SqlDataReader
            Try
                PubsConn.Open()
                Titles = TitlesCmd.ExecuteReader()
                Output.Text = "<table>"
                While Titles.Read()
                    Output.Text &= "<tr>"
                    Output.Text &= "<td>" & Titles.GetString(0) & "</td>"
                    Output.Text &= "<td>$" & _
                        Format(Titles.GetDecimal(1), "##0.00") & "</td>"
                    Output.Text &= "</tr>"
                End While
                Output.Text &= "</table>"
            Catch sqlEx As SqlException
                Response.Write("A SqlException has occurred.")
            Catch ex As Exception
                Response.Write("An Exception has occurred.")
            Finally
                If Not Titles Is Nothing Then
                    If Not Titles.IsClosed Then
                        Titles.Close()
                    End If
                End If
                If PubsConn.State = ConnectionState.Open Then
                    PubsConn.Close()
                End If
            End Try
            Response.Write("<br/>The current connection state is: " & _
                PubsConn.State.ToString() & ".")
        End Sub
    </script>
</head>
<body>
    <h1>SqlDataReader Example</h1>
    <asp:label id="Output" runat="server"/>
</body>
</html>
```

As you can see from the examples in this section, of the available exception-handling techniques, structured exception handling is likely to require the most code to implement. However, it also provides you with the ability to handle the exception transparently to the user in cases when it is possible to recover from the exception. For example, you could modify the code in Example 10-6 to test

---

whether the exception was related to the attempt to open the connection and, if so, retry the connection a predefined number of times. This way, if the exception is the result of a temporary network problem, the exception handling code can potentially handle this problem without the user ever being aware that a problem exists (apart from the slight delay in connecting).

Debugging

Debugging is the process of locating and eliminating errors in an application. Each error falls into one of three categories:

Syntax errors
> These errors result from writing code that violates the rules of the language. A good example of a syntax error is failing to end a statement in C# with a semicolon. Syntax errors are typically caught and reported by the compiler, and thus are the easiest to debug.

Crashing semantic errors
> These errors result when code that is syntactically correct results in a condition that causes the program to terminate unexpectedly or to hang (for example, looping code whose loop counter is never incremented). Depending on the condition that causes the program to terminate, you may get an error message indicating the cause and (if debugging is enabled for the page) the line number on which the error occurred.

Noncrashing semantic errors
> These errors result when code that is syntactically correct and does not cause the application to crash or hang nonetheless results in variables containing data outside of the range expected by the developer, or program code executing in an unexpected order. This type of error is the most difficult to debug.

Both types of semantic errors are most typically the target of debugging efforts, since syntax errors are fairly easy to fix once they are identified by the compiler.

Two main tools are useful for debugging ASP.NET applications: the ASP.NET trace feature (discussed later in this chapter) and debuggers.

Two debuggers are of primary interest to ASP.NET developers: the .NET Framework SDK debugger, which has the substantial advantage of being free, and the Visual Studio .NET debugger, which provides additional debugging features such as remote debugging and the ability to debug native Win32 applications. An important limitation of the SDK debugger is that you cannot use it to edit source files, so you need to use another editor to make changes as you debug. The debugger in Visual Studio .NET allows you to edit your source files (although you need to stop debugging before editing and rebuild the application before restarting the debugger).

To start a debugging session with either debugger, follow these basic steps:

1. Open the debugger (or the Visual Studio .NET IDE).

2. Open the project or files you wish to debug.

3. Ensure that debugging is enabled for all pages and classes that you wish to debug.

4. Set breakpoints in the source code that will halt execution at a chosen point and allow you to step through subsequent code.

5. Start the debugger, either by attaching to running processes for your application or by running the Debug → Start command in the Visual Studio .NET IDE. Note that you may need to set the desired start page as described in "Using the Visual Studio .NET Debugger," later in this chapter.

The key to debugging in either debugger is ensuring that all code to be debugged is compiled in debug mode. This mode inserts symbols into the compiled assemblies that allow the debuggers to attach to the running code and allows you to step through this code line by line.

In the next two sections we'll look at the specific steps taken to enable debug mode, start debugging sessions, and step through code in both debuggers.

Using the SDK Debugger

Debugging in the SDK debugger, *DbgCLR.exe*, is fairly straightforward. The program is located by default in the *\FrameworkSDK\GuiDebug* folder of either the Visual Studio .NET or .NET Framework install folder. Start by opening the debugger by double-clicking on its executable. The resulting window should look similar to Figure 10-2.

Figure 10-2. The .NET Framework SDK debugger

Now open the ASP.NET pages, code-behind files, and associated class files (for custom server controls, for example) that you wish to debug, using either the File → Open → File... menu command, or by clicking the Open File button on the toolbar.

Before you go any further, you should ensure that debugging is enabled for all of the pages and class files you've opened. For code contained in ASP.NET pages, enabling it is simple: just add the Debug attribute to the @ Page directive and set its value to True:

```
<%@ Page Language="VB" Debug="True" %>
```

This step will also enable debugging of code contained within a code-behind file that is referenced by the Src attribute of the @ Page directive, which is compiled dynamically the first time the page is requested.

For code contained within precompiled code-behind files or other precompiled assemblies, you must compile the assembly with the compiler's debug flag set to enable debugging.

Once you've ensured that all your code is ready for debugging, it's time to set a breakpoint. The easiest way to do this is to click in the lefthand margin next to the line of code at which you want the debugger to halt execution. Note that you can set breakpoints only on executable lines of code or procedure declarations. The result will look similar to Figure 10-3.

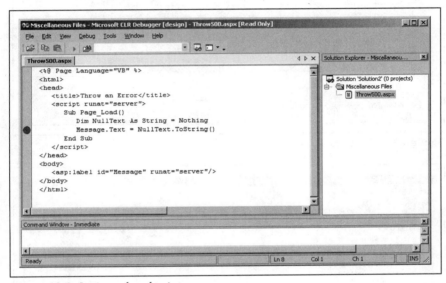

Figure 10-3. Setting a breakpoint

Once you've set your breakpoint, you'll need to open the desired page in Internet Explorer to start the processes to which the debugger will be attached. Once that's done, you can attach the debugger to the necessary processes by selecting Processes... from the Debug menu. This will open the Processes dialog. Select the *aspnet_wp.exe* process, and then click Attach... Next, locate the Internet Explorer process that corresponds to the page you loaded earlier, and attach that as well. At this point, the Processes dialog should look similar to Figure 10-4.

Now simply refresh the page in the browser, and assuming that the line on which you set the breakpoint is in the current flow of the application, the debugger should halt execution at the breakpoint, as shown in Figure 10-5. Then you can view the value of local variables using the Locals window (shown in Figure 10-5) or take advantage of other debugger features to examine your code.

Figure 10-4. Processes dialog

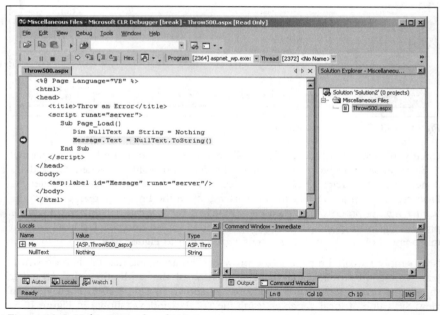

Figure 10-5. Halting on a breakpoint

Once program execution has halted at a breakpoint, you can also step through your code line by line using the Step Into, Step Over, and Step Out commands in the Debug menu (or their keyboard shortcuts). This allows you to examine the value of variables as you walk through your code, as well as better determine exactly where a given error is occurring.

In addition to setting breakpoints by clicking in the left margin, you can use the New Breakpoint dialog to set *conditional breakpoints* (i.e., breakpoints that only halt execution every *x* number of times they're hit). To open the New Breakpoint dialog, select New Breakpoint... from the Debug menu. The dialog appears in Figure 10-6.

Figure 10-6. New Breakpoint dialog

Using the Visual Studio .NET Debugger

Getting started with debugging in the Visual Studio .NET environment is simpler than with the SDK debugger, even though more debugging options and features are available, because projects are set up by default to support debugging. Assemblies generated for code-behind files in Visual Studio will be compiled in debug mode unless you explicitly tell the IDE to compile them in Release mode. Thus, as long as all of your code is in code-behind, you don't need to do anything further to enable debugging.

If you have a mix of code within server-side <script> blocks in your *.aspx* files and code-behind pages, you'll still need to add the Debug attribute to your *.aspx* files as described in the previous section.

To start debugging in Visual Studio .NET, open the project you want to debug, and then open the page (or pages), code-behind file(s), and/or class file(s) you want to debug. Because the Visual Studio .NET debugger can automatically attach itself to the correct processes when you want to start debugging, you don't need to explicitly attach the processes as described in the previous section (although you can still do it that way if you want to). However, in order to automatically attach the processes, you need to provide a starting point, which should be the first page you want to debug. Simply right-click that page in the Solution Explorer window and select Set As Start Page.

Next, set breakpoints as desired in your code-behind or class files. Setting breakpoints is done the same way in the Visual Studio .NET debugger and the SDK debugger (which is discussed in the previous section).

Once all your breakpoints are set, start debugging by selecting Start from the Debug menu. This should result in a new browser window being opened to the page that you set as the start page and the first breakpoint being hit. At this point, the IDE should look similar to Figure 10-7.

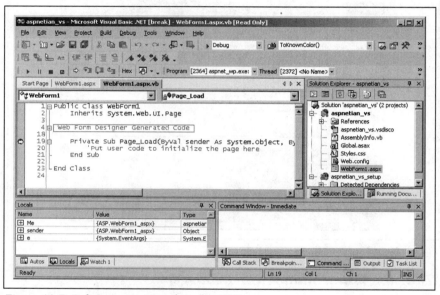

Figure 10-7. Debugging in Visual Studio .NET

Now you can walk through your code or examine local variables the way you can in the SDK debugger.

Tracing

The other useful tool provided by ASP.NET for debugging is the trace feature. Tracing allows you, through a simple configuration setting or page-level attribute, to have ASP.NET write a whole host of information about the currently executing request to the page or to a trace log. This information includes the SessionID; the time, type, and status code of the request; timing information for events such as Init, PreRender, SaveViewState, and Render; a Control Tree of all controls in the page; and the contents of the Cookies collection, the HTTP Headers, the QueryString collection (if any QueryString values were passed), the Form collection (if any form fields were passed), and the ServerVariables collection.

Essentially, tracing allows you to automatically write out the contents of all collections exposed by the classic ASP Request object, plus some really useful additional information. This allows you to examine a great deal of information about a request on a single page, which can assist greatly in debugging.

More importantly, you can also write to the trace output using the Trace.Write and Trace.Warn methods, which are exposed by the Trace property of the Page class. These methods can now be used in place of Response.Write when you determine the value of a variable on a page at a certain point in page execution or write out a notification that a certain point in the page has been hit. With Trace.Write or Trace.Warn, once you've disabled tracing, you can leave the statements in your code and you don't have to worry about anyone seeing the output. If you've ever deployed a page to production without removing or commenting out your Response.Write statements used for debugging, you'll be grateful for this feature.

Page-Level Tracing

Enabling tracing at the page level is very simple. Simply add the Trace attribute to the @ Page directive and set its value to True, as shown in the following code snippet:

```
<%@ Page Language="VB" Trace="True" %>
```

This provides a quick and easy way to get an overview of what's going on for a given page. The output from a page with tracing enabled looks similar to Figure 10-8.

One downside to enabling tracing at the page level is that if you use it with many pages, it's more work to add and remove the Trace attribute for each page (or to set the attributes to False). This can also make it more likely that you'll forget one and end up with trace information being written out in a production application. Not what you want.

Application-Level Tracing

ASP.NET provides the ability to enable tracing at the application level through the <trace> element in *web.config*. Application-level tracing makes it possible to disable tracing in a single location in your application and makes it easier to enable tracing for multiple pages. Example 10-8 shows a *web.config* file with tracing enabled at the application level.

While the <trace> element allows you to enable or disable tracing at the application level, the page-level Trace attribute overrides the setting in *web.config*. Thus, if any pages have the Trace attribute set to True, disabling tracing at the application level will not disable tracing for these pages.

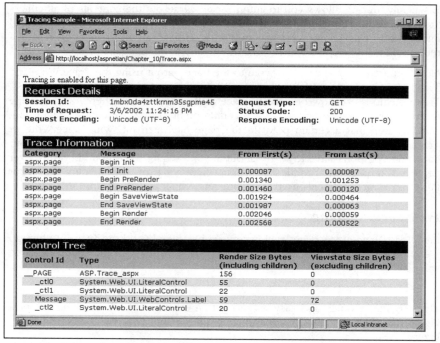

Figure 10-8. Page-level tracing

Example 10-8. The <trace> element

```
<configuration>
   <system.web>
      <trace enabled="true"
         localOnly="true"
         pageOutput="true"
         requestLimit="15"
         traceMode="SortByCategory" />
   <system.web>
</configuration>
```

In addition to providing a single point of control over enabling/disabling tracing, the <trace> element allows you to control several other factors: whether trace output is visible to machines other than the local host (using the localOnly attribute); whether the output is sent to the page or to a trace log (using the pageOutput attribute); the number of traces that are kept in the trace log (requestLimit); and how the Trace Information section of the trace output is sorted (traceMode).

If pageOutput is set to False, you can still view the trace output by entering the special URL *Trace.axd* (which isn't an actual file, but a URL that invokes an HttpHandler for the trace functionality) from the root of the application. *Trace.axd* lists all saved traces for the application. Note that once the number of traces specified by the requestLimit attribute is met, no more traces are saved until the trace log is cleared. *Trace.axd* provides a link for this purpose.

Using Trace.Write and Trace.Warn

Finally, as mentioned in the introduction to this section, instead of using Response. Write (as done in classic ASP) to write out variable values or flag certain points in your code, ASP.NET enables you to use *Trace.Write* and *Trace.Warn*. Both the Write and Warn methods are overloaded and can take one of the following sets of arguments:

- A single string argument containing the text to write to the trace output.

- One string argument containing a user-defined category for the entry and a second string argument containing the text to write to the trace output.

- One string argument containing a user-defined category for the entry, a second string argument containing the text to write to the trace output, and an Exception argument.

The only difference between Write and Warn is that entries written with the Warn method appear in red text, making them ideal for conditions that require special attention. Example 10-9 shows an ASP.NET page with tracing enabled that uses Trace.Write and Trace.Warn to write to the trace output. Figure 10-9 shows the output of this page.

Example 10-9. Trace.aspx

```
<%@ Page Language="VB" Trace="True" %>
<html>
<head>
    <title>Tracing Sample</title>
    <script runat="server">
        Sub Page_Load()
            Trace.Write("MyCategory", "Hello, Trace!")
            Trace.Warn("MyCategory", "This text will be red!")
            If Page.Trace.IsEnabled = True Then
                Message.Text = "Tracing is enabled for this page."
            Else
                Message.Text = "Tracing is not enabled for this page."
            End If
        End Sub
    </script>
</head>
<body>
    <asp:label id="Message" runat="server"/>
</body>
</html>
```

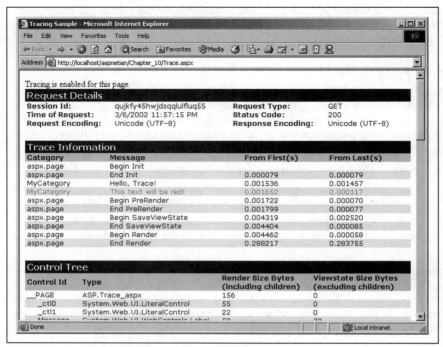

Figure 10-9. Output of Trace.aspx

Additional Resources

The following site provides additional information on the topics discussed in this chapter:

http://samples.gotdotnet.com/quickstart/aspplus/doc/debugcomsdk.aspx
  The ASP.NET QuickStart reference to the .NET Framework SDK Debugger.

CHAPTER 11

ASP.NET Deployment

To end Part 1 of the book, we've saved the best for last. Why do we call it the best? Because compared to classic ASP, deploying an ASP.NET application is extremely simple. In fact, in many cases, you can deploy an application by copying the entire application structure to a new IIS application folder on the target server.

This chapter discusses both simple deployment scenarios, for which the DOS XCOPY command or Windows Explorer are all you'll need. It also discusses more involved scenarios, such as using the Visual Studio Web Setup project type to deploy your application.

Deploying ASP.NET Applications

For most common applications, all you need to do to deploy the application is set up an IIS virtual directory on the target machine and copy the application's files to it. Assuming that the .NET Framework is installed on the target machine, the application should then run without further configuration or setup.

This type of scenario includes both ASP.NET applications written with their code inline in *.aspx* files and those that use code-behind files. Note, however, that deploying the code-behind files themselvesis not necessary, as long as you deploy the assembly or assemblies compiled from them.

To deploy an ASP.NET application:

1. Create a new IIS virtual directory (or web site) on the target machine using Internet Services Manager.

2. Use Windows Explorer, XCOPY, FTP, or another transfer mechanism to copy the files and folders contained in the application's root directory to the new directory on the target machine.

As long as any assemblies you're using are in the *bin* subdirectory of your application and you're not using COM components through COM Interop, it's really that simple. Because all application-specific configuration information is contained in your *web.config* file(s), this information is automatically copied with the application. In situations when you use shared assemblies, a little more work is necessary, as we'll discuss in the next section.

Deploying Assemblies

Assemblies are the basic unit of deployment for managed applications, including ASP.NET applications. Assemblies are used in ASP.NET in several ways, each of which has different implications for deployment. The three categories of assembly are described below. The steps required to deploy application-specific and global assemblies appear in subsequent sections.

Automatically generated assemblies
> Includes assemblies that are dynamically generated by the ASP.NET runtime for each *.aspx* page in your application, as well as for code-behind files identified by the src attribute of the @ Page directive. Because these assemblies are generated at runtime automatically, no action is required on the part of the developer at deployment time.

Application-specific assemblies
> Includes assemblies resulting from the compilation of code-behind files, whether through building an application in Visual Studio .NET or using the command-line compilers. This category also includes compiled assemblies containing business logic code, and/or assemblies containing custom server controls. All application-specific assemblies should reside in the application's *bin* subdirectory (also known as the local assembly cache), which allows your application to locate and use the assembly's members. There they are automatically loaded into memory by the ASP.NET runtime. Because these assemblies reside within the folder tree of the application, when you deploy the application using XCOPY, FTP, or Windows Explorer, they are copied with the rest of the files in your application and available to the deployed application automatically. Additionally, the ASP.NET runtime automatically modifies the IIS permissions on the local assembly cache directory to deny all HTTP access to the directory, which prevents anyone from reading or accessing assemblies directly.

Global assemblies
> Includes any assemblies that are shared across all applications on a machine by installing them in the global assembly cache (GAC). Assemblies must be strongly named in order to be installed in the GAC and can be versioned to support side-by-side installation of multiple versions of the same assembly.

Deploying Application-Specific Assemblies

As noted in the preceding section, deploying application-specific assemblies is as simple as deploying other application files. As long as the assemblies reside in the *bin* subdirectory of the application, no further action is required on the part of the developer apart from copying the application's files to the target server.

The magic of the *bin* directory is enabled by the `<assemblies>` configuration element in *machine.config*, which contains the following `<add>` element by default:

```
<add assembly="*" />
```

This element tells the ASP.NET runtime to load any assemblies residing in the *bin* subdirectory for use by the application.

Another important point is that when assemblies are loaded by the ASP.NET runtime, the actual physical DLL containing the assembly is never loaded into memory. Instead, the ASP.NET runtime makes a shadow copy of the DLL and loads and locks it on the disk instead (while setting up a file monitor on the original DLL file). This means that you can update the .NET assemblies associated with your application at any time, without the need to shut down IIS or restart the server. The ASP.NET runtime automatically detects when an assembly is updated and serves all new requests using the new version of the assembly. This makes it significantly easier to maintain and update applications with a minimum of downtime.

If you use code-behind for your page-specific logic, you can deploy only the *.aspx* pages and the precompiled assembly (or assemblies) for your code-behind files, without deploying the code-behind files. This allows you to run your application while protecting the source code contained in the actual code-behind files.

Some have argued that, as with Java bytecode, the Intermediate Language (IL) contained in .NET managed assemblies is readily decompiled into a managed language such as C#. Thus, even if you do not deploy the code-behind files for an application, it may still be possible for someone to derive this code from the assemblies by using an IL decompiler.

Application developers should consider the relative value represented by their code versus the effort required to decompile that code, and determine whether additional means for protecting the code are warranted. One such measure is a code obfuscator, which renders most member names meaningless to make understanding of decompiled code more difficult.

Deploying Global Assemblies

The global assembly cache (GAC) provides a centralized location for the storage of assemblies that are to be shared across applications on a given machine. As noted previously, to be stored in the GAC, an assembly must be named strongly. This process is outlined in this section. Because of this requirement, the extra deployment effort entailed, and the fact that global assemblies are available to all applications on a machine by default, you should only use the GAC for assemblies that fit the following profile:

- They need to be shared by many applications.

- The effort of maintaining and/or updating individual local copies of the assembly for each application outweighs the effort of strongly naming and deploying the assembly to the GAC.

The first step in deploying an assembly to the GAC is to provide the assembly with a strong name. This is a three-step process:

1. Generate a cryptographic key pair using the *sn.exe* command line tool:

   ```
   sn -k keyPair.snk
   ```

   To see all the options for the *sn.exe* tool, run `sn /?` at a command prompt.

2. Add an assembly-level `AssemblyKeyFile` attribute. You can also optionally add an `AssemblyVersion` attribute to provide a version number for the assembly. The `*` in the following version number example auto-increments the last two of the four version number parts with each compilation:

   ```
   ' VB.NET
   <Assembly: AssemblyKeyFile("keyfile.snk")>
   <Assembly: AssemblyVersion("0.1.*")>

   // C#
   [assembly: AssemblyKeyFile(@"..\..\sgKey.snk")]
   [Assembly: AssemblyVersion("0.1.*")]
   ```

3. Compile the assembly using the appropriate command-line compiler. Note that the key pair should be copied to the location of the code files to be compiled, since this location is where the compiler will look for the file based on the `AssemblyKeyFile` attribute shown previously.

Once the assembly has been strongly named, you can install it into the GAC in any one of three ways:

- Use the *gacutil.exe* command line tool to install (or uninstall) an assembly into the GAC, as follows:

  ```
  gacutil -i myAssembly.dll
  ```

  Note that this syntax assumes that *gacutil.exe* is called from the directory containing the assembly's physical file. The *gacutil.exe* utility is recommended only for development systems.

- Use Windows Explorer to drag and drop a copy of the assembly to the GAC. Access to the GAC is provided via a Windows Explorer shell extension, which displays the contents of the GAC as the folder *%windir%\Assembly*.

- Use Microsoft Windows Installer 2.0 to create an installation package that will install the assembly or assemblies to the GAC. This installation ensures easier rollback of assemblies and other benefits. See the Windows Installer 2.0 documentation for information on creating Installer packages.

Deploying Through Visual Studio .NET

If you are using Visual Studio .NET to create your web applications, you have some additional deployment options at your disposal. These options include simply using Visual Studio's Copy Project command to copy some or all project files to a new location and using a Web Setup project to create a Windows Installer package to install the web application, including creating the necessary IIS directories. These techniques are discussed in the following sections.

What About COM Components?

If you're using only managed assemblies in your application, the deployment picture is pretty rosy. It's considerably easier to deploy, update, and maintain managed assemblies than it was to maintain COM components in classic ASP. But what if your application requires you to use COM components through the .NET COM interoperability layer?

The good news is that if the version of the COM component you are using is already installed on the target machine, you should need to deploy only the runtime-callable wrapper (RCW) assembly for the component, since that assembly contains the information necessary to locate the component based on information in the registry.

However, if the COM component is a custom component or is not installed on the target system, you need to deploy the COM component to the target system and register it using *regsvr32.exe* as follows:

```
regsvr32 <dllname>
```

Note that you would replace *<dllname>* with the name of the component to register.

In addition to these options, Visual Studio .NET allows you to open a project directly from the Web, so you could theoretically create the project directly on the target server and edit it there. This is only recommended for development systems, since incorrect edits made using this technique on production systems could result in application errors or downtime. To open a project from the Web, simply open Visual Studio .NET and select File → Open → Project From Web....

Deploying Using Copy Project

The simplest option for deploying a project from Visual Studio is to use the Copy Project command. You can access Copy Project by either selecting Copy Project... from the Project menu or clicking the Copy Project button in the Solution Explorer toolbar, as shown in Figure 11-1.

Either method will open the Copy Project dialog, shown in Figure 11-2.

The Copy Project dialog gives you a number of options. The first is the destination folder for the project, which is expressed as a URL. You can either enter this URL manually or browse to the desired URL by clicking the ellipsis (...) button.

If you use the browse feature, however, you must select a resource that resolves to a valid URL, such as a web folder in My Network Places.

To copy the project files, you can use either File share access (for copying locally or to a network share) or FrontPage access. FrontPage access requires author permission on the destination web server. If you use FrontPage as the web access method, the destination project folder will be created automatically in IIS, while the File share method requires that you set up this folder manually.

Figure 11-1. Copy Project button in Solution Explorer

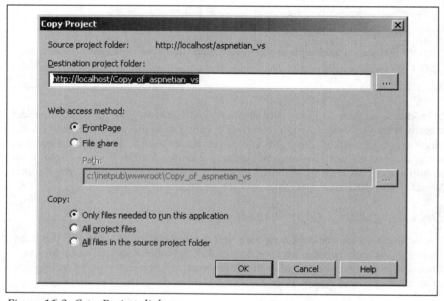

Figure 11-2. Copy Project dialog

Finally, you have three choices of which files to copy:

Only files needed to run this application
> Copies only the Web Forms, web services, and associated assemblies, without copying any code-behind files to the destination server. This allows you to copy and run your project on another machine without exposing the source code.

All project files
> Copies all files associated with the project to the destination machine, including code-behind files. This option will not copy files contained in the project folder that are not associated with the project. To keep a file from being copied, you can right-click the file in the Solution Explorer window and select Exclude From Project.

All files in the source project folder

Copies all files from the project folder, whether they are associated with the project or not. This option is useful for moving a project from one development machine to another, particularly if you will need to continue developing the application on the target machine.

Note that regardless of the options you choose, you must build your project before deploying it, so that any code in code-behind modules is compiled into assemblies.

Deploying Using a Web Setup Project

Visual Studio .NET also adds a completely new project type that now makes it possible to create an installation package for installing (and uninstalling) a web application as easily as any other application. The new project type is called the Web Setup Project, and it is available in the Setup and Deployment Projects folder in the New Project dialog, as shown in Figure 11-3. You can create a Web Setup Project in a standalone solution or as part of the solution containing your web application project. This section provides an overview of this project type and of how you can use it to deploy your web application.

Figure 11-3. New Project dialog

To create a Web Setup Project, select File → New → Project.... Then select the Setup and Deployment Projects folder in the lefthand pane of the New Project dialog. Next, select Web Setup Project in the righthand pane. Then fill in the Name and Location boxes and click OK. If you want to add the new project to an existing solution, you should open that solution first and then click the Add to Solution radio button in the New Project dialog.

Once the project is created, you'll be presented with the File System window (see Figure 11-4), which allows you to add files to be deployed to the target system. In addition to the File System window, the Web Setup Project type offers windows for adding Registry entries and File Type associations, as well as for modifying the user interface that will be displayed by the installer. These windows can be viewed by right-clicking the project name in the Solution Explorer and selecting View → *<windowname>*.

If you created your web setup project as part of the solution containing your web application, you can add all of the necessary files from the application to the setup project simply by right-clicking the Web Application Folder, selecting Add → Project Output..., and then selecting both Primary Output and Content Files, as shown in Figure 11-5.

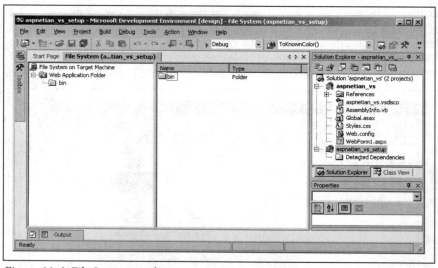

Figure 11-4. File System window

Now, if you build the setup project (note that you should create a fresh build of the web application project first), all necessary files for the web application will be included in the generated setup files.

These files will be located in either the Debug or Release subfolder of the project, depending on whether the Debug or Release configuration is selected in the solution's Configuration Manager.

If you created the web setup project in its own standalone solution, you'll need to add the files manually. Perhaps the easiest way to do this is to highlight the desired files in Windows Explorer and then drag and drop them from Windows Explorer onto the Web Application folder. This will add all selected files and folders to the web application. This step should work fine unless you need to mark any of the subfolders of the application as IIS applications.

Figure 11-5. Add Project Output dialog

In this case, you'll need to create separate folders for them by right-clicking the File System on Target Machine entry in the File System window, and then selecting Add Special Folder → Web Custom Folder. By default, the folder's IsApplication property, which determines whether the folder will be configured as an IIS Application, is set to True. You can use the Property Browser to modify this setting, if desired.

In addition to setting the IsApplication property for Web Custom Folders, you can use the property browser to set a variety of other IIS-specific configuration options for the folders in your setup project. For example, you can specify whether a given folder will allow read or write access or directory browsing, as well as whether the folder should be indexed. This way, you can provide all of the application configuration automatically, allowing the person installing the application to simply double-click the setup file generated by the project and follow a few brief wizard steps to install the application.

Once you've configured the application folders, you will need to build the project to create the setup files. Then you can copy or transfer those files to another machine, run *Setup.exe*, and the application should install and run normally.

Additional Resources

The following site provides additional information on the topics discussed in this chapter:

http://www.gotdotnet.com/quickstart/aspplus/doc/deployment.aspx
   The ASP.NET QuickStart reference for application deployment.

PART II

Intrinsic Class Reference

This section devotes a chapter to each of the following major classes that are available as part of the ASP.NET object model:

Page
HttpApplication and HttpApplicatonState
HttpContext
HttpException
HttpRequest
HttpResponse
HttpServerUtility
HttpSessionState

Each chapter adheres to a standardized format that includes the following elements:

- An introduction, which provides a background on the class and how it is used in an ASP.NET application.

- A list of the class members (properties, collections, methods, and events) documented in the chapter.

- A Comments/Troubleshooting section that provides helpful tips on using the class or discusses pitfalls commonly encountered when working with the class.

- Detailed documentation on class properties, with a separate entry devoted to each property.

- Detailed documentation on collections returned by properties of the class, if the class has any, with a separate entry devoted to each collection.

- Detailed documentation on class methods, with a separate entry devoted to each method

- Detailed documentation on events raised by the class, if the class exposes any, with a separate entry devoted to each event.

In addition, Chapter 20 documents configuration settings that can be found in either *machine.config* or *web.config*.

CHAPTER 12

The Page Class

In contrast to classic ASP, ASP.NET features a far richer object model that allows virtually every part of an ASP.NET application to be generated and modified dynamically. Central to this ability to generate—and particularly, to modify—content programmatically is the Page class, which is new to ASP.NET.

The Page class (or a class derived from the Page class) represents a request to an *.aspx* page that is processed by the ASP.NET extension to Internet Information Server or to another web server supporting the .NET Framework. The web page may contain simple HTML and text, .NET code, or a combination of both; in other words, the Page class represents a single Web Forms page. The requests for that page are served by the compiled object that sends HTML or other content back to the client.

The Page object is recompiled if any source files that form this page, such as a user control, a code-behind file, the *.aspx* page itself, or the application configuration file, are changed.

In the case of single-file ASP.NET pages (i.e., *.aspx* files that combine user interface elements with script), the *.aspx* page is compiled into an instance of a class that derives directly from the Page class. This is evident from the following code:

```
Public Sub Page_Load(o AS Object, e AS EventArgs)
    Dim oType As Type
    oType = Me.GetType
    Do
        Response.Write(oType.Name & "<BR />")
        oType = oType.BaseType
    Loop While Not oType Is Nothing
End Sub
```

The output produced by this code appears as follows:

```
Page1_aspx
Page
```

```
TemplateControl
Control
Object
```

Web Forms pages produced by Visual Studio, in contrast, consist of separate *.aspx* and code-behind files. In this case, the *.aspx* page is compiled into an instance of a class that derives from the class in the code-behind file, which in turn derives from the Page class. This is illustrated by the following code-behind file:

```
Option Strict On

Imports Microsoft.VisualBasic
Imports System
Imports System.ComponentModel
Imports System.Web
Imports System.Web.UI

Namespace AspNetPages
    Public Class Page2Class : Inherits Page
        Public Sub Page_Load(o AS Object, e AS EventArgs) _
                Handles MyBase.Load
        Dim oType As Type
        oType = Me.GetType
        Do
            Response.Write(oType.Name & "<BR />")
            oType = oType.BaseType
        Loop While Not oType Is Nothing
        End Sub
    End Class
End Namespace
```

The page produces the following output:

```
Page2_aspx
Page2Class
Page
TemplateControl
Control
Object
```

As the output from these two code examples shows, the Page class derives from the System.Web.UI.TemplateControl class, which defines the functionality common to both the Page class and the UserControl class. Such Page class members as the LoadControl method (which dynamically loads a control at runtime), the AbortTransaction and CommitTransaction events, and the Error event are all inherited from TemplateControl. The TemplateControl class in turn derives from the System.Web.UI.Control class, which defines the members common to all ASP.NET Server Controls. The Control class in turn derives from the Object class, the class from which all .NET reference types are derived directly or indirectly.

Because an object derived from the Page class is globally available whenever ASP. NET is processing a Web Forms page, you do not have to reference the Page object specifically in order to access its members. For example, to access the Session property of the Page class, we can use either:

```
Dim oSess As HttpSessionState = Page.Session
```

or:

```
Dim oSess As HttpSessionState = Session
```

In addition to representing the Web Form, the Page object is the container for all controls hosted by the page. All child controls on the page can be accessed through the Page object's Controls collection, which returns a ControlCollection object. For example, the following code iterates the ControlCollection collection and lists the name of each control:

```
Private Sub Page_Load(o As Object, e AS EventArgs)
    Dim ctl As Control
    For each ctl in Controls
        Response.Write(TypeName(ctl) & ": " & ctl.ID & "<BR />")
    Next
End Sub
```

Table 12-1 lists the properties, collections, and methods exposed by the Page class that are documented in this chapter.

Table 12-1. Page class summary

Properties	Collections	Methods	Events
Application	Controls	DataBind	Error
Cache	Validators	FindControl	Init
ClientTarget		HasControls	Load
Context		LoadControl	Unload
EnableViewState		MapPath	
ErrorPage		ResolveUrl	
IsPostBack		Validate	
IsValid			
Request			
Response			
Server			
Session			
SmartNavigation			
Trace			
User			
ViewState			

Comments/Troubleshooting

The ASP.NET equivalents of most classic ASP intrinsic objects are returned by properties of the ASP.NET Page class. These properties are shown in Table 12-2.

Table 12-2. ASP.NET equivalents of ASP intrinsic objects

ASP object	Equivalent ASP.NET class	Returned by
Application	HttpApplication and HttpApplication-State	Page.Application property
ASPError	None (ASP.NET uses Structured Exception Handling)	

Table 12-2. ASP.NET equivalents of ASP intrinsic objects (continued)

ASP object	Equivalent ASP.NET class	Returned by
ObjectContext	HttpContext	Page.Context property
Request	HttpRequest	Page.Request property
Response	HttpResponse	Page.Response property
Server	HttpServerUtility	Page.Server property
Session	HttpSessionState	Page.Session property

In this chapter, we'll use the following code listing as the basis for most examples. Unless otherwise noted, each example will consist of just the Page_Load event handler for that particular example. Any displayed output messages or return values will be shown as the Text property of the ASP.NET Label control named Message or displayed by calling Response.Write:

```
<%@ Page Language="vb" %>
<html>
   <head>
      <script runat="server">
         Sub Page_Load()
             'Example code will go here
         End Sub
      </script>
   </head>
<body>
   <asp:label id="Message" runat="server"/>
</body>
</html>
```

Properties Reference

Application

```
HttpApplicationState = Page.Application
```

Returns an instance of the HttpApplicationState class, which is the equivalent of the ASP intrinsic Application object. An instance of the HttpApplicationState class contains global information that can be shared across multiple sessions and requests within an ASP.NET application. For more information on the HttpApplicationState class and its members, see Chapter 13.

Parameters

HttpApplicationState
    A variable of type HttpApplicationState that receives the instance of the HttpApplicationState class.

Example

The following code example uses Page object's Application property to add a name/value pair to the Application object and display the value in a label control. Since all of the properties of the Page object are exposed directly to any code associated with the page, it is not necessary to explicitly name the Page class (i.e., Page.Application) to access the Application property.

```
Sub Page_Load()
    Application("Name") = "John Doe"
    Message.Text = "The value <em>" & CStr(Application("Name")) & _
        "</em> has been added to the Application collection."
End Sub
```

Notes

Although you can retrieve a local object reference to the HttpApplicationState instance for the application, the more common use of this property is to access it directly through the Application property, as shown in the example.

Cache

```
Cache = Page.Cache
```

Returns an instance of the Cache class, which represents the cache for an application domain. Using the Cache property, data can be added to and retrieved from the cache.

Parameters

Cache
    A variable of type Cache that will receive the Cache instance.

Example

The following code example adds two name/value pairs to the Cache object using the Cache property of the Page class and displays the values in a label control using the Page object's Cache property:

```
Sub Page_Load(o As Object, e As EventArgs)
    Cache("Name") = "John Doe"
    Cache("Age") = 42
    Message.Text = CStr(Cache.Item("Name")) & " is " & _
        CStr(Cache("Age")) & " years old."
End Sub
```

Notes

Like the Application object, the Cache object is more commonly accessed directly through the Cache property, rather than by obtaining a local object reference to the Cache instance for the application.

Chapter 13 discusses when you might use the ASP.NET Cache rather than the Application state collection, and vice-versa.

The Cache class includes the following members:

Cache member	Description
Add method	Adds an item to the cache
Count property	Indicates the number of items contained in the cache
Get method	Returns an object representing data in the cache with a particular key value

Cache member	Description
Insert method	Inserts an item into the cache and assigns it a key
Item property	Returns an object representing a cache item based on its key value or sets an item of data in the cache while assigning it a key value
Remove method	Removes an item with a particular key value from the cache

ClientTarget

```
String = Page.ClientTarget
```

Gets or sets a string value that allows you to override automatic browser detection in ASP.NET, force the page to be rendered for a browser type configured in *machine.config* or *web.config*, and specified by this property. The available preconfigured values for this property are:

downlevel

> The page will be rendered based on the browser capabilities defined for unknown browsers in the <browserCaps> element of *machine.config*.

ie4

> The page will be rendered based on the values for Internet Explorer 4.0 configured in the <browserCaps> element of *machine.config*.

ie5

> The page will be rendered based on the values for Internet Explorer 5.0 configured in the <browserCaps> element of *machine.config*.

Parameters

String

> A string that specifies the alias for the browser capabilities that the page will target.

Example

The following code example initializes the ClientTarget property of the Page class to downlevel, indicating that ASP.NET must render the page for an unknown browser type, which will result in HTML 3.2-compliant output. The example then displays a message indicating whether a set of features is supported. In the case of downlevel, none of the listed features is supported.

```
Sub Page_Load( )
    Page.ClientTarget = "downlevel"
       Message.Text = "Page is set to render for the " & _
    Page.ClientTarget & " alias.<br/>"
    Message.Text &= "Supported features:<br/>"
    Message.Text &= " - JavaScript: " & _
       Request.Browser.JavaScript & "<br/>"
    Message.Text &= " - ActiveX Controls: " & _
       Request.Browser.ActiveXControls & "<br/>"
    Message.Text &= " - Frames: " & _
       Request.Browser.Frames & "<br/>"
End Sub
```

Notes

The ClientTarget can also be specified by using the `ClientTarget` attribute of the `@ Page` directive.

Changing the value of the ClientTarget property in the example to `ie4` will result in output indicating that all of the listed features are supported.

While most server controls render HTML 3.2 for all browsers, the validation controls are an example of controls that render differently, depending on the value of ClientTarget. If the ClientTarget property is set to `downlevel`, then validation is performed on the server side, meaning that if we view the source, no client-side script will perform the validation.

If the ClientTarget is set to `uplevel`, then the validation controls emit client-side JavaScript to perform client-side validation.

Context

```
HttpContext = Page.Context
```

Returns an HttpContext instance containing context information for the current HTTP request.

Parameters

HttpContext
  A variable of type HttpContext that will receive the reference to the current HttpContext instance.

Example

The following code example uses the Context property to return the name of the currently logged in user. This information is also available from the User property of the `Page` class, which is derived from the HttpContext associated with the current request.

```
Sub Page_Load()
    Message.Text = "Currently logged in as: " & _
        Context.User.Identity.Name
End Sub
```

Notes

A common use of this property is to pass a reference to the HttpContext for the current request to a business object that needs access to the ASP.NET intrinsic objects (Request, Response, etc.). In addition to providing access to the Application, Request, Response, Server, and Session intrinsics, the HttpContext class provides access to the Trace and User information for the current HTTP request.

EnableViewState

```
Boolean = Page.EnableViewState
Page.EnableViewState = Boolean
```

Returns or sets a Boolean value that indicates whether the Page maintains its view state and that of server controls it contains. The default value of this property is True, which means that the page maintains its view state.

Parameters

Boolean

A Boolean value that indicates whether the page maintains its view state.

Example

The following code example sets EnableViewState to False using the EnableViewState attribute of the @ Page directive and displays its value on the page:

```
<%@ Page Language="vb" EnableViewState="True" %>
<html>
    <head>
        <title></title>
        <script runat="server">
            Sub Page_Load()
                If Page.EnableViewState = True Then
                    Message.Text = "ViewState is enabled."
                Else
                    Message.Text = "ViewState is disabled."
                End If
            End Sub
        </script>
    </head>
<body>
    <form runat="server">
        <asp:label id="Message" runat="server"/>
    </form>
</body>
</html>
```

Notes

The EnableViewState property can also be specified using the EnableViewState attribute of the @ Page directive, as shown in the example.

Examining a page's HTML source using a browser's View Source feature shows the effect of the EnableViewState property. If the EnableViewState property is set to False, the source will look similar to:

```
<input type="hidden" name="__VIEWSTATE"
        value="dDwxMDA3MzE2MzEyOzs+" />
```

If the EnableViewState property is set to True, the source will look similar to:

```
<input type="hidden" name="__VIEWSTATE"
value="dDwxMDA3MzE2MzEyO3Q8O2w8aTwxPjs+O2w8dDw7bDxpPDM+Oz47bDxOPHA8cDxsPF
RleHQ7PjtsPFZhbHVlIG9mIHRoZSBFbmFibGVWaWaWV3U3RhdGUgcHJvcGVydHkgaXMgVHJ1ZTs
+Pjs+Ozs+Oz4+Oz4=" />
```

The extra characters in the value of the __VIEWSTATE hidden field indicate the view state of the current page. The view state of a page includes the transient properties of server controls, such as BackColor or ForeColor.

Note that pages that do not contain a `<form>` element with the `runat="server"` attribute will not save view state, regardless of the value of the EnableViewState property.

ErrorPage

```
String = Page.ErrorPage
Page.ErrorPage = String
```

Returns or sets the name of the page to redirect to in the event of an unhandled page exception.

Parameters

String
> A String value that indicates the name of the page to redirect to in the event of an unhandled page exception.

Example

The example below changes the ErrorPage property and shows that executed page when an unhandled exception occurs in the page:

```
Sub Page_Load()
    Page.ErrorPage = "ErrorPage_Handler.aspx"
    Dim x, y, overflow As Integer
    x = 1
    y = 0
    overflow = x/y
    'This code will not be executed
    Message.Text = "Error Page is " & Page.ErrorPage & "."
End Sub
```

The Page_Load for *ErrorPage_Handler.aspx* is shown below:

```
Sub Page_Load()
    Message.Text = "We're sorry. An error occurred during the" & _
        " processing of your request. Please try again later."
End Sub
```

Notes

The ErrorPage property can also be specified using the ErrorPage attribute of the @ Page directive.

IsPostBack

```
Boolean = Page.IsPostBack
```

Returns a Boolean value that indicates if the page is loaded for the first time (False) or is loaded as a result of the client postback (True). This property comes handy for the logic that needs to be executed the first time the page is executed or every time the page is posted back to itself, depending on how you structure your If statement.

Parameters

Boolean

> A Boolean value that indicates if the page is loaded for the first time or is loaded as a result of the client postback.

Example

The code example below uses the IsPostBack property to display different messages in the Label control, depending on whether the page is loaded for the first time or is loaded as a result of the client postback. The first time the page is loaded, the IsPostBack property returns False, causing the string "Non-PostBack" to be displayed. Clicking the button posts the page back to itself, causing IsPostBack to return True and the string "PostBack" to be displayed.

```
<%@ Page Language="vb" %>
<html>
    <head>
        <title></title>
        <script runat="server">
            Sub Page_Load()
                If Page.IsPostBack Then
                    Message.Text = "PostBack"
                Else
                    Message.Text = "Non-PostBack"
                End If
            End Sub
        </script>
    </head>
<body>
    <form runat="server">
        <asp:button id="post" Text="Post page" runat="server"/>
        <asp:label id="Message" runat="server"/>
    </form>
</body>
</html>
```

Notes

The IsPostBack property will return True only for pages that contain a <form> element with the runat="server" attribute and at least one control that causes a postback. This can be a Button control, as shown in the example, or another control, such as a DropDownList control, whose AutoPostBack property is set to True.

IsValid

```
Boolean = Page.IsValid
```

Returns a Boolean value, indicating whether any validation controls on the page were unable to successfully validate user input.

Parameters

Boolean

A Boolean indicating whether the validation succeeded.

Example

The example uses the IsValid property to determine whether validation on the current page succeeded, and displays a message:

```
<%@ Page Language="vb" %>
<html>
    <head>
        <title></title>
        <script runat="server">
            Sub Page_Load()
                If IsPostBack Then
                    Page.Validate()
                    If Page.IsValid Then
                        Message.Text = "Page is valid."
                    Else
                        Message.Text = "Page is not valid."
                    End If
                End If
            End Sub
        </script>
    </head>
<body>
    <form runat="server">
        Enter your name:
        <asp:textbox id="name" runat="server"/>
        <asp:requiredfieldvalidator
            id="rfvName"
            controltovalidate="name"
            enableclientscript="false"
            errormessage="Required!"
            runat="server"/>
        <br/>
        <asp:button id="submit" Text="Submit" runat="server"/>
        <br/>
        <asp:label id="Message" runat="server"/>
    </form>
</body>
</html>
```

Notes

The IsValid property determines whether the overall validation performed by a form's validator controls has succeeded. If the page has no validator controls, the property's value is always True. Before checking the value of IsValid, you must either call the Page.Validate method, as shown in the example, or have submitted the page with a control (such as a Button, ImageButton, or LinkButton control) whose CausesValidation property is set to True. Otherwise, an exception will occur.

In the example, the EnableClientScript property of the RequiredFieldValidator control is set to False, which disables client-side validation. By default, client-side validation is enabled and the page is never submitted to the server if the validation fails. Uplevel browsers perform validation on the client using client-side scripts, and only when validation succeeds is the page submitted. Only when the page is submitted is the server-side event handler code executed and the message displayed based on the value of the IsValid property.

Checking the IsValid property is important whether client-side validation is enabled, since a malicious client could bypass client-side validation

---

Request

```
HttpRequest = Page.Request
```

Returns an instance of the HttpRequest class that allows us to access data from the incoming HTTP requests. It's the equivalent of the ASP intrinsic Request object. For more information on the HttpRequest class, see Chapter 16.

Parameters

HttpRequest
> An object of type HttpRequest that contains the data from the incoming HTTP requests.

Example

The following code example uses the ServerVariables collection of the HttpRequest object to display the IP address of the client making the request:

```
Sub Page_Load()
    Message.Text = "The current request is from: " & _
        CStr(Request.ServerVariables.Item("REMOTE_ADDRESS"))
End Sub
```

Notes

As with the Application and Cache properties, while you can retrieve a local reference to the HttpRequest instance associated with the request, it is more common to access this instance directly through the Request property, as shown in this example.

Response

```
HttpResponse = Page.Response
```

Returns an instance of the HttpResponse class that stores information about the response and allows us to send HTTP response data to a browser. It's the equivalent of the ASP intrinsic Response object. For information on the HttpResponse class, see Chapter 17.

Parameters

HttpResponse
> An object of type HttpResponse that receives the instance of the HttpResponse class.

Example

The following example uses the Response property of the page object to set the ContentType property of the HttpResponse class to text/xml. Setting this property will result in the output of the page being displayed as XML markup in Internet Explorer 5.0 or above.

```
Sub Page_Load()
    Response.ContentType = "text/xml"
    Message.Text = "This page will be displayed as XML in " & _
        "Internet Explorer 5.0 or above."
End Sub
```

Notes

As with the Application and Cache properties, while you can retrieve a local reference to the HttpResponse instance associated with the request, it is more common to access this instance directly through the Request property, as shown in this example.

Server

```
HttpServerUtility = Page.Server
```

Returns an instance of the HttpServerUtility class, which exposes useful methods for working with ASP.NET requests. For more information on the HttpServerUtility class, see Chapter 18.

Parameters

HttpServerUtility
> An object of type HttpServerUtility that may be used to access useful properties and methods exposed by this class.

Example

The following code example uses the Server property to access the HtmlEncode method of the HttpServerUtility class, which allows you to encode HTML tags and characters so that they will be displayed to the user, rather than interpreted and rendered by the browser:

```
Sub Page_Load()
    Message.Text = Server.HtmlEncode("<em>Hello, World!</em>")
End Sub
```

The HTML rendered from this page would look like the following:

```
<html>
    <head>
        <title>Server property example</title>
    </head>
<body>
    <span id="Message">&lt;em&gt;Hello, World!&lt;/em&gt;</span>
</body>
</html>
```

Notes

As with the Request and Response properties, while you can retrieve a local reference to the HttpServerUtility instance associated with the application, it is more common to access this instance directly through the Server property, as shown in this example.

Session

```
HttpSessionState = Page.Session
```

Returns an object that represents the current user session. A Session object is maintained for each user that requests a page from an ASP.NET application. You can store session-specific data in the Session object and then access it across multiple pages in an ASP.NET application. For more information on the HttpSessionState class, see Chapter 19.

Parameters

HttpSessionState
    An HttpSessionState object that represents the current user session.

Example

The example uses the Session object to display the value of the Mode property, which indicates where session state information is stored:

```
Sub Page_Load()
    Message.Text = "Current Session State Mode: " &_
            Session.Mode.ToString()
End Sub
```

Notes

As with the Request and Response properties, while you can retrieve a local reference to the HttpSessionState instance associated with the request, it is more common to access this instance directly through the Session property, as shown in this example.

SmartNavigation

```
Boolean = Page.SmartNavigation
Page.SmartNavigation = Boolean
```

Returns or sets a Boolean indicating whether the SmartNavigation feature is turned on. The SmartNavigation feature, which is compatible only with Internet Explorer, uses <iframe> elements to allow only portions of the page to be refreshed when the page is posted back. This can help eliminate the annoying visual flicker associated with postbacks.

Parameters

Boolean
    A Boolean value that indicates whether or not SmartNavigation is enabled.

Example

The following code example sets the SmartNavigation property to True using the SmartNavigation attribute of the @ Page directive. When the page is posted back, only the current page will be stored in the browser's history, so the Back button will be disabled.

```
<%@ Page Language="vb" SmartNavigation="True" %>
<html>
    <head>
        <title>SmartNavigation property example</title>
        <script runat="server">
            Sub Page_Load()
                Message.Text = "This Label will change."
                Message2.Text = "This Label will not change."
            End Sub
            Sub UpdateLabel(Sender As Object, e As EventArgs)
                Message.Text = "This Label has changed."
            End Sub
        </script>
    </head>
<body>
    <form runat="server">
        <asp:label id="Message" runat="server"/>
        <asp:button id="update"
          onClick="UpdateLabel"
          text="Click to update label text"
          runat="server"/>
    </form>
    <asp:label id="Message2" runat="server"/>
</body>
</html>
```

Page Class

Notes

In addition to eliminating flicker when navigating or posting back, SmartNavigation maintains the current scroll position when a page is posted back and maintains only a single page in the browser's history, which prevents users from clicking the browser's Back button to go to a previous state of the page.

While you can set this property from code, it is recommended that this property be set using the SmartNavigation attribute of the @ Page directive, as shown in this example.

Trace

```
TraceContext = Page.Trace
```

Returns the TraceContext object for the current web request. Tracing provides the details about the execution of the web request. The TraceContext class includes the following members:

Member	Description
IsEnabled	Indicates whether tracing is enabled for the current page.
TraceMode	A member of the TraceMode enumeration that indicates how items should be sorted. Possible values are `SortByCategory` and `SortByTime`. The latter is the default value defined in *machine.config*.
Warn method	Writes a message to the trace log using red text.
Write method	Writes a message to the trace log.

Parameters

`TraceContext`
  An instance of the `TraceContext` class.

Example

The example turns tracing on programmatically by using the Trace property of the Page class:

```
Sub Page_Load( )
    If Trace.IsEnabled = True Then
        Message.Text = "Tracing is enabled."
    Else
        Message.Text = "Tracing is not enabled."
    End If
End Sub
```

Notes

As with the Request and Response properties, while you can retrieve a local reference to the TraceContext instance associated with the request, it is more common to access this instance directly through the Trace property, as shown in the following example. For more information on application tracing, see Chapter 10.

User

`IPrincipal = Page.User`

Returns an instance of an object implementing the `IPrincipal` interface containing security information about the user making the page request. The `IPrincipal` interface implements the following members:

Member	Description
Identity property	Returns the IIdentity object representing the user requesting the page
IsInRole property	Indicates whether the user requesting the page is in a particular role

Parameters

`IPrincipal`
  An object variable that implements `IPrincipal`.

Example

The example obtains the user's authentication status and name using the User property and displays it in the browser:

```
Sub Page_Load()
    Message.Text = "Authenticated: " & _
        User.Identity.IsAuthenticated & "<br/>"
    Message.Text &= "User Name: " & User.Identity.Name
End Sub
```

Notes

In order for the IPrincipal object returned by the User property to be populated, some form of authentication must be configured in either *machine.config* or *web.config*, and at a minimum, an authorization rule must be configured that excludes anonymous users. If these conditions are not met, the IsAuthenticated property of the IIdentity object will return False and the Name property will return an empty string.

ViewState

```
StateBag = Page.ViewState
```

The ViewState property returns an instance of the StateBag class containing state information for server controls on the page. This StateBag instance can also be used to store arbitrary data that needs to be preserved across multiple requests for the same page.

Parameters

StateBag
> An object of type StateBag that contains the property values for server controls on the page. This StateBag instance can also be used to store arbitrary data that needs to be preserved across multiple requests for the same page.

Example

The following code example sets the ForeColor property of the Message control, and then stores the value of that color in the ViewState StateBag instance. If the page is posted back, the code retrieves the color that was stored, and depending on the name of the color, changes the color from Red to Black, or vice-versa.

```
<%@ Page Language="vb" %>
<html>
    <head>
        <title>ViewState property example</title>
        <script runat="server">
            Sub Page_Load()
                Dim LocalColor As System.Drawing.Color
                If IsPostBack Then
                    LocalColor = CType(ViewState("LabelColor"), _
                        System.Drawing.Color)
                    If LocalColor.Name = "Black" Then
                        LocalColor = System.Drawing.Color.Red
                    Else
```

```
                LocalColor = System.Drawing.Color.Black
            End If
            Message.ForeColor = LocalColor
            Message.Text = "Label color is " & LocalColor.Name
            ViewState("LabelColor") = LocalColor
        Else
            Message.ForeColor = System.Drawing.Color.Black
            LocalColor = Message.ForeColor
            Message.Text = "Label color is " & LocalColor.Name
            ViewState("LabelColor") = LocalColor
        End If
      End Sub
    </script>
  </head>
<body>
  <form runat="server">
    <asp:button id="button"
        text="Click to change label color"
        runat="server"/>
    <asp:label id="Message" runat="server"/>
  </form>
</body>
</html>
```

Notes

ViewState, in addition to managing state for server controls automatically, is a convenient place for ambient page state that needs to be maintained from request to request. In addition to storing primitive data types such as integers and strings, the StateBag class can be used to store objects, as long as those objects support serialization, as does the Color structure in the example. When you store an object that supports serialization in ViewState, the object's state is automatically serialized into a form that can be stored in ViewState and deserialized into an object instance when you reference the object again.

Because ViewState does not store type information with the object, you must cast the object retrieved from ViewState to the correct type. In the case of the example, this type is System.Drawing.Color.

Finally, think carefully before storing large objects (such as datasets) in ViewState. Because ViewState is stored as a hidden form field, it is sent to the browser with each request. Storing large objects in ViewState will result in slower page load times.

Collections Reference

Controls

```
ControlCollection = Page.Controls
```

Provides access to the ControlCollection instance associated with the page, with which you can add or manipulate controls at runtime.

Parameters

ControlCollection
> An object of type ControlCollection containing the controls associated with the page.

Example

The code example uses the Controls property to display the Count property of the `ControlCollection` class instance associated with the page. It then adds a new Label control to the collection and displays the updated Count property by using the new label.

```
Sub Page_Load( )
    Message.Text = "There are currently " & Controls.Count & _
        " controls on the page.<br/>"
    Dim Message2 As New Label
    Controls.AddAt(Controls.Count - 1, Message2)
    Message2.Text = "There are now " & Controls.Count & _
        " controls on the page."
End Sub
```

Notes

As with the Session and Trace properties, while you can retrieve a local reference to the Controls collection associated with the page, it is more common to access this instance directly through the Controls property, as shown in the example.

Note that when adding a control to a page that already contains controls, using the AddAt method of the `ControlCollection` class allows more precise placement of the control when compared to the Add method, which simply places the control at the end of the collection. In the example, using the Add method would result in the output from the added Label control appearing after the page's closing </html> tag, which is not well-formed HTML and could cause the page to render incorrectly in some browsers.

Validators

`ValidatorCollection = Page.Validators`

Returns an instance of the `ValidatorCollection` class containing all the validator controls contained on the requested page. We can access each validator control by iterating the ValidatorCollection collection.

Parameters

ValidatorCollection
> An object variable of type ValidatorCollection.

Example

The code example displays a Textbox control with a RequiredFieldValidator and RegularExpressionValidator control assigned to it. In Page_Load, the code iterates through the ValidatorCollection returned by the Validators property and displays the ID and ErrorMessage property of each validator in the collection:

```
<%@ Page Language="vb" %>
<html>
    <head>
        <title></title>
        <script runat="server">
            Sub Page_Load()
                Dim Validator as BaseValidator
                For Each Validator in Validators
                    Message.Text &= Validator.ID & " error message: "
                    Message.Text &= Validator.ErrorMessage & "<br/>"
                Next
            End Sub
        </script>
    </head>
<body>
    <form runat="server">
        Phone: <asp:textbox id="phone" runat="server"/>
        <asp:requiredfieldvalidator
            id="rfvPhone"
            controltovalidate="phone"
            display="dynamic"
            errormessage="Required!"
            runat="server"/>
        <asp:regularexpressionvalidator
            id="revPhone"
            controltovalidate="phone"
            display="dynamic"
            validationexpression="^[2-9]\d{2}-\d{3}-\d{4}$"
            errormessage="Enter a phone number in the form xxx-xxx-xxxx"
                runat="server"/>
        <br/>
        <asp:button id="submit" text="Submit" runat="server"/>
    </form>
    <br/>
    <asp:label id="Message" runat="server"/>
</body>
</html>
```

Notes

Because we are displaying only properties from the validator controls that are
inherited from the BaseValidator control (from which all validation controls are
derived), we don't need to cast the validator to its specific type before accessing
the properties. If, however, we wanted to display a property that was specific to
the type of validator used (such as the ValidationExpression property of the
RegularExpressionValidator class), we would need to cast the control to the
correct type. In Visual Basic .NET, this is done using the *CType* keyword.

Methods Reference

DataBind

```
Page.DataBind( )
```

Evaluates and resolves any data binding expressions in the page. It also calls DataBind on all child controls.

Parameters

None

Example

The following code example uses a data binding expression to set the ForeColor attribute of a label control tag to the value of local variable named color. When the DataBind method is called in Page_Load, the value of the Color variable is assigned to the ForeColor attribute (which is effectively the same as setting the ForeColor property in code):

```
<%@ Page Language="vb" %>
<html>
    <head>
        <title></title>
        <script runat="server">
            Dim Color As System.Drawing.Color = System.Drawing.Color.Red
            Sub Page_Load( )
                Message.Text = "ForeColor is: " & Color.Name
                DataBind( )
            End Sub
        </script>
    </head>
<body>
    <asp:label id="Message" ForeColor="<%# Color %>" runat="server"/>
</body>
</html>
```

Notes

If you want to perform data binding on a specific control on the page, such as a DataGrid or DataList control, it may be more efficient to call DataBind on that control rather than on the page, since calling it on the control will avoid any overhead in calling DataBind on controls for which data binding is not needed.

FindControl

```
Control = Page.FindControl(String)
```

Returns a reference to the control object whose name corresponds to a search string. The FindControl method is a member of the base Control class.

Parameters

Control

>An instance of the Control class that represents the control that is found using the FindControl method. This control must be cast to the correct control type to access members that are specific to the control type.

String

>A string containing the programmatic identifier of the control. This value is the same as the ID attribute of a declarative control, or in the case of controls created at runtime, is the same as the object name defined for the control.

Example

The example finds a control using its ID and changes its background color:

```
Sub Page_Load()
    Dim TheControl As Control = FindControl("Message")
    If Not TheControl Is Nothing Then
        Dim TheLabel As Label = CType(TheControl, Label)
        TheLabel.Text = "Found the label named Message!"
        TheLabel.BackColor = System.Drawing.Color.Blue
    End If
End Sub
```

Notes

The FindControl method, which is inherited from the Control class (from which the Page class is derived), is useful when dealing with nested controls or user controls that need to manipulate a control in their parent page. For example, code in a user control could call FindControl on the page containing the user control to locate and manipulate a control contained within the page (but outside the user control).

HasControls

```
Boolean = Page.HasControls()
```

Returns a Boolean value that indicates whether the page contains child controls.

Parameters

Boolean

>A Boolean value that indicates whether the page contains child controls.

Example

The code example displays a message indicating whether the page has controls in its Controls collection, based on the value returned by HasControls:

```
Sub Page_Load()
    If Page.HasControls = True Then
        Message.Text = "The page contains controls."
    Else
        Message.Text = "The page does not contain controls."
    End If
End Sub
```

LoadControl

```
objControl = Page.LoadControl(strPath)
```

Returns an instance of the user control defined in the *strPath* user control file. This allows dynamic loading of user controls instead of using the @ Register directive.

Parameters

objControl
> An object of type Control that represents the user control specified in the given path.

strPath
> The virtual path to a user control file.

Example

The example uses the LoadControl to load a user control at runtime and adds it to the page's Controls collection:

```
Sub Page_Load()
    Dim Hello As UserControl = LoadControl("hello.ascx")
    Page.Controls.Add(Hello)
End Sub
```

The user control *hello.ascx* is as follows:

```
<h1>Hello, World!</h1>
```

MapPath

```
String = Page.MapPath(virtualPath)
```

Returns the physical path that corresponds to a given virtual path.

Parameters

String
> A String containing the physical path that corresponds to *virtualPath*.

virtualPath
> A string containing an absolute or relative virtual path.

Example

The example maps the virtual path of the named page to its physical path:

```
Sub Page_Load()
    Message.Text = MapPath("MapPath.aspx")
End Sub
```

Notes

The Page.MapPath method duplicates the functionality of the Server.MapPath method.

ResolveUrl

```
String = Page.ResolveUrl(strRelativeUrl)
```

Returns an absolute URL corresponding to a relative URL.

Parameters

String
> A string containing the absolute URL.

strRelativeUrl
> A relative URL.

Example

The example maps the current relative URL to an absolute URL:

```
Sub Page_Load()
    Message.Text = Page.ResolveUrl("ResolveUrl.aspx")
End Sub
```

Validate

```
Page.Validate()
```

Invokes the validation logic for each validator control on the page. When this method is invoked, it iterates the Page object's ValidatorCollection collection and executes the validation logic associated with each validator control.

Example

See the example for the IsValid property.

Notes

The Validate method is called automatically when the user clicks any HTML or ASP button control whose CausesValidation property is True.

Events Reference

Error

```
Sub Page_Error(Sender As Object, e As EventArgs)
    'error handling code
End Sub
```

The Error event is fired when an unhandled exception occurs on the page. If no event handler is defined for this event, the Application_Error event is fired. If the exception is still not handled, control is passed to the page (or pages) defined in the <customErrors> element in *web.config*.

Parameters

Sender

An argument containing information about the object that raised the event.

e

An object of type EventArgs containing additional information about the event.

Example

The following code example deliberately causes an overflow exception and then handles that exception in the Page_Error handler, displaying the text of the exception and then clearing it:

```
Sub Page_Load( )
    Dim x, y, overflow As Integer
    x = 1
    y = 0
    overflow = x / y
End Sub

Sub Page_Error( )
    Response.Write(Server.GetLastError.ToString( ))
    Server.ClearError
End Sub
```

Notes

The current exception is obtained using the GetLastError method of the Server class. Once you've finished with your error handling, you can either clear the exception by calling Server.ClearError, as shown in the example, or allow the exception to bubble up to the next level of error handling.

Note that the *Sender* and *e* arguments are optional for this event, as shown in the example.

When the AutoEventWireup attribute of the @ Page directive is set to True (the default), ASP.NET will automatically call the event handler for this event, as long as it has the correct Page_Error signature.

Init

```
Sub Page_Init(Sender As Object, e As EventArgs)
    'initialization code
End Sub
```

Parameters

Sender

An argument containing information about the object that raised the event.

e

An object of type EventArgs containing additional information about the event.

Example

The code example initializes a variable for setting the ForeColor property of a label in Page_Init, and then modifies that value to set the ForeColor property of another label in Page_Load:

```
<%@ Page Language="vb" %>
<html>
    <head>
        <title>Init event example</title>
        <script runat="server">
            Dim TheColor As System.Drawing.Color
            Sub Page_Init()
                TheColor = System.Drawing.Color.Red
            End Sub
            Sub Page_Load()
                Message.ForeColor = TheColor
                Message.Text = "The color of the text was set in Page_Init."
                TheColor = System.Drawing.Color.Blue
                Message2.ForeColor = TheColor
                Message2.Text = "The color of the text was set in Page_Load."
            End Sub
        </script>
    </head>
<body>
    <asp:label id="Message" runat="server"/>
    <br/>
    <asp:label id="Message2" runat="server"/>
</body>
</html>
```

Notes

Note that the *Sender* and *e* arguments are optional for this event, as shown in the example.

When the AutoEventWireup attribute of the @ Page directive is set to True (the default), ASP.NET will automatically call the event handler for this event, as long as it has the signature Page_Init.

Load

```
Sub Page_Load(Sender As Object, e As EventArgs)
    'code
End Sub
```

Fired when the page is loaded. Since this event is fired on every page request, we can add any initialization code that needs to be executed at the page level, including the initialization of the page's child controls. When the Load event fires, the page's view state information is also accessible.

The Load event is passed the following arguments by ASP.NET:

Sender
    An argument containing information about the object that raised the event.

---

e

    An object of type EventArgs containing additional information about the event.

Example

See the example for Init.

Notes

Note that the *Sender* and *e* arguments are optional for this event, as shown in the example.

When the `AutoEventWireup` attribute of the `@ Page` directive is set to `True` (the default), ASP.NET will automatically call the event handler for this event, as long as it has the correct Page_Load event signature.

Unload

```
Sub Page_Unload(Sender As Object, e As EventArgs)
   'cleanup code
End Sub
```

Fired when the page is unloaded from memory. Since this event is fired before the page is unloaded, we can perform cleanup operations, such as closing open files and database connections.

The Unload event is passed the following arguments by ASP.NET:

Sender

    An argument containing information about the object that raised the event.

e

    An object of type EventArgs containing additional information about the event.

Example

The example demonstrates the Unload event by closing a file that was opened for display in the Page_Load event handler:

```
Dim TheFile As System.IO.StreamReader
Sub Page_Load()
   TheFile = System.IO.File.OpenText(MapPath("Init.aspx"))
   Message.Text = "<pre>" & _
      Server.HtmlEncode(TheFile.ReadToEnd()) & "</pre>"
End Sub

Sub Page_Unload()
   TheFile.Close()
End Sub
```

Notes

While the Unload event is useful for performing page-level cleanup tasks, for resources such as databases, for which it is possible that an exception will interrupt the normal flow of page processing, it may be better to place the cleanup

---

code for that resource in the Finally block of a Try...Catch...Finally statement, which will ensure that the cleanup code is always executed. For more information on Try...Catch...Finally, see Chapter 10.

Note that the *Sender* and *e* arguments are optional for this event, as shown in the example.

When the AutoEventWireup attribute of the @ Page directive is set to True (the default), ASP.NET will automatically call the event handler for this event, as long as it has the signature Page_Unload.

CHAPTER 13

The HttpApplicationState Class

Developers who are new to Web-based development encounter several challenges. Among the most serious is the realization that rather than a single monolithic application, web-based applications are just a series of pages. A web server is like an unusually inattentive waiter. Imagine sitting down for dinner and placing your order for drinks. When you next see the waiter, he asks you again what you would like to drink, as if he has never seen you before. Each request to the web browser is seen as a completely new request, totally unrelated to any previous request.

Several problems with the way Web-based applications are structured need to be resolved:

- Session data (data specific to a single user across all pages) needs to be available. While it is always a good idea to minimize session state, it is generally not possible to completely eliminate session state.

- Global data (data required across all pages and to all users) needs to be exposed. Traditional rich-client applications use global variables to store needed data application-wide. Classes instantiated on one page are not available to other pages, so creating global classes is not a solution.

Session data in ASP.NET can be managed in the `HttpSessionState` class, which will be covered in Chapter 19. Global data can be stored in the `HttpApplicationState` class, which is covered in this chapter.

ASP.NET creates the illusion that pages are grouped into an application. An instance of the `HttpApplicationState` class is created the first time any client requests a URL resource from within the virtual directory of a particular application. The `HttpContext` class (covered in Chapter 14) exposes a property named Application that provides access to the `HttpApplicationState` class for the application. The Application property and the HttpApplicationState object it returns are also available from the `Page` class. Since each ASP.NET page inherits from the `Page` class, the Application property is available to code on every page.

While this chapter covers the `HttpApplicationState` class, ASP.NET offers an alternative way to store information with an application global scope. The `Cache` class allows a developer to store data with an application scope. In addition to caching page output (a topic covered in Chapter 3), ASP.NET allows the developer to store other information within the Cache—in some ways similar to the way information can be stored in the `HttpApplicationState` class. There are, however, significant differences:

- Information stored in the HttpApplicationState object is stored for the life of the application. Information stored in the Cache may be stored for the life of the application (and in any event, may survive at most for the lifetime of the application), but might be purged sooner. The ASP.NET runtime can purge any cached item at any time if system memory becomes scarce. Cached items that are seldom used or unimportant (as the ASP.NET runtime defines these terms) are discarded using a technique called scavenging.

- Information stored in the Cache can be invalidated based upon a specific date and time or a time span. HttpApplicationState has no such ability.

- The developer can supply dependency rules to force the cache to be refreshed. For instance, you can use a Rube Goldberg-like setup, for which you cache a dataset and use a trigger in SQL Server to modify a file in the filesystem on the web server whenever the underlying table is modified. The cache for a given item can be invalidated based upon that file changing. Thus, you can cache a dataset and have the cached dataset refreshed whenever the underlying SQL Server table is changed. This is not possible with information stored in the HttpApplicationState object.

One significant limitation of both the Cache and the HttpApplicationState objects is that they are not shared across servers in a web farm. While classic ASP programmers will not be surprised by this, ASP.NET programmers who are familiar with the HttpSessionState object might be surprised, since in ASP.NET, session state *can* be shared across a server farm—either in a state server or a special SQL Server database. While having cached items available across all servers on a Web farm would be convenient, the nature of what is stored in the HttpApplicationState object makes the lack of a shared data store less critical.

The implications of the difference between HttpApplicationState and the Cache are clear:

- Large chunks of information that might be important should be stored in the cache. There is little harm in caching something because if it is not used and the memory is needed, the item will be scavenged and the memory used by it freed for the more pressing need.

- Information that can change frequently throughout the life of the application should be stored in the Cache rather than the HttpApplicationState object.

- Information that is stable during the life of the application is best stored in the HttpApplicationState object.

- Information that must always be available and must not be purged be stored in the HttpApplicationState object rather than the Cache.

- The Cache class is safe for multithreaded operations and does not require separate synchronization, unlike the Application collection (see the method references for the Lock and UnLock methods later in this chapter).

Classic ASP developers often used the Application object to store things like database connection strings. In ASP.NET, there is another alternative for storing small, possibly sensitive bits of information like connection strings. Inside the configuration files for the machine or applications, you can place values called appSettings within the <configuration> tag. For instance:

```
<appSettings>
    <add key="TestKey" value="TestValue" />
</appSettings>
```

Multiple add tags can be placed in the configuration file. To retrieve the value within code, you the System.Configuration.ConfigurationSettings class. Specifically, to retrieve the value saved in the TestKey key above, use the following code:

```
localVar = ConfigurationSettings.AppSettings("TestKey")
```

While you can place the appSettings section in *web.config* or *machine.config*, sensitive values are better stored in the *machine.config* file. *machine.config* is not located in a folder that is in any way mapped within the web-accessible space. Of course, this solution for storing application-level information is really only suitable for static information that does not need to change under program control as the application is running. Often, you can use AppSettings and Application state together, caching the value from AppSettings within the Application object. If a setting with the same key is contained in both the *machine.config* and *web.config* file, the value in *web.config* will be the value returned for the setting.

Much of HttpApplicationState will be familiar to classic ASP developers. The visible additions and changes from classic ASP are not dramatic. Most importantly, virtually all existing classic ASP code dealing with the Application object will work in ASP.NET.

When the first client requests a URL from the application, the Application object's start event is fired. This event can be handled by creating an event handler in the *global.asax* file (the ASP.NET equivalent of *global.asa*) with the following signature:

```
Sub Application_OnStart()
    'Application initialization code
End Sub
```

The Application start event is called only once within the lifetime of an application. This is where you would usually set Application variables. When the Application ends, a similar event is called with the following signature:

```
Sub Application_OnEnd()
    'Application cleanup code
End Sub
```

In the Application end event, you would dispose of any resources created in the Application start event. There are a few limitations to what you can do in the Application-level events, since the Response, Session, and Request objects are all unavailable.

The fact that the Application start event is called once within the lifetime of an application was mentioned above. However, what exactly is the lifetime of an application? Whenever the web server starts up, the first client to request a URL from an application marks the beginning of the application's lifetime. Similarly, as the web server stops, either because the underlying service is stopped or the server itself is restarted, the application's lifetime ends. Thus, can you presume that unless the Web service restarts or the server itself restarts, the application will continue running? The short answer is "No."

The longer answer is that to ensure that the Application start and Application end events called are coherent (i.e., that code has not been added to Application_End that would require changes to Application_Start after it had already fired, or vice-versa), any time the *global.asax* is changed, the ASP.NET framework detects that the file has changed. Upon sensing the file change, the framework completes any current requests and fires the Application end event (as it existed before the change to *global.asax*). Once the Application end event has fired, the application restarts, flushing all application information and client state information. When the next incoming client request is received, the ASP.NET framework reparses and recompiles the *global.asax* file and raises the Application start event as it appears in the newly saved version of *global.asax*. The moral of this story is that changes to the *global.asax* file should be infrequent, presuming the application must be available 24/7.

One question that sometimes arises is, "Can the Application state of one application be accessed from within another application?" The short answer is "No." The longer answer is that if the other application cooperates, you can create a page in one application that can be called by making an HTTP Request from the other application. There is no support within the ASP.NET Framework to do this explicitly.

Items can be stored in the Application collection in one of four ways:

- By calling the Add method, passing in the name (or key) to assign to the item, and the item's value. This value can be of any type supported by the CLR, including object instances, which are serialized automatically before being stored.

- By calling the Set method, passing in the name (or key) to assign to the item, and the item's value. This value can be any type supported by the CLR, including object instances, which are automatically serialized before being stored.

- By explicitly referring to the Item property, passing a name or index to assign to the new item.

- By implicitly referring to the Item property, passing a name to assign to the new item. This was the most common technique used in classic ASP.

Items can be accessed in one of four ways:

- By retrieving and iterating over the collection of keys in the Application collection (see the Keys collection description for an example).

- By calling the Get method, passing the name of the item to retrieve.

- By explicitly referring to the Item property, passing the name of the item to retrieve.

- By implicitly referring to the Item property, passing the name of the item to retrieve. This was the most common technique used in classic ASP.

Items can be removed from the Application collection in one of several ways:

- By calling the Clear method (clears all items).

- By calling the RemoveAll method (removes all items).

- By calling the Remove method, passing the name of the item to remove.

- By calling the RemoveAt method, passing the index of the item to remove.

Table 13-1 lists the properties, collections, and methods exposed by the HttpApplicationState class.

Table 13-1. HttpApplicationState class summary

Properties	Collections	Methods	Events*
Count	AllKeys	Add	Start
Item	Contents	Clear	End
	Keys	Get	
	StaticObjects	GetKey	
		Lock	
		Remove	
		RemoveAll	
		RemoveAt	
		Set	
		Unlock	
		Events	
		Start	
* Events are exposed by the HttpApplication class rather than the HttpApplicationState class.		End	

Comments/Troubleshooting

Understanding the scope of the Application collection for a given application is important. As mentioned above, the Application object is created the first time a client requests a URL within the application. The boundary of that ASP.NET application is defined by the boundary of an IIS application; the boundary of the ASP.NET application includes all of the ASP.NET pages within a single IIS Application and all of its subfolders and virtual directories. It does not, however, include any subfolders that are defined as IIS Applications. Figure 13-1 illustrates the different folder types in IIS. In Figure 13-1, the *SubApp* subfolder is a child folder of the *Chapter_13* application and shares Application state with it. If, however, the *SubApp* folder is configured as an IIS Application (by accessing the Virtual Directory tab of the Properties dialog for the folder and clicking the Create button in the Application Settings section), it will then define its own application boundaries, which will not be shared with the parent *Chapter_13* application.

Figure 13-1. IIS folder types

In classic ASP, a big no-no was storing non-thread-safe COM objects (which meant any COM object written in Visual Basic) in the Application collection. This was because such components would force IIS to process requests to the Application that stored the COM object only from the same thread that created the object, which substantially limited scalability. In ASP.NET, this is less of an issue, since all managed .NET components can be stored safely in the Application collection without impacting scalability due to threading model considerations.

When accessing any resource potentially shared by many clients, one concern is the synchronization of access to that resource. For instance, imagine that you declare a variable in the application collection to track the number of users currently logged into your application. To do so, in your Session start event handler (also defined in the *global.asax* file and covered completely in Chapter 19), you can place code such as this:

```
LocalVal = Application("Counter")
Application("Counter") = localVal + 1
```

This contrived example (don't use it in your application) shows a problem that can occur with global variables shared by multiple threads. Imagine that two sessions are created simultaneously. Each session gets its local copy of the Application variable, which will be the same since they were requested simultaneously. Then each thread sets the Application variable to its own local value plus one. In the end, though two clients incremented the value of our counter, the value will increase by only one.

Fortunately, a solution is provided within the HttpApplicationState class. The Lock and UnLock methods allow a developer to synchronize access to shared resources. Lock and UnLock must be called in matched pairs. The Lock method is entered only when no other client executes code between calls to Lock and UnLock. Win32 programmers may recognize the similarity between the use of Lock and Unlock in the HttpApplicationState class and Win32 critical sections.

The example above could be rewritten to be thread safe as follows:

```
Application.Lock()
LocalVal = Application("Counter")
```

```
Application("Counter") = LocalVal + 1
Application.UnLock()
```

While using Lock and UnLock solves the problem, their use should be absolutely essential. For instance, synchronization of Application-level variables is not required in the Application start or Application end event, since these events are called only once—just before the first client operation starts and just after the last client operation ends, respectively. Excessive use of Lock and UnLock can degrade both performance and scalability.

In addition to properties and methods provided for backwards compatibility with classic ASP, the ASP.NET version of the Application object adds several useful new properties and methods, including the AllKeys collection, the Count property, and the Clear, Get, GetKey, RemoveAll, RemoveAt, and Set methods.

In this chapter, we'll use the following code listing as the basis for most examples in the chapter. Unless otherwise noted, each example consists of just the Page_ Load event handler for that particular example. Any output messages or return values displayed are shown as the Text property of the ASP.NET Label control named Message or displayed by calling Response.Write.

```
<%@ Page Language="vb" %>
<html>
    <head>
        <script runat="server">
            Sub Page_Load()
                'Example code will go here
            End Sub
        </script>
    </head>
<body>
    <asp:label id="Message" runat="server"/>
</body>
</html>
```

Properties Reference

Count

```
Integer = Application.Count
```

Returns an Integer containing the number of items currently in the Application collection. The Count member is derived from the ICollection interface, which is implemented by the HttpApplicationState class.

Parameters

Integer
An Integer variable that will receive the Count property value.

Example

The example adds two values to the Application collection, displays the count of items in the Application collection, and then uses the Count property as a looping control value to display each item:

```
Sub Page_Load()
    Application.Clear()
    Application("foo") = "Hello, "
    Application("bar") = "World!"
    Message.Text = "The Application collection contains " & _
        Application.Count & " items: "
        Dim I as Integer
        For I = 0 To Application.Count - 1
            Message.Text &= Application(I)
        Next
End Sub
```

Notes

The Count property is new for ASP.NET. In addition to using the Count property for looping through the Application collection, you can use the property to keep track of how many items the Application stores at any given time. For example, you could write this information to a log for later review.

Item

```
Object = Application.Item(ByVal name As String)
Application.Item(ByVal name As String) = Object
Object = Application.Item(ByVal index As Integer)
Application.Item(ByVal index As Integer) = Object
```

Returns or sets an Object associated with a particular name or index.

Parameters

Object
> A variable of any type (since all .NET types are ultimately derived from Object) that will receive or set the item's value.

name
> A String argument containing the text key to apply to the item (or by which to retrieve the item).

index
> An Integer argument containing the index of the item whose value will be retrieved or modified.

Example

The example sets the values of two items in the Application collection. If these items do not already exist in the collection, they will be added. The example then displays the two values.

```
Sub Page_Load()
    Application.Clear()
```

```
    Application.Item("foo") = "foo"
    Application.Item("foo2") = "foo2"
    Message.Text = Application.Item("foo") & "<br/>"
    Message.Text &= Application.Item(1)
End Sub
```

Notes

The Item property is accessed implicitly when using the syntax:

```
Application("foo") = "foo"
```

This syntax is often seen in classic ASP code. Explicitly referencing the Item property is not required, but listing it may make your code more readable and understandable than accessing it implicitly.

Note that an index may only be used as an argument when modifying a value, not when creating a new item, and the index must be less than the number of items in the Application collection, or an exception will be thrown.

Collections Reference

AllKeys

```
Dim StateVars(Application.Count) As String
StateVars = Application.AllKeys
```

Returns a string array of key names stored in the HttpApplicationState object.

Parameters

StateVars
A variable of type String array that will receive the array of key names.

Example

The example displays all keys of data stored to the Application object:

```
Sub Page_Load()
    Dim I as Integer
    Dim StateVars(Application.Count - 1) As String
    StateVars = Application.AllKeys
    For I = 0 to StateVars.Length - 1
        Message.Text = Message.Text + StateVars(I) + "<br/>"
    Next I
End Sub
```

Notes

This property provides a list of key names assigned to all current Application variables.

Contents

```
HttpApplicationState = Application.Contents
```

Returns a reference to the current HttpApplicationState instance.

Parameters

```
HttpApplicationState
```
    A variable of type HttpApplicaitonState that will receive the Contents reference.

Example

The example below calls the RemoveAll method through the Contents collection reference and then writes a message:

```
Sub Page_Load()
Application.Contents.RemoveAll()
Message.Text = "Removed all items from current Application."
End Sub
```

Notes

This property is provided for backward compatibility with classic ASP. Properties such as the Item property and methods such as Remove and RemoveAll were accessed via the Contents property in classic ASP. In new ASP.NET development, you should access these members directly. For example, instead of calling the RemoveAll method through the Contents property, you can call RemoveAll method directly:

```
Application.RemoveAll()
```

Keys

```
KeysCollection = Application.Keys
```

Returns a NameObjectCollectionBase.KeysCollection containing the string keys associated with all values stored in the Application collection.

Parameters

```
KeysCollection
```
    A variable of type NameObjectCollectionBase.KeysCollection that will receive the Keys property value.

Example

The example loops through the collection of keys in the Application collection, and then displays the key name and the value associated with it by using the Text property of the Message control:

```
Sub Page_Load()
    Dim Key As String
    Message.Text = "Application Keys:"
    For Each Key in Application.Keys
```

```
        Message.Text &= "<br/>Key:   " & Key
        Message.Text &= "<br/>Value:   " & Application(Key)
    Next
  End Sub
```

Notes

The Keys property provides one of many ways to iterate over the contents of the Application collection.

StaticObjects

```
HttpStaticObjectsCollection = Application.StaticObjects
```

Returns an HttpStaticObjectsCollection containing all objects instantiated in *global.asax* using the `<object runat="server">` syntax whose scope attribute is set to `Application`.

Parameters

`HttpStaticObjectsCollection`
    A variable of type HttpStaticObjectsCollection that will receive the StaticObjects property value.

Example

The example uses the Count property of the `HttpStaticObjectsCollection` class to display the number of objects in the current application declared with the `<object scope="Application" runat="server"/>` syntax in *global.asax*. It then checks the type of each object, and if it is a Web TextBox control, adds it to the Controls collection of the current page.

```
Sub Page_Load()
    Message.Text = "There are " & Application.StaticObjects.Count & _
        " objects declared with the " & _
        "&lt;object runat=&quot;server&quot;&gt; syntax " & _
        "in Application scope."
    Dim myobj As Object
    For Each myObj in Application.StaticObjects
        If myObj.Value.GetType.ToString() = _
            "System.Web.UI.WebControls.TextBox" Then
            Page.Controls.Add(myObj.Value)
        End If
    Next
  End Sub
```

Notes

This property is provided for backward compatibility with classic ASP. You should think carefully before instantiating objects with Session or Application scope because of the impact such objects have on resource usage and application scalability. In most cases, it is advisable to limit objects to page scope.

Note that each object in the collection is represented by the DictionaryEntry structure, so its key and value are not directly accessible. To access the key and/or value, use the Key and/or Value members of the DictionaryEntry structure.

Methods Reference

Add

```
Application.Add(ByVal name As String, ByVal value As Object)
```

Adds a value to the Application collection.

Parameters

Name

A variable of type String that specifies the name of the item to be added to the Application collection.

Value

A variable of type Object that contains the value for the item to be added to the Application collection.

Example

The example adds an item to the Application collection and then displays it:

```
Sub Page_Load()
    Application.Add("Added", "AddedValue")
    Message.Text = Application("Added")
End Sub
```

Notes

The Add method, which is new in ASP.NET, provides a technique for adding items to the Application collection that is consistent with the technique used for adding items to other .NET collections. Of course, the classic ASP syntax of directly indexing the Application object by using the key name of index works correctly as well.

Clear

```
Application.Clear()
```

Clears the contents of the Application collection.

Parameters

None

Example

The example clears the contents of the Application collection and writes a message to the Text property of the Message control that includes the current count of the collection, which should be 0:

```
Sub Page_Load()
    Application.Clear()
    Message.Text = "There are " & Application.Count & _
        " items in the Application collection."
End Sub
```

The Clear method, which is new for ASP.NET, clears only the contents of the Application collection itself. It does not clear the contents of the StaticObjects collection.

Get

```
Application.Get(ByVal name As String)
Application.Get(ByVal Index As Integer)
```

Gets an element of the Application collection either by name or ordinal position (index) within the Application collection. Generally, the name is used in calls to Get unless you need to get members of the collection inside a loop.

Parameters

name
> A variable of type String that specifies the name of the item to be retrieved from the Application collection.

Index
> A variable of type Integer that specifies the index of the item to be retrieved from the Application collection.

Example

The example below sets and gets a value from the Application collection. It also uses the Get method to write a message to the Text property of the Message control that includes the current value of the newly added element of the Application collection.

```
Sub Page_Load()
    Application("GetTest") = "Got it!"
    Message.Text = "GetTest = " & Application.Get("GetTest")
End Sub
```

Notes

You can see whether a named value is saved in the Application collection by checking to ensure that its value is not null, as shown in the following code:

```
If Not Application("Foo") is Nothing then
    Message.Text = "Foo is set to " & Application.Get("Foo")
End If
```

GetKey

```
Application.GetKey(ByVal Index As Integer)
```

Retrieves the key name corresponding to the index of a data item stored to the Application object.

Parameters

Index

A variable of type Integer that specifies the index of the key to be retrieved from the Application collection.

Example

The example removes all values from the Application collection in order to start from a known state. Next, it writes a single value to the Application collection. Finally, it saves the key from the first element (index 0) retrieved by a call to GetKey into the Message control.

```
Sub Page_Load( )
    Application.RemoveAll( )
    Application("GetKeyTest") = "Got it!"
    Message.Text = "Key of Application(0) = " & _
                    Application.GetKey(0) & _
                    "<br/>(Should be GetKeyTest)"
End Sub
```

Notes

If *Index* is less than 0 or greater than Application.Count - 1, an ArgumentOutOf-RangeException exception will be thrown.

Lock

`Application.Lock`

Locks access to an Application collection to facilitate access synchronization.

Parameters

None

Example

The example locks the application, sets an application page load counter variable, unlocks the application, and displays the value:

```
Sub Page_Load( )
    Application.Lock( )
    Application("Counter") = Application("Counter") + 1
    Application.UnLock(.)
    Message.Text = "Counter = " & Application("Counter")
End Sub
```

Notes

In the example, note that we Lock the application, perform any operations that modify values within the Application collection, and UnLock the application as quickly as possible. Any read access to the Application collection can safely take place outside the Lock/UnLock method calls.

Remove

`Application.Remove(ByVal name As String)`

Removes an item by name from the Application collection.

Parameters

name
    A String argument containing the name (key) of the item to remove.

Example

The example determines whether the item with the key "foo" exists in the Application collection and, if it does, removes the item and displays an appropriate message:

```
Sub Page_Load()
    If Not Application("foo") Is Nothing Then
        Application.Remove("foo")
        Message.Text = "Item 'foo' was removed."
    Else
        Message.Text = "Item 'foo' does not exist."
    End If
End Sub
```

Notes

The Remove method is provided for backwards compatibility with classic ASP. In classic ASP, this method was accessed through the Contents collection. In ASP.NET, this method can be accessed either directly, as shown above, or through the Contents collection.

RemoveAll

`Application.RemoveAll()`

Removes all items from the Application collection.

Parameters

None

Example

The example checks to ensure that at least one item is in the Application collection, and if it is, it clears the collection by calling the RemoveAll method.

```
Sub Page_Load()
    If Application.Count > 0 Then
        Application.RemoveAll()
        Message.Text = "Application collection cleared."
    Else
        Message.Text = "Application collection is already empty."
    End If
End Sub
```

Notes

The RemoveAll method is provided for backwards compatibility with classic ASP. In classic ASP, this method was accessed through the Contents collection. In ASP. NET, this method can be accessed either directly, as shown above, or through the Contents collection.

RemoveAt

```
Application.RemoveAt(ByVal index As Integer)
```

Removes an item from the Application collection by index. This is a new companion to the Remove method, which removes an item by key.

Parameters
index
> An Integer argument containing the index location of the item to remove from the Application collection.

Example
```
Sub Page_Load()
    If Application.Count > 0 Then
        Application.RemoveAt(0)
        Message.Text = "The item at index 0 was removed."
    Else
        Message.Text = "The item at index 0 does not exist."
    End If
End Sub
```

Notes

The RemoveAt method allows items to be removed from the Application collection by index rather than by key. As in the example above, the items that follow the removed item will shift one position in the collection when the item is removed. If you remove an item by index and then call RemoveAt again with the same index, you will remove the item that immediately followed the original removed item. If a single item is in the Application collection and you call RemoveAt a second time, an ArgumentOutOfRangeException exception will be thrown.

Set

```
Application.Set(ByVal name As String, ByVal value As Object)
```

Updates the value of an object in the Application collection. This new method allows you to set objects in the Application collection.

Parameters
Name
> A String argument containing the name of the object in the Application collection to be updated.

Value

An Object argument containing the new value of the Application collection object to be updated.

Example

The example uses Set twice—once to set a new item in the Application collection and again to change that value.

```
Sub Page_Load()
    Application.RemoveAll()
    Application.Set("TotallyNewVariable","Test!")
    Message.Text = "First: " + Application("TotallyNewVariable") + "<br/>"
    Application.Set("TotallyNewVariable","Test again!")
    Message.Text = Message.Text & "First after Set: " +
    Application("TotallyNewVariable") + "<br/>"
End Sub
```

Notes

Set can be used to add values to the Application collection, but you will normally just use the simple syntax you are used to from classic ASP:

```
Application("TotallyNewVariable") = "Test!"
```

UnLock

```
Application.UnLock
```

Unlocks access to an Application collection to facilitate access synchronization.

Parameters

None

Example

The example locks the application, sets an application page load counter variable, unlocks the application, and displays the value:

```
Sub Page_Load()
    Application.Lock()
    Application("Counter") = Application("Counter") + 1
    Application.UnLock()
    Message.Text = "Counter = " & Application("Counter")
End Sub
```

Notes

In the example, note that we Lock the application, perform any operations that modify values within the Application collection, and UnLock the application as quickly as possible. Any read access to the Application collection can safely take place outside the Lock/UnLock method calls.

Events Reference

Start

```
Sub Application_OnStart()
    'Event handler logic
End Sub
```

Fired when the Application is created. The event handler for this event should be defined in the *global.asax* application file.

Parameters

None

Example

The example writes an entry to both the Application Event log and the IIS log for the application to indicate that the Start event has fired:

```
<Script language="VB" runat="server">
    Sub Application_OnStart()
        Dim EventLog1 As New System.Diagnostics.EventLog ("Application", _
            ".", "mySource")
        EventLog1.WriteEntry("Application_OnStart fired!")
        Context.Response.AppendToLog("Application_OnStart fired!")
    End Sub
</script>
```

There is one issue with the code above. Security in the released version of the .NET framework has been tightened, so writing to the event log will not work by default in an ASP.NET application.

Notes

The Start event is useful for performing initialization tasks when the application is initialized. You can initialize Application variables that are mostly static.

End

```
Sub Application_OnEnd()
    'Event handler logic
End Sub
```

Fired when the application is torn down, either when the web server is stopped or when the *global.asax* file is modified. The event handler for this event should be defined in the *global.asax* application file.

Parameters

None

Example

The example below writes an entry to the Application Event log to indicate that the End event has fired.

```
<Script language="VB" runat="server">
  Sub Application_OnEnd()
    Dim EventLog1 As New System.Diagnostics.EventLog ("Application", _
        ".", "mySource")
    EventLog1.WriteEntry("Application_OnEnd fired!")
  End Sub
</script>
```

Notes

The End event is useful for performing cleanup tasks when the Application ends, either because the web service stops or the *global.asax* file is changed.

CHAPTER 14

The HttpContext Class

With all the knowledge gained about the `HttpApplicationState` class covered in the last chapter, the next question is, "How you gain access to a copy of the `HttpApplicationState` within your application?" The good news is that within an ASP.NET page, the Application instance of the `HttpApplicationState` class is available exactly as it appears in a classic ASP page. The Response, Request and other objects familiar to classic ASP are also available. These and other objects are available by using the `HttpContext` class.

Unlike many classes within ASP.NET, the `HttpContext` class adds new methods and properties but does not contain any significant methods or properties carried over from classic ASP that are deprecated in ASP.NET. New properties include IsCustomErrorEnabled, IsDebuggingEnabled, SkipAuthorization, and Trace.

The `HttpContext` class encapsulates all the HTTP-specific information about a given HTTP request. The `HttpContext` class contains an Items collection that allows the developer to store information for the duration of the current request. In some ways, this class is similar to `HttpSessionState` (discussed in Chapter 19). However, information stored in the HttpContext collection is held only for the duration of the current request. While this might not initially seem useful, it is often helpful.

For instance, suppose an application is structured so that the user enters information into a form and clicks a button with a server-side event handler. When the button's Click handler is called, a different page must get the information. After placing the information gathered from the form in the `HttpContext` class, the click handler can use the server-side Server.Transfer method to go to the second page without requiring another round trip from the server to the client. In addition to other pages, HttpHandlers and HttpModules that might participate in a given request have access to the context.

The HttpContext object will seem a bit redundant for developers who only write traditional ASP.NET pages. Most of the properties and methods are duplicated in the Page object, so they might not seem important. However, if you are creating other types of ASP.NET code, such as HttpModules and HttpHandlers, the HttpContext class can be a lifesaver. Even developers creating only standard ASP. NET pages might need to use the HttpContext object if they are creating event handlers in the *global.asax* file. In some contexts, the traditional objects used within ASP.NET pages are not available within these *global.asax* event handlers.

Table 14-1 lists the properties, collections, and methods exposed by the HttpContext class.

Table 14-1. HttpContext class summary

Properties	Collections	Methods (instance)	Methods (static/shared)
Application	AllErrors	AddError	GetAppConfig
ApplicationInstance	Items	ClearError	
Cache		GetConfig	
Current		RewritePath	
Error			
Handler			
IsCustomErrorEnabled			
IsDebuggingEnabled			
Request			
Response			
Server			
Session			
SkipAuthorization			
Timestamp			
Trace			
User			

HttpContext Class

Comments/Troubleshooting

Many HttpContext class properties are topics in their own right. For instance, the Application, Response, Request and Session properties are accessible here, but covered in detail elsewhere in this book. A couple of methods within HttpContext, however, might require further explanation.

GetConfig sounds like it might be a way to get the appSettings configuration information mentioned in the previous chapter. While it is possible to use GetConfig("appSettings") for that purpose, it requires some casting. GetConfig returns an instance of System.Configuration.ReadOnlyNameValueCollection, which is a private class. To actually use the returned value, you need to cast it to a System.Collections.Specialized.NameValueCollection. Instead of doing this, using ConfigurationSettings.AppSettings is safer and easier. Why is GetConfig there, then? In addition to the appSettings section, a developer can place custom sections within the configuration files, which is what GetConfig is designed for.

The other somewhat unusual (although much more useful) method in HttpContext is RewritePath. The MSDN documentation on this method is, shall we say, sparse. The real use for this method is to silently redirect the user to a different URL.

In this chapter, as in others in the book, we'll use the following code listing as the basis for most examples in the chapter. Unless otherwise noted, each example will consist of the Page_Load event handler for just that particular example. Any output messages or return values displayed will be shown as the Text property of the ASP.NET Label control named Message or displayed by calling Response.Write.

```vb
<%@ Page Language="vb" %>
<html>
    <head>
        <script runat="server">
            Sub Page_Load()
                'Example code will go here
            End Sub
        </script>
    </head>
<body>
    <asp:label id="Message" runat="server"/>
</body>
</html>
```

Some examples will show Application handlers within *global.asax* rather than the Page_Load method of a page.

Properties Reference

Application

```
HttpApplicationState = Context.Application
```

Returns the current Application state object.

Parameters

`HttpApplicationState`
> An HttpApplicationState object that will receive the value of the property.

Example

The example sets an application value using the Application instance exposed by the Page class and gets the instance from Context. Finally, it displays the newly set value by using the HttpApplicationState instance retrieved from the Context object (proving they are the same object):

```vb
Sub Page_Load()
    Dim App as HttpApplicationState
    Page.Application("Test")="Value"
    App = Context.Application
    Message.Text = App("Test")
End Sub
```

Notes

Often, you will use the copy of Application from the Page class. However, for objects not derived from Page (for instance, HttpHandlers and HttpModules) this is a convenient way to access the Application state.

Do not confuse this property, which returns an instance of type HttpApplication-State, with the ApplicationInstance property, which returns an instance of type HttpApplication.

ApplicationInstance

```
Context.ApplicationInstance = HttpApplication
HttpApplication = Context.ApplicationInstance
```

Returns or sets the current HttpApplication object.

Parameters

HttpApplication
> An HttpApplication object that will receive or set the value of the Application-Instance property.

Notes

Generally, you do not need to use the HttpApplication object, since the properties it exposes are usually available through other objects. One exception is is when accessing all the methods that allow you to add event handlers for this request.

Cache

```
HttpCache = Context.Cache
```

Returns an instance of the Cache class.

Parameters

HttpCache
> An Object variable of type Cache.

Example

The example retrieves an instance of the Cache class into a local variable and then adds a value to the cache:

```
Sub Application_BeginRequest()
    Dim myCache As Cache
    myCache = Context.Cache
    myCache.Add("Test", "Test", Nothing, _
        System.DateTime.Now.AddHours(1), Nothing, _
        CacheItemPriority.High, Nothing)
End Sub
```

Notes

Note that rather than using the Page_Load event, the example above shows the Application_BeginRequest event handler in *global.asax*; a common use of the Cache property is to access the cache at points during request processing when the Cache property of the Page object is not available, such as before the Page object is instantiated.

Current

```
HttpContext = HttpContext.Current
```

Retrieves the current HttpContext instance.

Parameters

HttpContext
    The current context.

Example

This example uses the IsDebuggingEnabled property, described later in this chapter, to show whether debugging is enabled:

```
Sub Page_Load()
    Message.Text = HttpContext.Current.IsDebuggingEnabled.ToString()
End Sub
```

Notes

Current is a shared (static) property, indicating that you can access it without creating an instance of the HttpContext class.

Error

```
Exception = Context.Error
```

Returns the first error, if any, associated with the current request.

Parameters

Exception
    An Exception variable to receive the value of the property.

Example

The example checks to see if the Error property on the current context object is null (Nothing in VB.NET). If it is not null, it displays the error; otherwise, it displays a message indicating there is no error.

```
Sub Page_Load()
    If Not HttpContext.Current.Error Is Nothing then
        Message.Text = HttpContext.Current.Error.ToString()
    Else
        Message.Text = "No error detected"
    End If
End Sub
```

Handler

```
IHttpHandler = Context.Handler
Context.Handler = IHttpHandler
```

Sets or returns an instance of the IHttpHandler for the current request.

Parameters

IHttpHandler
> An Object variable of a type that implements the IHttpHandler interface.

Notes

The Handler property can be used to specify special handling for this request. To understand this idea, you need to understand how requests are processed in IIS. When a request comes in, unless the item requested is a simple HTML file, the request is generally handled by an Internet Server API (ISAPI) extension. For instance, classic ASP and ASP.NET pages are directed to ISAPI applications that process the request. ISAPI applications are reasonably easy to write in principal, but are very difficult to create in practice. The IHttpHandler interface is the .NET way of allowing the developer to write code to for requests to be handled in a way similar to ISAPI applications in IIS, without all of the problems of ISAPI.

IsCustomErrorEnabled

```
Boolean = Context.IsCustomErrorEnabled
```

Returns a Boolean value specifying whether custom errors are enabled for the current request.

Parameters

Boolean
> A Boolean variable to receive the value of this property.

Example

The following example displays True if custom errors are enabled; otherwise, it displays False.

```
Sub Page_Load()
    Message.Text = "Custom Error Enabled?" & _
        Context.IsCustomErrorEnabled
End Sub
```

Notes

This flag is controlled by the customErrors section in *web.config*. If the customErrors element's mode attribute is set to On,, IsCustomErrorEnabled returns True. If the customErrors element's mode attribute is set to False or RemoteOnly, this flag is False.

IsDebuggingEnabled

```
Boolean = Context.IsDebuggingEnabled
```

Returns a Boolean value specifying whether debugging is enabled for the current request.

Parameters

`Boolean`
> A Boolean variable to receive value of this flag.

Example

The example displays `True` if debugging enabled; otherwise, it displays `False`:

```
Sub Page_Load()
    Message.Text = "Debugging Enabled?" & _
        Context.IsDebuggingEnabled
End Sub
```

Notes

This flag is controlled by the `compilation` section in *web.config*. If the `compilation` section's debug attribute is set to `True`, IsDebuggingEnabled returns `True`. If the debug attribute in the compilation section is set to `False`, this property is `False`.

Request

`HttpRequest = Context.Request`

Returns the HttpRequest object for the current request.

Parameters

`HttpRequest`
> An HttpRequest variable to receive the current HttpRequest object.

Notes

This property is provided for applications other than ASP.NET pages (where the Page.Request property is normally used to retrieve the HttpRequest object). Code that does not have access to the properties of the `Page` class includes HttpHandlers and HttpModules, as well as event handlers in *global.asax*.

Response

`HttpResponse = Context.Response`

Returns the HttpResponse object for the current request.

Parameters

`HttpResponse`
> An HttpResponse variable to receive the current HttpResponse object.

Notes

This property is provided for applications other than ASP.NET pages (where the Page.Response property is normally used to retrieve the HttpResponse object). Code that does not have access to the properties of the `Page` class includes HttpHandlers and HttpModules, as well as *global.asax*. One common reason for using Context.Response is to write cookies in an HttpModule.

Session

```
HttpSessionState = Context.Session
```

Returns the HttpSession object for the current request.

Parameters

```
HttpSessionState
```
An HttpSessionState object to receive the current session.

Notes

This property is provided for applications other than ASP.NET pages (where the Page.Session property is normally used to retrieve the HttpSessionState object). Code that does not have access to the properties of the Page class includes HttpHandlers and HttpModules, as well as *global.asax*. When using Context. Session in the Application event handlers of *global.asax*, Session is not available in the Application BeginRequest event, but can be used in, for instance, the Application_PreRequestHandlerExecute event.

SkipAuthorization

```
Boolean = Context.SkipAuthorization
Context.SkipAuthentication = Boolean
```

Sets or returns a flag indicating whether the URLAuthorization module will skip the authorization check. The default is False.

Parameters

```
Boolean
```
A Boolean variable returning or setting the flag regarding authorization checks.

Example

The following example retrieves the status of the SkipAuthorization property and displays it in the Message label control:

```
Sub Page_Load()
    Message.Text = "SkipAuthorization? " _
        & Context.SkipAuthorization
End Sub
```

Notes

To set this value, the ControlPrincipal Flag must be set in the Flags property of the SecurityPermission object. This property is used internally by the Forms and Passport authentication modules.

Timestamp

```
timestamp = Context.Timestamp
```

Returns a DateTime object containing the date and time of the request on the server.

Parameters

timestamp
> An Object variable of type DateTime.

Example

The following example retrieves the date and time of the request and displays it in the Message label control:

```
Sub Page_Load()
    Message.Text = "Date/Time of Request: " _
    & Context.Timestamp
End Sub
```

Trace

```
TraceContext = Context.Trace
```

Returns the TraceContext for the current request. The members of the TraceContext class are listed in the entry for the Trace Property in Chapter 12.

Parameters

TraceContext
> A TraceContext variable to receive the TraceContext object for the current request.

Example

The example retrieves the date and time of the request and displays it in the Message label control.

```
Sub Page_Load()
    Message.Text = "Trace Enabled? " _
        & Context.Trace.IsEnabled
End Sub
```

Notes

Trace can be enabled by setting the Trace attribute of the @ Page directive to True.

User

```
IPrincipal = Context.User
Context.User = IPrincipal
```

Returns or sets the IPrincipal object for the current request.

Parameters

IPrincipal

> An object that implements the IPrincipal interface. The IPrincipal interface is implemented by the `GenericPrincipal` and the `WindowsPrincipal` classes. IPrincipal defines one property and one method.

Identity

> A property that returns a class that implements the IIdentity interface.

IsInRole(Role as String)

> A method that returns a Boolean indicating whether the current principal belongs to the specified Role.

The IIdentity interface provides several useful properties:

AuthenticationType

> A property that returns the type of authentication used, if the request is authenticated.

IsAuthenticated

> A property that returns a Boolean indicating if the user has been authenticated. This property should be checked (to ensure it is `True`) before checking for AuthenticationType or Name. IsAuthenticated returns `False` if anonymous authentication is enabled in Internet Information Server and neither Forms nor another authentication method is in use by ASP.NET.

Name

> A property that returns the Name of the current user. The user name format depends upon the type of authentication used. For Windows authentication, the name is in the format of `DOMAIN\UserName`.

Example

The example checks to see if the user is authenticated and if so, returns the name of the user:

```
Sub Page_Load()
    Message.Text = "User.Identity.IsAuthenticated?  " _
        & Context.User.Identity.IsAuthenticated & "<br/>"
    If Context.User.Identity.IsAuthenticated Then
        Message.Text = Message.Text & "User.Identity.Name?  " _
            & Context.User.Identity.Name & "<br/>"
    End If
End Sub
```

Notes

Understanding the values you receive back when checking the User property requires an understanding of ASP.NET and Internet Information Server, since the returned values depend on settings in both.

Collections Reference

The Context object in ASP.NET supports one collection, Items, and an array called AllErrors.

AllErrors

```
ExceptionArray = Context.AllErrors
```

Returns an array of Exception objects representing all accumulated errors that occurred in the current request.

As in classic ASP, the Server.GetLastError method returns an ASPError object. This mechanism is still available, though the returned value is now of type Exception rather than ASPError.

Parameters

None

Example

The example checks to see if the AllErrors array contains any elements and if so, displays them:

```
Sub Page_Load()
    Dim i as Integer
    Dim e As New Exception("A generalized error.")
    Context.AddError(e)
    If Not Context.AllErrors Is Nothing Then
        For i = 0 to Context.AllErrors.Length - 1
            Message.Text = Message.Text & _
                "Exception: " & _
                Context.AllErrors(i).ToString() & "<br/>"
        Next
    Else
        Message.Text = "No Errors to report."
    End if
End Sub
```

Notes

Unlike classic ASP, arrays in ASP.NET are zero-based, so the first element in any collection or array will be 0, not 1. Thus, in the example above, the array is indexed from 0 to Length - 1, not from 1 to Length.

Items

```
Context.Items(Name as String) = Value
Value = Context.Items(Index as Integer)
Value = Context.Items(Name as String)
```

The Items collection is a key-value collection that can contain any object the developer wishes to save for, at most, the duration of the request. Unlike Session- or Application-level collections that can be used to store values, this collection does not survive past the current request. This collection is the ideal place to store values that need not survive past the current request, especially if the items need to be stored or retrieved in places where the Session or Application objects are not available.

Parameters

Name
> The key name for the value to be stored.

Value
> The object to be stored in the Items collection, or the value to be retrieved.

Index
> The index of the value to be retrieved.

Example

The example adds two values to the Context.Items collection. The first is added traditionally, referring to the key in the Items collection directly. The second is added using the Item's collection's Add method. Finally, the Message label control displays whether the "Foo" value has been set. To display the string key used, you need to use two double quotes, which displays as the literal quote character. In C#, the quote character would need to be escaped by placing a backslash (\) in front of it.

```
Sub Page_Load()
    Context.Items("Foo")="Bar"
    Context.Items.Add("Bar","Foo")
    Message.Text = "Context.Items.Contains(""Foo"") is " & _
                    Context.Items.Contains("Foo")
End Sub
```

Notes

Unlike classic ASP, collections in ASP.NET are zero-based, so the first element in any collection or array is 0, not 1. While you can, as in the example above, use the Add method to add values to the Items collection; this is virtually never done. Values are almost always retrieved by referring to the Items collection directly, either by using a numeric index or indexing using a key string.

Methods Reference

AddError

```
Context.AddError(ByVal ErrorInfo As Exception)
```

Adds an Exception object to the array of exceptions returned by the AllErrors property.

Parameters

ErrorInfo
> An Exception object to be added to the array.

Example

The example shows how you can use AddError to add an error to the current request context. The exception is created within a Try block. In the Finally block, the ToString method is used to display the error and the ClearError method is used to clear the error so that the page will display properly.

```
Sub Page_Load()
    Try
        Context.AddError(New Exception("Test"))
    Finally
        Message.Text = "Context.Error.ToString() is " & _
            Context.Error.ToString()
        Context.ClearError()
    End Try
End Sub
```

Notes

Adding an exception by using AddError should not be confused with throwing an exception. Using AddError only adds the exception to the array returned by the AllErrors property and does not invoke any of the error handling mechanisms in the application.

ClearError

```
Context.ClearError()
```

Clears all errors for the current request. Note that even though ClearError is singular, it clears all errors for the current request.

Parameters

None

Example

The example checks whether there are any errors and then clears them. Finally, it reports if it has cleared any errors.

```
Sub Page_Load()
    If Not Context.AllErrors Is Nothing Then
        Context.ClearError()
        Message.Text = "Errors cleared."
    Else
        Message.Text = "No Errors to clear."
    End If
End Sub
```

GetAppConfig

```
Object = HttpContext.GetAppConfig(ByVal name As String)
```

Returns the collection of key/value pairs that are contained in the configuration specified by the *name* argument.

Parameters

Object

An object containing the keys and values in the configuration sections specified by *name*. This object is often of a type derived from NameValueCollection.

Name

The name of the section to retrieve.

Example

The example shows how you can use the GetAppConfig method to retrieve all items in a configuration by setting from the *web.config* or *machine.config* XML configuration file. While GetAppConfig returns an Object, you must cast the returned object to the NameValueCollection-derived type defined in the configuration section to actually access the information. This method is static, so an instance of the HttpContext class is not required.

```
Sub Page_Load( )
    Dim i As Integer
    Dim nv As NameValueCollection
    nv = CType(HttpContext.GetAppConfig("appSettings"), _
            NameValueCollection)
    For i = 0 To nv.Count - 1
        Response.Write(nv.GetKey(i) & " = " & nv(i) & "<br/>")
    Next
End Sub
```

Notes

Generally you will not use GetAppConfig to get the appSettings section from the configuration file. It is much easier and safer to use ConfigurationSettings.AppSettings to get at these values. This method, however, can be used to get information from custom configuration sections.

GetConfig

```
Object = Context.GetConfig(ByVal name As String)
```

Returns the collection of key/value pairs that are contained in the configuration specified by the *name* argument.

Parameters

Object

An object containing the keys and values in the configuration sections specified by *name*. This object is often of a type derived from NameValueCollection.

Name

The name of the section to retrieve.

Example

The example shows how you can use the GetConfig method to retrieve all items in a configuration setting from the *web.config* or *machine.config* XML configuration file. While GetAppConfig returns an object, you must cast the returned object to the NameValueCollection-derived type defined in the configuration section to actually access the information.

```
Sub Page_Load( )
    Dim i As Integer
    Dim nv As NameValueCollection
```

```
    nv = CType(Context.GetConfig("appSettings"), _
            NameValueCollection)
    For i = 0 To nv.Count - 1
        Response.Write(nv.GetKey(i) & " = " & nv(i) & "<br/>")
    Next
End Sub
```

Notes

Generally, you will not use GetConfig to get the appSettings section from the configuration file. It is much easier and safer to use ConfigurationSettings.AppSettings to get these values. This method, however, can be used to get information from custom configuration sections.

RewritePath

```
Context.RewritePath(ByVal newURL As String)
```

Assigns an internal rewrite path.

Parameters

newURL
    A String containing a local path to redirect the user silently.

Example

The example below shows how to change the path in a way that is completely transparent to the user. The URL shown in the address bar remains the original URL, and the redirection to the new page does not require a round trip to and from the server. RewritePath is almost always called from *global.asax* rather than an actual page. That is what this example shows.

```
Sub Application_BeginRequest(ByVal sender As Object, _
    ByVal e As EventArgs)
    ' No matter the URL, redirect to this URL...
    Context.RewritePath("/aspnetian/ShowGetConfig.aspx")
End Sub
```

Notes

This method seems to be redundant when compared with methods like Server.Transfer, which allow the developer to change the page being displayed. In fact, RewritePath serves a very unique purpose.

Perhaps you have seen or registered at Web sites that give registered users a unique URL. For instance, you might be given a URL like this:

```
http://www.SomeDomain.com/YourName/default.aspx
```

Implementing such a system that gives a virtual directory to each user is not practical unless you have very few registered users. Using RewritePath, the developer can essentially remove a level of directory hierarchy. This removal occurs without a redirect that would require a round trip to the server, and without changing the URL as it appears in the browser. Some information will be extracted and saved in

---

the Context Items collection for use by pages that will be displayed while translating from the URL entered by the user to the URL used for RewritePath.

In the example above, RewritePath might be sent a URL like this:

```
http://www.SomeDomain.com/default.aspx
```

The "YourName" folder name was removed from the URL, and the application can then be customized for the user identified as "YourName."

CHAPTER 15

The HttpException Class

The HttpException class provides a container for communicating error information from various classes used in ASP.NET. The Page, HttpRequest, HttpResponse, HttpServerUtility, and other classes all use the HttpException class to communicate information about errors that occur when calling their methods or properties.

The HttpException class is derived from the Exception class, the base class for all exceptions in the .NET Framework. HttpException adds two methods, GetHtmlErrorMessage and GetHttpCode, as well as other constructor overloads that create HttpException instances based on HTTP error codes.

In addition to its role in communicating error information from the Request, Response, and other ASP.NET intrinsic objects, the HttpException class can be useful in communicating error information from custom components or controls that communicate via HTTP. When an HTTP error occurs in such a component, you can use one of the constructor overloads for the HttpException class to create an instance of HttpException that contains the HTTP status code associated with the result, along with a custom error message, if desired, to the client of the component. This allows you to provide clients with rich, specific error information that they can handle as they choose. Table 15-1 lists the properties, collections, and methods exposed by the HttpException class.

Table 15-1. HttpException class summary

Properties	Methods (public instance)
ErrorCode (inherited from Exception)	GetBaseException (inherited from Exception)
HelpLink (inherited from Exception)	GetHtmlErrorMessage
InnerException (inherited from Exception)	GetHttpCode
Message (inherited from Exception)	ToString (inherited from Exception)
Source (inherited from Exception)	
StackTrace (inherited from Exception)	
TargetSite (inherited from Exception)	

Comments/Troubleshooting

In this chapter, as in others in the book, we'll use the following code listing as the basis for most examples in the chapter. Unless otherwise noted, each example will consist of just the Page_Load event handler for that particular example. Any displayed output messages or return values will be shown as the Text property of the ASP.NET Label control named Message or displayed by calling Response.Write:

```
<%@ Page Language="vb" %>
<html>
    <head>
        <script runat="server">
            Sub Page_Load( )
                'Example code will go here
            End Sub
        </script>
    </head>
<body>
    <asp:label id="Message" forecolor="red" runat="server"/>
</body>
</html>
```

Constructor Reference

The HttpException provides several overloaded constructors for communicating custom HTTP error information:

Dim MyHttpEx As New HttpException( )
> Creates an empty instance of HttpException.

Throw New HttpException(string)
> Throws an HttpException whose Message property is set to the value of the string passed into the constructor.

Throw New HttpException(integer, string)
> Throws an HttpException whose GetHttpCode method will return the integer value passed into the constructor, and whose Message property is set to the value of the string passed into the constructor.

Throw New HttpException(string, Exception)
> Throws an HttpException whose Message property is set to the value of the string passed into the constructor, and whose InnerException property is set to the Exception object passed into the constructor.

Throw New HttpException(string, integer)
> Throws an HttpException whose Message property is set to the value of the string passed into the constructor, and whose ErrorCode property is set to the value of the integer passed into the constructor.

Throw New HttpException(integer, string, Exception)
> Throws an HttpException whose GetHttpCode method returns the integer value passed into the constructor, whose Message property is set to the value of the string passed into the constructor, and whose InnerException property is set to the Exception object passed into the constructor.

```
Throw New HttpException(integer, string, integer)
```
Throws an HttpException whose GetHttpCode method returns the first integer value passed into the constructor, whose Message property is set to the value of the string passed into the constructor, and whose ErrorCode property is set to the value of the second integer passed into the constructor.

Properties Reference

ErrorCode

```
integer = HttpException.ErrorCode
```

Returns an integer representing the Win32 error code or HRESULT of the exception. This property is especially useful in situations when you are working with COM objects through COM Interop and need to return or evaluate the HRESULT returned from a COM object failure. When creating HttpException instances in your own code, you can use one of two overloaded constructors (shown earlier in the "Comments/Troubleshooting" section) to set this property for HttpExceptions that you throw.

Parameters

integer
    An integer that will receive the HRESULT or Win32 error code from the property.

Example

The code example uses the Page_Load event handler to throw an HttpException with a custom error message and error code, and then uses structured exception handling to catch the exception and display the error message and error code as the text of an ASP.NET Label control:

```
Sub Page_Load()
    Try
        Throw New HttpException("Threw an error from Page_Load", 100)
    Catch HttpEx As HttpException
        Message.Text = "ERROR:<br/>"
        Message.Text &= "Message: " & HttpEx.Message & "<br/>"
        Message.Text &= "Error Code: " & HttpEx.ErrorCode & "<br/>"
    End Try
End Sub
```

Notes

While the ErrorCode property is primarily useful when working with COM objects, this property is also set by the ASP.NET intrinsic objects when an exception is thrown.

HelpLink

```
string = HttpException.HelpLink
HttpException.HelpLink = string
```

Sets or returns a string containing the URN or URL to a help file containing information about the exception.

Parameters

string
> A string that will set the HelpLink property or receive the help link from the property.

Example

The code example will display the help link associated with a custom HttpException:

```
Sub Page_Load()
    Try
        Dim myHttpEx As _
            New HttpException("Threw an exception from Page_Load")
        myHttpEx.HelpLink = "file://C:/myHelpDir/myHelpFile.htm"
        Throw myHttpEx
    Catch HttpEx As HttpException
        Message.ForeColor = System.Drawing.Color.Red
        Message.Text = "ERROR:<br/>"
        Message.Text &= "Message: " & HttpEx.Message & "<br/>"
        Message.Text &= "Error Code: " & HttpEx.ErrorCode & "<br/>"
        Message.Text &= "Help Link: " & HttpEx.HelpLink & "<br/>"
    End Try
End Sub
```

Notes

The HelpLink is not always set by exceptions thrown from the ASP.NET intrinsic objects. For example, if you attempt to access the Session intrinsic object when Session state is disabled, an HttpException will be thrown, but its HelpLink property will return an empty string.

InnerException

```
Exception = HttpException.InnerException
```

Returns an Exception object containing the inner exception of the HttpException object.

Parameters

Exception
> An Exception instance that will be populated by the property.

Example

The code example creates two exceptions, the second of which is created with an overloaded constructor that sets the InnerException property to the first exception. The code throws the second exception, which is caught by the Catch statement. The Catch block then displays the error messages of both the outer and inner exceptions:

```
Sub Page_Load()
    Try
        Dim myHttpEx As _
            New HttpException("This is a nested exception")
        Throw New HttpException("Threw an exception from Page_Load", _
            myHttpEx)
    Catch HttpEx As HttpException
        Dim InnerHttpEx As HttpException
        InnerHttpEx = CType(HttpEx.InnerException, HttpException)
        Message.Text = "ERROR:<br/>"
        Message.Text &= "Message: " & HttpEx.Message & "<br/>"
        Message.Text &= "Inner Exception Message: " & _
            InnerHttpEx.Message & "<br/>"
    End Try
End Sub
```

Notes

The InnerException property allows exceptions to be nested, which can allow developers to track down the root cause of an exception, even when multiple exceptions are thrown. Because the InnerException property is inherited from the Exception class, other types of exceptions can be nested within an HttpException, and HttpExceptions can be nested within other exception types. The InnerException property can only be set manually through one of the overloaded constructors of the HttpException class.

Message

```
string = HttpException.Message
```

Returns a string representing the error message associated with the exception. The error message is the human-readable text description of the error.

Parameters

string
    A string that will receive the error message value from the property.

Example

The code example creates and throws an exception, passing the desired error message into the HttpException constructor, and then displays the Message property of the exception as the Text property of an ASP.NET Label control:

```
Sub Page_Load()
    Try
        Throw New HttpException("Threw an error from Page_Load")
```

```
        Catch HttpEx As HttpException
            Message.Text = "ERROR:<br/>"
            Message.Text &= "Message: " & HttpEx.Message & "<br/>"
        End Try
    End Sub
```

Notes

The ease with which the Message property can be accessed makes it temping to simply display this property when an error occurs. A better approach to error handling, however, is to log this information either in the NT Event Log or in your own private application log and handle the error to the user transparently. This provides you with better information to troubleshoot your applications and gives your users a more satisfying (and less frustrating) experience.

Source

```
string = HttpException.Source
HttpException.Source = string
```

Sets or returns a string representing the source of the exception. For custom exceptions that you create and throw, this code may be set to the name of the method and/or class from which the exception is thrown.

Parameters

string
> A string that will receive the value from the property.

Example

The code example causes an exception by attempting to set a Session value on a page for which the `enableSessionState` attribute of the `@ Page` directive has been set to `False`. The example code then displays the resulting error message and source:

```
<%@ Page Language="vb" EnableSessionState="false" %>

    ...

Sub Page_Load()
    Try
        Session("foo") = "Foo"
    Catch HttpEx As HttpException
        Message.Text = "ERROR:<br/>"
        Message.Text &= "Message: " & HttpEx.Message & "<br/>"
        Message.Text &= "Source: " & HttpEx.Source & "<br/>"
    End Try
End Sub
```

Notes

In the example, the Source property returns the value System.Web as the source of the Exception, which is not very specific. When creating and throwing your own custom exceptions, be as specific as possible with error messages and source descriptions. Just remember that providing specific information about an exception you're throwing is no substitute for handling the exception condition within your code instead of throwing an exception. If you have sufficient information about what went wrong to correct the problem, doing so is almost always preferable to throwing an exception that will interrupt the flow of the application from your users' standpoint.

StackTrace

```
string = HttpException.StackTrace
```

Returns a string containing a list of the methods in the current call stack in which the exception occurred. The method in which the exception occurred is listed first, followed by any additional methods in the call stack (methods that called the method in which the exception occurred), up to the point at which the exception was handled.

Parameters

string
    A string that will receive the stack trace value from the property.

Example

In the code example, the Page_Load event handler calls the ThrowMeAnException method, which throws an HttpException. The exception handler in Page_Load then displays the error message and stack trace:

```
Sub Page_Load()
    Try
        ThrowMeAnException
    Catch HttpEx As HttpException
        Message.Text = "ERROR:<br/>"
        Message.Text &= "Message: " & HttpEx.Message & "<br/>"
        Message.Text &= "Stack Trace: " & HttpEx.StackTrace & "<br/>"
    End Try
End Sub
Sub ThrowMeAnException()
    Throw New HttpException("Threw an error from ThrowMeAnException")
End Sub
```

Notes

The stack trace for the example first lists the ThrowMeAnException method, including the local path to the *.aspx* file containing the method and the line number at which the exception was thrown, and then lists the Page_Load method, including the path and line number where the exception originated.

TargetSite

```
MethodBase = HttpException.TargetSite
```

Returns a MethodBase instance (the MethodBase class resides in the System.Reflection namespace) representing the method from which the exception was thrown.

You can query the properties of MethodBase, such as the Name property, which returns the name of the method. You can also call ToString on the instance to return information about the method in a usable format.

Parameters

MethodBase
> An instance of the MethodBase class representing the method from which the exception was thrown.

Example

The code example causes an exception by attempting to set a Session value on a page for which the EnableSessionState attribute of the @ Page directive has been set to False. The example code then displays the resulting error message and uses the Name property of the MethodBase instance returned by the TargetSite property to display the name of the method from which the exception was thrown:

```
<%@ Page Language="vb" EnableSessionState="false" %>

...

Sub Page_Load()
    Try
        Session("foo") = "Foo"
    Catch HttpEx As HttpException
        Message.Text = "ERROR:<br/>"
        Message.Text &= "Message: " & HttpEx.Message & "<br/>"
        Message.Text &= "Target Site: " & HttpEx.TargetSite.Name & "<br/>"
    End Try
End Sub
```

Notes

In the example, we access the Name property of the MethodBase instance directly, without creating a separate local variable of type MethodBase. This direct access saves us the trouble of either adding an @ Import statement to import the System. Reflection namespace or explicitly declaring the local variable using syntax such as:

```
Dim myMethodBase As System.Reflection.MethodBase
myMethodBase = HttpEx.TargetSite
```

Accessing the Name property of MethodBase directly reduces the amount of code we need to write, but it does so at the expense of being less explicit about what we are actually doing. You should always keep such tradeoffs in mind when writing your code. Writing less code usually seems like a good idea, but if someone other than the original programmer needs to maintain the code, using such shortcuts can make it more difficult for the maintainer to understand what's going on in the code.

Methods Reference

GetBaseException

```
Exception = HttpException.GetBaseException( )
```

Returns an Exception object representing the original exception in a set of nested exceptions. This property provides a shortcut to the innermost exception accessible via the InnerException property.

Parameters

Exception
> An Exception instance that will be populated by the method.

Example

The following code example creates a set of three nested exceptions, the second and third of which are created with an overloaded constructor that sets the InnerException property to the prior exception. The code throws the third exception, which is caught by the Catch statement. The Catch block displays the error message of both the immediate inner exception by using the InnerException property and the original exception by using the Message property of the exception returned by the GetBaseException method:

```
Sub Page_Load( )
    Try
        Dim myHttpEx As _
            New HttpException("This is the original exception")
        Dim myHttpEx2 As _
            New HttpException("This is a nested exception", myHttpEx)
        Throw New HttpException("Threw an exception from Page_Load", _
            myHttpEx2)
    Catch HttpEx As HttpException
        Dim InnerHttpEx As HttpException
        InnerHttpEx = CType(HttpEx.InnerException, HttpException)
        Message.Text = "ERROR:<br/>"
        Message.Text &= "Message: " & HttpEx.Message & "<br/>"
        Message.Text &= "Inner Exception Message: " & _
            InnerHttpEx.Message & "<br/>"
        Message.Text &= "Base Exception Message: " & _
            InnerHttpEx.GetBaseException.Message & "<br/>"
    End Try
End Sub
```

Notes

Like the TargetSite property example, this example accesses a property of the instance returned by the GetBaseException method directly, rather than creating a local instance variable first. The same caveats about reduction in code versus readability apply here.

GetHtmlErrorMessage

```
string = HttpException.GetHtmlErrorMessage( )
```

Returns a string containing the HTTP error message (if any) set by the originator of the exception.

Parameters

string
> A string variable that will receive the value from the method.

Notes

This method will return a value only if the HttpException contains an HTTP error message.

GetHttpCode

```
integer = HttpException.GetHttpCode( )
```

Returns an integer containing the HTTP status code contained within the exception. For most exceptions thrown by the ASP.NET intrinsic objects, this integer will be 500, indicating an HTTP server error.

Parameters

integer
> An integer variable to receive the HTTP code from the method.

Example

The code example causes an exception by calling Server.Execute on a page that does not exist. The exception is then caught and the HTTP status code is displayed by calling GetHttpCode:

```
Sub Page_Load( )
    Try
        Server.Execute("Foo.aspx")
    Catch HttpEx As HttpException
        Message.Text = "ERROR:<br/>"
        Message.Text &= "Http Status Code: " & _
            HttpEx.GetHttpCode( ) & "<br/>"
    End Try
End Sub
```

Notes

This method is most useful for custom exceptions raised in methods that make HTTP calls, since it allows you to pass back the HTTP result code (404 for not found, 403 for access denied, etc.) to the calling client.

ToString

```
string = HttpException.ToString( )
```

Returns a string containing the fully qualified name of the exception, the error message (if available), the name of the inner exception, and the stack trace.

Parameters

string
> A string variable to receive the value from the method.

Example

The code example causes an exception by attempting to set a Session value on a page for which the EnableSessionState attribute of the @ Page directive has been set to False. The example code then displays the string representation of the resulting exception:

```
<%@ Page Language="vb" EnableSessionState="false" %>

Sub Page_Load( )
   Try
       Session("foo") = "Foo"
   Catch HttpEx As HttpException
       Message.Text = "ERROR:<br/>"
       Message.Text &= "String Representation of Exception: " & _
           HttpEx.ToString( ) & "<br/>"
   End Try
End Sub
```

Notes

This method provides a quick and easy shortcut for displaying the available information about a given exception without having to call the individual methods and properties of the HttpException object.

CHAPTER 16

The HttpRequest Class

The HttpRequest class is ASP.NET's replacement for ASP's Request intrinsic object. Because the HttpRequest class instance for a given ASP.NET page is exposed as the Request property of the Page class (from which all pages are derived), you can code to the HttpRequest class just as you did in ASP. Thus, your existing ASP code will be that much easier to migrate.

The HttpRequest class is used to access information related to a particular HTTP request made by a web client. The HttpRequest class provides access to this information through its properties, collections, and methods.

Each HTTP request from a client consists of an HTTP header and, optionally, a body. The header and body are separated by a blank line. The code following shows a typical HTTP request (without a body):

```
GET /ASPdotNET_iaN/Chapter_16/showHTTP.aspx HTTP/1.0
Connection: Keep-Alive
Accept: image/gif, image/x-xbitmap, image/jpeg, image/pjpeg, image/png,
*/*
Accept-Charset: iso-8859-1,*,utf-8
Accept-Encoding: gzip
Accept-Language: en
Host: localhost
User-Agent: Mozilla/4.08 [en] (WinNT; U ;Nav)
```

The first line of the HTTP header contains the request type, followed by a space, followed by the requested URL (URI), another space, and the HTTP version number. In the previous example, the request type is GET, the URL is */ASPdotNET_iaN/Chapter_16/showHTTP.aspx* (this URL is relative to the server or domain name), and the HTTP version is 1.0.

While we can gain much information from the text of an HTTP request header (which can be accessed either as a URL-encoded string in the Headers collection or by saving the request to disk by using the SaveAs method), having to parse the text each time we wanted to find a particular piece of information would be a pain.

HTTP Request Types

The current HTTP 1.1 standard (which can be found at *http://www.w3.org/Protocols/rfc2616/rfc2616.html*) defines the valid request types for an HTTP request. These types are:

- OPTIONS
- GET
- HEAD
- POST
- PUT
- DELETE
- TRACE
- CONNECT

While this list shows the valid request types, only the GET and HEAD are required to be supported by general-purpose servers. In practice, most, if not all, requests you'll deal with will be GET and POST type requests.

GET requests simply ask the server to return a resource (such as an HTML or ASP.NET page) specified by the URL passed with the request. GET requests can also pass data to the server by appending it to the URL in the following format:

```
GET /Chapter_16/showHTTP.aspx?name=andrew HTTP/1.0
```

This GET request fragment passes a key/value pair with the value "andrew" represented by the key "name." When more than one key/value pair is passed, each pair is separated by the ampersand (&) character. When using GET requests for passing data, in most cases, data passed with a GET request is limited to around 2K, which is limiting for complex or lengthy data. Pages using data passed by a GET request may be subject to alteration by a user before the request is made. Any data received via a GET request should be validated to ensure that processing or storing it will not cause an undesirable result.

POST requests are used to post data to the server. Like GET requests, this data is passed as one or more key/value pairs, separated by ampersands. Unlike GET requests, the key/value pairs in a POST request are passed in the request body:

```
POST /Chapter_16/showHTTP.aspx HTTP/1.0
name=andrew
```

The HttpRequest class does this work for us, allowing us to deal only with the specific piece(s) of information that we're interested in. Table 16-1 lists the properties, collections, and methods exposed by the HttpRequest class.

Table 16-1. HttpRequest class summary

Properties	Collections	Methods (public instance)
AcceptTypes	Cookies	BinaryRead
ApplicationPath	Files	MapPath
Browser	Form	SaveAs
ClientCertificate	Headers	
ContentEncoding	Params	
ContentLength	QueryString	
ContentType	ServerVariables	
FilePath		
HttpMethod		
InputStream		
IsAuthenticated		
IsSecureConnection		
Path		
PathInfo		
PhysicalApplicationPath		
PhysicalPath		
RawUrl		
RequestType		
TotalBytes		
Url		
UrlReferrer		
UserAgent		
UserHostAddress		
UserHostName		
UserLanguages		
Collections		

Comments/Troubleshooting

In ASP, the Request object provided relatively few properties and methods (one each, in fact), supplying most of the information from requests through its collections: ClientCertificate, Cookies, Form, QueryString, and in particular, the ServerVariables collection. With the exception of ClientCertificate (which now returns an instance of the HttpClientCertificate class representing the client's security certificate settings), all of these collections also exist in ASP.NET. A big difference is that the HttpRequest class exposes a substantial number of new properties (many of which are derived from information that was previously available only through the ServerVariables collection), as well as several new methods.

As was the case with ASP, you can request particular GET or POST values (or ServerVariable or Cookie values, for that matter) by passing the key for the value to the Request object (the current instance of the HttpRequest class):

```
Message.Text = Request("myKey")
```

If the key "myKey" exists in any of the collections that the HttpRequest class exposed, the previous code will return it.

 Although accessing values as shown in the previous example may seem easy, there are two very good reasons not to use this method.

First, accessing values without specifying the collection in which the value should be found requires ASP.NET to search through each collection until it finds the key (if it finds it). While ASP.NET generally performs significantly faster than ASP, there is still no reason to suffer the unnecessary overhead of this method of accessing values.

Second, using the method shown previously makes your code more difficult to understand, debug, and maintain. Someone attempting to understand how your page operates would not be able to figure out from this code whether the page was expected to be accessed via a GET request or a POST request. Explicitly specifying the desired collection clarifies your intent and makes it easier to track down a problem if your code doesn't work.

In this chapter, we'll use the following code listing as the basis for most examples in the chapter. Unless otherwise noted, each example will consist of only the Page_Load event handler for that particular example. Any displayed output messages or return values will be shown as the Text property of the ASP.NET Label control named Message or displayed by calling Response.Write:

```
<%@ Page Language="vb" %>
<html>
    <head>
        <script runat="server">
            Sub Page_Load()
                'Example code will go here
            End Sub
        </script>
    </head>
<body>
    <asp:label id="Message" runat="server"/>
</body>
</html>
```

Properties Reference

AcceptTypes

```
stringArray = Request.AcceptTypes
```

Returns a String array containing the Multipurpose Internet Mail Extension (MIME) types accepted by the client. You can use this property to determine whether a client can accept certain response types, including application types such as Word or Excel, which are supported only by Internet Explorer.

The following table lists some common MIME types:

MIME type	Description
text/html	HTML text content
text/xml	XML text content
image/gif	GIF-encoded image data
image/jpg	JPEG-encoded image data
application/msword	Binary data for Microsoft Word

Parameters

stringArray

A String array that receives the array of accept types from the property.

Example

The code example declares a string array and an integer counter variable and assigns the AcceptTypes property value to the array variable. It then iterates the array members using the counter variable, writing each value to the browser by using the Message label control:

```
Sub Page_Load()
    'Display Accept Types
    Dim MyArray() As String
    Dim I As Integer
    MyArray = Request.AcceptTypes
    For I = 0 To MyArray.GetUpperBound(0)
        Message.Text &= "Type " & CStr(I) & ": " & CStr(MyArray(I)) & _
            "<br/>"
    Next I
End Sub
```

The output of the code would look something like this:

Type 0: image/gif
Type 1: image/x-xbitmap
Type 2: image/jpeg
Type 3: image/pjpeg
Type 4: application/vnd.ms-powerpoint
Type 5: application/vnd.ms-excel
Type 6: application/msword
Type 7: */*

Notes

This property can prevent the server from wasting time sending responses to the client that the client cannot handle. For example, a request that would normally be fulfilled by returning an Excel spreadsheet could be fulfilled with an alternate response type for clients that do not support the Excel MIME type, application/vnd.ms-excel.

ApplicationPath

```
stringvar = Request.ApplicationPath
```

Returns a String containing the path to the virtual root of the current application.

Parameters

`stringvar`

A string variable to receive the value of the ApplicationPath property.

Example

The code example retrieves the ApplicationPath and writes it to the client using the Message label control:

```
Sub Page_Load()
    Message.Text = Request.ApplicationPath
End Sub
```

The output of the code should be the name of the virtual root of the application to which the request was sent.

Browser

```
bc = Request.Browser
```

Returns an instance of the HttpBrowserCapabilities class that describes the capabilities of the client browser. You can then use the class instance to determine what capabilities the client browser supports. The HttpBrowserCapabilities class exposes the capabilities of the client browser as a set of Boolean and String properties. Properties of the HttpBrowserCapabilities class include:

ActiveXControls

A Boolean indicating whether the browser supports ActiveX controls.

AOL

A Boolean indicating whether the browser is an AOL browser.

BackgroundSounds

A Boolean indicating whether the browser supports background sounds.

Beta

A Boolean indicating whether the browser is beta software.

Browser

A String containing the User-Agent header value.

CDF

A Boolean indicating whether the browser supports the Channel Definition Format for pushing content.

ClrVersion

Returns a System.Version object containing version information about the CLR (if any) installed on the client machine (from the User-Agent header). If ClrVersion is not Nothing, you can retrieve version information from four of its Integer properties: Major, Minor, Revision, and Build.

Cookies

A Boolean indicating whether the browser supports cookies.

Crawler

A Boolean indicating whether the browser is a search engine web crawler.

EcmaScriptVersion

Returns an instance of the `Version` class containing information about the version of ECMAScript supported by the client browser. If EcmaScriptVersion is not `Nothing`, you can retrieve version information from four of its Integer properties: Major, Minor, Revision, and Build.

Frames

A Boolean indicating whether the browser supports frames.

Item

A Dictionary interface to values (i.e., `Request.Browser.Item(keyname)`).

JavaApplets

A Boolean indicating whether the browser supports Java applets.

JavaScript

A Boolean indicating whether the browser supports JavaScript.

MajorVersion

An Integer representing the browser major version number (for example, for IE 3.01, the MajorVersion property would return 3).

MinorVersion

A Double representing the browser minor version number (for example, for IE 3.01, the MinorVersion property would return .01).

MSDomVersion

Returns an instance of the `Version` class containing information about the version of the Microsoft XML Document Object Model (DOM) supported by the client browser. If MSDomVersion is not `Nothing`, you can retrieve version information from four of its Integer properties: Major, Minor, Revision, and Build.

Platform

A String containing the platform name (if any) included in the User-Agent header.

Tables

A Boolean indicating whether the browser supports HTML tables.

Type

A String containing the name and major version of the client browser.

VBScript

A Boolean indicating whether the browser supports VBScript.

Version

A String containing both the major and minor version numbers of the client browser.

W3CDomVersion

Returns an instance of the `Version` class containing information about the version of the World Wide Web Consortium (W3C) XML DOM supported by the client browser. If W3CDomVersion is not Nothing, you can retrieve version information from four of its Integer properties: Major, Minor, Revision, and Build.

Win16

A Boolean indicating whether the client is a Win16 machine.

Win32

A Boolean indicating whether the client is a Win32 machine.

Parameters

bc

An Object variable of type HttpBrowserCapabilities.

Example

```
Sub Page_Load()
    Dim bc As HttpBrowserCapabilities
    bc = Request.Browser
    If bc.Cookies Then
        Message.Text = "Cookies are available with this browser"
    Else
        Message.Text = "Cookies are not available with this browser"
    End If
End Sub
```

Notes

You will probably use this property a lot if you plan to support multiple browsers and must provide the highest level of functionality on uplevel browsers such as Internet Explorer 5 or 6 or Netscape 6. For some properties, such as Cookies and JavaScript, the returned Boolean indicates only whether the browser version sending the request supports these features, not whether they are currently enabled in the current user's browser.

This property is especially important when developing custom server controls, since it allows you to have your custom controls automatically tailor their output to a specific browser (or class of browsers). See Chapter 6 for more information on custom control development.

ClientCertificate

```
cs = Request.ClientCertificate
```

Returns an instance of the HttpClientCertificate class, which exposes information about the client security certificate settings. These properties include issuer information, key size, and certificate validity dates.

Parameters

cs

An Object variable of type HttpClientCertificate.

Example

```
Sub Page_Load()
    Dim cs As HttpClientCertificate
```

```
cs = Request.ClientCertificate
Message.Text = "Certificate Issuer is: " & cs.Issuer & "."
End Sub
```

Notes

You will probably use this property in intranet settings, where you have provided a limited set of clients with certificates (issued from your own Certificate Server) for accessing your application, rather than requiring them to authenticate by using a set of credentials entered via the browser. In this case, client certificates are mapped to NT user accounts to provide secure access. Client certificates can also be issued by trusted third parties, but this method is rarely used. If no client certificate is installed on the requesting client, this property returns an HttpClientCertificate instance with no valid property values.

ContentEncoding

```
ce = Request.ContentEncoding
```

Returns an instance of the Encoding class (located in the System.Text namespace), which represents the character encoding of the body of the current request.

Parameters

ce
 An Object variable of type Encoding.

Example

The example demonstrates how to display the current ContentEncoding to the user:

```
Sub Page_Load( )
    Dim ce As System.Text.Encoding
    ce = Request.ContentEncoding
    Message.Text = "Current encoding is: " & ce.EncodingName & "."
End Sub
```

For a request using UTF-8 content encoding, the output of this example would be:

```
Current encoding is: Unicode (UTF-8).
```

ContentLength

```
intvar = Request.ContentLength
```

Returns an integer containing the length, in bytes, of the request sent from the client. This property includes only the content sent in the body of the HTTP request and does not include the length of the HTTP headers or of any data sent as part of an HTTP GET request (which would appear in the headers). If the HTTP request contains no body, its value is 0.

Parameters

intvar
 An Integer variable to receive the length, in bytes, of the content.

Example

This example demonstrates how to display the length of the current request in the browser:

```
Sub Page_Load()
    Dim length As Integer
    length = Request.ContentLength
    Message.Text = "Length of request was: " & length & " bytes."
End Sub
```

The following code can be used to post to the example page:

```
<html>
    <head>
        <title>Submit a named parameter via POST</title>
    </head>
<body>
    <form id="form1" action="ContentLength.aspx" method="POST">
        <h3>Name:</h3>
        <input type="text" name="name">
        <input type="submit">
    </form>
</body>
</html>
```

Notes

You can use this property to test the length of content posted via a POST request before acting on that content. For example, if your page receives files from a file input field, you could check the ContentLength property before saving or processing the uploaded file to prevent users from uploading files greater than a specific size. Note that in cases when you receive multiple form fields, you can get more specific data on the size of an uploaded file by referring to the PostedFile. ContentLength property of an HtmlInputFile control used for submitting files.

ContentType

```
stringvar = Request.ContentType
```

Returns a String containing the MIME type of the current client request. On GET requests, this property may return an empty string.

Parameters

stringvar
> A String variable to receive the content type.

Example

The example shows how you can take different actions in your page, depending on the ContentType of the request:

```
Sub Page_Load()
    Dim ct As String
    ct = Request.ContentType
```

```
If ct = "application/x-www-form-urlencoded" Then
    'Process form input
    Message.Text = "Form data was submitted."
Else
    Message.Text = "Content Type of request is: " & ct
End If
End Sub
```

The following code can be used to post to the example page:

```
<html>
    <head>
        <title>Submit a named parameter via POST</title>
    </head>
<body>
    <form id="form1" action="ContentType.aspx" method="POST">
        <h3>Name:</h3>
        <input type="text" name="name">
        <input type="submit">
    </form>
</body>
</html>
```

Notes

One potential use for this property is to ensure that the content type of the request is what you expect it to be. This can help avoid wasting processor time with invalid requests and prevent malicious users from attempting to forge requests to your application that send unexpected content.

FilePath

```
stringvar = Request.FilePath
```

Returns a String containing the virtual path of the current client request. The virtual path includes the name of the application root folder, any subfolders in the request path, and the requested filename.

Parameters

stringvar
    A String variable to receive the file path.

Example

The example displays the FilePath property to the user.

```
Sub Page_Load()
    Dim fp As String
    fp = Request.FilePath
    Message.Text = "The virtual path of the current request is: _
            & "<strong>" & fp & "</strong>"
End Sub
```

Notes

This property is identical to the Path property listed later in this chapter.

HttpMethod

```
stringvar = Request.HttpMethod
```

Returns a String containing the method (i.e., GET, POST, or HEAD) of the current request.

Parameters

stringvar
    A String variable to receive the HTTP method of the current request.

Example

The example uses the HttpMethod property to determine what action to take for a given request:

```
Sub Page_Load()
    Select Case Request.HttpMethod
        Case "POST"
            Response.Write("POST requests not allowed!<br/>")
            Response.End
        Case "HEAD"
            Response.Write("HEAD requests not allowed!<br/>")
            Response.End
        Case "GET"
            'Process request
            Message.Text = "GET requests are allowed!<br/>"
        Case Else
            Response.Write("Unknown request: not allowed!<br/>")
            Response.End
    End Select
End Sub
```

Note that we use Response.Write to send the message before calling Response. End. Calling Response.End will immediately terminate processing of the page, which will also prevent rendering of any server control output. The code for a page that makes a POST request to the example page is shown here:

```
<html>
    <head>
        <title>Submit a named parameter via POST</title>
    </head>
<body>
    <form id="form1" action="HttpMethod.aspx" method="POST">
        <h3>Name:</h3>
        <input type="text" name="name">
        <input type="submit">
    </form>
</body>
</html>
```

Notes

In classic ASP, the request method was typically retrieved using the REQUEST_METHOD key of the ServerVariables collection. Often, this key was used to create self-submitting form pages by displaying a set of form fields when the GET method was detected and processing the input received from the form fields when the POST method was detected. ASP.NET Web Forms provide built-in plumbing for self-submitting forms. By adding a form with the runat="server" attribute and adding one or more input type server controls to the form, the developer only needs to check the page's IsPostBack property to determine whether a POST or GET request has been received, and execute the desired code based on that property.

InputStream

```
inputstream = Request.InputStream
```

Returns a Stream object containing the body of the incoming HTTP request.

Parameters

inputstream
   An Object variable of type Stream.

Example

The example uses a byte array to search for a specified character and then copies that character and the remaining contents of the stream to a string. The @ Import directive shown in the example should be placed at the top of the page:

```
<% @ Import Namespace="System.IO" %>

Sub Page_Load()
    Dim InStream As Stream
    Dim iCounter, StreamLength, iRead As Integer
    Dim OutString As String
    Dim Found As Boolean

    InStream = Request.InputStream
    StreamLength = CInt(InStream.Length)
    Dim ByteArray(StreamLength) As Byte
    iRead = InStream.Read(ByteArray, 0, StreamLength)
    InStream.Close()

    For iCounter = 0 to StreamLength - 1
        If Found = True Then
            OutString &= Chr(ByteArray(iCounter))
        End If
        If Chr(ByteArray(iCounter)) = "A" Then
            Found = True
            OutString &= Chr(ByteArray(iCounter))
        End If
    Next iCounter

    Message.Text = "Output: " & OutString
End Sub
```

The following code can be used to post to the example page:

```html
<html>
    <head>
    </head>
<body>
    <form id="form1" action="InputStream.aspx" method="POST">
        <h3>Name:</h3>
        <input type="text" name="name">
        <input type="submit">
    </form>
</body>
</html>
```

The code returns as output the first capital A appearing in the request body. Any characters after it are returned to the end of the stream.

Notes

This property is useful if you wish to perform byte-level filtering of the request body. It works only with POST requests, since these requests are the only commonly used HTTP requests that provide a request body.

IsAuthenticated

```
boolvar = Request.IsAuthenticated
```

Returns a Boolean indicating whether the current request is coming from a user who is authenticated. This property refers to authentication against the NTLM account database.

Parameters

boolvar
   A Boolean variable to receive the authentication status of the user.

Example

The example checks to see if the current user is authenticated and it outputs one of two messages, depending on the authentication status of the user. Note that the message delivered to authenticated users utilizes the User property of the page to output the current user's name and domain.

```
Sub Page_Load()
    Dim boolAuth As Boolean

    boolAuth = Request.IsAuthenticated

    If boolAuth Then
        Message.Text = "User " & Page.User.Identity.Name & " is
authenticated."
    Else
        Message.Text = "Current user is not authenticated."
    End If
End Sub
```

In addition to the IsAuthenticated property that the HttpRequest class exposes, the FormsIdentity, WindowsIdentity, and PassportIdentity classes expose an IsAuthenticated property for much the same purpose as the HttpRequest class. Note that the IsAuthenticated property of the HttpRequest class returns the authentication status of the user regardless of the authentication method used.

IsSecureConnection

```
boolvar = Request.IsSecureConnection
```

Returns a Boolean indicating whether the current connection uses secure sockets (SSL) for communication.

Parameters

boolvar
> A Boolean variable to receive the SSL status of the current request.

Example

The example shows how you can take different actions depending on whether or not the current request was made via SSL:

```
Sub Page_Load()
    Dim boolvar As Boolean
    boolvar = Request.IsSecureConnection
    If boolvar = True Then
        Message.Text = "Connection is HTTPS."
    Else
        Message.Text = "Connection is HTTP."
    End If
End Sub
```

Notes

You would typically use this property to determine whether or not to fulfill a request that requires an SSL connection in order to encrypt sensitive data (such as credit card numbers) that might be submitted via the requested page. Additionally, you could use this property on a page that may or may not use SSL to determine how to render output to the page depending on the SSL status. Since encrypting and decrypting content for SSL communication exacts a performance penalty, reducing the number and/or size of graphics used on SSL-enabled pages is generally considered good practice. With this property, you could render more and/or higher-resolution graphics when SSL is not enabled for the request, and render fewer and/or lower-resolution graphics for SSL requests.

HttpRequest Class

Path

```
stringvar = Request.Path
```

Returns a String containing the virtual path of the current client request. The virtual path includes the name of the application root folder, subfolders in the request path, and the requested filename.

Parameters

```
stringvar
```
    A String variable to receive the file path.

Example

The example displays the Path property to the user:

```
Sub Page_Load()
    Dim path As String
    path = Request.FilePath
    Message.Text = "The virtual path of the current request is: " & path
End Sub
```

Notes

This property is identical to the FilePath property listed earlier in this chapter.

PathInfo

```
stringvar = Request.PathInfo
```

Returns a String containing any additional path information (including path information appended to a URL after the filename of the requested resource) passed with the current request.

Parameters

```
stringvar
```
    A String variable to receive the additional path information.

Example

The example writes both the Path and PathInfo properties to the client browser:

```
Sub Page_Load()
    Message.Text = "Path = " & Request.Path & "<br/>"
    Message.Text &= "Additional Path Info = " & Request.PathInfo & "<br/>"
End Sub
```

Notes

PathInfo does not return information such as query string values. PathInfo returns any characters following a forward-slash (/) after the resource (file) name, including the forward-slash itself.

PhysicalApplicationPath

```
stringvar = Request.PhysicalApplicationPath
```

Returns a String containing the physical path to the root of the current application.

Parameters

`stringvar`
> A String variable to receive the application path.

Example

The example writes the PhysicalApplicationPath property to the browser:

```
Sub Page_Load( )
    Dim physAppPath As String
    physAppPath = Request.PhysicalApplicationPath
    Message.Text = "Physical Application Path = " & physAppPath
End Sub
```

Notes

This property is useful when you need to create or write to a file within your web application. Rather than hardcoding a filesystem path in your page, you can use this property in combination with a filename to create or edit a file in the same folder as the page containing the code, regardless of the page's location.

PhysicalPath

```
stringvar = Request.PhysicalPath
```

Returns a String containing the physical path to the requested file.

Parameters

`stringvar`
> A String variable to receive the physical path.

Example

The example writes the PhysicalPath property to the browser:

```
Sub Page_Load( )
    Dim physicalPath As String
    physicalPath = Request.PhysicalPath
    Message.Text = "Physical Path = " & physicalPath
End Sub
```

Notes

Unlike the PhysicalApplicationPath, which returns only the path to the root of the application, the PhysicalPath property returns the full physical path of the requested resource, including any intervening folders and the resource's filename. This property may be useful in combination with ASP.NET's Trace functionality in troubleshooting situations when files you are attempting to write to or read from are not found, or when created files aren't located where you expect them to be.

Adding Trace.Write statements to your page to write the Path, PhysicalApplication-Path, and PhysicalPath properties to the trace log (which you can enable by adding the Trace="true" attribute to the @ Page directive) may help you track down such bugs.

RawUrl

```
stringvar = Request.RawUrl
```

Returns a String containing the raw URL of the current request. The raw URL consists of the portion of the URL following the domain information. Thus, for the URL *http://search.support.microsoft.com/kb/c.asp*, the raw URL is */kb/c.asp*. The raw URL includes the query string, if one is present.

Parameters

stringvar
> A String variable to receive the raw URL.

Example

The example writes the RawUrl property to the browser:

```
Sub Page_Load()
    Dim stringvar As String
    stringvar = Request.RawUrl
    Message.Text = "The raw URL is: " & stringvar
End Sub
```

RequestType

```
stringvar = Request.RequestType
```

The RequestType property returns a String containing the request type (i.e., GET or POST) of the current request.

Parameters

stringvar
> A String variable to receive the request type.

Example

The example writes the RequestType property to the browser:

```
Sub Page_Load()
    Dim stringvar As String
    stringvar = Request.RequestType
    Message.Text = "The request type is: " & stringvar
End Sub
```

Notes

This property is listed as read/write; however, there really aren't any situations where it would be useful to change its value. From the read standpoint, this property returns the same information as the read-only HttpMethod property listed earlier in this chapter. If you attempt to change its value, no corresponding change occurs in the value of HttpMethod.

TotalBytes

```
intvar = Request.TotalBytes
```

Returns an Integer representing the size of the HTTP request body. The Total-Bytes property does not include the size of the HTTP request headers, or the size of query string values passed with a GET request.

Parameters

intvar
> An Integer variable to receive the size, in bytes, of the current request body.

Example

The example writes the TotalBytes property to the browser:

```
Sub Page_Load()
    Dim intvar As Integer
    intvar = Request.TotalBytes
    Message.Text = "The size of the current request body is: <br/>"
    Message.Text &= intvar & " bytes."
End Sub
```

The following code can be used to post to the example page:

```
<html>
    <head>
        <title>Submit a named parameter via POST</title>
    </head>
    <body>
        <form id="form1" action="TotalBytes.aspx" method="POST">
            <h3>Name:</h3>
            <input type="text" name="name">
            <input type="submit">
        </form>
    </body>
</html>
```

Notes

This property's behavior is identical to that of the ContentLength property described earlier in this chapter.

Url

```
uriObj = Request.Url
```

Returns an instance of the Uri class containing properties that describe the current URL requested by the user. Properties exposed by the Uri class include Scheme (protocol), Port, and Host.

Parameters

uriObj

> An Object variable of type Uri.

Example

The example uses the Uri object that the Url property returns to write information about the URL for the current request to the browser:

```
Sub Page_Load( )
    Dim myUri As Uri
    myUri = Request.Url

    Message.Text = "Current request URL info - <br/><br/>"
    Message.Text &= "Protocol: " & myUri.Scheme & "<br/>"
    Message.Text &= "Port: " & myUri.Port & "<br/>"
    Message.Text &= "Host Name: " & myUri.Host & "<br/>"
End Sub
```

Notes

While the Uri class this property returns has methods as well as properties, you're more likely to use these methods (particularly the CheckHostName and Check-SchemeName methods) when creating your own Uri resource from scratch, rather than when receiving the Uri instance from the Url property.

A note on URIs: Uniform Resource Identifier (URI) (compare to Uniform Resource Locator, or URL) is a more general version of URLs and URNs. In most cases today, URI and URL are identical, although this may change as URNs are used more frequently. For the purposes of the Url property, the terms carry the same meaning.

UrlReferrer

```
uriObj = Request.UrlReferrer
```

Returns an instance of the Uri class containing properties that describe the URL for the resource from which the user navigated to the current requested resource. If the user did not navigate to the current resource (i.e., if the current resource is accessed directly), the UrlReferrer property returns Nothing.

Parameters

uriObj

> An Object variable of type Uri.

Example

The example uses the Uri object that the UrlReferrer property returned in order to write information about the URL for the referring resource to the browser:

```
Sub Page_Load( )
    Dim myUri As Uri
    myUri = Request.UrlReferrer

    If Not (myUri Is Nothing) Then
        Message.Text = "Referral URL info - <br/><br/>"
```

```
    Message.Text &= "Protocol: " & myUri.Scheme & "<br/>"
    Message.Text &= "Port: " & myUri.Port & "<br/>"
    Message.Text &= "Host Name: " & myUri.Host & "<br/>"
    Message.Text &= "App Path: " & myUri.AbsolutePath & "<br/>"
Else
    Message.Text = "No referral URL info available."
End If
End Sub
```

The following code can link to the example page:

```
<html>
    <head>
        <title>Link to UrlReferrer</title>
    </head>
<body>
    <a href="UrlReferrer.aspx">Go to UrlReferrer.aspx</a>
</body>
</html>
```

Notes

The example code makes sure that the UrlReferrer property returns a valid instance of the Uri class. The UrlReferrer property returns Nothing if the page is accessed directly, rather than from a link on another page.

UserAgent

```
stringvar = Request.UserAgent
```

Returns a String containing the User-Agent header. The User-Agent string identifies the browser (or other HTTP-capable client software, such as that used on mobile phones, etc.) the client uses to make the request. Depending on the browser and platform, this string may also identify the operating system the client uses, as well as the version of the installed .NET Framework (IE only).

Parameters

stringvar
  A String variable to receive the User-Agent string.

Example

The example writes the UserAgent property to the browser:

```
Sub Page_Load()
    Dim stringvar As String
    stringvar = Request.UserAgent
    Message.Text = "User Agent: " & stringvar
End Sub
```

Notes

When you attempt to discern the capabilities of the client browser, using the properties of the HttpBrowserCapabilities object returned by the Request.Browser property is generally easier. However, there may be cases in which the User-Agent for a given client returns information that is not checked for by the HttpBrowserCapabilities class. In this case, you could add the desired information to the <browserCaps> configuration section handler in *machine.config* (see Chapters 8 and 20 for more information on ASP.NET configuration) and then create your own version of the HttpBrowserCapabilities class by inheriting from the built-in class and adding your own property or properties for the User-Agent attribute you're looking for. Or, if you don't want to make that effort, you could simply parse the User-Agent string for the desired attribute by using the User-Agent property.

UserHostAddress

```
stringvar = Request.UserHostAddress
```

Returns the IP address of the client making the request.

Parameters

stringvar
    A String variable to receive the client IP address.

Example

The example writes the UserHostAddress, UserHostName, and UserLanguages properties to the browser:

```
Sub Page_Load()
    Dim HostAddress, HostName, Languages() As String
    Dim iCounter As Integer

    HostAddress = Request.UserHostAddress
    HostName = Request.UserHostName
    Languages = Request.UserLanguages

    Message.Text = "Client IP Address: " & HostAddress & "<br/>"
    Message.Text &= "Client Machine Name: " & HostName & "<br/>"
    For iCounter = 0 To Languages.GetUpperBound(0)
        Message.Text &= "Client Language " & iCounter & ": " & _
            CStr(Languages(iCounter)) & "<br/>"
    Next iCounter
End Sub
```

UserHostName

Parameters

```
stringvar = Request.UserHostName
```

Returns a string that contains the DNS hostname of the client making the request.

stringvar
    A String variable to receive the hostname.

Example

See the example for the UserHostAddress property.

Notes

If no DNS server is available that can resolve the client IP address to a DNS name, the UserHostName property returns the IP address of the client (just like the UserHostAddress property).

UserLanguages

```
stringArray = Request.UserLanguages
```

Returns a sorted String array containing the list of languages supported by the client.

Parameters

stringArray
A String array variable to receive the list of client-supported languages.

Example

See the example for the UserHostAddress property.

Notes

To test this property, you can set support for additional languages in your browser.

- In Internet Explorer 6, select Internet Options... from the Tools menu. On the General tab of the Internet Options dialog, click the Languages... button. Use the Language Preference dialog to add, remove, or move languages up or down on the list of preferred languages.

- In Netscape Navigator 6, select Preferences... from the Edit menu and then select the Languages node in the lefthand tree view. Use the options on the right to add, remove, or move languages up or down on the list.

Now if you browse a page containing the code in the UserHostAddress example, all languages you select will be listed in the order you chose.

Collections Reference

The Request object in ASP.NET supports seven collections, four of which were supported in ASP (Cookies, Forms, QueryString, and ServerVariables), and three of which are new (Files, Headers, and Params).

The collections of the Request class support the following common set of properties:

AllKeys
Returns a string array of all keys in the collection.

Count
Returns an integer count of name/value pairs in the collection.

Item(Index | Key)

Returns an instance of the collection class based on the index or passed-in key. This is the default property, which is why, for example, calling:

```
Response.Cookies (KeyVal)
```

returns the HttpCookie instance corresponding to *KeyVal*.

Keys

Returns a collection of the keys for the collection.

In addition, each collection class exposes the following methods:

CopyTo(Array, Index)

Copies the contents of the collection object to the provided *Array* argument, starting at the provided *Index* argument. Note that the array must be dimensioned to a sufficient size to contain the collection before calling CopyTo.

GetKey(Index)

Returns a string containing the key corresponding to the provided *Index* argument.

With the exception of the Cookies collection, the code used to access keys and values in the collections the Request class exposes is nearly identical in every case. This similarity makes it simple to create your own reusable classes or methods for manipulating the values from these collections, regardless of which collection you are working with.

Cookies

```
HttpCookieCollection = Request.Cookies
```

The Cookies collection returns an instance of the HttpCookieCollection class containing all cookies sent as a part of the current request. The HttpCookieCollection class contains an instance of the HttpCookie class for each cookie passed as part of the client request. The properties of these HttpCookie instances can be used to access information about the cookie(s).

As in classic ASP, the Cookies collection is still implemented as a collection (in fact, the HttpCookieCollection inherits from the .NET NameObjectCollectionBase class), but rather than a collection of string keys and string values, the ASP.NET implementation is a collection of string keys and objects (instances of the HttpCookie class). Individual cookies are retrieved into variables of type Http-Cookie, providing access to the cookies' values through class properties.

Dictionary-style cookies (cookies with more than one value) are accessible through the Values property of the HttpCookie class, which returns a NameValue-Collection containing the cookie subkeys and values. You can also retrieve individual values by their key with the following syntax:

```
HttpCookie.Values("keyname")
```

Parameters

HttpCookieCollection

An Object variable of type HttpCookieCollection.

Example

The example retrieves the collection of cookies from the Cookies property and writes out the key and value of each, along with any subkeys of dictionary cookies:

```
Sub Page_Load()
    Dim Counter1, Counter2 As Integer
    Dim Keys(), SubKeys() As String
    Dim CookieColl As HttpCookieCollection
    Dim Cookie As HttpCookie

    ' Get Cookie collection
    CookieColl = Request.Cookies

    ' Get Cookie keys
    Keys = CookieColl.AllKeys

    ' Get cookies by index
    For Counter1 = 0 To Keys.GetUpperBound(0)
        Cookie = CookieColl(Keys(Counter1))
        Message.Text = "Cookie: " & Cookie.Name & "<br/>"
        Message.Text &= "Expires: " & Cookie.Expires & "<br/>"

        ' Get keys for dictionary cookie into an array
        SubKeys = Cookie.Values.AllKeys
        ' Write dictionary cookie values to the browser
        For Counter2 = 0 To SubKeys.GetUpperBound(0)
            Message.Text &= "Key " & CStr(Counter2) + ": " & _
                SubKeys(Counter2) & "<br/>"
            Message.Text &= "Value " & CStr(Counter2) + ": " & _
                Cookie.Values(Counter2) & "<br/>"
        Next Counter2
        Message.Text &= "<br/>"
    Next Counter1
End Sub
```

Notes

The ASP implementation of the Cookies collection and the HttpCookieCollection class returned by the Cookies property expose a common set of properties; these properties are described in the "Collections Reference" section.

While it is still possible in ASP.NET to retrieve an individual cookie by its text key as well as its numerical index, the differences in the operation make wholesale migration of ASP cookie-handling code to ASP.NET impractical without significant changes. For example, the following code will raise exceptions:

```
For Each strKey In Request.Cookies
    Response.Write strKey & " = " & Request.Cookies(strKey) & _
                "<br/>"
    If Request.Cookies(strKey).HasKeys Then
        For Each strSubKey In Request.Cookies(strKey)
            Response.Write "->" & strKey & "(" & strSubKey & _
                ") = " & Request.Cookies(strKey)(strSubKey) & "<br/>"
```

```
      Next
    End If
  Next
```

Apart from the fact that this code does not explicitly declare its variables or their types (both of which are required by default in ASP.NET), the previous code fails because the Request.Cookies(*key*) property returns an instance of HttpCookie, rather than a string, and the HttpCookie instance cannot be implicitly converted to a string for the Response.Write statement, which expects a string. Additionally, the call to Request.Cookies(*key*) does not get the subkeys for a dictionary cookie. Fortunately, the modifications necessary to make the previous code work are fairly simple and are shown here:

```
For Each strKey In Request.Cookies
  Message.Text = strKey & " = " & _
    Request.Cookies(strKey).ToString() & "<br/>"
  If Request.Cookies(strKey).HasKeys Then
    For Each strSubKey In Request.Cookies(strKey).Values
      Message.Text = "->" & strKey & "(" & strSubKey & _
        ") = " & Request.Cookies(strKey)(strSubKey).ToString() _
        & "<br/>"
    Next
  End If
Next
```

To solve the first issue, we use the HttpCookie's Value method to get the value of the cookie as a string. The solution to the second issue is to call the Values property of the HttpCookie instance, which allows us to retrieve the subkeys of a dictionary cookie.

Another quirk of the change from the mostly text-based manipulation of cookie keys and values in ASP to class-based manipulation in ASP.NET is that the Expires property of the HttpCookie class is available whether you read or write to a cookie. In ASP, however, attempting to read the Expires property of a cookie would result in an error. Unfortunately, at the time of this writing, the Expires property of HttpCookie does not actually return the expiration of the cookie. Instead, it returns the value 12:00:00 AM, which suggests that despite its readability, the property is not designed to be read from.

Finally, unlike classic ASP, the collections in ASP.NET are zero-based, so the first element in any collection or array is 0, not 1. This is especially important to remember when retrieving values by their index.

Files

```
HttpFileCollection = Request.Files
```

The Files collection, which is new to ASP.NET, returns a collection of type HttpFileCollection that contains any files uploaded by the user's current request. This collection is especially useful in combination with the HtmlInputFile Server Control, which provides the basic plumbing necessary to upload files via an HTTP POST request. When a user submits one or more files (one per HtmlInputFile control on the submitting page), you can retrieve the files by using the Files collection.

Parameters

HttpFileCollection
    An Object variable of type HttpFileCollection.

Example

The example uses two HtmlInputFile server controls and a server-side <script> block to upload files and process them. The example shows both the <form> section of the page and its controls and the <script> block containing the UploadBtn_OnClick method called by the onServerClick event of the HtmlInput-Button control:

```
<!--Place between the <head> and </head> tags -->
<script runat="server">
    Sub UploadBtn_Click(Sender as Object, e as EventArgs)
        UploadForm.Visible = False
        If InStr(Request.ContentType, "multipart/form-data") Then
            Dim Counter1 As Integer
            Dim Keys() As String
            Dim Files As HttpFileCollection

            ' Load File collection
            Files = Request.Files
            ' Get names of all files into an array
            Keys = Files.AllKeys
            For Counter1 = 0 To Keys.GetUpperBound(0)
                Message.Text &= "File ID: " & Keys(Counter1) & "<br/>"
                Message.Text &= "File Name/Path: " & _
                    Files(Counter1).FileName & "<br/>"
            Next Counter1
        Else
            Message.Text = "Wrong content type!"
        End If
    End Sub
</script>

<!-- This section resides between the <body> and </body> tags -->
<form id="UploadForm" enctype="multipart/form-data" runat="server">
    Select File To Upload to Server:
    <br/>
    <%-- MyFile and MyFile2 are HtmlInputFile controls --%>
    <%-- note the runat attribute --%>
    <input id="MyFile" type="file" runat="server">
    <br/>
    <input id="MyFile2" type="file" runat="server">
    <br/>
    <input id="Submit1" type="submit" value="Upload!"
        onserverclick="UploadBtn_Click" runat="server" >
</form>
<asp:label id="Message" runat="server"/>
```

Notes

In classic ASP, file uploading was a painful process that usually involved finding and purchasing a third-party upload control to use on the receiving ASP page to parse and save uploaded files. Thanks to the Files collection, you no longer need to locate and learn how to use third-party controls to upload files. This is bad for the control developers (although we suspect they'll more than make up for the loss by writing new Server Controls), but great for ASP.NET developers.

Two important points to remember about the Files collection to successfully upload files:

- If using a client-side HTML form (no runat="server" attribute), set the method attribute of the form to POST.

- Set the enctype attribute of the form to multipart/form-data.

The upload will succeed only if you take both steps. Note that the code example checks to see if the incoming request is multipart/form-data before attempting to retrieve the files.

It is not necessary to use the HtmlInputFile control to upload files that can be retrieved via the Files collection. As long as the submitting page uses the POST method and the multipart/form-data enctype attribute, you can use the standard HTML file input tags:

```
<input type="file" id="myFile" name="myFile">
```

Note the use of the name attribute, without which the files collection will not contain the uploaded file for the control.

Form

```
NameValueCollection = Request.Form
```

The Form collection returns an instance of the NameValueCollection class containing all form fields passed along with an HTTP POST request. This collection will contain data only when the Content-Type of the HTTP request is either application/x-www-form-urlencoded or multipart/form-data.

The Form collection is one of two ways to retrieve data, depending on the HTTP method used to submit the data. The Form collection retrieves data submitted by an HTML form whose method attribute is set to POST, while the QueryString collection (covered later in this section) retrieves values submitted by HTML forms whose method attribute is set to GET.

Parameters

NameValueCollection
    An Object variable of type NameValueCollection.

Example

The example demonstrates how ASP.NET allows a single page to be used to submit values via HTTP POST and retrieve and display the values to the user. The example uses the IsPostBack property of the Page class to determine whether the request is a result of the form being submitted. If the request is not a postback, the

---

form fields are displayed to allow the user to enter values. If the request is a post-back, the page retrieves the Form collection and displays the name and value of each field in the browser.

```
Sub Page_Load()
    If IsPostBack Then
        Form1.Visible = False
        If Request.HttpMethod = "POST" Then
            Dim Counter1 As Integer
            Dim Keys() As String
            Dim FormElements As NameValueCollection

            ' Get Form keys/elements
            FormElements=Request.Form
            ' Get names of form fields into array
            Keys = FormElements.AllKeys
            For Counter1 = 0 To Keys.GetUpperBound(0)
                Message.Text &= "Form " & Counter1 & " name: " & _
                    Keys(Counter1) & "<br/>"
                Message.Text &= "Form " & Counter1 & " value: " & _
                    FormElements(Counter1) & "<br/>"
            Next Counter1
        End If
    Else
        Form1.Visible = True
    End If
End Sub

<!-- This section resides between the <body> and </body> tags -->
<form id="Form1" runat="server">
    First Name:
    <br/>
    <asp:Textbox id="txtFName" runat="server"/>
    <br/>
    Last Name:
    <br/>
    <asp:Textbox id="txtLName" runat="server"/>
    <br/>
    <asp:Button id="Submit" Text="Submit" runat="server"/>
</form>
<asp:label id="Message" runat="server"/>
```

Notes

The Form collection exposes the same properties and methods described in the "Collections Reference" section and adds the following methods:

Get(Index |Key)

Returns the contents of the specified item in the NameValueCollection as a comma-delimited String.

GetValues(Index |Key)

Returns the contents of the specified item in the NameValueCollection as a String array.

Headers

`NameValueCollection = Request.Headers`

The Headers collection returns an instance of the `NameValueCollection` class containing all HTTP headers sent with the current request. This collection provides the same information that is returned by calling the Request.ServerVariables collection with the `ALL_HTTP` key.

Parameters

`NameValueCollection`
> An Object variable of type NameValueCollection.

Example

The example writes the HTTP headers passed with the request to the browser, first by using the ServerVariables("ALL_HTTP") method and then by using the Headers collection:

```
Sub Page_Load()
    Dim AllHttp As String
    ' Get a String with all the HTTP headers
    AllHttp = Request.ServerVariables("ALL_HTTP")
    ' Use Replace to format the String
    AllHttp = Replace(AllHttp, "HTTP", "<br/>HTTP"
    Message.Text &= AllHttp & "<br/><br/>"

    Dim Counter1, Counter2 As Integer
    Dim Keys(), subKeys() As String
    Dim HeaderColl As NameValueCollection

    ' Load Headers into NameValueCollection
    HeaderColl=Request.Headers
    ' Get keys into an array
    Keys = HeaderColl.AllKeys
    For Counter1 = 0 To Keys.GetUpperBound(0)
        Message.Text &= "Key: " & Keys(Counter1) & "<br/>"
        ' Get all values under this key
        subKeys = HeaderColl.GetValues(Counter1)
        For Counter2 = 0 To subKeys.GetUpperBound(0)
            Message.Text &= "Value " & CStr(Counter2) & ": " & _
                subKeys(Counter2) & "<br/>"
        Next Counter2
    Next Counter1
End Sub
```

Notes

The Headers collection returns only the HTTP headers that were sent as a part of the current request, as opposed to the ServerVariables collection (described later in this section), which contains keys for every HTTP header, regardless of whether a value was passed.

If all you need to do is write the HTTP headers to a file or display them in the browser, it may be simpler to use the ServerVariables collection. In cases when you need to access a specific HTTP header by name or loop through the collection, the Headers collection is the way to go.

Params

```
NameValueCollection = Request.Params
```

The Params collection returns an instance of the `NameValueCollection` class containing key/value pairs for the QueryString, Form, ServerVariables, and Cookies collections. You can use the Params collection to dump all of these collections to a file or to the browser and to troubleshoot an application or track the form values your application receives, regardless of whether they come via GET (QueryString collection) or POST (Form collection).

Parameters

NameValueCollection
> An Object variable of type NameValueCollection.

Example

The example writes the keys and values contained in the Params collection to the browser:

```
Sub Page_Load()
    Dim Counter1, Counter2 As Integer
    Dim Keys(), subKeys() As String
    Dim ParamColl As NameValueCollection

    ' Load Params into NameValueCollection
    ParamColl=Request.Params
    ' Get keys into an array
    Keys = ParamColl.AllKeys
    For Counter1 = 0 To Keys.GetUpperBound(0)
        Message.Text &= "Key: " & Keys(Counter1) & "<br/>"
        ' Get all values under this key
        subKeys = ParamColl.GetValues(Counter1)
        For Counter2 = 0 To subKeys.GetUpperBound(0)
            Message.Text &= "Value " & CStr(Counter2) & ": " & _
                subKeys(Counter2) & "<br/>"
        Next Counter2
        Message.Text &= "<br/>"
    Next Counter1
End Sub
```

The following code can be used to post to the example page:

```
<html>
    <head>
        <title>Submit a named parameter via POST</title>
    </head>
<body>
    <form id="form1" action="Params.aspx" method="POST">
        <h3>Name:</h3>
```

HttpRequest Class

```
        <input type="text" name="name">
        <input type="submit">
    </form>
</body>
</html>
```

Notes

The collections are listed in the following order:

- QueryString
- Form
- Cookies
- ServerVariables

While it is possible to have both the Form and QueryString collections populated (for example, if a query string name/value pair is added to the URL for the action attribute of a form by using the POST method), you will normally see one or the other, not both.

QueryString

```
NameValueCollection = Request.QueryString
```

The QueryString collection returns an instance of the NameValueCollection class containing all the keys and values passed as a part of the query string (typically by submitting an HTML form that uses the GET method instead of POST).

Parameters

NameValueCollection
    An Object variable of type NameValueCollection.

Example

The example writes the contents of the QueryString collection to the browser:

```
Sub Page_Load()
    Dim Counter1, Counter2 As Integer
    Dim Keys(), subKeys() As String
    Dim QSColl As NameValueCollection

    ' Load QS into NameValueCollection
    QSColl=Request.QueryString
    ' Get keys into an array
    Keys = QSColl.AllKeys
    For Counter1 = 0 To Keys.GetUpperBound(0)
        Message.Text &= "Key: " & Keys(Counter1) & "<br/>"
        subKeys = QSColl.GetValues(Counter1) 'Get all values under this key
        For Counter2 = 0 To subKeys.GetUpperBound(0)
            Message.Text &= "Value " & CStr(Counter2) & ": " & _
                subKeys(Counter2) & "<br/>"
        Next Counter2
        Message.Text &= "<br/>"
```

```
    Next Counter1
  End Sub
```

The following code can be used to post to the example page (note that the form method attribute has been set to GET, which is required for the form value to be sent as part of the query string):

```
<html>
  <head>
    <title>Submit a named parameter via POST</title>
  </head>
<body>
    <form id="form1" action="QueryString.aspx" method="GET">
      <h3>Name:</h3>
      <input type="text" name="name">
      <input type="submit">
    </form>
</body>
</html>
```

Notes

One advantage that the QueryString collection has over the Form collection is that you do not always need to have the user submit a form to use it. Because the query string values are appended to the URL, it is relatively simple to statically add query strings to links within pages or dynamically create anchor tags with query string values appended. In fact, many online stores use this method to drive their catalog pages (by passing a product ID appended onto a link to the page designed to display the product). That page can then retrieve the ID by using the QueryString collection.

Because query string values are passed as plain text appended to the URL, they are more vulnerable to tampering than values passed as a result of a POST operation. If you need to pass important data or data that, if tampered with, could create problems for your application, you should consider encrypting values before adding them to the query string or using another method to pass the values.

Certain characters used in query string processing, including &, ?, %, and +, must be encoded to avoid confusion between their use in your key/value pair and their role as special characters in a query string. The following table lists the encoding for each of these special characters:

Character	Encoding
&	%26
?	%3f
%	%25
+	%2b
Space	%20

Rather than memorizing these values, you could make your life easier by simply using the UrlEncode method provided by the HttpServerUtility class (covered in Chapter 18), which automatically substitutes the appropriate encoding for any special characters in a string passed to it.

ServerVariables

```
NameValueCollection = Request.ServerVariables
```

Parameters

NameValueCollection
>   An Object variable of type NameValueCollection.

Example

The example, as in the previous collection-related examples, writes the contents of
the ServerVariables collection to the browser:

```
Sub Page_Load()
    Dim Counter1, Counter2 As Integer
    Dim Keys(), subKeys() As String
    Dim SVarsColl As NameValueCollection

    ' Load ServerVariables into NameValueCollection
    SVarsColl=Request.ServerVariables
    ' Get keys into an array
    Keys = SVarsColl.AllKeys
    For Counter1 = 0 To Keys.GetUpperBound(0)
        Message.Text &= "Key: " & Keys(Counter1) & "<br/>"
        subKeys = SVarsColl.GetValues(Counter1)
        ' Get all values under this key
        For Counter2 = 0 To subKeys.GetUpperBound(0)
            Message.Text &= "Value " & CStr(Counter2) & ": " & _
                subKeys(Counter2) & "<br/>"
        Next Counter2
        Message.Text &= "<br/>"
    Next Counter1
End Sub
```

Notes

In addition to retrieving all the values by looping through the Keys, you can
access individual values if you know their key. The following list shows the available keys for the ServerVariable collection:

ALL_HTTP
>   Returns a string containing all HTTP headers with each header name taking
>   the form HTTP_*headername*, for which *headername* is the name of an HTTP
>   header in all capital letters.

ALL_RAW
>   Provides the same information as ALL_HTTP, but header names are not all
>   capital letters and are not prefixed with HTTP_.

APPL_MD_PATH
>   Returns the path of the application in the IIS metabase.

APPL_PHYSICAL_PATH
>   Returns the physical path that corresponds to APPL_MD_PATH.

AUTH_TYPE

Returns the authentication method used to validate access to protected content.

AUTH_USER

Returns the username of the authenticated user in raw form.

AUTH_PASSWORD

Returns the password entered in the browser's authentication dialog, assuming Basic authentication was used.

LOGON_USER

Returns the name of the Windows account the current user is logged in to.

REMOTE_USER

Returns the username string sent by the browser before any authentication filtering has taken place.

CERT_COOKIE

Returns a unique string identifier for the client certificate.

CERT_FLAGS

Returns bit flags that represent whether a certificate is present (bit0) and whether the certificate authority for the client certificate is in the list of recognized certificate authorities on the server (bit1).

CERT_ISSUER

Returns the issuer of the client certificate.

CERT_KEYSIZE

Returns the number of bits for the SSL key (e.g., 40 or 128).

CERT_SECRETKEYSIZE

Returns the number of bits in the server's private key.

CERT_SERIALNUMBER

Returns the serial number of the client certificate.

CERT_SERVER_ISSUER

Returns the issuer of the server certificate.

CERT_SERVER_SUBJECT

Returns the subject field of the server certificate.

CERT_SUBJECT

Returns the subject field of the client certificate.

CONTENT_LENGTH

Returns the length of the content in the body of the HTTP request.

CONTENT_TYPE

Returns the MIME type of the content in the HTTP request.

GATEWAY_INTERFACE

Returns the revision number of the CGI specification used by the server.

HTTPS

Returns either on or off, depending on whether the request came through a secure socket (HTTPS) connection.

HTTPS_KEYSIZE

Returns the size, in bits, of the SSL key.

HTTPS_SECRETKEYSIZE

Returns the number of bits in the server's private key.

HTTPS_SERVER_ISSUER

Returns the issuer of the server certificate.

HTTPS_SERVER_SUBJECT

Returns the subject field of the server certificate.

INSTANCE_ID

Returns the ID for the IIS instance associated with the request. Unless more than one instance of IIS is running, this value is always 1.

INSTANCE_META_PATH

Returns the metabase path to the instance of IIS that responds to the current request.

LOCAL_ADDR

Returns the server address on which the request was received. Useful for servers with multiple NICs and IP addresses to determine which address received the request.

PATH_INFO

Returns any extra path information passed with the request. See the .PathInfo property earlier in the chapter for more information.

PATH_TRANSLATED

Returns the physical path corresponding to the virtual path for the request.

QUERY_STRING

Returns the raw query string (if any) passed with the request.

REMOTE_ADDR

Returns the IP address of the machine making the request.

REMOTE_HOST

Returns the DNS name of the machine making the request, if available. Otherwise, returns the IP address.

REQUEST_METHOD

Returns the HTTP request method (GET, POST, etc.) used in the request.

SCRIPT_NAME

Returns a virtual path to the page being executed.

SERVER_NAME

Returns the server name, DNS name, or IP address of the server.

SERVER_PORT

Returns the port number on which the request was received.

SERVER_PORT_SECURE

Returns a string containing either 0 or 1, depending on whether the request was received on a secure port (1) or not (0).

SERVER_PROTOCOL

Returns the name and version of the protocol used to handle the client request. For IE 5.5 and IIS 5, this name and version would be "HTTP/1.1".

SERVER_SOFTWARE

Returns the name and version of the web server software.

URL

    Returns the base URL of the request (i.e., everything after the domain name).

HTTP_CONNECTION

    Returns the type of connection established.

HTTP_ACCEPT

    Returns the value of the HTTP Accept header.

HTTP_ACCEPT_ENCODING

    Returns the value of the HTTP Accept-Encoding header.

HTTP_ACCEPT_LANGUAGE

    Returns the value of the HTTP Accept-Language header.

HTTP_HOST

    Returns the value of the HTTP Host header.

HTTP_USER_AGENT

    Returns the value of the HTTP User-Agent header.

Methods Reference

BinaryRead

```
byteArray = Request.BinaryRead(byteCount)
```

Returns a byte array containing the number of bytes specified by the *byteCount* argument.

Parameters

byteArray

    An Array variable of type Byte to receive the specified number of bytes from the method.

byteCount

    An integer specifying the number of bytes to return.

Notes

This method provides backward compatibility with classic ASP applications. For new development, using other means (such as the Files collection, etc.) is preferable to achieve the results that this method was used for.

MapPath

```
stringvar = Request.MapPath(virtualPath)
stringvar = Request.MapPath(virtualPath, _
            baseVirtualDirectory, allowCrossMapping)
```

The MapPath method, which the Server object exposed in classic ASP, allows you to retrieve a physical path on the server for a provided virtual path. In ASP.NET, this method is overloaded, meaning that it can be called with two different sets of arguments, as shown in the previous code. The first style, which is the same as in classic ASP, simply passes in a String containing the virtual path to be mapped.

The second adds the *baseVirtualDirectory* argument, which specifies a base from which to resolve relative paths, and the *allowCrossMapping* argument, which allows you to map virtual paths that belong to other applications.

Parameters

`stringvar`
> A String variable to receive the mapped physical path.

`virtualPath`
> A String argument containing the virtual path to map.

`baseVirtualDirectory`
> A String argument containing a base path to be used for resolving relative paths.

`allowCrossMapping`
> A Boolean argument specifying whether paths can be mapped across applications.

Example

The example maps the path of the .NET Framework SDK samples' */QuickStart* directory and writes the result to the browser:

```
Sub Page_Load()
    Dim VirPath, PhysPath, BasePath As String
    Dim BoolCross As Boolean = True

    VirPath = "/QuickStart"
    BasePath = ""

    Message.Text = Request.MapPath(VirPath, BasePath, BoolCross)
End Sub
```

Notes

In the previous example, if we had set the *BoolCross* variable to `False` and called the example code from outside the QuickStart application, an HttpException would be thrown, since this argument must be set to `True` to map paths across applications.

SaveAs

`Request.SaveAs(filename, includeHeaders)`

Saves the current HTTP request to disk, using the *filename* argument as the path and filename under which to save the request.

Parameters

`filename`
> A String argument containing the path and filename under which the request should be saved.

includeHeaders

A Boolean argument indicating whether to save the HTTP header information as part of the request. Note that unless this is a POST request (or other request type with a request body), no information is saved if this argument is set to False.

Example

The example writes the HTTP request headers to the browser (for comparison purposes) and then saves the current request both with and without header information:

```
Sub Page_Load()
    Message.Text = Request.Headers

    ' Save HTTP Request and Headers to a file
    Request.SaveAs((Request.PhysicalApplicationPath & _
        "HTTPRequest.txt"), True)
    ' Save HTTP Request to a file
    Request.SaveAs((Request.PhysicalApplicationPath & _
        "HTTPRequest_NoHeaders.txt"), False)
End Sub
```

Notes

This method can be very useful when debugging because it allows you to look at all the information sent in a given request (which is particularly useful in POST requests).

HttpRequest
Class

CHAPTER 17

The HttpResponse Class

Just as the HttpRequest class covered in Chapter 16 is the replacement for the classic ASP intrinsic Request object, the HttpResponse class is ASP.NET's replacement for ASP's intrinsic Response object. Like the HttpRequest class, the HttpResponse class instance for a given ASP.NET page is exposed as a property (the Response property) of the Page class (from which all pages are derived), so code for the HttpResponse class is the same as in classic ASP. For those of you with classic ASP applications that migrate to ASP.NET, this class will save you a lot of work.

The HttpResponse class controls a variety of factors related to ASP.NET's response to a given HTTP request and provides access to the output stream of the response, allowing the writing of text or binary content to the client browser programmatically. The HttpResponse class provides access to this functionality through its properties, collections, and methods, which are shown in Table 17-1.

The control over page output that the HttpResponse class provides includes the character set used and encoding of the response, as well as whether the response is buffered and sent all at once (the default) or sent as output is processed. Methods of the HttpResponse class provide granular control over output sent to the browser, including sending binary or text content and sending HTTP headers and cookies to the client.

Note that several properties and methods exposed by the Response object in classic ASP have been deprecated in ASP.NET in favor of new properties and methods exposed by the HttpResponse class (or, in some cases, by other functionality available in ASP.NET). For properties and methods that have been deprecated and/or replaced by new members in ASP.NET, that fact will be notated in the Notes section of the reference for that property or method.

Table 17-1. HttpResponse class summary

Properties	Collections	Methods (instance)
Buffer	Cookies	AddCacheItemDependencies
BufferOutput		AddCacheItemDependency
Cache		AddFileDependencies
CacheControl		AddFileDependency
Charset		AddHeader
ContentEncoding		AppendHeader
ContentType		AppendToLog
Expires		ApplyAppPathModifier
ExpiresAbsolute		BinaryWrite
IsClientConnected		Clear
Output		ClearContent
OutputStream		ClearHeaders
Status		Close
StatusCode		End
StatusDescription		Flush
SuppressContent		Pics
		Redirect
		Write
		WriteFile

Comments/Troubleshooting

The Response object provides control over both the format of the output sent to the browser and the content. In fact, an ASP.NET page can be written with no static HTML content whatsoever, and can generate that content exclusively through calls to the properties and methods of the response object, if desired. This provides the ability to programmatically generate not just HTML output dynamically, but any output the browser is capable of displaying, including image content and XML. This generation allows ASP.NET to be incredibly flexible in its response to user actions.

In classic ASP, the Response object's Write method was often used for quick and dirty debugging, such as to display a message indicating that a certain point in a page was reached or to display the value of variables used within the page. This simple and effective debugging technique had one major flaw: frequently, these calls to Response.Write were left in a page that was moved from a development server to a production server, resulting in end users seeing the debugging message—hardly a desirable outcome. In ASP.NET, the new Trace object (a property of the Page class) provides the ability to write messages to a central trace log rather than to the page itself (although trace output can optionally be directed to the page). This feature allows developers to use the same simple debugging techniques while significantly reducing the likelihood of end users inadvertently seeing debug messages. Tracing in ASP.NET is discussed in Chapter 10.

In this chapter, we'll use the following code listing as the basis for most examples in the chapter. Unless otherwise noted, each example will consist of only the Page_Load event handler for that particular example. Any output messages or return values displayed will be shown as the Text property of the ASP.NET Label control named Message or displayed by calling Response.Write:

```
<%@ Page Language="vb" %>
<html>
    <head>
        <script runat="server">
            Sub Page_Load()
                'Example code will go here
            End Sub
        </script>
    </head>
<body>
    <asp:label id="Message" runat="server"/>
</body>
</html>
```

Properties Reference

Buffer

```
Boolean = Response.Buffer
Response.Buffer = Boolean
```

Returns or sets a Boolean value that represents whether output is buffered on the server and sent when the request has completely finished processing, or when either the Response.Flush or Response.End methods are called. The default value is True.

Parameters

Boolean
    A Boolean that will receive or set the value of the property.

Notes

This property is supplied for backward compatibility with classic ASP and has been deprecated in favor of the BufferOutput property. New ASP.NET code should use BufferOutput in place of Buffer.

One important difference between Response.Buffer property in classic ASP and the Buffer and BufferOutput properties in ASP.NET is that in classic ASP, you could not modify the Buffer property beyond the point at which output had been sent to the browser without causing an error. In ASP.NET, because of its compiled (rather than interpreted) nature, you can modify the Buffer or BufferOutput property at any time, and the change only affects how buffering occurs. This gives developers much more flexibility over how and when their output is buffered. See the Buffer-Output example for a demonstration.

BufferOutput

```
Boolean = Response.BufferOutput
Response.BufferOutput = Boolean
```

Returns or sets a Boolean value that represents whether output is buffered on the server and sent when the request has completely finished processing, or when either the Response.Flush or Response.End methods are called. The default value is True.

Parameters

Boolean

A Boolean that will receive or set the value of the property.

Example

The example sets the BufferOutput property to False and then loops 50 times, writing a period to the HTTP output with each loop iteration. It also writes the same output to the Text property of the Message Label control. For the first 10 and the last 21 iterations, BufferOutput is set to False; for iterations 11 through 29, it is set to True.

```
Sub Page_Load()
    Response.BufferOutput = False
    Dim i As Integer
    For i = 1 To 50
        If (i > 10 And i < 30) Then
            Response.BufferOutput = True
        Else
            Response.BufferOutput = False
        End If
        System.Threading.Thread.Sleep(500)
        Response.Write(".")
        Message.Text &= "."
        'Response.Flush
    Next
    Response.Write("<br/>Done!<br/>")
    Message.Text &= "<br/>Done!<br/>"
End Sub
```

The output of the code would look something like this:

```
............................................... Done! ..............
................................. Done!
```

The first line of periods should appear one by one until ten have appeared, then pause, and then 20 more should appear, followed one by one by the rest and finally by the "Done!" statement. The identical output produced by the ASP.NET Label control (as an HTML <span>) will appear at once, since the output of controls on the server is not sent to the client until the control is rendered. This means that for each loop in the example, the code simply adds to a property of the control that will be rendered at a later time, while the text sent by the call to Response.Write is sent to the browser immediately after buffering is turned off.

You can see similar behavior by commenting out the Response.BufferOutput lines in the example (by prepending a single-quote (') character to the line), and uncommenting the Response.Flush line. This commenting and uncommenting will eliminate the pause in the output described previously.

The call to the Shared (static) Thread.Sleep method allows us to pause processing of an ASP.NET request for a given number of milliseconds. This can be useful when you need to wait during processing for whatever reason. However, using this method can impact the total time each request takes to process. In applications requiring high scalability, this may result in an unacceptable impact on the overall throughput of the application, since only a limited number of threads are available to process requests.

To avoid explicitly providing the namespace name when calling Thread.Sleep, add the following line to the page, immediately following the @ Page declaration:

```
<%@ Import Namespace="System.Threading" %>
```

Notes

This property is the ASP.NET equivalent of classic ASP's Buffer property and is preferred over Buffer for new development.

Cache

```
HttpCachePolicy = Response.Cache
```

Returns an instance of the HttpCachePolicy class that contains the cache policy of the page. You can use the methods exposed by the HttpCachePolicy class with this class instance to examine which headers or parameters (if any) have been set to vary the output cache, or to modify the current cache settings. The HttpCachePolicy class includes the following members:

HttpCachePolicy member	Description
SetCacheability method	Controls caching by setting the HTTP Cache-Control header.
SetExpires method	Sets the HTTP Expires header. This method takes a DateTime argument that represents the absolute expiration time for the header.
SetLastModified method	Sets the HTTP Last-Modified header. This method takes a DateTime argument that represents the absolute expiration time for the header.
Insert method	Inserts an item into the cache and assigns it a key.
Item property	Returns an Object representing a cache item based on its key value or sets an item of data in the cache while assigning it a key value.
Remove method	Removes an item with a particular key value from the cache.

Parameters

HttpCachePolicy
    An Object variable of type HttpCachePolicy.

Example

The example retrieves an instance of the HttpCachePolicy class into a local variable, sets the expiration time to two minutes after the page is processed, and then sets the cacheability of the of the page to Public. Finally, the Text property of the Message label control is set to the current time.

```
Sub Page_Load()
    Dim myCachePol As HttpCachePolicy
    myCachePol = Response.Cache
    myCachePol.SetExpires(DateTime.Now.AddSeconds(120))
    myCachePol.SetCacheability(HttpCacheability.Public)
    Message.Text = Now.ToString()
End Sub
```

The output of the page should be the current date and time. If refreshed, the output should not change until two minutes have elapsed.

Notes

The HttpCachePolicy object returned by this property is the preferred method in ASP.NET for modifying the cache policy for a given page. HttpCachePolicy provides the functionality provided by the classic ASP CacheControl, Expires, and ExpiresAbsolute properties. For example, the HttpCachePolicy class allows you to explicitly prevent the server from caching the response in question, but still allows downstream caching of the response.

You can also set the output caching policies for a page through the @ OutputCache directive and its attributes, although this provides less granular control than that provided by the methods of the HttpCachePolicy class. Caching through the @ OutputCache directive is discussed in Chapter 3.

CacheControl

```
Response.CacheControl = String
```

Sets the cacheability of the current page.

Parameters

String
> A string variable containing the value to set for the CacheControl property. Valid values include "Public" and "Private".

Example

```
Sub Page_Load()
    Response.CacheControl = "Public"
    Response.Expires = 2
    Message.Text = Now.ToString()
End Sub
```

The output of the code above should be identical to the previous example.

Notes

This property has been deprecated in favor of the HttpCacheability class methods.

Charset

```
String = Response.Charset
Response.Charset = String
```

Returns or sets a string representing the character set of the current response. When explicitly set, the value assigned to the Charset property is added to the HTTP Content-Type response header.

Parameters

String
    A string variable to receive or set the value of the property. The default is utf-8.

Example

The example below sets the character set for the HTTP response to Windows-1255 (note that as the name suggests, this character set is only available on Internet Explorer on Windows clients and may cause other browsers or browsers on other operating systems to display the page incorrectly). It then writes the value of the character set to the Text property of the Message label control. To see the difference between this character set and the default utf-8 character set, load the page into Internet Explorer, and comment out the line that sets the Charset property, save the page, and reload it in the browser.

```
Sub Page_Load()
    Response.Charset = "Windows-1255"
    Message.Text = "Current character set is " & Response.Charset
End Sub
```

Notes

Attempting to modify this property after the HTTP headers are sent to the browser results in an HttpException being thrown. This would most likely occur if you disabled output buffering by using the BufferOutput property and then wrote content to the browser by using Response.Write.

If the character set specified by the Charset property is not valid for the browser used by the client, it will be ignored and the default character set for that browser will be used instead. As mentioned above, using the default character set may cause the page to be displayed differently than intended.

ContentEncoding

```
Encoding = Response.ContentEncoding
Response.ContentEncoding = Encoding
```

Returns an instance of the Encoding class representing the encoding of the current response. The Encoding class exposes properties and methods that allow you to

---

examine and modify the system's character encoding—i.e., the way in which characters are stored internally in the system. For example, you can convert a Unicode string to ASCII, UTF-7, or UTF-8.

Parameters

Encoding
> An Object variable of type Encoding. Its EncodingName property provides the human-readable name of the encoding type.

Example

The example uses the properties of the Encoding class instance returned from the ContentEncoding property to display the human-readable name and the registered (IANA) name of the current encoding.

```
Sub Page_Load()
    Message.Text = "Current encoding is " & _
        Response.ContentEncoding.EncodingName & "<br/>"
    Message.Text &= "Current encoding IANA name is " & _
        Response.ContentEncoding.WebName & "<br/>"
End Sub
```

Notes

The ContentEncoding property is new in ASP.NET and provides a richer interface for examining and modifying character set and code page information for the current response. It also provides the only way to convert one character-encoded string to another character encoding (i.e., Unicode to ANSI).

ContentType

```
String = Response.ContentType
Response.ContentType = String
```

Returns or sets a String containing the MIME type of the current response. This allows you to retrieve or set the value of the HTTP Content-Type response header.

Parameters

String
> A string variable to receive or set the content type. The default is "text/html."

Example

The following example displays the current MIME content type in the client browser.

```
Sub Page_Load()
    Message.Text = "Current content type is " & _
        Response.ContentType & "<br/>"
End Sub
```

Notes

The ContentType property is very important, since it enables you to send content to the client browser other than the default HTML. For example, if you want to use the Response.BinaryWrite method to send binary image data to the client browser, you must also set the ContentType property to the appropriate MIME type ("image/jpg" or "image/gif", for example). See the BinaryWrite example for an example of how this is done.

Expires

```
Integer = Response.Expires
Response.Expires = Integer
```

Returns or sets an integer representing the number of minutes before a cached page expires. This property is used in concert with the CacheControl property to control caching of responses.

Parameters

Integer
    An Integer variable to receive or set the expiration in minutes.

Notes

This property is provided for backward compatibility with classic ASP. It has been deprecated in favor of the methods of the HttpCachePolicy instance returned by the Cache property.

ExpiresAbsolute

```
DateTime = Response.Expires
Response.Expires = DateTime
```

Returns or sets a DateTime value representing the date and time at which a cached response should expire.

Parameters

DateTime
    A DateTime variable to receive or set the absolute expiration.

Example

The following example makes the current response cacheable by using the Cache-Control property and then sets the absolute expiration to 30 seconds from the current time.

```
Sub Page_Load()
    Response.CacheControl = "Public"
    Response.ExpiresAbsolute = DateTime.Now.AddSeconds(30)
    Message.Text = Now.ToString()
End Sub
```

Notes

This property is provided for backward compatibility with classic ASP. It has been deprecated in favor of the methods of the HttpCachePolicy instance returned by the Cache property.

IsClientConnected

```
Boolean = Response.IsClientConnected
```

Returns a Boolean indicating whether the client is still connected. Returns False if the client is no longer connected.

Parameters

Boolean
> A Boolean variable to receive the value of the property.

Example

The example checks the IsClientConnected property before starting a long-running processing task in order to avoid the expense of running the task if the client is no longer connected. If the property returns False, the code calls the Response.End method. Even though the client has disconnected and can no longer receive the buffered output (which is sent when the End method is called), calling the End method is still a good idea, since it will halt further processing of the page and fire the Application_EndRequest event. If you have written cleanup code for the page that is run by the event handler for Application_EndRequest, calling Response.End will ensure that the cleanup code is executed, even if the client disconnects.

```
Sub Page_Load()
    'Check client connection status
    If Response.IsClientConnected = False Then
        Response.End
    Else
        'Start long-running processing task
    End If
End Sub
```

Notes

The IsClientConnected property is especially useful for long-running processes that require a significant amount of processing resources on the server. By querying the IsClientConnected property before starting an expensive processing task, or by querying the property periodically during processing, you can bypass further processing if the client has disconnected for some reason.

Output

```
TextWriter = Response.Output
```

Returns a write-only TextWriter object that can be used to write text directly to the output stream of the current response.

Parameters

TextWriter
> An Object variable of type TextWriter. The TextWriter class includes the following members:

Member	Description
Close method	Closes the text writer and releases its resources.
Flush method	Clears the text writer's buffer and writes output to its underlying device.
NewLine property	Gets or sets the new line character(s) used by the TextWriter object.
Write method	Writes data to the text stream.
WriteLine method	Writes data followed by a newline character to the text stream. The NewLine property defines the newline character.

Example

The example declares a local variable of type TextWriter, retrieves an instance of TextWriter from the Output property, and then uses the WriteLine method to write the text "Hello, World!" to the output stream. The WriteLine method writes the specified text (or text representation of nonstring data types), along with a line terminator, specified by setting the NewLine property of the TextWriter. Without setting the NewLine property, the line terminator would affect the formatting of the text sent to the browser. However, it would not alter the formatting of the output as rendered by the browser, since browsers typically ignore whitespace such as non-HTML line terminators when rendering HTML.

```
Sub Page_Load()
    Dim myWriter As System.IO.TextWriter
    myWriter = Response.Output
    myWriter.NewLine = "<br/>"
    myWriter.WriteLine("Hello, World!")
    myWriter.WriteLine("Hello, World, once again!")
End Sub
```

Notes

The Output property provides an alternative to the Response.Write method when outputting text to the output stream. You could also pass the TextWriter instance retrieved from the Output property to a method of a custom component to allow that component to write text directly to the output stream for the current response.

Like the Response.Write method, the result of writing text to the output stream by using the TextWriter returned from the Output property depends on the location of the code that writes the text. For example, in the code above, the text "Hello, World!" will appear before any static HTML in the page output. This is because the output of the TextWriter and the Response.Write method in this case is processed before the controls on the page are rendered. To make the output of the Text-Writer instance or Response.Write appear inline, you could put the code above in a <% %> render block where you want the output to appear. A better approach for locating output in ASP.NET precisely is to add an ASP.NET Literal Server Control at the point in the file where you wish the output to appear and pass the desired output text to the Text property of the Literal control.

To use the TextWriter class without explicitly adding the System.IO namespace to the variable declaration, you can add the @ Import directive directly below the @ Page directive with the namespace attribute set to System.IO, as shown here:

```
<% @ Import Namespace="System.IO" %>
```

OutputStream

```
Stream = Response.OutputStream
```

Returns a write-only Stream object that can be used to write binary content directly to the output stream of the current request.

Parameters

Stream

An Object variable of type Stream. The Stream class includes the following members:

Member	Description
BeginWrite method	Begins an asynchronous write operation.
Close method	Closes the stream and releases its resources.
EndWrite method	Ends an asynchronous write operation.
Write method	Writes data to the stream.
WriteByte method	Writes a single byte to the stream and advances the position within the stream one byte.

Notes

The OutputStream property provides an alternative to the Response.BinaryWrite method when outputting binary content to the output stream is desired. You could also pass the Stream instance retrieved from the OutputStream property to a method of a custom component to allow that component to write binary content directly to the output stream for the current response.

Status

```
String = Response.Status
Response.Status = String
```

Returns or sets a String that contains the HTTP status line that will be sent to the client browser.

Parameters

String

A String variable to set or receive the status code of the current request. The default is "200 OK."

Notes

This property is provided for backward compatibility with classic ASP and has been deprecated in ASP.NET in favor of the StatusDescription property. Unlike the Status property, the StatusCode and StatusDescription properties allow you to control the numeric status code portion of the status line and the text description individually.

StatusCode

```
Integer = Response.StatusCode
Response.StatusCode = Integer
```

Returns or sets an Integer that represents the HTTP status code that will be returned to the browser.

Parameters

Integer

> An integer variable to set or receive the status code. The default is 200. The possible status codes fall into the following ranges:

> *1xx*
>> The 100 range is for informational messages.

> *2xx*
>> The 200 range is for success messages.

> *3xx*
>> The 300 range is for redirection messages. The specific status code indicates whether a page has been moved temporarily or permanently.

> *4xx*
>> The 400 range is for client error messages. The best-known message is the 404 Not Found message, which indicates that the client has asked for a resource that does not exist on the server. This range also includes status error messages related to client authentication.

> *5xx*
>> The 500 range is for server error messages. For example, if more requests are received by IIS then can be processed or queued for later processing, clients will receive a 500-series status code with the "Server Too Busy" message.

Example

The example uses the StatusCode and StatusDescription properties to send an HTTP status message to the client. The Response.End method halts further processing and sends the currently buffered output to the client.

```
Sub Page_Load()
    Response.StatusCode = 542
    Response.StatusDescription = "Server Error - The code is the answer."
    Response.End()
End Sub
```

Notes

As with other properties that set HTTP response headers, this property cannot be set once HTTP body output is sent to the client using Response.Write or similar methods when buffering has been turned off.

StatusDescription

```
String = Response.StatusDescription
Response.StatusDescription = String
```

Returns or sets a String containing the text HTTP status message that will be sent to the browser along with the status code contained in the StatusCode property.

Parameters

String
    A string variable to set or receive the additional path information. The default is "OK."

Example

See the example for the StatusCode property.

Notes

As with other properties that set HTTP response headers, this property cannot be set once HTTP body output has been sent to the client (using Response.Write or similar methods) when buffering has been turned off.

SuppressContent

```
Boolean = Response.SuppressContent
Response.SuppressContent = Boolean
```

Returns or sets a Boolean indicating whether HTTP output should be sent to the client.

Parameters

Boolean
    A Boolean variable to receive or set the value of the property. The default is False; content is sent to the client.

Example

The following example writes the text "Hello, World!" to the output (which is buffered by default) and sets SuppressContent to True so that no output is sent to the client.

```
Sub Page_Load()
    Response.Write("Hello, World!")
    Response.SuppressContent = True
    If Response.SuppressContent Then Response.Close()
End Sub
```

Notes

Since SuppressContent prevents any output from being returned to the client (including any error messages), the Response.Close method (which closes the network connection to the client) must be called to prevent the client browser from hanging indefinitely.

Collections Reference

The Response object in ASP.NET supports only a single collection, the Cookies collection.

Cookies

```
HttpCookieCollection = Response.Cookies
```

The Cookies collection returns an instance of the `HttpCookieCollection` class containing all cookies sent as a part of the current request. The `HttpCookieCollection` class contains an instance of the `HttpCookie` class for each cookie passed as part of the client request. The properties of these HttpCookie instances can be used to access information about the cookie(s). The Cookies collection of the `Response` class supports the following set of properties:

AllKeys
> Returns a string array of all keys in the collection.

Count
> Returns an integer count of the number of name/value pairs in the collection.

Item(Index|Key)
> Returns an instance of the collection class based on the index or passed-in key. This is the default property, which is why calling:
>
> ```
> Response.Cookies (KeyVal)
> ```
>
> returns the HttpCookie instance corresponding to *KeyVal*.

Keys
> Returns a collection of the keys for the collection.

In addition, the `HttpCookieCollection` class exposes the following methods:

CopyTo(Array, Index)
> Copies the contents of the collection object to the provided *Array* argument, starting at the provided *Index* argument. Note that the array must be dimensioned to a sufficient size to contain the collection before calling CopyTo.

GetKey(Index)
> Returns a string containing the key corresponding to the provided *Index* argument.

As in classic ASP, the Cookies collection is still implemented as a collection (in fact, the `HttpCookieCollection` class inherits from the .NET `NameObjectCollectionBase` class), but rather than a collection of string keys and string values, the ASP.NET implementation is a collection of string keys and objects (instances of the `HttpCookie` class). Individual cookies are retrieved into variables of type Http-Cookie, providing access to the cookies values through class properties.

Dictionary-style cookies (cookies with more than one value) are accessible through the Values property of the `HttpCookie` class, which returns a NameValue-Collection containing the cookie subkeys and values. You can also set individual values by their key with the following syntax:

```
HttpCookie.Values("keyname") = "value"
```

Parameters

HttpCookieCollection
　　An Object variable of type HttpCookieCollection.

Example

The example creates a login cookie, sets the expiration of the cookie for 30 minutes from the current time, and adds the cookie to the Cookies collection.

```
Sub Page_Load()
    Dim myCookie As New HttpCookie("LoggedIn")
    myCookie.Value = "True"
    myCookie.Expires = DateTime.Now.AddMinutes(30)
    Response.Cookies.Add(myCookie)
End Sub
```

Notes

Unlike classic ASP, the collections in ASP.NET are zero-based, so the first element in any collection or array will be 0, not 1. This is especially important to remember when retrieving values by their index.

Methods Reference

AddCacheItemDependencies

```
Response.AddCacheItemDependencies(ByVal cacheKeys As ArrayList)
```

Adds a list of cache keys contained in an ArrayList to the list of Cache item keys upon which the output cache of the current response depends. If one of the cache items identified by the keys is modified, the output cache of the current response will be invalidated and a fresh response will be generated.

Parameters

cacheKeys
　　An ArrayList containing one or more Cache item key names.

Example

The example shows how you can use the AddCacheItemDependencies method to set a number of cache keys as dependencies for the output cache of the current response. If any of the cache items represented by these keys is modified, the output cache is invalidated and the page is refreshed by using Response.Redirect.

```
<%@ Page Language="vb" %>
<%@ OutputCache Duration="300" VaryByParam="None" %>
<html>
    <head>
        <title>Adding cache dependencies in ASP.NET</title>
        <script runat="server">
            Sub Page_Load()
                Dim myArrayList As New ArrayList
                myArrayList.Add("Key1")
                myArrayList.Add("Key2")
```

```
              Response.AddCacheItemDependencies(myArrayList)
              Message.Text = DateTime.Now.ToString()
          End Sub
          Sub Button1_Click(sender As Object, e As EventArgs)
              Cache("Key1") = "foo" & DateTime.Now.ToString()
              Response.Redirect("AddCacheItemDependencies.aspx")
          End Sub
          Sub Button2_Click(sender As Object, e As EventArgs)
              Cache("Key2") = "bar" & DateTime.Now.ToString()
              Response.Redirect("AddCacheItemDependencies.aspx")
          End Sub
      </script>
    </head>
<body>
    <form runat="server">
        <asp:label id="Message" runat="server"/>
        <asp:button id="Button1" text="Change Key 1"
           onClick="Button1_Click" runat="server"/>
        <asp:button id="Button2" text="Change Key 2"
           onClick="Button2_Click" runat="server"/>
    </form>
</body>
</html>
```

Notes

The AddCacheItemDependencies method is useful when you want to output cache a page, but the page depends on the value of several items stored in the ASP.NET cache. Rather than caching the page with a very short duration to avoid stale data, you can use AddCacheItemDependencies to automatically invalidate the output cache when the dependencies change.

AddCacheItemDependency

```
Response.AddCacheItemDependency(ByVal cacheKey As String)
```

Adds a cache item key to the list of cache keys upon which the output cache of the current response depends. If the cache item identified by the key is modified, the output cache of the current response will be invalidated and a fresh response will be generated.

Parameters

cacheKey
    A String containing the cache item key to add.

Example

The example shows how you can use the AddCacheItemDependency method to set a cache key as a dependency for the output cache of the current response. If the cache item represented by this key is modified, the output cache is invalidated and the page is refreshed by using Response.Redirect.

```
<%@ Page Language="vb" %>
<%@ OutputCache Duration="300" VaryByParam="None" %>
<html>
    <head>
        <title>Adding a cache dependency in ASP.NET</title>
        <script runat="server">
            Sub Page_Load()
                Response.AddCacheItemDependency("Key1")
                Message.Text = DateTime.Now.ToString()
            End Sub
            Sub Button1_Click(sender As Object, e As EventArgs)
                Cache("Key1") = "foo" & DateTime.Now.ToString()
                Response.Redirect("AddCacheItemDependency.aspx")
            End Sub
        </script>
    </head>
<body>
    <form runat="server">
        <asp:label id="Message" runat="server"/>
        <asp:button id="Button1" text="Change Key 1" onClick="Button1_
Click"            runat="server"/>
    </form>
</body>
</html>
```

Notes

The AddCacheItemDependency method provides the same functionality as the AddCacheItemDependencies method, but for a single cache item rather than multiple items.

AddFileDependencies

```
Response.AddFileDependencies(ByVal filenames As ArrayList)
```

Adds a list of files contained in an ArrayList to the list of files upon which the output cache of the current request depends. If any of these files is modified, the output cache is invalidated.

Parameters

filenames
    An ArrayList containing one or more path/filenames.

Example

The example shows how you can use the AddFileDependencies method to set a number of files as dependencies for the output cache of the current response. If any of these files is modified, the output cache is invalidated.

```
<%@ Page Language="vb" %>
<%@ OutputCache Duration="300" VaryByParam="None" %>
<html>
    <head>
        <title>Adding file dependencies in ASP.NET</title>
```

```
<script runat="server">
    Sub Page_Load()
        Dim myArrayList As New ArrayList
        myArrayList.Add(Server.MapPath("dep.txt"))
        myArrayList.Add(Server.MapPath("dep1.txt"))
        Response.AddFileDependencies(myArrayList)
        Message.Text = DateTime.Now.ToString()
    End Sub
</script>
    </head>
<body>
    <asp:label id="Message" runat="server"/>
</body>
</html>
```

Notes

The AddFileDependencies method is useful when you want to output cache a page, but the page depends on the value of several files on the web server (which can be accessed by a file path from the web server). Rather than caching the page with a very short duration to avoid stale data, you can use AddFileDependencies to automatically invalidate the output cache when the dependencies change.

AddFileDependency

```
Response.AddFileDependency(ByVal filename As String)
```

Adds a file to the list of files upon which the output cache of the current request depends. If the named by the filename argument is modified, the output cache is invalidated.

Parameters

filename
    A String containing the path and filename to add.

Example

The example below shows how you can use the AddFileDependency method to set a file as a dependency for the output cache of the current response. If the file is modified, the output cache is invalidated.

```
<%@ Page Language="vb" %>
<%@ OutputCache Duration="300" VaryByParam="None" %>
<html>
    <head>
        <title>Adding a file dependency in ASP.NET</title>
        <script runat="server">
            Sub Page_Load()
                Response.AddFileDependency(Server.MapPath("dep.txt"))
                Message.Text = DateTime.Now.ToString()
            End Sub
        </script>
    </head>
<body>
```

```
        <asp:label id="Message" runat="server"/>
    </body>
</html>
```

The *dep.txt* file named in the code above should reside in the same directory as the page. The contents of the page can be whatever you choose. If the file content is changed, the cache will be invalidated.

Notes

The AddFileDependency method provides the same functionality as the AddFile-Dependencies method, but for a single file rather than multiple files.

AddHeader

```
Response.AddHeader(ByVal name As String, ByVal value As String)
```

Adds an HTTP header with the specified name and value to the output stream.

Parameters

name
> A String argument containing the name for the header.

value
> A String argument containing the value for the header.

Notes

The AddHeader property provides for backward compatibility with classic ASP. This property has been deprecated in favor of the new AppendHeader method.

AppendHeader

```
Response.AppendHeader(ByVal name As String, _
                      ByVal value As String)
```

Adds an HTTP header with the specified name and value to the output stream. This method can be used to add custom HTTP headers or to modify the value of standard HTTP headers.

Parameters

name
> A String argument containing the name for the header.

value
> A String argument containing the value for the header.

Example

The example sets the HTTP Content-Type header to "text/xml" and then displays the new value by setting the Text property of the Message Label control to the value of the ContentType property. This causes the page output to be treated as XML.

```
Sub Page_Load()
```

```
Response.AppendHeader("Content-Type", "text/xml")
Message.Text = Response.ContentType
End Sub
```

Notes

When using this method with HTTP headers related to caching policy, if more restrictive settings are applied through the use of the ASP.NET cache APIs, the more restrictive settings will take priority over the settings applied using AppendHeader.

AppendToLog

```
Response.AppendToLog(ByVal param As String)
```

Appends the text specified by the *param* argument to the IIS log file for the current IIS application.

Parameters

param
> A String argument containing the text to be appended to the IIS log.

Example

The following example writes a message to the IIS log for the application the page is a part of, and then writes a message to the ASP.NET Message label control indicating that the message was written:

```
Sub Page_Load()
    Response.AppendToLog("Hello from Page_Load!")
    Message.Text = "Message written to IIS Log!"
End Sub
```

The IIS log entry generated by the example above looks similar to the following:

```
2001-10-14 00:13:14 127.0.0.1 - 127.0.0.1 80 GET
/ASPdotNET_iaN/Chapter_17/AppendToLog.aspx
Hello+from+Page_Load! 200 BrowserString
```

Notes

Unlike the AppendToLog method in classic ASP, which had a limit of 80 characters per call, you can write as much text as you wish to the log by using AppendToLog in ASP.NET. The IIS Log files are located by default in *%windir%*\System32\LogFiles\ W3SVC*x*\ex*date*.log, where *%windir%* is the name of the Windows directory, *x* is the number of the Web site for the log (this is the IIS Metabase name for the desired application), and *date* is the creation date of the log file.

ApplyAppPathModifier

```
String = Response.ApplyAppPathModifier(ByVal virtualPath _
                                      As String)
```

Given a virtual path to a resource, returns a string containing a new virtual path containing the SessionID. This new virtual path can be used to create absolute URLs for use in applications that use cookieless Sessions.

Parameters

`String`

A String argument that will receive the modified virtual path.

`virtualPath`

A String argument containing the virtual path to be modified.

Example

The following example retrieves a virtual path including the SessionID and displays the path by using the Text property of the Message label control:

```
Sub Page_Load()
    Dim NewPath As String
    NewPath = Response.ApplyAppPathModifier(Request.Path)
    Message.Text = "Modified virtual path = " & NewPath
End Sub
```

The *web.config* file to set the Session state handler to use cookieless Sessions is shown below:

```
<configuration>
    <system.web>
        <sessionState mode="InProc" cookieless="true"/>
    </system.web>
</configuration>
```

Notes

This method is very useful when making use of the cookieless Session state functionality introduced by ASP.NET. If the cookieless attribute of the `sessionState` config section in *web.config* is not set to `True`, this method will simply return the virtual path passed in without modification.

BinaryWrite

```
Response.BinaryWrite(ByVal buffer() As Byte)
```

Allows writing of binary content to the output stream. No modification of the output is performed before sending the binary content to the client.

Parameters

`buffer()`

A Byte array containing the binary data to be written to the output stream.

Example

Here is an example of BinaryWrite:

```
Sub Page_Load()
    Dim ImageStream As New FileStream(MapPath("aspnetian.jpg"), _
        FileMode.Open, FileAccess.Read)
    Dim ImageBytes(ImageStream.Length) As Byte
    ImageStream.Read(ImageBytes, 0, ImageStream.Length)
    ImageStream.Close()
    Response.ContentType = "image/bmp"
    Response.BinaryWrite(ImageBytes)
    Response.End()
End Sub
```

Notes

This method is especially useful for writing binary content retrieved from a database to the browser. When writing image or other nontext data to the browser, you should set the Response.ContentType property to the appropriate MIME type for the image type being sent (such as "image/jpg").

Clear

```
Response.Clear()
```

Clears the content of the current output stream.

Parameters

None

Notes

The Clear method clears all currently buffered output, but does not clear the HTTP response headers. If buffering of output is disabled by setting the BufferOutput property to False, this method will not have any effect, since it only clears buffered content. This behavior is different from classic ASP, in which calling Clear when buffering is disabled results in an error.

ClearContent

```
Response.ClearContent()
```

Clears the content of the current output stream.

Parameters

None

Example

The example writes a text message using Response.Write and then clears the buffered output by calling Response.Clear. If buffering is on, the text message will never be sent to the browser.

```
Sub Page_Load()
    Response.Write("This content will not be seen.")
    Response.Clear()
    Message.Text = _
        "Content written with <i>Response.Write</i> was cleared."
End Sub
```

Notes

The ClearContent method clears all currently buffered output, but does not clear the HTTP response headers. HTTP headers can be cleared by calling the ClearHeaders method. If buffering of output has been disabled by setting the BufferOutput property to `False`, the ClearContent method will not have any effect, since it only clears buffered content.

ClearHeaders

```
Response.ClearHeaders()
```

Clears the HTTP headers from the current output stream.

Parameters

None

Example

The example sets the HTTP Content-Type header to "text/xml", clears the HTTP headers by calling the ClearHeaders method, and then writes the value of the Response.ContentType property to the Text property of the Message ASP.NET Label control. The displayed Content-Type is the default of "text/html".

```
Sub Page_Load()
    Response.AppendHeader("Content-Type", "text/xml")
    Response.ClearHeaders()
    Message.Text = Response.ContentType
End Sub
```

Notes

The ClearHeaders method clears only the HTTP response headers, not the buffered content.

Close

```
Response.Close()
```

Closes the network socket for the current response.

Parameters

None

Example

See the example for the SuppressContent property.

Notes

The Close method can be used to immediately close the network socket for the current response. This closure will typically result in a browser error (such as "Cannot find server") being displayed to the client.

End

```
Response.End( )
```

Stops processing the current request and sends all buffered content to the client immediately.

Parameters

None

Example

The example below writes the text "Hello, World!" to the browser, calls Response. End, and then attempts to set the Text property of the Message ASP.NET Label control to "Hello, World!" However, that code will not be executed, as the End method immediately halts execution of page processing.

```
Sub Page_Load( )
    Response.Write("Hello, World!")
    Response.End( )
    Message.Text = "Hello, World!"
End Sub
```

In fact, the code above will result in only the "Hello, World!" text being output to the browser, as even the rendering of the static HTML and controls in the page will not occur.

Notes

When the End method is called, in addition to sending buffered output to the client and terminating processing, the Application_EndRequest event is fired.

Flush

```
Response.Flush( )
```

Immediately sends all buffered output to the client.

Parameters

None

Example

See the example for the BufferOutput property. If you comment out the lines that set BufferOutput to False and then uncomment the line that calls Response.Flush, you will see that the Flush method allows you to explicitly send buffered content to the browser.

Notes

Since buffering is on by default in ASP.NET, the Flush method becomes especially useful. Rather than turning off buffering, which results in any content sent from a Response.Write call being sent immediately to the browser, you can use Response. Flush to send content in discrete chunks or to ensure that an entire operation completes before sending the currently buffered content.

You can also combine calls to Response.Flush with calls to Response.Clear to allow you to perform preverification on content before it is sent to the browser. If a given set of calculations or output encounters an error, you can call Response. Clear to clear the problematic output and then replace it with an error message or with other replacement content. If there are no problems with the output, you can call Response.Flush to send the buffered output to the browser and then continue processing.

Pics

```
Response.Pics(ByVal value As String)
```

Adds a PICS-Label header to the output stream for the current response. The Platform for Internet Content Selection (PICS) is used to rate Internet content based on violence, sexual content, language, and nudity.

Parameters

value
 A String argument containing the text for the PICS-Label header.

Example

The following example sets a PICS header that specifies RSAC as the rating organization, sets the rating effective period from 8/1/2001 to 2/28/2002, and sets the ratings as follows:

- Violence - 1

- Sexual content - 2

- Adult Language - 3

- Nudity - 4

```
Sub Page_Load()
    Dim PICSLabel As String
    PICSLabel &= "(PICS-1.1 <http://www.rsac.org/ratingsv01.html> "
    PICSLabel &= "labels on " & Chr(34)
    PICSLabel &= "2001.08.01T06:00-0000" & Chr(34)
    PICSLabel &= " until " & Chr(34)
    PICSLabel &= "2002.02.28T23:59-0000" & Chr(34)
    PICSLabel &= " ratings (V 1 S 2 L 3 N 4))"
    Response.PICS(PICSLabel)
    Message.Text = PICSLabel
End Sub
```

Notes

The PICS-Label header is used for rating the content of a site. Users can configure their browsers to disallow viewing of sites that send PICS-Label headers, and whose ratings state that the site contains a higher level of content in one of the rated categories than the browser is configured to allow. Additional information on the PICS standard for content ratings is available at the World Wide Web Consortium web site at *http://www.w3c.org.*

Redirect

```
Response.Redirect(ByVal url As String)
Response.Redirect(ByVal url As String, _)
                  ByVal endResponse As Boolean)
```

Redirects the currently executing page to another page specified by the URL argument, optionally terminating the processing of the current page.

Parameters

url

A String argument containing the URL for the page to redirect to.

endResponse

A Boolean argument indicating whether to terminate processing of the current page. If the argument is omitted, the method call causes processing of the current page to be discontinued.

Example

The example redirects the current request to *BufferOutput.aspx* and directs ASP.NET to discontinue processing of the current page:

```
Sub Page_Load( )
    Response.Redirect("BufferOutput.aspx", True)
End Sub
```

Notes

Unless additional processing needs to be done in the page from which you call Response.Redirect, you should always pass True as the second argument to Response.Redirect to prevent server resources from being wasted by continuing to process the current page. This feature is new for ASP.NET. When calling Response.Redirect with only the *url* argument, processing of the current page is discontinued automatically.

Note that when redirecting to a page such as *BufferOutput.aspx* in which buffering is turned off, or to a page that calls Response.Flush, the redirect will not complete until the target page has completed processing. This means that all content on the target page will be seen at once, rather than as it is rendered or flushed from the buffer.

Write

```
Response.Write(ByVal ch As Char)
Response.Write(ByVal obj As Object)
Response.Write(ByVal s As String)
Response.Write(ByVal buffer() As Char, ByVal index As Integer, _
    ByVal count As Integer)
```

Allows writing of arbitrary content to the output stream. Content may be character data, an Object (using the object's ToString() method), or String data.

Parameters

ch

A Char argument containing a character to write to the output stream.

obj

An Object argument containing an object whose string representation will be written to the output stream.

s

A String argument containing text to write to the output stream.

buffer()

A Char array argument containing the characters to write to the output stream.

index

An Integer argument containing the starting point in the Char array from which to being writing.

count

An Integer argument containing the number of characters to write.

Example

The example creates an array of Chars, sets the values of the Chars, and then loops through the array and displays its contents by calling Response.Write:

```
Sub Page_Load()
    Dim MyChars(2) As Char
    Dim MyChar As Char
    MyChars(0) = CChar("A")
    MyChars(1) = CChar("B")
    MyChars(2) = CChar("C")
    For Each MyChar in MyChars
        Response.Write(MyChar)
    Next
End Sub
```

Notes

As shown above, the Write method in ASP.NET gains a number of new over-loaded implementations. The above code could also be written by using another overloaded implementation that accepts an array of Chars, a starting index, and the count of Chars to write, as follows:

```
Response.Write(MyChars, 0, 3)
```

The implementation of the Write method that takes an Object as an argument takes advantage of the built-in ToString method of the object class to display the string representation of the object. ToString is inherited by every .NET class and, by default, returns the namespace and class name of the object's class. Classes that wish to send other information about themselves can override the inherited implementation of ToString to send this information.

WriteFile

```
Response.WriteFile(ByVal fileName As String)
Response.WriteFile(ByVal fileName As String, _
    ByVal includeHeaders As Boolean)
Response.WriteFile(ByVal fileHandle As IntPtr, _
    ByVal offset As Long, ByVal size As Long)
Response.WriteFile(ByVal fileName As String, _
    ByVal offset As Long, ByVal size As Long)
```

Writes a file specified in one of the overloaded arguments to the output stream.

Parameters

fileName

A String argument containing the path and filename of the file whose content should be written to the output stream.

includeHeaders

A Boolean argument indicating whether the contents of the file should be written to a memory block.

fileHandle

An Argument of type IntPtr containing a handle to a file. You can get the handle by creating a new FileStream object from the file and then querying the FileStream's Handle property.

offset

An Argument of type Long containing the byte position in the file from which writing should start.

size

An Argument of type Long containing the number of bytes that should be written to the output stream.

Example

The example writes the contents of the file dep.txt to the output stream of the current response.

```
Sub Page_Load()
    Response.WriteFile("dep.txt")
End Sub
```

Notes

The WriteFile method can be used in a variety of ways to output text content directly from a file. Attempts to write other content types (such as image data) will fail.

CHAPTER 18

The HttpServerUtility Class

The HttpServerUtility class is ASP.NET's replacement for ASP's intrinsic Server object. Because the Server property of the Page class (from which all pages are derived) exposes the HttpServerUtility class instance for a given ASP.NET page, you can code to the HttpServerUtility class as you did in the Server object in classic ASP, meaning that your existing ASP code is much easier to migrate.

The HttpServerUtility class performs utility functions such as encoding and decoding strings for use in URLs or for plain-text display of content that may contain HTML markup tags. The HttpServerUtility class also provides access to limited error information and provides methods (Execute, Transfer) for modifying the execution of the current request. Table 18-1 lists the properties and methods exposed by the HttpServerUtility class.

Table 18-1. HttpServerUtility class summary

Properties	Collections	Methods (public instance)
MachineName	None	ClearError
ScriptTimeout		CreateObject
		CreateObjectFromClsid
		Execute
		GetLastError
		HtmlDecode
		HtmlEncode
		MapPath
		Transfer
		UrlDecode
		UrlEncode
		UrlPathEncode

Comments/Troubleshooting

In classic ASP, the Server object was used to create COM component instances by using the Server.CreateObject method. CreateObject still exists in ASP.NET, along with a new method, CreateObjectFromClsid, which uses a COM class ID (CLSID) instead of a ProgID to locate the object to create. You should use both methods only when necessary, since even though the details are handled for you, using these methods incurs the cost of interoperating between COM and .NET (unmanaged and managed) code. If there is a .NET alternative to using a COM object, you will get better performance by sticking with the .NET solution.

The ASP.NET version of the Server object also adds a number of useful new utility functions, including HtmlDecode, UrlDecode, and UrlPathEncode. HtmlDecode and UrlDecode are particularly welcome, given that classic ASP developers were stuck either manually implementing functionality to remove URL or HTML encoding from strings that they'd encoded on another page or relying on third party components or scripts to do so. Now this functionality is built in.

In this chapter, we'll use the following code listing as the basis for most examples in the chapter. Unless otherwise noted, each example will consist of the Page_ Load event handler for that particular example. Any output messages or return values displayed are shown as the Text property of the ASP.NET Label named Message, or displayed by calling Response.Write.

```
<%@ Page Language="vb" %>
<html>
    <head>
        <script runat="server">
            Sub Page_Load()
                'Example code will go here
            End Sub
        </script>
    </head>
<body>
    <asp:label id="Message" runat="server"/>
</body>
</html>
```

Properties Reference

MachineName

```
stringvar = Server.MachineName
```

Returns a String containing the name of the server on which the code is executing.

Parameters

stringvar
   A String variable that receives the machine name from the property.

Example

This code example declares a string variable, assigns the MachineName property value to the string variable, and then sets the text property of the Message label to the value of ServerName:

```
Sub Page_Load( )
    Dim ServerName As String
    ServerName = Server.MachineName
    Message.Text = "The name of the server is " & ServerName & ".<br/>"
End Sub
```

Notes

This property can be useful for code that needs to be easily portable, but needs to access resources that require the server name.

ScriptTimeout

```
intvar = Server.ScriptTimeout
```

Returns an Integer containing the length, in milliseconds, a request is allowed to run before timing out.

Parameters

intvar
    An Integer variable that receives the script timeout value.

Example

This code example declares an integer variable, sets the ScriptTimeout value to 120 seconds, assigns the ScriptTimeout property value to the variable, and then sets the text property of the Message label to the value of the variable:

```
Sub Page_Load( )
    Dim Timeout As String
    Server.ScriptTimeout = 120
    Timeout = CStr(Server.ScriptTimeout)
    Message.Text = "The current ScriptTimeout value is  " & _
        Timeout & ".<br/>"
End Sub
```

Notes

You can use this property to extend or reduce the timeout value in order to allow longer-running processes time to complete, or you can use ScriptTimeout to reduce the overhead associated with inefficient processes by terminating them before completion. The default for this value is set to an extremely high number so that a script will not time out by default. This is for backward compatibility with classic ASP.

Methods Reference

ClearError

```
Server.ClearError( )
```

Clears the last exception thrown.

Parameters

None

Notes

The ClearError method is new to ASP.NET. You can use this method at the beginning of page processing to clear the last exception so that the information provided by the GetLastError method is specific to an exception occurring on the current page.

CreateObject

```
objvar = Server.CreateObject(ProgID)
objvar = Server.CreateObject(Type)
```

Returns a reference to a COM object created based on the supplied ProgID.

Parameters

objvar
> A variable of type Object to receive the reference to the newly created object.

ProgID
> A String variable or literal containing the COM programmatic ID of the desired object.

Type
> The type name of a runtime callable wrapper (RCW) class that the *tlbimp.exe* utility generated to expose a COM object to managed code.

Example

The code example declares an object variable, uses Server.CreateObject to assign a reference to a newly created ADO Recordset object to the variable, and then opens the recordset and returns the RecordCount property to the browser by using the Message label control:

```
Sub Page_Load( )
    Dim rs1
    Dim ConnString As String
    ConnString = "driver={SQL Server};server=(local)\NetSDK;"
    ConnString =  ConnString & "database=Pubs;Trusted_Connection=yes"
    rs1 = Server.CreateObject("ADODB.Recordset")
    ' 1 and 3 are the values for adOpenKeyset and adLockOptimistic
    rs1.Open("SELECT * FROM Authors", ConnString, 1, 3)
    Message.Text = "There are " & rs1.RecordCount & _
```

```
        " records in the Authors table.<br/>"
    End Sub
```

Figure 18-1 shows the output of a page that combines the example for the CreateObject method with the example for the CreateObjectFromClsid method.

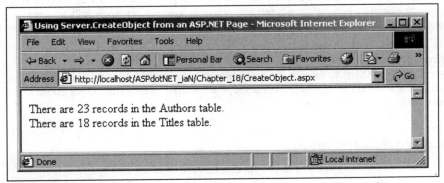

Figure 18-1. Output of CreateObject and CreateObjectFromClsid examples

Notes

This method enables backward compatibility with classic ASP applications and allows the late-bound use of COM components in ASP.NET applications. For new development, it is preferable to use other means to achieve the results that this method was used for in classic ASP. These means include:

- Using the *TlbImp.exe* utility to create a RCW for the component, which enables early binding and optimizes the performance of calls between managed and unmanaged code. If you add a reference to a COM component in the Visual Studio .NET IDE, the RCW is created for you automatically.

- Rewriting custom COM components to run in the managed environment. This method is preferable, as it entirely eliminates the marshalling cost of switching between managed and unmanaged code.

It is important for you to consider the second alternative for COM components that are called frequently and perform a little work each time they're called (as opposed to components that are called once and perform larger amounts of work per call). The distinction between these models is often referred to as "chatty" versus "chunky" communications. The cost of chatty components in marshalling between managed and unmanaged code tends to be significantly higher compared to the amount of work being done in each call. When upgrading COM components to run in the managed environment, you should convert chatty components first and then look at chunky components.

If you want ASP.NET to fire the OnStartPage and OnEndPage events used in some COM components to access the ASP intrinsics, you must add the ASPCompat attribute to the page's @ Page directive:

```
<%@ Page ASPCompat="true" %>
```

When ASPCompat is set to True, ASP.NET creates unmanaged intrinsic objects to pass to the component's OnStartPage method. ASP.NET also switches from executing in multithreaded apartment (MTA) to single-threaded apartment (STA) mode to ensure compatibility with COM components created in Visual Basic 5 or 6. This can have a significant negative impact on performance, so be sure to test your application carefully to determine whether the performance will be acceptable when using this attribute.

In ASP.NET, unlike in ASP, it isn't necessary to use the Set keyword with CreateObject, as shown in the previous example. It also isn't necessary to use Set objName = Nothing to release the reference to the object, since the managed reference is eventually garbage collected, at which point the COM object is dereferenced and destroyed.

CreateObjectFromClsid

```
objvar = Server.CreateObjectFromClsid(Clsid)
```

Returns a reference to a COM object created based on the supplied COM CLSID.

Parameters

objvar
> A variable of type Object to receive the reference to the newly created object.

Clsid
> A String variable or literal containing the COM CLSID (a type of globally unique identifier (GUID) for the component that is found in the Registry) of the desired object.

Example

The code example declares an object variable, uses Server.CreateObjectFromClsid to assign a reference to a newly created ADO Recordset object to the variable, and then opens the recordset and returns the RecordCount property to the browser using the Message label control.

```
Sub Page_Load()
    Dim rs1
    Dim ConnString As String
    ConnString = "driver={SQL Server};server=(local)\NetSDK;"
    ConnString = ConnString & "database=Pubs;Trusted_Connection=yes"
    rs1 = Server.CreateObjectFromClsid( _
        "00000535-0000-0010-8000-00AA006D2EA4")
    ' 1 and 3 are the values for adOpenKeyset and adLockOptimistic
    rs1.Open("SELECT * FROM Titles", ConnString, 1, 3)
    Message.Text &= "There are " & rs1.RecordCount & _
        " records in the Titles table.<br/>"
End Sub
```

Notes

This method is new to ASP.NET and, like the CreateObject method, it allows the late-bound use of COM components in ASP.NET applications.

The other notes relating to the CreateObject method also apply equally to the CreateObjectFromClsid method.

Execute

```
Server.Execute(Path)
Server.Execute(Path, Writer)
```

Executes a request on the URL passed by the *Path* argument and optionally captures the output of the requested page by using an instance of the TextWriter class supplied by the *Writer* argument.

Parameters

Path

> A String variable or literal specifying the URL to execute. The URL passed to the Execute method may be absolute (containing all the information needed to locate the resource, including the protocol type and server name) or relative (containing only the relative path of the resource).

Writer

> An instance of any class derived from the TextWriter class (found in the System.IO namespace); used to capture the output of the execution of the requested URL.

Example

The code example declares a string variable, creates a new TextWriter, and then calls Server.Execute to execute a page based on the CreateObject example code and capture its results. Figure 18-2 shows the output of the example.

```
Sub Page_Load()
    Dim Url As String = "CreateObject.aspx"
    Dim sw As New System.IO.StringWriter()
    Server.Execute(Url, sw)
    Message.Text = "Request output:<br/><br/>" & sw.ToString()
End Sub
```

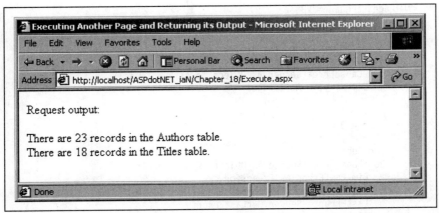

Figure 18-2. Output of CreateObject and CreateObjectFromClsid examples

Notes

The Execute method is a useful feature that first appeared in the IIS 5.0 version of Active Server Pages. ASP.NET includes an overloaded version of the method, adding the *Writer* argument for capturing, manipulating, and/or saving the output of the request being executed.

When called passing only the URL, the Execute method automatically inserts the output of the request into the HTML output stream of the calling page.

When called passing both the URL and an object reference derived from the TextWriter class (such as StringWriter, StreamWriter, or HtmlTextWriter), the output is not automatically added to the HTML output stream, but may be obtained, as in the previous example, by calling the ToString method of the writer class.

GetLastError

```
LastException = Server.GetLastError( )
```

Returns the last exception thrown.

Parameters

LastException
    An object of type Exception to receive the application's last exception.

Example

The code in *GetLastError.aspx* displays a button that, when clicked, calls a server-side event handler that declares three Integers and purposely divides by zero (a no-no) to cause an exception. The code in the Page_Error event handler declares an Exception object and a String, gets the Exception using GetLastError, tests whether the object reference is valid and assigns the Message property of the exception to the string variable, and then writes the value to the browser using the Response.Write method. You can also call the GetLastError method from the Application_Error event handler, which you can place in the *global.asax* file to catch errors that have not been handled at the page level.

```vb
<%@ Page Language="VB" %>
<html>
<head>
    <title>Examining the Last Error</title>
    <script runat="server">
        Sub CauseError(sender As Object, e As EventArgs)
            Dim x, y, z As Integer

            y = 1
            z = 0
            x = y / z
        End Sub
        Sub Page_Error(Source As Object, E As EventArgs)
            Dim LastError As Exception
            Dim ErrMessage As String
            LastError = Server.GetLastError( )
            If Not LastError Is Nothing Then
```

```
            ErrMessage = LastError.Message
        Else
            ErrMessage = "No Errors"
        End If
        Response.Write("Last Error = " & ErrMessage & "<br/><br/>")
        Server.ClearError()
    End Sub
  </script>
</head>
<body>
  <form runat="server">
    <h4><font face="verdana">Cause an Error to Occur...</font></h4>
    <asp:button text="CauseError" OnClick="CauseError" runat="server"/>
  </form>
</body>
</html>
```

Notes

You'll find this method useful for getting information about an error from a custom error-handling page. GetLastError returns information only when called in the Page_Error or Application_Error event handlers because once these events have been fired, the exception is cleared automatically.

HtmlDecode

```
returnstring = Server.HtmlDecode(s)
Server.HtmlDecode(s,output)
```

Returns a string in which any HTML information encoded by the HtmlEncode method (described later in this chapter) is decoded back into its standard HTML format.

Parameters

returnstring
> A String variable to receive the decoded string from the method.

s
> A string variable containing the encoded HTML that the method will decode.

output
> An instance of any class derived from the TextWriter class (found in the System.IO namespace) used to capture the decoded string.

Example

The code example declares two string variables, sets the value of *StrToDecode* to the encoded equivalent of <p>Hello, World!</p>, assigns the return value of the Server.HtmlDecode call to *StrToReturn*, and then writes the value to the browser using the Message label control:

```
Sub Page_Load()
    Dim StrToDecode As String
    Dim StrToReturn As String
    StrToDecode = "&lt;p&gt;Hello, World!&lt;/p&gt;"
```

```
        StrToReturn = Server.HtmlDecode(StrToDecode)
        Message.Text = StrToReturn
    End Sub
```

Notes

This method provides a simple way to undo the effects of calling HtmlEncode on
a given string. You can also use it as an educational tool to demonstrate the relationship between various characters used in HTML and ASP (such as the greater-
than (>) and less-than (<) symbols) and their encoded equivalents.

When called with only the *s* argument, this method returns a string. When called
with both an *s* argument and an *output* argument (such as a StringWriter or
HtmlTextWriter class instance), the method does not return a value; instead, you
can obtain the decoded string by calling the ToString method of the writer object.

While this method is useful, you probably won't use it as frequently as its cousin,
UrlDecode, which is described later in this chapter.

HtmlEncode

```
returnstring = Server.HtmlEncode(s)
Server.HtmlEncode(s, output)
```

Returns a string in which any HTML tags found are encoded by using the HTML
literal equivalents of symbols such as > (>), < (<), and even quotes
("). This allows developers to display HTML and ASP source code on the
page, rather than treating it as rendered output or code to execute.

Parameters

returnstring
    A String variable to receive the encoded string from the method.

s
    A string variable containing the HTML that the method will encode.

output
    An instance of any class derived from the TextWriter class, such as a
    StringWriter class instance (found in the System.IO namespace), used to
    capture the encoded string.

Example

The code example declares two string variables, sets the value of *StrToEncode*,
assigns the return value of the Server.HtmlEncode call to *StrToReturn*, and then
writes the value to the browser using the Message label control. Note that you
have to view the HTML source to see the actual string returned by the method call.

```
    Sub Page_Load()
        Dim StrToEncode As String
        Dim StrToReturn As String
        StrToEncode = "<%@ Page Language=""VB"" %>"
        StrToReturn = Server.HtmlEncode(StrToEncode)
        Message.Text = StrToReturn
    End Sub
```

Notes

This method is great for displaying the source of a page for educational purposes. It is also particularly useful for encoding text entered by users that may or may not be displayed or written to the browser. Without this encoding (or some form of filtering or validation of the input), it might be possible for the user to enter script or other code that the browser or server could execute. This possibility could pose a very large security risk.

Whether with HtmlEncode or with some form of filtering or validation, you should always ensure that text entered by your users that will be used or displayed by your application does not contain unexpected characters or content.

Like the HtmlDecode method, HtmlEncode is overloaded. It returns a string when called with the *s* argument alone, and it does not return a value when called with both an *s* and an *output* argument. Instead, it sends the encoded HTML to the *output* class instance.

MapPath

```
PhysicalPath = Server.MapPath(Path)
```

Returns a string containing the physical path in the server's filesystem that corresponds to the virtual or relative path specified by the *Path* argument.

Parameters

PhysicalPath
> A String variable to receive the physical path from the method.

Path
> A String variable containing the virtual or relative path to be mapped.

Example

The code example declares two string variables, sets the value of *RelativePath*, assigns the return value of the Server.MapPath call to *PhysicalPath*, and then writes the value to the browser by using the Message label control:

```
Sub Page_Load()
    Dim RelativePath As String
    Dim PhysicalPath As String
    RelativePath = "HtmlEncode.aspx"
    PhysicalPath = Server.MapPath(RelativePath)
    Message.Text = PhysicalPath
End Sub
```

Notes

You can use this method to determine the physical location for creating a new file in response to a user action or code event.

In classic ASP, attempting to use this method with the MS-DOS (.) and (..) relative directory syntax would result in an error. In ASP.NET, no error occurs. In the previous example, using `"../HtmlEncode.aspx"` for the *Path* returns a physical path mapping the file *HtmlEncode.aspx* to the parent folder of its physical location. Using "./HtmlEncode.aspx" for the *Path* returns the same physical path mapping as in the original example.

The MapPath method dynamically determines whether the provided path is a relative or virtual path based on whether the leading character is a slash (/) or backslash (\). If the leading character is either one, the path is assumed to be a complete virtual path. If not, the path is assumed to be relative to the physical path of the currently executing page.

If the last component in *Path* is a filename, the MapPath method does not verify its existence. In other words, the code example returns the same absolute path whether or not *HtmlEncode.aspx* exists.

A more flexible version of the MapPath method has been added to the Request object that enables you to specify a base directory for resolving mappings and lets you allow mapping of paths across different applications. You can read more about the Request.MapPath method in Chapter 16.

Transfer

```
Server.Transfer(Path)
Server.Transfer(Path, preserveForm)
```

Discontinues execution of the current page and transfers execution to the page specified by the *Path* argument. This allows control of an application to be redirected to the page specified by the *Path* argument without any response being sent to the client.

In contrast to the Execute method, which returns control to the page in which it is called once the page specified in the Execute method finishes processing, the Transfer method does not return control to the calling page.

Parameters

Path

    A String variable containing the path to the page to which execution will be transferred.

preserveForm

    A Boolean variable that indicates whether the Form and QueryString collections should be cleared before transferring control to the page that the *Path* argument specifies.

Example

The code example declares a string variable containing the name of the page to transfer control to, and then calls Server.Transfer. Note that the call that sets the Message.Text property will never be executed.

```
Sub Page_Load()
    Dim Url As String = "CreateObject.aspx"
    Server.Transfer(Url)
    Message.Text = "This code will never be executed!"
End Sub
```

Notes

The ability to clear the Form and QueryString collections prior to passing control to the page that the *Path* argument specifies is new in ASP.NET. This is convenient for passing control to pages that you did not create and that might break if they encounter unexpected values, or if you want to keep the Form or QueryString contents private. If you do not pass a *preserveForm* argument, the default behavior is for the Form and QueryString collections to be preserved.

Make sure that no code in your page must execute after a Server.Transfer. If you have such code, you may want to consider using Server.Execute instead.

UrlDecode

```
returnstring = Server.UrlDecode(s)
Server.UrlDecode(s,output)
```

Returns a string in which any special character sequences resulting from encoding by the UrlEncode method (described later in this chapter) are decoded back into the original format. For example, a URL with a query string such as:

```
http://localhost/ASPdotNET_iaN/Chapter_18/UrlDecode.
aspx?strtodecode=This%20is%20a%20good%20string.
```

would return the following string from the UrlDecode method:

```
This is a good string.
```

Parameters

returnstring
> A String variable to receive the decoded string from the method.

s
> A String variable containing the encoded URL to be decoded by the method.

output
> An instance of any class derived from the TextWriter class (found in the System.IO namespace) used to capture the decoded string. Examples are the StringWriter and HtmlTextWriter classes.

Example

The code example declares two string variables, sets the value of *StrToDecode* to the encoded equivalent of the QueryString's *StrToDecode* value, assigns the return value of the Server.UrlDecode call to *StrToReturn*, and then writes the value to the browser using the Message label control:

```
Sub Page_Load()
    Dim StrToDecode As String
    Dim StrToReturn As String
    StrToDecode = Request.QueryString("StrToDecode")
    StrToReturn = Server.UrlDecode(StrToDecode)
    Message.Text = StrToReturn
End Sub
```

Notes

New in ASP.NET, this method provides a simple way to undo the effects of calling UrlEncode on a given string. It is especially useful for retrieving values passed in the query string, since these values commonly contain characters, such as spaces and commas, that are not allowed in URLs.

When called with only the *s* argument, this method returns a string. When called with both the *s* argument and *output* argument, the method does not return a value; instead, the decoded string is sent to the *output* writer.

UrlEncode

```
returnstring = Server.UrlEncode(s)
Server.UrlEncode(s, output)
```

Returns a string in which any characters not allowed in URLs are encoded by using the URL literal equivalents, such as %2c for comma and + for space. This makes it very simple to pass any string as a query string value and, thanks to the new UrlDecode method, just as simple to retrieve the unencoded value.

Parameters

returnstring
> A String variable to receive the encoded string from the method.

s
> A String variable containing the value to be encoded by the method.

output
> An instance of any class derived from the TextWriter class (found in the System.IO namespace); used to capture the encoded string. Classes derived from TextWriter include StringWriter and HtmlTextWriter.

Example

The code example declares two string variables, sets the value of *StrToEncode*, assigns the return value of the Server.UrlEncode call to *StrToReturn*, and then writes the HTML anchor tag containing a query string with the encoded value to the browser using the Message label control:

```
Sub Page_Load()
    Dim StrToEncode As String
    Dim StrToReturn As String
    StrToEncode = "Hello, World!"
    StrToReturn = Server.UrlEncode(StrToEncode)
    Message.Text = "<a href=""UrlDecode.aspx?StrToDecode=" & StrToReturn
    Message.Text &= """>" & StrToReturn & " - Click to Decode!</a>"
End Sub
```

Notes

This method replaces non-URL-allowable characters in strings that need to be passed as part of a URL. For example, one of the most difficult things to pass as part of a URL is another URL. The UrlEncode method replaces all slash (/), dot (.), and colon (:) characters for you. Figure 18-3 shows the output of the previous example.

Figure 18-3. Output of server UrlEncode

Like the UrlDecode method, UrlEncode is overloaded. It returns a string when called with the *s* argument alone and does not return a value when called with both the *s* and *output* arguments. Instead, the encoded URL is sent to the writer object.

UrlPathEncode

```
returnstring = Server.UrlPathEncode(s)
```

Returns a string containing a URL whose path portion is encoded using the URL literal equivalents of symbols such as slash (/), colon (:), and dot (.). The method also encodes any spaces in the remaining portion of the URL, since spaces in the query string may be unexpectedly truncated by some browsers.

Parameters

returnstring
   A String variable to receive the encoded string from the method.

s
   A String variable containing the URL to be encoded by the method.

Example

The code example declares two string variables, sets the value of *StrToEncode*, assigns the return value of the Server.UrlPathEncode call to *StrToReturn*, and then writes the value to the browser as part of a hyperlink:

```
Sub Page_Load()
    Dim StrToEncode As String
    Dim StrToReturn As String
    StrToEncode = "http://www.aspnetian.com/Chapter18/UrlPathEncode.aspx"
    StrToReturn = Server.UrlPathEncode(StrToEncode)
    Message.Text = "<a href=""UrlPathEncode.aspx?target=" & _
        StrToReturn & """>" & StrToReturn & "</a><br/>"
    Message.Text &= "Target = " & Request("Target")
End Sub
```

Notes

This method existed in classic ASP, but was undocumented.

CHAPTER 19

The HttpSessionState Class

A significant challenge for any Web-based application is managing user state. Unlike rich client applications, in which user state can be stored in persistent variables local to the client application, web browsers do not have a comparable built-in facility for persistently storing user state locally. This is because HTTP, the basic communication protocol used in web applications, is essentially a connectionless protocol (the HTTP specification allows persistent connections, but problems with persistent HTTP connections prevent this specification from being widely used). Each HTTP request/response is treated as completely separate from every other request/response. As such, any local variable storage cannot be reliably mapped from the request/response in which they were created to any subsequent request/response.

An early solution to this challenge was the creation of cookies, which are bits of text that are stored either in memory (per-session cookies) or on disk (persistent cookies) and are associated with the domain name from which they originated. This solves the problem of being able to associate a bit of data with more than one request/response, but it has limitations that made it less than an ideal solution:

- Cookies can only store text (or a textual representation of other data), which means that cookie data cannot be made typesafe.

- Cookies are limited in size (the size limit depends on the browser, but is often 4k).

- Cookies can be manipulated on the client. If an application relying on cookies for user state does not take this into account, it is possible that a malicious user could use a manipulated cookie to breach the security of the application.

- Most browsers allow users to turn off or refuse cookies. If users do so, an application that relies on cookies for storing user state may not function correctly.

- Cookies present a potential performance and scalability problem, since all cookies for a given domain are sent with each request/response cycle. This means that sites making substantial use of cookies for state management will send a lot of information over the wire with each request/response cycle, whether that information is needed for that request/response or not.

For these reasons, classic ASP implemented state management through the Session intrinsic object, which provided a collection of key/value pairs for each user for storing user-specific state in memory on the web server. In classic ASP, each user session was identified by a unique identifier called the SessionID, which was sent as a per-session cookie. This alleviated several concerns of using cookies alone for storing user state, including the performance/scalability issue and cookie size limits. However, it still failed to address some issues, including the problem of users who disable cookies. ASP.NET addresses this issue by allowing both cookie-based and cookieless sessions, which are configurable at the application level.

The HttpSessionState class is ASP.NET's replacement for classic ASP's Session intrinsic object. Like the other classes that replace ASP intrinsics, HttpSessionState is exposed as a property of the Page class—in this case, the Session property. Since each ASP.NET page inherits from the Page class, these properties are available to any code in the page. This means that migrating classic ASP code that uses the Session object should be relatively painless.

The HttpSessionState class is used primarily for storing and accessing data that is shared across all the pages accessed by a particular user during a given session of interacting with the application. The HttpSessionState class provides properties and methods that map to the properties, methods, and collections of the classic ASP Session object for backward compatibility. It also adds a number of new properties and methods that increase the convenience of dealing with session state.

As in classic ASP, each user session in ASP.NET is identified by a unique SessionID, which is created at the same time as the user's session, is exposed as a property of the HttpSessionState class. In most cases, developers do not need to concern themselves with this SessionID, since ASP.NET handles it transparently.

A new SessionID is created the first time a user who does not have a current session accesses a page within an ASP.NET application whose session state has not been disabled by setting the enableSessionState attribute of the @ Page directive to False. If the page stores information in the Session collection, or if an event handler is defined for the Session.Start event in the *global.asax* file, then a new session is created and the newly created SessionID is assigned to that session. This delayed creation of the session until it is actually used helps conserve the limited resources of the web server and can help improve the scalability of ASP.NET applications.

When the session is created, the Session.Start event is fired. This event can be handled by creating an event handler in the *global.asax* file (the ASP.NET equivalent of *global.asa*) with the following signature:

```
Sub Session_OnStart()
    'Session initialization code
End Sub
```

By default, the lifetime of the session for a given user is 20 minutes from the time of the user's last request. This setting is configurable at the application level via the ASP.NET *web.config* configuration file or at the machine level via the *machine.config* configuration file. Refer to Chapter 20 for more information on configuring the session timeout value. When a session ends, either by exceeding the timeout value or by code that calls the Session.Abandon method, the Session.End event is fired. Like the Start event, you can handle this event by adding an event handler to *global.asax* with the following signature:

```
Sub Session_OnEnd()
    'Session cleanup code
End Sub
```

Note that the session does not end automatically when the user closes their browser, so if you want to explicitly end the session when a user is finished, you should implement some kind of logout feature that calls the Session.Abandon method.

In ASP.NET, session state is managed through the SessionStateModule class, which is an HttpModule. HttpModules are classes that derive from IHttpModule and that participate in each HTTP request in an ASP.NET application. The SessionStateModule class is responsible for generating and/or retrieving SessionIDs, firing the Start and End events of the Session object, and abstracting the underlying Session store from the HttpSessionState class.

Session state configuration is handled through the sessionState configuration section of the *machine.config* and *web.config* configuration files. (The sessionState configuration section of the Web.config configuration file will be discussed in detail in Chapter 20.) The *machine.config* file contains the default settings for all applications on the machine, and may be overridden by adding a sessionState section to the *web.config* file for an application. If no sessionState section appears in the application-level configuration file, the defaults in *machine.config* are inherited by the application. As installed, *machine.config* enables in-process session state by using cookies to track the SessionID by default.

ASP.NET adds two new configuration options in addition to the timeout value and enabling/disabling of sessions that were configurable in classic ASP. The first provides built-in support for cookieless sessions. Cookieless sessions are configured in the *web.config* (or *machine.config*) file and implemented through the SessionStateModule class, which automatically modifies all relative URLs in the application and embeds the SessionID, allowing the application to maintain user state without using cookies. ASP.NET also provides the Response.ApplyAppPath-Modifier method, which can create absolute URLs containing the embedded SessionID given a virtual path to a resource. This allows even applications to take advantage of cookieless sessions by using absolute URLs.

The second new configuration option allows session state in ASP.NET to span multiple servers through new out-of-process storage options. ASP.NET state can now be stored in-process (the same as classic ASP), in a special ASP.NET state NT service, or in a SQL Server database. The latter two options allow multiple machines to use the same state storage facility, albeit at the expense of making out-of-process calls to set and retrieve state information. More importantly, all storage options are transparent to the developer. Information is added to and retrieved from the session state store in exactly the same fashion, regardless of which underlying session state store is used. This allows applications to be developed by initially using in-process state storage for the best performance, and later moved to out-of process storage to facilitate scaling out by adding more web servers—all without changing a single line of code in the application.

Items can be stored in the Session collection in one of three ways:

- By calling the Add method, passing in the name to assign to the item and the item's value. This value can be of any type supported by the CLR, including object instances, which are automatically serialized before being stored. The Add method takes the form:

  ```
  Session.Add(itemName, itemValue)
  ```

- By explicitly referring to the Item property, passing a name or index to assign to the new item:

  ```
  Session.Item(itemName) = itemValue
  ```

- By implicitly referring to the Item property, passing a name to assign to the new item. This was the most common technique used in classic ASP.

  ```
  Session(itemName) = itemValue
  ```

Items in the Session collection can be accessed in one of three ways:

- By retrieving and iterating over the collection of keys in the Session collection (see the Keys collection description for an example).

- By explicitly referring to the Item property, passing the name of the item to retrieve:

  ```
  localVar = Session.Item(itemName)
  ```

- By implicitly referring to the Item property, passing the name of the item to retrieve. This was the most common technique used in classic ASP:

  ```
  localVar = Session(itemName)
  ```

Items can be removed from the Session collection in one of several ways:

- By calling the Clear method (clears all items).

- By calling the RemoveAll method (removes all items, which is effectively the same as calling the Clear method).

- By calling the Remove method, passing the name of the item to remove.

- By calling the RemoveAt method, passing the index of the item to remove.

Table 19-1 lists the properties, collections, methods, and events exposed by the HttpSessionState class.

Table 19-1. HttpSessionState class summary

Preoperties	Collections	Methods (public instance)	Events*
CodePage	Contents	Abandon	Start
Count	Keys	Add	End
IsCookieless	StaticObjects	Clear	
IsNewSession		CopyTo	
IsReadOnly		Remove	
Item		RemoveAll	
LCID		RemoveAt	
Mode			
SessionID			

Table 19-1. HttpSessionState class summary (continued)

Preoperties	Collections	Methods (public instance)	Events*
Timeout			
* These events are exposed by the SessionStateModule class, rather than the HttpSessionState class.			

Comments/Troubleshooting

Understanding both the scope and the lifetime of the Session collection for a given user is important when using the Session object. As mentioned above, a new session is created when a user first requests a page within an ASP.NET application for which session state is enabled (session state is enabled by default in in-process mode) and that stores a value in the Session collection. The boundary of that ASP.NET application is defined by the boundary of an IIS application. That is, the boundary of the ASP.NET session includes all ASP.NET pages within a single IIS application and all of its subfolders and virtual directories. It does not, however, include subfolders that are defined as IIS applications. Figure 19-1 illustrates the different folder types in IIS. In Figure 19-1, the *SessionWrite.aspx* file writes a value to the Session collection. Because the folder containing *SessionWrite.aspx* is a virtual directory that is a part of the *Chapter_19* application folder and is not defined as its own folder, the session value written by *SessionWrite.aspx* will be available to any page in either the *Chapter_19* folder or the *SubApp* subfolder. If, however, the *SubApp* folder is configured as an IIS Application (by accessing the Virtual Directory tab of the Properties dialog for the folder and clicking the Create button in the Application Settings section), it will then define its own session boundaries, which will not be shared with the parent *Chapter_19* application.

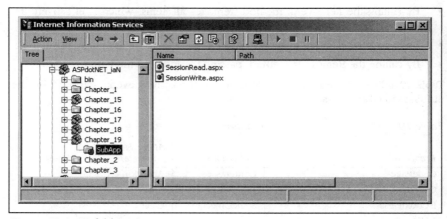

Figure 19-1. IIS folder types

The lifetime of an ASP.NET session is set by default to 20 minutes from the time of the last request to the application that created the session, or until the Session. Abandon method is called.

Keep this lifetime in mind for two reasons:

- Any information that you store at the session level will continue to consume resources (memory, in the case of in-process or state service storage; memory and/or disk space, in the case of SQL Server state storage) for a minimum of 20 minutes (or whatever length you've set for the timeout value), and possibly longer depending on the user's activity in the application. For this reason, you should always carefully consider the potential costs associated with storing an item (particularly object instances) in the Session collection.

- If code in your page relies on an item being in the Session collection, your code could break if and when the session timeout value is exceeded. For this reason, you should always check to make sure that the item exists by testing whether the item evaluates to Nothing (or null in C#) before attempting to access the item's value.

In classic ASP, a big no-no was storing non-thread-safe COM objects (i.e., *any* COM object written in Visual Basic) in the Session collection. This was because such components would force IIS to process requests only to the Session that stored the COM object from the same thread that created the object, which could limit scalability substantially. In ASP.NET, this is less of an issue, since all managed .NET components can be stored safely in the Session collection without the threading model impacting scalability. The concerns about resource usage and scalability still apply, however, so before storing objects in the Session collection, carefully consider just how much memory will probably be consumed by multiple serialized instances of the object being stored by multiple sessions.

The difference between objects added to the Session collection and objects created with Session scope using the <object> tag in *global.asax* is also important. While objects added to the Session collection can be removed by using the Remove, RemoveAll, or Clear methods, objects in the StaticObjects collection (those created in *global.asax*) are not affected by any of these methods.

In addition to properties and methods provided for backward compatibility with classic ASP, the ASP.NET version of the Session object also adds useful new properties and methods, including the Count, IsCookieless, IsNewSession, and IsReadOnly properties, and the Clear, CopyTo, and RemoveAt methods. The Count and CopyTo members are derived from the ICollection interface, which is implemented by the HttpSessionState class.

In this chapter, we'll use the following code listing as the basis for most examples in the chapter. Unless otherwise noted, each example will consist of the Page_ Load event handler for that particular example. Any displayed output messages or return values will be shown as the Text property of the ASP.NET Label named Message or by calling Response.Write.

```
<%@ Page Language="vb" %>
<html>
    <head>
        <script runat="server">
            Sub Page_Load()
                'Example code will go here
            End Sub
        </script>
```

```
    </head>
    <body>
        <asp:label id="Message" runat="server"/>
    </body>
    </html>
```

Properties Reference

CodePage

```
Integer = Session.CodePage
Session.CodePage = Integer
```

Returns or sets an Integer indicating the code page to be used in generating the page output. The code page is the character set that contains all characters and punctuation for a given locale setting.

Parameters
Integer
    An Integer variable that will receive or set the code page property value.

Example

The example writes the current code page value to the Text property of the Message label control:

```
Sub Page_Load( )
    Message.Text = "Current Code Page is: " & Session.CodePage
End Sub
```

Notes

The CodePage property is provided for compatibility with classic ASP. For new ASP.NET development, you should use the ContentEncoding property of the Response class for formatting output to a given code page, or configure globalization settings in *web.config* (see Chapters 8 and 20 for more information on globalization settings).

In the example above, although the property value is an Integer, ASP.NET automatically casts the Integer value to a String, which is then assigned to the Text property. This works because any .NET object or data type can be represented as a String.

Count

```
Integer = Session.Count
```

Returns an Integer containing the number of items currently in the Session collection.

Parameters
Integer
    An Integer variable that will receive the count property value.

Example

The example adds two values to the Session collection, displays the count of the items in the Session collection, and then displays each item, using the Count property as a looping control value:

```
Sub Page_Load()
    Session("foo") = "Hello, "
    Session("bar") = "World!"
    Message.Text = "The Session collection contains " & _
        Session.Count & " items.</br>"
        Dim I as Integer
        For I = 0 To Session.Count - 1
            Message.Text &= CStr(Session(I)) & "</br>"
        Next
End Sub
```

Notes

The Count property is new for ASP.NET. In addition to using the Count property for looping through the Session collection, you can use the property to keep track of how many items a given Session stores at any given time. For example, you could write this information to a log for later review.

IsCookieless

```
Boolean = Session.IsCookieless
```

Returns a Boolean indicating whether the application is configured for cookieless Session operation.

Parameters

Boolean
A Boolean variable that will receive the IsCookieless property value.

Example

The example displays a message indicating whether cookieless sessions have been enabled for the current session:

```
Sub Page_Load()
    If Session.IsCookieless Then
        Message.Text = "The current Session does not use cookies."
    Else
        Message.Text = "The current Session uses cookies."
    End If
End Sub
```

Notes

The IsCookieless property is new for ASP.NET, and is especially useful in combination with the Response.ApplyAppPathModifier method, which allows you to create absolute URLs containing the current SessionID for use with cookieless sessions.

IsNewSession

```
Boolean = Session.IsNewSession
```

Returns a Boolean indicating whether the current session was created as a result of the current request.

Parameters

Boolean

A Boolean variable that will receive the IsNewSession property value. Returns True on the request that creates a Session and False for each subsequent request from the same client.

Example

The example tests to see if the current request created a new session and if so, adds a value to the Session collection and then displays a message containing the SessionID of the current session:

```
Sub Page_Load()
    If Session.IsNewSession Then
        Session("foo") = "foo"
        Message.Text = "The current Session (SessionID: " & _
            Session.SessionID & ") was created with this request."
    Else
        Message.Text = "The current Session (SessionID: " & _
            Session.SessionID & ") existed prior to this request."
    End If
End Sub
```

Notes

The IsNewSession property is very useful when you want to initialize Session collection items for only certain pages. Unlike the Session_OnStart event handler in *global.asax*, which is called when a session is created, regardless of which page creates the session, this property gives you finer-grained control over initialization and session behavior.

As mentioned in the introduction to this chapter, while a new SessionID is generated for each request that does not already have a session, a new session is not created for a given request unless the requested page stores a value in the Session collection or an event handler exists in *global.asax* for the Session Start event.

Thus, if you commented out the line:

```
Session("foo") = "foo"
```

in the example above, and no Session_OnStart event handler was defined in *global.asax*, each request to the page would result in a new SessionID being generated, but no session would actually be created by the request.

IsReadOnly

```
Boolean = Session.IsReadOnly
```

Returns a Boolean indicating whether the current session can be written to from the current page. This property is set to `True` when the `EnableSessionState` attribute of the `@ Page` directive is set to `ReadOnly`.

Parameters

Boolean
> A Boolean variable that will receive the IsReadOnly property value. The default is `False`.

Example

The example tests whether the session is set to ReadOnly for the page and if so, displays an appropriate message. If not, it writes a value to the Session collection and then displays a different message:

```
Sub Page_Load()
    If Session.IsReadOnly Then
        Message.Text = "The current Session (SessionID: " & _
            Session.SessionID & ") is read-only for this page."
    Else
        Session("foo") = "foo"
        Message.Text = "The current Session (SessionID: " & _
            Session.SessionID & ") can be written to from this page."
    End If
End Sub
```

To test this page, add the `EnableSessionState` attribute to the `@ Page` directive for the page, setting its value to `ReadOnly`, as shown here:

```
<%@ Page Language="vb" EnableSessionState="ReadOnly" %>
```

Notes

Read-only session state is new in ASP.NET and is designed to improve the efficiency of pages that require only read access to the Session collection. Attempting to write to the Session collection from a page with the EnableSessionState attribute set to ReadOnly will result in an exception being thrown.

Item

```
Object = Session.Item(ByVal name As String)
Session.Item(ByVal name As String) = Object
Object = Session.Item(ByVal index As Integer)
Session.Item(ByVal index As Integer) = Object
```

Returns or sets an Object associated with a particular name or index.

Parameters

Object
> A variable of any type (since all .NET types are ultimately derived from Object) that will receive or set the item's value.

---

name

A String argument containing the text key to apply to the item or by which to retrieve the item.

index

An Integer argument containing the index of the item whose value will be retrieved or modified.

Example

The example sets the values of two items in the Session collection. If these items do not already exist in the collection, they will be added. The example then displays the two values:

```
Sub Page_Load()
    Session.Item("foo") = "foo"
    Session.Item("foo2") = "foo2"
    Message.Text = CStr(Session.Item("foo")) & "</br>"
    Message.Text &= CStr(Session.Item(1))
End Sub
```

Notes

The Item property is accessed implicitly when using the syntax:

```
Session("foo") = "foo"
```

which is commonly seen in classic ASP code. Using the Item property is not required, but it may make your code more readable and understandable than accessing it implicitly.

Note that an index may be used only as an argument when modifying a value, not to create a new item. The index must also be smaller than the number of items in the Session collection or an exception will be thrown.

LCID

```
Integer = Session.LCID
Session.LCID = Integer
```

Returns or sets an Integer containing the locale identifier for the session. The locale identifier determines how information such as date/time values is formatted.

Parameters

Integer

An Integer variable that will receive or set the LCID property value.

Example

The example displays the current LCID value and displays the current date and time formatted based on the current LCID. It then changes the LCID to the value for French, displays the LCID value, and displays the current date and time again, this time formatted based on the new LCID:

```
Sub Page_Load()
    Message.Text = "Current locale ID is: " & Session.LCID & "</br>"
```

```
  Message.Text &= "Current date and time is: " & DateTime.Now() & "</br>"
  Session.LCID = 1036 'France
  Message.Text &= "Current locale ID is: " & Session.LCID & "</br>"
  Message.Text &= "Current date and time is: " & DateTime.Now() & "</br>"
End Sub
```

Notes

The LCID property is provided for backward compatibility with classic ASP. For new ASP.NET development, you should use the System.Threading.CurrentThread. CurrentCulture.LCID property instead. ASP.NET stores and retrieves the Session. LCID property in System.Threading.CurrentThread.CurrentCulture.LCID.

Mode

```
SessionStateMode = Session.Mode
```

Returns one of the values of the `SessionStateMode` enumeration that describes the mode for which session state for the application has been configured.

Parameters

`SessionStateMode`

One of the following members of the `SessionStateMode` enumeration:

`InProc`

Indicates that session state is stored in-process. This setting provides the best performance when using session state storage, but cannot be shared across multiple servers.

`Off`

Indicates that session state is disabled. This setting provides the best performance overall, but at the expense of not using session state storage.

`SQLServer`

Indicates that session state is stored out-of-process in a SQL Server database. This setting allows state sharing across machines at the expense of some performance.

`StateServer`

Indicates that session state is stored out of process in a special NT service. This setting also allows state sharing across machines at the expense of some performance.

Example

The example writes a message containing the current Session state mode to the Text property of the Message ASP.NET Label control. To get the string representation of the enumeration value, call ToString on the Mode property value as shown:

```
Sub Page_Load()
  Message.Text = "The current Session state mode is: " & _
    Session.Mode.ToString() & ".</br>"
End Sub
```

Notes

The Mode property allows you to test the current mode of session state storage. One use for this property is to determine whether to store information in the Session collection, depending on the mode. Because both the StateServer and SQLServer modes require cross-process communication (which can be very expensive relative to in-process communication), you may wish to provide alternative means for storing certain information if one of these modes is used. Using the Mode property, you can write conditional statements that will decide at runtime whether or not to store a particular value based on the current session state mode. That way, if the session state mode is changed administratively, no change to your code is required.

SessionID

```
String = Session.SessionID
```

Returns a String containing the unique identifier for the current session.

Parameters

String
    A String variable that will receive the session ID property value.

Example

See the example for the IsReadOnly property.

Notes

The SessionID property value is generated the first time that a page for which session state has not been disabled is requested. As noted earlier, the actual session is not created unless either an event handler is provided in *global.asax* for the Session.Start event or a value is stored in the Session collection. The SessionID is stored on the client in a nonpersistent cookie, or if cookieless sessions are enabled, is passed as part of each URL request.

Note that if the client's browser is closed, the client will be unable to access their session (since the nonpersistent cookie will be destroyed when the browser is closed), but the session will continue to exist on the server until the configured timeout period has elapsed. If you want to explicitly expire a session, you can check the IsClientConnected property of the HttpResponse class, which returns a Boolean indicating whether the client has disconnected. If it returns False, you can then call Session.Abandon to expire the session.

While the SessionID value, which is a 120-bit ASCII string in ASP.NET, is unique to a given IIS application instance, it is not guaranteed to be universally unique and therefore should not be used for database identity values or for other purposes requiring universally unique values.

Timeout

```
Integer = Session.Timeout
Session. Timeout = Integer
```

Returns or sets an Integer containing the amount of time, in minutes, that can elapse between requests without the session being destroyed. If the timeout value is exceeded, the current session is destroyed and the Session.End event is fired.

Parameters

Integer
> An Integer variable that will receive or set the Timeout property value.

Example

The example writes the current value of the Timeout property to the Text property of the Message ASP.NET Label control:

```
Sub Page_Load( )
    Message.Text = "Current Session timeout value is " & _
        Session.Timeout & " minutes."
End Sub
```

Notes

You can use the Timeout property to temporarily override the timeout setting configured in *web.config* or *machine.config*, if you wish to make the value more restrictive for some reason.

Collections Reference

Contents

```
HttpSessionState = Session.Contents
```

Returns a reference to the current HttpSessionState instance.

Parameters

HttpSessionState
> A variable of type HttpSessionState that will receive the Contents reference.

Example

The example below calls the RemoveAll method through the Contents collection reference and then writes a message:

```
Sub Page_Load( )
    Session.Contents.RemoveAll( )
    Message.Text = "Removed all items from current Session."
End Sub
```

Notes

This property is provided for backward compatibility with classic ASP. Properties such as the Item property and methods such as Remove and RemoveAll were accessed via the Contents property in classic ASP. In new ASP.NET development, you should access these members directly.

Keys

```
KeysCollection = Session.Keys
```

Returns a NameObjectCollectionBase.KeysCollection containing the string keys associated with all of the values stored in the Session collection.

Parameters

KeysCollection
> A variable of type NameObjectCollectionBase.KeysCollection that will receive the Keys property value.

Example

The example loops through the collection of Keys in the Session collection and then displays the key name and the value associated with it by using the Text property of the Message label control:

```
Sub Page_Load()
    Dim Key As String
    Message.Text = "Session Keys:"
    For Each Key in Session.Keys
        Message.Text &= "<br/>Key:   " & Key
        Message.Text &= "<br/>Value:   " & _
                        CStr(Session(Key))
    Next
End Sub
```

Notes

The Keys property provides one of many ways to iterate over the contents of the Session collection.

StaticObjects

```
HttpStaticObjectsCollection = Session.StaticObjects
```

Returns an HttpStaticObjectsCollection containing all objects instantiated in *global. asax* by using the <object runat="server"> syntax whose scope is set to Session.

Parameters

HttpStaticObjectsCollection
> A variable of type HttpStaticObjectsCollection that will receive the StaticObjects property value.

Example

The example uses the Count property of the HttpStaticObjectsCollection class to display the number of objects in the current application declared with the `<object scope="session" runat="server"/>` syntax in *global.asax*. It then checks the type of each object and, if it is a TextBox web control, adds it to the Controls collection of the form:

```
Sub Page_Load()
    Message.Text = "There are " & Session.StaticObjects.Count & _
        " objects declared with the " & _
        "&lt;object runat=&quot;server&quot;&gt; syntax in Session scope."
    Dim myobj As Object
    For Each myObj in Session.StaticObjects
        If myObj.Value.GetType.ToString() = _
            "System.Web.UI.WebControls.TextBox" Then
            myForm.Controls.Add(myObj.Value)
        End If
    Next
End Sub
```

You also need to modify the `<body>` section of the document as follows:

```
<body>
    <form id="myForm" runat="server">
        <asp:label id="Message" runat="server"/>
    </form>
</body>
```

Notes

This property is provided for backward compatibility with classic ASP. You should think carefully before instantiating objects with Session or Application scope because of the impact such objects have on resource usage and application scalability. In most cases, it is advisable to limit objects to page scope.

Each object in the collection is represented by the DictionaryEntry structure, so its key and value are not directly accessible. To access the key and/or value, use the Key and/or Value members of the DictionaryEntry structure, as shown in the example.

Methods Reference

Abandon

`Session.Abandon()`

Immediately terminates the current user's session and causes the Session.End event to be fired.

Parameters

None

Example

The example examines the IsNewSession property to determine if the current request has resulted in a new session. If so, it adds a value to the Session collection and then displays a message indicating that a new session was created. If a session already exists, the example displays a button that, when clicked, causes a postback. This postback results in the Session.Abandon method being called and the session terminated:

```
If Not IsPostBack
    If Session.IsNewSession Then
        Session("foo") = "foo"
        Message.Text = "The current Session (SessionID: " & _
        Session.SessionID & ") was created with this request."
    Else
        Message.Text = "Click the button to abandon the current session."
        Dim AbandonButton As New Button
        AbandonButton.Text = "Abandon Session"
        myForm.Controls.Add(AbandonButton)
    End If
Else
    Session.Abandon()
    Message.Text = "Session abandoned."
End If
```

In order for the postback to work correctly, a server-side form needs to be added within the <body> tags, as shown below:

```
<form id="myForm" runat="server">
    <asp:label id="Message" runat="server"/>
</form>
```

Notes

The Abandon method is very important for controlling resource usage in ASP.NET applications that use session state. If you use session state for storing application data, you should implement a logout method that calls Session.Abandon and make it as easy as possible for your users to access this method (via a button or link on each page). Implementing this method will help prevent resources from being consumed for longer than necessary when a user has already quit using the application.

Note that the End event will be fired only when session state has been configured for in-process operation.

Add

```
Session.Add(ByVal name As String, ByVal value As Object)
```

Adds an item to the Session collection.

Parameters

name

A String argument containing the name that will be used to refer to the new item.

---

value
 An Object argument containing the value of the new item.

Example

The example declares a local variable, sets its value, and adds an item to the Session collection with the value of the local variable:

```
Sub Page_Load()
    Dim myBaz As String = "baz"
    Session.Add("baz", myBaz)
    Dim I as Integer
    For I = 0 To Session.Count - 1
        Message.Text &= CStr(Session(I)) & "<br/>"
    Next
End Sub
```

Notes

The Add method, which is new in ASP.NET, provides a technique for adding items to the Session collection, which is consistent with the technique used for adding items to other .NET collections.

Clear

```
Session.Clear()
```

Clears the contents of the Session collection for the current user.

Parameters

None

Example

The example clears the contents of the Session collection and writes a message to the Text property of the Message label control that includes the current count of the collection, which should be 0:

```
Sub Page_Load()
    Session.Clear()
    Message.Text = "There are " & Session.Count & _
        " items in the Session collection."
End Sub
```

Notes

The Clear method, which is new for ASP.NET, clears only the contents of the Session collection itself. It does not clear the contents of the StaticObjects collection.

CopyTo

```
Session.CopyTo(ByVal array As Array, ByVal index As Integer)
```

Copies the contents of the Session collection to a one-dimensional array.

Parameters

array
> An Array argument that will receive the session collection values.

index
> An Integer argument specifying the point in the array at which to begin copying.

Example

The example checks to ensure that at least one item is in the Session collection, and if there is, it creates a local object array, copies the contents of the Session collection to it, and displays the value of the first item:

```
Sub Page_Load()
    If Session.Count > 0 Then
        Dim myArray As Array = Array.CreateInstance(GetType(Object), _
            Session.Count)
        Session.CopyTo(myArray, 0)
        Message.Text = "The first item in the array is: " & _
            CStr(myArray(0))
    End If
End Sub
```

Notes

The CopyTo method is useful if you have a large number of items stored in the Session collection. In such cases, accessing values from a local array variable may be faster and more efficient than accessing the values from the Session collection, particularly when session state is configured to run out of process. The improved efficiency and performance comes at the cost of ease of use, since arrays do not provide the same feature richness as the Session collection.

Remove

```
Session.Remove(ByVal name As String)
```

Removes an item from the Session collection by name.

Parameters

name
> A String argument containing the name (key) of the item to remove.

Example

The example determines whether the item with the key "foo" exists in the Session collection and if it does, removes the item and displays an appropriate message:

```
Sub Page_Load()
    If Not Session("foo") Is Nothing Then
        Session.Remove("foo")
        Message.Text = "Item 'foo' was removed."
    Else
        Message.Text = "Item 'foo' does not exist."
    End If
End Sub
```

Notes

The Remove method is provided for backward compatibility with classic ASP. In classic ASP, this method was accessed through the Contents collection. In ASP. NET, this method can be accessed either directly, as shown above, or through the Contents collection.

RemoveAll

```
Session.RemoveAll( )
```

Removes all items from the Session collection.

Parameters

None

Example

The example checks to ensure that at least one item is in the Session collection (although if RemoveAll is called on an empty Session collection, no error will occur), and if it is, it clears the collection by calling the RemoveAll method:

```
Sub Page_Load( )
    If Session.Count > 0 Then
        Session.RemoveAll( )
        Message.Text = "Session collection cleared."
    Else
        Message.Text = "Session collection is already empty."
    End If
End Sub
```

Notes

The RemoveAll method is provided for backward compatibility with classic ASP. In classic ASP, this method was accessed through the Contents collection. In ASP. NET, this method can be accessed either directly, as shown above, or through the Contents collection.

RemoveAll has the same effect as calling the Clear method and like Clear, it clears the contents of the Session collection, but does not remove Session-scoped objects from the StaticObjects collection.

RemoveAt

```
Session.RemoveAt(ByVal index As Integer)
```

Removes an item from the Session collection by index. This is a new companion to the Remove method, which removes an item by key.

Parameters

index
> An Integer argument containing the index location of the item to remove from the Session collection.

Example

```
Sub Page_Load()
    If Session.Count > 0 Then
        Session.RemoveAt(0)
        Message.Text = "The item at index 0 was removed."
    Else
        Message.Text = "The item at index 0 does not exist."
    End If
End Sub
```

Notes

The RemoveAt method allows items to be removed from the Session collection by index rather than by key. As in the example above, the items that follow the removed item will shift one position in the collection when the item is removed. If you remove an item by index and call RemoveAt again with the same index, you will remove the item that immediately followed the original removed item.

Events Reference

Start

```
Sub Session_OnStart()
    'Event handler logic
End Sub
```

Fired when the session is created. The event handler for this event should be defined in the *global.asax* application file.

Parameters

None

Example

The example writes an entry to both the Application Event log and the IIS log for the application to indicate that the Start event has fired:

```
<Script language="VB" runat="server">
    Sub Session_OnStart()
        Dim EventLog1 As New System.Diagnostics.EventLog ("Application", _
            ".", "mySource")
        EventLog1.WriteEntry("Session_OnStart fired!")
        Context.Response.AppendToLog("Session_OnStart fired!")
    End Sub
</script>
```

Notes

The Start event is useful for performing initialization tasks for a new session. One limitation of classic ASP, the inability to access the Server.MapPath method in the Session_OnStart event handler, is eliminated in ASP.NET. You can now successfully call Server.MapPath from within this event handler.

End

```
Sub Session_OnEnd( )
    'Event handler logic
End Sub
```

Fired when the session is torn down—either by calling the Abandon method or when the Session.Timeout value expires. The event handler for this event should be defined in the *global.asax* application file.

Parameters

None

Example

The example below writes an entry to the Application Event log to indicate that the End event has fired:

```
<Script language="VB" runat="server">
    Sub Session_OnEnd( )
        Dim EventLog1 As New System.Diagnostics.EventLog ("Application", _
            ".", "mySource")
        EventLog1.WriteEntry("Session_OnEnd fired!")
        ' Response is not available in this event handler
        ' Context.Response.AppendToLog("Session_OnEnd fired!")
    End Sub
</script>
```

Notes

The End event is useful for performing cleanup tasks when the user's session ends—either when the Abandon method is called or when the session times out. Note that the Response object is not available in the context of the Session_OnEnd event handler. Unlike Session_OnStart, the Server.MapPath method is not available. Attempts to access the Response object or the Server.MapPath method from within this event handler will result in an exception being thrown. Since there is no context for displaying exception information, you will not see an error message. You can handle an exception thrown in the Session_OnEnd event handler by creating a handler for the Application.Error event, as shown below:

```
Sub Application_OnError( )
    Dim EventLog1 As New System.Diagnostics.EventLog ("Application", _
        ".", "mySource")
    EventLog1.WriteEntry("Error Occurred. Error info:" &    Server.
GetLastError( ).ToString( ))
    End Sub
```

Note that the End event will be fired only when session state has been configured for in-process operation.

CHAPTER 20

web.config Reference

ASP.NET provides a completely new model for configuring web applications. This greatly simplified process makes it considerably easier to deploy application configuration settings, the application's content, and its components. Central to this new configuration model is *web.config*, an XML-based file that contains the configuration settings for your application. Because the file is written in XML, it is both human- and machine-readable.

web.config files configure applications hierarchically—i.e., an application can contain more than one *web.config* file, with each file residing in a separate folder of the application. Settings in a *web.config* file in a child folder of the application root override the settings of the *web.config* file in the parent folder. Settings not defined in the child *web.config* file inherit the settings from the parent *web.config* file. Figure 20-1 demonstrates these rules of precedence.

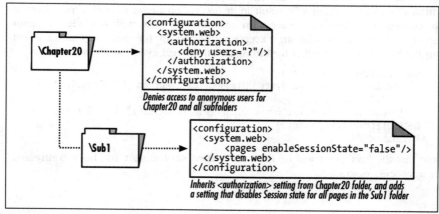

Figure 20-1. Inheriting and overriding web.config settings

In addition to inheriting settings from a *web.config* file defined in a parent folder, all applications on a given machine inherit settings from a file called *machine.config*. The *machine.config* file contains default ASP.NET configuration settings, as well as settings for other .NET application types. Thus, in Figure 20-1, the *Chapter20* folder inherits the *machine.config* setting for the enableSessionState attribute of the <pages> element, which is True by default. The *web.config* file in the *Chapter20* folder overrides the *machine.config* default settings for the <authorization> element, denying access to any anonymous user (any user who has not logged in). The *Sub1* subfolder inherits this setting (as well as all settings defined in *machine. config*) and adds a setting to override the *machine.config* setting for the <pages> element, disabling session state for all pages contained in the *Sub1* folder.

Web.config is made up of one or more of the elements listed in the "web.config Elements" section later in this section. The <configuration> element is required, as is its child, <system.web>. All child elements of <system.web> (i.e., the elements that actually provide the configuration information) are optional; however, the use of certain elements may require you to include other elements or child elements. Each element may also contain one or more attributes that affect the behavior of that element.

Certain elements are limited in the scope at which they can be used. Some elements can be used only at the Application level (in the *web.config* file at the root of the application), some only at the machine level (in *machine.config*), and some can be used at any scope (in *machine.config* or in any *web.config* file, whether at application root or subfolder level).

The elements in the table below are organized both functionally and hierarchically. That is, elements with related functions, such as <authentication> and <authorization>, are grouped together, and child elements immediately follow their parent elements. Thus, the <credentials> element immediately follows the <forms> element, which is its parent, and is immediately followed by <user>, which is a child of <credentials>. Table 20-1 summarizes the *web.config* elements covered in this chapter.

Table 20-1. web.config element summary

<configuration>	<case>	<clear>
<appSettings>	<clientTarget>	<httpModules>
<add>	<add>	<add>
<remove>	<remove>	<remove>
<clear>	<clear>	<clear>
<system.web>	<compilation>	<httpRuntime>
<authentication>	<compilers>	<identity>
<forms>	<compiler>	<machineKey>
<credentials>	<assemblies>	<pages>
<user>	<add>	<processModel>
<passport>	<remove>	<securityPolicy>
<authorization>	<clear>	<trustLevel>
<allow>	<customErrors>	<sessionState>
<deny>	<error>	<trace>

Table 20-1. web.config element summary (continued)

\<browserCaps\>	\<globalization\>	\<trust\>
\<result\>	\<httpHandlers\>	\<location\>
\<use\>	\<add\>	
\<filter\>	\<remove\>	

Comments/Troubleshooting

Probably the most common error that is encountered with *web.config* and *machine.config* relates to capitalization. Tags and elements within both these files are *case sensitive*. Tags and elements follow the naming convention referred to as camel-casing, in which the first letter of the first word of the element or attribute is lowercase, and the first letter of each subsequent word is uppercase. Attribute values are also case sensitive, but do not follow any particular naming convention.

While the ability of applications and folders to inherit settings from parent *web. config* files is very convenient, it presents security implications. For example, the \<appSettings\> element can be used to store key/value pairs for runtime retrieval from your application. If this element is used to store values in the *machine.config* file, these values are available to any application on that machine. In a shared server environment, this could potentially expose information to others in undesirable ways.

Another security issue with both *machine.config* and *web.config* is how to prevent modification of inherited settings. For example, a server administrator might want to configure authentication settings globally in the *machine.config* file and prevent application developers from overriding these settings in their applications. This can be accomplished by using the \<location\> element, setting its allowOverride attribute to False and optionally, setting the path attribute to an application path (if the locked-down settings are to apply only to a specific file or folder).

It is important to exercise caution when working with the *machine.config* file to avoid making changes if you are uncertain of their impact (particularly on other applications). Remember that *machine.config* contains configuration settings not only for all ASP.NET web applications for a given machine, but also for all .NET applications on that machine. Thus, changes to *machine.config* can have a broad impact. It's a good idea to back up the *machine.config* file before editing it, so that if your changes result in problems, you can always restore the previous copy. Another alternative is to place the *machine.config* file under a source code control system, such as Visual Source Safe, and require checkout of the file to make modifications. This provides the ability to roll back changes, as well as the additional ability to track who has made changes to the file.

Finally, your application is required to have a *web.config* file. If the default settings from *machine.config* (or a parent *web.config*) file serve your needs, then omitting this file will simplify your deployment and maintenance tasks. Only use *web.config* when you need to make changes to the default configuration provided by *machine.config*.

web.config Elements

<configuration>

```
<configuration>
</configuration>
```

The root element for all configuration files; it is required.

Scope

All

Attributes

None

<appSettings>

```
<appSettings>
</appSettings>
```

The <appSettings> element can be used to configure custom application settings as key/value pairs. These settings can later be retrieved at runtime using the AppSettings property of the ConfigurationSettings class, as shown in the example. This property is shared (static) and does not require the ConfigurationSettings class to be instantiated before accessing the property.

Scope

Any

Attributes

None

Child Elements

<add>
    The pattern to match.

<remove>
    The pattern to match.

<clear>
    The pattern to match.

Example

The following *web.config* section sets an application level key/value pair:

```
<configuration>
  <appSettings>
    <add key="applicationConfigKey" value="bar"/>
  </appSettings>
</configuration>
```

The following ASP.NET page retrieves the value set by the preceding code and also retrieves a value set at the *machine.config* level:

```
<%@ Page Language="VB" %>
<html>
<head>
    <script runat="server">
        Sub Page_Load( )
            Message1.Text &= _
                ConfigurationSettings.AppSettings("machineConfigKey")
            Message2.Text &= _
                ConfigurationSettings.AppSettings("applicationConfigKey")
        End Sub
    </script>
</head>
<body>
    <asp:label id="Message1" runat="server">Machine.Config setting: </
asp:label>
    <br/>
    <asp:label id="Message2" runat="server">Web.Config setting: </
asp:label>
</body>
</html>
```

Notes

As shown in the example, the <appSettings> element can be used separately from the <system.web> element and its children.

For security reasons, use caution when deciding what kinds of data to store using the <appSettings> element. Remember that while the ASP.NET runtime is set up to prevent an application's *web.config* file from being requested or read, this file could still be vulnerable if the security of the web server were breached in some other way. Thus, you should generally avoid storing sensitive information such as usernames and passwords, or connection strings containing usernames and passwords, in the *web.config* file. A better, although still moderately vulnerable, alternative is to store this information at the *machine.config* level, since this file is not within the web space of the application and is not as vulnerable to compromise through attacks on IIS. However, remember that this information will be available to any application on the machine.

<system.web>

```
<system.web>
</system.web>
```

Container element for all elements used in *web.config* files.

Scope

All

Attributes

None

Child Elements

<authentication>, <authorization>, <browserCaps>, <clientTarget>, <compilation>, <customErrors>, <globalization>, <httpHandlers>, <httpModules>, <httpRuntime>, <identity>, <iisFilter>, <machineKey>, <pages>, <processModel>, <securityPolicy>, <sessionState>, <trace>, <trust>, <webServices>

Notes

This element is required in order to use any of its child elements.

<authentication>

```
<authentication>
</authentication>
```

Provides attributes and contains child elements used to configure authentication options in ASP.NET.

Scope

Machine, Application

Attributes

Mode

> Determines the type of authentication that will be used by ASP.NET. Valid values are:

Windows *(default)*

> Uses credentials provided by IIS authentication methods (Basic, Digest, Integrated Windows Authentication, or Certificates) to authenticate user requests. Requests can then be permitted or denied based on settings contained within the <authorization> element, using the authenticated username (or an associated group/role name) to allow or deny the request. This is the default authentication mode defined in *machine.config.*

Forms

> Provides an infrastructure for performing custom authentication in situations when Windows authentication is not possible. When Forms authentication is enabled, users who have not logged in are automatically redirected to a login URL provided as an attribute of the <forms> element. Once logged in, a cookie is sent as an authentication token. Users can be authenticated against any credentials database the developer chooses—from Active Directory to a custom credentials database. This mode requires the inclusion of the <forms> child element.

Passport

> Takes advantage of Microsoft's Passport authentication service. This mode requires inclusion of the <passport> child element.

None

Specifies that no authentication be performed at the ASP.NET level. Requests can still be authenticated at the IIS level using one of the IIS authentication modes in combination with NTFS access control lists (ACLs).

Child Elements

`<forms>`, `<passport>`

Example

The example configures the pages within the scope of the configuration file to use ASP.NET forms-based authentication:

```
<configuration>
    <system.web>
        <authentication mode="Forms">
            <forms name="myAuthCookie"
                loginUrl="login.aspx"
                protection="All"
                timeout="30"
                path="/" />
        </authentication>
    </system.web>
</configuration>
```

Notes

The `<location>` element can be used to configure authentication at the machine level, if desired, and its `allowOverride` attribute can be used to prevent overriding these settings in individual applications.

Authentication can be a fairly involved topic. For more information on the various ASP.NET authentication methods and how they relate to IIS authentication, please see Chapter 9.

`<forms>`

```
<forms
    loginUrl=String
    name=String
    path=String
    protection="All|None|Encryption|Validation"
    timeout=Integer>
</forms>
```

Provides attributes and one child element (`<credentials>`) to configure ASP.NET to use forms-based authentication.

Scope

Machine, Application

---

name

Specifies the name of the authentication cookie. If this attribute is omitted, the value defaults to .ASPXAUTH. When running multiple applications that use forms-based authentication on the same server, it's usually a good idea to give each application its own authentication cookie name—to minimize the risk of authenticated users from one application being treated as authenticated in others.

loginUrl

Specifies the redirect URL for users who do not have a valid authentication cookie. If a user with no authentication cookie requests a page in the application, they will be redirected to this URL to log in. The login page can then redirect the user back to the originally requested page. If this attribute is omitted, the value defaults to login.aspx.

protection

Specifies the type of protection used to prevent the authentication cookie from being modified during transit. Valid values are:

All

Cookies are both encrypted (using triple DES encryption, if available) and subjected to data validation. Data validation is performed based on the settings of the <machineKey> element. All is the default value and is the recommended setting for securing the authentication cookie.

Encryption

Cookies are only encrypted. This reduces overhead associated with cookie protection, but may leave cookies vulnerable to plain-text attacks.

None

Neither encryption nor validation is enabled for cookie protection. This reduces overhead when using forms-based authentication, but provides no protection of the authentication cookie. This attribute is not recommended.

Validation

A validation key is concatenated with cookie data. This key is checked to ensure that cookie data has not been altered in transit.

timeout

Specifies the amount of time, in minutes, before the authentication cookie expires. This is a sliding value, which is reset when a request is received after more than half of the timeout period has elapsed. Note that this attribute does not apply to persistent cookies. The default value is 30.

path

Specifies the path for the authentication cookie. Because many browsers treat the path in a case-sensitive manner, the default is set to the backslash (\) character.

Child Elements

<credentials>

Example

See the example for the `<authentication>` element.

Notes

Forms-based authentication is only effective when used in conjunction with the `<authorization>` element to deny anonymous users access to pages within the application.

It's a good idea to use SSL encryption to protect the forms authentication credentials and cookie to prevent the possibility of these credentials being hijacked. If you can't (or don't want to) use SSL, you should at least reduce the default timeout value to lessen the likelihood of someone capturing and impersonating the authentication cookie.

<credentials>

```
<credentials
    passwordFormat="Clear|SHA1|MD5">
</credentials>
```

Allows you to store one or more sets of credentials in the application (or machine) configuration file for later use in authenticating requests. The child `<user>` element is used to store the actual credentials.

Scope

Machine, Application

Attributes

passwordFormat
Specifies the format in which passwords will be stored (and compared). Valid options are Clear, SHA1, and MD5.

Child Elements

`<user>`

Example

The example shows the `<credentials>` element, which is used to store two user accounts to authenticate against:

```
<credentials passwordFormat = "SHA1">
    <user name="foo" password="794ED3D18464BAFF93F8DED1CFD00D9A2D9FE316"/>
    <user name="bar" password="B7CDD2A2B0F05E6948E5CEED22FA9A38EB28DEC8"/>
</credentials>
```

Notes

Once you've stored the credentials, you can authenticate against them by calling the static (shared) Authenticate method of the FormsAuthentication helper class. You can use the static (shared) HashPasswordForStoringInConfigFile method of FormsAuthentication to create an MD5 or SHA1 hash of the password for storing in the `<user>` element. When using the `<credentials>` element to store

---

credentials, you should always hash passwords, since storing them in readable text presents a potential security risk. Although theoretically, no one should be able to read the configuration file, a server misconfiguration or security vulnerability could conceivably expose this file.

`<user>`

Stores the username and password for each user defined in the `<credentials>` element.

Scope

Machine, Application

Attributes

`name`
> The username to be authenticated against.

`password`
> The password to be authenticated against.

Child Elements

None

Example

See the example for the `<credentials>` element.

Notes

You should always use the HashPasswordForStoringInConfigFile method to hash passwords stored in the password attribute. A utility page that creates SHA1 or MD5 hashes of plain text passwords is provided in the examples for Chapter 9.

`<passport>`

`<passport redirectUrl=Url />`

This optional element configures an internal URL to which unauthenticated requests will be redirected when using Microsoft's Passport authentication provider. This element should be used only when the `<authentication>` element's mode attribute is set to Passport.

Scope

Machine, Application

Attributes

`redirectUrl`
> A URL in the application to which requests lacking a Passport authentication token are redirected.

Child Elements

None

Example

This example shows a *web.config* file that configures an application for Passport authentication:

```
<configuration>
  <system.web>
    <authentication mode="Passport">
      <passport redirectUrl="Login.aspx"/>
    </authentication>
  </system.web>
</configuration>
```

Notes

For more information on configuring Passport authentication, see the Passport SDK documentation, which is available from *http://www.passport.com*.

<authorization>

Provides two child elements, <allow> and <deny>, that allow you to configure the users, roles, or HTTP verbs that can be used to access application resources.

Scope

Any

Attributes

None

Child Elements

<allow>, <deny>

Example

The example allows users Mary and John to access application resources using any HTTP verb, while denying POST access to nonauthenticated users:

```
<configuration>
  <system.web>
    <authorization>
      <allow users="Mary, John" />
      <deny users="?" verbs="POST" />
    </authorization>
  </system.web>
</configuration>
```

The type of authorization implemented by the `<authorization>` element is referred to as *URL authorization*. You can read more about URL authorization in Chapter 9.

You can specify authorization settings for a specific file or directory in your application that differs from the defaults configured in the root *web.config* file for the application in either of two ways:

- By adding an `<authorization>` element to the *web.config* file of the desired child directory, as shown in the example.

- By using a `<location>` tag in the root *web.config* file and setting its path attribute to the desired path, as follows:

```
<configuration>
    <location path="files">
        <system.web>
            <authorization>
                <deny users="?" />
            </authorization>
        </system.web>
    </location>
    <system.web>
        <!--other configuration settings -->
    </system.web>
</configuration>
```

<allow>

Specifies users, roles, and/or HTTP verbs to be authorized for the application.

Scope

Any

Attributes

`users`
   A comma-delimited list of authorized usernames.

`roles`
   A comma-delimited list of authorized roles (NT groups).

`verbs`
   A comma-delimited list of authorized HTTP verbs (GET, HEAD, POST, or DEBUG).

Child Elements

None

Example

See the example for the `<authorization>` element.

Notes

You can use two wildcards to specify special groups of users:

*
> When used for the value of the user attribute, allows access for all users. This is the default configuration setting, as defined in *machine.config*.

?
> When used for the value of the user attribute, allows access to anonymous users. This wildcard is more commonly used with the <deny> element.

<deny>

Specifies users, roles, and/or HTTP verbs to be denied authorization for the application.

Scope

Any

Attributes

users
> A comma-delimited list of authorized usernames.

roles
> A comma-delimited list of authorized roles (NT groups).

verbs
> A comma-delimited list of authorized HTTP verbs (GET, HEAD, POST, or DEBUG).

Child Elements

None

Example

See the example for the <authorization> element.

Notes

The same wildcards used by the <allow> element also apply to the deny element. To deny access to anonymous (non-authenticated) users, set the value of the users attribute of the <deny> element to ?.

<browserCaps>

```
<browserCaps>
    <result type=className />
    <use var=serverVarName />
        property1=value
        property2=value
        propertyN=value
```

```
<filter match=string>
    property1=value
    property2=value
    propertyN=value
</filter>
<filter match=string>
    <filter match=string with=expressionToSearch>
        property1=value
        property2=value
        propertyN=value
    </filter>
</filter>
<filter>
    <case match=string>
        property1=value
        property2=value
        propertyN=value
    </case>
    <case match=string>
        property1=value
        property2=value
        propertyN=value
    </case>
</filter>
</browserCaps>
```

Controls the configuration of the browser capabilities component returned by the Response.Browser property. The property/value pairs under the <use> element configure the default values of the browser capabilities component properties; the property/value pairs in the <filter> elements update these properties based on a match between the string value specified for the match attribute of the <case> element and the value of the var attribute of the <use> element (which is typically set to HTTP_USER_AGENT).

Scope

Any

Attributes

None

Child Elements

<result>, <use>, <filter>

Example

The *machine.config* configuration file contains the default settings for the <browserCaps> element. The default settings provide the best example for modifying or updating this element.

Notes

The primary purpose of this configuration element and its children is to allow the addition of new browser types and updating the capabilities of these browsers. Thus, when a page calls the browser capabilities component, it will receive accurate information about the capabilities of the browser used for the current request.

<result>

```
<result type=className />
```

Specifies the class.

Scope

Any

Attributes

type

> The class name, and optionally, version, culture, and key information that specifies the class that will contain the results of the browser capabilities analysis. This class must derive from HttpCapabilitiesBase. The default (set in *machine.config*) is System.Web.HttpBrowserCapabilities.

Child Elements

None

Notes

The default type of System.Web.HttpBrowserCapabilities is fine in most cases. If you want to add additional properties beyond those defined by the HttpBrowserCapabilities class, you can create your own class (derived from HttpCapabilitiesBase or HttpBrowserCapabilities) and use the <result> element to substitute it.

<use>

```
<use var=serverVariableName as=aliasName />
```

Sets the name of the server variable to use when evaluating browser capabilities.

Scope

Any

Attributes

var

> The name of the server variable to use. The default is HTTP_USER_AGENT.

as

> The string containing a name by which the server variable can be referenced in <case> elements and regular expressions.

Child Elements

None

Notes

The <use> element is followed by property/value pairs that specify the default properties for the browser capabilities component if no match is found with a <filter> element's match attribute (or that of its child <case> element). This usage is demonstrated in the entry for the <browserCaps> element.

<filter>

```
<filter match=string>
    property1=value
    property2=value
    propertyN=value
</filter>
<filter match=string>
    <filter match=string with=expressionToSearch>
        property1=value
        property2=value
        propertyN=value
    </filter>
</filter>
<filter>
    <case match=string>
        property1=value
        property2=value
        propertyN=value
    </case>
    <case match=string>
        property1=value
        property2=value
        propertyN=value
    </case>
</filter>
```

Specifies a regular expression pattern to search for in the server variable given in the <use> element (or optionally, another expression). Multiple <filter> elements can be contained in the <browserCaps> element; likewise, each <filter> element can contain <case> elements or other <filter> elements. All property assignments for matching <filter> elements will be executed, regardless of their order.

Scope

Any

Attributes

`match`

> The pattern to match. Uses .NET Framework regular expression syntax. This attribute is optional. If omitted, all requests will be assumed to match and any property/value assignments contained within the `<filter>` element will be executed.

`with`

> The regular expression or string to search for. This attribute is optional. If omitted, the server variable specified in the `<use>` element will be searched.

Child Elements

`<case>`

Notes

The fact that `<filter>` elements can be nested makes them very flexible in terms of locating subsets of information. For example, the default `<browserCaps>` element in *machine.config* uses nested `<filter>` elements to locate both the major and minor browser versions contained in the `HTTP_USER_AGENT` server variable so that it can assign specific properties that vary among minor versions (i.e., the x in 4.x) of a browser.

<case>

```
<case match=string>
   property1=value
   property2=value
   propertyN=value
</case>
```

Specifies one of a group of exclusive matching cases for which property assignments will be executed. Only the first matching `<case>` element within a given `<filter>` element will be executed. The rest will be ignored.

Scope

Any

Attributes

`match`

> The pattern to match. Uses the .NET Framework regular expression syntax. This attribute is optional. If omitted, all requests will be assumed to match, and any property/value assignments contained within the `<filter>` element will be executed.

`with`

> The regular expression or string to search for. This attribute is optional. If omitted, the server variable specified in the `<use>` element will be searched.

Child Elements

None

Notes

This element is useful in situations when you only want a single match. For example, the default <browserCaps> configuration in *machine.config* uses the <case> element to assign the platform, win16, and win32 attributes.

<clientTarget>

```
<clientTarget>
    <add alias=aliasName
        userAgent=userAgentString />
    <remove alias=aliasName />
    <clear />
</clientTarget>
```

Assigns aliases for specified browser user agent strings to be used by ASP.NET Server Controls in deciding what type of content to render.

Scope

Any

Attributes

None

Child Elements

<add>
> Adds an alias with the name specified by the alias attribute for the User Agent string specified by the userAgent attribute.

<remove>
> Removes a previously configured alias with the name specified by the alias attribute.

<clear>
> Clears all previously configured aliases.

Example

This example comes from the default <clientTarget> element:

```
<clientTarget>
    <add alias="ie5"
        userAgent="Mozilla/4.0 (compatible; MSIE 5.5; Windows NT 4.0)" />
    <add alias="ie4"
        userAgent="Mozilla/4.0 (compatible; MSIE 4.0; Windows NT 4.0)" />
    <add alias="uplevel"
        userAgent="Mozilla/4.0 (compatible; MSIE 4.0; Windows NT 4.0)" />
    <add alias="downlevel"
        userAgent="Unknown" />
</clientTarget>
```

Notes

This element is used primarily by the built-in ASP.NET Server Controls. Thus, you should avoid making changes to the existing aliases to avoid preventing these controls from rendering uplevel content.

<compilation>

```
<compilation
   batch=boolean
   batchTimeout=numSeconds
   debug=boolean
   defaultLanguage=languageAlias
   explicit=boolean
   maxBatchSize=maxPages
   maxBatchGeneratedFileSize=maxSize
   numRecompilesBeforeAppRestart=numRecompiles
   strict=boolean
   tempDirectory=dirName >
   <compilers>
      <compiler language=languageAlias
         extension=fileExt
         type=typeName
         warningLevel=number
         compilerOptions=optionString />
   </compilers>
   <assemblies>
      <add assembly=assemblyName />
      <remove assembly=assemblyName />
      <clear />
   </assemblies>
</compilation>
```

Provides attributes and child elements for configuring the compilation options of ASP.NET applications. All attributes are optional.

Scope

Any

Attributes

batch

Specifies whether ASP.NET should attempt to batch compile all pages in the application when the first request for a page is made. The default is True.

batchTimeout

Specifies the amount of time, in seconds, that the compiler will spend attempting to batch compile pages in the application. If the timeout is exceeded, pages will be compiled as they are requested for the first time. The default is 15.

---

debug

> Specifies whether pages will be compiled with debug symbols. The default is False.

defaultLanguage

> Specifies the language compiler that will be used to compile inline code in ASP.NET pages for which no language is specified. The default is VB (Visual Basic .NET).

explicit

> Specifies whether the Visual Basic .NET Option Explicit compiler option is enabled. The default is True.

maxBatchSize

> Specifies the maximum number of classes generated during batch compilation. The default is 1000.

maxBatchGeneratedFileSize

> Specifies the maximum combined size in KB of generated source files created during batch compilation. The default is 3000.

numRecompilesBeforeAppRestart

> Specifies the number of recompiles before the appDomain containing the application is cycled (a new appDomain is created and the old one is torn down). The default is 15.

strict

> Specifies whether the Visual Basic .NET Option Strict compiler option (which disallows implicit narrowing conversions) is enabled. The default is False.

tempDirectory

> Specifies the directory in which temporary files from dynamically compiled code for the application will be stored. The default is *%windir%\Microsoft. NET\Framework\%version%\Temporary ASP.NET Files.*

Child Elements

<assemblies>, <compilers>

Example

The example enables the Visual Basic .NET Option Strict compiler option and disables batch compilation:

```
<configuration>
    <system.web>
        <compilation
            batch="false"
            strict="true">
        </compilation>
    </system.web>
</configuration>
```

Notes

Make sure you understand the impact of changes to this element before making modifications. For example, setting the debug attribute to True will have a significant negative impact on performance. While setting the `strict` attribute to `True` will reduce the likelihood of bugs from implicit data type conversion, it could also increase the number of compiler errors you get while developing your code.

\<assemblies\>

```
<assemblies>
    <add assembly=assemblyInfo />
    <remove assembly=assemblyInfo />
    <clear />
</assemblies>
```

Adds or removes assemblies to be referenced and linked during dynamic compilation of ASP.NET pages. By default, the mscorlib, System, System.Drawing, System. EnterpriseServices, System.Web, System.Data, System.Web.Services, and System. Xml assemblies are referenced during dynamic compilation, as are any assemblies located in the application directory's *bin* subdirectory.

Scope

Any

Attributes

None

Child Elements

`<add>`

> Adds an assembly specified by the `assembly` attribute to the list of assemblies to be linked during dynamic resource compilation.

`<remove>`

> Removes a previously configured assembly specified by the `assembly` attribute from the list of assemblies to be linked during dynamic resource compilation.

`<clear>`

> Clears all previously configured assemblies.

Example

This example shows the `<add>` element used by the Mobile Internet Toolkit to add the assembly System.Web.Mobile to the list of assemblies for dynamic compilation:

```
<assemblies>
    <add assembly="System.Web.Mobile,
        Version=1.0.3300.0,
        Culture=neutral,
        PublicKeyToken=b03f5f7f11d50a3a" />
</assemblies>
```

Notes

The asterisk (*) wildcard is used with the `<add>` element to indicate that all assemblies in the application's private assembly cache (by default, the *bin* subdirectory of the application) should be added to the list of assemblies linked during

---

dynamic compilation. This ensures that all members of these assemblies will be available to all the pages in your application automatically.

<compilers>

```
<compilers>
   <compiler language=languageAlias
      extension=fileExt
      type=typeName
      warningLevel=number
      compilerOptions=optionString />
</compilers>
```

Contains one or more <compiler> elements, each of which defines configuration options for a particular compiler to be used with ASP.NET.

Scope

Any

Attributes

None

Child Elements

<compiler>

Notes

Thanks to the <compilers> and <compiler> elements, adding support for a new .NET language in ASP.NET is as simple as adding a new <compiler> element specifying the language aliases, the file extension for class files for the language, and the type information for the language compiler.

<compiler>

```
<compiler language=languageAlias
   extension=fileExt
   type=typeName
   warningLevel=number
   compilerOptions=optionString />
```

Specifies configuration options for a given language.

Scope

Any

Attributes

language

Specifies the name or names by which the language will be specified in the language attribute of the @ Page directive. Multiple names should be separated by semicolons. This attribute is required.

extension

Specifies the extension(s) used by code-behind files for the specified language. Multiple entries should be separated by semicolons. This attribute is required.

type

Specifies the .NET type information for the class to be used to compile resources for the specified language. This attribute is required.

warningLevel

Specifies the compiler warning level for the language. This attribute is optional and may not be supported for all compilers.

compilerOptions

Specifies a string containing valid compiler options to be passed to the compiler.

Child Elements

None

Notes

The `<compilers>` element in *machine.config* provides a good example of the use of this element. Review that configuration section to see how the Visual Basic .NET, C#, and JScript .NET compilers are configured.

<customErrors>

```
<customErrors
    defaultRedirect=Url
    mode=mode >
    <error statusCode=httpStatusCode
        redirect=Url />
</customErrors>
```

Specifies one or more pages to which users should be redirected if an unhandled exception is detected in an ASP.NET application. A default error page can be specified, as well as one or more error pages for specific HTTP error codes.

Scope

Any

Attributes

defaultRedirect

Specifies the URL of the page to which all errors should be redirected when no specific error page is configured for the HTTP status code of the error. This attribute is optional.

mode

Specifies the custom errors mode. Valid values are Off, On, and RemoteOnly. Off disables custom error handling, On enables custom error pages for both local and remote requests. RemoteOnly enables custom error pages for remote requests, while sending detailed error messages for local requests. This attribute is required.

Child Elements

<error>

Example

The example configures a default page to be displayed to remote clients when an unhandled exception is encountered:

```
<configuration>
    <system.web>
        <customErrors
            defaultRedirect="Error.aspx" />
    </system.web>
</configuration>
```

Notes

If you set the mode attribute to RemoteOnly, you will only be able to see detailed error information from the local machine on which the pages are running. Remote requests will return the custom error page (if any) configured for the status code of the error that occurred.

If you want to see the debug information provided by ASP.NET when an error occurs, the mode attribute should be set to Off.

<error>

```
<error statusCode=httpStatusCode
    redirect=Url />
```

Specifies a custom error page to handle redirections for a specific HTTP status code.

Scope

Any

Attributes

statusCode
> Specifies the HTTP status code (such as 404 for a "Not Found" error) for the specified custom error page. This attribute is optional.

redirect
> Specifies the URL of the page to which requests with a matching HTTP status code should be redirected. This attribute is optional.

Child Elements

None

Example

The example configures a custom error page for 404 errors, and the default error page configured in the previous example:

```
<configuration>
    <system.web>
```

```
    <customErrors
        defaultRedirect="Error.aspx">
        <error statusCode="404" redirect="My404ErrorPage.aspx"/>
    </customErrors>
  </system.web>
</configuration>
```

Notes

While custom error pages provide a convenient way to prevent users from seeing raw error messages (and perhaps provide more helpful messages), they are not a substitute for proper exception handling. By the time an error reaches a custom error page, recovering from the error gracefully will be much more difficult, which can degrade the experience of your users.

<globalization>

```
<globalization
    requestEncoding=encodingString
    responseEncoding=encodingString
    fileEncoding=encodingString
    culture=cultureString
    uiCulture=cultureString />
```

Provides attributes for configuring encoding and culture settings. These attributes are used as the basis for the expected encoding of requests, responses, and files for internationalization.

Scope

Any

Attributes

requestEncoding
> Specifies the assumed encoding of incoming requests. This can be any valid encoding string and should match the responseEncoding attribute. The default is UTF-8. This attribute is optional.

responseEncoding
> Specifies the content encoding of responses. This can be any valid encoding string and should match the requestEncoding attribute. The default is UTF-8. This attribute is optional.

fileEncoding
> Specifies the encoding used to parse *.aspx*, *.asmx*, and *.asax* files. This attribute is optional.

culture
> Specifies the assumed culture for incoming requests. The value can be any valid culture string. This attribute is optional.

uiCulture
> Specifies the culture for locale-specific resource searches. The value can be any valid culture string. This attribute is optional.

Child Elements

None

Example

This example shows how the default <globalization> settings are configured in *web.config*:

```
<configuration>
    <system.web>
        <globalization
            requestEncoding="utf-8"
            responseEncoding="utf-8" />
    </system.web>
</configuration>
```

Notes

A list of valid culture strings can be found in the .NET Framework documentation for the System.Globalization.CultureInfo class.

<httpHandlers>

```
<httpHandlers>
    <add verb=httpVerbs
        path=pathInfo
        type=typeInfo
        validate=boolean />
    <remove verb=httpVerbs
        path=pathInfo />
    <clear />
</httpHandlers>
```

Adds or removes HttpHandlers, which are used to provide request processing for a specified HTTP verb and/or file type or path. ASP.NET itself is set up as an HttpHandler for *.aspx* and *.asmx* files, and HttpHandlers are used to prevent downloading of source code for other ASP.NET file types, such as *global.asax*.

Scope

Any

Attributes

None

Child Elements

<add>

Adds an HttpHandler. The HTTP verbs (GET, POST, etc.) handled by the HttpHandler are specified by the verb attribute; the asterisk (*) wildcard is used to specify all verbs. The path or file extension to be handled by the HttpHandler is specified by the path attribute. The class used to process the request is specified by the type attribute. This class must implement the

IHttpHandler interface. Finally, the `validate` attribute tells ASP.NET whether or not to attempt to load the class specified by the `type` attribute before a matching request comes in.

`<remove>`

Removes a previously configured HttpHandler, based on the specified `verb` and `path` attributes. The attributes must match a previously configured `<add>` element.

`<clear>`

Clears all previously configured HttpHandlers.

Example

The example configures a custom HttpHandler for the file extension *.aspnetian*:

```
<configuration>
    <system.web>
        <httpHandlers>
            <add verb="*"
                path="*.aspnetian"
                type="aspnetian.aspnetianHandler" />
        </httpHandlers>
    </system.web>
</configuration>
```

Notes

To make the example work properly, you need to map the file extension *.aspnetian* to the ASP.NET ISAPI handler, Otherwise, the request would never be handed to the custom HttpHandler. Chapter 9 has a step-by-step walkthrough of the process for mapping additional file types to the ASP.NET ISAPI handler.

<httpModules>

```
<httpModules>
    <add
        name=moduleName
        type=typeInfo />
    <remove name=moduleName />
    <clear />
</httpModules>
```

Adds or removes HttpModules. HttpModules are special classes that participate in the processing of all application requests. Both ASP.NET caching and session state are implemented as HttpModules, as are the authentication and authorization features of ASP.NET.

Scope

Any

Attributes

None

Child Elements

`<add>`

> Adds an HttpModule. The class that implements the HttpModule is specified by the `type` attribute. This class must implement the IHttpModule interface. The `name` attribute provides an alias by which the HttpModule can be referred to—for example, in a later `<remove>` element.

`<remove>`

> Removes a previously configured HttpModule, based on the specified `name` attribute. The attribute must match a previously configured `<add>` element.

`<clear>`

> Clears all previously configured HttpModules.

Example

The example removes the HttpModule for the Session state provider, which can be useful if you're not using it:

```
<configuration>
    <system.web>
        <httpModules>
            <remove name="Session" />
        </httpModules>
    </system.web>
</configuration>
```

Notes

If you're not using a particular HttpModule, such as the Session state module or authentication modules, you may be able to save overhead by removing these HttpModules from an application's *web.config* file by using the `<remove>` element.

`<httpRuntime>`

```
<httpRuntime
    appRequestQueueLimit=numRequests
    executionTimeout=numSeconds
    maxRequestLength=numKBytes
    minFreeLocalRequestFreeThreads=numThreads
    minFreeThreads=numThreads
    useFullyQualifiedRedirectUrl=boolean />
```

Contains attributes used to configure the settings for the ASP.NET HTTP runtime.

Scope

Any

Attributes

`appRequestQueueLimit`

> Specifies the upper limit for request queuing. Once this limit has been reached, additional requests will receive a response of "503 - Server Too Busy". The default is 100.

executionTimeout

Specifies the amount of time, in seconds, that a request can execute before being terminated by the runtime. The default is 90.

maxRequestLength

Specifies the maximum file size, in KB, that can be uploaded by a client to an ASP.NET application. This attribute is used primarily to prevent denial of launched service attacks by attempting to upload very large files to the server. The default is 4096.

minFreeLocalRequestFreeThreads

Specifies the minimum number of threads that will be reserved for requests from the local host that require additional threads. The default is 4.

minFreeThreads

Specifies the minimum number of threads that will be reserved for requests that require additional threads. The default is 8.

useFullyQualifiedRedirectUrl

Specifies whether URLs sent to the client for redirects are fully qualified or relative. The default is False, which specifies that the URL is relative.

Child Elements

None

Example

This example forces client-side redirect URLs to be fully qualified, which is required for some of the mobile controls supplied in the Microsoft Mobile Internet Toolkit:

```
<configuration>
    <system.web>
        <httpRuntime
            useFullyQualifiedRedirectUrl="true" />
    </system.web>
</configuration>
```

Notes

One of the most commonly customized attributes is maxRequestLength, since for sites that need to upload files, 4MB can be fairly limiting. Use caution when increasing this value, however; only increase it as much as necessary for the maximum file size you expect. Making this value too large can make your site vulnerable to denial-of-service attacks.

<identity>

```
<identity
    impersonate=boolean
    userName=string
    password=string />
```

Specifies whether request impersonation is enabled, as well as the identity to be used for requests made from the ASP.NET worker process and the password for that identity.

Scope

Any

Attributes

`impersonate`
> Specifies whether impersonation is enabled for the application. If `True`, requests made by the ASP.NET worker process will be made with the security context of the account specified by the `userName` attribute; if that attribute is blank, the context of the account of the logged on user. The default is `False`.

`userName`
> Specifies the username of the Windows account to use for impersonation. If the value is left blank or is omitted, requests will be made in the context of the logged-in user.

`password`
> Specifies the password for the account named in the `userName` attribute. This password is stored in clear text.

Child Elements

None

Example

The example turns on impersonation for the logged-in user authenticated by IIS:

```
<configuration>
   <system.web>
      <identity
          impersonate="true"
          userName="" />
   </system.web>
</configuration>
```

Notes

Because the `password` attribute stores passwords in readable text, you should carefully consider whether it makes sense to use this functionality. Storing sensitive information such as passwords in text files presents a potential security risk.

<machineKey>

```
<machineKey
   validationKey="autogenerate|value"
   decryptionKey="autogenerate|value"
   validation="SHA1|MD5|3DES" />
```

Specifies the settings for cryptographic keys used for validation and decryption of Forms Authentication cookies.

Scope

All

Attributes

validationKey

> The key used for validation of forms authentication cookie data, MAC checking of ViewState, and session state cookies. The default is autogenerate, which generates and stores a random key. For web farm implementations, you can set this value to the same 40 to 128-character key value on each server to ensure that all servers can validate successfully.

decryptionKey

> The key used for decryption of forms authentication cookie data. The default is autogenerate, which generates and stores a random key. For web farm implementations, you can set this value to the same 40 to 128-character key value on each server to ensure that all servers can validate successfully.

validation

> Specifies the type of encryption used for data validation.

Child Elements

None

Notes

For web farms, ensuring that the validationKey and decryptionKey values are synchronized across all servers in the farm is important. If they are not synchronized, you may get errors in Forms Authentication, ViewState errors, or problems with session state.

<pages>

```
<pages
   buffer=boolean
   enableSessionState="true|false|ReadOnly"
   enableViewState=boolean
   enableViewStateMac=boolean
   autoEventWireup=boolean
   smartNavigation=boolean
   pageBaseType=typeInfo
   userControlBaseType=typeInfo />
```

Contains attributes used to configure the default settings for ASP.NET pages and user controls. These settings can be overridden by attributes on the @ Page or @ Control directive.

Scope

Any

Attributes

buffer

> Specifies whether buffering of page output is on or off. The default is True.

`enableSessionState`

Specifies whether a page has access to the Session state module. Acceptable values include `True`, `False`, and `ReadOnly`. The default is `True`.

`enableViewState`

Specifies whether ViewState is enabled at the page level. The default is `True`.

`enableViewStateMac`

Specifies at the page level whether a machine authentication check (MAC) is performed on the ViewState hidden field. This specification can help identify client-side tampering with the ViewState. The default is `True`.

`autoEventWireup`

Specifies whether ASP.NET will automatically support specific page events, such as Page_Load. The default is `True`.

`smartNavigation`

Specifies whether the Smart Navigation feature, for which IE 5 or above provides support for posting back and refreshing only portions of a page, is turned on at the page level. The default is `False`.

`pageBaseType`

Specifies the base class from which all pages are derived. The default is `System.Web.UI.Page`.

`userControlBaseType`

Specifies the base class from which all user controls are derived. The default is `System.Web.UI.UserControl`.

Child Elements

None

Example

The example disables both Session state and ViewState at the page level:

```
<configuration>
    <system.web>
        <pages
            enableSessionState="false"
            enableViewState="false" />
    </system.web>
</configuration>
```

Notes

The <pages> element is very useful for setting application-level (or folder-level) defaults for pages in your application. One possible use is to place pages that do not require access to session state in a separate folder and use the <pages> element to disable session state for that folder. In this case, a session will not be created for a user until the user requests a page in your application for which `EnableSessionState` is `True`.

The default setting of `EnableViewStateMac` is `True`. It's important to remember this because the MAC check uses the settings in the <machineKey> element to create an encrypted version of the ViewState hidden field. In a web farm scenario, the <machineKey> settings for each server in the farm must match. Otherwise, the MAC check will fail when a user's initial request is handled by one server, while a subsequent postback is handled by another server with different settings for <machineKey>.

<processModel>

```
<processModel
    enable=boolean
    timeout="Infinite"|HH:MM:SS
    idleTimeout="Infinite"|HH:MM:SS
    shutdownTimeout="Infinite"|HH:MM:SS
    requestLimit=numRequests
    requestQueueLimit="Infinite"|numRequests
    restartQueueLimit="Infinite"|numRequests
    memoryLimit=percentMemory
    cpuMask=cpuNumBitMask
    webGarden=boolean
    userName=username
    password=password
    logLevel="All|None|Errors"
    clientConnectedCheck=HH:MM:SS
    comAuthenticationLevel="Default|None|Connect|Call|Pkt|
        PktIntegrity|PktPrivacy"
comImpersonationLevel="Default|Anonymous|Identify|Impersonate|
    Delegate"
    responseRestartDeadlockInterval="Infinite"|HH:MM:SS
    responseDeadlockInterval="Infinite"|HH:MM:SS
    maxWorkerThreads=numThreads
    maxIoThreads=numThreads
    serverErrorMessageFile=fileName />
```

Contains attributes used to configure the ASP.NET worker process in IIS 5.

Scope

Machine only

Attributes

enable
: Specifies whether the <processModel> settings are enabled. The default is True.

timeout
: Specifies the life span, in the format *hh:mm:ss*, of the process. When this value expires, a new process is started and the current process is shut down. To disable the timeout, use the value Infinite. The default is Infinite.

idleTimeout
: Specifies the life span of the process, when idle, in the format *hh:mm:ss*. When this value expires, the current process is shut down. To disable the timeout, use the value Infinite. The default is Infinite.

shutdownTimeout

Specifies the amount of time, in the format *hh:mm:ss*, that the process is given to shut down gracefully. When this value expires, the process will be killed. To disable the timeout, use the value Infinite. The default is 0:00:05.

requestLimit

Specifies the number of requests that can be served by the ASP.NET process before it is shut down and restarted. This attribute can be used to proactively restart the ASP.NET process to compensate for memory leaks or other problems that may be associated with legacy resources (such as COM components) that you need to use in your applications. The default is Infinite, which disables this feature.

requestQueueLimit

Specifies the number of requests that can be queued by ASP.NET before it is shut down and restarted. This attribute can be used to proactively remedy situations in which resource contention causes requests to be queued. The default is 5000.

restartQueueLimit

Specifies the number of requests that will remain in the request queue while a process restart based on the requestQueueLimit setting occurs. The default is 10.

memoryLimit

Specifies the upper limit, as a percentage, of the server's physical memory that the ASP.NET process will be allowed to use. If this value is exceeded, a new process will be started up and the current process will be shut down. The default is 60.

cpuMask

Used in web garden scenarios to specify the CPU or CPUs in a multiprocessor server that will run the ASP.NET process. This value is a bitmask. The default is 0xffffffff, which specifies that a worker process should be created for every CPU.

webGarden

Specifies whether web gardening, in which worker processes are tied to specific processors within a multiprocessor server, is enabled. The default is False.

userName

Specifies the identity under which the ASP.NET worker process will be run. This can be a valid NT account or one of two special values:

SYSTEM

Runs the ASP.NET process as the SYSTEM account, which is a highly privileged administrative account.

machine

Runs the ASP.NET process as the ASPNET account (installed with the .NET Framework), which is a special account with few privileges. This process is the default and provides superior out-of-the box security for web applications written with ASP.NET. Note that the documentation for the <processModel> element incorrectly states that SYSTEM is the default.

password

Specifies the password of the account specified by the userName attribute. Use the value AutoGenerate (the default) when using the SYSTEM or machine accounts.

logLevel

Specifies the type of process events that are logged to the NT event log. Valid values are:

All

All process events will be logged.

Errors

Only errors will be logged; this is the default.

None

No process events will be logged.

clientConnectedCheck

Specifies the amount of time, in the format hh:mm:ss, that a request remains in the queue before the ASP.NET process checks to ensure that the client is still connected. The default is 0:00:05.

comAuthenticationLevel

Specifies the authentication level used for DCOM security. The default is Connect.

comImpersonationLevel

Specifies the authentication level used for COM security. The default is Impersonate.

responseRestartDeadlockInterval

Specifies the amount of time, in the format hh:mm:ss, that will be allowed to elapse between process restarts due to the responseDeadlockInterval attribute value. This specification prevents constant process cycling due to deadlocks. To disable this feature, use the value Infinite. The default is 0:09:00.

responseDeadlockInterval

Specifies the amount of time, in the format hh:mm:ss, that may elapse without a response when requests are queued. When this value expires, the process will be shut down and restarted. To disable this feature, use the value Infinite. The default is 0:03:00.

maxWorkerThreads

Specifies the upper limit for worker threads per CPU in the thread pool. The default is 25.

maxIoThreads

Specifies the upper limit for IO threads per CPU in the thread pool. The default is 25.

serverErrorMessageFile

Specifies the filename of a file to be displayed when a "Server Unavailable" error occurs.

Child Elements

None

Notes

In IIS 6 native mode, the settings in the <processModel> element will be ignored.

Because the settings in the <processModel> element are read by and applied to the unmanaged *aspnet_isapi.dll* handler that passes requests to the managed *aspnet_wp.exe* worker process (rather than by managed code), changes to the <processModel> element will not be applied until IIS is restarted.

<securityPolicy>

```
<securityPolicy>
   <trustLevel
      name=trustLevelName
      policyFile=fileName />
</securityPolicy>
```

Configures mappings of trust names (used by the <trust> element) to security policy files. The security policy files contain elements that configure the code access security permissions that are specific to that trust level. <securityPolicy> can contain one or more <trustLevel> elements.

Scope

Machine, Application

Attributes

None

Child Elements

<trustLevel>
    Each <trustLevel> element maps a trust-level name to a specific policy file that implements the code access security permissions for that trust level. The name attribute specifies the name by which the trust level will be referred in the <trust> element, while the policyFile attribute specifies the name of the policy file to map to the name.

Example

This example comes from the default <securityPolicy> element in *machine.config*:

```
<securityPolicy>
   <trustLevel
      name="Full"
      policyFile="internal" />
   <trustLevel
      name="High"
      policyFile="web_hightrust.config" />
   <trustLevel
```

```
        name="Low"
        policyFile="web_lowtrust.config" />
    <trustLevel
        name="None"
        policyFile="web_notrust.config" />
  </securityPolicy>
```

Notes

For a specific application, if you want to modify the code access security permissions applied, you could create a new CAS policy file and map that file to a custom trust level by using the <trustLevel> element. To implement the new security policy, you would add a <trust> element to the *web.config* file of the desired application and use it to specify the mapped policy file by name.

<sessionState>

```
<sessionState
    mode="Off|Inproc|StateServer|SQLServer"
    cookieless=boolean
    timeout=numMinutes
    stateNetworkTimeout=numSeconds
    stateConnectionString="tcpip=server:port"
    sqlConnectionString=connString />
```

Scope

Machine, Application

Attributes

mode

Specifies whether session state is enabled, and if so, how the state data will be stored. Valid values are:

Off

The session state is disabled.

InProc

The session state data will be stored in memory on the local server. This is the same model as session state in classic ASP. This session state mode does not allow session state to be shared across servers in a web farm.

StateServer

The session state data will be stored in memory in a special NT state service on a designated state server. This session state mode allows session state to be shared across servers in a web farm.

SQLServer

The session state data will be stored in a special SQL Server database on a designated SQL Server. This session state mode allows session state to be shared across servers in a web farm. This mode also requires running a SQL query (which is included with the .NET Framework SDK) to set up the SQL Server database.

The default is InProc.

---

cookieless

Specifies whether or not cookies will be used to associate users with specific sessions. If set to True, the session identifier will be automatically munged into the URL for each request. This requires that your application use relative URLs to work correctly. The default is False.

timeout

Specifies the amount of time, in minutes, before the session will time out when inactive (no requests are received with that SessionID). The default is 20.

stateNetworkTimeout

Specifies the amount of time, in seconds, that network operations will time out when working with the StateServer session state mode. The default is 10.

stateConnectionString

Specifies the server name or IP address and TCP port number for the session state server when using StateServer mode. This attribute is required when the mode attribute is StateServer. The default is tcpip=127.0.0.1:42424.

sqlConnectionString

Specifies the SQL Server name and authentication credentials when using SQLServer session mode. This attribute is required when the mode attribute is SQLServer. The default is data source=127.0.0.1;user id=sa;password=. Where possible, this value should use trusted connections to avoid storing a SQL userID and password in the *web.config* or *machine.config* file. To support SQL Server state mode, you need to run the *InstallSqlState.sql* batch file on the target SQL server to create the ASPState database and its associated tables and stored procedures. This file is installed by default in the *%windir%\Microsoft.NET\Framework\%version%* folder.

Child Elements

None

Example

The example configures session state to run in SQL Server mode without cookies:

```
<configuration>
    <system.web>
        <sessionState
            mode="SQLServer"
            cookieless="true"
            sqlConnectionString="data source=myServer;trusted_
connection=true" />
    </system.web>
</configuration>
```

Notes

To use SQL Server mode with a trusted connection, the account identity of the ASP.NET worker process must have a login to the SQL Server database and must have permission to access the ASPState and TempDB databases. If you cannot use a trusted connection, you should create a special account specifically to access the state database, and use that account for the *sqlConnectionString* attribute.

Note that when using either of the out-of-process session state modes, it's wise to use the `EnableSessionState` attribute of the `@ Page` directive to disable session state for pages in your application that do not use it. Otherwise, these pages will make unnecessary cross-machine calls to retrieve unused session state information. If you have a page that reads session data but does not alter it, you can also set the `EnableSessionState` attribute to `ReadOnly` to avoid the cross-machine call to store updated session data.

<trace>

```
<trace
    enabled=boolean
    localOnly=boolean
    pageOutput=boolean
    requestLimit=numRequests
    traceMode="SortByTime|SortByCategory" />
```

Scope

Any

Attributes

`enabled`

Specifies whether tracing is enabled. The default is `False`.

`localOnly`

Specifies whether or not trace output can be viewed by machines other than the local host. The default is `True`.

`pageOutput`

Specifies whether trace output is rendered to the page or stored in memory and made accessible by the special *Trace.axd* URL. *Trace.axd* maps to an HttpHandler that displays all currently stored traces for a given application. The default is `False`.

`requestLimit`

Specifies the number of requests that can be stored in the trace buffer read by *Trace.axd*. Once the total number of request traces specified by this attribute has been stored, no more traces will be stored until the trace log has been cleared. The page displayed by *Trace.axd* includes a link for clearing the trace log. The default is 10.

`traceMode`

Specifies the sort order of items in the Trace Information section of the trace. Valid values are `SortByTime` and `SortByCategory`. `SortByCategory` is useful when you are using Trace.Write and Trace.Warn with your own category names passed as parameters. The default is `SortByTime`.

Child Elements

None

Example

This example turns tracing on at the application level:

```
<configuration>
    <system.web>
        <trace enabled="true" />
    </system.web>
</configuration>
```

Notes

Chapter 10 provides an overview of how to use the trace functionality of ASP.NET.

<trust>

```
<trust
    level="Full|High|Low|None"
    originUrl=URL />
```

Assigns a named trust level created with the <trustLevel> child element of the <securityPolicy> element to a machine, a site, or an application.

Scope

Machine, Application

Attributes

level
> Specifies the trust level to be applied. This attribute can be any value defined by the <securityPolicy> element. The default is Full. This attribute is required.

originUrl
> Specifies URL of origin of an application. This attribute allows classes such as WebRequest, which may need the origin host information for certain security permissions, to work properly. This attribute is optional.

Child Elements

None

Example

This example sets the application CAS permissions, based on a custom trust level:

```
<configuration>
    <system.web>
        <trust level="myTrustLevel" />
    </system.web>
</configuration>
```

Notes

Make sure that you understand the security implications of using custom security policy mappings before using this element. Incorrect permissions can cause major problems for your application.

<location>

```
<location
   path=pathToConfigure
   allowOverride=boolean >
   <system.web>
      <!-- Configuration settings -->
   </system.web>
</location>
```

Allows you to prevent settings in *machine.config* or *web.config* from being overridden in child configuration files. You can also use it to configure settings for
specific files or folders from a configuration file in a parent folder.

Scope

Any

Attributes

path
> Specifies the path to the file or folder to which the configuration settings
> contained in the <location> tag pair should be applied.

allowOverride
> Specifies whether child configuration files can override values configured within
> the <location> tag pair. This attribute locks down configuration settings (i.e., at
> the *machine.config* level) for which you want to enforce uniformity.

Child Elements

<system.web>

Example

The example, if used in *machine.config*, would force all applications on the
machine to use Windows authentication:

```
<configuration>
   <location
      allowOverride="false">
      <system.web>
         <authentication mode="Windows">
      </system.web>
   </location>
   <system.web>
      <!-- Other configuration settings -->
   </system.web>
</configuration>
```

Notes

This tag provides powerful control over configuration. In addition to the scenario
of enforcing an authentication method across all applications, you can also use the
path attribute to configure multiple child folders or files from the *web.config* file in
the root of the application. Using this configuration can avoid having a large
number of child *web.config* files to manage for a larger application.

PART III

Namespace Reference

The quick-reference section that follows packs a lot of information into a small space. This introductory section explains how to get the most out of that information: it describes how the quick reference is organized and how to read the individual quick reference entries.

CHAPTER 21

Namespace Reference

The quick reference is organized into chapters-one per namespace. Each chapter begins with an overview of the namespace and includes a hierarchy diagram for the types (classes, interfaces, enumerations, delegates, and structs) in the namespace. Quick-reference entries for all the types in the namespace follow the overview.

Figure 21-1 is a sample diagram showing the notation used in this book. This notation is similar to that used in O'Reilly's *Java in a Nutshell*, but it borrows some features from UML.

Classes marked as MustInherit are shown as a slanted rectangle; classes marked as NonInheritable are shown as an octagonal rectangle. Inheritance is shown as a solid line from the subtype, ending with a hollow triangle that points to the base class. Two notations indicate interface implementation. The lollipop notation is used most of the time, since it is easier to read. In some cases, especially when many types implement a given interface, the shaded box notation with the dashed line is used.

Important relationships between types (associations) are shown with a dashed line ending with an arrow. The figures don't show every possible association. Some types have strong containing relationships with one another. For example, a System.Net.WebException object instance includes a System.Net.WebResponse object instance that represents the HTTP response containing the error details (HTTP status code and error message). To show this relationship, a filled diamond is attached to the containing type with a solid line that points to the contained type.

Entries are organized alphabetically by type and namespace so that related types are grouped near one another. Thus, in order to look up a quick reference entry for a particular type, you must also know the name of the namespace that contains that type. Usually, the namespace is obvious from the context, and you should have no trouble looking up the quick-reference entry you want. Use the tabs on the outside edge of the book and the dictionary-style headers on the upper corner of each page to help you find the namespace and type you are looking for.

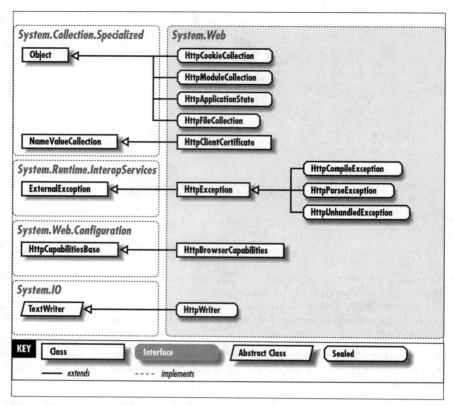

Figure 21–1: Class hierarchy notation

Occasionally, you may need to look up a type for which you do not already know the namespace. In this case, refer to the Appendix at the end of this book. This index allows you to look up a type by its name and identify what namespace it is part of.

Reading a Quick-Reference Entry

Each quick-reference entry contains quite a bit of information. The sections that follow describe the structure of a quick-reference entry, explaining what information is available, where it is found, and what it means. While reading the descriptions that follow, you will find it helpful to flip through the reference section itself to find examples of the described features.

Type Name, Namespace, Assembly, Type Category, and Flags

Each quick-reference entry begins with a four-part title that specifies the name, namespace (followed by the assembly in parentheses), and type category of the type, and may also specify various additional flags that describe the type. The type name appears in bold at the upper-left side of the title. The namespace and assembly appear in smaller print in the lower-left side, below the type name.

The upper-right portion of the title indicates the type category of the type (class, delegate, enum, interface, or struct). The "class" category may include modifiers such as NonInheritable or MustInherit.

In the lower-right corner of the title, you may find a list of flags that describe the type. The possible flags and their meanings are as follows:

ECMA
> Specifies that the type is part of the ECMA CLI specification.

serializable
> Specifies that the type, or a base class, implements System.Runtime.Serialization.ISerializable or has been flagged with the System.Serializable attribute.

marshal by reference
> This class, or a superclass, derives from System.MarshalByRefObject.

context bound
> This class, or a superclass, derives from System.ContextBoundObject.

disposable
> Specifies that the type implements the System.IDisposable interface.

flag
> Specifies that the enumeration be marked with the System.FlagsAttribute attribute.

Description

The title of each quick-reference entry is followed by a short description of the most important features of the type. This description may be anywhere from a couple of sentences to several paragraphs long.

Synopsis

The most important part of every quick-reference entry is the synopsis, which follows the title and description. The synopsis for a type looks much like its source code, except that the member bodies are omitted and some additional annotations are added. If you know VB.NET syntax, you know how to read the type synopsis.

The first line of the synopsis contains information about the type itself. It begins with a list of type modifiers, such as MustInherit and NonInheritable. These modifiers are followed by the Class, Delegate, Enum, Interface, or Struct keyword and then by the name of the type. The type name may be followed by a colon (:) and a base class or interfaces that the type implements.

The type definition line is followed by a list of the members that the type defines. This list includes only members that are explicitly declared in the type, are overridden from a base class, or are implementations of an interface member. Members that are simply inherited from a base class are not shown; you will need to look up the base class definition to find those members.

Once again, if you understand basic VB.NET syntax, you should have no trouble making sense of these lines. The listing for each member includes the modifiers, type, and name of the member. For methods, the synopsis also includes the type and name of each method parameter. The member names are in boldface, so it is easy to scan the list of members looking for the one you want. The names of method parameters are in italics to indicate that they should not be used literally. The member listings are printed on alternating gray and white backgrounds to keep them visually separate.

Member Availability and Flags

Each member listing is a single line that defines the syntax for that member. These listings use VB.NET syntax, so their meaning is immediately clear to any VB.NET programmer. Some auxiliary information associated with each member synopsis, however, requires explanation.

The area to the right of the member synopsis displays a variety of flags that provide additional information about the member. Some flags indicate additional specification details that do not appear in the member syntax itself.

The following flags may be displayed to the right of a member synopsis:

Overrides
> Indicates that a method overrides a method in one of its base classes. The flag is followed by the name of the base class that the method overrides.

Implements
> Indicates that a method implements a method in an interface. The flag is followed by the name of the implemented interface.

= For enumeration fields and constant fields, this flag is followed by the constant value of the field. Only constants of primitive and String types and constants with the value Nothing are displayed. Some constant values are specification details, while others are implementation details. Some constants, such as System.BitConverter.IsLittleEndian, are platform dependent. Platform-dependent values shown in this book conform to the System.PlatformID.Win32NT platform (32-bit Windows NT, 2000, or XP). The reason why symbolic constants are defined, however, is so you can write code that does not rely directly upon the constant value. Use this flag to help you understand the type, but do not rely upon the constant values in your own programs.

Functional Grouping of Members

Within a type synopsis, the members are not listed in strict alphabetical order. Instead, they are broken down into functional groups and listed alphabetically within each group. Constructors, events, fields, methods, and properties are all listed separately. Instance methods are kept separate from shared (class) methods. Public members are listed separately from protected members. Grouping members by category breaks a type down into smaller, more comprehensible segments, making the type easier to understand. This grouping also makes it easier for you to find a desired member.

Functional groups are separated from one another in a type synopsis with VB.NET comments, such as:

Public Constructors

or:

' Protected Instance Properties

or:

' Events

The various functional categories follow below (in the order in which they appear in a type synopsis):

Constructors
> Displays the constructors for the type. Public and protected constructors are displayed separately in subgroupings. If a type defines no constructor at all, the VB.NET compiler adds a default parameterless constructor that is displayed here. If a type defines only private constructors, it cannot be instantiated, so no constructor appears. Constructors are listed first because the first thing you do with most types is instantiate them by calling a constructor.

Fields
> Displays all fields defined by the type, including constants. Public and protected fields are displayed in separate subgroups. Fields are listed here, near the top of the synopsis, because constant values are often used throughout the type as legal values for method parameters and return values.

Properties
> Lists all the properties of the type, breaking them down into subgroups for public and protected shared properties and public and protected instance properties. After the property name, its accessors (get or set) are shown.

Shared methods
> Lists the shared methods (class methods) of the type, broken down into subgroups for public shared methods and protected shared methods.

Public instance methods
> Contains all public instance methods.

Protected instance methods
> Contains all protected instance methods.

Class Hierarchy

For any type that has a nontrivial inheritance hierarchy, the synopsis is followed by a "Hierarchy" section. This section lists all of the base classes of the type, as well as any interfaces implemented by those base classes. It also lists any interfaces implemented by an interface. In the hierarchy listing, arrows indicate base class to derived class relationships, while the interfaces implemented by a type follow the type name in parentheses. For example, the following hierarchy indicates that System.IO.Stream implements IDisposable and extends MarshalByRefObject, which itself extends Object:

If a type has subtypes, the "Hierarchy" section is followed by a "Subtypes" section that lists those subtypes. If an interface has implementations, the "Hierarchy" section is followed by an "Implementations" section that lists those implementations. While the "Hierarchy" section shows ancestors of the type, the "Subtypes" or "Implementations" section shows descendants.

Cross References

The hierarchy section of a quick-reference entry is followed by optional cross reference sections that indicate other related types and methods that may be of interest. These sections include:

Passed to
> This section lists all members (from other types) that are passed an object of this type as an argument, including properties whose values can be set to this type. It is useful when you have an object of a given type and want to know where it can be used.

Returned by
> This section lists all members that return an object of this type, including properties whose values can take on this type. It is useful when you know that you want to work with an object of this type, but don't know how to obtain one.

Valid on
> For attributes, this section lists the attribute targets that the attribute can be applied to.

Associated events
> For delegates, this section lists the events it can handle.

A Note About Type Names

Throughout the quick reference, you'll notice that types are sometimes referred to by type name alone, and at other times are referred to by type name and namespace. If namespaces were always used, the type synopses would become long and hard to read. On the other hand, if namespaces were never used, it would sometimes be difficult to know what type was being referred to. The rules for including or omitting the namespace name are complex. However, they can be summarized as follows:

- If the type name alone is ambiguous, the namespace name is always used.

- If the type is part of the System namespace or is a commonly used type like System.Collection.ICollection, the namespace is omitted.

- If the type being referred to is part of the current namespace (and has a quick-reference entry in the current chapter), the namespace is omitted. The namespace is also omitted if the type being referred to is part of a namespace that contains the current namespace.

CHAPTER 22

The System.Web Namespace

The System.Web namespace contains some of the fundamental ingredients for ASP.NET applications. These ingredients include the classes used for the original built-in ASP objects (Request, Response, Application, and Server), as well as classes for managing cookies, configuring page caching, implementing tracing, and retrieving information about the web server and client browser. Aside from the classes required for web services and the Web Forms user interface, the System.Web namespace contains the heart of ASP.NET's functionality. Figure 22-1 and Figure 22-2 show the types in this namespace.

One confusing aspect about the System.Web namespace is Microsoft's "all roads lead to Rome" approach to backward compatibility. For example, the HttpRequest class can be accessed on a Web Form through the Page class (Page.Request), the HttpContext class (Page.Context.Request), and the HttpApplication class (Page.Context.ApplicationInstance.Request). In all cases, the reference is pointing to the same object. Essentially, the HttpContext class encapsulates the fundamental types that relate to an HTTP request. The HttpContext object is made available to all IHttpModule and IHttpHandler instances (which includes HttpApplication, System.Web.UI.Page, and System.Web.UI.UserControl), and some of its properties are "magically" copied into these classes for convenience and backward compatibility. When you use the built-in Request object on a Web Forms page, for example, you use the Request property from the Page class.

Due to backward compatibility, some class names don't match the name of the corresponding built-in object. For example, the Application object is an instance of the HttpApplicationState class, not the HttpApplication class. Similarly, the built-in Response.Cache object references an instance of the HttpCachePolicy class, while the built-in Cache object references the System.Web.Caching.Cache class.

BeginEventHandler

Delegate

System.Web (system.web.dll)

serializable

This class is used to connect an event handler to an HttpApplication event. It is used transparently by the ASP.NET framework.

Public Delegate Function **BeginEventHandler**(ByVal sender As Object, ByVal e As EventArgs, _
    ByVal cb As AsyncCallback, ByVal extraData As Object) As IAsyncResult

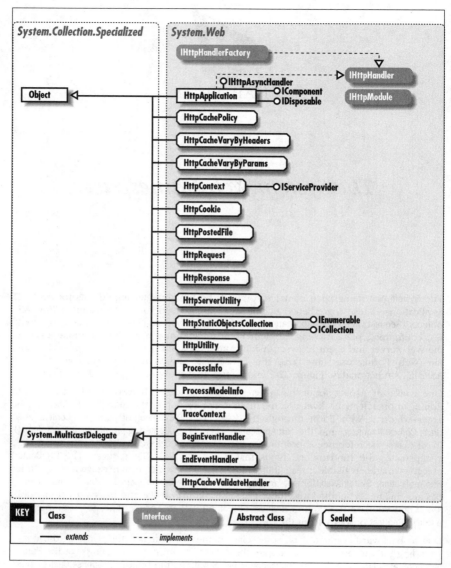

Figure 22-1: Fundamental types from System.Web

EndEventHandler

Delegate

System.Web (system.web.dll)

serializable

This class is used to connect an event handler to an HttpApplication event. It is used transparently by the ASP.NET framework.

Public Delegate Sub **EndEventHandler**(ByVal ar As IAsyncResult)

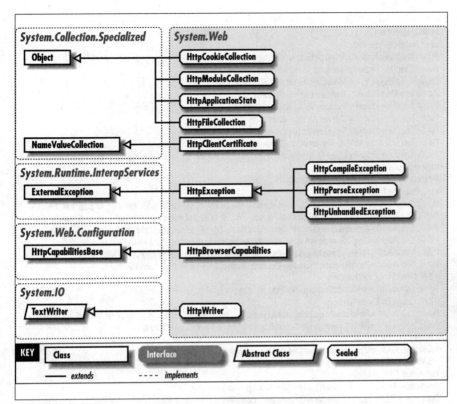

Figure 22-2: More System.Web types, including collections and exceptions

HttpApplication
Class

System.Web (system.web.dll)
disposable

HttpApplication is the default base class from which your web application derives. This class is most notable for the application-level events it provides. You can code event handlers that react to global application events in the *global.asax* file. If you use Visual Studio .NET to create a code-behind class (like *global.asax.vb*), the event handler code will be created in a class called Global, which inherits from HttpApplication. Note that the application event handlers are not connected with a Handles keyword or AddHandler() statement. Instead, they are recognized by their method names, which must match the event name and be preceded by "Application_" (as in Application_AuthenticateRequest or Application_EndRequest).

The first time a user navigates to a page in your application, the ASP.NET engine creates a pool of HttpApplication objects. Whenever your application receives a request, the ASP.NET engine automatically assigns one of these HttpApplication instances to serve the request. This HttpApplication instance will be reused, but only once the request is complete.

```
Public Class HttpApplication : Implements IHttpAsyncHandler, IHttpHandler , System.ComponentModel.IComponent, _
    IDisposable
' Public Constructors
```

```
      Public Sub New()
' Public Instance Properties
      Public ReadOnly Property Application As HttpApplicationState
      Public ReadOnly Property Context As HttpContext
      Public ReadOnly Property Modules As HttpModuleCollection
      Public ReadOnly Property Request As HttpRequest
      Public ReadOnly Property Response As HttpResponse
      Public ReadOnly Property Server As HttpServerUtility
      Public ReadOnly Property Session As HttpSessionState
      Public Property Site As ISite Implements IComponent.Site
      Public ReadOnly Property User As IPrincipal
' Protected Instance Properties
      Protected Property Events As EventHandlerList
' Public Instance Methods
      Public Sub AddOnAcquireRequestStateAsync(ByVal bh As BeginEventHandler, ByVal eh As EndEventHandler)
      Public Sub AddOnAuthenticateRequestAsync(ByVal bh As BeginEventHandler, ByVal eh As EndEventHandler)
      Public Sub AddOnAuthorizeRequestAsync(ByVal bh As BeginEventHandler, ByVal eh As EndEventHandler)
      Public Sub AddOnBeginRequestAsync(ByVal bh As BeginEventHandler, ByVal eh As EndEventHandler)
      Public Sub AddOnEndRequestAsync(ByVal bh As BeginEventHandler, ByVal eh As EndEventHandler)
      Public Sub AddOnPostRequestHandlerExecuteAsync(ByVal bh As BeginEventHandler, _
        ByVal eh As EndEventHandler)
      Public Sub AddOnPreRequestHandlerExecuteAsync(ByVal bh As BeginEventHandler, _
        ByVal eh As EndEventHandler)
      Public Sub AddOnReleaseRequestStateAsync(ByVal bh As BeginEventHandler, ByVal eh As EndEventHandler)
      Public Sub AddOnResolveRequestCacheAsync(ByVal bh As BeginEventHandler, _
        ByVal eh As EndEventHandler)
      Public Sub AddOnUpdateRequestCacheAsync(ByVal bh As BeginEventHandler, _
        ByVal eh As EndEventHandler)
      Public Sub CompleteRequest()
      Overridable Public Sub Dispose() Implements IDisposable.Dispose
      Overridable Public Function GetVaryByCustomString(ByVal context As HttpContext, ByVal custom As String) _
        As String
      Overridable Public Sub Init()
' Events
      Public Event AcquireRequestState As EventHandler
      Public Event AuthenticateRequest As EventHandler
      Public Event AuthorizeRequest As EventHandler
      Public Event BeginRequest As EventHandler
      Public Event Disposed As EventHandler Implements IComponent.Disposed
      Public Event EndRequest As EventHandler
      Public Event Error As EventHandler
      Public Event PostRequestHandlerExecute As EventHandler
      Public Event PreRequestHandlerExecute As EventHandler
      Public Event PreSendRequestContent As EventHandler
      Public Event PreSendRequestHeaders As EventHandler
      Public Event ReleaseRequestState As EventHandler
      Public Event ResolveRequestCache As EventHandler
      Public Event UpdateRequestCache As EventHandler
End Class
```

HttpApplicationState
NotInheritable Class

System.Web (system.web.dll)

This class provides server-side state management that is available globally across all client sessions in an ASP.NET application. Application state is not shared across multiple ASP.NET applications, or across multiple processes or multiple computers in a single application (for example, proxy load balancing in a web farm can thwart this type of state management).

The HttpApplicationState class exposes a name/value collection of items that can store simple value types or instances of .NET objects. A single instance of the class is created automatically the first time a client requests a page in the ASP.NET virtual directory. A reference is provided through the built-in Application object.

The HttpApplicationState class combines two state collections: Contents and StaticObjects. The StaticObjects collection contains the application state objects that are defined in the *global.asax* file with <object runat=server> tags. This collection is immutable. The Contents collection contains all the state objects added at runtime.

The Item collection is the default indexer for HttpApplicationState, so you can use the name of a state object as an index, as in: Application("globalcounter") = 1. If you assign a value to a state object that does not exist, it is created automatically. Items are stored as the generic System.Object type and must be cast to the appropriate types when you retrieve them.

Multiple clients or threads can access application state values simultaneously. To avoid synchronization problems, use the Lock() method to gain exclusive access before writing to a property, followed by the UnLock() method. This approach can result in performance degradation, which makes this type of state management unsuitable for frequently modified values. Using another form of state management or a relational database is usually a better alternative. HttpApplicationState objects should also be thread-safe, or you should use synchronization techniques (like the SyncLock statement).

```
Public NotInheritable Class HttpApplicationState : Inherits    _
          System.Collections.Specialized.NameObjectCollectionBase
' Public Instance Properties
    Public ReadOnly Property AllKeys As String()
    Public ReadOnly Property Contents As HttpApplicationState
    Overrides Public ReadOnly Property Count As Integer
    Public Default Property Item (ByVal name As String) As Object
    Public Default ReadOnly Property Item (ByVal index As Integer) As Object
    Public ReadOnly Property StaticObjects As HttpStaticObjectsCollection
' Public Instance Methods
    Public Sub Add(ByVal name As String, ByVal value As Object)
    Public Sub Clear()
    Public Function Get(ByVal index As Integer) As Object
    Public Function Get(ByVal name As String) As Object
    Public Function GetKey(ByVal index As Integer) As String
    Public Sub Lock()
    Public Sub Remove(ByVal name As String)
    Public Sub RemoveAll()
    Public Sub RemoveAt(ByVal index As Integer)
    Public Sub Set(ByVal name As String, ByVal value As Object)
    Public Sub UnLock()
End Class
```

Hierarchy: System.Object → System.Collections.Specialized.NameObjectCollectionBase (System.Collections.ICollection , System.Collections.IEnumerable , System.Runtime.Serialization.ISerializable , System.Runtime.Serialization.IDeserializationCallback) → HttpApplicationState

HttpBrowserCapabilities

System.Web (system.web.dll)

This class allows you to take advantage of features enabled in the client's browser. It is automatically available through the Browser property of the built-in Request object and corresponds roughly to the MSWC.BrowserCapabilities component that existed in ASP.

Essentially, the HttpBrowserCapabilities class is a list of properties that describe the client's browser. Many properties return True or False, depending on whether a given capability is enabled in the browser, such as ActiveXControls, BackgroundSounds, CDF (the channel definition format used in webcasting), Cookies, Frames, JavaApplets, JavaScript, and VBScript. Other Boolean values tell you whether or not the browser is AOL-based, a beta, and running on the Win16 or Win32 platform (the AOL, Beta, Win16, and Win32 properties, respectively). Additionally, you can retrieve information such as version number (MajorVersion and MinorVersion), the Platform name (e.g., "Win32"), the browser Type (e.g., "Microsoft Internet Explorer 5"), and the full Version number as a string.

```
Public Class HttpBrowserCapabilities : Inherits System.Web.Configuration.HttpCapabilitiesBase
' Public Constructors
   Public Sub New()
' Public Instance Properties
   Public ReadOnly Property ActiveXControls As Boolean
   Public ReadOnly Property AOL As Boolean
   Public ReadOnly Property BackgroundSounds As Boolean
   Public ReadOnly Property Beta As Boolean
   Public ReadOnly Property Browser As String
   Public ReadOnly Property CDF As Boolean
   Public ReadOnly Property ClrVersion As Version
   Public ReadOnly Property Cookies As Boolean
   Public ReadOnly Property Crawler As Boolean
   Public ReadOnly Property EcmaScriptVersion As Version
   Public ReadOnly Property Frames As Boolean
   Public ReadOnly Property JavaApplets As Boolean
   Public ReadOnly Property JavaScript As Boolean
   Public ReadOnly Property MajorVersion As Integer
   Public ReadOnly Property MinorVersion As Double
   Public ReadOnly Property MSDomVersion As Version
   Public ReadOnly Property Platform As String
   Public ReadOnly Property Tables As Boolean
   Public ReadOnly Property TagWriter As Type
   Public ReadOnly Property Type As String
   Public ReadOnly Property VBScript As Boolean
   Public ReadOnly Property Version As String
   Public ReadOnly Property W3CDomVersion As Version
   Public ReadOnly Property Win16 As Boolean
   Public ReadOnly Property Win32 As Boolean
End Class
```

Hierarchy: System.Object → System.Web.Configuration.HttpCapabilitiesBase → HttpBrowserCapabilities

HttpCacheability

System.Web (system.web.dll)

This enumeration is used by the HttpCachePolicy.SetCacheability() method of the HttpCachePolicy class. It allows you to configure how a cached page is shared among users. A value of Public means that the page can be stored in shared caches on a proxy server, or ASP.NET's own output cache, and made available to all clients. Private means that the page can be cached only on the client's computer, will not be stored in the ASP.NET output cache or on a proxy server, and cannot benefit other users.

```
Public Enum HttpCacheability
    NoCache = 1
    Private = 2
    Server = 3
    Public = 4
End Enum
```

Hierarchy: System.Object → System.ValueType → System.Enum (System.IComparable , System.IFormattable , System.IConvertible)→ HttpCacheability

HttpCachePolicy   NotInheritable Class

System.Web (system.web.dll)

This class allows you to configure "page" or output caching for an ASP.NET application, which stores a fully rendered page for automatic reuse. A cached page will be used for GET requests until it expires, as long as the URL request does not have different query string arguments. A cached page will not be used for POST requests, so postbacks (such as when a user clicks on button) will bypass the cached page. (This behavior is slightly and mysteriously different than just using the <OutputCache> page directive, which always reuses the cached page for any type of request when the VaryByParam attribute is set to None.) To specifically modify this behavior, you can use the VaryBy-Params property and the HttpCacheVaryByParams class.

To enable caching for a page, use the SetCacheability() method to set the page's visibility to Public so it can be stored in the shared cache. Then use the SetExpires() method to determine the lifetime of the page in the cache. For example, Response.Cache.SetEx-pires(DateTime.Now.AddSeconds(60)) will keep a page for 60 seconds, which is enough to make a substantial performance difference. By default, the cache uses absolute expira-tion. You can also invoke the SetSlidingExpiration() method, with the parameter True, to enable sliding expiration. In sliding expiration, the time limit is compared to the time elapsed since the most recent request, not the time since the first request. You can also use the AddValidationCallback() method to add a callback that decides on a page-by-page basis whether to allow a cached page to be served. Finally, you can use fragment caching by developing a Web Form user control for a portion of a page, and caching just that portion using page directives or the methods of this class.

If your page requires customization based on Session variables or user- specific details other than a query string, you shouldn't cache the page! In these cases, data caching will be more useful. With data caching, you manually store specific information, such as binary data or recordsets. For more information on data caching, refer to the Sys-tem.Web.Caching.Cache class.

The HttpCachePolicy class is available through the Cache property of the built-in Response object. It replaces properties of the Response object that were used to configure caching in ASP (like CacheControl and Expires). Microsoft uses somewhat confusing nomenclature. An instance of the HttpCachePolicy class (used to configure page caching) is available through the built-in Response.Cache object, and the System.Web.Caching.Cache class (used for data caching) is available through the built-in Cache object. Cache and Response.Cache are not the same!

```
Public NotInheritable Class HttpCachePolicy
' Public Instance Properties
```

System.Web Namespace

Public ReadOnly Property **VaryByHeaders** As HttpCacheVaryByHeaders
Public ReadOnly Property **VaryByParams** As HttpCacheVaryByParams
' *Public Instance Methods*
Public Sub **AddValidationCallback**(ByVal handler As HttpCacheValidateHandler, ByVal data As Object)
Public Sub **AppendCacheExtension**(ByVal extension As String)
Public Sub **SetCacheability**(ByVal cacheability As HttpCacheability)
Public Sub **SetCacheability**(ByVal cacheability As HttpCacheability, ByVal field As String)
Public Sub **SetETag**(ByVal etag As String)
Public Sub **SetETagFromFileDependencies**()
Public Sub **SetExpires**(ByVal date As Date)
Public Sub **SetLastModified**(ByVal date As Date)
Public Sub **SetLastModifiedFromFileDependencies**()
Public Sub **SetMaxAge**(ByVal delta As TimeSpan)
Public Sub **SetNoServerCaching**()
Public Sub **SetNoStore**()
Public Sub **SetNoTransforms**()
Public Sub **SetProxyMaxAge**(ByVal delta As TimeSpan)
Public Sub **SetRevalidation**(ByVal revalidation As HttpCacheRevalidation)
Public Sub **SetSlidingExpiration**(ByVal slide As Boolean)
Public Sub **SetValidUntilExpires**(ByVal validUntilExpires As Boolean)
Public Sub **SetVaryByCustom**(ByVal custom As String)
End Class

HttpCacheRevalidation

Enum

System.Web (system.web.dll)   *serializable*

This enumeration is used by the SetRevalidation() method of the HttpCachePolicy class, which programmatically forces the revalidation of a page. If you use ProxyCaches with this method, the page will be dropped from all shared caches, but potentially left in the client's local cache. If you use AllCaches, the page will be dropped from all caches.

Public Enum **HttpCacheRevalidation**
    AllCaches = 1
    ProxyCaches = 2
    None = 3
End Enum

Hierarchy: System.Object → System.ValueType → System.Enum (System.IComparable , System.IFormattable , System.IConvertible) → HttpCacheRevalidation

HttpCacheValidateHandler

Delegate

System.Web (system.web.dll)   *serializable*

A function with this signature can be used for the AddValidationCallback() method of the HttpCachePolicy class. Using this signature gives you the opportunity to check other dependencies that a cached page may have and either allow the page to be served or invalidate it and require the page to be recompiled. To invalidate a page, set the validationStatus parameter to HttpValidationStatus.Invalid.

Public Delegate Sub **HttpCacheValidateHandler**(ByVal context As HttpContext, ByVal data As Object, _
    ByRef validationStatus As HttpValidationStatus)

HttpCacheVaryByHeaders
NotInheritable Class

System.Web (system.web.dll)

This class is used to set the VaryByHeaders property of the HttpCachePolicy class. It allows you to specify that separate versions of a page should be cached for different languages or character sets. For example, if you set the UserCharSet property of this class to True, the "Accept-Charset" field will be included in the HTTP Vary header and a separate version of the page will be cached for each request that has a different character set. The cache page will be reused only among requests that have the same Accept-Charset header.

Alternatively, if type safety is not important, you can set the default Item property to a string that contains the name of a header, or a list of header names separated by semi-colons (;). Cached pages will then be reused only among requests that have the same values for the headers you identify.

```
Public NotInheritable Class HttpCacheVaryByHeaders
' Public Instance Properties
    Public Property AcceptTypes As Boolean
    Public Default Property Item (ByVal header As String) As Boolean
    Public Property UserAgent As Boolean
    Public Property UserCharSet As Boolean
    Public Property UserLanguage As Boolean
' Public Instance Methods
    Public Sub VaryByUnspecifiedParameters()
End Class
```

HttpCacheVaryByParams
NotInheritable Class

System.Web (system.web.dll)

This class is used to set the VaryByParams property of the HttpCachePolicy class. By default, cached pages will be reused only for GET requests with identical query string arguments. However, if you supply an instance of an HttpCacheVaryByParams class, the parameters that you specify will be the only criteria that determine whether or not a cached page can be reused. For example, if you specify ProductID, a separate copy of the page's output will be cached every time ASP.NET receives a request for the page with a different ProductID value. You can also use the wildcard asterisk (*) to indicate that all variables will be used to determine whether a page should be cached. This technique is discouraged because it could lead to excesssive copies of the page being stored in the cache, which could cause ASP.NET to clear out other, more useful data.

To specify parameters, set the default item property to a string that contains the name of a variable or to a list of variable names separated by semi-colons (;). Cached pages will be reused among requests that have the same values for these variables (in either the query string or form POST collection). All other variables will be ignored and will not stop a cached page from being reused.

```
Public NotInheritable Class HttpCacheVaryByParams
' Public Instance Properties
    Public Property IgnoreParams As Boolean
    Public Default Property Item (ByVal header As String) As Boolean
End Class
```

HttpClientCertificate
Class

System.Web (system.web.dll)

This class exposes a name/value collection of certification fields specified in the X.509 standard. To get the certification fields for the current request, use the ClientCertificate property of the HttpRequest class. Note that the certification fields are sent only if the client browser is accessing the page through SSL (indicated by a URL starting with *https://* instead of *http://*).

Public Class **HttpClientCertificate** : Inherits System.Collections.Specialized.NameValueCollection
' *Public Instance Properties*
  Public ReadOnly Property **BinaryIssuer** As Byte()
  Public ReadOnly Property **CertEncoding** As Integer
  Public ReadOnly Property **Certificate** As Byte()
  Public ReadOnly Property **Cookie** As String
  Public ReadOnly Property **Flags** As Integer
  Public ReadOnly Property **IsPresent** As Boolean
  Public ReadOnly Property **Issuer** As String
  Public ReadOnly Property **IsValid** As Boolean
  Public ReadOnly Property **KeySize** As Integer
  Public ReadOnly Property **PublicKey** As Byte()
  Public ReadOnly Property **SecretKeySize** As Integer
  Public ReadOnly Property **SerialNumber** As String
  Public ReadOnly Property **ServerIssuer** As String
  Public ReadOnly Property **ServerSubject** As String
  Public ReadOnly Property **Subject** As String
  Public ReadOnly Property **ValidFrom** As Date
  Public ReadOnly Property **ValidUntil** As Date
' *Public Instance Methods*
  Overrides Public Function **Get**(ByVal field As String) As String
End Class

Hierarchy: System.Object → System.Collections.Specialized.NameObjectCollectionBase (System.Collections.ICollection , System.Collections.IEnumerable , System.Runtime.Serialization.ISerializable , System.Runtime.Serialization.IDeserializationCallback) → System.Collections.Specialized.NameValueCollection → HttpClientCertificate

HttpCompileException
NotInheritable Class

System.Web (system.web.dll)

This class represents an HTTP compiler exception.

Public NotInheritable Class **HttpCompileException** : Inherits HttpException
' *Public Instance Properties*
  Public ReadOnly Property **Results** As CompilerResults
  Public ReadOnly Property **SourceCode** As String
End Class

Hierarchy: System.Object → System.Exception (System.Runtime.Serialization.ISerializable) → System.SystemException → System.Runtime.InteropServices.ExternalException → HttpException → HttpCompileException

HttpContext

System.Web (system.web.dll)

The HttpContext class represents the "operating context" of an ASP.NET application. It provides references to instances of fundamental classes like HttpApplicationState and HttpRequest, which are known as intrinsic or "built-in" objects. The HttpContext class is provided to IHttpModule and IHttpHandler instances (like System.Web.UI.Page and HttpApplication), which provide these classes through their own properties. The shared (static) property Current returns the current HttpContext, and is useful if you need to access the built-in ASP.NET objects from another code module like a class (where you won't have access to the System.Web.UI.Page properties). One example is a web service that doesn't inherit from System.Web.Services.WebService. You can also use the shared GetAppConfig() method to retrieve a collection object from the *web.config* file that contains configuration information. Just specify the configuration section you want to examine as a parameter (like "appSettings").

If you are creating your own IHttpHandler class, you will receive the current instance of the HttpContext class as a parameter of the IHttpHandler.ProcessRequest() method. To use the Session property of the HttpContext lass, you must also implement either the System.Web.SessionState.IReadOnlySessionState interface or the System.Web.SessionState.IRequiresSessionState interface.

```
Public NotInheritable Class HttpContext : Implements IServiceProvider
' Public Constructors
    Public Sub New(ByVal request As HttpRequest, ByVal response As HttpResponse)
    Public Sub New(ByVal wr As HttpWorkerRequest)
' Public Shared Properties
    Public Shared ReadOnly Property Current As HttpContext
' Public Instance Properties
    Public ReadOnly Property AllErrors As Exception()
    Public ReadOnly Property Application As HttpApplicationState
    Public Property ApplicationInstance As HttpApplication
    Public ReadOnly Property Cache As Cache
    Public ReadOnly Property Error As Exception
    Public Property Handler As IHttpHandler
    Public ReadOnly Property IsCustomErrorEnabled As Boolean
    Public ReadOnly Property IsDebuggingEnabled As Boolean
    Public ReadOnly Property Items As IDictionary
    Public ReadOnly Property Request As HttpRequest
    Public ReadOnly Property Response As HttpResponse
    Public ReadOnly Property Server As HttpServerUtility
    Public ReadOnly Property Session As HttpSessionState
    Public Property SkipAuthorization As Boolean
    Public ReadOnly Property Timestamp As Date
    Public ReadOnly Property Trace As TraceContext
    Public Property User As IPrincipal
' Public Shared Methods
    Public Shared Function GetAppConfig(ByVal name As String) As Object
' Public Instance Methods
    Public Sub AddError(ByVal errorInfo As Exception)
    Public Sub ClearError()
    Public Function GetConfig(ByVal name As String) As Object
    Public Sub RewritePath(ByVal path As String)
End Class
```

HttpCookie
NotInheritable Class

System.Web (system.web.dll)

Use this class to create a client-side cookie. The HttpCookie constructor takes a string representing the name of the cookie. After creating a cookie, you can add information to it in the form of name/value pairs by using the HttpCookieCollection.Add() method as follows: objCookies.Values.Add("Name", "John"). Values can be retrieved by using their name with a syntax like strName = objCookies.Values("Name").

To send the cookie to the client browser as part of the HTTP response, use the Append-Cookie() method of the HttpResponse class. This method stores the cookie on the client browser. You can then retrieve a cookie from the HttpResponse class's cookie collection on other pages by using the cookie name, as in Response.Cookies("NameList"). To ensure compatibility with all browsers, you should not store more than 4096 bytes in a single cookie.

To make a cookie persist between sessions, set the Expires property for the HttpCookie to a date in the future. You can also set the Secure property to True to restrict the cookie to Secure Socket Layer (SSL) transmission. A cookie is usually considered less secure than Application or Session state variables, as information is maintained on the client and transmitted back and forth continuously.

```
Public NotInheritable Class HttpCookie
' Public Constructors
    Public Sub New(ByVal name As String)
    Public Sub New(ByVal name As String, ByVal value As String)
' Public Instance Properties
    Public Property Domain As String
    Public Property Expires As Date
    Public ReadOnly Property HasKeys As Boolean
    Public Default Property Item (ByVal key As String) As String
    Public Property Name As String
    Public Property Path As String
    Public Property Secure As Boolean
    Public Property Value As String
    Public ReadOnly Property Values As NameValueCollection
End Class
```

HttpCookieCollection
NotInheritable Class

System.Web (system.web.dll)

HttpCookieCollection is a name/value collection of HttpCookie objects. The Cookies property of the HttpResponse class contains the cookies sent from the client with the current request. The Cookies property of the HttpRequest class contains the cookies sent back from the server.

These collections contain all the transmitted cookies, including those you have created automatically in code, and other cookies used by the ASP.NET framework like the Forms Authentication cookie and the Session state cookie (named ASP.NET_SessionId).

```
Public NotInheritable Class HttpCookieCollection : Inherits
        System.Collections.Specialized.NameObjectCollectionBase
' Public Constructors
    Public Sub New()
' Public Instance Properties
    Public ReadOnly Property AllKeys As String()
    Public Default ReadOnly Property Item (ByVal index As Integer) As HttpCookie
    Public Default ReadOnly Property Item (ByVal name As String) As HttpCookie
```

' *Public Instance Methods*
   Public Sub **Add**(ByVal cookie As HttpCookie)
   Public Sub **Clear**()
   Public Sub **CopyTo**(ByVal dest As Array, ByVal index As Integer) Implements ICollection.CopyTo
   Public Function **Get**(ByVal index As Integer) As HttpCookie
   Public Function **Get**(ByVal name As String) As HttpCookie
   Public Function **GetKey**(ByVal index As Integer) As String
   Public Sub **Remove**(ByVal name As String)
   Public Sub **Set**(ByVal cookie As HttpCookie)
End Class

Hierarchy: System.Object → System.Collections.Specialized.NameObjectCollectionBase (
System.Collections.ICollection , System.Collections.IEnumerable ,
System.Runtime.Serialization.ISerializable , System.Runtime.Serialization.IDeserializationCallback) →
HttpCookieCollection

HttpException   Class

System.Web (system.web.dll)

This class encapsulates an ASP.NET exception. It is a standard exception object, with
the addition of the GetHtmlErrorMessage() method and the GetHttpCode() method, that
returns the HTTP error code representing the error (like 404 for file not found) as an
integer. If no HTTP error code exists for the current exception or the InnerException, the
status code 500 is returned.

Public Class **HttpException** : Inherits System.Runtime.InteropServices.ExternalException
' *Public Constructors*
   Public Sub **New**()
   Public Sub **New**(ByVal httpCode As Integer, ByVal message As String)
   Public Sub **New**(ByVal httpCode As Integer, ByVal message As String, ByVal innerException As Exception)
   Public Sub **New**(ByVal httpCode As Integer, ByVal message As String, ByVal hr As Integer)
   Public Sub **New**(ByVal message As String)
   Public Sub **New**(ByVal message As String, ByVal innerException As Exception)
   Public Sub **New**(ByVal message As String, ByVal hr As Integer)
' *Public Shared Methods*
   Public Shared Function **CreateFromLastError**(ByVal message As String) As HttpException
' *Public Instance Methods*
   Public Function **GetHtmlErrorMessage**() As String
   Public Function **GetHttpCode**() As Integer
End Class

Hierarchy: System.Object → System.Exception (System.Runtime.Serialization.ISerializable) →
System.SystemException → System.Runtime.InteropServices.ExternalException → HttpException

HttpFileCollection   NotInheritable Class

System.Web (system.web.dll)

This class is a name/value collection of HttpPostedFile instances, which represents incoming files uploaded by a client (using multipart MIME and the HTTP content type of mul-
tipart/formdata). The HtmlInputFile class in the System.Web.UI.HtmlControls namespace
provides an easier way to allow a user to upload files.

Public NotInheritable Class **HttpFileCollection** : Inherits System.Collections.Specialized.NameObjectCollectionBase
' *Public Instance Properties*

```
   Public ReadOnly Property AllKeys As String()
   Public Default ReadOnly Property Item (ByVal index As Integer) As HttpPostedFile
   Public Default ReadOnly Property Item (ByVal name As String) As HttpPostedFile
' Public Instance Methods
   Public Sub CopyTo(ByVal dest As Array, ByVal index As Integer)  Implements ICollection.CopyTo
   Public Function Get(ByVal index As Integer) As HttpPostedFile
   Public Function Get(ByVal name As String) As HttpPostedFile
   Public Function GetKey(ByVal index As Integer) As String
End Class
```

Hierarchy: System.Object → System.Collections.Specialized.NameObjectCollectionBase (
System.Collections.ICollection , System.Collections.IEnumerable ,
System.Runtime.Serialization.ISerializable , System.Runtime.Serialization.IDeserializationCallback) →
HttpFileCollection

HttpModuleCollection
NotInheritable Class

System.Web (system.web.dll)

This is a name/value collection of IHttpModule instances. It's used by the Modules property of the HttpApplication class to provide a collection of all modules used by your application (as defined in the <httpmodules> section of the application's *web.config* file).

```
Public NotInheritable Class HttpModuleCollection : Inherits
         System.Collections.Specialized.NameObjectCollectionBase
' Public Instance Properties
   Public ReadOnly Property AllKeys As String()
   Public Default ReadOnly Property Item (ByVal index As Integer) As IHttpModule
   Public Default ReadOnly Property Item (ByVal name As String) As IHttpModule
' Public Instance Methods
   Public Sub CopyTo(ByVal dest As Array, ByVal index As Integer)  Implements ICollection.CopyTo
   Public Function Get(ByVal index As Integer) As IHttpModule
   Public Function Get(ByVal name As String) As IHttpModule
   Public Function GetKey(ByVal index As Integer) As String
End Class
```

Hierarchy: System.Object → System.Collections.Specialized.NameObjectCollectionBase (
System.Collections.ICollection , System.Collections.IEnumerable ,
System.Runtime.Serialization.ISerializable , System.Runtime.Serialization.IDeserializationCallback) →
HttpModuleCollection

HttpParseException
NotInheritable Class

System.Web (system.web.dll)

This class represents an exception generated when parsing an ASP.NET file.

```
Public NotInheritable Class HttpParseException : Inherits HttpException
' Public Instance Properties
   Public ReadOnly Property FileName As String
   Public ReadOnly Property Line As Integer
End Class
```

Hierarchy: System.Object → System.Exception (System.Runtime.Serialization.ISerializable) →
System.SystemException → System.Runtime.InteropServices.ExternalException → HttpException →
HttpParseException

HttpPostedFile
NotInheritable Class

System.Web (system.web.dll)

The HttpPostedFile class allows you to easily manipulate files that are uploaded by the client. An HttpPostedFile instance is provided by the PostedFile property of the System.Web.UI.HtmlControls.HtmlInputFile control.

You can use the SaveAs() method to save a posted file to disk synchronously. The method will return once the file is completely uploaded. Alternatively, you can get a System.IO.Stream object containing the file from the InputStream property and use it to work with the file asynchronously (while it is being uploaded).

```
Public NotInheritable Class HttpPostedFile
' Public Instance Properties
   Public ReadOnly Property ContentLength As Integer
   Public ReadOnly Property ContentType As String
   Public ReadOnly Property FileName As String
   Public ReadOnly Property InputStream As Stream
' Public Instance Methods
   Public Sub SaveAs(ByVal filename As String)
End Class
```

HttpRequest
NotInheritable Class

System.Web (system.web.dll)

The HttpRequest class wraps all information that a client browser passes to the server during an HTTP request. It includes client certificates, cookies, and values submitted through HTML form elements. You can access this information in its entirety as a System.IO.Stream object through the InputStream property, or you can use one of the more useful higher-level properties.

The QueryString property allows you to retrieve values from the URL's query string, which can transfer information from one ASP.NET page to another. This query string takes the form of a series of name/value pairs appended to the URL after a question mark (for example, the client request *http://www.myapp.com/mypage.aspx?var1=hi* will result in a value of "hi" for Request.QueryString("var1")). The QueryString collection is limited to string data and should not contain sensitive information, as it is clearly visible to the user. To ensure compatibility with all browsers, you should not store more than about 1000 bytes in the query string.

The HttpRequest class also exposes an HttpCookieCollection object in the Cookies property. This is a collection of client-side cookies that your script (or other scripts on your server) have created. They are transmitted to the server with each request in the HTTP Cookie header. This collection is read-only. If you want to modify or add a cookie, use the HttpResponse.Cookies property instead.

The HttpRequestClass class provides some frequently used, lower-level properties. For example, the Form collection wraps the information returned from the HTML form elements, which you will typically access through the higher-level web control abstraction. Similarly, the Headers and ServerVariables collections allow you to access HTML headers and server variables directly, provided you know their names. Many of these variables now have corresponding read-only properties that you can use more easily, like HttpMethod (the data transfer method like GET or POST), UserHostAddress (the IP address of the client), and UserHostName (the DNS name of remote client). The Browser property is a reference to an HttpBrowserCapabilities object with full information about the user's browser.

Additional information available in the HttpRequest class includes the currently requested URL (Url), the URL from which the request is being made (UrlReferrer), and the root path for the current ASP.NET application as a virtual path (ApplicationPath) or physical filesystem path (PhysicalApplicationPath).

```
Public NotInheritable Class HttpRequest
' Public Constructors
   Public Sub New(ByVal filename As String, ByVal url As String, ByVal queryString As String)
' Public Instance Properties
   Public ReadOnly Property AcceptTypes As String()
   Public ReadOnly Property ApplicationPath As String
   Public Property Browser As HttpBrowserCapabilities
   Public ReadOnly Property ClientCertificate As HttpClientCertificate
   Public Property ContentEncoding As Encoding
   Public Property ContentLength As Integer
   Public ReadOnly Property ContentType As String
   Public ReadOnly Property Cookies As HttpCookieCollection
   Public ReadOnly Property CurrentExecutionFilePath As String
   Public ReadOnly Property FilePath As String
   Public ReadOnly Property Files As HttpFileCollection
   Public Property Filter As Stream
   Public ReadOnly Property Form As NameValueCollection
   Public ReadOnly Property Headers As NameValueCollection
   Public ReadOnly Property HttpMethod As String
   Public ReadOnly Property InputStream As Stream
   Public ReadOnly Property IsAuthenticated As Boolean
   Public ReadOnly Property IsSecureConnection As Boolean
   Public Default ReadOnly Property Item (ByVal key As String) As String
   Public ReadOnly Property Params As NameValueCollection
   Public ReadOnly Property Path As String
   Public ReadOnly Property PathInfo As String
   Public ReadOnly Property PhysicalApplicationPath As String
   Public ReadOnly Property PhysicalPath As String
   Public ReadOnly Property QueryString As NameValueCollection
   Public ReadOnly Property RawUrl As String
   Public Property RequestType As String
   Public ReadOnly Property ServerVariables As NameValueCollection
   Public ReadOnly Property TotalBytes As Integer
   Public ReadOnly Property Url As Uri
   Public ReadOnly Property UrlReferrer As Uri
   Public ReadOnly Property UserAgent As String
   Public ReadOnly Property UserHostAddress As String
   Public ReadOnly Property UserHostName As String
   Public ReadOnly Property UserLanguages As String()
' Public Instance Methods
   Public Function BinaryRead(ByVal count As Integer) As Byte()
   Public Function MapImageCoordinates(ByVal imageFieldName As String) As Integer()
   Public Function MapPath(ByVal virtualPath As String) As String
   Public Function MapPath(ByVal virtualPath As String, ByVal baseVirtualDir As String, _
       ByVal allowCrossAppMapping As Boolean) As String
   Public Sub SaveAs(ByVal filename As String, ByVal includeHeaders As Boolean)
End Class
```

HttpResponse   NotInheritable Class

System.Web (system.web.dll)

The HttpResponse class is used to send information to the client's browser, including HTML content, HTML headers, and customized cookies. Its name derives from the fact that it is used to "respond" to an HTTP request.

The Redirect() method of the HttpResponse class provides the easiest way to programmatically send the user to another web page. You supply the name of the HTML or ASPX file as an argument (e.g., Response.Redirect ("newpage.aspx")). As long as the file is in the same directory as the current page, you don't need to provide a full URL (like *http://www.mysite/myapplication/newpage.aspx*), although you can use a relative path or fully-qualified URL. Other ways to transfer a user between pages in an ASP.NET program include the HttpServerUtility.Transfer() method and the System.Web.UI.WebControls.HyperLink web control.

The Cookies property of the HttpResponse class provides a reference to the application's HttpCookieCollection, which can send custom cookies to the client. The Cache property provides a reference to the application's HttpCachePolicy settings. Both classes are described separately. These properties, along with the Redirect() method, are the most commonly used members of HttpResponse.

In traditional ASP development, the Write() method was often used to append HTML to a web page (e.g., Reponse.Write "<h1>Hello World</h1>"). ASP.NET programs will rarely use this method because it is much easier to handle dynamic content by changing the properties of full-featured web controls on Web Forms. Similarly, the BinaryWrite() method, which allows you to write binary information into the HTTP text stream by supplying a byte array, or the WriteFile() method, which allows you to write the content from a named text file into the output stream, are rarely used.

The BufferOutput property is a Boolean value that determines whether or not the HTTP output is buffered. It is sent to the client only when it is fully rendered and all code has executed. The default is True. The HttpResponse class also provides low-level control over the management of the output buffer, with the Clear(), Flush(), and End() methods. You can also use the AppendToLog() method to write a string of information to the IIS log file on the web server. This method should not be used for debugging, as better options are provided by the TraceContext class.

Public NotInheritable Class **HttpResponse**
' Public Constructors
    Public Sub **New**(ByVal writer As System.IO.TextWriter)
' Public Instance Properties
    Public Property **Buffer** As Boolean
    Public Property **BufferOutput** As Boolean
    Public ReadOnly Property **Cache** As HttpCachePolicy
    Public Property **CacheControl** As String
    Public Property **Charset** As String
    Public Property **ContentEncoding** As Encoding
    Public Property **ContentType** As String
    Public ReadOnly Property **Cookies** As HttpCookieCollection
    Public Property **Expires** As Integer
    Public Property **ExpiresAbsolute** As Date
    Public Property **Filter** As Stream
    Public ReadOnly Property **IsClientConnected** As Boolean
    Public ReadOnly Property **Output** As TextWriter
    Public ReadOnly Property **OutputStream** As Stream
    Public Property **Status** As String
    Public Property **StatusCode** As Integer
    Public Property **StatusDescription** As String
    Public Property **SuppressContent** As Boolean
' Public Shared Methods
    Public Shared Sub **RemoveOutputCacheItem**(ByVal path As String)
' Public Instance Methods
    Public Sub **AddCacheItemDependencies**(ByVal cacheKeys As System.Collections.ArrayList)

Public Sub **AddCacheItemDependency**(ByVal cacheKey As String)
Public Sub **AddFileDependencies**(ByVal filenames As System.Collections.ArrayList)
Public Sub **AddFileDependency**(ByVal filename As String)
Public Sub **AddHeader**(ByVal name As String, ByVal value As String)
Public Sub **AppendCookie**(ByVal cookie As HttpCookie)
Public Sub **AppendHeader**(ByVal name As String, ByVal value As String)
Public Sub **AppendToLog**(ByVal param As String)
Public Function **ApplyAppPathModifier**(ByVal virtualPath As String) As String
Public Sub **BinaryWrite**(ByVal buffer As Byte())
Public Sub **Clear**()
Public Sub **ClearContent**()
Public Sub **ClearHeaders**()
Public Sub **Close**()
Public Sub **End**()
Public Sub **Flush**()
Public Sub **Pics**(ByVal value As String)
Public Sub **Redirect**(ByVal url As String)
Public Sub **Redirect**(ByVal url As String, ByVal endResponse As Boolean)
Public Sub **SetCookie**(ByVal cookie As HttpCookie)
Public Sub **Write**(ByVal ch As Char)
Public Sub **Write**(ByVal buffer As Char(), ByVal index As Integer, ByVal count As Integer)
Public Sub **Write**(ByVal obj As Object)
Public Sub **Write**(ByVal s As String)
Public Sub **WriteFile**(ByVal fileHandle As IntPtr, ByVal offset As Long, ByVal size As Long)
Public Sub **WriteFile**(ByVal filename As String)
Public Sub **WriteFile**(ByVal filename As String, ByVal readIntoMemory As Boolean)
Public Sub **WriteFile**(ByVal filename As String, ByVal offset As Long, ByVal size As Long)
End Class

HttpRuntime
NotInheritable Class

System.Web (system.web.dll)

The HttpRuntime class provides ASP.NET runtime services and is used transparently by the ASP.NET framework. In some rare cases, you may want to use it. For example, you can use the ProcessRequest() static (shared) method to process an ASP.NET request outside of Internet Information Server and Close() to clear the cache and shutdown the Common Language Runtime.

Public NotInheritable Class **HttpRuntime**
' Public Constructors
Public Sub **New**()
' Public Shared Properties
Public Shared ReadOnly Property **AppDomainAppId** As String
Public Shared ReadOnly Property **AppDomainAppPath** As String
Public Shared ReadOnly Property **AppDomainAppVirtualPath** As String
Public Shared ReadOnly Property **AppDomainId** As String
Public Shared ReadOnly Property **AspInstallDirectory** As String
Public Shared ReadOnly Property **BinDirectory** As String
Public Shared ReadOnly Property **Cache** As Cache
Public Shared ReadOnly Property **ClrInstallDirectory** As String
Public Shared ReadOnly Property **CodegenDir** As String
Public Shared ReadOnly Property **IsOnUNCShare** As Boolean
Public Shared ReadOnly Property **MachineConfigurationDirectory** As String
' Public Shared Methods
Public Shared Sub **Close**()

```
    Public Shared Sub ProcessRequest(ByVal wr As HttpWorkerRequest)
End Class
```

HttpServerUtility

NotInheritable Class

System.Web (system.web.dll)

This class provides helper methods and is available through the built-in Server object. It provides the useful UrlEncode() method, which converts a string into a form suitable for use as a query string variable, and the HtmlEncode() method, which converts nonlegal HTML characters in a string into the equivalent HTML entity (i.e., "<" is converted to <) so they can be displayed on a page. Some ASP.NET web controls (like buttons) do not require this conversion, but label controls do. You may need to use the HtmlEncode() method manually if you bind a field with URL information from a database.

The HttpServerUtility class provides the MapPath() method, which takes a string representing a virtual path and returns the real (physical) path (for example, it could convert "/myapp/index.html" to "E:\Inetpub\wwwroot\myapp\index.html"). It also provides a CreateObject() method for instantiating a COM object by using its ProgID (i.e., objInfo=Server.CreateObject ("MSWC.MyInfo")) and the two flow control methods Execute() and Transfer(). The Execute() method, which runs the script in a separate ASP.NET page and then returns control to the current page, is rarely used in class-based ASP.NET programming. The Transfer() method halts the execution of the current page and transfers execution to the specified page. It is similar to the HttpResponse.Redirect() method, but does not require a roundtrip to the client and back and cannot transfer execution to a page on another server (or from an ASP.NET page to an ASP page).

```
Public NotInheritable Class HttpServerUtility
' Public Instance Properties
   Public ReadOnly Property MachineName As String
   Public Property ScriptTimeout As Integer
' Public Instance Methods
   Public Sub ClearError()
   Public Function CreateObject(ByVal progID As String) As Object
   Public Function CreateObject(ByVal type As Type) As Object
   Public Function CreateObjectFromClsid(ByVal clsid As String) As Object
   Public Sub Execute(ByVal path As String)
   Public Sub Execute(ByVal path As String, ByVal writer As System.IO.TextWriter)
   Public Function GetLastError() As Exception
   Public Function HtmlDecode(ByVal s As String) As String
   Public Sub HtmlDecode(ByVal s As String, ByVal output As System.IO.TextWriter)
   Public Function HtmlEncode(ByVal s As String) As String
   Public Sub HtmlEncode(ByVal s As String, ByVal output As System.IO.TextWriter)
   Public Function MapPath(ByVal path As String) As String
   Public Sub Transfer(ByVal path As String)
   Public Sub Transfer(ByVal path As String, ByVal preserveForm As Boolean)
   Public Function UrlDecode(ByVal s As String) As String
   Public Sub UrlDecode(ByVal s As String, ByVal output As System.IO.TextWriter)
   Public Function UrlEncode(ByVal s As String) As String
   Public Sub UrlEncode(ByVal s As String, ByVal output As System.IO.TextWriter)
   Public Function UrlPathEncode(ByVal s As String) As String
End Class
```

System.Web Namespace

HttpStaticObjectsCollection

NotInheritable Class

System.Web (system.web.dll)

This class provides an immutable name/value collection of objects that is used for the HttpApplicationState.StaticObjects and System.Web.SessionState.HttpSessionState.StaticObjects collections.

Public NotInheritable Class **HttpStaticObjectsCollection** : Implements ICollection, IEnumerable
' *Public Constructors*
   Public Sub **New**()
' *Public Instance Properties*
   Public ReadOnly Property **Count** As Integer Implements ICollection.Count
   Public ReadOnly Property **IsReadOnly** As Boolean
   Public ReadOnly Property **IsSynchronized** As Boolean Implements ICollection.IsSynchronized
   Public Default ReadOnly Property **Item** (ByVal name As String) As Object
   Public ReadOnly Property **SyncRoot** As Object Implements ICollection.SyncRoot
' *Public Instance Methods*
   Public Sub **CopyTo**(ByVal array As Array, ByVal index As Integer) Implements ICollection.CopyTo
   Public Function **GetEnumerator**() As IEnumerator Implements IEnumerable.GetEnumerator
   Public Function **GetObject**(ByVal name As String) As Object
End Class

HttpUnhandledException

NotInheritable Class

System.Web (system.web.dll)

This class represents a generic HTTP exception.

Public NotInheritable Class **HttpUnhandledException** : Inherits HttpException
' *No public or protected members*
End Class

Hierarchy: System.Object → System.Exception (System.Runtime.Serialization.ISerializable) → System.SystemException → System.Runtime.InteropServices.ExternalException → HttpException → HttpUnhandledException

HttpUtility

NotInheritable Class

System.Web (system.web.dll)

This class provides static (shared) helper methods. The UrlEncode() and UrlDecode() methods are the same as those provided by the HttpServerUtility class for encoding a string into a format that's safe for use in a URL. Additionally, a UrlEncodeToBytes() method is provided to convert a string into an array of bytes and a UrlEncodeUnicode() method converts a string into a Unicode (wide-character) string.

Public NotInheritable Class **HttpUtility**
' *Public Constructors*
   Public Sub **New**()
' *Public Shared Methods*
   Public Shared Function **HtmlAttributeEncode**(ByVal s As String) As String
   Public Shared Sub **HtmlAttributeEncode**(ByVal s As String, ByVal output As System.IO.TextWriter)
   Public Shared Function **HtmlDecode**(ByVal s As String) As String
   Public Shared Sub **HtmlDecode**(ByVal s As String, ByVal output As System.IO.TextWriter)
   Public Shared Function **HtmlEncode**(ByVal s As String) As String
   Public Shared Sub **HtmlEncode**(ByVal s As String, ByVal output As System.IO.TextWriter)
   Public Shared Function **UrlDecode**(ByVal bytes As Byte(), ByVal e As System.Text.Encoding) As String
   Public Shared Function **UrlDecode**(ByVal bytes As Byte(), ByVal offset As Integer, ByVal count As Integer, _
     ByVal e As System.Text.Encoding) As String

Public Shared Function **UrlDecode**(ByVal str As String) As String
Public Shared Function **UrlDecode**(ByVal str As String, ByVal e As System.Text.Encoding) As String
Public Shared Function **UrlDecodeToBytes**(ByVal bytes As Byte()) As Byte()
Public Shared Function **UrlDecodeToBytes**(ByVal bytes As Byte(), ByVal offset As Integer, ByVal count As Integer) _
    As Byte()
Public Shared Function **UrlDecodeToBytes**(ByVal str As String) As Byte()
Public Shared Function **UrlDecodeToBytes**(ByVal str As String, ByVal e As System.Text.Encoding) As Byte()
Public Shared Function **UrlEncode**(ByVal bytes As Byte()) As String
Public Shared Function **UrlEncode**(ByVal bytes As Byte(), ByVal offset As Integer, ByVal count As Integer) As String
Public Shared Function **UrlEncode**(ByVal str As String) As String
Public Shared Function **UrlEncode**(ByVal str As String, ByVal e As System.Text.Encoding) As String
Public Shared Function **UrlEncodeToBytes**(ByVal bytes As Byte()) As Byte()
Public Shared Function **UrlEncodeToBytes**(ByVal bytes As Byte(), ByVal offset As Integer, ByVal count As Integer) _
    As Byte()
Public Shared Function **UrlEncodeToBytes**(ByVal str As String) As Byte()
Public Shared Function **UrlEncodeToBytes**(ByVal str As String, ByVal e As System.Text.Encoding) As Byte()
Public Shared Function **UrlEncodeUnicode**(ByVal str As String) As String
Public Shared Function **UrlEncodeUnicodeToBytes**(ByVal str As String) As Byte()
End Class

HttpValidationStatus

Enum

System.Web (system.web.dll)

serializable

This enumeration is used by the HttpCacheValidateHandler delegate. It allows you to specify whether a cached page should remain valid or be invalidated (and then recreated).

Public Enum **HttpValidationStatus**
    Invalid = 1
    IgnoreThisRequest = 2
    Valid = 3
End Enum

Hierarchy: System.Object → System.ValueType → System.Enum (System.IComparable , System.IFormattable , System.IConvertible) → HttpValidationStatus

HttpWorkerRequest

MustInherit Class

System.Web (system.web.dll)

This abstract class defines the base worker methods and enumerations used for request processing by the ASP.NET engine. It is used by the HttpContext constructor and the ProcessRequest() method of the HttpRuntime class. You will not need to use it directly in your code because ASP.NET provides higher-level objects like HttpResponse and HttpRequest. However, you can use the System.Web.Hosting.SimpleWorkerRequest class, which extends HttpWorkerRequest and allows you to host ASP.NET outside of IIS.

Public MustInherit Class **HttpWorkerRequest** : Implements IHttpMapPath
' *Protected Constructors*
    Protected Sub **New**()
' *Public Shared Fields*
    public const **HeaderAccept** As Integer   =20
    public const **HeaderAcceptCharset** As Integer   =21
    public const **HeaderAcceptEncoding** As Integer   =22
    public const **HeaderAcceptLanguage** As Integer   =23
    public const **HeaderAcceptRanges** As Integer   =20

```
public const HeaderAge As Integer                              =21
public const HeaderAllow As Integer                            =10
public const HeaderAuthorization As Integer                    =24
public const HeaderCacheControl As Integer                     =0
public const HeaderConnection As Integer                       =1
public const HeaderContentEncoding As Integer                  =13
public const HeaderContentLanguage As Integer                  =14
public const HeaderContentLength As Integer                    =11
public const HeaderContentLocation As Integer                  =15
public const HeaderContentMd5 As Integer                       =16
public const HeaderContentRange As Integer                     =17
public const HeaderContentType As Integer                      =12
public const HeaderCookie As Integer                           =25
public const HeaderDate As Integer                             =2
public const HeaderEtag As Integer                             =22
public const HeaderExpect As Integer                           =26
public const HeaderExpires As Integer                          =18
public const HeaderFrom As Integer                             =27
public const HeaderHost As Integer                             =28
public const HeaderIfMatch As Integer                          =29
public const HeaderIfModifiedSince As Integer                  =30
public const HeaderIfNoneMatch As Integer                      =31
public const HeaderIfRange As Integer                          =32
public const HeaderIfUnmodifiedSince As Integer                =33
public const HeaderKeepAlive As Integer                        =3
public const HeaderLastModified As Integer                     =19
public const HeaderLocation As Integer                         =23
public const HeaderMaxForwards As Integer                      =34
public const HeaderPragma As Integer                           =4
public const HeaderProxyAuthenticate As Integer                =24
public const HeaderProxyAuthorization As Integer               =35
public const HeaderRange As Integer                            =37
public const HeaderReferer As Integer                          =36
public const HeaderRetryAfter As Integer                       =25
public const HeaderServer As Integer                           =26
public const HeaderSetCookie As Integer                        =27
public const HeaderTe As Integer                               =38
public const HeaderTrailer As Integer                          =5
public const HeaderTransferEncoding As Integer                 =6
public const HeaderUpgrade As Integer                          =7
public const HeaderUserAgent As Integer                        =39
public const HeaderVary As Integer                             =28
public const HeaderVia As Integer                              =8
public const HeaderWarning As Integer                          =9
public const HeaderWwwAuthenticate As Integer                  =29
public const ReasonCachePolicy As Integer                      =2
public const ReasonCacheSecurity As Integer                    =3
public const ReasonClientDisconnect As Integer                 =4
public const ReasonDefault As Integer                          =0
public const ReasonFileHandleCacheMiss As Integer              =1
public const ReasonResponseCacheMiss As Integer                =0
public const RequestHeaderMaximum As Integer                   =40
public const ResponseHeaderMaximum As Integer                  =30
' Public Instance Properties
   Overridable Public ReadOnly Property MachineConfigPath As String _
      Implements IHttpMapPath.MachineConfigPath
```

Overridable Public ReadOnly Property **MachineInstallDirectory** As String
' *Public Shared Methods*
Public Shared Function **GetKnownRequestHeaderIndex**(ByVal header As String) As Integer
Public Shared Function **GetKnownRequestHeaderName**(ByVal index As Integer) As String
Public Shared Function **GetKnownResponseHeaderIndex**(ByVal header As String) As Integer
Public Shared Function **GetKnownResponseHeaderName**(ByVal index As Integer) As String
Public Shared Function **GetStatusDescription**(ByVal code As Integer) As String
' *Public Instance Methods*
Overridable Public Sub **CloseConnection**()
MustInherit Public Sub **EndOfRequest**()
MustInherit Public Sub **FlushResponse**(ByVal finalFlush As Boolean)
Overridable Public Function **GetAppPath**() As String
Overridable Public Function **GetAppPathTranslated**() As String
Overridable Public Function **GetAppPoolID**() As String
Overridable Public Function **GetBytesRead**() As Long
Overridable Public Function **GetClientCertificate**() As Byte()
Overridable Public Function **GetClientCertificateBinaryIssuer**() As Byte()
Overridable Public Function **GetClientCertificateEncoding**() As Integer
Overridable Public Function **GetClientCertificatePublicKey**() As Byte()
Overridable Public Function **GetClientCertificateValidFrom**() As Date
Overridable Public Function **GetClientCertificateValidUntil**() As Date
Overridable Public Function **GetConnectionID**() As Long
Overridable Public Function **GetFilePath**() As String
Overridable Public Function **GetFilePathTranslated**() As String
MustInherit Public Function **GetHttpVerbName**() As String
MustInherit Public Function **GetHttpVersion**() As String
Overridable Public Function **GetKnownRequestHeader**(ByVal index As Integer) As String
MustInherit Public Function **GetLocalAddress**() As String
MustInherit Public Function **GetLocalPort**() As Integer
Overridable Public Function **GetPathInfo**() As String
Overridable Public Function **GetPreloadedEntityBody**() As Byte()
Overridable Public Function **GetProtocol**() As String
MustInherit Public Function **GetQueryString**() As String
Overridable Public Function **GetQueryStringRawBytes**() As Byte()
MustInherit Public Function **GetRawUrl**() As String
MustInherit Public Function **GetRemoteAddress**() As String
Overridable Public Function **GetRemoteName**() As String
MustInherit Public Function **GetRemotePort**() As Integer
Overridable Public Function **GetRequestReason**() As Integer
Overridable Public Function **GetServerName**() As String
Overridable Public Function **GetServerVariable**(ByVal name As String) As String
Overridable Public Function **GetUnknownRequestHeader**(ByVal name As String) As String
Overridable Public Function **GetUnknownRequestHeaders**() As String()()
MustInherit Public Function **GetUriPath**() As String
Overridable Public Function **GetUrlContextID**() As Long
Overridable Public Function **GetUserToken**() As IntPtr
Overridable Public Function **GetVirtualPathToken**() As IntPtr
Public Function **HasEntityBody**() As Boolean
Overridable Public Function **HeadersSent**() As Boolean
Overridable Public Function **IsClientConnected**() As Boolean
Overridable Public Function **IsEntireEntityBodyIsPreloaded**() As Boolean
Overridable Public Function **IsSecure**() As Boolean
Overridable Public Function **MapPath**(ByVal virtualPath As String) As String Implements IHttpMapPath.MapPath
Overridable Public Function **ReadEntityBody**(ByVal buffer As Byte(), ByVal size As Integer) As Integer
Overridable Public Sub **SendCalculatedContentLength**(ByVal contentLength As Integer)

MustInherit Public Sub **SendKnownResponseHeader**(ByVal index As Integer, ByVal value As String)
MustInherit Public Sub **SendResponseFromFile**(ByVal handle As IntPtr, ByVal offset As Long, _
ByVal length As Long)
MustInherit Public Sub **SendResponseFromFile**(ByVal filename As String, ByVal offset As Long, _
ByVal length As Long)
MustInherit Public Sub **SendResponseFromMemory**(ByVal data As Byte(), ByVal length As Integer)
Overridable Public Sub **SendResponseFromMemory**(ByVal data As IntPtr, ByVal length As Integer)
MustInherit Public Sub **SendStatus**(ByVal statusCode As Integer, ByVal statusDescription As String)
MustInherit Public Sub **SendUnknownResponseHeader**(ByVal name As String, ByVal value As String)
Overridable Public Sub **SetEndOfSendNotification**(ByVal callback As EndOfSendNotification, _
ByVal extraData As Object)
End Class

HttpWorkerRequest.EndOfSendNotification

Delegate

System.Web (system.web.dll)
serializable

This delegate is used by the SetEndOfSendNotification() method of the HttpWorkerRequest class.

Public Delegate Sub **HttpWorkerRequest.EndOfSendNotification**(ByVal wr As HttpWorkerRequest, _
ByVal extraData As Object)

HttpWriter

NotInheritable Class

System.Web (system.web.dll)
marshal by reference, disposable

This is System.IO.TextWriter object that is used to write directly to an HTTP output stream. It is used transparently by the Write() method of the HttpResponse class.

Public NotInheritable Class **HttpWriter** : Inherits System.IO.TextWriter
' Public Instance Properties
Overrides Public ReadOnly Property **Encoding** As Encoding
Public ReadOnly Property **OutputStream** As Stream
' Public Instance Methods
Overrides Public Sub **Close**()
Overrides Public Sub **Flush**()
Overrides Public Sub **Write**(ByVal ch As Char)
Overrides Public Sub **Write**(ByVal buffer As Char(), ByVal index As Integer, ByVal count As Integer)
Overrides Public Sub **Write**(ByVal obj As Object)
Overrides Public Sub **Write**(ByVal s As String)
Public Sub **WriteBytes**(ByVal buffer As Byte(), ByVal index As Integer, ByVal count As Integer)
Overrides Public Sub **WriteLine**()
Public Sub **WriteString**(ByVal s As String, ByVal index As Integer, ByVal count As Integer)
End Class

Hierarchy: System.Object → System.MarshalByRefObject → System.IO.TextWriter (System.IDisposable) → HttpWriter

IHttpAsyncHandler

Interface

System.Web (system.web.dll)

This interface is implemented by the HttpApplication class and defines the requirements for asynchronous processing. It is an integral part of the ASP.NET framework and is not used directly by ASP.NET application code.

Public Interface **IHttpAsyncHandler** : Implements IHttpHandler

' *Public Instance Methods*
  Public Function **BeginProcessRequest**(ByVal context As HttpContext, ByVal cb As AsyncCallback, _
    ByVal extraData As Object) As IAsyncResult
  Public Sub **EndProcessRequest**(ByVal result As IAsyncResult)
End Interface

IHttpHandler

Interface

System.Web (system.web.dll)

This interface is required to process HTTP requests. It's implemented by the System.Web.UI.Page and HttpApplication classes, but you can use IHttpHandler to create a custom HttpHandler for a lower-level programming model. You can still access the HttpContext object (and, through its properties, built in objects like HttpRequest and HttpResponse), but you cannot use the higher-level Page abstraction. Common uses of handlers include filters and CGI-like applications, especially those returning binary data.

When using the IHttpHandler interface, you must implement the ProcessRequest() method and IsReusable property. The ProcessRequest() method receives an HttpContext object, which gives you access to ASP.NET's built-in objects. Use the IsReusable property to declare whether a single instance of your handler can serve multiple requests.

You will also need to modify <httphandlers> section of the *web.config* file to make your custom handler a target for HTTP requests. You can map requests based on the requested page, file type, or HTTP method (GET, PUT, or POST). If you want to create a handler that can process all requests, you should create a custom HttpModule using the IHttpModule interface.

Public Interface **IHttpHandler**
' *Public Instance Properties*
  Public ReadOnly Property **IsReusable** As Boolean
' *Public Instance Methods*
  Public Sub **ProcessRequest**(ByVal context As HttpContext)
End Interface

IHttpHandlerFactory

Interface

System.Web (system.web.dll)

You can implement this interface to create a factory class that can create IHttpHandler instances dynamically. ASP.NET includes standard IHttpHandlerFactory classes like PageHandlerFactory, RestrictedResourceFactory, and WebServiceHandlerFactory (which are not shown in the class library documentation because they are private types).

Using the <httphandlers> section of the *web.config* file, you can map specific requests to directly to an IHttpHandler class or to an IHttpHandlerFactory class, which will dynamically create an appropriate IHttpHandler class by using the GetHandler() method.

Note that the standard factory classes used by ASP.NET do not appear in the MSDN help or this reference. These classes are marked Private and are used exclusively by the ASP.NET framework.

Public Interface **IHttpHandlerFactory**
' *Public Instance Methods*
  Public Function **GetHandler**(ByVal context As HttpContext, ByVal requestType As String, ByVal url As String, _
    ByVal pathTranslated As String) As IHttpHandler
  Public Sub **ReleaseHandler**(ByVal handler As IHttpHandler)
End Interface

IHttpModule
Interface

System.Web (system.web.dll)

You can use this interface to create custom HttpModules. HttpModules are added through the <httpmodules> section of the *web.config* file. Some HttpModules that are available to you include FormsAuthenticationModule, PassportAuthenticationModule, and other security modules in the System.Web.Security namespace.

HttpModules are often used for security or logging because they can participate in the processing of every request into an application. HttpModules work by reacting to ASP.NET events. For example, if you want an HttpModule to participate in every web request, you could react to the HttpApplication.BeginRequest event. You can also specify that a HttpModule process other files (for example, JPEG and BMP) rather than just ASP.NET file types by updating the Application Extension Mapping to use *asp-net_ISAPI.dll* to manage the appropriate extension.

```
Public Interface IHttpModule
' Public Instance Methods
   Public Sub Dispose()
   Public Sub Init(ByVal context As HttpApplication)
End Interface
```

ProcessInfo
Class

System.Web (system.web.dll)

This class encapsulates information about the ASP.NET worker process on the server. It is returned by the ProcessModelInfo class. It includes properties such as the time the process started (StartTime), how long it has been running (Age), and the most memory used so far in bytes (PeakMemoryUsed). The Status property indicates the current state of a process; the ShutdownReason property indicates why the process was terminated, unless it is the current process.

```
Public Class ProcessInfo
' Public Constructors
   Public Sub New()
   Public Sub New(ByVal startTime As Date, ByVal age As TimeSpan, ByVal processID As Integer, _
      ByVal requestCount As Integer, ByVal status As ProcessStatus),
      ByVal shutdownReason As ProcessShutdownReason, ByVal peakMemoryUsed As Integer)
' Public Instance Properties
   Public ReadOnly Property Age As TimeSpan
   Public ReadOnly Property PeakMemoryUsed As Integer
   Public ReadOnly Property ProcessID As Integer
   Public ReadOnly Property RequestCount As Integer
   Public ReadOnly Property ShutdownReason As ProcessShutdownReason
   Public ReadOnly Property StartTime As Date
   Public ReadOnly Property Status As ProcessStatus
' Public Instance Methods
   Public Sub SetAll(ByVal startTime As Date, ByVal age As TimeSpan, ByVal processID As Integer, _
      ByVal requestCount As Integer, ByVal status As ProcessStatus),
      ByVal shutdownReason As ProcessShutdownReason, ByVal peakMemoryUsed As Integer)
End Class
```

ProcessModelInfo
Class

System.Web (system.web.dll)

ASP.NET includes automated features for restarting a process when memory leaks or crashes occur. This class allows you to retrieve information about how the ASP.NET worker process is performing, along with the history of approximately the last 100 process restarts (a process restart may be in response to an unrecoverble error, blocked thread, or just automatic maintaince when a certain time or memory threshold is reached, according to *machine.config* settings). This gives you a basic idea about the health of your web application and the ASP.NET service.

You can use the static (shared) GetCurrentProcessInfo() method to retrieve a ProcessInfo object representing the current process. You can also use the static GetHistory() method and supply the number of ProcessInfo objects that you want as an argument. The method will return an array of ProcessInfo objects, starting with the most recent (current) process.

```
Public Class ProcessModelInfo
' Public Constructors
    Public Sub New()
' Public Shared Methods
    Public Shared Function GetCurrentProcessInfo() As ProcessInfo
    Public Shared Function GetHistory(ByVal numRecords As Integer) As ProcessInfo()
End Class
```

ProcessShutdownReason

Enum

System.Web (system.web.dll)   *serializable*

This enumeration defines constants used by the ProcessInfo class that indicate the reason a process was ended (or None if it is the current process).

```
Public Enum ProcessShutdownReason
    None = 0
    Unexpected = 1
    RequestsLimit = 2
    RequestQueueLimit = 3
    Timeout = 4
    IdleTimeout = 5
    MemoryLimitExceeded = 6
    PingFailed = 7
    DeadlockSuspected = 8
End Enum
```

Hierarchy: System.Object → System.ValueType → System.Enum (System.IComparable , System.IFormattable , System.IConvertible) → ProcessShutdownReason

ProcessStatus

Enum

System.Web (system.web.dll)   *serializable*

This enumeration is used by the ProcessInfo class to indicate the status of a process.

```
Public Enum ProcessStatus
    Alive = 1
    ShuttingDown = 2
    ShutDown = 3
    Terminated = 4
End Enum
```

Hierarchy: System.Object → System.ValueType → System.Enum (System.IComparable , System.IFormattable , System.IConvertible) → ProcessStatus

TraceContext

System.Web (system.web.dll)

The TraceContext class allows you display trace messages that can help you debug ASP.NET applications. To enable tracing for a specific page, insert the page directive Trace="True" in the ASPX file or set the IsEnabled property of the TraceContext class in your code-behind module.

The TraceContext class provides two methods: Write() and Warn(). Both display a message in the current page's trace log, but Warn() uses red lettering that is meant to indicate exception information. You can invoke the Write() or Warn() method with a category string and message string. Often, the category string indicates the position in the code ("In FunctionA"), while the message string indicates specific information ("Exception while opening database"). Additionally, an overloaded version of Write() and Warn() allows you supply an exception object that ASP.NET will use to extract the appropriate information. Even if you don't use the Write() and Warn() methods, ASP.NET automatically inserts trace log entries to indicate standard events, and appends a great deal of information after the list of trace message, including performance data, tree-structure information, and state management content.

The TraceContext class is provided as the built-in Trace object. You can use the *web.config* file to set additional tracing options like the default TraceMode, and enable application-wide tracing. Application-wide tracing can be displayed on the page or cached exclusively in memory.

```
Public NotInheritable Class TraceContext
' Public Constructors
    Public Sub New(ByVal context As HttpContext)
' Public Instance Properties
    Public Property IsEnabled As Boolean
    Public Property TraceMode As TraceMode
' Public Instance Methods
    Public Sub Warn(ByVal message As String)
    Public Sub Warn(ByVal category As String, ByVal message As String)
    Public Sub Warn(ByVal category As String, ByVal message As String, ByVal errorInfo As Exception)
    Public Sub Write(ByVal message As String)
    Public Sub Write(ByVal category As String, ByVal message As String)
    Public Sub Write(ByVal category As String, ByVal message As String, ByVal errorInfo As Exception)
End Class
```

TraceMode

System.Web (system.web.dll)

serializable

This enumeration is used to set the TraceMode property of the TraceContext class. It specifies whether entries in the trace log will be listed alphabetically (SortByCategory) or chronologically (SortByTime).

```
Public Enum TraceMode
    SortByTime = 0
    SortByCategory = 1
    Default = 2
End Enum
```

Hierarchy: System.Object → System.ValueType → System.Enum (System.IComparable , System.IFormattable , System.IConvertible)→ TraceMode

The System.Web.Caching Namespace

The System.Web.Caching namespace includes types used for ASP.NET caching. The Cache class is the focal point of this namespace; it contains a collection of cached objects and allows you to set expiration policies and dependencies for each item in the cache. The CacheDependency class encapsulates a cache dependency and allows you to link the validity of a cache item to another item or a file on the web server. The CacheItemRemovedCallback delegate allows you to respond when an object is dropped from the cache. Both types work in conjunction with the Cache class. Together, they allow you to implement sophisticated data caching.

ASP.NET also supports page caching, which stores entire compiled pages for automatic reuse. To configure settings for page caching, you must use the System.Web.HttpCachePolicy class. Figure 23-1 shows the types in this namespace.

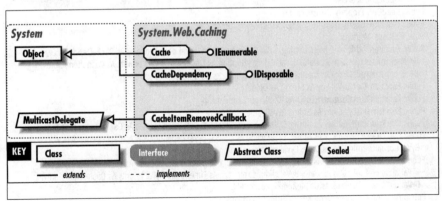

Figure 23-1: The System.Web.Caching namespace

Cache   NotInheritable Class
System.Web.Caching (system.web.dll)

The Cache class allows your application to use data caching. The Cache class works by exposing a key-value collection where you can store objects that are expensive to create or frequently used. Its use is analogous to the System.Web.HttpApplicationState class, although you use the System.Web.HttpApplicationState to store information that must be retained for long periods of time and the Cache class for volatile objects that may quickly expire and can be dropped automatically when memory declines.

Much like the System.Web.HttpApplicationState class, the Cache class is globally accessible to all clients on a single web server, persists for the lifetime of the ASP.NET application, and has only one instance per application. Unlike the System.Web.HttpApplicationState class, the Cache class is thread-safe.

You can add items to the cache as you would with other state collections like System.Web.HttpApplicationState (for example, Cache("myobject") = rsCustomerData). However, using the overloaded Insert() method allows much more control. For example, you can set an absolute expiration policy in which an item will be removed after a specified time (Cache.Insert("Data", rsData, Nothing, DateTime.Now.AddMinutes(10), NoSlidingExpiration) or a sliding expiration policy in which an item will be removed after a specified interval of disuse (Cache.Insert("Data", rsData, Nothing, NoAbsoluteExpiration, TimeSpan.FromMinutes(10)). Note that the NoAbsoluteExpiration and NoSlidingExpiration fields from the Cache class allow you to disable the type of caching you don't want to use. Attempts to retrieve a removed cached item will return Nothing (or null).

You can also use a version of the Insert() method with additional parameters for setting cache dependencies (by supplying an instance of a CacheDependency class), priorities (by using the CacheItemPriority enumeration), and a callback (by supplying a CacheItemRemovedCallback delegate).

The Cache class is available through the built-in Cache object and shouldn't be confused with the System.Web.HttpCachePolicy class, which is used to configure page caching and is available through the Response.Cache reference.

```
Public NotInheritable Class Cache : Implements IEnumerable
' Public Constructors
    Public Sub New()
' Public Shared Fields
    public Shared ReadOnly NoAbsoluteExpiration As Date          =12/31/9999 11:59:59 PM
    public Shared ReadOnly NoSlidingExpiration As TimeSpan       =00:00:00
' Public Instance Properties
    Public ReadOnly Property Count As Integer
    Public Default Property Item (ByVal key As String) As Object
' Public Instance Methods
    Public Function Add(ByVal key As String, ByVal value As Object, ByVal dependencies As CacheDependency, _
        ByVal absoluteExpiration As Date, ByVal slidingExpiration As TimeSpan), ByVal priority As CacheItemPriority, _
        ByVal onRemoveCallback As CacheItemRemovedCallback)  As Object
    Public Function Get(ByVal key As String) As Object
    Public Function GetEnumerator() As IDictionaryEnumerator
    Public Sub Insert(ByVal key As String, ByVal value As Object)
    Public Sub Insert(ByVal key As String, ByVal value As Object, ByVal dependencies As CacheDependency)
    Public Sub Insert(ByVal key As String, ByVal value As Object, ByVal dependencies As CacheDependency, _
        ByVal absoluteExpiration As Date, ByVal slidingExpiration As TimeSpan)
    Public Sub Insert(ByVal key As String, ByVal value As Object, ByVal dependencies As CacheDependency, _
        ByVal absoluteExpiration As Date, ByVal slidingExpiration As TimeSpan), ByVal priority As CacheItemPriority, _
        ByVal onRemoveCallback As CacheItemRemovedCallback)
    Public Function Remove(ByVal key As String) As Object
End Class
```

CacheDependency
NotInheritable Class

System.Web.Caching (system.web.dll)
disposable

Cache dependencies allow the validity of a cache item to be based on a file or directory on the web server, or on another cache item. When the dependency object changes, the dependent cache item is invalidated and removed automatically. To set up a dependency, you first create a CacheDependency object that references the file, directory, or cache item upon which the dependency will be based. You then use the Cache.Insert() method to add the dependent cache item, with the CacheDependency object supplied as a parameter.

The overloaded constructor of the CacheDependency class determines the type of dependency. You can pass a single string argument to set up a dependency on a file or directory (CacheDependency(Server.MapPath("data.xml")) or you can use a second string argument with the key of another cache item (CacheDependency(Nothing, "MyData")). Other versions of the constructor allow you to specify an array of strings specifying files or cache objects. If any one file or object changes, the dependent cache item will be invalidated.

The CacheDependency object begins to monitor for changes as soon as it is created to account for changes that may occur in the brief delay before the dependent cache item is added to the Cache class.

```
Public NotInheritable Class CacheDependency : Implements IDisposable
' Public Constructors
    Public Sub New(ByVal filename As String)
    Public Sub New(ByVal filenames As String())
    Public Sub New(ByVal filenames As String(), ByVal start As Date)
    Public Sub New(ByVal filenames As String(), ByVal cachekeys As String())
    Public Sub New(ByVal filenames As String(), ByVal cachekeys As String(), ByVal dependency As CacheDependency)
    Public Sub New(ByVal filenames As String(), ByVal cachekeys As String(), ByVal dependency As CacheDependency, _
        ByVal start As Date)
    Public Sub New(ByVal filenames As String(), ByVal cachekeys As String(), ByVal start As Date)
    Public Sub New(ByVal filename As String, ByVal start As Date)
' Public Instance Properties
    Public ReadOnly Property HasChanged As Boolean
' Public Instance Methods
    Public Sub Dispose()  Implements IDisposable.Dispose
End Class
```

Caching Namespace

CacheItemPriority
Enum

System.Web.Caching (system.web.dll)
serializable

Priorities are hints that can optimize cache scavenging. Essentially, if the ASP.NET engine decides to remove cache items because memory is scarce, it will remove items with a lower priority cost first. The CacheItemPriority enumeration also includes a NotRemovable member that you can use to prevent ASP.NET from removing an object from the cache automatically when memory is low.

```
Public Enum CacheItemPriority
    Low = 1
    BelowNormal = 2
    Normal = 3
    Default = 3
    AboveNormal = 4
    High = 5
    NotRemovable = 6
End Enum
```

Hierarchy: System.Object → System.ValueType → System.Enum (System.IComparable , System.IFormattable , System.IConvertible) → CacheItemPriority

CacheItemRemovedCallback

Delegate

System.Web.Caching (system.web.dll)

serializable

Functions with the CacheItemRemovedCallback signature can be used to respond to the onRemoveCallback event when an item is dropped from the cache. For example, this could allow you to perform related cleanup tasks. You are provided with the cache object, its key, and the reason why it was removed (using the CacheItemRemovedReason enumeration).

To use this event, pass the function name as an argument in the Cache.Insert() method.

Public Delegate Sub **CacheItemRemovedCallback**(ByVal key As String, ByVal value As Object, _
    ByVal reason As CacheItemRemovedReason)

CacheItemRemovedReason

Enum

System.Web.Caching (system.web.dll)

serializable

If you have set a callback to occur when a cached item is removed, you will be provided with a CacheItemRemovedReason argument. The CacheItemRemovedReason will be Expired if the sliding or absolute expiration time interval passed, Removed if the object was removed programmatically with the Cache.Remove() method or by an Cache.Insert() method with the same key, DependencyChanged if the object was invalidated because of a dependency, or Underused if it has been removed to free memory.

Public Enum **CacheItemRemovedReason**
        Removed = 1
        Expired = 2
        Underused = 3
        DependencyChanged = 4
End Enum

Hierarchy: System.Object → System.ValueType → System.Enum (System.IComparable , System.IFormattable , System.IConvertible) → CacheItemRemovedReason

The System. Web. Configuration Namespace

The System.Web.Configuration namespace includes a few miscellaneous types used in ASP.NET configuration with the *web.config* file; AuthenticationMode, FormsAuthPasswordFormat, and FormsProtectionEnum are all involved in ASP.NET security services. It also provides a ClientTargetSectionHandler class, which provides the basic functionality for processing tags in the *web.config* file, and HttpCapabilitiesBase, which stores a collection of client browser information used by the System.Web.HttpBrowserCapabilities class.

If you've explored the *machine.config* file, you have probably noticed that many other types referenced there don't appear in the ASP.NET reference (including configuration types like HttpCapabilitiesSectionHandler and AuthenticationConfigHandler). These private types aren't available to the client programmer and are part of the low-level ASP.NET infrastructure. Figure 24-1 shows the types in this namespace.

Figure 24-1: The System.Web.Configuration namespace

AuthenticationMode

Enum

System.Web.Configuration (system.web.dll)   *serializable*

This enumeration allows you to specify a type of ASP.NET authentication. It is not used in ASP.NET code, but in the *web.config* file by the mode attribute in the authentication tag (for example, <authentication mode="Forms">). The authentication mode you select determines which HttpModule from the System.Web.Security namespace is used to validate a user's credentials.

```
Public Enum AuthenticationMode
    None = 0
    Windows = 1
    Passport = 2
    Forms = 3
End Enum
```

Hierarchy: System.Object → System.ValueType → System.Enum (System.IComparable , System.IFormattable , System.IConvertible) → AuthenticationMode

ClientTargetSectionHandler   Class

System.Web.Configuration (system.web.dll)

ASP.NET delegates the processing of *web.config* data to configuration section handlers. Section handlers are declared in the *web.config* file using "add" directives inside the <configsections> element. Each element identifies a specific section of configuration data, and the associated System.Configuration.IConfigurationSectionHandler class is used to process it. By inheriting from this class, you could create your own custom section handler. Note that you do not need to create your own custom section handler just to add application-specific constants to your *web.config* file; these constants can be added to the <appSettings> section and retrieved through the System.Configuration.ConfigurationSettings class.

```
Class ClientTargetSectionHandler : Inherits  System.Configuration.NameValueSectionHandler
' Public Constructors
    Public Sub New()
' Protected Instance Properties
    Overrides Protected Property KeyAttributeName As String
    Overrides Protected Property ValueAttributeName As String
End Class
```

Hierarchy: System.Object → System.Configuration.NameValueSectionHandler (System.Configuration.IConfigurationSectionHandler) → ClientTargetSectionHandler

FormsAuthPasswordFormat   Enum

System.Web.Configuration (system.web.dll)   *serializable*

This enumeration specifies the format that ASP.NET uses for encrypting passwords (if you are using Forms Authentication and the System.Web.Security.FormsAuthenticationModule). It is not used in ASP.NET code, but in the *web.config* file by the passwordFormat attribute in the <credentials> element (for example, <credentials passwordFormat="Clear">). When using any format other than clear, the user's password is hashed with an appropriate algorithm and compared to the value stored in the *web.config* file each time authentication is performed. No matter what encryption you use for the password, usernames will still be transmitted in clear text.

```
Public Enum FormsAuthPasswordFormat
    Clear = 0
    SHA1 = 1
    MD5 = 2
End Enum
```

Hierarchy: System.Object → System.ValueType → System.Enum (System.IComparable , System.IFormattable , System.IConvertible) → FormsAuthPasswordFormat

FormsProtectionEnum

System.Web.Configuration (system.web.dll)

This enumeration specifies how ASP.NET protects the Forms Authentication cookie. It is not used in ASP.NET code, but in the *web.config* file by the protection attribute of the forms element (for example, <forms name="name" loginUrl="url" protection="None ">). Encryption uses Triple-DES or DES to encode the cookie before it is transmitted. Validation verifies the cookie hasn't been altered in transit by appending a validation key and then a Message Authentication Code (MAC) to the cookie.

```
Public Enum FormsProtectionEnum
    All = 0
    None = 1
    Encryption = 2
    Validation = 3
End Enum
```

Hierarchy: System.Object → System.ValueType → System.Enum (System.IComparable , System.IFormattable , System.IConvertible)→ FormsProtectionEnum

HttpCapabilitiesBase

System.Web.Configuration (system.web.dll)

This is the base class for the System.Web.HttpBrowserCapabilities class. HttpCapabilitiesBase is weakly typed with a name/value collection of browser settings. These settings are provided (more usefully) as properties by the System.Web.HttpBrowserCapabilities class.

```
Public Class HttpCapabilitiesBase
' Public Constructors
    Public Sub New()
' Public Instance Properties
    Overridable Public Default ReadOnly Property Item (ByVal key As String) As String
' Public Shared Methods
    Public Shared Function GetConfigCapabilities(ByVal configKey As String, _
      ByVal request As System.Web.HttpRequest) As HttpCapabilitiesBase
' Protected Instance Methods
    Overridable Protected Sub Init()
End Class
```

HttpConfigurationContext

System.Web.Configuration (system.web.dll)

This class supplies the current context information to configuration section handlers in ASP.NET applications. The single VirtualPath property provides the path to the current *web.config* file that is evaluated, unless it is the root *web.config* for the site or the *machine.config* file is being evaluated instead (in which case, it will return an empty string).

You don't need to use this class directly in your code.

```
Public Class HttpConfigurationContext
' Public Instance Properties
    Public ReadOnly Property VirtualPath As String
End Class
```

CHAPTER 25

The System.Web.Hosting Namespace

The System.Web.Hosting namespace is not used in ASP.NET web applications; instead, it provides support for hosting the ASP.NET service outside of Internet Information Services (IIS) in a custom hosting application (which you would write using .NET). The two important classes in this namespace are ApplicationHost and SimpleWorkerRequest. The other classes provide lower-level framework support and are not used directly in an application. Figure 25-1 shows the types in this namespace.

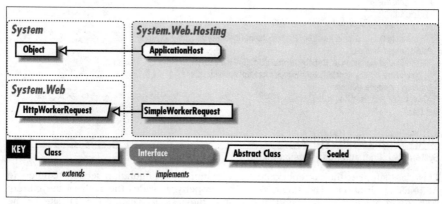

Figure 25-1: The System.Web.Hosting namespace

AppDomainFactory
NotInheritable Class

System.Web.Hosting (system.web.dll)

This class supports the .NET Framework infrastructure. You do not need to use it directly in your code.

Public NotInheritable Class **AppDomainFactory** : Implements IAppDomainFactory
' *Public Constructors*
  Public Sub **New**()
' *Public Instance Methods*
  Public Function **Create**(ByVal module As String, ByVal typeName As String, ByVal appId As String, _
    ByVal appPath As String, ByVal strUrlOfAppOrigin As String, ByVal iZone As Integer) As Object   _
    Implements IAppDomainFactory.Create
End Class

ApplicationHost

NotInheritable Class

System.Web.Hosting (system.web.dll)

This class exposes a single shared CreateApplicationHost() method, which allows you to create an application domain that will be used to process ASP.NET requests. This method accepts three parameters—the hostType (your request-handling class, which will be created in the new domain), virtualDir (the virtual directory for the application domain, such as "/MyApp"), and physicalDir (the physical directory for the application domain where the ASP.NET pages are located, such as "c:\MyApp"). The CreateApplicationHost() method returns the live instance of the hostType class.

Public NotInheritable Class **ApplicationHost**
' *Public Shared Methods*
  Public Shared Function **CreateApplicationHost**(ByVal hostType As Type, ByVal virtualDir As String, _
    ByVal physicalDir As String) As Object
End Class

IAppDomainFactory

Interface

System.Web.Hosting (system.web.dll)

This interface supports the .NET Framework infrastructure. You do not need to use it directly in your code.

Public Interface **IAppDomainFactory**
' *Public Instance Methods*
  Public Function **Create**(ByVal module As String, ByVal typeName As String, ByVal appId As String, _
    ByVal appPath As String, ByVal strUrlOfAppOrigin As String, ByVal iZone As Integer) As Object
End Interface

IISAPIRuntime

Interface

System.Web.Hosting (system.web.dll)

This interface supports the .NET Framework infrastructure. You do not need to use it directly in your code.

Public Interface **IISAPIRuntime**
' *Public Instance Methods*
  Public Sub **DoGCCollect**()
  Public Function **ProcessRequest**(ByVal ecb As IntPtr, ByVal useProcessModel As Integer) As Integer
  Public Sub **StartProcessing**()
  Public Sub **StopProcessing**()
End Interface

ISAPIRuntime

NotInheritable Class

System.Web.Hosting (system.web.dll)

This class supports the .NET Framework infrastructure. You do not need to use it directly in your code.

```
Public NotInheritable Class ISAPIRuntime : Implements IISAPIRuntime
' Public Constructors
    Public Sub New()
' Public Instance Methods
    Public Sub DoGCCollect() Implements IISAPIRuntime.DoGCCollect
    Public Function ProcessRequest(ByVal ecb As IntPtr, ByVal iWRType As Integer) As Integer _
        Implements IISAPIRuntime.ProcessRequest
    Public Sub StartProcessing() Implements IISAPIRuntime.StartProcessing
    Public Sub StopProcessing() Implements IISAPIRuntime.StopProcessing
End Class
```

SimpleWorkerRequest   Class

System.Web.Hosting (system.web.dll)

This class extends the abstract System.Web.HttpWorkerRequest class. It provides features that
allow you to read the incoming HTTP request and send an appropriate HTTP response.
You can retrieve the URL request with the query string appended (through GetRawUrl()),
a server variable by name from a dictionary collection (GetServerVariable()), and the physical file path of the requested URL (GetFilePathTranslated()). You send a response as series
of bytes with the SendResponseFromFile() or SendResponseFromMemory() methods. Use
FlushResponse() to send all pending data to the client. If you want to provide higher-level
methods or properties, such as those found in the System.Web.HttpResponse and Sys-
tem.Web.HttpRequest classes, you should extend SimpleWorkerRequest.

```
Public Class SimpleWorkerRequest : Inherits System.Web.HttpWorkerRequest
' Public Constructors
    Public Sub New(ByVal appVirtualDir As String, ByVal appPhysicalDir As String, ByVal page As String, _
        ByVal query As String, ByVal output As System.IO.TextWriter)
    Public Sub New(ByVal page As String, ByVal query As String, ByVal output As System.IO.TextWriter)
' Public Instance Properties
    Overrides Public ReadOnly Property MachineConfigPath As String
    Overrides Public ReadOnly Property MachineInstallDirectory As String
' Public Instance Methods
    Overrides Public Sub EndOfRequest()
    Overrides Public Sub FlushResponse(ByVal finalFlush As Boolean)
    Overrides Public Function GetAppPath() As String
    Overrides Public Function GetAppPathTranslated() As String
    Overrides Public Function GetFilePath() As String
    Overrides Public Function GetFilePathTranslated() As String
    Overrides Public Function GetHttpVerbName() As String
    Overrides Public Function GetHttpVersion() As String
    Overrides Public Function GetLocalAddress() As String
    Overrides Public Function GetLocalPort() As Integer
    Overrides Public Function GetPathInfo() As String
    Overrides Public Function GetQueryString() As String
    Overrides Public Function GetRawUrl() As String
    Overrides Public Function GetRemoteAddress() As String
    Overrides Public Function GetRemotePort() As Integer
    Overrides Public Function GetServerVariable(ByVal name As String) As String
    Overrides Public Function GetUriPath() As String
    Overrides Public Function GetUserToken() As IntPtr
    Overrides Public Function MapPath(ByVal path As String) As String
    Overrides Public Sub SendKnownResponseHeader(ByVal index As Integer, ByVal value As String)
    Overrides Public Sub SendResponseFromFile(ByVal handle As IntPtr, ByVal offset As Long, _
        ByVal length As Long)
```

```
Overrides Public Sub SendResponseFromFile(ByVal filename As String, ByVal offset As Long, _
   ByVal length As Long)
Overrides Public Sub SendResponseFromMemory(ByVal data As Byte(), ByVal length As Integer)
Overrides Public Sub SendStatus(ByVal statusCode As Integer, ByVal statusDescription As String)
Overrides Public Sub SendUnknownResponseHeader(ByVal name As String, ByVal value As String)
End Class
```

Hierarchy: System.Object → System.Web.HttpWorkerRequest (System.Web.IHttpMapPath) →
SimpleWorkerRequest

CHAPTER 26

The System.Web.Mail Namespace

The System.Web.Mail namespace allows you to send email messages from your ASP.NET application. This capability uses the built-in SMTP service included with IIS, and is similar to the CDO component used in traditional ASP development. The SMTP service maps its Inbox and Outbox to directories on the server. Message transfer is handled so that the Outbox is always empty and the Inbox never has an incoming queue.

Messages and attachments are encapsulated in MailMessage and MailAttachment objects and sent using the SmtpMail helper class, which provides a single Send() method. Figure 26-1 shows the types in this namespace.

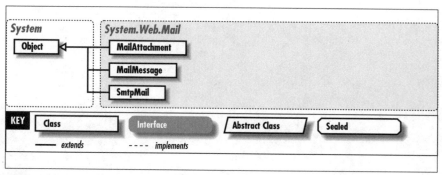

Figure 26-1: The System.Web.Mail namespace

MailAttachment   Class

System.Web.Mail (system.web.dll)

This class encapsulates an attachment to an email message. The constructor takes a string argument that identifies the local path to the file, as in MailAttachment("c:\temp\report.pdf"). An optional second argument lets you set the encoding (which will be System.Web.Mail.Encoding.UUEncode if omitted). Once you create an instance of MailAttachment, you can add it to an instance of the MailMessage class with the MailMessage.Attachments collection. The easiest way to do this is through the Add() method of the MailMessage.Attachments class, like this: objMessage.Attachments.Add(objAttachment).

```
Public Class MailAttachment
' Public Constructors
    Public Sub New(ByVal filename As String)
    Public Sub New(ByVal filename As String, ByVal encoding As MailEncoding)
' Public Instance Properties
    Public ReadOnly Property Encoding As MailEncoding
    Public ReadOnly Property Filename As String
End Class
```

MailEncoding
Enum

System.Web.Mail (system.web.dll)
serializable

This enumeration sets the BodyEncoding property of the MailMessage class and the Encoding property of the MailAttachment class.

```
Public Enum MailEncoding
    UUEncode = 0
    Base64 = 1
End Enum
```

Hierarchy: System.Object → System.ValueType → System.Enum (System.IComparable , System.IFormattable , System.IConvertible)→ MailEncoding

MailFormat
Enum

System.Web.Mail (system.web.dll)
serializable

This enumeration sets the BodyFormat property of the MailMessage class. If you use Html, you can include standard HTML markup tags in the Body property of a MailMessage instance and they will be rendered in the recepient's email program, if supported.

```
Public Enum MailFormat
    Text = 0
    Html = 1
End Enum
```

Hierarchy: System.Object → System.ValueType → System.Enum (System.IComparable , System.IFormattable , System.IConvertible)→ MailFormat

MailMessage
Class

System.Web.Mail (system.web.dll)

This class encapsulates an email message. To send an email message programmatically, create a MailMessage object, set the appropriate properties and use the SmtpMail.Send() method.

The properties of the MailMessage class are fairly straightforward and include all the typical details entered in an email program, such as subject, priority, and the email addresses for the sender, recipient, and any carbon-copied recipients (all as strings). You can also use the Attachments collection to add MailAttachment objects to a message.

The actual body of the email message is set as a string through the Body property. You will have to add line return characters (for example msg.Body = "Hi Bob," & System.Environment.NewLine & "This is it!") as required. If you set the BodyFormat property to MailFormat.Html, you can also insert standard HTML markup tags.

Mail Namespace

```
Public Class MailMessage
' Public Constructors
   Public Sub New()
' Public Instance Properties
   Public ReadOnly Property Attachments As IList
   Public Property Bcc As String
   Public Property Body As String
   Public Property BodyEncoding As Encoding
   Public Property BodyFormat As MailFormat
   Public Property Cc As String
   Public Property From As String
   Public ReadOnly Property Headers As IDictionary
   Public Property Priority As MailPriority
   Public Property Subject As String
   Public Property To As String
   Public Property UrlContentBase As String
   Public Property UrlContentLocation As String
End Class
```

MailPriority

Enum

System.Web.Mail (system.web.dll)

serializable

This enumeration sets the Priority property of a MailMessage object.

```
Public Enum MailPriority
      Normal = 0
      Low = 1
      High = 2
End Enum
```

Hierarchy: System.Object → System.ValueType → System.Enum (System.IComparable , System.IFormattable , System.IConvertible) → MailPriority

SmtpMail

Class

System.Web.Mail (system.web.dll)

The SmtpMail class represents the SMTP Server. It includes a shared (static) Send() method that you can use to send email programmatically. There are two versions of the Send() method: one accepts a MailMessage object, and the other provides a quick and simple way to send an e-mail message without creating a MailMessage instance (by specifying the sender's e-mail address, the recipient, the subject, and the body text as string parameters).

```
Public Class SmtpMail
' Public Shared Properties
   Public Shared Property SmtpServer As String
' Public Shared Methods
   Public Shared Sub Send(ByVal message As MailMessage)
   Public Shared Sub Send(ByVal from As String, ByVal to As String, ByVal subject As String, _
      ByVal messageText As String)
End Class
```

CHAPTER 27

The System.Web.Security Namespace

The System.Web.Security namespace includes the modules that implement various types of ASP.NET authentication, such as WindowsAuthenticationModule, FormsAuthenticationModule, and PassportAuthenticationModule. You don't interact directly with these modules in an ASP.NET application; instead, the ASP.NET framework uses the appropriate module (based on the options you have set in the *web.config* file) to authenticate the user. After this point, ASP.NET provides identity information in the System.Web.HttpContext.User property and uses this identity to authorize access to resources such as files and URLs (using modules like UrlAuthorizationModule and FileAuthorizationModule, which are also found in this namespace).

One reason you might use the types in this namespace is to handle authentication events. Generic security events, like System.Web.HttpApplication.AuthenticateRequest and System.Web.HttpApplication.AuthorizeRequest are already available in the *global.asax* file. However, each authentication module also provides its own Authenticate event, which can be used to validate a user programmatically or attach a new System.Security.Principal.IIdentity instance. Event handlers for Authenticate events are coded in the *global.asax* file, but defined in this namespace.

Another important class in this namespace is FormsAuthentication. This class provides the shared methods you need to use in your login page if you use ASP.NET's forms-based security. These methods let you authenticate a user, instruct ASP.NET to issue the authenticated forms cookie, and redirect the user to the original requested page.

Note that many security options are not reflected in these classes. When implementing a custom authorization/authentication scheme, you should first examine all the security options provided in the *web.config* file. Internet Information Server (IIS) also provides an additional layer of security configuration. Figure 27-1 and Figure 27-2 show the types in this namespace.

DefaultAuthenticationEventArgs   NotInheritable Class

System.Web.Security (system.web.dll)

This class provides a reference to the System.Web.HttpContext object for the DefaultAuthenticationModule.Authenticate event. Unlike all other Authenticate events, this event does not provide objects that allow you to set or examine user identity information; the DefaultAuthenticationModule is used only when the authentication mode is set to "None."

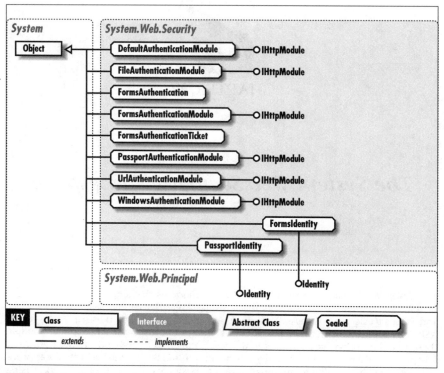

Figure 27-1: Core types from the System.Web.Security namespace

Public NotInheritable Class **DefaultAuthenticationEventArgs** : Inherits EventArgs
  ' Public Constructors
    Public Sub **New**(ByVal context As System.Web.HttpContext)
  ' Public Instance Properties
    Public ReadOnly Property **Context** As HttpContext
End Class

Hierarchy: System.Object → System.EventArgs → DefaultAuthenticationEventArgs

DefaultAuthenticationEventHandler

Delegate

System.Web.Security (system.web.dll)

serializable

This delegate represents an event handler for the DefaultAuthenticationModule.Authenticate event. It provides a custom DefaultAuthenticationEventArgs object with a reference to the current System.Web.HttpContext. This event handler must be coded in the *global.asax*, using the event name DefaultAuthentication_OnAuthenticate (and it does not need to be connected with a Handles keyword or the AddHandler() command).

Public Delegate Sub **DefaultAuthenticationEventHandler**(ByVal sender As Object, _
  ByVal e As DefaultAuthenticationEventArgs)

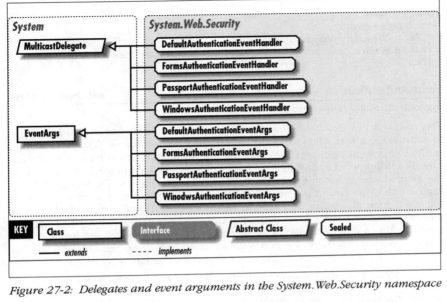

Figure 27-2: Delegates and event arguments in the System.Web.Security namespace

DefaultAuthenticationModule

NotInheritable Class

System.Web.Security (system.web.dll)

The ASP.NET framework uses this authentication module automatically when no other authentication module is specified in the current context (for example, when you set <authentication mode="None"> in the *web.config* file. This is similar to how many traditional ASP applications work. IIS authentication is still used and access to local system resources is provided in the context of a local system process account (or the IUSR_MACHINENAME account) according to the IIS settings. However, ASP.NET page requests will not require additional authentication.

```
Public NotInheritable Class DefaultAuthenticationModule : Implements System.Web.IHttpModule
' Public Constructors
    Public Sub New()
' Public Instance Methods
    Public Sub Dispose()  Implements IHttpModule.Dispose
    Public Sub Init(ByVal app As System.Web.HttpApplication)  Implements  IHttpModule.Init
' Events
    Public Event Authenticate As DefaultAuthenticationEventHandler
End Class
```

FileAuthorizationModule

NotInheritable Class

System.Web.Security (system.web.dll)

This class is used automatically when you use the WindowsAuthenticationModule class. ASP.NET uses FileAuthorizationModule to determine whether a specified file operation should be allowed or denied, based on the currently authenticated NT user account (and using Access Control Lists (ACLs)).

```
Public NotInheritable Class FileAuthorizationModule : Implements  System.Web.IHttpModule
' Public Constructors
```

```
    Public Sub New()
  ' Public Instance Methods
    Public Sub Dispose() Implements IHttpModule.Dispose
    Public Sub Init(ByVal app As System.Web.HttpApplication) Implements IHttpModule.Init
End Class
```

FormsAuthentication
NotInheritable Class

System.Web.Security (system.web.dll)

This class contains the shared (static) methods that you use in your custom login page to authenticate a user when using the FormsAuthenticationModule class. Typically, the first method your login page uses is the Authenticate() method, which compares a supplied user ID and password against the list of allowed logins defined in the *web.config* file. If this method returns True, the information is valid and you can use the RedirectFromLogin-Page() method to issue the Forms cookie and redirect the user to the previously requested page, all at once. You need to supply the user ID to this method, along with a boolean createPersistentCookie parameter. If createPersistentCookie is set to True, a "permanent" cookie (with an expiration date of fifty years into the future) will be created so that the user never needs to log in when they return to the site. This cookie is suitable only for applications that use authentication for personalization rather than security.

Other methods you might want to use in this class include SignOut(), which removes the current Forms cookie, and SetAuthCookie(), which creates the Forms cookie but does not redirect the user. (You could then retrieve the original requested URL by using the GetRedirectUrl() method and make a decision about whether to redirect the user to this page or to a default main page.)

You can also use the GetAuthCookie() method, which returns the Forms cookie as a System.Web.HttpCookie object. In this case, the user is not authenticated (and won't be able to access other pages in your application) until the cookie is added to the System.Web.HttpResponse.Cookies collection. You can work with this cookie on a lower level by using methods like Decrypt().

```
Public NotInheritable Class FormsAuthentication
' Public Constructors
    Public Sub New()
' Public Shared Properties
    Public Shared ReadOnly Property FormsCookieName As String
    Public Shared ReadOnly Property FormsCookiePath As String
' Public Shared Methods
    Public Shared Function Authenticate(ByVal name As String, ByVal password As String) As Boolean
    Public Shared Function Decrypt(ByVal encryptedTicket As String) As FormsAuthenticationTicket
    Public Shared Function Encrypt(ByVal ticket As FormsAuthenticationTicket) As String
    Public Shared Function GetAuthCookie(ByVal userName As String, ByVal createPersistentCookie As Boolean) _
      As HttpCookie
    Public Shared Function GetAuthCookie(ByVal userName As String, ByVal createPersistentCookie As Boolean, _
      ByVal strCookiePath As String) As HttpCookie
    Public Shared Function GetRedirectUrl(ByVal userName As String, ByVal createPersistentCookie As Boolean) _
      As String
    Public Shared Function HashPasswordForStoringInConfigFile(ByVal password As String, _
      ByVal passwordFormat As String) As String
    Public Shared Sub Initialize()
    Public Shared Sub RedirectFromLoginPage(ByVal userName As String, _
      ByVal createPersistentCookie As Boolean)
    Public Shared Sub RedirectFromLoginPage(ByVal userName As String, _
      ByVal createPersistentCookie As Boolean, ByVal strCookiePath As String)
```

```
Public Shared Function RenewTicketIfOld(ByVal tOld As FormsAuthenticationTicket) _
    As FormsAuthenticationTicket
  Public Shared Sub SetAuthCookie(ByVal userName As String, ByVal createPersistentCookie As Boolean)
  Public Shared Sub SetAuthCookie(ByVal userName As String, ByVal createPersistentCookie As Boolean, _
    ByVal strCookiePath As String)
  Public Shared Sub SignOut()
End Class
```

FormsAuthenticationEventArgs   NotInheritable Class

System.Web.Security (system.web.dll)

This class is a custom System.EventArgs that is used in the event handler for the Form-sAuthenticationModule.Authenticate event. It provides two properties—Context, which pro-vides a reference to the current System.Web.HttpContext, and User, which will be a null reference (Nothing) because information is not yet retrieved from the Forms authentica-tion cookie. This event is not typically used because Forms authentication already uses the custom code you have created for the login page.

```
Public NotInheritable Class FormsAuthenticationEventArgs : Inherits EventArgs
' Public Constructors
  Public Sub New(ByVal context As System.Web.HttpContext)
' Public Instance Properties
  Public ReadOnly Property Context As HttpContext
  Public Property User As IPrincipal
End Class
```

Hierarchy: System.Object → System.EventArgs → FormsAuthenticationEventArgs

FormsAuthenticationEventHandler   Delegate

System.Web.Security (system.web.dll)   *serializable*

This delegate represents the event handler that can be used to handle the FormsAuthenti-cationModule.Authenticate event. This event handler must be coded in *global.asax*, using the event name WindowsAuthentication_OnAuthenticate (and it does not need to be con-nected with a Handles keyword or the AddHandler() command).

```
Public Delegate Sub FormsAuthenticationEventHandler(ByVal sender As Object, _
    ByVal e As FormsAuthenticationEventArgs)
```

FormsAuthenticationModule   NotInheritable Class

System.Web.Security (system.web.dll)

This module, when loaded through the *web.config* file (<authentication mode="Forms">), provides Forms-based authentication. In this model, the ASP.NET framework uses a special authentication cookie. If it is not present, users are redirected to a custom ASP.NET page where they can acquire the cookie once they log in successfully. If the cookie is present, ASP.NET fires the Authenticate event, places identity information in the System.Web.HttpContext.User property, and allows access. You can react to this event by creating an event handler called FormsAuthentication_OnAuthenticate in the *global.asax* file.

Several additional settings, including the URL for the login page and the length of time before the cookie expires, can be set in the *web.config* file. The actual authentication for the user is performed in the custom code you create for the login page. This code uses the helper methods in the FormsAuthentication class to authenticate the user and assign the Forms authentication cookie.

```
Public NotInheritable Class FormsAuthenticationModule : Implements System.Web.IHttpModule
' Public Constructors
   Public Sub New()
' Public Instance Methods
   Public Sub Dispose() Implements IHttpModule.Dispose
   Public Sub Init(ByVal app As System.Web.HttpApplication) Implements IHttpModule.Init
' Events
   Public Event Authenticate As FormsAuthenticationEventHandler
End Class
```

FormsAuthenticationTicket
NotInheritable Class

System.Web.Security (system.web.dll)
serializable

This class wraps the information in the Forms authentication cookie. This information includes the expiration and issue date (Expiration and IssueDate), the username (Name), and an application-defined string that can be stored in the cookie (UserData). An instance of this class is provided through the FormsIdentity.Ticket property.

```
Public NotInheritable Class FormsAuthenticationTicket
' Public Constructors
   Public Sub New(ByVal version As Integer, ByVal name As String, ByVal issueDate As Date, ByVal expiration As Date, _
      ByVal isPersistent As Boolean, ByVal userData As String)
   Public Sub New(ByVal version As Integer, ByVal name As String, ByVal issueDate As Date, ByVal expiration As Date, _
      ByVal isPersistent As Boolean), ByVal userData As String, ByVal cookiePath As String)
   Public Sub New(ByVal name As String, ByVal isPersistent As Boolean, ByVal timeout As Integer)
' Public Instance Properties
   Public ReadOnly Property CookiePath As String
   Public ReadOnly Property Expiration As Date
   Public ReadOnly Property Expired As Boolean
   Public ReadOnly Property IsPersistent As Boolean
   Public ReadOnly Property IssueDate As Date
   Public ReadOnly Property Name As String
   Public ReadOnly Property UserData As String
   Public ReadOnly Property Version As Integer
End Class
```

FormsIdentity
NotInheritable Class

System.Web.Security (system.web.dll)
serializable

This System.Security.Principal.IIdentity instance provides information to the FormsAuthenticationModule about the current user identity. This information consists of the username (Name), the type of authentication (AuthenticationType), which will always be "Forms," and the corresponding ticket object (Ticket).

```
Public NotInheritable Class FormsIdentity : Implements System.Security.Principal.IIdentity
' Public Constructors
   Public Sub New(ByVal ticket As FormsAuthenticationTicket)
' Public Instance Properties
   Public ReadOnly Property AuthenticationType As String Implements IIdentity.AuthenticationType
   Public ReadOnly Property IsAuthenticated As Boolean Implements IIdentity.IsAuthenticated
   Public ReadOnly Property Name As String Implements IIdentity.Name
   Public ReadOnly Property Ticket As FormsAuthenticationTicket
End Class
```

PassportAuthenticationEventArgs

NotInheritable Class

System.Web.Security (system.web.dll)

This class is a custom System.EventArgs object that is used in the event handler for the PassportAuthenticationModule.Authenticate event. It provides three properties: Context, which provides a reference to the current System.Web.HttpContext; User, which will be a null reference (Nothing); and Identity, which will contain the information received from Passport as a PassportIdentity object.

You can implement a custom authentication scheme and set the User value programmatically to the appropriate user identity. If you do not set it to a non-null value, the PassportAuthenticationModule will create a System.Security.Principal.WindowsPrincipal object based on the information supplied in the PassportIdentity object and assign it to the System.Web.HttpContext.User property.

```
Public NotInheritable Class PassportAuthenticationEventArgs : Inherits EventArgs
' Public Constructors
   Public Sub New(ByVal identity As PassportIdentity, ByVal context As System.Web.HttpContext)
' Public Instance Properties
   Public ReadOnly Property Context As HttpContext
   Public ReadOnly Property Identity As PassportIdentity
   Public Property User As IPrincipal
End Class
```

Hierarchy: System.Object → System.EventArgs → PassportAuthenticationEventArgs

PassportAuthenticationEventHandler

Delegate

System.Web.Security (system.web.dll)

serializable

This delegate represents the event handler that can be used to handle the PassportAuthenticationModule.Authenticate event. This event handler must be coded in the *global.asax* file, using the event handler name PassportAuthentication_OnAuthenticate (and it does not need to be connected with a Handles keyword or the AddHandler() command).

```
Public Delegate Sub PassportAuthenticationEventHandler(ByVal sender As Object, _
   ByVal e As PassportAuthenticationEventArgs)
```

PassportAuthenticationModule

NotInheritable Class

System.Web.Security (system.web.dll)

This module, when loaded through the *web.config* file (<authentication mode="Passport">), provides authentication using Microsoft's Passport service. In this model, the ASP.NET framework will check for the Passport "ticket" (an encrypted value in a cookie or the query string) and use it to authenticate the user. If no ticket is present, or if it has expired, the user will be redirected to the Passport service's login page. The user will be redirected automatically to the original ASP.NET page with the correct ticket after logging in. At this point, the Authenticate event will be fired. You can handle this event with an event handler named PassportAuthentication_OnAuthenticate in the *global.asax* file.

The location of the Passport login page is set using the <passport redirectUrl> element in the *web.config* file.

```
Public NotInheritable Class PassportAuthenticationModule : Implements System.Web.IHttpModule
' Public Constructors
   Public Sub New()
' Public Instance Methods
   Public Sub Dispose() Implements IHttpModule.Dispose
```

```
    Public Sub Init(ByVal app As System.Web.HttpApplication) Implements IHttpModule.Init
' Events
    Public Event Authenticate As PassportAuthenticationEventHandler
End Class
```

PassportIdentity   NotInheritable Class

System.Web.Security (system.web.dll)

This class wraps information from the Passport user profile. For example, you can retrieve the 64-bit Passport User ID (PUID) from the Name property, along with information about how long the user has been signed in (TimeSinceSignIn), how old the current ticket is (TicketAge), and whether the password is currently saved on the user's Passport login page (HasSavedPassword). Additionally, you can get information about any error associated with the current ticket (Error), although you must compare the number to values in the Passport documentation, as no enumeration is currently supplied. Other information from the Passport profile (including everything from the user's birth date to the user's language preference) is available through the Item key/value collection. For information on valid attribute names, consult the Passport documentation.

The PassportIdentity class also provides several methods, many of which are shared and available without a PassportIdentity instance (such as those used for encryption and compression). You can use LoginUser() to redirect a user to the Passport sign-in page, initiate a Passport-aware client authentication exchange. You can also use SignOut() to end the user's session.

Note that you can pass -1 to any Passport method in place of an optional integer parameter. This indicates that Passport should use the default value from the registry and is equivalent to omitting optional parameters.

```
Public NotInheritable Class PassportIdentity : Implements System.Security.Principal.IIdentity
' Public Constructors
    Public Sub New()
' Public Instance Properties
    Public ReadOnly Property AuthenticationType As String Implements IIdentity.AuthenticationType
    Public ReadOnly Property Error As Integer
    Public ReadOnly Property GetFromNetworkServer As Boolean
    Public ReadOnly Property HasSavedPassword As Boolean
    Public ReadOnly Property HasTicket As Boolean
    Public ReadOnly Property HexPUID As String
    Public ReadOnly Property IsAuthenticated As Boolean Implements IIdentity.IsAuthenticated
    Public Default ReadOnly Property Item (ByVal strProfileName As String) As String
    Public ReadOnly Property Name As String Implements IIdentity.Name
    Public ReadOnly Property TicketAge As Integer
    Public ReadOnly Property TimeSinceSignIn As Integer
' Public Shared Methods
    Public Shared Function Compress(ByVal strData As String) As String
    Public Shared Function CryptIsValid() As Boolean
    Public Shared Function CryptPutHost(ByVal strHost As String) As Integer
    Public Shared Function CryptPutSite(ByVal strSite As String) As Integer
    Public Shared Function Decompress(ByVal strData As String) As String
    Public Shared Function Decrypt(ByVal strData As String) As String
    Public Shared Function Encrypt(ByVal strData As String) As String
    Public Shared Sub SignOut(ByVal strSignOutDotGifFileName As String)
' Public Instance Methods
    Public Function AuthUrl() As String
    Public Function AuthUrl(ByVal strReturnUrl As String, ByVal iTimeWindow As Integer, ByVal fForceLogin As Boolean, _
        ByVal strCoBrandedArgs As String, ByVal iLangID As Integer, ByVal strNameSpace As String, ByVal iKPP As Integer, _
```

ByVal bUseSecureAuth As Boolean) As String
Public Function **AuthUrl**(ByVal strReturnUrl As String, ByVal iTimeWindow As Integer, ByVal iForceLogin As Integer, _
  ByVal strCoBrandedArgs As String, ByVal iLangID As Integer, ByVal strNameSpace As String, ByVal iKPP As Integer, _
  ByVal iUseSecureAuth As Integer) As String

Public Function **AuthUrl2**() As String

Public Function **AuthUrl2**(ByVal strReturnUrl As String, ByVal iTimeWindow As Integer,   _
  ByVal fForceLogin As Boolean, ByVal strCoBrandedArgs As String, ByVal iLangID As Integer,   _
  ByVal strNameSpace As String, ByVal iKPP As Integer, ByVal bUseSecureAuth As Boolean) As String

Public Function **AuthUrl2**(ByVal strReturnUrl As String, ByVal iTimeWindow As Integer, ByVal iForceLogin As Integer _
  , ByVal strCoBrandedArgs As String, ByVal iLangID As Integer, ByVal strNameSpace As String, ByVal iKPP As Integer, _
  ByVal iUseSecureAuth As Integer) As String

Public Function **GetCurrentConfig**(ByVal strAttribute As String) As Object

Public Function **GetDomainAttribute**(ByVal strAttribute As String, ByVal iLCID As Integer, _
  ByVal strDomain As String) As String

Public Function **GetDomainFromMemberName**(ByVal strMemberName As String) As String

Public Function **GetIsAuthenticated**(ByVal iTimeWindow As Integer, ByVal bForceLogin As Boolean, _
  ByVal bCheckSecure As Boolean) As Boolean

Public Function **GetIsAuthenticated**(ByVal iTimeWindow As Integer, ByVal iForceLogin As Integer, _
  ByVal iCheckSecure As Integer) As Boolean

Public Function **GetLoginChallenge**() As String

Public Function **GetLoginChallenge**(ByVal szRetURL As String, ByVal iTimeWindow As Integer, _
  ByVal fForceLogin As Integer, ByVal szCOBrandArgs As String, ByVal iLangID As Integer,   _
  ByVal strNameSpace As String, ByVal iKPP As Integer, ByVal iUseSecureAuth As Integer,   _
  ByVal oExtraParams As Object) As String

Public Function **GetOption**(ByVal strOpt As String) As Object

Public Function **GetProfileObject**(ByVal strProfileName As String) As Object

Public Function **HasFlag**(ByVal iFlagMask As Integer) As Boolean

Public Function **HasProfile**(ByVal strProfile As String) As Boolean

Public Function **HaveConsent**(ByVal bNeedFullConsent As Boolean, ByVal bNeedBirthdate As Boolean) _
As Boolean

Public Function **LoginUser**() As Integer

Public Function **LoginUser**(ByVal szRetURL As String, ByVal iTimeWindow As Integer, ByVal fForceLogin As Boolean, _
  ByVal szCOBrandArgs As String, ByVal iLangID As Integer, ByVal strNameSpace As String, ByVal iKPP As Integer, _
  ByVal fUseSecureAuth As Boolean, ByVal oExtraParams As Object) As Integer

Public Function **LoginUser**(ByVal szRetURL As String, ByVal iTimeWindow As Integer, ByVal fForceLogin As Integer, _
  ByVal szCOBrandArgs As String, ByVal iLangID As Integer, ByVal strNameSpace As String, ByVal iKPP As Integer,   _
  ByVal iUseSecureAuth As Integer, ByVal oExtraParams As Object) As Integer

Public Function **LogoTag**() As String

Public Function **LogoTag**(ByVal strReturnUrl As String, ByVal iTimeWindow As Integer, ByVal fForceLogin As Boolean _
  , ByVal strCoBrandedArgs As String, ByVal iLangID As Integer, ByVal fSecure As Boolean,   —
  ByVal strNameSpace As String, ByVal iKPP As Integer, ByVal bUseSecureAuth As Boolean) As String

Public Function **LogoTag**(ByVal strReturnUrl As String, ByVal iTimeWindow As Integer, ByVal iForceLogin As Integer, _
  ByVal strCoBrandedArgs As String, ByVal iLangID As Integer, ByVal iSecure As Integer,   —
  ByVal strNameSpace As String, ByVal iKPP As Integer, ByVal iUseSecureAuth As Integer) As String

Public Function **LogoTag2**() As String

Public Function **LogoTag2**(ByVal strReturnUrl As String, ByVal iTimeWindow As Integer,   _
  ByVal fForceLogin As Boolean, ByVal strCoBrandedArgs As String, ByVal iLangID As Integer, _
  ByVal fSecure As Boolean, ByVal strNameSpace As String, ByVal iKPP As Integer,   —
  ByVal bUseSecureAuth As Boolean) As String

Public Function **LogoTag2**(ByVal strReturnUrl As String, ByVal iTimeWindow As Integer, ByVal iForceLogin As Integer _
  , ByVal strCoBrandedArgs As String, ByVal iLangID As Integer, ByVal iSecure As Integer,   —
  ByVal strNameSpace As String, ByVal iKPP As Integer, ByVal iUseSecureAuth As Integer) As String

Public Function **LogoutURL**() As String

Public Function **LogoutURL**(ByVal szReturnURL As String, ByVal szCOBrandArgs As String, ByVal iLangID As Integer, _
  ByVal strDomain As String, ByVal iUseSecureAuth As Integer) As String

Public Sub **SetOption**(ByVal strOpt As String, ByVal vOpt As Object)

```
Public Function Ticket(ByVal strAttribute As String) As Object
' Protected Instance Methods
    Overrides Protected Sub Finalize()
End Class
```

UrlAuthorizationModule
NotInheritable Class

System.Web.Security (system.web.dll)

ASP.NET uses this class automatically to determine whether access to a specified resource (a URL requested by the client) should be allowed or denied, based on the identity of the currently authenticated user. This class is used as needed, but is not directly referenced in the *web.config* file. You can configure URL authorization by adding a list of users or roles in the <allow> or <deny> elements of the <authorization> section of a configuration file.

Both the FormsAuthenticationModule and PassportAuthenticationModule set the System.Web.Http-Context.SkipAuthorization property to True when redirecting the client to a login page so they can bypass the UrlAuthorizationModule checks.

```
Public NotInheritable Class UrlAuthorizationModule : Implements System.Web.IHttpModule
' Public Constructors
    Public Sub New()
' Public Instance Methods
    Public Sub Dispose() Implements IHttpModule.Dispose
    Public Sub Init(ByVal app As System.Web.HttpApplication) Implements IHttpModule.Init
End Class
```

WindowsAuthenticationEventArgs
NotInheritable Class

System.Web.Security (system.web.dll)

This class is a custom System.EventArgs that is used in the event handler for the WindowsAuthenticationModule.Authenticate event. It provides three properties: Context, which provides a reference to the current System.Web.HttpContext; User, which will be a null reference (Nothing); and Identity, which will contain the information received from IIS. You can implement a custom authentication scheme and set the User property programmatically to the appropriate user identity. If you don't set it to a non-null value, the WindowsAuthenticationModule creates a System.Security.Principal.WindowsPrincipal object based on the information supplied by IIS and assign it to the System.Web.HttpContext.User property.

The easiest way to set a default identity for impersonation is by using the settings in the *web.config* file. You should use this event only if you need to implement a custom authentication scheme.

```
Public NotInheritable Class WindowsAuthenticationEventArgs : Inherits EventArgs
' Public Constructors
    Public Sub New(ByVal identity As System.Security.Principal.WindowsIdentity, _
        ByVal context As System.Web.HttpContext)
' Public Instance Properties
    Public ReadOnly Property Context As HttpContext
    Public ReadOnly Property Identity As WindowsIdentity
    Public Property User As IPrincipal
End Class
```

Hierarchy: System.Object → System.EventArgs → WindowsAuthenticationEventArgs

WindowsAuthenticationEventHandler

Delegate

System.Web.Security (system.web.dll)

serializable

This delegate represents the event handler that can be used to handle the WindowsAuthenticationModule.Authenticate event. This event handler must be coded in *global.asax*, using an event handler named WindowsAuthentication_OnAuthenticate (and it does not need to be connected with a Handles keyword or the AddHandler() command.

```
Public Delegate Sub WindowsAuthenticationEventHandler(ByVal sender As Object, _
    ByVal e As WindowsAuthenticationEventArgs)
```

WindowsAuthenticationModule

NotInheritable Class

System.Web.Security (system.web.dll)

This module, when loaded through the *web.config* file (<authentication mode="Windows">), provides Windows/IIS authentication. In this model, IIS authenticates the user identity for the current web request using any supported method (including Basic, Digest, or Integrated Windows), and then passes that account to the ASP.NET application, which it uses to access the resources it needs. The WindowsAuthenticationModule uses a System.Security.Principal.WindowsIdentity object to hold user information received from IIS and constructs a System.Security.Principal.WindowsPrincipal object to provide information about group memberships. The System.Security.Principal.WindowsPrincipal object is attached to the application context and provided through the System.Web.HttpContext.User property. This module also provides a single event, Authenticate, which you can access through the WindowsAuthentication_OnAuthenticate event handler in the *global.asax* file.

This type of authentication scheme is particularly useful in corporate intranet scenarios, where IIS can be set to Integrated Windows authentication and all users can access the application under their network accounts.

```
Public NotInheritable Class WindowsAuthenticationModule : Implements System.Web.IHttpModule
' Public Constructors
    Public Sub New()
' Public Instance Methods
    Public Sub Dispose() Implements IHttpModule.Dispose
    Public Sub Init(ByVal app As System.Web.HttpApplication) Implements IHttpModule.Init
' Events
    Public Event Authenticate As WindowsAuthenticationEventHandler
End Class
```

CHAPTER 28

The System.Web.Services Namespace

The System.Web.Services namespace contains the types used for creating web services. Web services are "component-like" units of programming logic that exist on a web server as *.asmx* files. Web services can be incorporated seamlessly into Windows or ASP.NET applications. Web services differ from many other methods of remote method invocation (like DCOM) in that they use open XML-based standards, work over normal text HTTP channels, and can be consumed (with a little more programming work) from applications on other platforms and non-Windows operating systems.

The System.Web.Services namespace is the starting point for creating web services. It contains a WebService class that custom web services can inherit from and the WebMethodAttribute and WebServiceAttribute, which are used to mark web service classes and methods and add additional information. Most types in other web service namespaces are used seamlessly by the .NET framework and are not used directly by the .NET programmer. Figure 28-1 shows the types in this namespace.

Figure 28-1: The System.Web.Services namespace

WebMethodAttribute

System.Web.Services (system.web.services.dll)

Use the WebMethodAttribute to mark all the methods that should be made available to web service clients. All methods marked with this attribute will be accessible automatically and will be included in the WSDL document (and the proxy class) that .NET generates. Methods that are not marked with this attribute will not visible or usable, even if they are public.

You can set various properties when you use this attribute. For example, the Description property contains a string of information about a web method and is used for automatically generated description documents and the Internet Explorer test page. CacheDuration specifies (in seconds) how long a response will be cached and reused for web method requests with identical parameter values. EnableSession allows you to configure whether session support is enabled for your web method. By default, a web service method will not be cached at all, and session support will not be enabled. The BufferResponse property is rarely used, as it only applies to HTTP requests. By default, BufferResponse is True, all as responses are serialized to memory and transferred only when complete.

The MessageName property is used to add an alias to a method. This property is most commonly used with polymorphic (overloaded) methods, which must be given unique names, or "disambiguated" before you can use them as web methods. When adding overloaded methods, the original method should retain its name for compatibility with existing clients.

The TransactionOption property allows a web method to take part in a COM+ transaction. Due to the stateless nature of the HTTP protocol, web service methods can only participate as the root object in a transaction. This means that both System.EnterpriseServices.TransactionOption.RequiresNew and System.EnterpriseServices.TransactionOption.Required will have the same effect, causing the web method to start a new transaction when it is invoked. Other COM objects that require transactions can then be created and used by the web method. A transaction started in this way is committed automatically when the method ends, unless the method explicitly calls System.EnterpriseServices.ContextUtil.SetAbort() or an unhandled exception occurs.

To set a property of the WebMethodAttribute, specify it by name in the attribute declaration (as in <WebMethod(EnableSession := True)>).

```
Public NotInheritable Class WebMethodAttribute : Inherits Attribute
' Public Constructors
   Public Sub New()
   Public Sub New(ByVal enableSession As Boolean)
   Public Sub New(ByVal enableSession As Boolean,             _
     ByVal transactionOption As System.EnterpriseServices.TransactionOption)
   Public Sub New(ByVal enableSession As Boolean,                               _
     ByVal transactionOption As System.EnterpriseServices.TransactionOption, ByVal cacheDuration As Integer)
   Public Sub New(ByVal enableSession As Boolean,                               _
     ByVal transactionOption As System.EnterpriseServices.TransactionOption, ByVal cacheDuration As Integer, _
     ByVal bufferResponse As Boolean)
' Public Instance Properties
   Public Property BufferResponse As Boolean
   Public Property CacheDuration As Integer
   Public Property Description As String
   Public Property EnableSession As Boolean
   Public Property MessageName As String
   Public Property TransactionOption As TransactionOption
End Class
```

Hierarchy: System.Object → System.Attribute → WebMethodAttribute

Valid On: Method

WebService Class

System.Web.Services (system.web.services.dll) *disposable*

When creating a web service, you can inherit from this class to gain access to the built-in ASP.NET objects Application (the current System.Web.HttpApplicationState collection), Server, Session, User, and Context (which provides access to the built-in Request and Response objects). If you don't need to access these objects (or if you choose to go through the System.Web.HttpContext.Context property) you don't need to derive your web service from this class.

When creating a web service class, all web methods must be marked with the WebMethodAttribute. To configure additional activities, you should also add the WebServiceAttribute to the class declaration.

```
Public Class WebService : Inherits System.ComponentModel.MarshalByValueComponent
' Public Constructors
    Public Sub New()
' Public Instance Properties
    Public ReadOnly Property Application As HttpApplicationState
    Public ReadOnly Property Context As HttpContext
    Public ReadOnly Property Server As HttpServerUtility
    Public ReadOnly Property Session As HttpSessionState
    Public ReadOnly Property User As IPrincipal
End Class
```

Hierarchy: System.Object → System.ComponentModel.MarshalByValueComponent (System.ComponentModel.IComponent , System.IDisposable , System.IServiceProvider)→ WebService

WebServiceAttribute NotInheritable Class

System.Web.Services (system.web.services.dll)

This attribute is not required to create a web service, but it should be used before a web service is deployed to specify a unique XML namespace and allow clients to distinguish your web service from others on the Web. By default, if you do not use this attribute, the default namespace *http://tempuri.org/* is used. Namespaces look like URLs, but they do not actually need to correspond to valid locations on the Web. In a web service, the XML namespace is used to uniquely identify parts of the Service Description (WSDL) file that specifically pertain to the web service. The Name property identifies the local portion of the XML qualified name, which will be the web service class name by default. Elements of the WSDL contract that are specific to WSDL use the *http://schemas.xmlsoap.org/wsdl/* namespace.

Ideally, you should use a namespace that you control, such as your company's web site address. This XML namespace should not be confused with the .NET namespace used programmatically by clients. For more information on XML qualified names, see *http://www.w3.org/TR/REC-xml-names*.

You can also set a Description property, which contains information about your web service that will be displayed in automatically generated description documents and the Internet Explorer test page.

Public NotInheritable Class **WebServiceAttribute** : Inherits Attribute
' *Public Constructors*
   Public Sub **New**()
' *Public Shared Fields*
   public const **DefaultNamespace** As String   =*http://tempuri.org/*
' *Public Instance Properties*
   Public Property **Description** As String
   Public Property **Name** As String
   Public Property **Namespace** As String
End Class

Hierarchy: System.Object → System.Attribute → WebServiceAttribute

Valid On: Class

WebServiceBindingAttribute   NotInheritable Class

System.Web.Services (system.web.services.dll)

This attribute is used to mark the class declaration of the proxy class that allows communication between a client and a web service. It defines a Web Service Description Language (WSDL) binding. The Name and the Namespace properties must be set to the name and XML namespace of the Web Service. An example is <WebServiceBinding(Name := "StockQuote", Namespace := "http://www.mysite.com/MyServices")>. These properties match the corresponding properties in the WebServiceAttribute.

You must also use a System.Web.Services.Protocols.SoapDocumentMethodAttribute or System.Web.Services.Protocols.SoapRpcMethodAttribute to describe the binding for each individual web service method represented in the proxy class. This code is generated automatically in the proxy class by adding a Visual Studio .NET web reference or using the *WSDL.exe* utility included with ASP.NET.

Public NotInheritable Class **WebServiceBindingAttribute** : Inherits Attribute
' *Public Constructors*
   Public Sub **New**()
   Public Sub **New**(ByVal name As String)
   Public Sub **New**(ByVal name As String, ByVal ns As String)
   Public Sub **New**(ByVal name As String, ByVal ns As String, ByVal location As String)
' *Public Instance Properties*
   Public Property **Location** As String
   Public Property **Name** As String
   Public Property **Namespace** As String
End Class

Hierarchy: System.Object → System.Attribute → WebServiceBindingAttribute

Valid On: Class

CHAPTER 29

The System.Web.Services.Configuration Namespace

The System.Web.Services.Configuration namespace contains three .NET attributes that are useful if you want to add custom format extensions to your web services (in other words, if you want to insert additional XML elements to your web service's WSDL service description). One practical reason to use a format extension is if your web service requires a SOAP extension that runs at both the server and the client end. By default, no information about SOAP extensions is added to the service description, meaning that clients may not be aware that they need to use a given extension (for example, a security or encryption extension) before they can use the web service.

To use a format extension in this way, you need to start by deriving a custom class from System.Web.Services.Description.ServiceDescriptionFormatExtension, which represents the actual format extension. Next, you use the XmlFormatExtensionAttribute in this namespace with the class to define the extension points where the extension should apply. Optionally, you can use the XmlFormatExtensionPointAttribute class with the custom format extension class to specify a member in the class that will act as a new extension point, and the XmlFormatExtensionPrefixAttribute to set an XML namespace for the elements generated by the format extension. Finally, you configure your format extension to run within the <serviceDescriptionFormatExtensionTypes> section of the configuration file. Figure 29-1 shows the types in this namespace.

XmlFormatExtensionAttribute   NotInheritable Class

System.Web.Services.Configuration (system.web.services.dll)

This attribute is applied to the declaraction of a custom System.Web.Services.Description.ServiceDescriptionFormatExtension class. It specifes that the format extension runs at one or more extension points. The constructors specify the name of the XML element that will be added to the WSDL document by the service description format extension (element-Name) and the XML namespace for this element (ns). Depending on the constructor you use, you can supply up to four points where the format extension should run (extension-Point).

Public NotInheritable Class **XmlFormatExtensionAttribute** : Inherits Attribute
' *Public Constructors*
  Public Sub **New**()
  Public Sub **New**(ByVal elementName As String, ByVal ns As String, ByVal extensionPoint1 As Type)

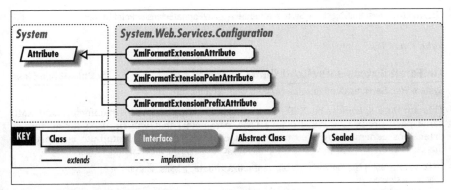

Figure 29-1: The System.Web.Services.Configuration namespace

```
Public Sub New(ByVal elementName As String, ByVal ns As String, ByVal extensionPoints As Type())
Public Sub New(ByVal elementName As String, ByVal ns As String, ByVal extensionPoint1 As Type, _
    ByVal extensionPoint2 As Type)
Public Sub New(ByVal elementName As String, ByVal ns As String, ByVal extensionPoint1 As Type, _
    ByVal extensionPoint2 As Type, ByVal extensionPoint3 As Type)
Public Sub New(ByVal elementName As String, ByVal ns As String, ByVal extensionPoint1 As Type, _
    ByVal extensionPoint2 As Type, ByVal extensionPoint3 As Type, ByVal extensionPoint4 As Type)
' Public Instance Properties
Public Property ElementName As String
Public Property ExtensionPoints As Type()
Public Property Namespace As String
End Class
```

Hierarchy: System.Object → System.Attribute → XmlFormatExtensionAttribute

Valid On: Class

XmlFormatExtensionPointAttribute   NotInheritable Class

System.Web.Services.Configuration (system.web.services.dll)

Like all the attributes in this namespace, the XmlFormatExtensionPointAttribute is applied to the custom System.Web.Services.Description.ServiceDescriptionFormatExtension class. Use this attribute to specifiy that a member of the custom format extension class should have its own custom format extension associated with it. MemberName specifies the member of the format extension class (as a string) that has its own format extension. AllowElements is True (the default) if the member of the class implementing the format extension can accept raw XML elements.

```
Public NotInheritable Class XmlFormatExtensionPointAttribute : Inherits Attribute
' Public Constructors
Public Sub New(ByVal memberName As String)
' Public Instance Properties
Public Property AllowElements As Boolean
Public Property MemberName As String
End Class
```

Hierarchy: System.Object → System.Attribute → XmlFormatExtensionPointAttribute

Valid On: Class

XmlFormatExtensionPrefixAttribute   NotInheritable Class

System.Web.Services.Configuration (system.web.services.dll)

This attribute specifies the XML namespace (the constructor's ns parameter) and XML namespace prefix (the constructor's prefix parameter) that will be used for all format extensions generated by a custom format extension class. This attribute is applied to the custom System.Web.Services.Description.ServiceDescriptionFormatExtension class.

Public NotInheritable Class **XmlFormatExtensionPrefixAttribute** : Inherits Attribute
' *Public Constructors*
   Public Sub **New**()
   Public Sub **New**(ByVal prefix As String, ByVal ns As String)
' *Public Instance Properties*
   Public Property **Namespace** As String
   Public Property **Prefix** As String
End Class

Hierarchy: System.Object → System.Attribute → XmlFormatExtensionPrefixAttribute

Valid On: Class

CHAPTER 30

The System.Web.Services.Description Namespace

The System.Web.Services.Description namespace includes types used to represent the elements of Web Service Description Language (WSDL), an XML grammar that describes web services and specifies how to interact with them. Web services created with ASP.NET automatically generate their own WSDL documents, which contain all the information a client needs to interact with them and invoke their methods. You can retrieve this document by requesting the appropriate *.asmx* file with *?WSDL* appended to the end of the URL (as in *http://www.mysite.com/myservice.asmx?WSDL*).

The starting point for understanding this namespace is the ServiceDescription class, which represents the complete WSDL document and provides collections of Binding, Message, Types, and Service objects. The ServiceDescription class also provides Read() and Write() methods, which allow you to convert between actual WSDL documents and their object representation. Finally, you can also use the ServiceDescriptionReflector class to create a ServiceDescription object based on an existing web service by supplying the web service's URL.

Another interesting class in this namespace is ServiceDescriptionImporter, which provides the functionality .NET uses to create proxy classes based on WSDL documents. Most other classes represent a paticular portion of a WSDL document, and you do not provide any additional functionality.

All details of WSDL implementation are "abstracted away" from you when creating or consuming a web service with .NET. For that reason, you may have little need to use the types in this namespace. To learn more about the specifics of the WSDL standard on which these types are based, refer to *http://www.w3.org/TR/wsdl*. Figure 30-1 shows ServiceDescriptionFormatDescription-derived types and Figure 30-2 shows other types. Figure 30-3 contains the collections in this namespace.

Binding   NotInheritable Class

System.Web.Services.Description (system.web.services.dll)

A WSDL document defines abstract information for data types, messages, and operations. A binding bridges the gap between abstract, protocol-independent information, and the encoding of that information (the concrete physical representation of messages on the wire). The Binding class represents the WSDL <binding> element, which provides binding information for a single protocol. For example, the WSDL document ASP.NET

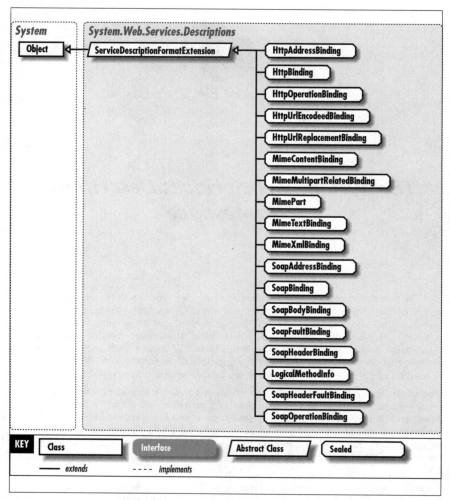

Figure 30-1: ServiceDescriptionFormatDescription-derived types

generates for a web service called StockQuotes would have three bindings: Stock-QuotesHttpGet, StockQuotesHttpPost, and StockQuotesSoap.

A Binding contains a collection of OperationBinding objects (provided through the Operations property). Bindings must define WSDL ports (represented by the Port class).

```
Public NotInheritable Class Binding : Inherits DocumentableItem
' Public Constructors
   Public Sub New()
' Public Instance Properties
   Public ReadOnly Property Extensions As ServiceDescriptionFormatExtensionCollection
   Public Property Name As String
   Public ReadOnly Property Operations As OperationBindingCollection
   Public ReadOnly Property ServiceDescription As ServiceDescription
   Public Property Type As XmlQualifiedName
End Class
```

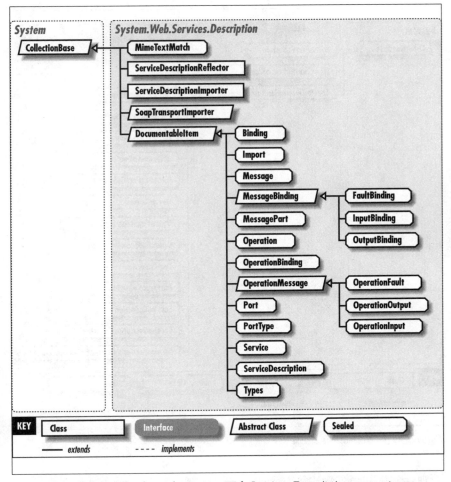

Figure 30-2: More types from the System.Web.Services.Description namespace

Hierarchy: System.Object → DocumentableItem → Binding

BindingCollection

NotInheritable Class

System.Web.Services.Description (system.web.services.dll)

This collection of Binding objects is used by the Bindings property of the ServiceDescription class. Bindings can be accessed by name or by position (index number).

Public NotInheritable Class **BindingCollection** : Inherits ServiceDescriptionBaseCollection
' *Public Instance Properties*
  Public Default ReadOnly Property **Item** (ByVal name As String) As Binding
  Public Default Property **Item** (ByVal index As Integer) As Binding
' *Public Instance Methods*
  Public Function **Add**(ByVal binding As Binding) As Integer
  Public Function **Contains**(ByVal binding As Binding) As Boolean
  Public Sub **CopyTo**(ByVal array As Binding(), ByVal index As Integer)

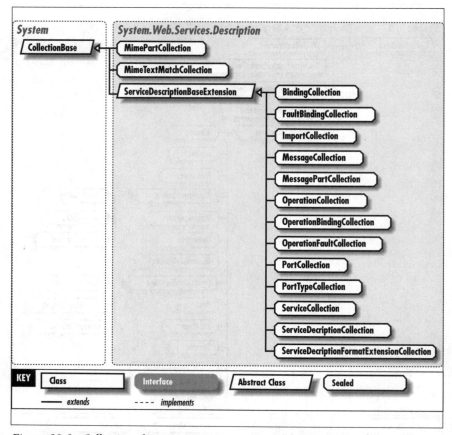

Figure 30-3: Collection classes

```
Public Function IndexOf(ByVal binding As Binding) As Integer
Public Sub Insert(ByVal index As Integer, ByVal binding As Binding)
Public Sub Remove(ByVal binding As Binding)
' Protected Instance Methods
Overrides Protected Function GetKey(ByVal value As Object) As String
Overrides Protected Sub SetParent(ByVal value As Object, ByVal parent As Object)
End Class
```

Hierarchy: System.Object → System.Collections.CollectionBase (System.Collections.IList ,
System.Collections.ICollection , System.Collections.IEnumerable)→ ServiceDescriptionBaseCollection
→ BindingCollection

DocumentableItem   MustInherit Class

System.Web.Services.Description (system.web.services.dll)

This abstract base class is used by several different classes in the System.Web.Ser-
vices.Description namespace. It provides only one property, Documentation, which represents the <documentation> element that can be added inside other WSDL language

elements to provide human-readable information (like a descriptive comment). This tag is generated automatically when you use the Description property of the System.Web.Services.WebMethodAttribute or System.Web.Services.WebServiceAttribute.

```
Public MustInherit Class Documentableltem
' Protected Constructors
   Protected Sub New()
' Public Instance Properties
   Public Property Documentation As String
End Class
```

FaultBinding   NotInheritable Class

System.Web.Services.Description (system.web.services.dll)

This binding specifies the concrete transmission format for any error messages that occur during an operation. It maps to the WSDL <fault> element in the <binding> element.

```
Public NotInheritable Class FaultBinding : Inherits MessageBinding
' Public Constructors
   Public Sub New()
' Public Instance Properties
   Overrides Public ReadOnly Property Extensions As ServiceDescriptionFormatExtensionCollection
End Class
```

Hierarchy: System.Object → DocumentableItem → MessageBinding → FaultBinding

FaultBindingCollection   NotInheritable Class

System.Web.Services.Description (system.web.services.dll)

This collection of FaultBinding objects is used by the OperationBinding.Faults property. Each FaultBinding can be accessed by name or position (index number).

```
Public NotInheritable Class FaultBindingCollection : Inherits ServiceDescriptionBaseCollection
' Public Instance Properties
   Public Default ReadOnly Property Item (ByVal name As String) As FaultBinding
   Public Default Property Item (ByVal index As Integer) As FaultBinding
' Public Instance Methods
   Public Function Add(ByVal bindingOperationFault As FaultBinding) As Integer
   Public Function Contains(ByVal bindingOperationFault As FaultBinding) As Boolean
   Public Sub CopyTo(ByVal array As FaultBinding(), ByVal index As Integer)
   Public Function IndexOf(ByVal bindingOperationFault As FaultBinding) As Integer
   Public Sub Insert(ByVal index As Integer, ByVal bindingOperationFault As FaultBinding)
   Public Sub Remove(ByVal bindingOperationFault As FaultBinding)
' Protected Instance Methods
   Overrides Protected Function GetKey(ByVal value As Object) As String
   Overrides Protected Sub SetParent(ByVal value As Object, ByVal parent As Object)
End Class
```

Hierarchy: System.Object → System.Collections.CollectionBase (System.Collections.IList , System.Collections.ICollection , System.Collections.IEnumerable)→ ServiceDescriptionBaseCollection → FaultBindingCollection

HttpAddressBinding
NotInheritable Class

System.Web.Services.Description (system.web.services.dll)

Represents an extensibility element added to the WSDL \<port\> element, which enables HTTP binding to a specific web service address. The Location property specifies the base URL address for the web service.

Public NotInheritable Class **HttpAddressBinding** : Inherits ServiceDescriptionFormatExtension
' *Public Constructors*
   Public Sub **New**()
' *Public Instance Properties*
   Public Property **Location** As String
End Class

Hierarchy: System.Object → ServiceDescriptionFormatExtension → HttpAddressBinding

HttpBinding
NotInheritable Class

System.Web.Services.Description (system.web.services.dll)

Represents an extensibility element added to the WSDL \<binding\> element, which allows information to be transmitted by HTTP. The Verb property is a string that can have three values: an empty string (the default), "POST" (which specifies that requests will use HTTP POST), or "GET" (which specifies that requests will use HTTP GET).

Public NotInheritable Class **HttpBinding** : Inherits ServiceDescriptionFormatExtension
' *Public Constructors*
   Public Sub **New**()
' *Public Shared Fields*
   public const **Namespace** As String   *=http://schemas.xmlsoap.org/wsdl/http/*
' *Public Instance Properties*
   Public Property **Verb** As String
End Class

Hierarchy: System.Object → ServiceDescriptionFormatExtension → HttpBinding

HttpOperationBinding
NotInheritable Class

System.Web.Services.Description (system.web.services.dll)

Represents an extensibility element added to the WSDL \<operation\> element, which allows a web service method to be invoked over HTTP. The Location property specifes the relative URL of a web service operation (using the base specified by HttpOperationBinding).

Public NotInheritable Class **HttpOperationBinding** : Inherits ServiceDescriptionFormatExtension
' *Public Constructors*
   Public Sub **New**()
' *Public Instance Properties*
   Public Property **Location** As String
End Class

Hierarchy: System.Object → ServiceDescriptionFormatExtension → HttpOperationBinding

HttpUrlEncodedBinding

NotInheritable Class

System.Web.Services.Description (system.web.services.dll)

Represents an extensibility element added to a WSDL InputBinding object. It indicates that the request will send data using the standard URL encoding format ("name=value&name2=value2") over HTTP. This class does not provide any properties.

Public NotInheritable Class **HttpUrlEncodedBinding** : Inherits ServiceDescriptionFormatExtension
' *Public Constructors*
   Public Sub **New**()
End Class

Hierarchy: System.Object → ServiceDescriptionFormatExtension → HttpUrlEncodedBinding

HttpUrlReplacementBinding

NotInheritable Class

System.Web.Services.Description (system.web.services.dll)

Represents an extensibility element added to a WSDL InputBinding object. It indicates that the request will send data using a custom format over HTTP.

Public NotInheritable Class **HttpUrlReplacementBinding** : Inherits ServiceDescriptionFormatExtension
' *Public Constructors*
   Public Sub **New**()
End Class

Hierarchy: System.Object → ServiceDescriptionFormatExtension → HttpUrlReplacementBinding

Import

NotInheritable Class

System.Web.Services.Description (system.web.services.dll)

This class represents the WSDL <import> element, which associates an XML namespace with a document location. The familiar XML equivalent is <import namespace="uri" location="uri"/>. This equivalent allows a WSDL document to be split into multiple subdocuments, each with a unique XML namespace, which can then be imported as needed.

Public NotInheritable Class **Import** : Inherits DocumentableItem
' *Public Constructors*
   Public Sub **New**()
' *Public Instance Properties*
   Public Property **Location** As String
   Public Property **Namespace** As String
   Public ReadOnly Property **ServiceDescription** As ServiceDescription
End Class

Hierarchy: System.Object → DocumentableItem → Import

ImportCollection

NotInheritable Class

System.Web.Services.Description (system.web.services.dll)

This collection of Import objects is used by the Imports property of the ServiceDescription class to specify XML namespaces for a WSDL document. You can retrieve an individual Import object by index number.

Public NotInheritable Class **ImportCollection** : Inherits ServiceDescriptionBaseCollection
' *Public Instance Properties*
   Public Default Property **Item** (ByVal index As Integer) As Import

' *Public Instance Methods*
Public Function **Add**(ByVal import As Import) As Integer
Public Function **Contains**(ByVal import As Import) As Boolean
Public Sub **CopyTo**(ByVal array As Import(), ByVal index As Integer)
Public Function **IndexOf**(ByVal import As Import) As Integer
Public Sub **Insert**(ByVal index As Integer, ByVal import As Import)
Public Sub **Remove**(ByVal import As Import)
' *Protected Instance Methods*
Overrides Protected Sub **SetParent**(ByVal value As Object, ByVal parent As Object)
End Class

Hierarchy: System.Object → System.Collections.CollectionBase (System.Collections.IList , System.Collections.ICollection , System.Collections.IEnumerable)→ ServiceDescriptionBaseCollection → ImportCollection

InputBinding   NotInheritable Class
System.Web.Services.Description (system.web.services.dll)

This specific binding is used to specify the encoding of an input message. The InputBinding class provides a Extensions property, which contains a collection consisting of a single binding. This binding varies depending on the type of protocol that this element applies to (HTTP POST, HTTP GET, or SOAP). For example, this collection would contain a HttpUrlEncodedBinding for HTTP GET messages, a MimeContentBinding for HTTP POST messages, or a SoapBodyBinding for SOAP messages.

Public NotInheritable Class **InputBinding** : Inherits MessageBinding
' *Public Constructors*
Public Sub **New**()
' *Public Instance Properties*
Overrides Public ReadOnly Property **Extensions** As ServiceDescriptionFormatExtensionCollection
End Class

Hierarchy: System.Object → DocumentableItem → MessageBinding → InputBinding

Message   NotInheritable Class
System.Web.Services.Description (system.web.services.dll)

This class represents the WSDL <message> element, which is used to describe the contents of message exchanged between a client and the Web Service. For every method in a web service, a WSDL document contains an input and output message. There are also separate message definitions for every protocol type. For example, for a method called GetInfo, ASP.NET would generate GetInfoHttpPostIn and GetInfoHttpPostOut messages, along with corresponding messages for HTTP GET and SOAP. Messages consist of zero or more MessagePart objects, which specify method parameters and return values.

Public NotInheritable Class **Message** : Inherits DocumentableItem
' *Public Constructors*
Public Sub **New**()
' *Public Instance Properties*
Public Property **Name** As String
Public ReadOnly Property **Parts** As MessagePartCollection
Public ReadOnly Property **ServiceDescription** As ServiceDescription
' *Public Instance Methods*
Public Function **FindPartByName**(ByVal partName As String) As MessagePart

```
Public Function FindPartsByName(ByVal partNames As String()) As MessagePart()
End Class
```

Hierarchy: System.Object → DocumentableItem → Message

MessageBinding   **MustInherit Class**

System.Web.Services.Description (system.web.services.dll)

This abstract class is implemented by FaultBinding, InputBinding, and OutputBinding. Binding specifies how abstract data formats are mapped to the concrete protocol used for transmission.

```
Public MustInherit Class MessageBinding : Inherits DocumentableItem
' Protected Constructors
   Protected Sub New()
' Public Instance Properties
   MustInherit Public ReadOnly Property Extensions As ServiceDescriptionFormatExtensionCollection
   Public Property Name As String
   Public ReadOnly Property OperationBinding As OperationBinding
End Class
```

Hierarchy: System.Object → DocumentableItem → MessageBinding

MessageCollection   **NotInheritable Class**

System.Web.Services.Description (system.web.services.dll)

This collection of Message objects is used by the Messages property of the ServiceDescription class to represent all <message> elements in a WSDL document. You can access an invidual Message by name or position (index number).

```
Public NotInheritable Class MessageCollection : Inherits ServiceDescriptionBaseCollection
' Public Instance Properties
   Public Default ReadOnly Property Item (ByVal name As String) As Message
   Public Default Property Item (ByVal index As Integer) As Message
' Public Instance Methods
   Public Function Add(ByVal message As Message) As Integer
   Public Function Contains(ByVal message As Message) As Boolean
   Public Sub CopyTo(ByVal array As Message(), ByVal index As Integer)
   Public Function IndexOf(ByVal message As Message) As Integer
   Public Sub Insert(ByVal index As Integer, ByVal message As Message)
   Public Sub Remove(ByVal message As Message)
' Protected Instance Methods
   Overrides Protected Function GetKey(ByVal value As Object) As String
   Overrides Protected Sub SetParent(ByVal value As Object, ByVal parent As Object)
End Class
```

Hierarchy: System.Object → System.Collections.CollectionBase (System.Collections.IList , System.Collections.ICollection , System.Collections.IEnumerable)→ ServiceDescriptionBaseCollection → MessageCollection

MessagePart
NotInheritable Class

System.Web.Services.Description (system.web.services.dll)

This class represents a WSDL <part> element, which is contained in a <message> element. Each MessagePart object corresponds to a single parameter or a return value for a function, and specifies the variable's Name and either an XML Type or an XML Element, which refers to an element from the Types collection.

For example, a GetStockQuote method would have several messages, including GetStockQuoteHttpGetOut, and would have a single MessagePart representing the return value. Return values are given the Name "parameters" for a SOAP request or "Body" for an HTTP request.

```
Public NotInheritable Class MessagePart : Inherits DocumentableItem
' Public Constructors
    Public Sub New()
' Public Instance Properties
    Public Property Element As XmlQualifiedName
    Public ReadOnly Property Message As Message
    Public Property Name As String
    Public Property Type As XmlQualifiedName
End Class
```

Hierarchy: System.Object → DocumentableItem → MessagePart

MessagePartCollection
NotInheritable Class

System.Web.Services.Description (system.web.services.dll)

This collection of MessagePart objects is used by the Parts property of the Message class to represent the return value and parameters of a message. You can access an invidual MessagePart by name or position (index number).

```
Public NotInheritable Class MessagePartCollection : Inherits ServiceDescriptionBaseCollection
' Public Instance Properties
    Public Default ReadOnly Property Item (ByVal name As String) As MessagePart
    Public Default Property Item (ByVal index As Integer) As MessagePart
' Public Instance Methods
    Public Function Add(ByVal messagePart As MessagePart) As Integer
    Public Function Contains(ByVal messagePart As MessagePart) As Boolean
    Public Sub CopyTo(ByVal array As MessagePart(), ByVal index As Integer)
    Public Function IndexOf(ByVal messagePart As MessagePart) As Integer
    Public Sub Insert(ByVal index As Integer, ByVal messagePart As MessagePart)
    Public Sub Remove(ByVal messagePart As MessagePart)
' Protected Instance Methods
    Overrides Protected Function GetKey(ByVal value As Object) As String
    Overrides Protected Sub SetParent(ByVal value As Object, ByVal parent As Object)
End Class
```

Hierarchy: System.Object → System.Collections.CollectionBase (System.Collections.IList , System.Collections.ICollection , System.Collections.IEnumerable)→ ServiceDescriptionBaseCollection → MessagePartCollection

MimeContentBinding   **NotInheritable Class**

System.Web.Services.Description (system.web.services.dll)

This binding represents an extensibility element added to an InputBinding or an Output-Binding element.

This binding is generally used for an HTTP POST input message (represented by OperationInput). It includes a Type property, which specifies the MIME encoding type (typically application/x-www-form-urlencoded) used for encoding data for HTTP transmission. The Part property specifes the name of the message part to which the binding applies.

```
Public NotInheritable Class MimeContentBinding : Inherits ServiceDescriptionFormatExtension
' Public Constructors
   Public Sub New()
' Public Shared Fields
   public const Namespace As String                    =http://schemas.xmlsoap.org/wsdl/mime/
' Public Instance Properties
   Public Property Part As String
   Public Property Type As String
End Class
```

Hierarchy: System.Object → ServiceDescriptionFormatExtension → MimeContentBinding

MimeMultipartRelatedBinding   **NotInheritable Class**

System.Web.Services.Description (system.web.services.dll)

Represents an extensibility element added to an InputBinding or an OutputBinding element. This class supports multipart MIME messages that use different MIME types for different portions of the message body.

The Parts property provides a collection of MessagePart objects. Each one represents an extensibility element added to the MimeMultipartRelatedBinding to specify the MIME format for a single portion of the MIME message.

```
Public NotInheritable Class MimeMultipartRelatedBinding : Inherits ServiceDescriptionFormatExtension
' Public Constructors
   Public Sub New()
' Public Instance Properties
   Public ReadOnly Property Parts As MimePartCollection
End Class
```

Hierarchy: System.Object → ServiceDescriptionFormatExtension → MimeMultipartRelatedBinding

MimePart   **NotInheritable Class**

System.Web.Services.Description (system.web.services.dll)

This class represents an extensibility element added to a MimeMultipartRelatedBinding object. The Extensions collection can include MimeContentBinding, MimeXmlBinding, and Soap-BodyBinding objects. Each one specifies the concrete MIME type for a portion of the multipart MIME message (these classes all provide a Part property that references the MessagePart object to which the MIME binding applies).

```
Public NotInheritable Class MimePart : Inherits ServiceDescriptionFormatExtension
' Public Constructors
   Public Sub New()
' Public Instance Properties
   Public ReadOnly Property Extensions As ServiceDescriptionFormatExtensionCollection
```

End Class

Hierarchy: System.Object → ServiceDescriptionFormatExtension → MimePart

MimePartCollection   NotInheritable Class

System.Web.Services.Description (system.web.services.dll)

This class provides a collection of MimePart objects used by the MimeMultipartRelatedBinding class. Individual MimePart objects can be retrieved only by index number.

Public NotInheritable Class **MimePartCollection** : Inherits CollectionBase
' Public Constructors
    Public Sub **New**()
' Public Instance Properties
    Public Default Property **Item** (ByVal index As Integer) As MimePart
' Public Instance Methods
    Public Function **Add**(ByVal mimePart As MimePart) As Integer
    Public Function **Contains**(ByVal mimePart As MimePart) As Boolean
    Public Sub **CopyTo**(ByVal array As MimePart(), ByVal index As Integer)
    Public Function **IndexOf**(ByVal mimePart As MimePart) As Integer
    Public Sub **Insert**(ByVal index As Integer, ByVal mimePart As MimePart)
    Public Sub **Remove**(ByVal mimePart As MimePart)
End Class

Hierarchy: System.Object → System.Collections.CollectionBase (System.Collections.IList ,
System.Collections.ICollection , System.Collections.IEnumerable)→ MimePartCollection

MimeTextBinding   NotInheritable Class

System.Web.Services.Description (system.web.services.dll)

This class represents an extensibility element added to an InputBinding, an OutputBinding, or a MimePart object. It includes a single Matches property, which specifies the text patterns for which the HTTP transmission is searched.

Public NotInheritable Class **MimeTextBinding** : Inherits ServiceDescriptionFormatExtension
' Public Constructors
    Public Sub **New**()
' Public Shared Fields
    public const **Namespace** As String   =http://microsoft.com/wsdl/mime/textMatching/
' Public Instance Properties
    Public ReadOnly Property **Matches** As MimeTextMatchCollection
End Class

Hierarchy: System.Object → ServiceDescriptionFormatExtension → MimeTextBinding

MimeTextMatch   NotInheritable Class

System.Web.Services.Description (system.web.services.dll)

This class represents a text pattern that will be searched for in the HTTP transmission. Type specifies the MIME type of the message, Pattern specifies the pattern, and Repeats sets the number of times the search will be performed (the default is 1, but you can specify System.Int32.MaxValue to get all matches.)

Public NotInheritable Class **MimeTextMatch**

' *Public Constructors*
Public Sub **New**()
' *Public Instance Properties*
Public Property **Capture** As Integer
Public Property **Group** As Integer
Public Property **IgnoreCase** As Boolean
Public ReadOnly Property **Matches** As MimeTextMatchCollection
Public Property **Name** As String
Public Property **Pattern** As String
Public Property **Repeats** As Integer
Public Property **RepeatsString** As String
Public Property **Type** As String
End Class

MimeTextMatchCollection

NotInheritable Class

System.Web.Services.Description (system.web.services.dll)

This class provides a collection of MimeTextMatch objects used by the MimeTextBinding class. Individual MimePart objects can be retrieved only by index number.

Public NotInheritable Class **MimeTextMatchCollection** : Inherits CollectionBase
' *Public Constructors*
Public Sub **New**()
' *Public Instance Properties*
Public Default Property **Item** (ByVal index As Integer) As MimeTextMatch
' *Public Instance Methods*
Public Function **Add**(ByVal match As MimeTextMatch) As Integer
Public Function **Contains**(ByVal match As MimeTextMatch) As Boolean
Public Sub **CopyTo**(ByVal array As MimeTextMatch(), ByVal index As Integer)
Public Function **IndexOf**(ByVal match As MimeTextMatch) As Integer
Public Sub **Insert**(ByVal index As Integer, ByVal match As MimeTextMatch)
Public Sub **Remove**(ByVal match As MimeTextMatch)
End Class

Hierarchy: System.Object → System.Collections.CollectionBase (System.Collections.IList , System.Collections.ICollection , System.Collections.IEnumerable)→ MimeTextMatchCollection

MimeXmlBinding

NotInheritable Class

System.Web.Services.Description (system.web.services.dll)

This class represents an extensibility element added to an InputBinding, an OutputBinding, or a MimePart object. It specifies an XML schema for messages, but is not SOAP-compliant. By default, ASP.NET uses this binding for HTTP GET and POST output messages, which are represented by the OperationOutput class.

Public NotInheritable Class **MimeXmlBinding** : Inherits ServiceDescriptionFormatExtension
' *Public Constructors*
Public Sub **New**()
' *Public Instance Properties*
Public Property **Part** As String
End Class

Hierarchy: System.Object → ServiceDescriptionFormatExtension → MimeXmlBinding

Operation
NotInheritable Class

System.Web.Services.Description (system.web.services.dll)

This class represents the WSDL <operation> element. It describes an operation, which consists of one or more OperationMessage objects. In a WSDL document, an <operation> element exists for every method in your web service. (Actually, there will be three copies of this set of operation elements—one for each different type of transmission, contained in differently named <portType> elements.)

Every operation is associated with exactly one OperationInput and one OperationOutput object.

```
Public NotInheritable Class Operation : Inherits DocumentableItem
' Public Constructors
    Public Sub New()
' Public Instance Properties
    Public ReadOnly Property Faults As OperationFaultCollection
    Public ReadOnly Property Messages As OperationMessageCollection
    Public Property Name As String
    Public Property ParameterOrder As String()
    Public Property ParameterOrderString As String
    Public ReadOnly Property PortType As PortType
' Public Instance Methods
    Public Function IsBoundBy(ByVal operationBinding As OperationBinding) As Boolean
End Class
```

Hierarchy: System.Object → DocumentableItem → Operation

OperationBinding
NotInheritable Class

System.Web.Services.Description (system.web.services.dll)

This class represents the <operation> element in the <binding> element of a WSDL document. Each OperationBinding specifies how the abstract data for input and output messages is encoded. The binding thus consists of InputBinding and OutputBinding objects, and optionally, a FaultBinding object.

```
Public NotInheritable Class OperationBinding : Inherits DocumentableItem
' Public Constructors
    Public Sub New()
' Public Instance Properties
    Public ReadOnly Property Binding As Binding
    Public ReadOnly Property Extensions As ServiceDescriptionFormatExtensionCollection
    Public ReadOnly Property Faults As FaultBindingCollection
    Public Property Input As InputBinding
    Public Property Name As String
    Public Property Output As OutputBinding
End Class
```

Hierarchy: System.Object → DocumentableItem → OperationBinding

OperationBindingCollection
NotInheritable Class

System.Web.Services.Description (system.web.services.dll)

This collection of OperationBinding objects is used for the Operations property of the Binding class. You can access each OperationBinding element by position (index number).

Public NotInheritable Class **OperationBindingCollection** : Inherits ServiceDescriptionBaseCollection
' *Public Instance Properties*
  Public Default Property **Item** (ByVal index As Integer) As OperationBinding
' *Public Instance Methods*
  Public Function **Add**(ByVal bindingOperation As OperationBinding) As Integer
  Public Function **Contains**(ByVal bindingOperation As OperationBinding) As Boolean
  Public Sub **CopyTo**(ByVal array As OperationBinding(), ByVal index As Integer)
  Public Function **IndexOf**(ByVal bindingOperation As OperationBinding) As Integer
  Public Sub **Insert**(ByVal index As Integer, ByVal bindingOperation As OperationBinding)
  Public Sub **Remove**(ByVal bindingOperation As OperationBinding)
' *Protected Instance Methods*
  Overrides Protected Sub **SetParent**(ByVal value As Object, ByVal parent As Object)
End Class

Hierarchy: System.Object → System.Collections.CollectionBase (System.Collections.IList , System.Collections.ICollection , System.Collections.IEnumerable)→ ServiceDescriptionBaseCollection → OperationBindingCollection

OperationCollection
NotInheritable Class

System.Web.Services.Description (system.web.services.dll)

This collection of Operation objects is used by the Operations property of the PortType class. You can access each Operation element by position (index number).

Public NotInheritable Class **OperationCollection** : Inherits ServiceDescriptionBaseCollection
' *Public Instance Properties*
  Public Default Property **Item** (ByVal index As Integer) As Operation
' *Public Instance Methods*
  Public Function **Add**(ByVal operation As Operation) As Integer
  Public Function **Contains**(ByVal operation As Operation) As Boolean
  Public Sub **CopyTo**(ByVal array As Operation(), ByVal index As Integer)
  Public Function **IndexOf**(ByVal operation As Operation) As Integer
  Public Sub **Insert**(ByVal index As Integer, ByVal operation As Operation)
  Public Sub **Remove**(ByVal operation As Operation)
' *Protected Instance Methods*
  Overrides Protected Sub **SetParent**(ByVal value As Object, ByVal parent As Object)
End Class

Hierarchy: System.Object → System.Collections.CollectionBase (System.Collections.IList , System.Collections.ICollection , System.Collections.IEnumerable)→ ServiceDescriptionBaseCollection → OperationCollection

OperationFault
NotInheritable Class

System.Web.Services.Description (system.web.services.dll)

This class represents a OperationMessage object that defines the specifications for error messages returned by a Web Service.

Public NotInheritable Class **OperationFault** : Inherits OperationMessage
' *Public Constructors*
  Public Sub **New**()
End Class

Hierarchy: System.Object → DocumentableItem → OperationMessage → OperationFault

OperationFaultCollection

NotInheritable Class

System.Web.Services.Description (system.web.services.dll)

This collection of OperationFault objects is used by the Operation.Faults property. You can access each OperationFault element by name or position (index number).

Public NotInheritable Class **OperationFaultCollection** : Inherits ServiceDescriptionBaseCollection
' Public Instance Properties
   Public Default ReadOnly Property **Item** (ByVal name As String) As OperationFault
   Public Default Property **Item** (ByVal index As Integer) As OperationFault
' Public Instance Methods
   Public Function **Add**(ByVal operationFaultMessage As OperationFault) As Integer
   Public Function **Contains**(ByVal operationFaultMessage As OperationFault) As Boolean
   Public Sub **CopyTo**(ByVal array As OperationFault(), ByVal index As Integer)
   Public Function **IndexOf**(ByVal operationFaultMessage As OperationFault) As Integer
   Public Sub **Insert**(ByVal index As Integer, ByVal operationFaultMessage As OperationFault)
   Public Sub **Remove**(ByVal operationFaultMessage As OperationFault)
' Protected Instance Methods
   Overrides Protected Function **GetKey**(ByVal value As Object) As String
   Overrides Protected Sub **SetParent**(ByVal value As Object, ByVal parent As Object)
End Class

Hierarchy: System.Object → System.Collections.CollectionBase (System.Collections.IList , System.Collections.ICollection , System.Collections.IEnumerable)→ ServiceDescriptionBaseCollection → OperationFaultCollection

OperationFlow

Enum

System.Web.Services.Description (system.web.services.dll)

serializable

This enumeration is used for the OperationMessageCollection.Flow property. It indicates the direction of message transmission. Notification indicates that an endpoint or service sends a message. OneWay indicates that the endpoint or service receives a message. RequestResponse indicates that an endpoint or services receives the message, and then sends a response, while SolicitResponse indicates the reverse.

Public Enum **OperationFlow**
   None = 0
   OneWay = 1
   Notification = 2
   RequestResponse = 3
   SolicitResponse = 4
End Enum

Hierarchy: System.Object → System.ValueType → System.Enum (System.IComparable , System.IFormattable , System.IConvertible)→ OperationFlow

OperationInput

NotInheritable Class

System.Web.Services.Description (system.web.services.dll)

This class represents the WSDL <input> element. It defines an abstract message format for sending information to a specific web method by referring to the appropriate Message object.

Public NotInheritable Class **OperationInput** : Inherits OperationMessage
' Public Constructors

```
  Public Sub New()
End Class
```

Hierarchy: System.Object → DocumentableItem → OperationMessage → OperationInput

OperationMessage   **MustInherit Class**

System.Web.Services.Description (system.web.services.dll)

This abstract class represents the WSDL <message> element. There are two types of operations recognized in WSDL, input and output. These operations are represented specifically by the classes OperationInput and OperationOutput, both of which derive from this class. OperationFault also derives from this class.

```
Public MustInherit Class OperationMessage : Inherits DocumentableItem
' Protected Constructors
  Protected Sub New()
' Public Instance Properties
  Public Property Message As XmlQualifiedName
  Public Property Name As String
  Public ReadOnly Property Operation As Operation
End Class
```

Hierarchy: System.Object → DocumentableItem → OperationMessage

OperationMessageCollection   **NotInheritable Class**

System.Web.Services.Description (system.web.services.dll)

This collection of OperationMessage objects is used by the Messages property of the Operation class. You can access each OperationMessage element by position (index number).

```
Public NotInheritable Class OperationMessageCollection : Inherits ServiceDescriptionBaseCollection
' Public Instance Properties
  Public ReadOnly Property Flow As OperationFlow
  Public ReadOnly Property Input As OperationInput
  Public Default Property Item (ByVal index As Integer) As OperationMessage
  Public ReadOnly Property Output As OperationOutput
' Public Instance Methods
  Public Function Add(ByVal operationMessage As OperationMessage) As Integer
  Public Function Contains(ByVal operationMessage As OperationMessage) As Boolean
  Public Sub CopyTo(ByVal array As OperationMessage(), ByVal index As Integer)
  Public Function IndexOf(ByVal operationMessage As OperationMessage) As Integer
  Public Sub Insert(ByVal index As Integer, ByVal operationMessage As OperationMessage)
  Public Sub Remove(ByVal operationMessage As OperationMessage)
' Protected Instance Methods
  Overrides Protected Sub OnInsert(ByVal index As Integer, ByVal value As Object)
  Overrides Protected Sub OnSet(ByVal index As Integer, ByVal oldValue As Object, ByVal newValue As Object)
  Overrides Protected Sub OnValidate(ByVal value As Object)
  Overrides Protected Sub SetParent(ByVal value As Object, ByVal parent As Object)
End Class
```

Hierarchy: System.Object → System.Collections.CollectionBase (System.Collections.IList , System.Collections.ICollection , System.Collections.IEnumerable)→ ServiceDescriptionBaseCollection → OperationMessageCollection

OperationOutput
NotInheritable Class

System.Web.Services.Description (system.web.services.dll)

This class represents the WSDL <output> element. It defines an abstract message format for retrieving information from a specific web method (by referring to the appropriate Message object).

Public NotInheritable Class **OperationOutput** : Inherits OperationMessage
' *Public Constructors*
   Public Sub **New**()
End Class

Hierarchy: System.Object → DocumentableItem → OperationMessage → OperationOutput

OutputBinding
NotInheritable Class

System.Web.Services.Description (system.web.services.dll)

This specific binding is used to specify the encoding of an output message. The Output-Binding class provides a Extensions property, which contains a collection of one binding. This binding varies depending on the type of protocol that this element applies to (HTTP POST, HTTP GET, or SOAP). For example, this collection would contain a MimeXmlBinding for HTTP messages and a SoapBodyBinding for SOAP messages.

Public NotInheritable Class **OutputBinding** : Inherits MessageBinding
' *Public Constructors*
   Public Sub **New**()
' *Public Instance Properties*
   Overrides Public ReadOnly Property **Extensions** As ServiceDescriptionFormatExtensionCollection
End Class

Hierarchy: System.Object → DocumentableItem → MessageBinding → OutputBinding

Port
NotInheritable Class

System.Web.Services.Description (system.web.services.dll)

This class represents the WSDL <port> element. It defines a service endpoint, which is the URL required to access the web service. In a WSDL document generated by ASP.NET, you will find three <port> elements—one for each type of transmission (HTTP GET, HTTP POST, and SOAP). Each element will point to the same URL, which is the fully qualified location of your *.asmx* file (for example, *http://www.mysite.com/ws/MyService.asmx*)

Public NotInheritable Class **Port** : Inherits DocumentableItem
' *Public Constructors*
   Public Sub **New**()
' *Public Instance Properties*
   Public Property **Binding** As XmlQualifiedName
   Public ReadOnly Property **Extensions** As ServiceDescriptionFormatExtensionCollection
   Public Property **Name** As String
   Public ReadOnly Property **Service** As Service
End Class

Hierarchy: System.Object → DocumentableItem → Port

PortCollection
NotInheritable Class

System.Web.Services.Description (system.web.services.dll)

This collection of Port objects is used by the Ports property of the Service class to represent all the <port> elements in a WSDL document. You can access each Port element by name or position (index number).

```
Public NotInheritable Class PortCollection : Inherits ServiceDescriptionBaseCollection
' Public Instance Properties
   Public Default ReadOnly Property Item (ByVal name As String) As Port
   Public Default Property Item (ByVal index As Integer) As Port
' Public Instance Methods
   Public Function Add(ByVal port As Port) As Integer
   Public Function Contains(ByVal port As Port) As Boolean
   Public Sub CopyTo(ByVal array As Port(), ByVal index As Integer)
   Public Function IndexOf(ByVal port As Port) As Integer
   Public Sub Insert(ByVal index As Integer, ByVal port As Port)
   Public Sub Remove(ByVal port As Port)
' Protected Instance Methods
   Overrides Protected Function GetKey(ByVal value As Object) As String
   Overrides Protected Sub SetParent(ByVal value As Object, ByVal parent As Object)
End Class
```

Hierarchy: System.Object → System.Collections.CollectionBase (System.Collections.IList , System.Collections.ICollection , System.Collections.IEnumerable) → ServiceDescriptionBaseCollection → PortCollection

PortType
NotInheritable Class

System.Web.Services.Description (system.web.services.dll)

This class represents the WSDL <portType> element. It groups a set of related Operation objects, and identifies them with a Name. In a WSDL document generated by ASP.NET, there are three <portType> elements—one relating to HTTP GET, another for HTTP POST, and one for SOAP transmissions. ASP.NET creates these elements using the name of your web service and adding a suffix describing the type of transmission (for example, MyWebServiceHttpGet).

```
Public NotInheritable Class PortType : Inherits DocumentableItem
' Public Constructors
   Public Sub New()
' Public Instance Properties
   Public Property Name As String
   Public ReadOnly Property Operations As OperationCollection
   Public ReadOnly Property ServiceDescription As ServiceDescription
End Class
```

Hierarchy: System.Object → DocumentableItem → PortType

PortTypeCollection
NotInheritable Class

System.Web.Services.Description (system.web.services.dll)

This collection of PortType objects (which are themselves collections of Operation objects) is used by the PortTypes property of the ServiceDescription class to represent all <portType> elements in a WSDL document. You can access each PortType element by name or position (index number).

```
Public NotInheritable Class PortTypeCollection : Inherits ServiceDescriptionBaseCollection
' Public Instance Properties
    Public Default ReadOnly Property Item (ByVal name As String) As PortType
    Public Default Property Item (ByVal index As Integer) As PortType
' Public Instance Methods
    Public Function Add(ByVal portType As PortType) As Integer
    Public Function Contains(ByVal portType As PortType) As Boolean
    Public Sub CopyTo(ByVal array As PortType(), ByVal index As Integer)
    Public Function IndexOf(ByVal portType As PortType) As Integer
    Public Sub Insert(ByVal index As Integer, ByVal portType As PortType)
    Public Sub Remove(ByVal portType As PortType)
' Protected Instance Methods
    Overrides Protected Function GetKey(ByVal value As Object) As String
    Overrides Protected Sub SetParent(ByVal value As Object, ByVal parent As Object)
End Class
```

Hierarchy: System.Object → System.Collections.CollectionBase (System.Collections.IList , System.Collections.ICollection , System.Collections.IEnumerable) → ServiceDescriptionBaseCollection → PortTypeCollection

ProtocolImporter

MustInherit Class

System.Web.Services.Description (system.web.services.dll)

This type supports the .NET Framework infrastructure. You don't need to use it directly in your code.

```
Public MustInherit Class ProtocolImporter
' Protected Constructors
    Protected Sub New()
' Public Instance Properties
    Public ReadOnly Property AbstractSchemas As XmlSchemas
    Public ReadOnly Property Binding As Binding
    Public ReadOnly Property ClassName As String
    Public ReadOnly Property ClassNames As CodeIdentifiers
    Public ReadOnly Property CodeNamespace As CodeNamespace
    Public ReadOnly Property CodeTypeDeclaration As CodeTypeDeclaration
    Public ReadOnly Property ConcreteSchemas As XmlSchemas
    Public ReadOnly Property InputMessage As Message
    Public ReadOnly Property MethodName As String
    Public ReadOnly Property Operation As Operation
    Public ReadOnly Property OperationBinding As OperationBinding
    Public ReadOnly Property OutputMessage As Message
    Public ReadOnly Property Port As Port
    Public ReadOnly Property PortType As PortType
    MustInherit Public ReadOnly Property ProtocolName As String
    Public ReadOnly Property Schemas As XmlSchemas
    Public ReadOnly Property Service As Service
    Public ReadOnly Property ServiceDescriptions As ServiceDescriptionCollection
    Public ReadOnly Property Style As ServiceDescriptionImportStyle
    Public Property Warnings As ServiceDescriptionImportWarnings
' Public Instance Methods
    Public Sub AddExtensionWarningComments(                               _
      ByVal comments As System.CodeDom.CodeCommentStatementCollection, _
      ByVal extensions As ServiceDescriptionFormatExtensionCollection)
    Public Function OperationBindingSyntaxException(ByVal text As String) As Exception
```

Public Function **OperationSyntaxException**(ByVal text As String) As Exception
Public Sub **UnsupportedBindingWarning**(ByVal text As String)
Public Sub **UnsupportedOperationBindingWarning**(ByVal text As String)
Public Sub **UnsupportedOperationWarning**(ByVal text As String)
' *Protected Instance Methods*
MustInherit Protected Function **BeginClass**() As CodeTypeDeclaration
Overridable Protected Sub **BeginNamespace**()
Overridable Protected Sub **EndClass**()
Overridable Protected Sub **EndNamespace**()
MustInherit Protected Function **GenerateMethod**() As CodeMemberMethod
MustInherit Protected Function **IsBindingSupported**() As Boolean
MustInherit Protected Function **IsOperationFlowSupported**(ByVal flow As OperationFlow) As Boolean
End Class

ProtocolReflector   MustInherit Class

System.Web.Services.Description (system.web.services.dll)

This type supports the .NET Framework infrastructure. You don't need to use it directly in your code.

Public MustInherit Class **ProtocolReflector**
' *Protected Constructors*
Protected Sub **New**()
' *Public Instance Properties*
Public ReadOnly Property **Binding** As Binding
Public ReadOnly Property **DefaultNamespace** As String
Public ReadOnly Property **HeaderMessages** As MessageCollection
Public ReadOnly Property **InputMessage** As Message
Public ReadOnly Property **Method** As LogicalMethodInfo
Public ReadOnly Property **MethodAttribute** As WebMethodAttribute
Public ReadOnly Property **Methods** As LogicalMethodInfo()
Public ReadOnly Property **Operation** As Operation
Public ReadOnly Property **OperationBinding** As OperationBinding
Public ReadOnly Property **OutputMessage** As Message
Public ReadOnly Property **Port** As Port
Public ReadOnly Property **PortType** As PortType
MustInherit Public ReadOnly Property **ProtocolName** As String
Public ReadOnly Property **ReflectionImporter** As XmlReflectionImporter
Public ReadOnly Property **SchemaExporter** As XmlSchemaExporter
Public ReadOnly Property **Schemas** As XmlSchemas
Public ReadOnly Property **Service** As Service
Public ReadOnly Property **ServiceDescription** As ServiceDescription
Public ReadOnly Property **ServiceDescriptions** As ServiceDescriptionCollection
Public ReadOnly Property **ServiceType** As Type
Public ReadOnly Property **ServiceUrl** As String
' *Public Instance Methods*
Public Function **GetServiceDescription**(ByVal ns As String) As ServiceDescription
' *Protected Instance Methods*
Overridable Protected Sub **BeginClass**()
Overridable Protected Sub **EndClass**()
MustInherit Protected Function **ReflectMethod**() As Boolean
Overridable Protected Function **ReflectMethodBinding**() As String
End Class

Service
NotInheritable Class

System.Web.Services.Description (system.web.services.dll)

This class represents the WSDL <service> element. It groups multiple related Port objects and identifies them with a Name. To invoke a web service method, a client sends a SOAP request identifying the service, the port in that service, and the operation it wants executed along with the input parameter values.

```
Public NotInheritable Class Service : Inherits DocumentableItem
' Public Constructors
    Public Sub New()
' Public Instance Properties
    Public ReadOnly Property Extensions As ServiceDescriptionFormatExtensionCollection
    Public Property Name As String
    Public ReadOnly Property Ports As PortCollection
    Public ReadOnly Property ServiceDescription As ServiceDescription
End Class
```

Hierarchy: System.Object → DocumentableItem → Service

ServiceCollection
NotInheritable Class

System.Web.Services.Description (system.web.services.dll)

This collection of Service objects is used by the Services property of the ServiceDescription class to represent all <service> elements in a WSDL document. You can access each Service element by name or position (index number).

```
Public NotInheritable Class ServiceCollection : Inherits ServiceDescriptionBaseCollection
' Public Instance Properties
    Public Default ReadOnly Property Item (ByVal name As String) As Service
    Public Default Property Item (ByVal index As Integer) As Service
' Public Instance Methods
    Public Function Add(ByVal service As Service) As Integer
    Public Function Contains(ByVal service As Service) As Boolean
    Public Sub CopyTo(ByVal array As Service(), ByVal index As Integer)
    Public Function IndexOf(ByVal service As Service) As Integer
    Public Sub Insert(ByVal index As Integer, ByVal service As Service)
    Public Sub Remove(ByVal service As Service)
' Protected Instance Methods
    Overrides Protected Function GetKey(ByVal value As Object) As String
    Overrides Protected Sub SetParent(ByVal value As Object, ByVal parent As Object)
End Class
```

Hierarchy: System.Object → System.Collections.CollectionBase (System.Collections.IList , System.Collections.ICollection , System.Collections.IEnumerable)→ ServiceDescriptionBaseCollection → ServiceCollection

ServiceDescription
NotInheritable Class

System.Web.Services.Description (system.web.services.dll)

The ServiceDescription class represents a valid WSDL document, complete with appropriate namespaces, elements and attributes. The elements of the WSDL file are all represented by other, distinct classes in the System.Web.Services.Description namespace, and provided through the properties of the ServiceDescription class. At the top level, a WSDL document contains a series of definitions in a <definitions> element. These definitions define Types, Message, PortType, Binding, and Service elements.

The ServiceDescription class also provides a Read() and Write() method. Both methods are overloaded to allow you serialize information to or from a System.IO.Stream, a System.IO.TextReader, a System.IO.TextWriter, a System.Xml.XmlReader, a System.Xml.XmlWriter, or a string containing a fully qualified path and filename.

There are three ways to create a ServiceDescription object. You can use the New keyword and create one manually, you can use the ServiceDescriptionReflector to create one from a live web service, or you can use the shared Read() method to create one from a WSDL file. For example, you can create a ServiceDescription object with all its fully populated subobjects by using a syntax like MyServiceDesc = ServiceDescription.Read("MyFile.xml").

```
Public NotInheritable Class ServiceDescription : Inherits DocumentableItem
' Public Constructors
   Public Sub New()
' Public Shared Fields
   public const Namespace As String                                    =http://schemas.xmlsoap.org/wsdl/
' Public Shared Properties
   Public Shared ReadOnly Property Serializer As XmlSerializer
' Public Instance Properties
   Public ReadOnly Property Bindings As BindingCollection
   Public ReadOnly Property Extensions As ServiceDescriptionFormatExtensionCollection
   Public ReadOnly Property Imports As ImportCollection
   Public ReadOnly Property Messages As MessageCollection
   Public Property Name As String
   Public ReadOnly Property PortTypes As PortTypeCollection
   Public Property RetrievalUrl As String
   Public ReadOnly Property ServiceDescriptions As ServiceDescriptionCollection
   Public ReadOnly Property Services As ServiceCollection
   Public Property TargetNamespace As String
   Public Property Types As Types
' Public Shared Methods
   Public Shared Function CanRead(ByVal reader As System.Xml.XmlReader) As Boolean
   Public Shared Function Read(ByVal stream As System.IO.Stream) As ServiceDescription
   Public Shared Function Read(ByVal fileName As String) As ServiceDescription
   Public Shared Function Read(ByVal textReader As System.IO.TextReader) As ServiceDescription
   Public Shared Function Read(ByVal reader As System.Xml.XmlReader) As ServiceDescription
' Public Instance Methods
   Public Sub Write(ByVal stream As System.IO.Stream)
   Public Sub Write(ByVal fileName As String)
   Public Sub Write(ByVal writer As System.IO.TextWriter)
   Public Sub Write(ByVal writer As System.Xml.XmlWriter)
End Class
```

Hierarchy: System.Object → DocumentableItem → ServiceDescription

ServiceDescriptionBaseCollection   MustInherit Class

System.Web.Services.Description (system.web.services.dll)

This is the base class for many of the strongly typed collection classes in this namespace. Classes that derive from ServiceDescriptionBaseCollection end with the word "Collection," as in PortCollection. These classes are strongly typed, but not named. This differs from the classes that represent WSDL language elements. For example, the PortType class represents a WSDL language element, contains other elements as Operation objects, and does not inherit from ServiceDescriptionBaseCollection.

```
Public MustInherit Class ServiceDescriptionBaseCollection : Inherits CollectionBase
```

```
' Protected Instance Properties
    Overridable Protected Property Table As IDictionary
' Protected Instance Methods
    Overridable Protected Function GetKey(ByVal value As Object) As String
    Overrides Protected Sub OnClear()
    Overrides Protected Sub OnInsertComplete(ByVal index As Integer, ByVal value As Object)
    Overrides Protected Sub OnRemove(ByVal index As Integer, ByVal value As Object)
    Overrides Protected Sub OnSet(ByVal index As Integer, ByVal oldValue As Object, ByVal newValue As Object)
    Overridable Protected Sub SetParent(ByVal value As Object, ByVal parent As Object)
End Class
```

Hierarchy: System.Object → System.Collections.CollectionBase (System.Collections.IList , System.Collections.ICollection , System.Collections.IEnumerable)→ ServiceDescriptionBaseCollection

ServiceDescriptionCollection   NotInheritable Class

System.Web.Services.Description (system.web.services.dll)

This is a collection of ServiceDescription objects. Every ServiceDescription object provides a reference to the ServiceDescriptionCollection that it is a part of in its ServiceDescription.ServiceDescriptions property. You can access each ServiceDescription element by name or position (index number).

```
Public NotInheritable Class ServiceDescriptionCollection : Inherits ServiceDescriptionBaseCollection
' Public Constructors
    Public Sub New()
' Public Instance Properties
    Public Default ReadOnly Property Item (ByVal ns As String) As ServiceDescription
    Public Default Property Item (ByVal index As Integer) As ServiceDescription
' Public Instance Methods
    Public Function Add(ByVal serviceDescription As ServiceDescription) As Integer
    Public Function Contains(ByVal serviceDescription As ServiceDescription) As Boolean
    Public Sub CopyTo(ByVal array As ServiceDescription(), ByVal index As Integer)
    Public Function GetBinding(ByVal name As System.Xml.XmlQualifiedName) As Binding
    Public Function GetMessage(ByVal name As System.Xml.XmlQualifiedName) As Message
    Public Function GetPortType(ByVal name As System.Xml.XmlQualifiedName) As PortType
    Public Function GetService(ByVal name As System.Xml.XmlQualifiedName) As Service
    Public Function IndexOf(ByVal serviceDescription As ServiceDescription) As Integer
    Public Sub Insert(ByVal index As Integer, ByVal serviceDescription As ServiceDescription)
    Public Sub Remove(ByVal serviceDescription As ServiceDescription)
' Protected Instance Methods
    Overrides Protected Function GetKey(ByVal value As Object) As String
End Class
```

Hierarchy: System.Object → System.Collections.CollectionBase (System.Collections.IList , System.Collections.ICollection , System.Collections.IEnumerable)→ ServiceDescriptionBaseCollection → ServiceDescriptionCollection

ServiceDescriptionFormatExtension   MustInherit Class

System.Web.Services.Description (system.web.services.dll)

This abstract class allows you to create a WSDL extensibility element. Extensibility elements can be added at many levels by adding a ServiceDescriptionFormatExtension object to the Extensions collection of a class in this namespace. Note that you will also need to derive your own SoapExtensionImporter class if you need to extend the import process to use your extensibility element when generating a proxy class.

Public MustInherit Class **ServiceDescriptionFormatExtension**
' Protected Constructors
   Protected Sub **New**()
' Public Instance Properties
   Public Property **Handled** As Boolean
   Public ReadOnly Property **Parent** As Object
   Public Property **Required** As Boolean
End Class

ServiceDescriptionFormatExtensionCollection   NotInheritable Class

System.Web.Services.Description (system.web.services.dll)

This collection of objects is derived from ServiceDescriptionFormatExtension. It is used in various classes in this namespace, including Types, Port, Service, and Binding, allowing you to implement type extensions at several different levels. For example, the InputBinding.Extensions property provides a ServiceDescriptionFormatExtensionCollection that could contain a HttpUrlEncodedBinding or SoapBodyBinding.

Public NotInheritable Class **ServiceDescriptionFormatExtensionCollection** : Inherits _
    ServiceDescriptionBaseCollection
' Public Constructors
   Public Sub **New**(ByVal parent As Object)
' Public Instance Properties
   Public Default Property **Item** (ByVal index As Integer) As Object Implements IList.Item
' Public Instance Methods
   Public Function **Add**(ByVal extension As Object) As Integer Implements IList.Add
   Public Function **Contains**(ByVal extension As Object) As Boolean Implements IList.Contains
   Public Sub **CopyTo**(ByVal array As Object(), ByVal index As Integer)
   Public Function **Find**(ByVal type As Type) As Object
   Public Function **Find**(ByVal name As String, ByVal ns As String) As XmlElement
   Public Function **FindAll**(ByVal type As Type) As Object()
   Public Function **FindAll**(ByVal name As String, ByVal ns As String) As XmlElement()
   Public Function **IndexOf**(ByVal extension As Object) As Integer Implements IList.IndexOf
   Public Sub **Insert**(ByVal index As Integer, ByVal extension As Object) Implements IList.Insert
   Public Function **IsHandled**(ByVal item As Object) As Boolean
   Public Function **IsRequired**(ByVal item As Object) As Boolean
   Public Sub **Remove**(ByVal extension As Object) Implements IList.Remove
' Protected Instance Methods
   Overrides Protected Sub **OnValidate**(ByVal value As Object)
   Overrides Protected Sub **SetParent**(ByVal value As Object, ByVal parent As Object)
End Class

Hierarchy: System.Object → System.Collections.CollectionBase (System.Collections.IList , System.Collections.ICollection , System.Collections.IEnumerable)→ ServiceDescriptionBaseCollection → ServiceDescriptionFormatExtensionCollection

ServiceDescriptionImporter   Class

System.Web.Services.Description (system.web.services.dll)

The ServiceDescriptionImporter is used to programmatically create a proxy class for a web service. Clients invoke web service methods by creating an instance of the proxy class and invoking the corresponding method on the proxy class.

To create a proxy class, first use the AddServiceDescription() method to add a ServiceDescription to the ServiceDescriptions collection. Then create the proxy class with the Import() method.

When using the AddServiceDescription() method, use the appSettingUrlKey and appSetting-BaseUrl parameters to specify how the Url property will be generated for the web service proxy class.

Public Class **ServiceDescriptionImporter**
' *Public Constructors*
   Public Sub **New**()
' *Public Instance Properties*
   Public Property **ProtocolName** As String
   Public ReadOnly Property **Schemas** As XmlSchemas
   Public ReadOnly Property **ServiceDescriptions** As ServiceDescriptionCollection
   Public Property **Style** As ServiceDescriptionImportStyle
' *Public Instance Methods*
   Public Sub **AddServiceDescription**(ByVal serviceDescription As ServiceDescription, _
     ByVal appSettingUrlKey As String, ByVal appSettingBaseUrl As String)
   Public Function **Import**(ByVal codeNamespace As System.CodeDom.CodeNamespace,   _
     ByVal codeCompileUnit As System.CodeDom.CodeCompileUnit) As ServiceDescriptionImportWarnings
End Class

ServiceDescriptionImportStyle Enum

System.Web.Services.Description (system.web.services.dll)   *serializable*

This enumeration is used for the ServiceDescriptionImporter.Style property; it specifies whether a ServiceDescriptionImporter.Import() method call will be made to the server or client. When you import to the client computer, you will receive a proxy class with synchronous and asynchronous methods for invoking each method within the web service, just as if .NET generated the proxy class for you automatically. A server import, however, will generate an abstract class with abstract members, which you must override to provide the appropriate implementation.

Public Enum **ServiceDescriptionImportStyle**
     Client = 0
     Server = 1
End Enum

Hierarchy: System.Object → System.ValueType → System.Enum (System.IComparable , System.IFormattable , System.IConvertible) → ServiceDescriptionImportStyle

ServiceDescriptionImportWarnings Enum

System.Web.Services.Description (system.web.services.dll)   *serializable*

This enumeration is used for the return value from the ServiceDescriptionImporter.Import() method. It can indicate common problems creating the proxy class, including the failure to create a required or optional ServiceDescriptionFormatExtension or an unsupported type of Binding or Operation.

Public Enum **ServiceDescriptionImportWarnings**
     NoCodeGenerated = 1
     OptionalExtensionsIgnored = 2
     RequiredExtensionsIgnored = 4
     UnsupportedOperationsIgnored = 8
     UnsupportedBindingsIgnored = 16
     NoMethodsGenerated = 32
End Enum

Hierarchy: System.Object → System.ValueType → System.Enum (System.IComparable , System.IFormattable , System.IConvertible)→ ServiceDescriptionImportWarnings

ServiceDescriptionReflector
Class

System.Web.Services.Description (system.web.services.dll)

This class allows you to dynamically create a ServiceDescription object that represents a "live" web service. To use this class, invoke the Reflect() method with the web service URL as a string. The WSDL document for the web service will be added to the ServiceDescriptions collection. You can also retrieve any associated XML schemas from the Schemas collection.

```
Public Class ServiceDescriptionReflector
' Public Constructors
    Public Sub New()
' Public Instance Properties
    Public ReadOnly Property Schemas As XmlSchemas
    Public ReadOnly Property ServiceDescriptions As ServiceDescriptionCollection
' Public Instance Methods
    Public Sub Reflect(ByVal type As Type, ByVal url As String)
End Class
```

SoapAddressBinding
NotInheritable Class

System.Web.Services.Description (system.web.services.dll)

This class epresents an extensibility element added to the WSDL <port> element, which enables SOAP binding to a specific web service address. The Location property specifies the base URI for the web service port.

```
Public NotInheritable Class SoapAddressBinding : Inherits ServiceDescriptionFormatExtension
' Public Constructors
    Public Sub New()
' Public Instance Properties
    Public Property Location As String
End Class
```

Hierarchy: System.Object → ServiceDescriptionFormatExtension → SoapAddressBinding

SoapBinding
NotInheritable Class

System.Web.Services.Description (system.web.services.dll)

This class represents an extensibility element added to the WSDL <binding> element, which allows information to be transmitted via SOAP encoding. The Style property specifies whether Document or RPC encoding is used, and the Transport property specifies a URI (such as "SMTP" or "HTTP").

```
Public NotInheritable Class SoapBinding : Inherits ServiceDescriptionFormatExtension
' Public Constructors
    Public Sub New()
' Public Shared Fields
    public const HttpTransport As String                    =http://schemas.xmlsoap.org/soap/http
    public const Namespace As String                        =http://schemas.xmlsoap.org/wsdl/soap/
' Public Instance Properties
    Public Property Style As SoapBindingStyle
    Public Property Transport As String
```

End Class

Hierarchy: System.Object → ServiceDescriptionFormatExtension → SoapBinding

SoapBindingStyle   Enum

System.Web.Services.Description (system.web.services.dll)   *serializable*

This enumeration provides different SOAP transport options. Procedure-oriented messages use the Rpc value and can contain parameters and return values. Document-oriented messages, however, use the value Document and typically contain documents.

```
Public Enum SoapBindingStyle
    Default = 0
    Document = 1
    Rpc = 2
End Enum
```

Hierarchy: System.Object → System.ValueType → System.Enum (System.IComparable , System.IFormattable , System.IConvertible)→ SoapBindingStyle

SoapBindingUse   Enum

System.Web.Services.Description (system.web.services.dll)   *serializable*

This enumeration applies to SOAP extensibility elements and specifies the XML encoding of a message. Encoded specifies that the message parts are encoded using the given encoding rules (which are usually specified in a corresponding Encoding property), while Literal indicates that the message parts represent a concrete schema and Default specifies an empty string for the corresponding XML use attribute. Classes that use this enumeration expose a Use property (as in SoapBodyBinding.Use and SoapFaultBinding.Use).

```
Public Enum SoapBindingUse
    Default = 0
    Encoded = 1
    Literal = 2
End Enum
```

Hierarchy: System.Object → System.ValueType → System.Enum (System.IComparable , System.IFormattable , System.IConvertible)→ SoapBindingUse

SoapBodyBinding   NotInheritable Class

System.Web.Services.Description (system.web.services.dll)

This class represents an extensibility element added to an InputBinding or an OutputBinding object. This binding is used for an SOAP input and output messages (represented by OperationInput and OperationOutput objects). It specifies that data is encoded for SOAP transmission and does not provide any properties.

```
Public NotInheritable Class SoapBodyBinding : Inherits ServiceDescriptionFormatExtension
' Public Constructors
    Public Sub New()
' Public Instance Properties
    Public Property Encoding As String
    Public Property Namespace As String
```

```
    Public Property Parts As String()
    Public Property PartsString As String
    Public Property Use As SoapBindingUse
End Class
```

Hierarchy: System.Object → ServiceDescriptionFormatExtension → SoapBodyBinding

SoapExtensionImporter   MustInherit Class

System.Web.Services.Description (system.web.services.dll)

This class is used by the .NET framework, not directly by your code.

```
Public MustInherit Class SoapExtensionImporter
' Protected Constructors
    Protected Sub New()
' Public Instance Properties
    Public Property ImportContext As SoapProtocolImporter
' Public Instance Methods
    MustInherit Public Sub ImportMethod(ByVal metadata As System.CodeDom.CodeAttributeDeclarationCollection)
End Class
```

SoapExtensionReflector   MustInherit Class

System.Web.Services.Description (system.web.services.dll)

This class is used by the .NET framework, not directly by your code.

```
Public MustInherit Class SoapExtensionReflector
' Protected Constructors
    Protected Sub New()
' Public Instance Properties
    Public Property ReflectionContext As ProtocolReflector
' Public Instance Methods
    MustInherit Public Sub ReflectMethod()
End Class
```

SoapFaultBinding   NotInheritable Class

System.Web.Services.Description (system.web.services.dll)

This class represents an extensibility element added to the WSDL <fault> element (enclosed in the <operation> element) that allows information to be transmitted via SOAP. The encoding is indicated with the Encoding and Use properties and the namespace with the Namespace property.

```
Public NotInheritable Class SoapFaultBinding : Inherits ServiceDescriptionFormatExtension
' Public Constructors
    Public Sub New()
' Public Instance Properties
    Public Property Encoding As String
    Public Property Namespace As String
    Public Property Use As SoapBindingUse
End Class
```

Hierarchy: System.Object → ServiceDescriptionFormatExtension → SoapFaultBinding

SoapHeaderBinding
NotInheritable Class

System.Web.Services.Description (system.web.services.dll)

This class represents an extensibility element added to the WSDL <input> or <output> element (enclosed in the <operation> element), which allows information to be transmitted via SOAP. The encoding is indicated with the SoapFaultBinding.Encoding and SoapFaultBinding.Use properties, and the namespace is indicated with the SoapFaultBinding.Namespace property.

Public NotInheritable Class **SoapHeaderBinding** : Inherits ServiceDescriptionFormatExtension
' *Public Constructors*
   Public Sub **New**()
' *Public Instance Properties*
   Public Property **Encoding** As String
   Public Property **MapToProperty** As Boolean
   Public Property **Message** As XmlQualifiedName
   Public Property **Namespace** As String
   Public Property **Part** As String
   Public Property **Use** As SoapBindingUse
End Class

Hierarchy: System.Object → ServiceDescriptionFormatExtension → SoapHeaderBinding

SoapHeaderFaultBinding
NotInheritable Class

System.Web.Services.Description (system.web.services.dll)

This class represents an extensibility element added to the WSDL <input> or <output> element (enclosed in the <operation> element) that allows information to be transmitted via SOAP. It specifies the SOAP header types used to transmit error information within the SOAP header. The encoding is indicated with the SoapFaultBinding.Encoding and SoapFaultBinding.Use properties and the namespace with the SoapFaultBinding.Namespace property.

Public NotInheritable Class **SoapHeaderFaultBinding** : Inherits ServiceDescriptionFormatExtension
' *Public Constructors*
   Public Sub **New**()
' *Public Instance Properties*
   Public Property **Encoding** As String
   Public Property **Message** As XmlQualifiedName
   Public Property **Namespace** As String
   Public Property **Part** As String
   Public Property **Use** As SoapBindingUse
End Class

Hierarchy: System.Object → ServiceDescriptionFormatExtension → SoapHeaderFaultBinding

SoapOperationBinding
NotInheritable Class

System.Web.Services.Description (system.web.services.dll)

This class represents an extensibility element added to the WSDL <operation> element, which allows information to be transmitted via SOAP encoding. The Style property specifies whether Document or RPC encoding is used, and the SoapAction property contains a string with the URI for the SOAP header.

Public NotInheritable Class **SoapOperationBinding** : Inherits ServiceDescriptionFormatExtension
' *Public Constructors*

```
   Public Sub New()
' Public Instance Properties
   Public Property SoapAction As String
   Public Property Style As SoapBindingStyle
End Class
```

Hierarchy: System.Object → ServiceDescriptionFormatExtension → SoapOperationBinding

SoapProtocolImporter   **NotInheritable Class**

System.Web.Services.Description (system.web.services.dll)

This class is used by the .NET framework, not directly by your code.

```
Public NotInheritable Class SoapProtocolImporter : Inherits ProtocolImporter
' Public Constructors
   Public Sub New()
' Public Instance Properties
   Overrides Public ReadOnly Property ProtocolName As String
   Public ReadOnly Property SoapBinding As SoapBinding
   Public ReadOnly Property SoapExporter As SoapCodeExporter
   Public ReadOnly Property SoapImporter As SoapSchemaImporter
   Public ReadOnly Property XmlExporter As XmlCodeExporter
   Public ReadOnly Property XmlImporter As XmlSchemaImporter
' Protected Instance Methods
   Overrides Protected Function BeginClass() As CodeTypeDeclaration
   Overrides Protected Sub BeginNamespace()
   Overrides Protected Sub EndClass()
   Overrides Protected Sub EndNamespace()
   Overrides Protected Function GenerateMethod() As CodeMemberMethod
   Overrides Protected Function IsBindingSupported() As Boolean
   Overrides Protected Function IsOperationFlowSupported(ByVal flow As OperationFlow) As Boolean
End Class
```

Hierarchy: System.Object → ProtocolImporter → SoapProtocolImporter

SoapTransportImporter   **MustInherit Class**

System.Web.Services.Description (system.web.services.dll)

This class serves as a base class for custom classes that import SOAP transmission protocols into web services. Note, however, that the current implementation of web services does not support these user-defined classes.

```
Public MustInherit Class SoapTransportImporter
' Protected Constructors
   Protected Sub New()
' Public Instance Properties
   Public Property ImportContext As SoapProtocolImporter
' Public Instance Methods
   MustInherit Public Sub ImportClass()
   MustInherit Public Function IsSupportedTransport(ByVal transport As String) As Boolean
End Class
```

Types

System.Web.Services.Description (system.web.services.dll)

This class represents the WSDL <types> element. It provides abstract data type definitions that can be used for the WSDL messages. You can access them through the Schemas property. The preferred (and default) type system used with WSDL is XSD. You can also add type extensibility elements, which are represented in this class by the Extensions property. This property will contain an empty collection in the default implementation of this class.

When ASP.NET generates a WSDL document for your web service, it includes an entry in the <types> element for every method, specifying the input parameter information. It also specifies the return value information, if applicable, in an entry that has your method name with the word "Response" added (for example, GetStockQuoteResponse). Additionally, if your Web Method accepts or returns a custom class or structure, a separate entry will be added to the <types> element to describe the data members of that class.

```
Public NotInheritable Class Types : Inherits DocumentableItem
' Public Constructors
    Public Sub New()
' Public Instance Properties
    Public ReadOnly Property Extensions As ServiceDescriptionFormatExtensionCollection
    Public ReadOnly Property Schemas As XmlSchemas
End Class
```

Hierarchy: System.Object → DocumentableItem → Types

CHAPTER 31

The System.Web.Services.Discovery Namespace

The System.Web.Services.Discovery namespace includes the classes that model .NET web service discovery documents (usually seen as *.disco* or *.vsdisco* files). These classes are generally not used directly, as the discovery process is automated in tools such as Visual Studio .NET. However, they could be used to create programs that worked with discovery documents for reasons other than consuming a given web service. For example, you could create a utility that parses multiple discovery documents and retrieves aggregate information.

The discovery process has little to do with Universal Description, Design, Discovery, and Integration (UDDI), the cross-vendor initiative for publishing information about business and their web services in an online repository. (In fact, UDDI repositories can provide links to web services or discovery documents.) Discovery documents are a simple approach—essentially nothing more than a collection of links without any associated documentation or categorization. These "links" can point to WSDL service descriptions, XSD schemas, or other discovery documents.

A good starting point to understanding this namespace is the DiscoveryDocument class, which represents a single *.disco* or *.vsdisco* file. The most useful type in this namespace is the DiscoveryClientProtocol class, which allows you to invoke web service discovery programmatically. Figure 31-1 shows the types in this namespace.

ContractReference   Class

System.Web.Services.Discovery (system.web.services.dll)

This class represents a discovery document reference to a WSDL service description. This is the most common type of reference in a discovery document and the most useful, as it directly corresponds to a web service that the client can consume. The Contract property returns the System.Web.Services.Description.ServiceDescription object that represents the service description. Ref provides the URL to the WSDL document as a string, while DocRef provides the URL to the web service that the WSDL document describes.

```
Public Class ContractReference : Inherits DiscoveryReference
' Public Constructors
   Public Sub New()
   Public Sub New(ByVal href As String)
   Public Sub New(ByVal href As String, ByVal docRef As String)
```

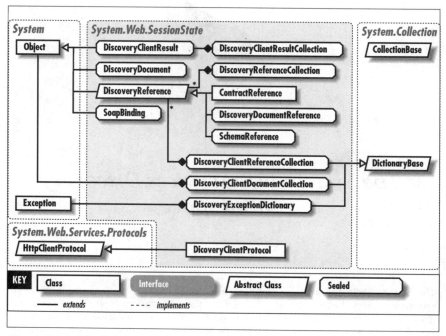

Figure 31-1: The System.Web.Services.Discovery namespace

```
' Public Shared Fields
   public const Namespace As String                                    =http://schemas.xmlsoap.org/disco/scl/
' Public Instance Properties
   Public ReadOnly Property Contract As ServiceDescription
   Overrides Public ReadOnly Property DefaultFilename As String
   Public Property DocRef As String
   Public Property Ref As String
   Overrides Public Property Url As String
' Public Instance Methods
   Overrides Public Function ReadDocument(ByVal stream As System.IO.Stream) As Object
   Overrides Public Sub WriteDocument(ByVal document As Object, ByVal stream As System.IO.Stream)
' Protected Instance Methods
   Overrides Protected Friend Sub Resolve(ByVal contentType As String, ByVal stream As System.IO.Stream)
End Class
```

Hierarchy: System.Object → DiscoveryReference → ContractReference

ContractSearchPattern   NotInheritable Class

System.Web.Services.Discovery (system.web.services.dll)

This type is used by the .NET framework and is never used directly by your code.

```
Public NotInheritable Class ContractSearchPattern : Inherits DiscoverySearchPattern
' Public Constructors
   Public Sub New()
' Public Instance Properties
```

Overrides Public ReadOnly Property **Pattern** As String
' Public Instance Methods
    Overrides Public Function **GetDiscoveryReference**(ByVal filename As String) As DiscoveryReference
End Class

Hierarchy: System.Object → DiscoverySearchPattern → ContractSearchPattern

DiscoveryClientDocumentCollection   NotInheritable Class

System.Web.Services.Discovery (system.web.services.dll)

This class is a collection of DiscoveryDocument instances. It can be used to represent the discovery documents that are downloaded to a client during the discovery process.

Public NotInheritable Class **DiscoveryClientDocumentCollection** : Inherits DictionaryBase
' Public Constructors
    Public Sub **New**()
' Public Instance Properties
    Public Default Property **Item** (ByVal url As String) As Object
    Public ReadOnly Property **Keys** As ICollection Implements IDictionary.Keys
    Public ReadOnly Property **Values** As ICollection Implements IDictionary.Values
' Public Instance Methods
    Public Sub **Add**(ByVal url As String, ByVal value As Object)
    Public Function **Contains**(ByVal url As String) As Boolean
    Public Sub **Remove**(ByVal url As String)
End Class

Hierarchy: System.Object → System.Collections.DictionaryBase (System.Collections.IDictionary , System.Collections.ICollection , System.Collections.IEnumerable)→ DiscoveryClientDocumentCollection

DiscoveryClientProtocol   Class

System.Web.Services.Discovery (system.web.services.dll)   *marshal by reference, disposable*

Most types in this namespace are used for modelling discovery documents. This class provides the utility methods that allow you to reflect on URLs and create the appropriate discovery document objects. This class is based on two properties: Documents, which contains a collection of discovery documents, and the References, which will contain a collection of disovery document references when the discovery process is complete.

To start the discovery process, you need to know the location of the discovery document you want to process (which could have been retrieved through a service like UDDI). You can then use the Discover() method and supply the appropriate URL as a string. (Alternatively, you can use the DiscoverAny() method if you are not sure whether the URL points to a discovery document, WSDL service description, or XSD file). If the document is valid, the document will be added to the References and Documents collection. In addition, all references contained in the discovery document are added to the References collection, but they are not validated.

To verify the discovery document's references (the next stage of the discovery process), you should use the ResolveOneLevel() method, which moves through the References collection and ensures that all valid references are added to the Documents collection. Alternatively, you can use the ResolveAll() method, which will examine any nested discovery documents. For example, if you have a discovery document that references another discovery document, which references a third discovery document, the ResolveAll() method will burrow through all the levels. Errors found during the reference resolving process are not thrown and caught in your code, but added to the Errors collection. Additional information found in the discovery document (such as SOAP bindings), will be added to the AdditionalInformation collection.

The DiscoveryClientProtocol class also contains methods that let you download discovery documents to files on the client computer. You can use the Download() method to send the discovery document at a specified URL to a System.IO.Stream, and the WriteAll() method writes all discovery documents, XSD files, and Service Descriptions in the Documents property to the supplied directory. In this case, the file designated by the topLevelFileName argument is used to store a map of saved documents, which you can read to recreate the DiscoveryClientProtocol instance by using the ReadAll() method. The format used in this file is XML.

```
Public Class DiscoveryClientProtocol : Inherits System.Web.Services.Protocols.HttpWebClientProtocol
' Public Constructors
   Public Sub New()
' Public Instance Properties
   Public ReadOnly Property AdditionalInformation As IList
   Public ReadOnly Property Documents As DiscoveryClientDocumentCollection
   Public ReadOnly Property Errors As DiscoveryExceptionDictionary
   Public ReadOnly Property References As DiscoveryClientReferenceCollection
' Public Instance Methods
   Public Function Discover(ByVal url As String) As DiscoveryDocument
   Public Function DiscoverAny(ByVal url As String) As DiscoveryDocument
   Public Function Download(ByRef url As String) As Stream
   Public Function Download(ByRef url As String, ByRef contentType As String) As Stream
   Public Function ReadAll(ByVal topLevelFilename As String) As DiscoveryClientResultCollection
   Public Sub ResolveAll()
   Public Sub ResolveOneLevel()
   Public Function WriteAll(ByVal directory As String, ByVal topLevelFilename As String) _
       As DiscoveryClientResultCollection
End Class
```

Hierarchy: System.Object → System.MarshalByRefObject → System.ComponentModel.Component (System.ComponentModel.IComponent , System.IDisposable)→ System.Web.Services.Protocols.WebClientProtocol → System.Web.Services.Protocols.HttpWebClientProtocol → DiscoveryClientProtocol

DiscoveryClientProtocol.DiscoveryClientResultsFile   NotInheritable Class

System.Web.Services.Discovery (system.web.services.dll)

This class provides the results of the DiscoveryClientProtocol.WriteAll() method. The System.Web.Services.Discovery.DiscoveryClientProtocol.DiscoveryClientResultsFile.Results property provides a collection of DiscoveryClientResult objects with information about all references that were written to disk.

```
Public NotInheritable Class DiscoveryClientProtocol.DiscoveryClientResultsFile
' Public Constructors
   Public Sub New()
' Public Instance Properties
   Public ReadOnly Property Results As DiscoveryClientResultCollection
End Class
```

DiscoveryClientReferenceCollection

System.Web.Services.Discovery (system.web.services.dll)

This class represents a collection of discovery document references (links to WSDL service descriptions, XSD files, or other discovery documents), much like the DiscoveryClientResultCollection class. However, the DiscoveryClientResultCollection class provides the discovery references from a single discovery document, while DiscoveryClientReferenceCollection is usually used to provide the aggregated references from multiple documents. The DiscoveryClientReferenceCollection class is used by the DiscoveryClientProtocol.References property.

```
Public NotInheritable Class DiscoveryClientReferenceCollection : Inherits DictionaryBase
' Public Constructors
    Public Sub New()
' Public Instance Properties
    Public Default Property Item (ByVal url As String) As DiscoveryReference
    Public ReadOnly Property Keys As ICollection Implements IDictionary.Keys
    Public ReadOnly Property Values As ICollection Implements IDictionary.Values
' Public Instance Methods
    Public Sub Add(ByVal value As DiscoveryReference)
    Public Sub Add(ByVal url As String, ByVal value As DiscoveryReference)
    Public Function Contains(ByVal url As String) As Boolean
    Public Sub Remove(ByVal url As String)
End Class
```

Hierarchy: System.Object → System.Collections.DictionaryBase (System.Collections.IDictionary , System.Collections.ICollection , System.Collections.IEnumerable)→ DiscoveryClientReferenceCollection

DiscoveryClientResult

System.Web.Services.Discovery (system.web.services.dll)

This class represents some of the details in a discovery document reference. It's used in conjunction with the DiscoveryClientProtocol.WriteAll() method, which writes the references from multiple discovery documents to disk in one batch operation, and summarizes the results with a collection of DiscoveryClientResult objects. You can use the Filename property to determine the file that the corresponding discovery reference is saved in.

```
Public NotInheritable Class DiscoveryClientResult
' Public Constructors
    Public Sub New()
    Public Sub New(ByVal referenceType As Type, ByVal url As String, ByVal filename As String)
' Public Instance Properties
    Public Property Filename As String
    Public Property ReferenceTypeName As String
    Public Property Url As String
End Class
```

DiscoveryClientResultCollection

System.Web.Services.Discovery (system.web.services.dll)

This class contains a collection of DiscoveryClientResult objects. It's used by the the System.Web.Services.Discovery.DiscoveryClientProtocol.DiscoveryClientResultsFile.Results property in conjunction with the DiscoveryClientProtocol.WriteAll() method, and can contain information about the references from multiple discovery documents.

```
Public NotInheritable Class DiscoveryClientResultCollection : Inherits CollectionBase
' Public Constructors
    Public Sub New()
' Public Instance Properties
    Public Default Property Item (ByVal i As Integer) As DiscoveryClientResult
' Public Instance Methods
    Public Function Add(ByVal value As DiscoveryClientResult) As Integer
    Public Function Contains(ByVal value As DiscoveryClientResult) As Boolean
    Public Sub Remove(ByVal value As DiscoveryClientResult)
End Class
```

Hierarchy: System.Object → System.Collections.CollectionBase (System.Collections.IList , System.Collections.ICollection , System.Collections.IEnumerable)→ DiscoveryClientResultCollection

DiscoveryDocument
NotInheritable Class

System.Web.Services.Discovery (system.web.services.dll)

This class represents a discovery document (usually found as a *.disco* or *.vsdisco* file). The discovery document is an XML document that contains references to any number of web services (actually, it points to their WSDL service descriptions), XSD files, or other discovery documents. The References property contains a list of the discover document references. The Read() and Write() methods serialize or deserialize the DiscoveryDocument to or from a System.IO.Stream, System.IO.TextWriter, or System.Xml.XmlWriter.

```
Public NotInheritable Class DiscoveryDocument
' Public Constructors
    Public Sub New()
' Public Shared Fields
    public const Namespace As String                        =http://schemas.xmlsoap.org/disco/
' Public Instance Properties
    Public ReadOnly Property References As IList
' Public Shared Methods
    Public Shared Function CanRead(ByVal xmlReader As System.Xml.XmlReader) As Boolean
    Public Shared Function Read(ByVal stream As System.IO.Stream) As DiscoveryDocument
    Public Shared Function Read(ByVal reader As System.IO.TextReader) As DiscoveryDocument
    Public Shared Function Read(ByVal xmlReader As System.Xml.XmlReader) As DiscoveryDocument
' Public Instance Methods
    Public Sub Write(ByVal stream As System.IO.Stream)
    Public Sub Write(ByVal writer As System.IO.TextWriter)
    Public Sub Write(ByVal writer As System.Xml.XmlWriter)
End Class
```

DiscoveryDocumentLinksPattern
Class

System.Web.Services.Discovery (system.web.services.dll)

This type is used by the .NET framework and is never used directly by your code.

```
Public Class DiscoveryDocumentLinksPattern : Inherits DiscoverySearchPattern
' Public Constructors
    Public Sub New()
' Public Instance Properties
    Overrides Public ReadOnly Property Pattern As String
' Public Instance Methods
    Overrides Public Function GetDiscoveryReference(ByVal filename As String) As DiscoveryReference
End Class
```

DiscoveryDocumentReference

NotInheritable Class

System.Web.Services.Discovery (system.web.services.dll)

This class represents a discovery document reference to another discovery document. The Ref property provides a string with the discovery document's URL. The System.Web.Services.DiscoveryDocumentReference.Documents property returns another DiscoveryDocument object that represents the discovery document and its references.

```
Public NotInheritable Class DiscoveryDocumentReference : Inherits DiscoveryReference
' Public Constructors
   Public Sub New()
   Public Sub New(ByVal href As String)
' Public Instance Properties
   Overrides Public ReadOnly Property DefaultFilename As String
   Public ReadOnly Property Document As DiscoveryDocument
   Public Property Ref As String
   Overrides Public Property Url As String
' Public Instance Methods
   Overrides Public Function ReadDocument(ByVal stream As System.IO.Stream) As Object
   Public Sub ResolveAll()
   Overrides Public Sub WriteDocument(ByVal document As Object, ByVal stream As System.IO.Stream)
' Protected Instance Methods
   Overrides Protected Friend Sub Resolve(ByVal contentType As String, ByVal stream As System.IO.Stream)
End Class
```

Hierarchy: System.Object → DiscoveryReference → DiscoveryDocumentReference

DiscoveryDocumentSearchPattern

NotInheritable Class

System.Web.Services.Discovery (system.web.services.dll)

This type is used by the .NET framework and is never used directly by your code.

```
Public NotInheritable Class DiscoveryDocumentSearchPattern : Inherits DiscoverySearchPattern
' Public Constructors
   Public Sub New()
' Public Instance Properties
   Overrides Public ReadOnly Property Pattern As String
' Public Instance Methods
   Overrides Public Function GetDiscoveryReference(ByVal filename As String) As DiscoveryReference
End Class
```

Hierarchy: System.Object → DiscoverySearchPattern → DiscoveryDocumentSearchPattern

DiscoveryExceptionDictionary

NotInheritable Class

System.Web.Services.Discovery (system.web.services.dll)

This class is a collection of exception objects. It is used by the DiscoveryClientProtocol.Errors property to represent all errors that occured during the discovery process.

```
Public NotInheritable Class DiscoveryExceptionDictionary : Inherits DictionaryBase
' Public Constructors
   Public Sub New()
' Public Instance Properties
```

```
    Public Default Property Item (ByVal url As String) As Exception
    Public ReadOnly Property Keys As ICollection Implements IDictionary.Keys
    Public ReadOnly Property Values As ICollection Implements IDictionary.Values
' Public Instance Methods
    Public Sub Add(ByVal url As String, ByVal value As Exception)
    Public Function Contains(ByVal url As String) As Boolean
    Public Sub Remove(ByVal url As String)
End Class
```

Hierarchy: System.Object → System.Collections.DictionaryBase (System.Collections.IDictionary , System.Collections.ICollection , System.Collections.IEnumerable) → DiscoveryExceptionDictionary

DiscoveryReference   MustInherit Class

System.Web.Services.Discovery (system.web.services.dll)

A discovery document can refer to three things: WSDL service descriptions, XSD documents, or other discovery files. These references are represented by three different classes in this namespace (ContractReference, DiscoveryDocumentReference, and SchemaReference), all of which inherit from this abstract base class.

```
Public MustInherit Class DiscoveryReference
' Protected Constructors
    Protected Sub New()
' Public Instance Properties
    Public Property ClientProtocol As DiscoveryClientProtocol
    Overridable Public ReadOnly Property DefaultFilename As String
    MustInherit Public Property Url As String
' Protected Shared Methods
    Shared Protected Function FilenameFromUrl(ByVal url As String) As String
' Public Instance Methods
    MustInherit Public Function ReadDocument(ByVal stream As System.IO.Stream) As Object
    Public Sub Resolve()
    MustInherit Public Sub WriteDocument(ByVal document As Object, ByVal stream As System.IO.Stream)
' Protected Instance Methods
    MustInherit Protected Friend Sub Resolve(ByVal contentType As String, ByVal stream As System.IO.Stream)
End Class
```

DiscoveryReferenceCollection   NotInheritable Class

System.Web.Services.Discovery (system.web.services.dll)

This class provides a collection of discovery references (instances of one of the three classes that inherit from DiscoveryReference). It can be used to represent all the references in a given discovery document.

```
Public NotInheritable Class DiscoveryReferenceCollection : Inherits CollectionBase
' Public Constructors
    Public Sub New()
' Public Instance Properties
    Public Default Property Item (ByVal i As Integer) As DiscoveryReference
' Public Instance Methods
    Public Function Add(ByVal value As DiscoveryReference) As Integer
    Public Function Contains(ByVal value As DiscoveryReference) As Boolean
    Public Sub Remove(ByVal value As DiscoveryReference)
End Class
```

Hierarchy: System.Object → System.Collections.CollectionBase (System.Collections.IList , System.Collections.ICollection , System.Collections.IEnumerable) → DiscoveryReferenceCollection

DiscoveryRequestHandler   NotInheritable Class

System.Web.Services.Discovery (system.web.services.dll)

This type is used by the .NET framework and is never used directly by your code.

Public NotInheritable Class **DiscoveryRequestHandler** : Implements System.Web.IHttpHandler
' Public Constructors
  Public Sub **New**()
' Public Instance Properties
  Public ReadOnly Property **IsReusable** As Boolean Implements IHttpHandler.IsReusable
' Public Instance Methods
  Public Sub **ProcessRequest**(ByVal context As System.Web.HttpContext) _
    Implements IHttpHandler.ProcessRequest
End Class

DiscoverySearchPattern   MustInherit Class

System.Web.Services.Discovery (system.web.services.dll)

This type is used by the .NET framework and is never used directly by your code.

Public MustInherit Class **DiscoverySearchPattern**
' Protected Constructors
  Protected Sub **New**()
' Public Instance Properties
  MustInherit Public ReadOnly Property **Pattern** As String
' Public Instance Methods
  MustInherit Public Function **GetDiscoveryReference**(ByVal filename As String) As DiscoveryReference
End Class

DynamicDiscoveryDocument   NotInheritable Class

System.Web.Services.Discovery (system.web.services.dll)

This type is used by the .NET framework and is never used directly by your code.

Public NotInheritable Class **DynamicDiscoveryDocument**
' Public Constructors
  Public Sub **New**()
' Public Shared Fields
  public const **Namespace** As String   =urn:schemas-dynamicdiscovery:disco.2000-03-17
' Public Instance Properties
  Public Property **ExcludePaths** As ExcludePathInfo()
' Public Shared Methods
  Public Shared Function **Load**(ByVal stream As System.IO.Stream) As DynamicDiscoveryDocument
' Public Instance Methods
  Public Sub **Write**(ByVal stream As System.IO.Stream)
End Class

ExcludePathInfo   NotInheritable Class

System.Web.Services.Discovery (system.web.services.dll)

This type is used by the .NET framework and is never used directly by your code.

Public NotInheritable Class **ExcludePathInfo**

```
' Public Constructors
   Public Sub New()
   Public Sub New(ByVal path As String)
' Public Instance Properties
   Public Property Path As String
End Class
```

SchemaReference   NotInheritable Class

System.Web.Services.Discovery (system.web.services.dll)

This class represents a discovery document reference to an XML Schema Definition (XSD) document. This is the least common type of reference in a discovery document. The Ref property provides a string with the XSD file's URL. The System.Web.Services.Discovery.Schema property returns a full System.Xml.Schema.XmlSchema object that represents the XSD document.

```
Public NotInheritable Class SchemaReference : Inherits DiscoveryReference
' Public Constructors
   Public Sub New()
   Public Sub New(ByVal url As String)
' Public Shared Fields
   public const Namespace As String                =http://schemas.xmlsoap.org/disco/schema/
' Public Instance Properties
   Overrides Public ReadOnly Property DefaultFilename As String
   Public Property Ref As String
   Public ReadOnly Property Schema As XmlSchema
   Public Property TargetNamespace As String
   Overrides Public Property Url As String
' Public Instance Methods
   Overrides Public Function ReadDocument(ByVal stream As System.IO.Stream) As Object
   Overrides Public Sub WriteDocument(ByVal document As Object, ByVal stream As System.IO.Stream)
' Protected Instance Methods
   Overrides Protected Friend Sub Resolve(ByVal contentType As String, ByVal stream As System.IO.Stream)
End Class
```

Hierarchy: System.Object → DiscoveryReference → SchemaReference

SoapBinding   NotInheritable Class

System.Web.Services.Discovery (system.web.services.dll)

This class represents a SOAP binding in a discovery document. You could add a SOAP binding for versioning (or to indicate additional information about a group of web services). SOAP bindings are specified in the discovery document by adding a SOAP XML element with an XML namespace equal to the Namespace constant.

```
Public NotInheritable Class SoapBinding
' Public Constructors
   Public Sub New()
' Public Shared Fields
   public const Namespace As String                =http://schemas.xmlsoap.org/disco/soap/
' Public Instance Properties
   Public Property Address As String
   Public Property Binding As XmlQualifiedName
End Class
```

XmlSchemaSearchPattern

System.Web.Services.Discovery (system.web.services.dll)

This type is used by the .NET framework and is never used directly by your code.

Public NotInheritable Class **XmlSchemaSearchPattern** : Inherits DiscoverySearchPattern

' Public Constructors

   Public Sub **New**()

' Public Instance Properties

   Overrides Public ReadOnly Property **Pattern** As String

' Public Instance Methods

   Overrides Public Function **GetDiscoveryReference**(ByVal filename As String) As DiscoveryReference

End Class

Hierarchy: System.Object → DiscoverySearchPattern → XmlSchemaSearchPattern

CHAPTER 32

The System.Web.Services.Protocols Namespace

The System.Web.Services.Protocols namespace contains types that support communication between a client and a web service. They define protocols that encode and transmit data across an Internet connection, including HTTP GET, HTTP POST, and SOAP.

The primary use of these types is to support the proxy class that manages the communication between web service and client. You can create this proxy class automatically by using the Visual Studio .NET IDE or the *WSDL.exe* command-line utility, or you can code it by hand. This class will inherit from HttpGetClientProtocol, HttpPostClientProtocol, or SoapHttpClientProtocol (which is the most common choice and the default for automatically generated proxy classes). Other important types in this namespace include the attributes that you use to set the encoding for SOAP request and response messages, such as SoapDocumentMethodAttribute.

This class also provides types you can use to create SOAP extensions. Typically, SOAP extensions are used to directly access the SOAP messages exchanged between web services and clients before they are sent or deserialized into objects. The SoapExtension class and SoapExtensionAttribute are the basic building blocks for SOAP extensions. You can also use SoapHeader and SoapHeaderAttribute classes to create custom SOAP headers for your message. You can then create web service methods that require specific custom SOAP headers. Figure 32-1 and Figure 32-2 show the types in this namespace.

AnyReturnReader   Class

System.Web.Services.Protocols (system.web.services.dll)

This class supports the .NET Framework infrastructure. You do not need to use it directly in your code.

```
Public Class AnyReturnReader : Inherits MimeReturnReader
' Public Constructors
   Public Sub New()
' Public Instance Methods
   Overrides Public Function GetInitializer(ByVal methodInfo As LogicalMethodInfo) As Object
   Overrides Public Sub Initialize(ByVal o As Object)
   Overrides Public Function Read(ByVal response As System.Net.WebResponse, _
      ByVal responseStream As System.IO.Stream) As Object
End Class
```

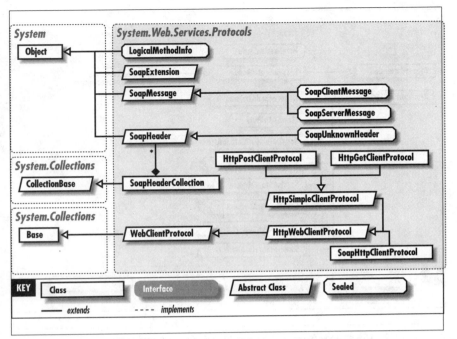

Figure 32-1: Some types from the System.Web.Services.Protocols namespace

Hierarchy: System.Object → MimeFormatter → MimeReturnReader → AnyReturnReader

HtmlFormParameterReader
Class

System.Web.Services.Protocols (system.web.services.dll)

This class supports the .NET Framework infrastructure. You do not need to use it directly in your code.

```
Public Class HtmlFormParameterReader : Inherits ValueCollectionParameterReader
' Public Constructors
   Public Sub New()
' Public Instance Methods
   Overrides Public Function Read(ByVal request As System.Web.HttpRequest) As Object()
End Class
```

Hierarchy: System.Object → MimeFormatter → MimeParameterReader → ValueCollectionParameterReader → HtmlFormParameterReader

HtmlFormParameterWriter
Class

System.Web.Services.Protocols (system.web.services.dll)

This class supports the .NET Framework infrastructure. You do not need to use it directly in your code.

```
Public Class HtmlFormParameterWriter : Inherits UrlEncodedParameterWriter
' Public Constructors
   Public Sub New()
```

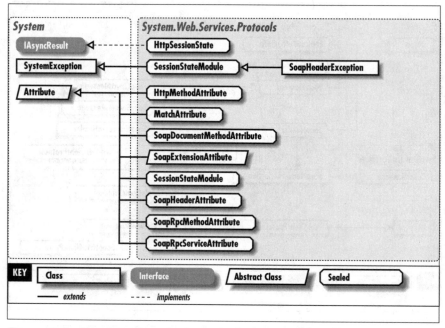

Figure 32-2: More types from the System.Web.Services.Protocols namespace

```
' Public Instance Properties
    Overrides Public ReadOnly Property UsesWriteRequest As Boolean
' Public Instance Methods
    Overrides Public Sub InitializeRequest(ByVal request As System.Net.WebRequest, ByVal values As Object())
    Overrides Public Sub WriteRequest(ByVal requestStream As System.IO.Stream, ByVal values As Object())
End Class
```

Hierarchy: System.Object → MimeFormatter → MimeParameterWriter →
UrlEncodedParameterWriter → HtmlFormParameterWriter

HttpGetClientProtocol
Class

System.Web.Services.Protocols (system.web.services.dll)　　　*marshal by reference, disposable*

You can inherit from this class to create a proxy class that communicates by using the
HTTP GET protocol, which sends parameters in the query string portion of the URL.
When using this class, you must use the corresponding HttpMethodAttribute to bind proxy
class methods to web service methods.

```
Public Class HttpGetClientProtocol : Inherits HttpSimpleClientProtocol
' Public Constructors
    Public Sub New()
' Protected Instance Methods
    Overrides Protected Function GetWebRequest(ByVal uri As Uri) As WebRequest
End Class
```

Hierarchy: System.Object → System.MarshalByRefObject → System.ComponentModel.Component
(System.ComponentModel.IComponent , System.IDisposable)→ WebClientProtocol →
HttpWebClientProtocol → HttpSimpleClientProtocol → HttpGetClientProtocol

HttpMethodAttribute
NotInheritable Class

System.Web.Services.Protocols (system.web.services.dll)

This attribute is used to bind methods in an HttpGetClientProtocol or HttpPostClientProtocol proxy class to web service methods.

The ParameterFormatter property specifies how the proxy encodes parameters before sending them to a web service method. The ReturnFormatter property specifies how the proxy class decodes the web method's return value. Both values must be set, as there is no default value. Set ReturnFormatter to the UrlParameterWriter type if you are using HTTP GET or the HtmlFormParameterWriter type if you are using HTTP POST. Always set ParameterFormatter to the XmlReturnReader type. An example attribute declaration for HTTP GET is <HttpMethodAttribute(GetType(XmlReturnReader), GetType(UrlParameterWriter))>.

```
Public NotInheritable Class HttpMethodAttribute : Inherits Attribute
' Public Constructors
   Public Sub New()
   Public Sub New(ByVal returnFormatter As Type, ByVal parameterFormatter As Type)
' Public Instance Properties
   Public Property ParameterFormatter As Type
   Public Property ReturnFormatter As Type
End Class
```

Hierarchy: System.Object → System.Attribute → HttpMethodAttribute

Valid On: Method

HttpPostClientProtocol
Class

System.Web.Services.Protocols (system.web.services.dll)   *marshal by reference, disposable*

You can inherit from this class to create a proxy class that communicates by using the HTTP POST protocol, which encodes parameters in the body of the HTTP request. When using this class, you must use the corresponding HttpMethodAttribute to bind proxy class methods to web service methods.

```
Public Class HttpPostClientProtocol : Inherits HttpSimpleClientProtocol
' Public Constructors
   Public Sub New()
' Protected Instance Methods
   Overrides Protected Function GetWebRequest(ByVal uri As Uri) As WebRequest
End Class
```

Hierarchy: System.Object → System.MarshalByRefObject → System.ComponentModel.Component (System.ComponentModel.IComponent , System.IDisposable)→ WebClientProtocol → HttpWebClientProtocol → HttpSimpleClientProtocol → HttpPostClientProtocol

HttpSimpleClientProtocol
MustInherit Class

System.Web.Services.Protocols (system.web.services.dll)   *marshal by reference, disposable*

This abstract class provides basic functionality for communicating with a web service over HTTP. This class is inherited by HttpGetClientProtocol and HttpPostClientProtocol, both of which your proxy classes can derive from directly. Parameters for an HTTP proxy are encoded by using application/x-www-form-urlencoded content type.

```
Public MustInherit Class HttpSimpleClientProtocol : Inherits HttpWebClientProtocol
' Protected Constructors
   Protected Sub New()
```

' *Protected Instance Methods*
    Protected Function **BeginInvoke**(ByVal methodName As String, ByVal requestUrl As String, _
    ByVal parameters As Object(), ByVal callback As AsyncCallback, ByVal asyncState As Object) As IAsyncResult
    Protected Function **EndInvoke**(ByVal asyncResult As IAsyncResult) As Object
    Protected Function **Invoke**(ByVal methodName As String, ByVal requestUrl As String, ByVal parameters As Object()) _
    As Object
End Class

Hierarchy: System.Object → System.MarshalByRefObject → System.ComponentModel.Component
(System.ComponentModel.IComponent , System.IDisposable)→ WebClientProtocol →
HttpWebClientProtocol → HttpSimpleClientProtocol

HttpWebClientProtocol   MustInherit Class

System.Web.Services.Protocols (system.web.services.dll)   *marshal by reference, disposable*

This abstract base class provides basic functionality for communication between a web
service and proxy class. The System.Web.Services.Discovery.DiscoveryClientProtocol, HttpSimple-
ClientProtocol, and SoapHttpClientProtocol classes all inherit from HttpWebClientProtocol. The
proxy class inherits from one of these derived classes, depending on which transmission protocol it uses.

You can use the Proxy property to connect to a web service through a firewall, as in
WS.Proxy = New WebProxy("http://proxyserver:80", True). This property will override the computer's default Internet settings. You can also set the AllowAutoRedirect property to allow a
client to follow server redirects. This is False by default for security reasons. The UserA-
gent property is automatically set to something like "MS Web Services Client Protocol
1.0.2509.0," where 1.0.2509.0 is the Common Language Runtime version.

The CookieContainer property is important when connecting to a web service that uses
ASP.NET's session state facility. To allow a proxy class to reuse the same session on
subsequent calls, you must explicitly create a new (empty) System.Net.CookieContainer
object and assign it to the CookieContainer property. This allows the proxy class to store
the session cookie with each call. If you want multiple proxy class instances to access
the same session, or if you want to recreate a proxy class and use a previous session
that has not yet timed out, you must take extra steps to transfer or store the Sys-
tem.Net.CookieContainer object.

Public MustInherit Class **HttpWebClientProtocol** : Inherits WebClientProtocol
' *Protected Constructors*
    Protected Sub **New**()
' *Public Instance Properties*
    Public Property **AllowAutoRedirect** As Boolean
    Public ReadOnly Property **ClientCertificates** As X509CertificateCollection
    Public Property **CookieContainer** As CookieContainer
    Public Property **Proxy** As IWebProxy
    Public Property **UserAgent** As String
' *Protected Instance Methods*
    Overrides Protected Function **GetWebRequest**(ByVal uri As Uri) As WebRequest
    Overrides Protected Function **GetWebResponse**(ByVal request As System.Net.WebRequest) As WebResponse
    Overrides Protected Function **GetWebResponse**(ByVal request As System.Net.WebRequest, _
    ByVal result As IAsyncResult) As WebResponse
End Class

Hierarchy: System.Object → System.MarshalByRefObject → System.ComponentModel.Component
(System.ComponentModel.IComponent , System.IDisposable)→ WebClientProtocol →
HttpWebClientProtocol

LogicalMethodInfo

System.Web.Services.Protocols (system.web.services.dll)

A LogicalMethodInfo object is provided to the SoapExtension.GetInitializer() method. This object contains information about the web service or proxy class method where the custom SoapExtensionAttribute is applied.

```
Public NotInheritable Class LogicalMethodInfo
' Public Constructors
    Public Sub New(ByVal methodInfo As System.Reflection.MethodInfo)
' Public Instance Properties
    Public ReadOnly Property AsyncCallbackParameter As ParameterInfo
    Public ReadOnly Property AsyncResultParameter As ParameterInfo
    Public ReadOnly Property AsyncStateParameter As ParameterInfo
    Public ReadOnly Property BeginMethodInfo As MethodInfo
    Public ReadOnly Property CustomAttributeProvider As ICustomAttributeProvider
    Public ReadOnly Property DeclaringType As Type
    Public ReadOnly Property EndMethodInfo As MethodInfo
    Public ReadOnly Property InParameters As ParameterInfo()
    Public ReadOnly Property IsAsync As Boolean
    Public ReadOnly Property IsVoid As Boolean
    Public ReadOnly Property MethodInfo As MethodInfo
    Public ReadOnly Property Name As String
    Public ReadOnly Property OutParameters As ParameterInfo()
    Public ReadOnly Property Parameters As ParameterInfo()
    Public ReadOnly Property ReturnType As Type
    Public ReadOnly Property ReturnTypeCustomAttributeProvider As ICustomAttributeProvider
' Public Shared Methods
    Public Shared Function Create(ByVal methodInfos As System.Reflection.MethodInfo()) As LogicalMethodInfo()
    Public Shared Function Create(ByVal methodInfos As System.Reflection.MethodInfo(), _
        ByVal types As LogicalMethodTypes) As LogicalMethodInfo()
    Public Shared Function IsBeginMethod(ByVal methodInfo As System.Reflection.MethodInfo) As Boolean
    Public Shared Function IsEndMethod(ByVal methodInfo As System.Reflection.MethodInfo) As Boolean
' Public Instance Methods
    Public Function BeginInvoke(ByVal target As Object, ByVal values As Object(), ByVal callback As AsyncCallback, _
        ByVal asyncState As Object) As IAsyncResult
    Public Function EndInvoke(ByVal target As Object, ByVal asyncResult As IAsyncResult) As Object()
    Public Function GetCustomAttribute(ByVal type As Type) As Object
    Public Function GetCustomAttributes(ByVal type As Type) As Object()
    Public Function Invoke(ByVal target As Object, ByVal values As Object()) As Object()
    Overrides Public Function ToString() As String
End Class
```

LogicalMethodTypes

System.Web.Services.Protocols (system.web.services.dll)

This enumeration specifies whether a web service method was invoked synchronously or asynchronously with the corresponding "Begin" method.

```
Public Enum LogicalMethodTypes
    Sync = 1
    Async = 2
End Enum
```

Hierarchy: System.Object → System.ValueType → System.Enum (System.IComparable , System.IFormattable , System.IConvertible) → LogicalMethodTypes

MatchAttribute
NotInheritable Class

System.Web.Services.Protocols (system.web.services.dll)

.NET allows you to create screen-scraping web services that search the HTML content on a web page by using a regular expression. To create a pattern matching web service, you need to create a WSDL document with <match> elements. These match elements specify the regular expression to use when parsing the contents of the page and how many matches should be returned. When the client builds the proxy class for a pattern-matching web service, it will include a MatchAttribute that describes the match elements you added to the WSDL document.

The Pattern property specfies the regular expression pattern to use when searching the web page. IgnoreCase specifies whether the regular expression should be run in case-sensitive mode (the default). MaxRepeats specifies the maximum number of matches that will be returned (-1, the default, indicates all). Finally, Group specifies a grouping of related matches, while Capture specifies the index of a match within a group.

```
Public NotInheritable Class MatchAttribute : Inherits Attribute
' Public Constructors
   Public Sub New(ByVal pattern As String)
' Public Instance Properties
   Public Property Capture As Integer
   Public Property Group As Integer
   Public Property IgnoreCase As Boolean
   Public Property MaxRepeats As Integer
   Public Property Pattern As String
End Class
```

Hierarchy: System.Object → System.Attribute → MatchAttribute

Valid On: All

MimeFormatter
MustInherit Class

System.Web.Services.Protocols (system.web.services.dll)

This class supports the .NET Framework infrastructure. You do not need to use it directly in your code.

```
Public MustInherit Class MimeFormatter
' Protected Constructors
   Protected Sub New()
' Public Shared Methods
   Public Shared Function CreateInstance(ByVal type As Type, ByVal initializer As Object) As MimeFormatter
   Public Shared Function GetInitializer(ByVal type As Type, ByVal methodInfo As LogicalMethodInfo) As Object
   Public Shared Function GetInitializers(ByVal type As Type, ByVal methodInfos As LogicalMethodInfo()) _
      As Object()
' Public Instance Methods
   MustInherit Public Function GetInitializer(ByVal methodInfo As LogicalMethodInfo) As Object
   Overridable Public Function GetInitializers(ByVal methodInfos As LogicalMethodInfo()) As Object()
   MustInherit Public Sub Initialize(ByVal initializer As Object)
End Class
```

MimeParameterReader
MustInherit Class

System.Web.Services.Protocols (system.web.services.dll)

This class supports the .NET Framework infrastructure. You do not need to use it directly in your code.

Public MustInherit Class **MimeParameterReader** : Inherits MimeFormatter
' *Protected Constructors*
   Protected Sub **New**()
' *Public Instance Methods*
   MustInherit Public Function **Read**(ByVal request As System.Web.HttpRequest) As Object()
End Class

Hierarchy: System.Object → MimeFormatter → MimeParameterReader

MimeParameterWriter
MustInherit Class

System.Web.Services.Protocols (system.web.services.dll)

This class supports the .NET Framework infrastructure. You do not need to use it directly in your code.

Public MustInherit Class **MimeParameterWriter** : Inherits MimeFormatter
' *Protected Constructors*
   Protected Sub **New**()
' *Public Instance Properties*
   Overridable Public Property **RequestEncoding** As Encoding
   Overridable Public ReadOnly Property **UsesWriteRequest** As Boolean
' *Public Instance Methods*
   Overridable Public Function **GetRequestUrl**(ByVal url As String, ByVal parameters As Object()) As String
   Overridable Public Sub **InitializeRequest**(ByVal request As System.Net.WebRequest, ByVal values As Object())
   Overridable Public Sub **WriteRequest**(ByVal requestStream As System.IO.Stream, ByVal values As Object())
End Class

Hierarchy: System.Object → MimeFormatter → MimeParameterWriter

MimeReturnReader
MustInherit Class

System.Web.Services.Protocols (system.web.services.dll)

This class supports the .NET Framework infrastructure. You do not need to use it directly in your code.

Public MustInherit Class **MimeReturnReader** : Inherits MimeFormatter
' *Protected Constructors*
   Protected Sub **New**()
' *Public Instance Methods*
   MustInherit Public Function **Read**(ByVal response As System.Net.WebResponse, _
      ByVal responseStream As System.IO.Stream) As Object
End Class

Hierarchy: System.Object → MimeFormatter → MimeReturnReader

NopReturnReader
Class

System.Web.Services.Protocols (system.web.services.dll)

This class supports the .NET Framework infrastructure. You do not need to use it directly in your code.

Public Class **NopReturnReader** : Inherits MimeReturnReader
' *Public Constructors*
   Public Sub **New**()

' *Public Instance Methods*
   Overrides Public Function **GetInitializer**(ByVal methodInfo As LogicalMethodInfo) As Object
   Overrides Public Sub **Initialize**(ByVal initializer As Object)
   Overrides Public Function **Read**(ByVal response As System.Net.WebResponse, _
     ByVal responseStream As System.IO.Stream) As Object
End Class

Hierarchy: System.Object → MimeFormatter → MimeReturnReader → NopReturnReader

PatternMatcher
NotInheritable Class

System.Web.Services.Protocols (system.web.services.dll)

This class supports the .NET Framework infrastructure. You do not need to use it directly in your code.

Public NotInheritable Class **PatternMatcher**
' *Public Constructors*
   Public Sub **New**(ByVal type As Type)
' *Public Instance Methods*
   Public Function **Match**(ByVal text As String) As Object
End Class

SoapClientMessage
NotInheritable Class

System.Web.Services.Protocols (system.web.services.dll)

This class represents a SOAP request sent by a proxy client or SOAP response received by a proxy client. It inherits from SoapMessage, which defines most of the functionality used for SOAP messages.

Public NotInheritable Class **SoapClientMessage** : Inherits SoapMessage
' *Public Instance Properties*
   Overrides Public ReadOnly Property **Action** As String
   Public ReadOnly Property **Client** As SoapHttpClientProtocol
   Overrides Public ReadOnly Property **MethodInfo** As LogicalMethodInfo
   Overrides Public ReadOnly Property **OneWay** As Boolean
   Overrides Public ReadOnly Property **Url** As String
' *Protected Instance Methods*
   Overrides Protected Sub **EnsureInStage**()
   Overrides Protected Sub **EnsureOutStage**()
End Class

Hierarchy: System.Object → SoapMessage → SoapClientMessage

SoapDocumentMethodAttribute
NotInheritable Class

System.Web.Services.Protocols (system.web.services.dll)

This attribute is used to specify the encoding for SOAP request and response messages. You can apply this attribute to methods in a web service or in methods in a proxy class that derives from SoapHttpClientProtocol (where it's required to bind the messages to the appropriate web method). You use this attribute, instead of SoapRpcMethodAttribute, when you want to use the Document encoding standard.

There are two options for encoding XML information in a SOAP message: RPC and Document. ASP.NET's default is Document. The Document style specifies that messages are encoded as described in an XSD schema. When Document style is used, the WSDL document defines the XSD schemas for SOAP requests and SOAP responses. For more information on the SOAP specification, see *http://www.w3.org/TR/SOAP/*.

One reason you might want to apply this attribute to a web method is to explicitly set the OneWay property. For example, by adding <SoapDocumentMethod(OneWay := True)> before a web method, you ensure that the method will return immediately and can finish processing asynchronously. This ensures that the client doesn't need to wait for the method to return or call it asynchronously. However, this web method will not be able to access the System.Web.HttpContext for the client and will not be able to set a return value. If the client needs to know about the success or result of such a web method, you will have to implement a second method and use some type of ticket-issuing system to keep track of the outstanding request.

```
Public NotInheritable Class SoapDocumentMethodAttribute : Inherits Attribute
' Public Constructors
   Public Sub New()
   Public Sub New(ByVal action As String)
' Public Instance Properties
   Public Property Action As String
   Public Property Binding As String
   Public Property OneWay As Boolean
   Public Property ParameterStyle As SoapParameterStyle
   Public Property RequestElementName As String
   Public Property RequestNamespace As String
   Public Property ResponseElementName As String
   Public Property ResponseNamespace As String
   Public Property Use As SoapBindingUse
End Class
```

Hierarchy: System.Object → System.Attribute → SoapDocumentMethodAttribute

Valid On: Method

SoapDocumentServiceAttribute   NotInheritable Class

System.Web.Services.Protocols (system.web.services.dll)

This attribute can be applied to web service's class declaration. It specifies that the default encoding for SOAP request and response messages will be Document. The client can override this default by using the SoapRpcMethodAttribute. This attribute is rarely used because the default in ASP.NET proxy classes is already Document encoding.

```
Public NotInheritable Class SoapDocumentServiceAttribute : Inherits Attribute
' Public Constructors
   Public Sub New()
   Public Sub New(ByVal use As System.Web.Services.Description.SoapBindingUse)
   Public Sub New(ByVal use As System.Web.Services.Description.SoapBindingUse, _
      ByVal paramStyle As SoapParameterStyle)
' Public Instance Properties
   Public Property ParameterStyle As SoapParameterStyle
   Public Property RoutingStyle As SoapServiceRoutingStyle
   Public Property Use As SoapBindingUse
End Class
```

Protocols Namespace

Hierarchy: System.Object → System.Attribute → SoapDocumentServiceAttribute

Valid On: Class

SoapException Class

System.Web.Services.Protocols (system.web.services.dll)

This class is a generic exception for SOAP-related problems. The Common Language Runtime can throw a SoapException when it encounters an incorrectly formatted SOAP message. Also, any error that occurs inside a web service method is caught on the server and returned to the client as a SoapException. ASP.NET will then set the SoapException property (which identifies the web service URL) and the Code property (using one of the fault code fields) automatically.

When you are creating your own web methods, you may need to provide more information about exceptions. To do so, catch any server errors and create and throw a corresponding SoapException object. You can specify application-specific details about the error by adding custom XML content to the Detail property.

```
Public Class SoapException : Inherits SystemException
' Public Constructors
    Public Sub New(ByVal message As String, ByVal code As System.Xml.XmlQualifiedName)
    Public Sub New(ByVal message As String, ByVal code As System.Xml.XmlQualifiedName, _
        ByVal innerException As Exception)
    Public Sub New(ByVal message As String, ByVal code As System.Xml.XmlQualifiedName, ByVal actor As String)
    Public Sub New(ByVal message As String, ByVal code As System.Xml.XmlQualifiedName, ByVal actor As String, _
        ByVal innerException As Exception)
    Public Sub New(ByVal message As String, ByVal code As System.Xml.XmlQualifiedName, ByVal actor As String, _
        ByVal detail As System.Xml.XmlNode)
    Public Sub New(ByVal message As String, ByVal code As System.Xml.XmlQualifiedName, ByVal actor As String, _
        ByVal detail As System.Xml.XmlNode, ByVal innerException As Exception)
' Public Shared Fields
    public Shared ReadOnly ClientFaultCode                    =http://schemas.xmlsoap.org/soap/envelope/:Client _
        As XmlQualifiedName
    public Shared ReadOnly DetailElementName As XmlQualifiedName                           =detail
    public Shared ReadOnly                     =http://schemas.xmlsoap.org/soap/envelope/:MustUnderstand _
        MustUnderstandFaultCode                                                              _
        As XmlQualifiedName
    public Shared ReadOnly ServerFaultCode                   =http://schemas.xmlsoap.org/soap/envelope/:Server _
        As XmlQualifiedName
    public Shared ReadOnly                     =http://schemas.xmlsoap.org/soap/envelope/:VersionMismatch _
        VersionMismatchFaultCode                                                             _
        As XmlQualifiedName
' Public Instance Properties
    Public ReadOnly Property Actor As String
    Public ReadOnly Property Code As XmlQualifiedName
    Public ReadOnly Property Detail As XmlNode
End Class
```

Hierarchy: System.Object → System.Exception (System.Runtime.Serialization.ISerializable)→ System.SystemException → SoapException

SoapExtension
MustInherit Class

System.Web.Services.Protocols (system.web.services.dll)

You can inherit from this class to create a custom SOAP extension, which allows you to access and manipulate SOAP messages before they are sent or converted into objects. SOAP extensions can be used to implement additional encryption, compression, or tracing. They can also be applied to web wervices or web service clients.

The key to using a derived SoapExtension class is overriding the ProcessMessage() method. This method is called automatically by the ASP.NET framework at several different SoapMessageStages and provides you with the current SoapMessage object. You also connect your SoapExtension to a proxy class or web service method by using a custom SoapExtensionAttribute.

You can initialize a SoapExtension with a constructor method and the Initialize() and GetInitializer() methods. The GetInitializer() method is called only once the first time a SOAP request is made. It gives you the opportunity to retrieve information about the web service or proxy method (in the methodInfo parameter) and custom SoapExtensionAttribute and return an appropriate initialization object. This object will be cached and provided to the Initialize() method, which is called every time a SOAP request is made.

```
Public MustInherit Class SoapExtension
' Protected Constructors
   Protected Sub New()
' Public Instance Methods
   Overridable Public Function ChainStream(ByVal stream As System.IO.Stream) As Stream
   MustInherit Public Function GetInitializer(ByVal methodInfo As LogicalMethodInfo, _
      ByVal attribute As SoapExtensionAttribute) As Object
   MustInherit Public Function GetInitializer(ByVal serviceType As Type) As Object
   MustInherit Public Sub Initialize(ByVal initializer As Object)
   MustInherit Public Sub ProcessMessage(ByVal message As SoapMessage)
End Class
```

SoapExtensionAttribute
MustInherit Class

System.Web.Services.Protocols (system.web.services.dll)

When using a SoapExtension, you must also derive a custom SoapExtensionAttribute. This attribute is used to "connect" methods in your web service or proxy class to the corresponding extension.

When creating a custom SoapExtensionAttribute, you need to override the ExtensionType property so that it returns the type of your custom SoapExtension class. You can then use your custom attribute to mark methods in your web service or proxy class. ASP.NET will automatically use the specified SoapExtension when the associated method is invoked.

```
Public MustInherit Class SoapExtensionAttribute : Inherits Attribute
' Protected Constructors
   Protected Sub New()
' Public Instance Properties
   MustInherit Public ReadOnly Property ExtensionType As Type
   MustInherit Public Property Priority As Integer
End Class
```

Hierarchy: System.Object → System.Attribute → SoapExtensionAttribute

Valid On: All

SoapHeader
MustInherit Class

System.Web.Services.Protocols (system.web.services.dll)

This class allows you to create custom SOAP headers, which are used to send additional information to or from a web service. For example, rather than require an extra security parameter to authenticate every web service method, you could use a custom SoapHeader. The client could then set a simple property of the proxy class, and the header would be sent automatically with every web method request.

To use a custom SoapHeader, create a class that inherits from SoapHeader, and add the member variables you need to contain additional information (in this case, some sort of security credentials). When invoking a method, instantiate your custom SoapHeader, set its properties accordingly, and send it to the web service or proxy class. The web service must provide a member variable to receive the SoapHeader and must indicate which methods will process the custom header. It marks these methods with a SoapHeaderAttribute.

The Actor property is specified by the SOAP standard and should be set to the URL of the web service. If you set the MustUnderstand property to True, the method in the class receiving the message must set the DidUnderstand property to True, or a SoapHeaderException will be thrown. Note that ASP.NET automatically defaults MustUnderstand to True and automatically defaults DidUnderstand to True as long as the recipient (for example, the web service) contains the custom header class definition. The only time DidUnderstand will not be automatically set to True is when you explicitly retrieve unknown SOAP headers.

```
Public MustInherit Class SoapHeader
' Protected Constructors
    Protected Sub New()
' Public Instance Properties
    Public Property Actor As String
    Public Property DidUnderstand As Boolean
    Public Property EncodedMustUnderstand As String
    Public Property MustUnderstand As Boolean
End Class
```

SoapHeaderAttribute
NotInheritable Class

System.Web.Services.Protocols (system.web.services.dll)

This attribute is used to receive a custom SoapHeader. Before you can use this attribute, you need to add a member variable of the appropriate SoapHeader type to your web service or proxy class (for example, Public ReceivedHeader As MyCustomHeader). Before invoking a method, the client will set this member to the appropriate header object. You must also add a SoapHeaderAttribute to each method that wants to process the custom header. This declaration specifies the class member that received the custom header object, as in SoapHeader(MemberName := "ReceivedHeader").

If a method will process more than one SoapHeader, just add multiple SoapHeaderAttribute declarations. You can also receive all headers that are not defined in the web service by creating a member array of SoapUnknownHeader objects and using it in the SoapHeaderAttribute declaration.

```
Public NotInheritable Class SoapHeaderAttribute : Inherits Attribute
' Public Constructors
    Public Sub New(ByVal memberName As String)
' Public Instance Properties
    Public Property Direction As SoapHeaderDirection
```

Public Property **MemberName** As String
Public Property **Required** As Boolean
End Class

Hierarchy: System.Object → System.Attribute → SoapHeaderAttribute

Valid On: Method

SoapHeaderCollection

Class

System.Web.Services.Protocols (system.web.services.dll)

This class contains a collection of SoapHeader objects. It is used for the SoapMessage.Headers property, which contains all the headers in a single SOAP request or response message.

Public Class **SoapHeaderCollection** : Inherits CollectionBase
' *Public Constructors*
    Public Sub **New**()
' *Public Instance Properties*
    Public Default Property **Item** (ByVal index As Integer) As SoapHeader
' *Public Instance Methods*
    Public Function **Add**(ByVal header As SoapHeader) As Integer
    Public Function **Contains**(ByVal header As SoapHeader) As Boolean
    Public Sub **CopyTo**(ByVal array As SoapHeader(), ByVal index As Integer)
    Public Function **IndexOf**(ByVal header As SoapHeader) As Integer
    Public Sub **Insert**(ByVal index As Integer, ByVal header As SoapHeader)
    Public Sub **Remove**(ByVal header As SoapHeader)
End Class

Hierarchy: System.Object → System.Collections.CollectionBase (System.Collections.IList , System.Collections.ICollection , System.Collections.IEnumerable)→ SoapHeaderCollection

SoapHeaderDirection

Enum

serializable, flag

System.Web.Services.Protocols (system.web.services.dll)

This enumeration is used to set the SoapHeaderAttribute.Direction property. The direction is relative to the receiving method where the attribute is placed. A value of InOut on a web method specifies that the SoapHeader is sent to the method and back to the client with possible modifications.

Public Enum **SoapHeaderDirection**
    In = &H000000001
    Out = &H000000002
    InOut = &H000000003
End Enum

Hierarchy: System.Object → System.ValueType → System.Enum (System.IComparable , System.IFormattable , System.IConvertible)→ SoapHeaderDirection

SoapHeaderException

Class

System.Web.Services.Protocols (system.web.services.dll)

This class represents an error processing a SoapHeader. Typically, it results when a header with a SoapHeader.MustUnderstand property of True is processed by the receiving method, but the corresponding SoapHeader.DidUnderstand property is not set to True.

Public Class **SoapHeaderException** : Inherits SoapException
' *Public Constructors*
  Public Sub **New**(ByVal message As String, ByVal code As System.Xml.XmlQualifiedName)
  Public Sub **New**(ByVal message As String, ByVal code As System.Xml.XmlQualifiedName, _
    ByVal innerException As Exception)
  Public Sub **New**(ByVal message As String, ByVal code As System.Xml.XmlQualifiedName, ByVal actor As String)
  Public Sub **New**(ByVal message As String, ByVal code As System.Xml.XmlQualifiedName, ByVal actor As String, _
    ByVal innerException As Exception)
End Class

Hierarchy: System.Object → System.Exception (System.Runtime.Serialization.ISerializable)→
System.SystemException → SoapException → SoapHeaderException

SoapHttpClientProtocol   Class

System.Web.Services.Protocols (system.web.services.dll)   *marshal by reference, disposable*

You can inherit from this class to create a proxy class that communicates by using the
SOAP protocol over HTTP. This is the most commonly used class for creating proxies,
and the default in proxy classes .NET generates automatically. When using this class,
you must also use the corresponding SoapDocumentMethodAttribute or SoapRpcMethodAttribute to bind a proxy class method to a web service method.

Public Class **SoapHttpClientProtocol** : Inherits HttpWebClientProtocol
' *Public Constructors*
  Public Sub **New**()
' *Public Instance Methods*
  Public Sub **Discover**()
' *Protected Instance Methods*
  Protected Function **BeginInvoke**(ByVal methodName As String, ByVal parameters As Object(), _
    ByVal callback As AsyncCallback, ByVal asyncState As Object) As IAsyncResult
  Protected Function **EndInvoke**(ByVal asyncResult As IAsyncResult) As Object()
  Overrides Protected Function **GetWebRequest**(ByVal uri As Uri) As WebRequest
  Protected Function **Invoke**(ByVal methodName As String, ByVal parameters As Object()) As Object()
End Class

Hierarchy: System.Object → System.MarshalByRefObject → System.ComponentModel.Component
(System.ComponentModel.IComponent , System.IDisposable)→ WebClientProtocol →
HttpWebClientProtocol → SoapHttpClientProtocol

SoapMessage   MustInherit Class

System.Web.Services.Protocols (system.web.services.dll)

This class represents a SOAP request or SOAP response used to communicate between
a web service and proxy class. The SoapMessage class is used primarily for SOAP extensions. SOAP extensions, which derive from SoapExtension, receive a SoapMessage object at
each SoapMessageStage as an argument to SoapExtension.ProcessMessage() method, which is
called automatically by the ASP.NET framework.

The SoapMessage class provides methods that allow you to retrieve the web service
method parameters and the return value encoded in the SOAP message. For a Soap-
ClientMessage, you should use the GetInParameterValue() method if the SOAP message is in
the SoapMessageStage.BeforeSerialize stage, or the GetOutParameterValue() method if it's in the
SoapMessageStage.AfterSerialize stage. For a SoapServerMessage, the reverse is true.

To verify that the parameters are available, you can use the EnsureInStage() or EnsureOut-Stage() method (a System.InvalidOperationException will be thrown if the message is not in a compatible stage). Alternatively, you can use the Stage property to determine the state when the SoapMessage was generated.

```
Public MustInherit Class SoapMessage
' Public Instance Properties
    MustInherit Public ReadOnly Property Action As String
    Public Property ContentType As String
    Public ReadOnly Property Exception As SoapException
    Public ReadOnly Property Headers As SoapHeaderCollection
    MustInherit Public ReadOnly Property MethodInfo As LogicalMethodInfo
    MustInherit Public ReadOnly Property OneWay As Boolean
    Public ReadOnly Property Stage As SoapMessageStage
    Public ReadOnly Property Stream As Stream
    MustInherit Public ReadOnly Property Url As String
' Public Instance Methods
    Public Function GetInParameterValue(ByVal index As Integer) As Object
    Public Function GetOutParameterValue(ByVal index As Integer) As Object
    Public Function GetReturnValue() As Object
' Protected Instance Methods
    MustInherit Protected Sub EnsureInStage()
    MustInherit Protected Sub EnsureOutStage()
    Protected Sub EnsureStage(ByVal stage As SoapMessageStage)
End Class
```

SoapMessageStage

Enum

System.Web.Services.Protocols (system.web.services.dll)

serializable

This enumeration indicates the stage that a SoapMessage is in. Messages are serialized into SOAP before they are transmitted over the Internet and deserialized when they are received. Both the web service and the proxy client send and receive messages, so both participate in the serialization and deserialization process.

```
Public Enum SoapMessageStage
    BeforeSerialize = 1
    AfterSerialize = 2
    BeforeDeserialize = 4
    AfterDeserialize = 8
End Enum
```

Hierarchy: System.Object → System.ValueType → System.Enum (System.IComparable , System.IFormattable , System.IConvertible) → SoapMessageStage

SoapParameterStyle

Enum

System.Web.Services.Protocols (system.web.services.dll)

serializable

This enumeration is used when applying a SoapDocumentMethodAttribute or SoapDocumentServiceAttribute. It specifies how web service parameter information is encoded in a SOAP message. If you use Bare, parameter information will be placed in multiple elements under the Body element. If you specify Wrapped, all parameters will be wrapped in a single element beneath the Body element. Default uses the default web service parameter style, which will be Wrapped unless the web service includes a SoapDocumentServiceAttribute in its class declaration that specifies differently.

```
Public Enum SoapParameterStyle
    Default = 0
    Bare = 1
    Wrapped = 2
End Enum
```

Hierarchy: System.Object → System.ValueType → System.Enum (System.IComparable , System.IFormattable , System.IConvertible) → SoapParameterStyle

SoapRpcMethodAttribute

NotInheritable Class

System.Web.Services.Protocols (system.web.services.dll)

This attribute is used to specify the encoding for SOAP request and response messages. You can apply this attribute to methods in a web service or in methods in a proxy class that derives from SoapHttpClientProtocol (where it's required to bind the messages to the appropriate web method). You use this attribute, instead of SoapDocumentMethodAttribute, when you want to use the RPC encoding standard.

There are two options for encoding XML information in a SOAP message: RPC and Document. ASP.NET's default is Document. RPC (found in section 7 of the SOAP specification) specifies that all method parameters be wrapped in a single element named after the web service method and that each element be named after their respective parameter name. If you apply this attribute to a web method, it will not be able to return objects because no XSD schema will be generated.

```
Public NotInheritable Class SoapRpcMethodAttribute : Inherits Attribute
' Public Constructors
    Public Sub New()
    Public Sub New(ByVal action As String)
' Public Instance Properties
    Public Property Action As String
    Public Property Binding As String
    Public Property OneWay As Boolean
    Public Property RequestElementName As String
    Public Property RequestNamespace As String
    Public Property ResponseElementName As String
    Public Property ResponseNamespace As String
End Class
```

Hierarchy: System.Object → System.Attribute → SoapRpcMethodAttribute

Valid On: Method

SoapRpcServiceAttribute

NotInheritable Class

System.Web.Services.Protocols (system.web.services.dll)

This attribute can be applied to a web service's class declaration. It specifies that the default encoding for SOAP request and response messages will be RPC. The client can override this default by using the SoapDocumentMethodAttribute. If you apply this attribute, the web service will not be able to return objects because no XSD schema will be generated.

```
Public NotInheritable Class SoapRpcServiceAttribute : Inherits Attribute
' Public Constructors
    Public Sub New()
```

' *Public Instance Properties*
   Public Property **RoutingStyle** As SoapServiceRoutingStyle
End Class

Hierarchy: System.Object → System.Attribute → SoapRpcServiceAttribute

Valid On: Class

SoapServerMessage   **NotInheritable Class**

System.Web.Services.Protocols (system.web.services.dll)

This class represents a SOAP request sent by a web service or SOAP response received by a web service. It inherits from the SoapMessage class, which contains most of the functionality for SOAP messages.

Public NotInheritable Class **SoapServerMessage** : Inherits SoapMessage
' *Public Instance Properties*
   Overrides Public ReadOnly Property **Action** As String
   Overrides Public ReadOnly Property **MethodInfo** As LogicalMethodInfo
   Overrides Public ReadOnly Property **OneWay** As Boolean
   Public ReadOnly Property **Server** As Object
   Overrides Public ReadOnly Property **Url** As String
' *Protected Instance Methods*
   Overrides Protected Sub **EnsureInStage**()
   Overrides Protected Sub **EnsureOutStage**()
End Class

Hierarchy: System.Object → SoapMessage → SoapServerMessage

SoapServiceRoutingStyle   **Enum**

System.Web.Services.Protocols (system.web.services.dll)   *serializable*

This enumeration is used to specify the SoapDocumentServiceAttribute.RoutingStyle and the SoapRpcServiceAttribute.RoutingStyle properties. Allowed values are RequestElement (the message is routed based on the first child element in the body of the SOAP message) and SoapAction (the SOAP message is routed based on the SOAPAction HTTP header).

Public Enum **SoapServiceRoutingStyle**
   SoapAction = 0
   RequestElement = 1
End Enum

Hierarchy: System.Object → System.ValueType → System.Enum (System.IComparable , System.IFormattable , System.IConvertible) → SoapServiceRoutingStyle

SoapUnknownHeader   **NotInheritable Class**

System.Web.Services.Protocols (system.web.services.dll)

This class represents a SoapHeader that was not understood by the receiving method in the web service or proxy class. You can receive all unknown headers by creating an array of SoapUnknownHeader objects and using it with the SoapHeaderAttribute.

Public NotInheritable Class **SoapUnknownHeader** : Inherits SoapHeader
' *Public Constructors*

```
      Public Sub New()
    ' Public Instance Properties
      Public Property Element As XmlElement
End Class
```

Hierarchy: System.Object → SoapHeader → SoapUnknownHeader

TextReturnReader   Class

System.Web.Services.Protocols (system.web.services.dll)

This class supports the .NET Framework infrastructure. You do not need to use it directly in your code.

```
Public Class TextReturnReader : Inherits MimeReturnReader
' Public Constructors
      Public Sub New()
' Public Instance Methods
      Overrides Public Function GetInitializer(ByVal methodInfo As LogicalMethodInfo) As Object
      Overrides Public Sub Initialize(ByVal o As Object)
      Overrides Public Function Read(ByVal response As System.Net.WebResponse, _
        ByVal responseStream As System.IO.Stream) As Object
End Class
```

Hierarchy: System.Object → MimeFormatter → MimeReturnReader → TextReturnReader

UrlEncodedParameterWriter   MustInherit Class

System.Web.Services.Protocols (system.web.services.dll)

This class supports the .NET Framework infrastructure. You do not need to use it directly in your code.

```
Public MustInherit Class UrlEncodedParameterWriter : Inherits MimeParameterWriter
' Protected Constructors
      Protected Sub New()
' Public Instance Properties
      Overrides Public Property RequestEncoding As Encoding
' Public Instance Methods
      Overrides Public Function GetInitializer(ByVal methodInfo As LogicalMethodInfo) As Object
      Overrides Public Sub Initialize(ByVal initializer As Object)
' Protected Instance Methods
      Protected Sub Encode(ByVal writer As System.IO.TextWriter, ByVal values As Object())
      Protected Sub Encode(ByVal writer As System.IO.TextWriter, ByVal name As String, ByVal value As Object)
End Class
```

Hierarchy: System.Object → MimeFormatter → MimeParameterWriter →
UrlEncodedParameterWriter

UrlParameterReader   Class

System.Web.Services.Protocols (system.web.services.dll)

This class supports the .NET Framework infrastructure. You do not need to use it directly in your code.

Public Class **UrlParameterReader** : Inherits ValueCollectionParameterReader
' *Public Constructors*
   Public Sub **New**()
' *Public Instance Methods*
   Overrides Public Function **Read**(ByVal request As System.Web.HttpRequest) As Object()
End Class

Hierarchy: System.Object → MimeFormatter → MimeParameterReader →
ValueCollectionParameterReader → UrlParameterReader

UrlParameterWriter Class

System.Web.Services.Protocols (system.web.services.dll)

This class supports the .NET Framework infrastructure. You do not need to use it directly in your code.

Public Class **UrlParameterWriter** : Inherits UrlEncodedParameterWriter
' *Public Constructors*
   Public Sub **New**()
' *Public Instance Methods*
   Overrides Public Function **GetRequestUrl**(ByVal url As String, ByVal parameters As Object()) As String
End Class

Hierarchy: System.Object → MimeFormatter → MimeParameterWriter →
UrlEncodedParameterWriter → UrlParameterWriter

ValueCollectionParameterReader MustInherit Class

System.Web.Services.Protocols (system.web.services.dll)

This class supports the .NET Framework infrastructure. You do not need to use it directly in your code.

Public MustInherit Class **ValueCollectionParameterReader** : Inherits MimeParameterReader
' *Protected Constructors*
   Protected Sub **New**()
' *Public Shared Methods*
   Public Shared Function **IsSupported**(ByVal methodInfo As LogicalMethodInfo) As Boolean
   Public Shared Function **IsSupported**(ByVal paramInfo As System.Reflection.ParameterInfo) As Boolean
' *Public Instance Methods*
   Overrides Public Function **GetInitializer**(ByVal methodInfo As LogicalMethodInfo) As Object
   Overrides Public Sub **Initialize**(ByVal o As Object)
' *Protected Instance Methods*
   Protected Function **Read**(ByVal collection As System.Collections.Specialized.NameValueCollection) As Object()
End Class

Hierarchy: System.Object → MimeFormatter → MimeParameterReader →
ValueCollectionParameterReader

WebClientAsyncResult Class

System.Web.Services.Protocols (system.web.services.dll)

This class is used to return a result when invoking a web service method asynchronously, through the corresponding "Begin" and "End" methods. These method variants are created for you when you generate a proxy automatically by using Visual Studio .NET or *WSDL.exe*.

```
Public Class WebClientAsyncResult : Implements IAsyncResult
' Public Instance Properties
   Public ReadOnly Property AsyncState As Object Implements IAsyncResult.AsyncState
   Public ReadOnly Property AsyncWaitHandle As WaitHandle Implements IAsyncResult.AsyncWaitHandle
   Public ReadOnly Property CompletedSynchronously As Boolean _
      Implements IAsyncResult.CompletedSynchronously
   Public ReadOnly Property IsCompleted As Boolean Implements IAsyncResult.IsCompleted
' Public Instance Methods
   Public Sub Abort()
End Class
```

WebClientProtocol
MustInherit Class

System.Web.Services.Protocols (system.web.services.dll)   *marshal by reference, disposable*

This is the base class for all web server proxy classes. It includes basic properties like Url, which is usually set to the appropriate web service address in the proxy class's constructor, and Timeout, which specifies a value in milliseconds. By default, the proxy class uses a Timeout of -1, which represents infinity, although the web server can still time out the request on the server side. The RequestEncoding property is overridden by derived classes to provide the appropriate character encoding.

To set Credentials, you must use an System.Net.ICredentials object like System.Net.NetworkCredential and set the credentials that are specific to the type of authentication you are using. You can also set the PreAuthenticate property to True, which will cause the proxy class to automatically send authentication information with every request.

```
Public MustInherit Class WebClientProtocol : Inherits System.ComponentModel.Component
' Protected Constructors
   Protected Sub New()
' Public Instance Properties
   Public Property ConnectionGroupName As String
   Public Property Credentials As ICredentials
   Public Property PreAuthenticate As Boolean
   Public Property RequestEncoding As Encoding
   Public Property Timeout As Integer
   Public Property Url As String
' Protected Shared Methods
   Shared Protected Sub AddToCache(ByVal type As Type, ByVal value As Object)
   Shared Protected Function GetFromCache(ByVal type As Type) As Object
' Public Instance Methods
   Overridable Public Sub Abort()
' Protected Instance Methods
   Overridable Protected Function GetWebRequest(ByVal uri As Uri) As WebRequest
   Overridable Protected Function GetWebResponse(ByVal request As System.Net.WebRequest) As WebResponse
   Overridable Protected Function GetWebResponse(ByVal request As System.Net.WebRequest, _
      ByVal result As IAsyncResult) As WebResponse
End Class
```

Hierarchy: System.Object → System.MarshalByRefObject → System.ComponentModel.Component
(System.ComponentModel.IComponent , System.IDisposable)→ WebClientProtocol

WebServiceHandlerFactory
Class

System.Web.Services.Protocols (system.web.services.dll)

This class is used by ASP.NET to instantiate an appropriate HttpHandler for handling web service requests. You do not need to use this class directly in your code.

Public Class **WebServiceHandlerFactory** : Implements System.Web.IHttpHandlerFactory
' *Public Constructors*
  Public Sub **New**()
' *Public Instance Methods*
  Public Function **GetHandler**(ByVal context As System.Web.HttpContext, ByVal verb As String, ByVal url As String, _
    ByVal filePath As String) As IHttpHandler Implements IHttpHandlerFactory.GetHandler
  Public Sub **ReleaseHandler**(ByVal handler As System.Web.IHttpHandler) _
    Implements IHttpHandlerFactory.ReleaseHandler
End Class

XmlReturnReader   Class

System.Web.Services.Protocols (system.web.services.dll)

This class supports the .NET Framework infrastructure. You do not need to use it directly in your code.

Public Class **XmlReturnReader** : Inherits MimeReturnReader
' *Public Constructors*
  Public Sub **New**()
' *Public Instance Methods*
  Overrides Public Function **GetInitializer**(ByVal methodInfo As LogicalMethodInfo) As Object
  Overrides Public Function **GetInitializers**(ByVal methodInfos As LogicalMethodInfo()) As Object()
  Overrides Public Sub **Initialize**(ByVal o As Object)
  Overrides Public Function **Read**(ByVal response As System.Net.WebResponse, _
    ByVal responseStream As System.IO.Stream) As Object
End Class

Hierarchy: System.Object → MimeFormatter → MimeReturnReader → XmlReturnReader

Protocols
Namespace

CHAPTER 33

The System.Web.SessionState Namespace

The System.Web.SessionState namespace provides the types used for session state management, which stores information that is specific to one session or client. Each user accessing an ASP.NET application has a separate session state collection. Session state is ideal for sensitive data (like credit card numbers and mailing addresses) because it is stored exclusively on the server. It is also well suited for complex data (like recordsets, .NET class instances, or COM objects) that cannot be easily serialized to a client-side cookie.

To support session state, each active ASP.NET session is identified and tracked with a unique 120-bit session ID string. Session ID values are created and managed automatically by the ASP.NET framework by using an algorithm that guarantees uniqueness and randomness so that they can't be regenerated by a malicious user. When a client requests an ASP.NET page, the appropriate ID is transmitted from the client by a cookie or a modified ("munged") URL. ASP.NET worker processes then retrieve the serialized data from the state server as a binary stream, convert it into live objects, and place these objects into the HttpSessionState class's key/value collection. This class is the core of the System.Web.SessionState namespace. Most other classes in this namespace are used transparently by the ASP.NET framework, except the IReadOnlySessionState and IRequiresSessionState interfaces, which allow custom System.Web.IHttpHandler instances to access session data.

Session state is typically removed if no requests are received within a specified timeframe (typically about 20 minutes). This is the main trade-off of session state storage: you must choose a timeframe short enough to allow valuable memory to be reclaimed on the server, but long enough to allow a user to continue a session after a short delay.

Note that most session state settings, including the method session ID transmission, the type of storage, and the timeout, are all configured through the <sessionstate> section of the *web.config* file. Figure 33-1 shows the types in this namespace.

HttpSessionState   NotInheritable Class

System.Web.SessionState (system.web.dll)

The HttpSessionState class provides server-side state management that is stored on a per-client basis. The HttpSessionState class exposes a key/value collection of items that can store simple value types or instances of .NET objects. You can add and access items in

582

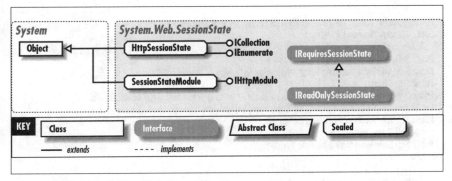

Figure 33-1: The System.Web.SessionState namespace

the HttpSessionState collection as you would with other ASP.NET collections, including System.Web.HttpApplicationState and System.Web.Caching.Cache. Unlike these classes, session state can be stored outside of the main ASP.NET process. This allows it to be shared across multiple computers in a web farm and persist after server restarts.

The HttpSessionState class combines two state collections: Contents and StaticObjects. The StaticObjects collection contains the application state objects that are defined in the *global.asax* file with <object runat="server"> tags. This collection is immutable. The Contents collection contains all the state objects added at runtime.

The Item collection is the default indexer for HttpSessionState, so you can use the name of a state object as an index, as in: Session("userName") = "Lucy". If you assign a value to a state object that does not exist, it is created automatically. Items are stored as the generic System.Object type and must be cast to the appropriate types when you retrieve them.

Other properties allow you to get information about whether or not the session has just been created with the current request (IsNewSession) and what type of session ID transmission (IsCookieless) and session storage (Mode) is being used. You can use the SessionID property to retrieve the session ID string, but you will not need to, as it is created and managed automatically by the ASP.NET framework. A reference is provided to the HttpSessionState class through the built-in Session object. Use Abandon() to end a session immediately and release memory occupied by session state objects without waiting for the session to time out.

Public NotInheritable Class **HttpSessionState** : Implements ICollection, IEnumerable
' *Public Instance Properties*
  Public Property **CodePage** As Integer
  Public ReadOnly Property **Contents** As HttpSessionState
  Public ReadOnly Property **Count** As Integer Implements ICollection.Count
  Public ReadOnly Property **IsCookieless** As Boolean
  Public ReadOnly Property **IsNewSession** As Boolean
  Public ReadOnly Property **IsReadOnly** As Boolean
  Public ReadOnly Property **IsSynchronized** As Boolean Implements ICollection.IsSynchronized
  Public Default Property **Item** (ByVal name As String) As Object
  Public Default Property **Item** (ByVal index As Integer) As Object
  Public ReadOnly Property **Keys** As KeysCollection
  Public Property **LCID** As Integer
  Public ReadOnly Property **Mode** As SessionStateMode
  Public ReadOnly Property **SessionID** As String
  Public ReadOnly Property **StaticObjects** As HttpStaticObjectsCollection

Public ReadOnly Property **SyncRoot** As Object Implements ICollection.SyncRoot
Public Property **Timeout** As Integer
' *Public Instance Methods*
Public Sub **Abandon**()
Public Sub **Add**(ByVal name As String, ByVal value As Object)
Public Sub **Clear**()
Public Sub **CopyTo**(ByVal array As Array, ByVal index As Integer) Implements ICollection.CopyTo
Public Function **GetEnumerator**() As IEnumerator Implements IEnumerable.GetEnumerator
Public Sub **Remove**(ByVal name As String)
Public Sub **RemoveAll**()
Public Sub **RemoveAt**(ByVal index As Integer)
End Class

IReadOnlySessionState
Interface

System.Web.SessionState (system.web.dll)

This interface should be implemented by a custom HttpHandler (any class that interprets web requests and implements System.Web.IHttpHandler). The IReadOnlySessionState interface contains no members and is used only as a marker. When present, it tells ASP.NET that the HttpHandler should be given readonly access to the HttpSessionState collection.

Every HttpHandler should implement either IReadOnlySessionState or IRequiresSessionState, or session state variables will not be accessible.

Public Interface **IReadOnlySessionState** : Implements IRequiresSessionState
' *No public or protected members*
End Interface

IRequiresSessionState
Interface

System.Web.SessionState (system.web.dll)

This interface should be implemented by a custom HttpHandler. This interface contains no members and is used only as a marker. When present, it tells ASP.NET that the HttpHandler should be given read and write access to the HttpSessionState collection.

Every HttpHandler should implement either IReadOnlySessionState or IRequiresSessionState, or session state variables will not be accessible.

Public Interface **IRequiresSessionState**
' *No public or protected members*
End Interface

IStateRuntime
Interface

System.Web.SessionState (system.web.dll)

This interface defines a contract for the StateRuntime class.

Public Interface **IStateRuntime**
' *Public Instance Methods*
Public Sub **ProcessRequest**(ByVal tracker As IntPtr, ByVal verb As Integer, ByVal uri As String, _
  ByVal exclusive As Integer, ByVal timeout As Integer, ByVal lockCookieExists As Integer, ByVal lockCookie As Integer _
  , ByVal contentLength As Integer, ByVal content As IntPtr)
Public Sub **StopProcessing**()
End Interface

SessionStateMode

System.Web.SessionState (system.web.dll)

This enumeration allows you to identify the type of ASP.NET session storage by using the HttpSessionState.Mode property. It also allows you to specify it by using the mode attribute of the <sessionState> tag in the *web.config* file (for example, <sessionState mode="SQLServer">).

Session state can be stored locally in the ASP.NET process (InProc, the method used in traditional ASP applications), in a separate server (StateServer), or serialized to a temporary table in an SQL Server database (SQLServer), which the ASP.NET worker processes access and manage automatically. Note that both StateServer and SQLServer methods allow state to be shared across servers in web farm/web garden scenarios and retained in the case of a server restart.

```
Public Enum SessionStateMode
    Off = 0
    InProc = 1
    StateServer = 2
    SQLServer = 3
End Enum
```

Hierarchy: System.Object → System.ValueType → System.Enum (System.IComparable , System.IFormattable , System.IConvertible) → SessionStateMode

SessionStateModule

NotInheritable Class

System.Web.SessionState (system.web.dll)

This class implements session state storage, taking care of tasks like the generation of unique session IDs and the storage and retrieval of state information from an external state provider, as directed by the ASP.NET framework. It is not used directly in your code, but is specified in the *machine.config* file.

```
Public NotInheritable Class SessionStateModule : Implements System.Web.IHttpModule
' Public Constructors
    Public Sub New()
' Public Instance Methods
    Public Sub Dispose() Implements IHttpModule.Dispose
    Public Sub Init(ByVal app As System.Web.HttpApplication) Implements IHttpModule.Init
' Events
    Public Event End As EventHandler
    Public Event Start As EventHandler
End Class
```

SessionStateSectionHandler

Class

System.Web.SessionState (system.web.dll)

The SessionStateSectionHandler class, like all section handlers, is responsible for parsing a portion of the *web.config* file and applying ASP.NET settings accordingly. The SessionStateSectionHandler considers the data in the <sessionstate> sections. This class is used transparently by the ASP.NET framework and is not used directly in your code.

```
Class SessionStateSectionHandler : Implements System.Configuration.IConfigurationSectionHandler
' Public Constructors
    Public Sub New()
' Public Instance Methods
```

```
    Public Function Create(ByVal parent As Object, ByVal contextObject As Object,
      ByVal section As System.Xml.XmlNode) As Object Implements  IConfigurationSectionHandler.Create
End Class
```

StateRuntime

NotInheritable Class

System.Web.SessionState (system.web.dll)

This class is used by the ASP.NET framework to provide session state support. It is not used directly in your code.

```
Public NotInheritable Class StateRuntime : Implements IStateRuntime
' Public Constructors
    Public Sub New()
' Public Instance Methods
    Public Sub ProcessRequest(ByVal tracker As IntPtr, ByVal verb As Integer, ByVal uri As String,
      ByVal exclusive As Integer, ByVal timeout As Integer, ByVal lockCookieExists As Integer, ByVal lockCookie As Integer
      , ByVal contentLength As Integer, ByVal content As IntPtr)  Implements  IStateRuntime.ProcessRequest
    Public Sub StopProcessing() Implements  IStateRuntime.StopProcessing
End Class
```

CHAPTER 34

The System.Web.UI Namespace

The System.Web.UI namespace provides types that allow you to create controls and Web Forms (*.aspx* pages). Many of these types provide support for controls in the System.Web.UI.HtmlControls and System.Web.UI.WebControls namespaces and are not used directly in your code. Some of these types provide parsing, data binding, and template functionality. The System.Web.UI namespace also includes a number of fundamental classes like Control (the base class for all HTML, Web, and user controls), Page (the base class for every *.aspx* Web Forms page you create), and UserControl (the class representing all *.ascx* user controls).

Many of the types in this namespace are useful if you want to create your own custom controls. These types include the IPostBackDataHandler and IPostBackEventHandler interfaces (used to access postback data and raise control events), the HtmlTextWriter class (used to create a control's HTML user interface), the INamingContainer interface (used to create composite controls), and the ITemplate interface (used to create templated controls with configurable HTML). Additionally, the System.Web.UI namespace also contains types used for control styles (AttributeCollection and CssStyleCollection) and view state management (StateBag and StateItem).

Figure 34-1 shows the controls and control builders for this namespace. Figure 34-2 shows attributes as well as a delegate and its related event arguments. Figure 34-3 shows the remaining types.

AttributeCollection   NotInheritable Class

System.Web.UI (system.web.dll)

AttributeCollection is a name/value collection of all attributes declared in the opening tag of an ASP.NET server control (which should not be confused with .NET metadata attributes). For example, an HTML text area element has rows and cols attributes that specify its size. You can access and modify the collection of control attributes for any HTML server control through the System.Web.UI.HtmlControls.HtmlControl.Attributes collection. You can also access most important attributes as control properties. Note that you cannot iterate through the AttributeCollection class because it does not directly implement the System.Collections.IEnumerable interface. Use the read-only Keys collection instead.

Web Controls also provide an attribute collection through the System.Web.UI.WebControls.WebControl.Attributes property. However, because web controls are "abstracted away"

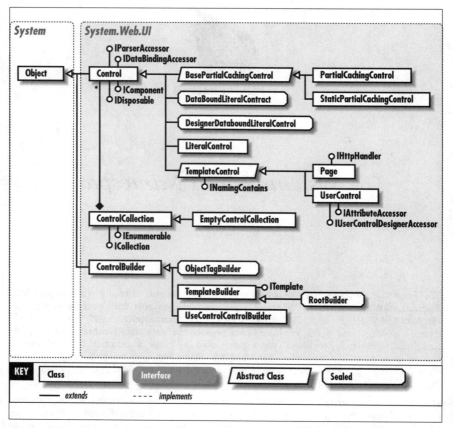

Figure 34-1: Controls and control builders

from the underlying HTML interface code, you cannot directly access the underlying attributes for the composite HTML elements of a control. Instead, this collection will typically contain a single style attribute. You can still add your own attributes to the collection (for example, TextBox1.Attributes("key") = strKey).

One useful way to use the AttributeCollection class is to add a JavaScript event to a control. For example, TextBox1.Attributes("onblur") = "javascript:alert('Focus lost!);" adds a "lost focus" JavaScript event. This will work for HTML controls and some simple Web Controls (like System.Web.UI.WebControls.TextBox), but not for others (like System.Web.UI.WebControls.Calendar).

Public NotInheritable Class **AttributeCollection**
' Public Constructors
   Public Sub **New**(ByVal bag As StateBag)
' Public Instance Properties
   Public ReadOnly Property **Count** As Integer
   Public ReadOnly Property **CssStyle** As CssStyleCollection
   Public Default Property **Item** (ByVal key As String) As String
   Public ReadOnly Property **Keys** As ICollection
' Public Instance Methods
   Public Sub **Add**(ByVal key As String, ByVal value As String)

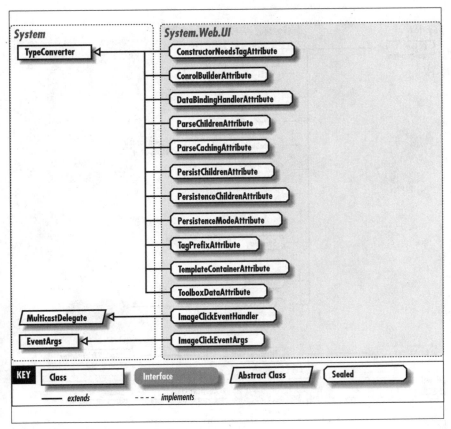

Figure 34-2: Attributes and other types

```
Public Sub AddAttributes(ByVal writer As HtmlTextWriter)
Public Sub Clear()
Public Sub Remove(ByVal key As String)
Public Sub Render(ByVal writer As HtmlTextWriter)
End Class
```

BaseParser   Class

System.Web.UI (system.web.dll)

This class is used transparently by the .NET framework. It is the base class used for parsing—the process by which code in an *.aspx* file is interpreted and ultimately rendered as HTML.

```
Public Class BaseParser
' Public Constructors
   Public Sub New()
End Class
```

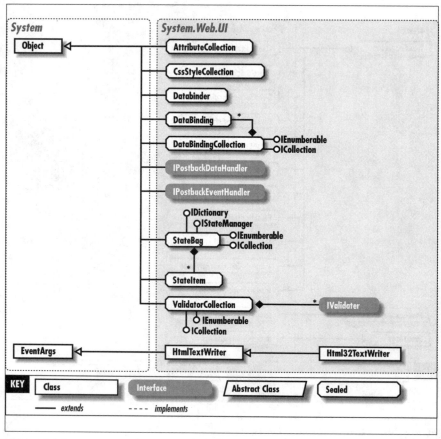

Figure 34-3: More types from System.Web.UI

BasePartialCachingControl

MustInherit Class

System.Web.UI (system.web.dll)

disposable

This base class supports fragment caching, which allows portions of an ASP.NET page to be cached. This page is inherited by the PartialCachingControl and StaticPartialCachingControl classes.

```
Public MustInherit Class BasePartialCachingControl : Inherits Control
' Protected Constructors
   Protected Sub New()
' Public Instance Properties
   Public Property Dependency As CacheDependency
' Public Instance Methods
   Overrides Public Sub Dispose()
' Protected Instance Methods
   Overrides Protected Sub OnInit(ByVal e As EventArgs)
   Overrides Protected Sub Render(ByVal output As HtmlTextWriter)
End Class
```

Hierarchy: System.Object → Control (System.ComponentModel.IComponent , System.IDisposable , IParserAccessor , IDataBindingsAccessor) → BasePartialCachingControl

BuildMethod
Delegate

System.Web.UI (system.web.dll)
serializable

This delegate is used exclusively by the ASP.NET framework. It specifies the signature for a method used to build a control and is used in the StaticPartialCachingControl.Build-CachedControl() method. It is not used in your code.

Public Delegate Function **BuildMethod**() As Control

BuildTemplateMethod
Delegate

System.Web.UI (system.web.dll)
serializable

This delegate is used exclusively by the ASP.NET framework. It specifies the signature for a method used to build a template-based control like a Page and is used by the CompiledTemplateBuilder class. It is not used in your code.

Public Delegate Sub **BuildTemplateMethod**(ByVal control As Control)

CompiledTemplateBuilder
NotInheritable Class

System.Web.UI (system.web.dll)

This utility class is used exclusively by the ASP.NET framework when generating controls. It is not used in your code.

Public NotInheritable Class **CompiledTemplateBuilder** : Implements ITemplate
' *Public Constructors*
   Public Sub **New**(ByVal buildTemplateMethod As BuildTemplateMethod)
' *Public Instance Methods*
   Public Sub **InstantiateIn**(ByVal container As Control) Implements ITemplate.InstantiateIn
End Class

ConstructorNeedsTagAttribute
NotInheritable Class

System.Web.UI (system.web.dll)

This attribute is used in the class declaration for a control. You add it, with the parameter set to True, to indicate that a control's constructor requires an HTML tag. This tag is used for the System.Web.UI.HtmlControls.HtmlTableCell and System.Web.UI.HtmlControls.HtmlGenericControl classes, which can represent different HTML elements. For example, a System.Web.UI.HtmlControls.HtmlTableCell could represent a <td> or <th> tag, depending on what tag is provided in the constructor.

Public NotInheritable Class **ConstructorNeedsTagAttribute** : Inherits Attribute
' *Public Constructors*
   Public Sub **New**()
   Public Sub **New**(ByVal needsTag As Boolean)
' *Public Instance Properties*
   Public ReadOnly Property **NeedsTag** As Boolean
End Class

Hierarchy: System.Object → System.Attribute → ConstructorNeedsTagAttribute

Valid On: Class

Control

Class

System.Web.UI (system.web.dll)

disposable

The Control class defines properties, methods, and events that all server controls in ASP.NET require. ASP.NET controls do not inherit directly from this class; instead, they inherit from either the System.Web.UI.HtmlControls.HtmlControl or the System.Web.UI.WebControls.WebControl class, both of which inherit from the Control class. Similarly, the Page and UserControl classes inherit from TemplateControl, which inherits from this class.

The Control class contains many of the typical members you would expect in a control, including properties that reference the parent Web Form (Page) and a collection of contained controls (Controls). The EnableViewState property determines whether ASP.NET maintains the control's state automatically by using a hidden field. The ViewState property provides the StateBag collection of state information.

Most Control methods are used transparently by the ASP.NET framework, such as Render(), which generates the HTML output of a control, and LoadViewState() and SaveViewState(), which manage view state automatically. One interesting method is DataBind(), which binds controls to arrays or data tables. If you are creating a page that interacts with information from a database, you may need to use this method frequently.

You can inherit from the Control class to create a simple ASP.NET control. Override the Render() method so that the control can generate its own output by using the supplied HtmlTextWriter. If you are creating a composite control, you must also override the CreateChildControls() method. Use this method to instantiate new server-based ASP.NET controls or LiteralControl objects and add them by using the System.Web.UI.Control.Controls.Add() method. If you need to access child controls from another procedure and you are not sure if they have been created yet, you can use the EnsureChildControls() method, which automatically calls CreateChildControls(), if needed. You should also implement the INamingContainer interface to ensure that child controls are created in a distinct namespace.

Usually, it is easier to derive from System.Web.UI.WebControls.WebControl when creating a custom control, as this class provides basic style and color options and manages the state for these properties automatically.

```
Public Class Control : Implements System.ComponentModel.IComponent, IDisposable, IParserAccessor, _
     IDataBindingsAccessor
' Public Constructors
   Public Sub New()
' Public Instance Properties
   Public ReadOnly Property BindingContainer As Control
   Overridable Public ReadOnly Property ClientID As String
   Overridable Public ReadOnly Property Controls As ControlCollection
   Overridable Public Property EnableViewState As Boolean
   Overridable Public Property ID As String
   Overridable Public ReadOnly Property NamingContainer As Control
   Overridable Public Property Page As Page
   Overridable Public ReadOnly Property Parent As Control
   Public Property Site As ISite Implements IComponent.Site
   Overridable Public ReadOnly Property TemplateSourceDirectory As String
   Overridable Public ReadOnly Property UniqueID As String
   Overridable Public Property Visible As Boolean
' Protected Instance Properties
   Protected Property ChildControlsCreated As Boolean
   Overridable Protected Property Context As HttpContext
   Protected Property Events As EventHandlerList
   Protected Property HasChildViewState As Boolean
   Protected Property IsTrackingViewState As Boolean
```

Overridable Protected Property **ViewState** As StateBag
Overridable Protected Property **ViewStateIgnoresCase** As Boolean
' *Public Instance Methods*
Overridable Public Sub **DataBind**()
Overridable Public Sub **Dispose**() Implements IDisposable.Dispose
Overridable Public Function **FindControl**(ByVal id As String) As Control
Overridable Public Function **HasControls**() As Boolean
Public Sub **RenderControl**(ByVal writer As HtmlTextWriter)
Public Function **ResolveUrl**(ByVal relativeUrl As String) As String
Public Sub **SetRenderMethodDelegate**(ByVal renderMethod As RenderMethod)
' *Protected Instance Methods*
Overridable Protected Friend Sub **AddedControl**(ByVal control As Control, ByVal index As Integer)
Overridable Protected Sub **AddParsedSubObject**(ByVal obj As Object) _
  Implements IParserAccessor.AddParsedSubObject
Protected Sub **BuildProfileTree**(ByVal parentId As String, ByVal calcViewState As Boolean)
Protected Sub **ClearChildViewState**()
Overridable Protected Sub **CreateChildControls**()
Overridable Protected Function **CreateControlCollection**() As ControlCollection
Overridable Protected Sub **EnsureChildControls**()
Overridable Protected Function **FindControl**(ByVal id As String, ByVal pathOffset As Integer) As Control
Protected Function **IsLiteralContent**() As Boolean
Overridable Protected Sub **LoadViewState**(ByVal savedState As Object)
Protected Function **MapPathSecure**(ByVal virtualPath As String) As String
Overridable Protected Function **OnBubbleEvent**(ByVal source As Object, ByVal args As EventArgs) As Boolean
Overridable Protected Sub **OnDataBinding**(ByVal e As EventArgs)
Overridable Protected Sub **OnInit**(ByVal e As EventArgs)
Overridable Protected Sub **OnLoad**(ByVal e As EventArgs)
Overridable Protected Sub **OnPreRender**(ByVal e As EventArgs)
Overridable Protected Sub **OnUnload**(ByVal e As EventArgs)
Protected Sub **RaiseBubbleEvent**(ByVal source As Object, ByVal args As EventArgs)
Overridable Protected Friend Sub **RemovedControl**(ByVal control As Control)
Overridable Protected Sub **Render**(ByVal writer As HtmlTextWriter)
Overridable Protected Sub **RenderChildren**(ByVal writer As HtmlTextWriter)
Overridable Protected Function **SaveViewState**() As Object
Overridable Protected Sub **TrackViewState**()
' *Events*
Public Event **DataBinding** As EventHandler
Public Event **Disposed** As EventHandler Implements IComponent.Disposed
Public Event **Init** As EventHandler
Public Event **Load** As EventHandler
Public Event **PreRender** As EventHandler
Public Event **Unload** As EventHandler
End Class

ControlBuilder

Class

System.Web.UI (system.web.dll)

This class is used transparently by the ASP.NET network when generating a Web Forms page. It works with the appropriate parser object to build the relevant controls. You can derive from this class to create your custom control builders for your custom controls. Just override the appropriate methods and apply the ControlBuilderAttribute to your control class to instruct ASP.NET to use your custom ControlBuilder. For example, you could override the AllowWhitespaceLiterals() method to return False. This override instructs ASP.NET to refrain from creating LiteralControl objects for any whitespace it finds inside a control. Note, however, that it is easiest and most common to use the standard Control-Builder for your custom controls.

*UI
Namespace*

```
Public Class ControlBuilder
' Public Constructors
   Public Sub New()
' Public Instance Properties
   Public ReadOnly Property ControlType As Type
   Public ReadOnly Property HasAspCode As Boolean
   Public Property ID As String
   Public ReadOnly Property NamingContainerType As Type
   Public ReadOnly Property TagName As String
' Protected Instance Properties
   Protected Property FChildrenAsProperties As Boolean
   Protected Property FIsNonParserAccessor As Boolean
   Protected Property InDesigner As Boolean
   Protected Property Parser As TemplateParser
' Public Shared Methods
   Public Shared Function CreateBuilderFromType(ByVal parser As TemplateParser,
      ByVal parentBuilder As ControlBuilder, ByVal type As Type, ByVal tagName As String, ByVal id As String, _
      ByVal attribs As System.Collections.IDictionary, ByVal line As Integer, ByVal sourceFileName As String) _
      As ControlBuilder
' Public Instance Methods
   Overridable Public Function AllowWhitespaceLiterals() As Boolean
   Overridable Public Sub AppendLiteralString(ByVal s As String)
   Overridable Public Sub AppendSubBuilder(ByVal subBuilder As ControlBuilder)
   Overridable Public Sub CloseControl()
   Overridable Public Function GetChildControlType(ByVal tagName As String, _
      ByVal attribs As System.Collections.IDictionary) As Type
   Overridable Public Function HasBody() As Boolean
   Overridable Public Function HtmlDecodeLiterals() As Boolean
   Overridable Public Sub Init(ByVal parser As TemplateParser, ByVal parentBuilder As ControlBuilder,
      ByVal type As Type, ByVal tagName As String, ByVal id As String, ByVal attribs As System.Collections.IDictionary)
   Overridable Public Function NeedsTagInnerText() As Boolean
   Overridable Public Sub OnAppendToParentBuilder(ByVal parentBuilder As ControlBuilder)
   Overridable Public Sub SetTagInnerText(ByVal text As String)
End Class
```

ControlBuilderAttribute

NotInheritable Class

System.Web.UI (system.web.dll)

This attribute specifies the control builder that a custom control should use. If you want your control to use the standard control builder, you do not need to use this attribute. If you have created a custom ControlBuilder class, you can instruct ASP.NET to use it to create a control by adding this attribute to the control's class declaration, as in <ControlBuilder(GetType(MyControlBuilder))>.

```
Public NotInheritable Class ControlBuilderAttribute : Inherits Attribute
' Public Constructors
   Public Sub New(ByVal builderType As Type)
' Public Shared Fields
   public Shared ReadOnly Default As ControlBuilderAttribute            =System.Web.UI.ControlBuilderAttribute
' Public Instance Properties
   Public ReadOnly Property BuilderType As Type
' Public Instance Methods
   Overrides Public Function Equals(ByVal obj As Object) As Boolean
   Overrides Public Function GetHashCode() As Integer
```

Overrides Public Function **IsDefaultAttribute**() As Boolean
End Class

Hierarchy: System.Object → System.Attribute → ControlBuilderAttribute

Valid On: Class

ControlCollection

Class

System.Web.UI (system.web.dll)

This class represents a collection of controls. It allows pages and other controls to specify their child controls (as with the Page.Controls Property).

Public Class **ControlCollection** : Implements ICollection, IEnumerable
' *Public Constructors*
  Public Sub **New**(ByVal owner As Control)
' *Public Instance Properties*
  Public ReadOnly Property **Count** As Integer Implements ICollection.Count
  Public ReadOnly Property **IsReadOnly** As Boolean
  Public ReadOnly Property **IsSynchronized** As Boolean Implements ICollection.IsSynchronized
  Overridable Public Default ReadOnly Property **Item** (ByVal index As Integer) As Control
  Public ReadOnly Property **SyncRoot** As Object Implements ICollection.SyncRoot
' *Protected Instance Properties*
  Protected Property **Owner** As Control
' *Public Instance Methods*
  Overridable Public Sub **Add**(ByVal child As Control)
  Overridable Public Sub **AddAt**(ByVal index As Integer, ByVal child As Control)
  Overridable Public Sub **Clear**()
  Overridable Public Function **Contains**(ByVal c As Control) As Boolean
  Public Sub **CopyTo**(ByVal array As Array, ByVal index As Integer) Implements ICollection.CopyTo
  Public Function **GetEnumerator**() As IEnumerator Implements IEnumerable.GetEnumerator
  Overridable Public Function **IndexOf**(ByVal value As Control) As Integer
  Overridable Public Sub **Remove**(ByVal value As Control)
  Overridable Public Sub **RemoveAt**(ByVal index As Integer)
End Class

CssStyleCollection

NotInheritable Class

System.Web.UI (system.web.dll)

This class contains a name-value collection of cascading style sheet (CSS) attributes for a specific control. CSS styles are used to configure many aspects of a control's appearance (such as font and color) and are supported for both web controls and HTML controls. A CssStyleCollection is provided through the System.Web.UI.HtmlControls.HtmlControl.Style and System.Web.UI.WebControls.WebControl.Style properties. This collection is similar to the AttributeCollection class, and you can retrieve values by using the specific attribute name or enumerating through the read-only Keys collection.

Public NotInheritable Class **CssStyleCollection**
' *Public Instance Properties*
  Public ReadOnly Property **Count** As Integer
  Public Default Property **Item** (ByVal key As String) As String
  Public ReadOnly Property **Keys** As ICollection
' *Public Instance Methods*
  Public Sub **Add**(ByVal key As String, ByVal value As String)
  Public Sub **Clear**()

```
      Public Sub Remove(ByVal key As String)
End Class
```

DataBinder

NotInheritable Class

System.Web.UI (system.web.dll)

This class contains a single shared utility method, Eval(), which allows you to specify data binding for controls like System.Web.UI.WebControls.DataList and System.Web.UI.WebControls.Repeater. The Eval() method accepts a string that identifies a field in the control's data source and uses it to retrieve the corresponding information. For example, the statement <%# DataBinder.Eval(Container.DataItem, "Name") %> in a template for a data control would retrieve data from the Name field of the control's bound data table. Note that you don't need to use this method to create a data binding expression (you can just use the <%# Container.DataItem("Name") %> syntax, which is faster). However, using the DataBinder method gives you the chance to supply a format string to configure date or numeric values.

```
Public NotInheritable Class DataBinder
' Public Constructors
    Public Sub New()
' Public Shared Methods
    Public Shared Function Eval(ByVal container As Object, ByVal expression As String) As Object
    Public Shared Function Eval(ByVal container As Object, ByVal expression As String, ByVal format As String) _
        As String
    Public Shared Function GetIndexedPropertyValue(ByVal container As Object, ByVal expr As String) As Object
    Public Shared Function GetIndexedPropertyValue(ByVal container As Object, ByVal propName As String, _
        ByVal format As String) As String
    Public Shared Function GetPropertyValue(ByVal container As Object, ByVal propName As String) As Object
    Public Shared Function GetPropertyValue(ByVal container As Object, ByVal propName As String, _
        ByVal format As String) As String
End Class
```

DataBinding

NotInheritable Class

System.Web.UI (system.web.dll)

This class represents a design-time data binding, which is contained in the DataBindingCollection. Generally, most developers will create data bindings at runtime instead, which allows increased flexibility and more transparent code.

You can configure data binding expressions by clicking the ellipsis (...) next to the (DataBindings) option in the Visual Studio .NET Properties window. Every data binding consists of an expression identifying the source (Expression), the bound property (PropertyName), and the data type (PropertyType).

```
Public NotInheritable Class DataBinding
' Public Constructors
    Public Sub New(ByVal propertyName As String, ByVal propertyType As Type, ByVal expression As String)
' Public Instance Properties
    Public Property Expression As String
    Public ReadOnly Property PropertyName As String
    Public ReadOnly Property PropertyType As Type
' Public Instance Methods
    Overrides Public Function Equals(ByVal obj As Object) As Boolean
    Overrides Public Function GetHashCode() As Integer
End Class
```

DataBindingCollection

System.Web.UI (system.web.dll)

This collection of DataBinding objects represents data binding expressions configured at design time.

```
Public NotInheritable Class DataBindingCollection : Implements ICollection, IEnumerable
' Public Constructors
   Public Sub New()
' Public Instance Properties
   Public ReadOnly Property Count As Integer Implements ICollection.Count
   Public ReadOnly Property IsReadOnly As Boolean
   Public ReadOnly Property IsSynchronized As Boolean Implements ICollection.IsSynchronized
   Public Default ReadOnly Property Item (ByVal propertyName As String) As DataBinding
   Public ReadOnly Property RemovedBindings As String()
   Public ReadOnly Property SyncRoot As Object Implements ICollection.SyncRoot
' Public Instance Methods
   Public Sub Add(ByVal binding As DataBinding)
   Public Sub Clear()
   Public Sub CopyTo(ByVal array As Array, ByVal index As Integer) Implements ICollection.CopyTo
   Public Function GetEnumerator() As IEnumerator Implements IEnumerable.GetEnumerator
   Public Sub Remove(ByVal binding As DataBinding)
   Public Sub Remove(ByVal propertyName As String)
   Public Sub Remove(ByVal propertyName As String, ByVal addToRemovedList As Boolean)
End Class
```

DataBindingHandlerAttribute

System.Web.UI (system.web.dll)

This class is used for controls requiring special data binding handlers. For example, the System.Web.UI.WebControls.Calendar control uses a System.Web.UI.Design.CalendarDataBindingHandler class that derives from System.Web.UI.Design.DataBindingHandler. This custom data binding handler is specified by using the DataBindingHandlerAttribute in the control's class declaration.

```
Public NotInheritable Class DataBindingHandlerAttribute : Inherits Attribute
' Public Constructors
   Public Sub New()
   Public Sub New(ByVal typeName As String)
   Public Sub New(ByVal type As Type)
' Public Shared Fields
   public Shared ReadOnly Default As DataBindingHandlerAttribute      =System.Web.UI.DataBindingHandlerAttribute
' Public Instance Properties
   Public ReadOnly Property HandlerTypeName As String
End Class
```

Hierarchy: System.Object → System.Attribute → DataBindingHandlerAttribute

Valid On: Class

DataBoundLiteralControl

System.Web.UI (system.web.dll)

ASP.NET creates a DataBoundLiteralControl for each data binding expression it finds on a page (such as <%# Container.DataItem("Name") %>). You do not need to create this control directly.

```
Public NotInheritable Class DataBoundLiteralControl : Inherits Control
' Public Constructors
    Public Sub New(ByVal staticLiteralsCount As Integer, ByVal dataBoundLiteralCount As Integer)
' Public Instance Properties
    Public ReadOnly Property Text As String
' Public Instance Methods
    Public Sub SetDataBoundString(ByVal index As Integer, ByVal s As String)
    Public Sub SetStaticString(ByVal index As Integer, ByVal s As String)
' Protected Instance Methods
    Overrides Protected Function CreateControlCollection() As ControlCollection
    Overrides Protected Sub LoadViewState(ByVal savedState As Object)
    Overrides Protected Sub Render(ByVal output As HtmlTextWriter)
    Overrides Protected Function SaveViewState() As Object
End Class
```

Hierarchy: System.Object → Control (System.ComponentModel.IComponent , System.IDisposable , IParserAccessor , IDataBindingsAccessor)→ DataBoundLiteralControl

DesignTimeParseData   NotInheritable Class
System.Web.UI (system.web.dll)

This class is used by the ASP.NET framework to parse *.aspx* files at design time. You do not use it in your code.

```
Public NotInheritable Class DesignTimeParseData
' Public Constructors
    Public Sub New(ByVal designerHost As System.ComponentModel.Design.IDesignerHost, ByVal parseText As String)
' Public Instance Properties
    Public Property DataBindingHandler As EventHandler
    Public ReadOnly Property DesignerHost As IDesignerHost
    Public Property DocumentUrl As String
    Public ReadOnly Property ParseText As String
End Class
```

DesignTimeTemplateParser   NotInheritable Class
System.Web.UI (system.web.dll)

This control is used by the ASP.NET framework to parse templated controls in *.aspx* files at design time. You do not use it in your code.

```
Public NotInheritable Class DesignTimeTemplateParser
' Public Shared Methods
    Public Shared Function ParseControl(ByVal data As DesignTimeParseData) As Control
    Public Shared Function ParseTemplate(ByVal data As DesignTimeParseData) As ITemplate
End Class
```

EmptyControlCollection   Class
System.Web.UI (system.web.dll)

This class represents a collection of controls that is always empty. Using the Add() method will trigger an exception.

```
Public Class EmptyControlCollection : Inherits ControlCollection
' Public Constructors
    Public Sub New(ByVal owner As Control)
```

' Public Instance Methods
Overrides Public Sub **Add**(ByVal child As Control)
Overrides Public Sub **AddAt**(ByVal index As Integer, ByVal child As Control)
End Class

Hierarchy: System.Object → ControlCollection (System.Collections.ICollection ,
System.Collections.IEnumerable)→ EmptyControlCollection

Html32TextWriter   Class

System.Web.UI (system.web.dll)   *marshal by reference, disposable*

This class derives from HtmlTextWriter and is used by the ASP.NET framework to generate
HTML output for ASP.NET controls.

Public Class **Html32TextWriter** : Inherits HtmlTextWriter
' Public Constructors
Public Sub **New**(ByVal writer As System.IO.TextWriter)
Public Sub **New**(ByVal writer As System.IO.TextWriter, ByVal tabString As String)
' Protected Instance Properties
Protected Property **FontStack** As Stack
' Public Instance Methods
Overrides Public Sub **RenderBeginTag**(ByVal tagKey As HtmlTextWriterTag)
Overrides Public Sub **RenderEndTag**()
' Protected Instance Methods
Overrides Protected Function **GetTagName**(ByVal tagKey As HtmlTextWriterTag) As String
Overrides Protected Function **OnStyleAttributeRender**(ByVal name As String, ByVal value As String, _
    ByVal key As HtmlTextWriterStyle) As Boolean
Overrides Protected Function **OnTagRender**(ByVal name As String, ByVal key As HtmlTextWriterTag) As Boolean
Overrides Protected Function **RenderAfterContent**() As String
Overrides Protected Function **RenderAfterTag**() As String
Overrides Protected Function **RenderBeforeContent**() As String
Overrides Protected Function **RenderBeforeTag**() As String
End Class

Hierarchy: System.Object → System.MarshalByRefObject → System.IO.TextWriter (
System.IDisposable)→ HtmlTextWriter → Html32TextWriter

HtmlTextWriter   Class

System.Web.UI (system.web.dll)   *marshal by reference, disposable*

The ASP.NET framework uses this class when writing the client-side HTML for a Web
Forms page. It contains a wealth of methods for rendering the appropriate content, and
derives from the more generic System.IO.TextWriter. Typically, you will not use this class
directly in your code, unless you are a control developer.

When deriving custom controls from Control or System.Web.UI.WebControls.WebControl, you
can override the Render() or RenderContents() method and create the control's output by
using the supplied HtmlTextWriter. Commonly used methods include Write(), which can
output text or HTML tags, AddStyleAttribute(), which specifies a CSS style attribute for the
next tag, and RenderBeginTag() and RenderEndTag(), which make it easy to insert open and
closing HTML tags while keeping the code readable. The HtmlTextWriter also performs
automatic indentation of the HTML output.

Public Class **HtmlTextWriter** : Inherits System.IO.TextWriter
' Public Constructors

UI Namespace

Public Sub **New**(ByVal writer As System.IO.TextWriter)	
Public Sub **New**(ByVal writer As System.IO.TextWriter, ByVal tabString As String)	

' Public Shared Fields

public const **DefaultTabString** As String	=
public const **DoubleQuoteChar** As Char	= [amp] H000000022
public const **EndTagLeftChars** As String	= [lt]/
public const **EqualsChar** As Char	= [amp] H00000003D
public const **EqualsDoubleQuoteString** As String	== [quot]
public const **SelfClosingChars** As String	= /
public const **SelfClosingTagEnd** As String	= / [gt]
public const **SemicolonChar** As Char	= [amp] H00000003B
public const **SingleQuoteChar** As Char	= [amp] H000000027
public const **SlashChar** As Char	= [amp] H00000002F
public const **SpaceChar** As Char	= [amp] H000000020
public const **StyleEqualsChar** As Char	= [amp] H00000003A
public const **TagLeftChar** As Char	= [amp] H00000003C
public const **TagRightChar** As Char	= [amp] H00000003E

' Public Instance Properties

Overrides Public ReadOnly Property **Encoding** As Encoding
Public Property **Indent** As Integer
Public Property **InnerWriter** As TextWriter
Overrides Public Property **NewLine** As String

' Protected Instance Properties

Protected Property **TagKey** As HtmlTextWriterTag
Protected Property **TagName** As String

' Protected Shared Methods

Shared Protected Sub **RegisterAttribute**(ByVal name As String, ByVal key As HtmlTextWriterAttribute)
Shared Protected Sub **RegisterStyle**(ByVal name As String, ByVal key As HtmlTextWriterStyle)
Shared Protected Sub **RegisterTag**(ByVal name As String, ByVal key As HtmlTextWriterTag)

' Public Instance Methods

Overridable Public Sub **AddAttribute**(ByVal key As HtmlTextWriterAttribute, ByVal value As String)
Overridable Public Sub **AddAttribute**(ByVal key As HtmlTextWriterAttribute, ByVal value As String, _
  ByVal fEncode As Boolean)
Overridable Public Sub **AddAttribute**(ByVal name As String, ByVal value As String)
Overridable Public Sub **AddAttribute**(ByVal name As String, ByVal value As String, ByVal fEndode As Boolean)
Overridable Public Sub **AddStyleAttribute**(ByVal key As HtmlTextWriterStyle, ByVal value As String)
Overridable Public Sub **AddStyleAttribute**(ByVal name As String, ByVal value As String)
Overrides Public Sub **Close**()
Overrides Public Sub **Flush**()
Overridable Public Sub **RenderBeginTag**(ByVal tagKey As HtmlTextWriterTag)
Overridable Public Sub **RenderBeginTag**(ByVal tagName As String)
Overridable Public Sub **RenderEndTag**()
Overrides Public Sub **Write**(ByVal value As Boolean)
Overrides Public Sub **Write**(ByVal value As Char)
Overrides Public Sub **Write**(ByVal buffer As Char())
Overrides Public Sub **Write**(ByVal buffer As Char(), ByVal index As Integer, ByVal count As Integer)
Overrides Public Sub **Write**(ByVal value As Double)
Overrides Public Sub **Write**(ByVal value As Integer)
Overrides Public Sub **Write**(ByVal value As Long)
Overrides Public Sub **Write**(ByVal value As Object)
Overrides Public Sub **Write**(ByVal value As Single)
Overrides Public Sub **Write**(ByVal s As String)
Overrides Public Sub **Write**(ByVal format As String, ByVal arg0 As Object)
Overrides Public Sub **Write**(ByVal format As String, ParamArray arg As Object())
Overrides Public Sub **Write**(ByVal format As String, ByVal arg0 As Object, ByVal arg1 As Object)

Overridable Public Sub **WriteAttribute**(ByVal name As String, ByVal value As String)
Overridable Public Sub **WriteAttribute**(ByVal name As String, ByVal value As String, ByVal fEncode As Boolean)
Overridable Public Sub **WriteBeginTag**(ByVal tagName As String)
Overridable Public Sub **WriteEndTag**(ByVal tagName As String)
Overridable Public Sub **WriteFullBeginTag**(ByVal tagName As String)
Overrides Public Sub **WriteLine**()
Overrides Public Sub **WriteLine**(ByVal value As Boolean)
Overrides Public Sub **WriteLine**(ByVal value As Char)
Overrides Public Sub **WriteLine**(ByVal buffer As Char())
Overrides Public Sub **WriteLine**(ByVal buffer As Char(), ByVal index As Integer, ByVal count As Integer)
Overrides Public Sub **WriteLine**(ByVal value As Double)
Overrides Public Sub **WriteLine**(ByVal value As Integer)
Overrides Public Sub **WriteLine**(ByVal value As Long)
Overrides Public Sub **WriteLine**(ByVal value As Object)
Overrides Public Sub **WriteLine**(ByVal value As Single)
Overrides Public Sub **WriteLine**(ByVal s As String)
Overrides Public Sub **WriteLine**(ByVal format As String, ByVal arg0 As Object)
Overrides Public Sub **WriteLine**(ByVal format As String, ParamArray arg As Object())
Overrides Public Sub **WriteLine**(ByVal format As String, ByVal arg0 As Object, ByVal arg1 As Object)
Overrides Public Sub **WriteLine**(ByVal value As UInt32)
Public Sub **WriteLineNoTabs**(ByVal s As String)
Overridable Public Sub **WriteStyleAttribute**(ByVal name As String, ByVal value As String)
Overridable Public Sub **WriteStyleAttribute**(ByVal name As String, ByVal value As String, _
  ByVal fEncode As Boolean)
' *Protected Instance Methods*
Overridable Protected Sub **AddAttribute**(ByVal name As String, ByVal value As String, _
  ByVal key As HtmlTextWriterAttribute)
Overridable Protected Sub **AddStyleAttribute**(ByVal name As String, ByVal value As String, _
  ByVal key As HtmlTextWriterStyle)
Overridable Protected Function **EncodeAttributeValue**(ByVal attrKey As HtmlTextWriterAttribute, _
  ByVal value As String) As String
Protected Function **EncodeAttributeValue**(ByVal value As String, ByVal fEncode As Boolean) As String
Protected Function **EncodeUrl**(ByVal url As String) As String
Overridable Protected Sub **FilterAttributes**()
Protected Function **GetAttributeKey**(ByVal attrName As String) As HtmlTextWriterAttribute
Protected Function **GetAttributeName**(ByVal attrKey As HtmlTextWriterAttribute) As String
Protected Function **GetStyleKey**(ByVal styleName As String) As HtmlTextWriterStyle
Protected Function **GetStyleName**(ByVal styleKey As HtmlTextWriterStyle) As String
Overridable Protected Function **GetTagKey**(ByVal tagName As String) As HtmlTextWriterTag
Overridable Protected Function **GetTagName**(ByVal tagKey As HtmlTextWriterTag) As String
Protected Function **IsAttributeDefined**(ByVal key As HtmlTextWriterAttribute) As Boolean
Protected Function **IsAttributeDefined**(ByVal key As HtmlTextWriterAttribute, ByRef value As String) As Boolean
Protected Function **IsStyleAttributeDefined**(ByVal key As HtmlTextWriterStyle) As Boolean
Protected Function **IsStyleAttributeDefined**(ByVal key As HtmlTextWriterStyle, ByRef value As String) _
  As Boolean
Overridable Protected Function **OnAttributeRender**(ByVal name As String, ByVal value As String, _
  ByVal key As HtmlTextWriterAttribute) As Boolean
Overridable Protected Function **OnStyleAttributeRender**(ByVal name As String, ByVal value As String, _
  ByVal key As HtmlTextWriterStyle) As Boolean
Overridable Protected Function **OnTagRender**(ByVal name As String, ByVal key As HtmlTextWriterTag) As Boolean
Overridable Protected Sub **OutputTabs**()
Protected Function **PopEndTag**() As String
Protected Sub **PushEndTag**(ByVal endTag As String)
Overridable Protected Function **RenderAfterContent**() As String
Overridable Protected Function **RenderAfterTag**() As String

---

Overridable Protected Function **RenderBeforeContent**() As String
Overridable Protected Function **RenderBeforeTag**() As String
End Class

Hierarchy: System.Object → System.MarshalByRefObject → System.IO.TextWriter (
System.IDisposable)→ HtmlTextWriter

HtmlTextWriterAttribute

Enum

System.Web.UI (system.web.dll)

serializable

This enumeration specifies the HTML attributes that should be written to the opening
tag of an HTML element when a client request is processed. It is used by several methods in the HtmlTextWriter class.

Public Enum **HtmlTextWriterAttribute**
    Accesskey = 0
    Align = 1
    Alt = 2
    Background = 3
    Bgcolor = 4
    Border = 5
    Bordercolor = 6
    Cellpadding = 7
    Cellspacing = 8
    Checked = 9
    Class = 10
    Cols = 11
    Colspan = 12
    Disabled = 13
    For = 14
    Height = 15
    Href = 16
    Id = 17
    Maxlength = 18
    Multiple = 19
    Name = 20
    Nowrap = 21
    Onchange = 22
    Onclick = 23
    ReadOnly = 24
    Rows = 25
    Rowspan = 26
    Rules = 27
    Selected = 28
    Size = 29
    Src = 30
    Style = 31
    Tabindex = 32
    Target = 33
    Title = 34
    Type = 35
    Valign = 36
    Value = 37
    Width = 38
    Wrap = 39

End Enum

Hierarchy: System.Object → System.ValueType → System.Enum (System.IComparable , System.IFormattable , System.IConvertible) → HtmlTextWriterAttribute

HtmlTextWriterStyle
System.Web.UI (system.web.dll)

Enum

serializable

This enumeration specifies HTML styles that the methods in the HtmlTextWriter class can use to create output.

```
Public Enum HtmlTextWriterStyle
      BackgroundColor = 0
      BackgroundImage = 1
      BorderCollapse = 2
      BorderColor = 3
      BorderStyle = 4
      BorderWidth = 5
      Color = 6
      FontFamily = 7
      FontSize = 8
      FontStyle = 9
      FontWeight = 10
      Height = 11
      TextDecoration = 12
      Width = 13
End Enum
```

Hierarchy: System.Object → System.ValueType → System.Enum (System.IComparable , System.IFormattable , System.IConvertible) → HtmlTextWriterStyle

HtmlTextWriterTag
System.Web.UI (system.web.dll)

Enum

serializable

This enumeration represents different HTML tags for the HtmlTextWriter class. For example, you can use a value from this enumeration as a parameter for the HtmlTextWriter.RenderBeginTag() method to specify what tag should be written to the output stream.

```
Public Enum HtmlTextWriterTag
      Unknown = 0
      A = 1
      Acronym = 2
      Address = 3
      Area = 4
      B = 5
      Base = 6
      Basefont = 7
      Bdo = 8
      Bgsound = 9
      Big = 10
      Blockquote = 11
      Body = 12
      Br = 13
      Button = 14
```

```
Caption = 15
Center = 16
Cite = 17
Code = 18
Col = 19
Colgroup = 20
Dd = 21
Del = 22
Dfn = 23
Dir = 24
Div = 25
Dl = 26
Dt = 27
Em = 28
Embed = 29
Fieldset = 30
Font = 31
Form = 32
Frame = 33
Frameset = 34
H1 = 35
H2 = 36
H3 = 37
H4 = 38
H5 = 39
H6 = 40
Head = 41
Hr = 42
Html = 43
I = 44
Iframe = 45
Img = 46
Input = 47
Ins = 48
Isindex = 49
Kbd = 50
Label = 51
Legend = 52
Li = 53
Link = 54
Map = 55
Marquee = 56
Menu = 57
Meta = 58
Nobr = 59
Noframes = 60
Noscript = 61
Object = 62
Ol = 63
Option = 64
P = 65
Param = 66
Pre = 67
Q = 68
Rt = 69
```

Ruby = 70	
S = 71	
Samp = 72	
Script = 73	
Select = 74	
Small = 75	
Span = 76	
Strike = 77	
Strong = 78	
Style = 79	
Sub = 80	
Sup = 81	
Table = 82	
Tbody = 83	
Td = 84	
Textarea = 85	
Tfoot = 86	
Th = 87	
Thead = 88	
Title = 89	
Tr = 90	
Tt = 91	
U = 92	
Ul = 93	
Var = 94	
Wbr = 95	
Xml = 96	

End Enum

Hierarchy: System.Object → System.ValueType → System.Enum (System.IComparable , System.IFormattable , System.IConvertible)→ HtmlTextWriterTag

IAttributeAccessor   Interface

System.Web.UI (system.web.dll)

This interface defines a GetAttribute() and a SetAttribute() method that provide programmatic access to the style attributes defined in the opening tag for a server control. This interface is implemented by System.Web.UI.WebControls.WebControl and System.Web.UI.HtmlControls.HtmlControl, both of which also provide an AttributeCollection through the Style property. Although you can use this interface if you create a custom control that derives from Control, it is easier to just inherit directly from System.Web.UI.WebControls.WebControl.

Public Interface **IAttributeAccessor**
' *Public Instance Methods*
    Public Function **GetAttribute**(ByVal key As String) As String
    Public Sub **SetAttribute**(ByVal key As String, ByVal value As String)
End Interface

IDataBindingsAccessor   Interface

System.Web.UI (system.web.dll)

This interface is implemented by all controls that derive from Control. It allows access to the corresponding DataBindingCollection through the DataBindings property. As the DataBindingCollection represents data bindings created in the IDE, the properties in this interface are only valid at design time.

```
Public Interface IDataBindingsAccessor
' Public Instance Properties
    Public ReadOnly Property DataBindings As DataBindingCollection
    Public ReadOnly Property HasDataBindings As Boolean
End Interface
```

ImageClickEventArgs   NotInheritable Class
System.Web.UI (system.web.dll)

This custom System.EventArgs object provides extra information for some image-click events. These include the System.Web.UI.WebControls.ImageButton.Click and System.Web.UI.HtmlControls.HtmlInputImage.ServerClick events. Note that the System.Web.UI.WebControls.Image and System.Web.UI.HtmlControls.HtmlImage controls do not use this class.

The extra information consists of two coordinates indicating the exact position where the image was clicked: X and Y. These coordinates are measured from the top-left corner, which has the coordinates (0, 0) by convention.

```
Public NotInheritable Class ImageClickEventArgs : Inherits EventArgs
' Public Constructors
    Public Sub New(ByVal x As Integer, ByVal y As Integer)
' Public Instance Fields
    public X As Integer
    public Y As Integer
End Class
```

Hierarchy: System.Object → System.EventArgs → ImageClickEventArgs

ImageClickEventHandler   Delegate
System.Web.UI (system.web.dll)   *serializable*

This delegate specifies the signature for the event handler that handles the System.Web.UI.WebControls.ImageButton.Click and System.Web.UI.HtmlControls.HtmlInputImage.ServerClick events. This event handler receives extra information about the exact coordinates where the image was clicked.

```
Public Delegate Sub ImageClickEventHandler(ByVal sender As Object, ByVal e As ImageClickEventArgs)
```

INamingContainer   Interface
System.Web.UI (system.web.dll)

This is a marker interface. When ASP.NET renders a control that implements INamingContainer, it creates a new namespace and uses it for any child controls. This guarantees that the child control IDs will be unique on the page. This interface is used for controls that dynamically generate a series of similar controls, such as System.Web.UI.WebControls.Repeater and System.Web.UI.WebControls.RadioButtonList. If you are developing your own composite control, you will also need to implement this interface.

```
Public Interface INamingContainer
' No public or protected members
End Interface
```

IParserAccessor
Interface

System.Web.UI (system.web.dll)

This interface is implemented by the Control class. It allows the ASP.NET framework to access the parser for the control.

```
Public Interface IParserAccessor
' Public Instance Methods
   Public Sub AddParsedSubObject(ByVal obj As Object)
End Interface
```

IPostBackDataHandler
Interface

System.Web.UI (system.web.dll)

This interface, which is implemented by many ASP.NET Server Controls, allows a control to receive and process postback data. It consists of two methods. The first, LoadPost-Data(), allows a control to receive the form data and update its properties as required. ASP.NET calls this method automatically on postback. It provides form data as a collection in the postCollection argument and a postDataKey argument identifying the control's key (i.e., postCollection(postDataKey) will contain the posted information for the control). The control returns True from this method to indicate that its state has changed, or False if it hasn't. ASP.NET calls the second method, RaisePostDataChangedEvent(), automatically after LoadPostData() if the control's state is changed. The control can use this method to raise any required events. Events should never be raised from the LoadPostData() method because other controls may not have loaded their state information yet.

```
Public Interface IPostBackDataHandler
' Public Instance Methods
   Public Function LoadPostData(ByVal postDataKey As String,          _
     ByVal postCollection As System.Collections.Specialized.NameValueCollection) As Boolean
   Public Sub RaisePostDataChangedEvent()
End Interface
```

IPostBackEventHandler
Interface

System.Web.UI (system.web.dll)

This interface allows a control to raise events in response to a postback operation. This interface is commonly used for button controls like System.Web.UI.WebControls.Button and System.Web.UI.WebControls.ImageButton. It can be used instead of, or in conjunction with, the IPostBackDataHandler interface. The distinction is that the RaisePostBackEvent() method is always called when a postback event occurs. The IPostBackDataHandler.RaisePostDataChangedEvent() method is called only if the control's state has changed, and is thus more suited for a "Change" event than a "Click" event.

```
Public Interface IPostBackEventHandler
' Public Instance Methods
   Public Sub RaisePostBackEvent(ByVal eventArgument As String)
End Interface
```

IStateManager
Interface

System.Web.UI (system.web.dll)

This interface provides methods that are used to manage view state, which is the set of information that describes a control's current state. View state is stored in a hidden field on a Web Forms page, so it can be maintained across postbacks. State management is built into the Control class, and you can write values into the Control.ViewState collection to store any information you need without using IStateManager. However, you can also create a custom control that implements this interface to customize how state management works. The IStateManager consists of three methods: SaveViewState(), which stores changes to an object, LoadViewState(), which retrieves and applies previously stored values, and TrackViewState(), which sets the IsTrackingViewState property to True and instructs ASP.NET to track changes to the control's view state.

```
Public Interface IStateManager
' Public Instance Properties
    Public ReadOnly Property IsTrackingViewState As Boolean
' Public Instance Methods
    Public Sub LoadViewState(ByVal state As Object)
    Public Function SaveViewState() As Object
    Public Sub TrackViewState()
End Interface
```

ITagNameToTypeMapper   Interface
System.Web.UI (system.web.dll)

This interface consists of a single method GetControlType(), which accepts a string containing a control tag and returns a System.Type object identifying the corresponding control class.

```
Interface ITagNameToTypeMapper
' Public Instance Methods
    Public Function GetControlType(ByVal tagName As String, ByVal attribs As System.Collections.IDictionary) _
    As Type
End Interface
```

ITemplate   Interface
System.Web.UI (system.web.dll)

Templates allow controls to make portions of their user interface configurable. Templates are used in classes like System.Web.UI.WebControls.DataList and can be added in your own custom controls by declaring properties of type ITemplate (for example, an ItemStyle or HeaderStyle property). This allows the user to specify a template for a portion of your control.

Your custom control code uses a supplied template by invoking the InstantiateIn() method. This method accepts a control reference and populates its Control.Controls collection with one or more server controls that represent the user interface defined in the template. The control you supply to the InstantiateIn() method could be the current control, or one of the current control's children. Note that you do not need to write the implementation code for this method, as the .NET framework provides it intrinsically.

```
Public Interface ITemplate
' Public Instance Methods
    Public Sub InstantiateIn(ByVal container As Control)
End Interface
```

IValidator   Interface
System.Web.UI (system.web.dll)

This interface defines members used for validation controls. The Validate() method is used to examine supplied information, compare it with the valid parameters, and update IsValid property appropriately. The ErrorMessage contains the message that should be generated for the user when the supplied information is not valid.

When creating a custom validation control, you do not need to implement this interface. Instead, you should inherit from one of the validation classes in the System.Web.UI.WebControls namespace. The base class, System.Web.UI.WebControls.BaseValidator, implements this interface.

```
Public Interface IValidator
' Public Instance Properties
    Public Property ErrorMessage As String
    Public Property IsValid As Boolean
' Public Instance Methods
    Public Sub Validate()
End Interface
```

LiteralControl
Class

System.Web.UI (system.web.dll)
disposable

The ASP.NET parser automatically creates LiteralControl instances for any text or HTML it finds in a page that does not correspond to a server control, and then adds them to the containing control's Control.Controls collection. You should not confuse this class with the System.Web.UI.WebControls.Literal control class, which can be used to add simple text to a web page (much like an unformatted Label control).

```
Public Class LiteralControl : Inherits Control
' Public Constructors
    Public Sub New()
    Public Sub New(ByVal text As String)
' Public Instance Properties
    Overridable Public Property Text As String
' Protected Instance Methods
    Overrides Protected Function CreateControlCollection() As ControlCollection
    Overrides Protected Sub Render(ByVal output As HtmlTextWriter)
End Class
```

Hierarchy: System.Object → Control (System.ComponentModel.IComponent , System.IDisposable , IParserAccessor , IDataBindingsAccessor)→ LiteralControl

LosFormatter
NotInheritable Class

System.Web.UI (system.web.dll)

This class is used by ASP.NET to implement Limited Object Serialization (LOS) for view state. It converts the data stored in every control's StateBag into a lightly encrypted, condensed ASCII field that is added to the page as a hidden input control. While you can store complex information in the StateBag, the LosFormatter is optimized for strings, arrays, hashtables, and other primitive .NET types defined in the System namespace. This class provides functionality through the methods Serialize() and Deserialize().

```
Public NotInheritable Class LosFormatter
' Public Constructors
    Public Sub New()
' Public Instance Methods
    Public Function Deserialize(ByVal stream As System.IO.Stream) As Object
    Public Function Deserialize(ByVal input As String) As Object
    Public Function Deserialize(ByVal input As System.IO.TextReader) As Object
    Public Sub Serialize(ByVal stream As System.IO.Stream, ByVal value As Object)
    Public Sub Serialize(ByVal output As System.IO.TextWriter, ByVal value As Object)
End Class
```

UI Namespace

ObjectConverter
Notinheritable Class

System.Web.UI (system.web.dll)

This class is used automatically by the ASP.NET framework and never used directly in your code.

```
Public NotInheritable Class ObjectConverter
' Public Constructors
   Public Sub New()
' Public Shared Methods
   Public Shared Function ConvertValue(ByVal value As Object, ByVal toType As Type, ByVal formatString As String) _
   As Object
End Class
```

ObjectTagBuilder
Notinheritable Class

System.Web.UI (system.web.dll)

This class is used automatically by the ASP.NET framework and never used directly in your code.

```
Public NotInheritable Class ObjectTagBuilder : Inherits ControlBuilder
' Public Constructors
   Public Sub New()
' Public Instance Methods
   Overrides Public Sub AppendLiteralString(ByVal s As String)
   Overrides Public Sub AppendSubBuilder(ByVal subBuilder As ControlBuilder)
   Overrides Public Sub Init(ByVal parser As TemplateParser, ByVal parentBuilder As ControlBuilder, ByVal type As Type _
   , ByVal tagName As String, ByVal id As String, ByVal attribs As System.Collections.IDictionary)
End Class
```

Hierarchy: System.Object → ControlBuilder → ObjectTagBuilder

OutputCacheLocation
Enum

System.Web.UI (system.web.dll)
serializable

You can enable output caching for an ASP.NET page by using the System.Web.HttpCachePolicy class or adding a page directive. This enumeration is used by ASP.NET when it calls the Page.InitOutputCache() method. It specifies whether the page is cached locally on the client (Client), on the web server (Server), or on another server between the client and the web server (Downstream).

```
Public Enum OutputCacheLocation
      Any = 0
      Client = 1
      Downstream = 2
      Server = 3
      None = 4
End Enum
```

Hierarchy: System.Object → System.ValueType → System.Enum (System.IComparable , System.IFormattable , System.IConvertible)→ OutputCacheLocation

Page

System.Web.UI (system.web.dll)

All Web Forms you create for an ASP.NET application derive implicitly or explicitly from Page. This class, which is a special subclass of Control, adds additional page-specific functionality. For example, rather than simply providing the Control.Context property, the Page class provides the traditional built-in objects through references like Response, Request, and Application. The Page class also provides properties that allow you to use tracing (Trace and TraceEnabled) and access all the validation controls and information about whether their validation was successful (Validators and IsValid).

Another useful property is IsPostBack, which you can test in the Load event. Typically, you will skip control initialization if this property returns True, indicating that the page has already been displayed and the control values will be persisted in view state. You can also set AspCompatMode to True so the Page will be executed on a single-threaded apartment (STA) thread. This setting allows the page to call other STA components, such as those you may have developed with Visual Basic 6 (although it can hamper performance significantly).

Most Page methods are used by the ASP.NET framework and will never be used in your code. One exception is MapPath(), which returns the physical path on the server that corresponds to a specified virtual path (URL).

```
Public Class Page : Inherits TemplateControl : Implements System.Web.IHttpHandler
' Public Constructors
   Public Sub New()
' Protected Shared Fields
   protected const postEventArgumentID As String                              =__EVENTARGUMENT
   protected const postEventSourceID As String                                =__EVENTTARGET
' Public Instance Properties
   Public ReadOnly Property Application As HttpApplicationState
   Public ReadOnly Property Cache As Cache
   Public Property ClientTarget As String
   Overrides Public Property EnableViewState As Boolean
   Public Property ErrorPage As String
   Overrides Public Property ID As String
   Public ReadOnly Property IsPostBack As Boolean
   Public ReadOnly Property IsReusable As Boolean Implements IHttpHandler.IsReusable
   Public ReadOnly Property IsValid As Boolean
   Public ReadOnly Property Request As HttpRequest
   Public ReadOnly Property Response As HttpResponse
   Public ReadOnly Property Server As HttpServerUtility
   Overridable Public ReadOnly Property Session As HttpSessionState
   Public Property SmartNavigation As Boolean
   Public ReadOnly Property Trace As TraceContext
   Public ReadOnly Property User As IPrincipal
   Public ReadOnly Property Validators As ValidatorCollection
   Overrides Public Property Visible As Boolean
' Protected Instance Properties
   Protected Property AspCompatMode As Boolean
   Protected Property Buffer As Boolean
   Protected Property CodePage As Integer
   Protected Property ContentType As String
   Overrides Protected Property Context As HttpContext
   Protected Property Culture As String
   Protected Property EnableViewStateMac As Boolean
   Protected Property FileDependencies As ArrayList
```

Protected Property **LCID** As Integer
Protected Property **ResponseEncoding** As String
Protected Property **TraceEnabled** As Boolean
Protected Property **TraceModeValue** As TraceMode
Protected Property **TransactionMode** As Integer
Protected Property **UICulture** As String
' *Public Instance Methods*
Public Sub **DesignerInitialize**()
Public Function **GetPostBackClientEvent**(ByVal control As Control, ByVal argument As String) As String
Public Function **GetPostBackClientHyperlink**(ByVal control As Control, ByVal argument As String) As String
Public Function **GetPostBackEventReference**(ByVal control As Control) As String
Public Function **GetPostBackEventReference**(ByVal control As Control, ByVal argument As String) As String
Overridable Public Function **GetTypeHashCode**() As Integer
Public Function **IsClientScriptBlockRegistered**(ByVal key As String) As Boolean
Public Function **IsStartupScriptRegistered**(ByVal key As String) As Boolean
Public Function **MapPath**(ByVal virtualPath As String) As String
Public Sub **ProcessRequest**(ByVal context As System.Web.HttpContext) _
    Implements IHttpHandler.ProcessRequest
Public Sub **RegisterArrayDeclaration**(ByVal arrayName As String, ByVal arrayValue As String)
Overridable Public Sub **RegisterClientScriptBlock**(ByVal key As String, ByVal script As String)
Overridable Public Sub **RegisterHiddenField**(ByVal hiddenFieldName As String, _
    ByVal hiddenFieldInitialValue As String)
Public Sub **RegisterOnSubmitStatement**(ByVal key As String, ByVal script As String)
Public Sub **RegisterRequiresPostBack**(ByVal control As Control)
Overridable Public Sub **RegisterRequiresRaiseEvent**(ByVal control As IPostBackEventHandler)
Overridable Public Sub **RegisterStartupScript**(ByVal key As String, ByVal script As String)
Public Sub **RegisterViewStateHandler**()
Overridable Public Sub **Validate**()
Overridable Public Sub **VerifyRenderingInServerForm**(ByVal control As Control)
' *Protected Instance Methods*
Protected Function **AspCompatBeginProcessRequest**(ByVal context As System.Web.HttpContext, _
    ByVal cb As AsyncCallback, ByVal extraData As Object) As IAsyncResult
Protected Sub **AspCompatEndProcessRequest**(ByVal result As IAsyncResult)
Overridable Protected Function **CreateHtmlTextWriter**(ByVal tw As System.IO.TextWriter) As HtmlTextWriter
Overridable Protected Function **DeterminePostBackMode**() As NameValueCollection
Overridable Protected Sub **InitOutputCache**(ByVal duration As Integer, ByVal varyByHeader As String, _
    ByVal varyByCustom As String, ByVal location As OutputCacheLocation, ByVal varyByParam As String)
Overridable Protected Function **LoadPageStateFromPersistenceMedium**() As Object
Overridable Protected Sub **RaisePostBackEvent**(ByVal sourceControl As IPostBackEventHandler, _
    ByVal eventArgument As String)
Overridable Protected Sub **SavePageStateToPersistenceMedium**(ByVal viewState As Object)
End Class

Hierarchy: System.Object → Control (System.ComponentModel.IComponent , System.IDisposable
, IParserAccessor , IDataBindingsAccessor)→ TemplateControl (INamingContainer)→ Page (
System.Web.IHttpHandler)

PageParser
NotInheritable Class

System.Web.UI (system.web.dll)

This class provides a page parser that compiles an *.aspx* file into a custom Page object.

Public NotInheritable Class **PageParser** : Inherits TemplateControlParser
' *Public Constructors*
Public Sub **New**()
' *Public Shared Methods*

```
Public Shared Function GetCompiledPageInstance(ByVal virtualPath As String, ByVal inputFile As String, _
    ByVal context As System.Web.HttpContext) As IHttpHandler
' Protected Instance Methods
    Overrides Protected Function CompileIntoType() As Type
End Class
```

Hierarchy: System.Object → BaseParser → TemplateParser → TemplateControlParser →
PageParser

Pair   Class

System.Web.UI (system.web.dll)

This class is used internally for the LosFormatter. It contains two types that can be serialized into view state.

```
Public Class Pair
' Public Constructors
    Public Sub New()
    Public Sub New(ByVal x As Object, ByVal y As Object)
' Public Instance Fields
    public First As Object
    public Second As Object
End Class
```

ParseChildrenAttribute   NotInheritable Class

System.Web.UI (system.web.dll)

You can use this attribute to mark the class declaration for any custom controls that you create. If you specify True for the ChildrenAsProperties property, the ASP.NET parser will treat any subelements inside your control tag as object properties. If you do not use this attribute or you specify False, ASP.NET will assume that nested elements should be added as child controls. In this case, you can still set object properties by using the "object walker" syntax, where properties are split by using a dash (as in <MyControls MyObject-MyProperty="Value" />).

```
Public NotInheritable Class ParseChildrenAttribute : Inherits Attribute
' Public Constructors
    Public Sub New()
    Public Sub New(ByVal childrenAsProperties As Boolean)
    Public Sub New(ByVal childrenAsProperties As Boolean, ByVal defaultProperty As String)
' Public Shared Fields
    public Shared ReadOnly Default As ParseChildrenAttribute        =System.Web.UI.ParseChildrenAttribute
' Public Instance Properties
    Public Property ChildrenAsProperties As Boolean
    Public Property DefaultProperty As String
' Public Instance Methods
    Overrides Public Function Equals(ByVal obj As Object) As Boolean
    Overrides Public Function GetHashCode() As Integer
    Overrides Public Function IsDefaultAttribute() As Boolean
End Class
```

Hierarchy: System.Object → System.Attribute → ParseChildrenAttribute

Valid On: Class

PartialCachingAttribute

NotInheritable Class

System.Web.UI (system.web.dll)

This class specifies the attributes that can be set on user controls for fragment caching. To enable fragment caching, use the <OutputCache> directive at the beginning of the appropriate *.ascx* file. ASP.NET will automatically generate this attribute when the user control is requested. Alternatively, you can leave out the directive and use this attribute in the code-behind class for the user control.

Public NotInheritable Class **PartialCachingAttribute** : Inherits Attribute
' Public Constructors
   Public Sub **New**(ByVal duration As Integer)
   Public Sub **New**(ByVal duration As Integer, ByVal varyByParams As String, ByVal varyByControls As String, _
    ByVal varyByCustom As String)
' Public Instance Properties
   Public ReadOnly Property **Duration** As Integer
   Public ReadOnly Property **VaryByControls** As String
   Public ReadOnly Property **VaryByCustom** As String
   Public ReadOnly Property **VaryByParams** As String
End Class

Hierarchy: System.Object → System.Attribute → PartialCachingAttribute

Valid On: Class

PartialCachingControl

Class

System.Web.UI (system.web.dll)

disposable

This class is utilized by the ASP.NET framework to use fragment caching with user controls. You can enable fragment caching by using the <OutputCache> directive at the beginning of the appropriate *.ascx* file.

Public Class **PartialCachingControl** : Inherits BasePartialCachingControl
' Public Instance Properties
   Public ReadOnly Property **CachedControl** As Control
End Class

Hierarchy: System.Object → Control (System.ComponentModel.IComponent , System.IDisposable , IParserAccessor , IDataBindingsAccessor)→ BasePartialCachingControl → PartialCachingControl

PersistChildrenAttribute

NotInheritable Class

System.Web.UI (system.web.dll)

This attribute indicates how the child controls of an ASP.NET Server Control should be persisted at design time. If set to True, the child controls are persisted as nested inner server control tags. If False, the properties of the control may be persisted as inner tags.

Public NotInheritable Class **PersistChildrenAttribute** : Inherits Attribute
' Public Constructors
   Public Sub **New**(ByVal persist As Boolean)
' Public Shared Fields
   public Shared ReadOnly **Default** As PersistChildrenAttribute   *=System.Web.UI.PersistChildrenAttribute*
   public Shared ReadOnly **No** As PersistChildrenAttribute   *=System.Web.UI.PersistChildrenAttribute*
   public Shared ReadOnly **Yes** As PersistChildrenAttribute   *=System.Web.UI.PersistChildrenAttribute*
' Public Instance Properties
   Public ReadOnly Property **Persist** As Boolean

' *Public Instance Methods*

Overrides Public Function **Equals**(ByVal obj As Object) As Boolean
Overrides Public Function **GetHashCode**() As Integer
Overrides Public Function **IsDefaultAttribute**() As Boolean
End Class

Hierarchy: System.Object → System.Attribute → PersistChildrenAttribute

Valid On: Class

PersistenceMode   Enum

System.Web.UI (system.web.dll)   *serializable*

This enumeration provides values for the PersistenceModeAttribute. PersistenceModeAttribute.Attribute instructs ASP.NET to persist a property in a control's HTML tag as an attribute. This is the default and does not require the use of the PersistenceModeAttribute. You can also use PersistenceModeAttribute.InnerDefaultProperty or PersistenceModeAttribute.EncodedInnerDefaultProperty to designate a property as the inner content of control tag. Only one property can be used in this way, and the only difference between these two options is whether the ASP.NET framework will automatically perform HTML encoding before persisting the value. Finally, PersistenceModeAttribute.InnerProperty persists the property as a nested tag inside the control tag.

Public Enum **PersistenceMode**
    Attribute = 0
    InnerProperty = 1
    InnerDefaultProperty = 2
    EncodedInnerDefaultProperty = 3
End Enum

Hierarchy: System.Object → System.ValueType → System.Enum (System.IComparable , System.IFormattable , System.IConvertible) → PersistenceMode

PersistenceModeAttribute   NotInheritable Class

System.Web.UI (system.web.dll)

This attribute specifies how a control property should be persisted in the opening tag in the *.aspx* file, using one of the PersistenceMode values. You can use this attribute for the properties in any custom controls that you make.

Public NotInheritable Class **PersistenceModeAttribute** : Inherits Attribute
' *Public Constructors*
  Public Sub **New**(ByVal mode As PersistenceMode)
' *Public Shared Fields*
  public Shared ReadOnly **Attribute** As PersistenceModeAttribute   =*System.Web.UI.PersistenceModeAttribute*
  public Shared ReadOnly **Default** As PersistenceModeAttribute   =*System.Web.UI.PersistenceModeAttribute*
  public Shared ReadOnly **EncodedInnerDefaultProperty**   =*System.Web.UI.PersistenceModeAttribute* _
       As PersistenceModeAttribute
  public Shared ReadOnly **InnerDefaultProperty**   =*System.Web.UI.PersistenceModeAttribute* _
       As PersistenceModeAttribute
  public Shared ReadOnly **InnerProperty** As PersistenceModeAttribute   =*System.Web.UI.PersistenceModeAttribute*
' *Public Instance Properties*
  Public ReadOnly Property **Mode** As PersistenceMode
' *Public Instance Methods*

UI
Namespace

```
Overrides Public Function Equals(ByVal obj As Object) As Boolean
Overrides Public Function GetHashCode() As Integer
Overrides Public Function IsDefaultAttribute() As Boolean
End Class
```

Hierarchy: System.Object → System.Attribute → PersistenceModeAttribute

Valid On: All

PropertyConverter
NotInheritable Class

System.Web.UI (system.web.dll)

This class is used by the .NET framework, not directly by your own code.

```
Public NotInheritable Class PropertyConverter
' Public Shared Methods
    Public Shared Function EnumFromString(ByVal enumType As Type, ByVal value As String) As Object
    Public Shared Function EnumToString(ByVal enumType As Type, ByVal enumValue As Object) As String
    Public Shared Function ObjectFromString(ByVal objType As Type, _
      ByVal propertyInfo As System.Reflection.MemberInfo, ByVal value As String) As Object
End Class
```

RenderMethod
Delegate

System.Web.UI (system.web.dll)
serializable

This delegate is used exclusively by the ASP.NET framework. It specifies the signature for a method used to render a control.

```
Public Delegate Sub RenderMethod(ByVal output As HtmlTextWriter, ByVal container As Control)
```

RootBuilder
NotInheritable Class

System.Web.UI (system.web.dll)

This class is used by the .NET framework, not directly by your own code.

```
Public NotInheritable Class RootBuilder : Inherits TemplateBuilder
' Public Constructors
    Public Sub New(ByVal parser As TemplateParser)
' Public Instance Methods
    Overrides Public Function GetChildControlType(ByVal tagName As String, _
      ByVal attribs As System.Collections.IDictionary) As Type
End Class
```

Hierarchy: System.Object → ControlBuilder → TemplateBuilder (ITemplate)→ RootBuilder

SimpleWebHandlerParser
MustInherit Class

System.Web.UI (system.web.dll)

This class provides basic functionality used to parse web handler files. It is used by the .NET framework, not directly by your own code.

```
Public MustInherit Class SimpleWebHandlerParser
' Protected Constructors
    Protected Sub New(ByVal context As System.Web.HttpContext, ByVal virtualPath As String, _
      ByVal physicalPath As String)
' Protected Instance Properties
```

MustInherit Protected Property **DefaultDirectiveName** As String
' *Protected Instance Methods*
   Protected Function **GetCompiledTypeFromCache**() As Type
End Class

StateBag   **NotInheritable Class**

System.Web.UI (system.web.dll)

Every control stores view state information in a StateBag provided in the Control.ViewState property, if you enabled the Control.EnableViewState property. View state includes information representing all properties of a control or page and any custom items you added. Information is provided in a key/value collection and is accessed much like the System.Web.SessionState.HttpSessionState or System.Web.Caching.Cache class. You can add a value to the StateBag collection like this: ViewState("NewObject") = dsNorthwind.

The StateBag can contain primitive types or full-fledged serializable objects. When retrieving an object, you will have to cast it to the correct type. Also note that you can enumerate through the StateBag collection by using the StateItem enumerator.

Public NotInheritable Class **StateBag** : Implements IStateManager, IDictionary, ICollection, IEnumerable
' *Public Constructors*
   Public Sub **New**()
   Public Sub **New**(ByVal ignoreCase As Boolean)
' *Public Instance Properties*
   Public ReadOnly Property **Count** As Integer Implements ICollection.Count
   Public Default Property **Item** (ByVal key As String) As Object
   Public ReadOnly Property **Keys** As ICollection Implements IDictionary.Keys
   Public ReadOnly Property **Values** As ICollection Implements IDictionary.Values
' *Public Instance Methods*
   Public Function **Add**(ByVal key As String, ByVal value As Object) As StateItem
   Public Sub **Clear**() Implements IDictionary.Clear
   Public Function **GetEnumerator**() As IDictionaryEnumerator Implements IDictionary.GetEnumerator
   Public Function **IsItemDirty**(ByVal key As String) As Boolean
   Public Sub **Remove**(ByVal key As String)
   Public Sub **SetItemDirty**(ByVal key As String, ByVal dirty As Boolean)
End Class

StateItem   **NotInheritable Class**

System.Web.UI (system.web.dll)

This class represents an item in the StateBag collection and is used to track changes to that item. The actual stored object is contained in the Value property. An additional piece of information is provided in the IsDirty property, which is True if the item has been changed since being saved into the StateBag collection. Changes to an item in the StateBag are saved when the ASP.NET framework calls the Control.SaveViewState() method.

When you retrieve an option from the StateBag collection using the default indexer StateBag.Item, you will receive the actual object. If, however, you want to enumerate through the StateBag collection using for each syntax, you should create a StateItem enumerator. You can also retrieve a StateItem object from the StateBag.Add() method.

Public NotInheritable Class **StateItem**
' *Public Instance Properties*
   Public Property **IsDirty** As Boolean
   Public Property **Value** As Object
End Class

UI Namespace

StaticPartialCachingControl
Class

System.Web.UI (system.web.dll)
disposable

When you include a user control on your page, and specify that it should be cached (either by using the standard <OutputCache> directive in the *.ascx* file, or the PartialCachingAttribute in the the user control's code-behind file), an instance of the StaticPartialCachingControl class will be placed in the control hierarchy of the page as a parent to the cached user control.

Public Class **StaticPartialCachingControl** : Inherits BasePartialCachingControl
' *Public Constructors*
   Public Sub **New**(ByVal ctrlID As String, ByVal guid As String, ByVal duration As Integer, ByVal varyByParams As String _
   , ByVal varyByControls As String), ByVal varyByCustom As String, ByVal buildMethod As BuildMethod)
' *Public Shared Methods*
   Public Shared Sub **BuildCachedControl**(ByVal parent As Control, ByVal ctrlID As String, ByVal guid As String, _
   ByVal duration As Integer, ByVal varyByParams As String, ByVal varyByControls As String,
   ByVal varyByCustom As String, ByVal buildMethod As BuildMethod)
End Class

Hierarchy: System.Object → Control (System.ComponentModel.IComponent , System.IDisposable , IParserAccessor , IDataBindingsAccessor)→ BasePartialCachingControl → StaticPartialCachingControl

TagPrefixAttribute
NotInheritable Class

System.Web.UI (system.web.dll)

Tag prefixes are used to identify control elements in an *.aspx* file. For example, all prebuilt ASP.NET controls have a tag prefix of asp:, as in <asp:Label />. You can use the TagPrefixAttribute for your custom controls to define a different tag, which can help you distinguish your controls easily. The portion of the tag after the tag prefix is the control class name. Alternatively, you can use the <Register> directive in the *.aspx* file (not the code-behind file).

Public NotInheritable Class **TagPrefixAttribute** : Inherits Attribute
' *Public Constructors*
   Public Sub **New**(ByVal namespaceName As String, ByVal tagPrefix As String)
' *Public Instance Properties*
   Public ReadOnly Property **NamespaceName** As String
   Public ReadOnly Property **TagPrefix** As String
End Class

Hierarchy: System.Object → System.Attribute → TagPrefixAttribute

Valid On: Assembly

TemplateBuilder
Class

System.Web.UI (system.web.dll)

This class works with the ASP.NET framework to parse and build a templated control when a request is made for a Web Forms page. It is not used in your code.

Public Class **TemplateBuilder** : Inherits ControlBuilder : Implements ITemplate
' *Public Constructors*
   Public Sub **New**()
' *Public Instance Properties*
   Overridable Public Property **Text** As String

' Public Instance Methods

Overrides Public Sub **Init**(ByVal parser As TemplateParser, ByVal parentBuilder As ControlBuilder, ByVal type As Type _
, ByVal tagName As String, ByVal ID As String, ByVal attribs As System.Collections.IDictionary)
Overridable Public Sub **InstantiateIn**(ByVal container As Control) Implements ITemplate.InstantiateIn
Overrides Public Function **NeedsTagInnerText**() As Boolean
Overrides Public Sub **SetTagInnerText**(ByVal text As String)
End Class

Hierarchy: System.Object → ControlBuilder → TemplateBuilder (ITemplate)

TemplateContainerAttribute   NotInheritable Class

System.Web.UI (system.web.dll)

This attribute is used when creating templated controls, which allow the control user to specify a portion of the control's user interface. This functionality is implemented in controls like System.Web.UI.WebControls.Repeater and System.Web.UI.WebControls.DataList, which format bound data according to specified templates. In these controls, and in any custom templated controls you make, the TemplateContainerAttribute is applied to every ITemplate property. The attribute specifies the type of the container control the template will be instantiated in, so that casting is not required to evaluate data binding expressions. For example, the System.Web.UI.WebControls.DataList.ItemTemplate property is a ITemplate property that allows you to set or retrieve the template for items in the list. This particular property has the attribute <TemplateContainer(typeof(System.Web.UI.WebControls.DataListItem))>.

Public NotInheritable Class **TemplateContainerAttribute** : Inherits Attribute
' Public Constructors
Public Sub **New**(ByVal containerType As Type)
' Public Instance Properties
Public ReadOnly Property **ContainerType** As Type
End Class

Hierarchy: System.Object → System.Attribute → TemplateContainerAttribute

Valid On: Property

TemplateControl   MustInherit Class

System.Web.UI (system.web.dll)   *disposable*

This abstract class provides basic functionality for template controls, which include Page and UserControl. This functionality includes transaction support and various properties, methods, and events that are used and managed transparently by the ASP.NET framework.

Public MustInherit Class **TemplateControl** : Inherits Control : Implements INamingContainer
' Protected Constructors
Protected Sub **New**()
' Protected Instance Properties
Overridable Protected Property **AutoHandlers** As Integer
Overridable Protected Property **SupportAutoEvents** As Boolean
' Public Shared Methods
Public Shared Function **ReadStringResource**(ByVal t As Type) As Object
' Public Instance Methods
Public Function **LoadControl**(ByVal virtualPath As String) As Control
Public Function **LoadTemplate**(ByVal virtualPath As String) As ITemplate
Public Function **ParseControl**(ByVal content As String) As Control

```
' Protected Instance Methods
   Overridable Protected Sub Construct()
   Protected Function CreateResourceBasedLiteralControl(ByVal offset As Integer, ByVal size As Integer, _
      ByVal fAsciiOnly As Boolean) As LiteralControl
   Overridable Protected Sub FrameworkInitialize()
   Overridable Protected Sub OnAbortTransaction(ByVal e As EventArgs)
   Overridable Protected Sub OnCommitTransaction(ByVal e As EventArgs)
   Overridable Protected Sub OnError(ByVal e As EventArgs)
   Protected Sub SetStringResourcePointer(ByVal stringResourcePointer As Object, _
      ByVal maxResourceOffset As Integer)
   Protected Sub WriteUTF8ResourceString(ByVal output As HtmlTextWriter, ByVal offset As Integer, _
      ByVal size As Integer, ByVal fAsciiOnly As Boolean)
' Events
   Public Event AbortTransaction As EventHandler
   Public Event CommitTransaction As EventHandler
   Public Event Error As EventHandler
End Class
```

Hierarchy: System.Object → Control (System.ComponentModel.IComponent , System.IDisposable , IParserAccessor , IDataBindingsAccessor) → TemplateControl (INamingContainer)

TemplateControlParser   MustInherit Class

System.Web.UI (system.web.dll)

This abstract class includes some of the functionality for parsing ASP.NET files and interpreting tags as controls. PageParser derives from this class. It is not used in your code.

```
Public MustInherit Class TemplateControlParser : Inherits TemplateParser
' Protected Constructors
   Protected Sub New()
End Class
```

Hierarchy: System.Object → BaseParser → TemplateParser → TemplateControlParser

TemplateParser   MustInherit Class

System.Web.UI (system.web.dll)

This abstract class includes some of the functionality for parsing ASP.NET files. Template-ControlParser derives directly from this class. It is not used in your code.

```
Public MustInherit Class TemplateParser : Inherits BaseParser
' Protected Instance Methods
   MustInherit Protected Function CompileIntoType() As Type
End Class
```

Hierarchy: System.Object → BaseParser → TemplateParser

ToolboxDataAttribute   NotInheritable Class

System.Web.UI (system.web.dll)

This attribute is used when you are creating your own custom controls (typically by inheriting from System.Web.UI.WebControls.WebControl or Control). By default, designers like Visual Studio .NET will create an empty tag when you drag a control from the toolbox onto the design surface. This empty tag represents a control in its default state. Rather than using the empty tag, you can specify initial values and default HTML will be placed inside the control tag by using this attribute. For example, the attribute <Toolbox-Data("<{0}:MyLabel Text='MyLabel' BackColor='Yellow' runat='server'></{0}:MyLabel>")> configures the initial tag for a custom label control with a yellow background. Note that all occurences of {0} in the supplied Data string will be replaced, by the designer, with the tag prefix associated with the MyLabel class.

```
Public NotInheritable Class ToolboxDataAttribute : Inherits Attribute
' Public Constructors
   Public Sub New(ByVal data As String)
' Public Shared Fields
   public Shared ReadOnly Default As ToolboxDataAttribute          =System.Web.UI.ToolboxDataAttribute
' Public Instance Properties
   Public ReadOnly Property Data As String
' Public Instance Methods
   Overrides Public Function Equals(ByVal obj As Object) As Boolean
   Overrides Public Function GetHashCode() As Integer
   Overrides Public Function IsDefaultAttribute() As Boolean
End Class
```

Hierarchy: System.Object → System.Attribute → ToolboxDataAttribute

Valid On: Class

Triplet   Class

System.Web.UI (system.web.dll)

This class is used internally for the LosFormatter. It contains three types that can be combined and serialized into view state.

```
Public Class Triplet
' Public Constructors
   Public Sub New()
   Public Sub New(ByVal x As Object, ByVal y As Object)
   Public Sub New(ByVal x As Object, ByVal y As Object, ByVal z As Object)
' Public Instance Fields
   public First As Object
   public Second As Object
   public Third As Object
End Class
```

UserControl   Class

System.Web.UI (system.web.dll)   *disposable*

This class represents a user control, or *.ascx* file, inside a Web Form. A user control allows you to share commonly used portions of user interface. User controls are similar to *.aspx* pages and can contain HTML, server controls, and event handling logic. They are instantiated and cached in much the same was as Page objects and contain many of the same properties. The difference is that user controls must be situated inside a Web Forms page. User controls should not be confused with custom web controls, which you can create by inheriting from System.Web.UI.WebControls.WebControl.

When using fragment caching with user controls, remember that you will not be able to modify any of the properties of the UserControl; the cached control will be loaded as straight HTML rather than a UserControl object.

```
Public Class UserControl : Inherits TemplateControl : Implements IAttributeAccessor, IUserControlDesignerAccessor
' Public Constructors
```

```
    Public Sub New()
' Public Instance Properties
    Public ReadOnly Property Application As HttpApplicationState
    Public ReadOnly Property Attributes As AttributeCollection
    Public ReadOnly Property Cache As Cache
    Public ReadOnly Property IsPostBack As Boolean
    Public ReadOnly Property Request As HttpRequest
    Public ReadOnly Property Response As HttpResponse
    Public ReadOnly Property Server As HttpServerUtility
    Public ReadOnly Property Session As HttpSessionState
    Public ReadOnly Property Trace As TraceContext
' Public Instance Methods
    Public Sub DesignerInitialize()
    Public Sub InitializeAsUserControl(ByVal page As Page)
    Public Function MapPath(ByVal virtualPath As String) As String
' Protected Instance Methods
    Overrides Protected Sub LoadViewState(ByVal savedState As Object)
    Overrides Protected Sub OnInit(ByVal e As EventArgs)
    Overrides Protected Function SaveViewState() As Object
End Class
```

Hierarchy: System.Object → Control (System.ComponentModel.IComponent , System.IDisposable , IParserAccessor , IDataBindingsAccessor)→ TemplateControl (INamingContainer)→ UserControl (IAttributeAccessor , IUserControlDesignerAccessor)

ValidationPropertyAttribute   NotInheritable Class
System.Web.UI (system.web.dll)

This attribute specifies which property of a server control should be used for validation. Typically, this is a property like Text, Value, or SelectedItem. The ValidationPropertyAttribute is used only when you create custom controls; existing ASP.NET controls use it intrinsically.

This attribute is applied to the class declaration, not a specific property. You can specify the property to validate through the attribute's Name property, as in: <ValidationProperty("Text")>.

```
Public NotInheritable Class ValidationPropertyAttribute : Inherits Attribute
' Public Constructors
    Public Sub New(ByVal name As String)
' Public Instance Properties
    Public ReadOnly Property Name As String
End Class
```

Hierarchy: System.Object → System.Attribute → ValidationPropertyAttribute

Valid On: Class

ValidatorCollection   NotInheritable Class
System.Web.UI (system.web.dll)

This class contains a collection of validation controls (controls that implement IValidator, usually by deriving from System.Web.UI.WebControls.BaseValidator). It is used for the Page.Validators property, which provides a collection of all validation controls on a Web Forms page. For more information about validation controls, refer to the System.Web.UI.WebControls namespace.

```
Public NotInheritable Class ValidatorCollection : Implements ICollection, IEnumerable
' Public Constructors
  Public Sub New()
' Public Instance Properties
  Public ReadOnly Property Count As Integer Implements ICollection.Count
  Public ReadOnly Property IsReadOnly As Boolean
  Public ReadOnly Property IsSynchronized As Boolean Implements ICollection.IsSynchronized
  Public Default ReadOnly Property Item (ByVal index As Integer) As IValidator
  Public ReadOnly Property SyncRoot As Object Implements ICollection.SyncRoot
' Public Instance Methods
  Public Sub Add(ByVal validator As IValidator)
  Public Function Contains(ByVal validator As IValidator) As Boolean
  Public Sub CopyTo(ByVal array As Array, ByVal index As Integer)  Implements ICollection.CopyTo
  Public Function GetEnumerator() As IEnumerator Implements IEnumerable.GetEnumerator
  Public Sub Remove(ByVal validator As IValidator)
End Class
```

WebServiceParser   Class

System.Web.UI (system.web.dll)

This class is used by the ASP.NET framework when handling web service requests. It is not used directly in your code.

```
Public Class WebServiceParser : Inherits SimpleWebHandlerParser
' Protected Instance Properties
  Overrides Protected Property DefaultDirectiveName As String
' Public Shared Methods
  Public Shared Function GetCompiledType(ByVal inputFile As String, ByVal context As System.Web.HttpContext) _
    As Type
End Class
```

Hierarchy: System.Object → SimpleWebHandlerParser → WebServiceParser

UI Namespace

CHAPTER 35

The System.Web.UI.Design Namespace

The System.Web.UI.Design namespace contains types used for providing design-time support for the Web Forms user interface. These types fall into four basic categories: type converters, UI type editors, designers, and other helper classes (such as classes that provide ASP.NET data binding support). Type converters allow control properties to be converted to and from base data types, which allows them to be displayed and edited in the Properties Window. Type converters also extend runtime support, but they are only used implicitly and never instantiated directly. Type converter classes derive from System.ComponentModel.TypeConverter and end with the word "Converter" by convention. Unlike type converters, UI type editors are used exclusively in the design environment. They provide the custom user interface that is used to select special property values from the Properties Window (like a control's color). UI type editors derive from System.Drawing.Design.UITypeEditor and end with the word "Editor."

Designers help provide the design-time representation of a control. They derive from System.ComponentModel.Design.ComponentDesigner and end with the word "Designer." The System.Web.UI.Design namespace contains the base designers used for ASP.NET controls. ASP.NET controls use different designers than Windows Form controls because they are rendered by using HTML rather than Windows-specific GDI+ functions. For custom designers that extend specific controls, refer to the System.Web.UI.Design.WebControls namespace.

Generally, the types in the System.Web.UI.Design namespace are never used directly in the runtime logic of an application. However, they are useful for ASP.NET control designers. For example, if you are creating a custom Web Forms control from scratch, you may want to derive from ControlDesigner to create a custom designer. However, you may find it more convenient to extend an existing web control—in which case, you would continue using the default designers, type converters, and UI type editors, or derive custom versions from the corresponding control-specific class in the System.Web.UI.Design.WebControls namespace, if it exists.

Figure 35-1 shows the fundamental types in this namespace, and Figure 35-2 shows the remaining types.

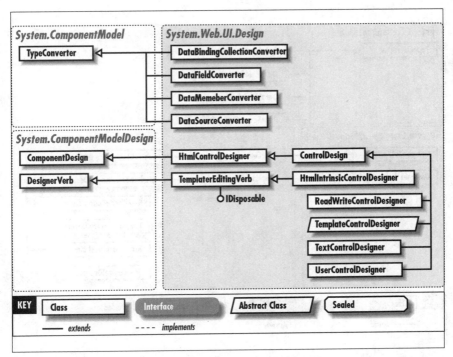

Figure 35-1: Fundamental types from the System.Web.UI.Design namespace

CalendarDataBindingHandler

Class

System.Web.UI.Design (system.design.dll)

Provides the type of data binding used by the System.Web.UI.WebControls.Calendar control.

```
Public Class CalendarDataBindingHandler : Inherits DataBindingHandler
' Public Constructors
   Public Sub New()
' Public Instance Methods
   Overrides Public Sub DataBindControl(ByVal designerHost As System.ComponentModel.Design.IDesignerHost, _
      ByVal control As System.Web.UI.Control)
End Class
```

Hierarchy: System.Object → DataBindingHandler → CalendarDataBindingHandler

ColorBuilder

NotInheritable Class

System.Web.UI.Design (system.design.dll)

This class launches the graphical color editor you see when you modify a control property like System.Web.UI.WebControls.WebControl.ForeColor in the Properties Window. The shared BuildColor() method launches the color builder for the appropriate control.

```
Public NotInheritable Class ColorBuilder
' Public Shared Methods
   Public Shared Function BuildColor(ByVal component As System.ComponentModel.IComponent, _
      ByVal owner As System.Windows.Forms.Control, ByVal initialColor As String) As String
End Class
```

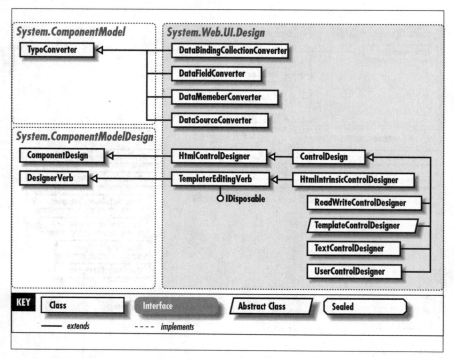

Figure 35-2: *More types from the System.Web.UI.Design namespace.*

ControlDesigner

Class

System.Web.UI.Design (system.design.dll)

disposable

This is base class for web control designers like System.Web.UI.Design.WebControls.AdRotatorDesigner. These designers create the design-time appearance that a control provides to the design editor (like Visual Studio .NET). This HTML code is provided through the GetDesignTimeHtml() method, which is called by the host. The base implementation of the GetDesignTimeHtml() method invokes the System.Web.UI.Control.Render() method of the appropriate control to create the same HTML at design time as at runtime. A custom designer modifies this behavior by overriding the GetDesignTimeHtml() to provide HTML that is more suitable for a design-time representation.

You can create your own custom designer to use with a custom System.Web.UI.WebControls.WebControl. In this case, you use the System.ComponentModel.DesignerAttribute on the class declaration of your control to connect it with the appropriate designer. You can set various ControlDesigner properties—the most useful of which is AllowResize, which restricts your control to a fixed size. When your control is resized, the designer will call corresponding methods like OnControlResize() to give you a chance to refresh the appearance of your control accordingly.

The GetDesignTimeHtml() method should call GetEmptyDesignTimeHtml() if the rendered HTML string is empty (for example, when required control properties are not set). The base implementation of GetEmptyDesignTimeHtml() returns the fully qualified name of the control. Alternatively, you may want to override this property to supply a place holder using the CreatePlaceHolderDesignTimeHtml(). You may also want to override GetErrorDesignTimeHtml() method with specific information based on the exception object that is provided.

```
Public Class ControlDesigner : Inherits HtmlControlDesigner
' Public Constructors
  Public Sub New()
' Public Instance Properties
  Overridable Public ReadOnly Property AllowResize As Boolean
  Overridable Public ReadOnly Property DesignTimeHtmlRequiresLoadComplete As Boolean
  Overridable Public Property ID As String
  Public Property IsDirty As Boolean
  Public Property ReadOnly As Boolean
' Protected Instance Properties
  Protected Property DesignTimeElementView As Object
' Public Instance Methods
  Overridable Public Function GetDesignTimeHtml() As String
  Overridable Public Function GetPersistInnerHtml() As String
  Overrides Public Sub Initialize(ByVal component As System.ComponentModel.IComponent)
  Public Function IsPropertyBound(ByVal propName As String) As Boolean
  Overridable Public Sub OnComponentChanged(ByVal sender As Object, _
    ByVal ce As System.ComponentModel.Design.ComponentChangedEventArgs)
  Public Sub RaiseResizeEvent()
  Overridable Public Sub UpdateDesignTimeHtml()
' Protected Instance Methods
  Protected Function CreatePlaceHolderDesignTimeHtml() As String
  Protected Function CreatePlaceHolderDesignTimeHtml(ByVal instruction As String) As String
  Overridable Protected Function GetEmptyDesignTimeHtml() As String
  Overridable Protected Function GetErrorDesignTimeHtml(ByVal e As Exception) As String
  Overrides Protected Sub OnBehaviorAttached()
  Overrides Protected Sub OnBindingsCollectionChanged(ByVal propName As String)
  Overridable Protected Sub OnControlResize()
  Overrides Protected Sub PreFilterProperties(ByVal properties As System.Collections.IDictionary)
End Class
```

Hierarchy: System.Object → System.ComponentModel.Design.ComponentDesigner (
System.ComponentModel.Design.IDesigner , System.IDisposable ,
System.ComponentModel.Design.IDesignerFilter)→ HtmlControlDesigner → ControlDesigner

ControlParser   NotInheritable Class

System.Web.UI.Design (system.design.dll)

This class is used by the ASP.NET framework. It provides basic functionality used to parse the code for a Web Forms control.

```
Public NotInheritable Class ControlParser
' Public Shared Methods
  Public Shared Function ParseControl(ByVal designerHost As System.ComponentModel.Design.IDesignerHost, _
    ByVal controlText As String) As Control
  Public Shared Function ParseControl(ByVal designerHost As System.ComponentModel.Design.IDesignerHost, _
    ByVal controlText As String, ByVal directives As String) As Control
  Public Shared Function ParseTemplate(ByVal designerHost As System.ComponentModel.Design.IDesignerHost, _
    ByVal templateText As String) As ITemplate
  Public Shared Function ParseTemplate(ByVal designerHost As System.ComponentModel.Design.IDesignerHost, _
    ByVal templateText As String, ByVal directives As String) As ITemplate
End Class
```

UI.Design Namespace

ControlPersister

NotInheritable Class

System.Web.UI.Design (system.design.dll)

This class provides shared (static) helper methods that retrieve the information used to persist a control and its state. For example, the PersistControl() method returns a string that looks very similar to the control tag used in the *.aspx* file, with the named class used instead of the "asp:" prefix. Typically, this class is used only by the IDE.

```
Public NotInheritable Class ControlPersister
' Public Shared Methods
   Public Shared Function PersistControl(ByVal control As System.Web.UI.Control) As String
   Public Shared Function PersistControl(ByVal control As System.Web.UI.Control, _
      ByVal host As System.ComponentModel.Design.IDesignerHost) As String
   Public Shared Sub PersistControl(ByVal sw As System.IO.TextWriter, ByVal control As System.Web.UI.Control)
   Public Shared Sub PersistControl(ByVal sw As System.IO.TextWriter, ByVal control As System.Web.UI.Control, _
      ByVal host As System.ComponentModel.Design.IDesignerHost)
   Public Shared Function PersistInnerProperties(ByVal component As Object, _
      ByVal host As System.ComponentModel.Design.IDesignerHost) As String
   Public Shared Sub PersistInnerProperties(ByVal sw As System.IO.TextWriter, ByVal component As Object, _
      ByVal host As System.ComponentModel.Design.IDesignerHost)
End Class
```

DataBindingCollectionConverter

Class

System.Web.UI.Design (system.design.dll)

This custom System.ComponentModel.TypeConverter class provides a single method, ConvertTo(), which is used to convert System.Web.UI.DataBindingCollection objects.

```
Public Class DataBindingCollectionConverter : Inherits System.ComponentModel.TypeConverter
' Public Constructors
   Public Sub New()
' Public Instance Methods
   Overrides Public Function ConvertTo(ByVal context As System.ComponentModel.ITypeDescriptorContext, _
      ByVal culture As System.Globalization.CultureInfo, ByVal value As Object, ByVal destinationType As Type) _
      As Object
End Class
```

Hierarchy: System.Object → System.ComponentModel.TypeConverter → DataBindingCollectionConverter

DataBindingCollectionEditor

Class

System.Web.UI.Design (system.design.dll)

This class is a custom System.Drawing.Design.UITypeEditor used for editing data binding collections.

```
Public Class DataBindingCollectionEditor : Inherits System.Drawing.Design.UITypeEditor
' Public Constructors
   Public Sub New()
' Public Instance Methods
   Overrides Public Function EditValue(ByVal context As System.ComponentModel.ITypeDescriptorContext, _
      ByVal provider As IServiceProvider, ByVal value As Object) As Object
   Overrides Public Function GetEditStyle(ByVal context As System.ComponentModel.ITypeDescriptorContext) _
      As UITypeEditorEditStyle
End Class
```

Hierarchy: System.Object → System.Drawing.Design.UITypeEditor → DataBindingCollectionEditor

DataBindingHandler   MustInherit Class

System.Web.UI.Design (system.design.dll)

This a base class for all design-time data-binding handlers. In provides a single method, DataBindControl(), which binds the specified control.

```
Public MustInherit Class DataBindingHandler
' Protected Constructors
   Protected Sub New()
' Public Instance Methods
   MustInherit Public Sub DataBindControl(ByVal designerHost As System.ComponentModel.Design.IDesignerHost, _
   ByVal control As System.Web.UI.Control)
End Class
```

DataBindingValueUIHandler   Class

System.Web.UI.Design (system.design.dll)

This class helps create a user interface for editing control data binding. The OnGetUIValueItem() method adds the actual binding.

```
Public Class DataBindingValueUIHandler
' Public Constructors
   Public Sub New()
' Public Instance Methods
   Public Sub OnGetUIValueItem(ByVal context As System.ComponentModel.ITypeDescriptorContext, _
   ByVal propDesc As System.ComponentModel.PropertyDescriptor,                                    _
   ByVal valueUIItemList As System.Collections.ArrayList)
End Class
```

DataFieldConverter   Class

System.Web.UI.Design (system.design.dll)

This class provides a System.ComponentModel.TypeConverter that can be used to convert a string to and from a data field. You will not need to access this class directly, unless you want to use it for a custom ASP.NET control—in which case, you can bind it to the appropriate property by using the System.ComponentModel.TypeConverterAttribute.

```
Public Class DataFieldConverter : Inherits System.ComponentModel.TypeConverter
' Public Constructors
   Public Sub New()
' Public Instance Methods
   Overrides Public Function CanConvertFrom(ByVal context As System.ComponentModel.ITypeDescriptorContext, _
   ByVal sourceType As Type) As Boolean
   Overrides Public Function ConvertFrom(ByVal context As System.ComponentModel.ITypeDescriptorContext, _
   ByVal culture As System.Globalization.CultureInfo, ByVal value As Object) As Object
   Overrides Public Function GetStandardValues(                                    _
   ByVal context As System.ComponentModel.ITypeDescriptorContext) As StandardValuesCollection
   Overrides Public Function GetStandardValuesExclusive(                                    _
   ByVal context As System.ComponentModel.ITypeDescriptorContext) As Boolean
   Overrides Public Function GetStandardValuesSupported(                                    _
   ByVal context As System.ComponentModel.ITypeDescriptorContext) As Boolean
End Class
```

Hierarchy: System.Object → System.ComponentModel.TypeConverter → DataFieldConverter

DataMemberConverter

Class

System.Web.UI.Design (system.design.dll)

This class provides a System.ComponentModel.TypeConverter that can be used to convert a string to a database table name, and vice versa. You will not need to access this class directly, unless you want to use it for a custom ASP.NET control—in which case you can bind it to the DataMember property by using the System.ComponentModel.TypeConverterAttribute.

Public Class **DataMemberConverter** : Inherits System.ComponentModel.TypeConverter
```
' Public Constructors
    Public Sub New()
' Public Instance Methods
    Overrides Public Function CanConvertFrom(ByVal context As System.ComponentModel.ITypeDescriptorContext, _
        ByVal sourceType As Type) As Boolean
    Overrides Public Function ConvertFrom(ByVal context As System.ComponentModel.ITypeDescriptorContext, _
        ByVal culture As System.Globalization.CultureInfo, ByVal value As Object) As Object
    Overrides Public Function GetStandardValues(
        ByVal context As System.ComponentModel.ITypeDescriptorContext) As StandardValuesCollection
    Overrides Public Function GetStandardValuesExclusive(
        ByVal context As System.ComponentModel.ITypeDescriptorContext) As Boolean
    Overrides Public Function GetStandardValuesSupported(
        ByVal context As System.ComponentModel.ITypeDescriptorContext) As Boolean
End Class
```

Hierarchy: System.Object → System.ComponentModel.TypeConverter → DataMemberConverter

DataSourceConverter

Class

System.Web.UI.Design (system.design.dll)

This class provides a System.ComponentModel.TypeConverter that can be used to convert a string to a data source object and vice versa. You will not need to access this class directly, unless you want to use it for a custom ASP.NET control—in which case you can bind it to the DataSource property by using the System.ComponentModel.TypeConverterAttribute.

Public Class **DataSourceConverter** : Inherits System.ComponentModel.TypeConverter
```
' Public Constructors
    Public Sub New()
' Public Instance Methods
    Overrides Public Function CanConvertFrom(ByVal context As System.ComponentModel.ITypeDescriptorContext, _
        ByVal sourceType As Type) As Boolean
    Overrides Public Function ConvertFrom(ByVal context As System.ComponentModel.ITypeDescriptorContext, _
        ByVal culture As System.Globalization.CultureInfo, ByVal value As Object) As Object
    Overrides Public Function GetStandardValues(
        ByVal context As System.ComponentModel.ITypeDescriptorContext) As StandardValuesCollection
    Overrides Public Function GetStandardValuesExclusive(
        ByVal context As System.ComponentModel.ITypeDescriptorContext) As Boolean
    Overrides Public Function GetStandardValuesSupported(
        ByVal context As System.ComponentModel.ITypeDescriptorContext) As Boolean
End Class
```

Hierarchy: System.Object → System.ComponentModel.TypeConverter → DataSourceConverter

DesignTimeData **NotInheritable Class**

System.Web.UI.Design (system.design.dll)

This class provides shared helper methods that the design-time host (IDE) can use to generate "dummy" information for a sample rendering of a complex control. Typically, this class is used with table controls, as maintaining a database connection in design mode would be too resource intensive, and the data source provider may not even be available. Using the CreateDummyDataTable() method, a default table is created that uses no information from the actual data source. This table could be used before a control's DataSource property is set.

Visual Studio .NET can also use a minimum amount of information to help present a design-time rendering of data tables. The GetDataFields() and GetDataMembers() methods retrieve a basic amount of information about the structure of the data source, which is then used when a dummy table is created with CreateSampleDataTable(). The GetDesign-TimeDataSource() method adds sample rows into the specified data table control.

```
Public NotInheritable Class DesignTimeData
' Public Shared Fields
    public Shared ReadOnly DataBindingHandler As EventHandler                =System.EventHandler
' Public Shared Methods
    Public Shared Function CreateDummyDataTable() As DataTable
    Public Shared Function CreateSampleDataTable(ByVal referenceData As System.Collections.IEnumerable) _
        As DataTable
    Public Shared Function GetDataFields(ByVal dataSource As System.Collections.IEnumerable) _
        As PropertyDescriptorCollection
    Public Shared Function GetDataMember(ByVal dataSource As System.ComponentModel.IListSource, _
        ByVal dataMember As String) As IEnumerable
    Public Shared Function GetDataMembers(ByVal dataSource As Object) As String()
    Public Shared Function GetDesignTimeDataSource(ByVal dataTable As System.Data.DataTable, _
        ByVal minimumRows As Integer) As IEnumerable
    Public Shared Function GetSelectedDataSource(ByVal component As System.ComponentModel.IComponent, _
        ByVal dataSource As String, ByVal dataMember As String) As IEnumerable
    Public Shared Function GetSelectedDataSource(ByVal component As System.ComponentModel.IComponent, _
        ByVal dataSource As String) As Object
End Class
```

HtmlControlDesigner **Class**

System.Web.UI.Design (system.design.dll) *disposable*

This class provides basic functionality for all ASP.NET control designers. If you want to create your own control designer, inherit instead from ControlDesigner, which derives from HtmlControlDesigner.

```
Public Class HtmlControlDesigner : Inherits System.ComponentModel.Design.ComponentDesigner
' Public Constructors
    Public Sub New()
' Public Instance Properties
    Public Property Behavior As IHtmlControlDesignerBehavior
    Public ReadOnly Property DataBindings As DataBindingCollection
    Overridable Public Property ShouldCodeSerialize As Boolean
' Protected Instance Properties
    Protected Property DesignTimeElement As Object
' Public Instance Methods
    Overridable Public Sub OnSetParent()
' Protected Instance Methods
    Overrides Protected Sub Dispose(ByVal disposing As Boolean)
```

Overridable Protected Sub **OnBehaviorAttached**()
Overridable Protected Sub **OnBehaviorDetaching**()
Overridable Protected Sub **OnBindingsCollectionChanged**(ByVal propName As String)
Overrides Protected Sub **PreFilterEvents**(ByVal events As System.Collections.IDictionary)
Overrides Protected Sub **PreFilterProperties**(ByVal properties As System.Collections.IDictionary)
End Class

Hierarchy: System.Object → System.ComponentModel.Design.ComponentDesigner (
System.ComponentModel.Design.IDesigner , System.IDisposable ,
System.ComponentModel.Design.IDesignerFilter)→ HtmlControlDesigner

HtmlIntrinsicControlDesigner   Class

System.Web.UI.Design (system.design.dll)   *disposable*

This base class provides a basic designer for HTML controls (the controls contained in
the System.Web.UI.HtmlControls namespace).

Public Class **HtmlIntrinsicControlDesigner** : Inherits HtmlControlDesigner
' *Public Constructors*
  Public Sub **New**()
End Class

Hierarchy: System.Object → System.ComponentModel.Design.ComponentDesigner (
System.ComponentModel.Design.IDesigner , System.IDisposable ,
System.ComponentModel.Design.IDesignerFilter)→ HtmlControlDesigner →
HtmlIntrinsicControlDesigner

HyperLinkDataBindingHandler   Class

System.Web.UI.Design (system.design.dll)

This class provides a data-binding handler for the hyperlink property used in some
ASP.NET controls.

Public Class **HyperLinkDataBindingHandler** : Inherits DataBindingHandler
' *Public Constructors*
  Public Sub **New**()
' *Public Instance Methods*
  Overrides Public Sub **DataBindControl**(ByVal designerHost As System.ComponentModel.Design.IDesignerHost, _
    ByVal control As System.Web.UI.Control)
End Class

Hierarchy: System.Object → DataBindingHandler → HyperLinkDataBindingHandler

IControlDesignerBehavior   Interface

System.Web.UI.Design (system.design.dll)

IControlDesignerBehavior defines an interface that enables the extension of specific behaviors of a control designer.

Public Interface **IControlDesignerBehavior**
' *Public Instance Properties*
  Public ReadOnly Property **DesignTimeElementView** As Object
  Public Property **DesignTimeHtml** As String
' *Public Instance Methods*

```
Public Sub OnTemplateModeChanged()
End Interface
```

IDataSourceProvider   Interface

System.Web.UI.Design (system.design.dll)

This interface specifies the behavior required for designers that interact with a data source, such as System.Web.UI.Design.WebControls.ListControlDesigner and System.Web.UI.Design.WebControls.DataGridDesigner. The interface provides two methods designed to convert a data source to a more useful object. GetSelectedDataSource() retrieves the selected data source object as a loosely typed System.Object. GetResolvedSelectedDataSource() retrieves the resolved data source as a System.Collections.IEnumerable object, like a System.Array or a System.Data.DataView instance.

```
Public Interface IDataSourceProvider
' Public Instance Methods
   Public Function GetResolvedSelectedDataSource() As IEnumerable
   Public Function GetSelectedDataSource() As Object
End Interface
```

IHtmlControlDesignerBehavior   Interface

System.Web.UI.Design (system.design.dll)

IHtmlControlDesignerBehavior defines an interface that enables the extension of specific behaviors of an HTML control designer.

```
Public Interface IHtmlControlDesignerBehavior
' Public Instance Properties
   Public Property Designer As HtmlControlDesigner
   Public ReadOnly Property DesignTimeElement As Object
' Public Instance Methods
   Public Function GetAttribute(ByVal attribute As String, ByVal ignoreCase As Boolean) As Object
   Public Function GetStyleAttribute(ByVal attribute As String, ByVal designTimeOnly As Boolean, _
      ByVal ignoreCase As Boolean) As Object
   Public Sub RemoveAttribute(ByVal attribute As String, ByVal ignoreCase As Boolean)
   Public Sub RemoveStyleAttribute(ByVal attribute As String, ByVal designTimeOnly As Boolean, _
      ByVal ignoreCase As Boolean)
   Public Sub SetAttribute(ByVal attribute As String, ByVal value As Object, ByVal ignoreCase As Boolean)
   Public Sub SetStyleAttribute(ByVal attribute As String, ByVal designTimeOnly As Boolean, ByVal value As Object, _
      ByVal ignoreCase As Boolean)
End Interface
```

ImageUrlEditor   Class

System.Web.UI.Design (system.design.dll)

This class provides a System.Drawing.Design.UITypeEditor that can be used when modifying properties that correspond to Internet URLs. This class extends on the basic UrlEditor class and is customized for creating URLs that point to image files. The differences are minor: the Filter property is overridden to provide the "*.gif; *.jpg; *.jpeg; *.bmp; *.wmf; *.pgn" file filter, and the Caption of the designer window is modified to "Select Image File." This class is used, for example, by the ImageUrl property of the System.Web.UI.WebControls.HyperLink control.

```
Public Class ImageUrlEditor : Inherits UrlEditor
' Public Constructors
```

```
    Public Sub New()
  ' Protected Instance Properties
    Overrides Protected Property Caption As String
    Overrides Protected Property Filter As String
End Class
```

Hierarchy: System.Object → System.Drawing.Design.UITypeEditor → UrlEditor → ImageUrlEditor

ITemplateEditingFrame

Interface

System.Web.UI.Design (system.design.dll)

disposable

This interface is implemented by System.Web.UI.Design.WebControls.DataListDesigner and System.Web.UI.Design.WebControls.DataGridDesigner. It allows them to support in-place editing of a control template at design time. The properties of this interface represent the characteristics of the template editing area (like InitialHeight, InitialWidth, and ControlStyle). The methods are used to manage the template editing area (like Save() and Resize()).

Note that a System.Web.UI.WebControls.DataGrid control uses templates (and hence template editing) only if you have added a System.Web.UI.WebControls.TemplateColumn.

```
Public Interface ITemplateEditingFrame : Implements IDisposable
  ' Public Instance Properties
    Public ReadOnly Property ControlStyle As Style
    Public Property InitialHeight As Integer
    Public Property InitialWidth As Integer
    Public ReadOnly Property Name As String
    Public ReadOnly Property TemplateNames As String()
    Public ReadOnly Property TemplateStyles As Style()
    Public Property Verb As TemplateEditingVerb
  ' Public Instance Methods
    Public Sub Close(ByVal saveChanges As Boolean)
    Public Sub Open()
    Public Sub Resize(ByVal width As Integer, ByVal height As Integer)
    Public Sub Save()
    Public Sub UpdateControlName(ByVal newName As String)
End Interface
```

ITemplateEditingService

Interface

System.Web.UI.Design (system.design.dll)

This class supports design-time control template editing.

```
Public Interface ITemplateEditingService
  ' Public Instance Properties
    Public ReadOnly Property SupportsNestedTemplateEditing As Boolean
  ' Public Instance Methods
    Public Function CreateFrame(ByVal designer As TemplatedControlDesigner, ByVal frameName As String, _
      ByVal templateNames As String()) As ITemplateEditingFrame
    Public Function CreateFrame(ByVal designer As TemplatedControlDesigner, ByVal frameName As String, _
      ByVal templateNames As String(), ByVal controlStyle As System.Web.UI.WebControls.Style,
      ByVal templateStyles As System.Web.UI.WebControls.Style()) As ITemplateEditingFrame
    Public Function GetContainingTemplateName(ByVal control As System.Web.UI.Control) As String
End Interface
```

IWebFormReferenceManager Interface

System.Web.UI.Design (system.design.dll)

This interface allows the IDE to look up and manage references (to .NET types) used in a web form.

```
Public Interface IWebFormReferenceManager
' Public Instance Methods
    Public Function GetObjectType(ByVal tagPrefix As String, ByVal typeName As String) As Type
    Public Function GetRegisterDirectives() As String
    Public Function GetTagPrefix(ByVal objectType As Type) As String
End Interface
```

IWebFormsBuilderUIService Interface

System.Web.UI.Design (system.design.dll)

This interface defines methods that can be used to launch a custom System.Drawing.Design.UITypeEditor object for assigning URLs (BuildUrl()) or colors (BuildColor()).

```
Public Interface IWebFormsBuilderUIService
' Public Instance Methods
    Public Function BuildColor(ByVal owner As System.Windows.Forms.Control, ByVal initialColor As String) As String
    Public Function BuildUrl(ByVal owner As System.Windows.Forms.Control, ByVal initialUrl As String, _
    ByVal baseUrl As String, ByVal caption As String, ByVal filter As String, ByVal options As UrlBuilderOptions) _
    As String
End Interface
```

IWebFormsDocumentService Interface

System.Web.UI.Design (system.design.dll)

This interface provides methods for tracking the state of a Web Forms document, handling load-time events, determining a document's location, setting a document selection, and managing a document's "Undo" service.

```
Public Interface IWebFormsDocumentService
' Public Instance Properties
    Public ReadOnly Property DocumentUrl As String
    Public ReadOnly Property IsLoading As Boolean
' Public Instance Methods
    Public Function CreateDiscardableUndoUnit() As Object
    Public Sub DiscardUndoUnit(ByVal discardableUndoUnit As Object)
    Public Sub EnableUndo(ByVal enable As Boolean)
    Public Sub UpdateSelection()
' Events
    Public Event LoadComplete As EventHandler
End Interface
```

ReadWriteControlDesigner Class
disposable

System.Web.UI.Design (system.design.dll)

This class provides functionality for designers. In the .NET framework, only the System.Web.UI.Design.WebControls.PanelDesigner derives from this class. It uses read/write functionality to provide a design-time surface where you can directly type static inner text for the Panel control.

```
Public Class ReadWriteControlDesigner : Inherits ControlDesigner
' Public Constructors
```

*UI.Design
Namespace*

```
   Public Sub New()
' Public Instance Methods
   Overrides Public Sub OnComponentChanged(ByVal sender As Object,      _
      ByVal ce As System.ComponentModel.Design.ComponentChangedEventArgs)
' Protected Instance Methods
   Overridable Protected Sub MapPropertyToStyle(ByVal propName As String, ByVal varPropValue As Object)
   Overrides Protected Sub OnBehaviorAttached()
End Class
```

Hierarchy: System.Object → System.ComponentModel.Design.ComponentDesigner (
System.ComponentModel.Design.IDesigner , System.IDisposable ,
System.ComponentModel.Design.IDesignerFilter)→ HtmlControlDesigner → ControlDesigner →
ReadWriteControlDesigner

TemplatedControlDesigner
MustInherit Class

System.Web.UI.Design (system.design.dll)
disposable

This designer supports the template editing features that allow you to enter template information into a control at design-time. These features include a slew of methods for creating a template-editing frame, updating the control properties and design-time HTML accordingly, and providing context menu verbs. System.Web.UI.Design.WebControls.BaseDataListDesigner inherits from this class.

```
Public MustInherit Class TemplatedControlDesigner : Inherits ControlDesigner
' Public Constructors
   Public Sub New()
' Public Instance Properties
   Public ReadOnly Property ActiveTemplateEditingFrame As ITemplateEditingFrame
   Public ReadOnly Property CanEnterTemplateMode As Boolean
   Public ReadOnly Property InTemplateMode As Boolean
' Protected Instance Properties
   Overridable Protected Property HidePropertiesInTemplateMode As Boolean
' Public Instance Methods
   Public Sub EnterTemplateMode(ByVal newTemplateEditingFrame As ITemplateEditingFrame)
   Public Sub ExitTemplateMode(ByVal fSwitchingTemplates As Boolean, ByVal fNested As Boolean, _
      ByVal fSave As Boolean)
   Overrides Public Function GetPersistInnerHtml() As String
   Overridable Public Function GetTemplateContainerDataItemProperty(ByVal templateName As String) _
      As String
   Overridable Public Function GetTemplateContainerDataSource(ByVal templateName As String) _
      As IEnumerable
   MustInherit Public Function GetTemplateContent(ByVal editingFrame As ITemplateEditingFrame, _
      ByVal templateName As String, ByRef allowEditing As Boolean) As String
   Public Function GetTemplateEditingVerbs() As TemplateEditingVerb()
   Overridable Public Function GetTemplatePropertyParentType(ByVal templateName As String) As Type
   Overrides Public Sub OnComponentChanged(ByVal sender As Object,      _
      ByVal ce As System.ComponentModel.Design.ComponentChangedEventArgs)
   Overrides Public Sub OnSetParent()
   MustInherit Public Sub SetTemplateContent(ByVal editingFrame As ITemplateEditingFrame, _
      ByVal templateName As String, ByVal templateContent As String)
   Overrides Public Sub UpdateDesignTimeHtml()
' Protected Instance Methods
   MustInherit Protected Function CreateTemplateEditingFrame(ByVal verb As TemplateEditingVerb) _
      As ITemplateEditingFrame
   MustInherit Protected Function GetCachedTemplateEditingVerbs() As TemplateEditingVerb()
```

Protected Function **GetTemplateFromText**(ByVal text As String) As ITemplate
Protected Function **GetTextFromTemplate**(ByVal template As System.Web.UI.ITemplate) As String
Overrides Protected Sub **OnBehaviorAttached**()
Overridable Protected Sub **OnTemplateModeChanged**()
Overrides Protected Sub **PreFilterProperties**(ByVal properties As System.Collections.IDictionary)
Protected Sub **SaveActiveTemplateEditingFrame**()
End Class

Hierarchy: System.Object → System.ComponentModel.Design.ComponentDesigner (
System.ComponentModel.Design.IDesigner , System.IDisposable ,
System.ComponentModel.Design.IDesignerFilter)→ HtmlControlDesigner → ControlDesigner →
TemplatedControlDesigner

TemplateEditingService

NotInheritable Class

System.Web.UI.Design (system.design.dll)

disposable

This class implements the ITemplateEditingService interface and provides IDE functionality
for editing the templates for controls like System.Web.UI.WebControls.DataList and Sys-
tem.Web.UI.WebControls.DataGrid. This class offers a CreateFrame() method, which takes a
reference to a TemplatedControlDesigner and returns an ITemplateEditingFrame instance for it.

Public NotInheritable Class **TemplateEditingService** : Implements ITemplateEditingService, IDisposable
' *Public Constructors*
Public Sub **New**(ByVal designerHost As System.ComponentModel.Design.IDesignerHost)
' *Public Instance Properties*
Public ReadOnly Property **SupportsNestedTemplateEditing** As Boolean _
Implements ITemplateEditingService.SupportsNestedTemplateEditing
' *Public Instance Methods*
Public Function **CreateFrame**(ByVal designer As TemplatedControlDesigner, ByVal frameName As String,   _
ByVal templateNames As String()) As ITemplateEditingFrame Implements ITemplateEditingService.CreateFrame
Public Function **CreateFrame**(ByVal designer As TemplatedControlDesigner, ByVal frameName As String, _
ByVal templateNames As String(), ByVal controlStyle As System.Web.UI.WebControls.Style,   _
ByVal templateStyles As System.Web.UI.WebControls.Style()) As ITemplateEditingFrame   _
Implements ITemplateEditingService.CreateFrame
Public Sub **Dispose**() Implements IDisposable.Dispose
Public Function **GetContainingTemplateName**(ByVal control As System.Web.UI.Control) As String _
Implements ITemplateEditingService.GetContainingTemplateName
' *Protected Instance Methods*
Overrides Protected Sub **Finalize**()
End Class

TemplateEditingVerb

Class

System.Web.UI.Design (system.design.dll)

disposable

This class represents a type of verb that can be invoked only by a template editor (like
TemplatedControlDesigner,   System.Web.UI.Design.WebControls.DataListDesigner,   and   Sys-
tem.Web.UI.Design.WebControls.DataGridDesigner). A verb is a menu command that appears in
the context menu when you right-click a control.

Public Class **TemplateEditingVerb** : Inherits System.ComponentModel.Design.DesignerVerb: Implements _
IDisposable
' *Public Constructors*
Public Sub **New**(ByVal text As String, ByVal index As Integer, ByVal designer As TemplatedControlDesigner)
' *Public Instance Properties*
Public ReadOnly Property **Index** As Integer

```
' Public Instance Methods
    Public Sub Dispose() Implements IDisposable.Dispose
' Protected Instance Methods
    Overridable Protected Sub Dispose(ByVal disposing As Boolean)
    Overrides Protected Sub Finalize()
End Class
```

Hierarchy: System.Object → System.ComponentModel.Design.MenuCommand →
System.ComponentModel.Design.DesignerVerb → TemplateEditingVerb (System.IDisposable)

TextDataBindingHandler

Class

System.Web.UI.Design (system.design.dll)

This DataBindingHandler class provides data binding for the Text property of a control, using an overridden DataBindingHandler.DataBindControl() method.

```
Public Class TextDataBindingHandler : Inherits DataBindingHandler
' Public Constructors
    Public Sub New()
' Public Instance Methods
    Overrides Public Sub DataBindControl(ByVal designerHost As System.ComponentModel.Design.IDesignerHost, _
        ByVal control As System.Web.UI.Control)
End Class
```

Hierarchy: System.Object → DataBindingHandler → TextDataBindingHandler

UrlBuilder

NotInheritable Class

System.Web.UI.Design (system.design.dll)

This class contains shared (static) helper methods that support the various UrlEditor classes. Essentially, the UrlEditor class provides the user interface used for choosing a URL for a property at design time, and the BuildUrl() method is invoked to create a string representing the selected URL.

```
Public NotInheritable Class UrlBuilder
' Public Shared Methods
    Public Shared Function BuildUrl(ByVal component As System.ComponentModel.IComponent, _
        ByVal owner As System.Windows.Forms.Control, ByVal initialUrl As String, ByVal caption As String, _
        ByVal filter As String) As String
    Public Shared Function BuildUrl(ByVal component As System.ComponentModel.IComponent, _
        ByVal owner As System.Windows.Forms.Control, ByVal initialUrl As String, ByVal caption As String, _
        ByVal filter As String, ByVal options As UrlBuilderOptions) As String
End Class
```

UrlBuilderOptions

Enum

serializable, flag

System.Web.UI.Design (system.design.dll)

This enumeration specifies whether a URL is fully qualified (None) or relative to the current document (NoAbsolute). This enumeration is set by the various UrlEditor classes and ultimately used by UrlBuilder.BuildUrl() to create a string representing the specified URL.

```
Public Enum UrlBuilderOptions
    None = &H000000000
    NoAbsolute = &H000000001
End Enum
```

Hierarchy: System.Object → System.ValueType → System.Enum (System.IComparable , System.IFormattable , System.IConvertible) → UrlBuilderOptions

UrlEditor
Class

System.Web.UI.Design (system.design.dll)

This class provides a System.Drawing.Design.UITypeEditor that can be used when modifying properties that correspond to Internet URLs. An example is the System.Web.UI.WebControls.HyperLink.NavigateUrl property of the System.Web.UI.WebControls.HyperLink control. Note that this class, like all type editors, implements the user interface linked to the appropriate property in the Properties Window. The actual construction of the URL is supported by the methods in the UrlBuilder class.

```
Public Class UrlEditor : Inherits System.Drawing.Design.UITypeEditor
' Public Constructors
   Public Sub New()
' Protected Instance Properties
   Overridable Protected Property Caption As String
   Overridable Protected Property Filter As String
   Overridable Protected Property Options As UrlBuilderOptions
' Public Instance Methods
   Overrides Public Function EditValue(ByVal context As System.ComponentModel.ITypeDescriptorContext, _
      ByVal provider As IServiceProvider, ByVal value As Object) As Object
   Overrides Public Function GetEditStyle(ByVal context As System.ComponentModel.ITypeDescriptorContext) _
      As UITypeEditorEditStyle
End Class
```

Hierarchy: System.Object → System.Drawing.Design.UITypeEditor → UrlEditor

UserControlDesigner
Class

System.Web.UI.Design (system.design.dll)
disposable

This class provides a custom designer for user controls (page-like groups of text, controls, and scripting contained in *.ascx* files). This designer provides the design-time HTML used when you insert a user control onto a Web Forms page. This design-time HTML consists of a generic, labeled gray box that does not render any of the actual content.

```
Public Class UserControlDesigner : Inherits ControlDesigner
' Public Constructors
   Public Sub New()
' Public Instance Properties
   Overrides Public ReadOnly Property AllowResize As Boolean
   Overrides Public Property ShouldCodeSerialize As Boolean
' Public Instance Methods
   Overrides Public Function GetDesignTimeHtml() As String
   Overrides Public Function GetPersistInnerHtml() As String
End Class
```

Hierarchy: System.Object → System.ComponentModel.Design.ComponentDesigner (System.ComponentModel.Design.IDesigner , System.IDisposable , System.ComponentModel.Design.IDesignerFilter) → HtmlControlDesigner → ControlDesigner → UserControlDesigner

WebControlToolboxItem

Class

System.Web.UI.Design (system.design.dll)   *serializable*

This class represents a toolbox item for a web control. Toolbox items are the icons you use to insert controls when designing a Web Forms page.

```
Public Class WebControlToolboxItem : Inherits System.Drawing.Design.ToolboxItem
' Public Constructors
   Public Sub New()
   Public Sub New(ByVal type As Type)
' Public Instance Methods
   Public Function GetToolAttributeValue(ByVal host As System.ComponentModel.Design.IDesignerHost, _
      ByVal attributeType As Type) As Object
   Public Function GetToolHtml(ByVal host As System.ComponentModel.Design.IDesignerHost) As String
   Public Function GetToolType(ByVal host As System.ComponentModel.Design.IDesignerHost) As Type
   Overrides Public Sub Initialize(ByVal type As Type)
' Protected Instance Methods
   Overrides Protected Function CreateComponentsCore(                                        _
      ByVal host As System.ComponentModel.Design.IDesignerHost) As IComponent()
   Overrides Protected Sub Deserialize(ByVal info As System.Runtime.Serialization.SerializationInfo, _
      ByVal context As System.Runtime.Serialization.StreamingContext)
   Overrides Protected Sub Serialize(ByVal info As System.Runtime.Serialization.SerializationInfo, _
      ByVal context As System.Runtime.Serialization.StreamingContext)
End Class
```

Hierarchy: System.Object → System.Drawing.Design.ToolboxItem (System.Runtime.Serialization.ISerializable)→ WebControlToolboxItem

XmlFileEditor

Class

System.Web.UI.Design (system.design.dll)

This class provides the interface used for selecting an XML file from the standard open file dialog. It works in conjunction with XmlUrlEditor.

```
Public Class XmlFileEditor : Inherits System.Drawing.Design.UITypeEditor
' Public Constructors
   Public Sub New()
' Public Instance Methods
   Overrides Public Function EditValue(ByVal context As System.ComponentModel.ITypeDescriptorContext, _
      ByVal provider As IServiceProvider, ByVal value As Object) As Object
   Overrides Public Function GetEditStyle(ByVal context As System.ComponentModel.ITypeDescriptorContext) _
      As UITypeEditorEditStyle
End Class
```

Hierarchy: System.Object → System.Drawing.Design.UITypeEditor → XmlFileEditor

XmlUrlEditor

Class

System.Web.UI.Design (system.design.dll)

This class provides a System.Drawing.Design.UITypeEditor that can be used when modifying properties that correspond to Internet URLs. This class extends on the basic UrlEditor, and is customized for creating URLs that point to XML files. The differences are minor: the ImageUrlEditor.Filter property is overridden to provide the "*.xml" file filter and the ImageUrlEditor.Caption of the designer window is modified to "Select XML File." This class is used, for example, by the DocumentSource property of the System.Web.UI.WebControls.Xml control.

```
Public Class XmlUrlEditor : Inherits UrlEditor
' Public Constructors
   Public Sub New()
' Protected Instance Properties
   Overrides Protected Property Caption As String
   Overrides Protected Property Filter As String
   Overrides Protected Property Options As UrlBuilderOptions
End Class
```

Hierarchy: System.Object → System.Drawing.Design.UITypeEditor → UrlEditor → XmlUrlEditor

XslUrlEditor

Class

System.Web.UI.Design (system.design.dll)

This class provides a System.Drawing.Design.UITypeEditor that can be used when modifying properties that correspond to Internet URLs. This class extends on the basic UrlEditor and is customized for creating URLs that point to XSL transform files. The differences are minor: the ImageUrlEditor.Filter property is overridden to provide the "*.xsl; *.xslt" file filter and the ImageUrlEditor.Caption of the designer window is modified to "Select XSL Transform File." This class is used, for example, by the TransformSource property of the System.Web.UI.WebControls.Xml control.

```
Public Class XslUrlEditor : Inherits UrlEditor
' Public Constructors
   Public Sub New()
' Protected Instance Properties
   Overrides Protected Property Caption As String
   Overrides Protected Property Filter As String
   Overrides Protected Property Options As UrlBuilderOptions
End Class
```

Hierarchy: System.Object → System.Drawing.Design.UITypeEditor → UrlEditor → XslUrlEditor

CHAPTER 36

The System.Web.UI.Design.WebControls Namespace

The types in the System.Web.UI.Design.WebControls namespace extend Visual Studio's design-time support for creating web controls. Most types in this namespace are designers that provide special design-time specific HTML (which may be only slightly different than runtime HTML) and custom System.Drawing.Design.UITypeEditor classes that provide the graphic interface for modifying some special properties. The most detailed implementations of these features can be found in the types used for the System.Web.UI.WebControls.DataGrid and System.Web.UI.WebControls.DataList controls, such as DataGridComponentEditor and DataGridDesigner. These classes provide sophisticated property builders that offer complete design-time customization in a multipage "applet."

These designers, UI type editors, and component editors have no effect on the runtime capabilities of a control. They are also not used directly in code. That means that the System.Web.UI.Design.WebControls namespace is probably of most interest to developers who are interested in creating controls and add-ins of their own and want to review Microsoft's examples. Unfortunately, while you can review the interfaces these types have and extend them in your own code, the implementation details are not provided.

Figure 36-1 and Figure 36-2 show the types in this namespace.

AdRotatorDesigner   Class
System.Web.UI.Design.WebControls (system.design.dll)   *disposable*

This class provides the design-time representation of a System.Web.UI.WebControls.AdRotator control, using an overridden GetDesignTimeHtml() method. This control ignores the System.Web.UI.WebControls.AdRotator.AdvertisementFile property at design time and just displays the control's name and a blank picture icon in the corner.

```
Public Class AdRotatorDesigner : Inherits System.Web.UI.Design.ControlDesigner
' Public Constructors
    Public Sub New()
' Public Instance Methods
    Overrides Public Function GetDesignTimeHtml() As String
End Class
```

Hierarchy: System.Object → System.ComponentModel.Design.ComponentDesigner (System.ComponentModel.Design.IDesigner , System.IDisposable , System.ComponentModel.Design.IDesignerFilter) → System.Web.UI.Design.HtmlControlDesigner →

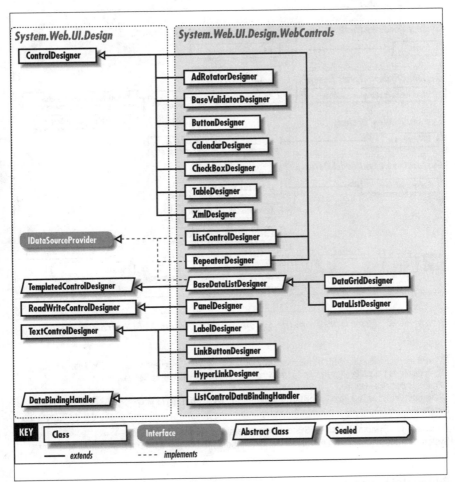

Figure 36-1: Some types from the System.Web.UI.Design.WebControls namespace

System.Web.UI.Design.ControlDesigner
→ AdRotatorDesigner

BaseDataListComponentEditor   MustInherit Class

System.Web.UI.Design.WebControls (system.design.dll)

This abstract class provides basic functionality for the DataListComponentEditor and Data-GridComponentEditor classes, which provide the Property Builder user interface for editing complex properties for these controls.

```
Public MustInherit Class BaseDataListComponentEditor : Inherits _
    System.Windows.Forms.Design.WindowsFormsComponentEditor
' Public Constructors
    Public Sub New(ByVal initialPage As Integer)
' Public Instance Methods
```

Design WebControls

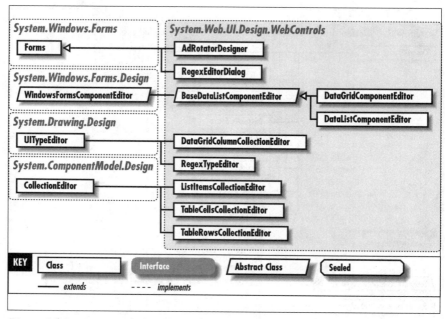

Figure 36-2: More types from the System.Web.UI.Design.WebControls namespace

```
Overrides Public Function EditComponent(ByVal context As System.ComponentModel.ITypeDescriptorContext, _
    ByVal obj As Object, ByVal parent As System.Windows.Forms.IWin32Window) As Boolean
' Protected Instance Methods
    Overrides Protected Function GetInitialComponentEditorPageIndex() As Integer
End Class
```

Hierarchy: System.Object → System.ComponentModel.ComponentEditor →
System.Windows.Forms.Design.WindowsFormsComponentEditor → BaseDataListComponentEditor

BaseDataListDesigner   **MustInherit Class**

System.Web.UI.Design.WebControls (system.design.dll)   *disposable*

This abstract class provides basic functionality for the DataListDesigner and DataGridDesigner classes. This includes functionality for styles, additional verbs for the context menu, and other helper methods for data binding.

```
Public MustInherit Class BaseDataListDesigner : Inherits                                    _
        System.Web.UI.Design.TemplatedControlDesigner: Implements  System.Web.UI.Design.IDataSourceProvider
' Public Constructors
    Public Sub New()
' Public Instance Properties
    Public Property DataKeyField As String
    Public Property DataMember As String
    Public Property DataSource As String
    Overrides Public ReadOnly Property DesignTimeHtmlRequiresLoadComplete As Boolean
    Overrides Public ReadOnly Property Verbs As DesignerVerbCollection
' Public Instance Methods
```

Public Function **GetResolvedSelectedDataSource**() As IEnumerable _
    Implements IDataSourceProvider.GetResolvedSelectedDataSource
Public Function **GetSelectedDataSource**() As Object _
    Implements IDataSourceProvider.GetSelectedDataSource
Overrides Public Function **GetTemplateContainerDataSource**(ByVal templateName As String) _
    As IEnumerable
Overrides Public Sub **Initialize**(ByVal component As System.ComponentModel.IComponent)
Overrides Public Sub **OnComponentChanged**(ByVal sender As Object, _
    ByVal e As System.ComponentModel.Design.ComponentChangedEventArgs)
' *Protected Instance Methods*
Overrides Protected Sub **Dispose**(ByVal disposing As Boolean)
Protected Function **GetDesignTimeDataSource**(ByVal selectedDataSource As System.Collections.IEnumerable, _
    ByVal minimumRows As Integer, ByRef dummyDataSource As Boolean) As IEnumerable
Protected Function **GetDesignTimeDataSource**(ByVal minimumRows As Integer, _
    ByRef dummyDataSource As Boolean) As IEnumerable
Protected Friend Sub **InvokePropertyBuilder**(ByVal initialPage As Integer)
Protected Sub **OnAutoFormat**(ByVal sender As Object, ByVal e As EventArgs)
Overridable Protected Friend Sub **OnDataSourceChanged**()
Protected Sub **OnPropertyBuilder**(ByVal sender As Object, ByVal e As EventArgs)
Protected Friend Sub **OnStylesChanged**()
MustInherit Protected Sub **OnTemplateEditingVerbsChanged**()
Overrides Protected Sub **PreFilterProperties**(ByVal properties As System.Collections.IDictionary)
End Class

Hierarchy: System.Object → System.ComponentModel.Design.ComponentDesigner (
System.ComponentModel.Design.IDesigner , System.IDisposable ,
System.ComponentModel.Design.IDesignerFilter)→ System.Web.UI.Design.HtmlControlDesigner →
System.Web.UI.Design.ControlDesigner → System.Web.UI.Design.TemplatedControlDesigner →
BaseDataListDesigner (System.Web.UI.Design.IDataSourceProvider)

BaseValidatorDesigner
                               Class

System.Web.UI.Design.WebControls (system.design.dll)   *disposable*

This class provides the design-time representation of controls that inherit from the System.Web.UI.WebControls.BaseValidator control, including System.Web.UI.WebControls.CompareValidator, System.Web.UI.WebControls.CustomValidator, System.Web.UI.WebControls.RangeValidator, System.Web.UI.WebControls.RegularExpressionValidator, and System.Web.UI.WebControls.RequiredFieldValidator. It uses an overridden GetDesignTimeHtml() method. Validation controls display the control class name in red lettering at design time.

Public Class **BaseValidatorDesigner** : Inherits System.Web.UI.Design.ControlDesigner
' *Public Constructors*
Public Sub **New**()
' *Public Instance Methods*
Overrides Public Function **GetDesignTimeHtml**() As String
End Class

Hierarchy: System.Object → System.ComponentModel.Design.ComponentDesigner (
System.ComponentModel.Design.IDesigner , System.IDisposable ,
System.ComponentModel.Design.IDesignerFilter)→ System.Web.UI.Design.HtmlControlDesigner →
System.Web.UI.Design.ControlDesigner → BaseValidatorDesigner

ButtonDesigner
Class

System.Web.UI.Design.WebControls (system.design.dll)
disposable

This class provides the design-time representation of a System.Web.UI.WebControls.Button control, using an overridden GetDesignTimeHtml() method. If the System.Web.UI.WebControls.Button.Text property is empty, you will see the control's name displayed in square brackets.

```
Public Class ButtonDesigner : Inherits System.Web.UI.Design.ControlDesigner
' Public Constructors
    Public Sub New()
' Public Instance Methods
    Overrides Public Function GetDesignTimeHtml() As String
End Class
```

Hierarchy: System.Object → System.ComponentModel.Design.ComponentDesigner (System.ComponentModel.Design.IDesigner , System.IDisposable , System.ComponentModel.Design.IDesignerFilter)→ System.Web.UI.Design.HtmlControlDesigner → System.Web.UI.Design.ControlDesigner → ButtonDesigner

CalendarAutoFormatDialog
Class

System.Web.UI.Design.WebControls (system.design.dll)
marshal by reference, disposable

This class works in conjunction with the CalendarDesigner class. It displays an "auto format" window that allows the user to change several formatting-related properties at once by choosing one of the presets it provides.

```
Public Class CalendarAutoFormatDialog : Inherits System.Windows.Forms.Form
' Public Constructors
    Public Sub New(ByVal calendar As System.Web.UI.WebControls.Calendar)
' Protected Instance Methods
    Protected Sub DoDelayLoadActions()
    Protected Sub OnActivated(ByVal source As Object, ByVal e As EventArgs)
    Protected Sub OnOKClicked(ByVal source As Object, ByVal e As EventArgs)
    Protected Sub OnSelChangedScheme(ByVal source As Object, ByVal e As EventArgs)
    Protected Sub SaveComponent()
End Class
```

Hierarchy: System.Object → System.MarshalByRefObject → System.ComponentModel.Component (System.ComponentModel.IComponent , System.IDisposable)→ System.Windows.Forms.Control (System.Windows.Forms.IOleControl , System.Windows.Forms.IOleObject , System.Windows.Forms.IOleInPlaceObject , System.Windows.Forms.IOleInPlaceActiveObject , System.Windows.Forms.IOleWindow , System.Windows.Forms.IViewObject , System.Windows.Forms.IViewObject2 , System.Windows.Forms.IPersist , System.Windows.Forms.IPersistStreamInit , System.Windows.Forms.IPersistPropertyBag , System.Windows.Forms.IPersistStorage , System.Windows.Forms.IQuickActivate , System.ComponentModel.ISynchronizeInvoke , System.Windows.Forms.IWin32Window)→ System.Windows.Forms.ScrollableControl → System.Windows.Forms.ContainerControl (System.Windows.Forms.IContainerControl)→ System.Windows.Forms.Form → CalendarAutoFormatDialog

CalendarDesigner
Class

System.Web.UI.Design.WebControls (system.design.dll)
disposable

This class provides the design-time representation for the System.Web.UI.WebControls.Calendar control. It works in conjunction with the CalendarAutoFormatDialog class to provide an "auto format" window, adding a special verb to the context menu and responding to format changes by updating the corresponding properties.

```
Public Class CalendarDesigner : Inherits System.Web.UI.Design.ControlDesigner
' Public Constructors
   Public Sub New()
' Public Instance Properties
   Overrides Public ReadOnly Property Verbs As DesignerVerbCollection
' Public Instance Methods
   Overrides Public Sub Initialize(ByVal component As System.ComponentModel.IComponent)
' Protected Instance Methods
   Protected Sub OnAutoFormat(ByVal sender As Object, ByVal e As EventArgs)
End Class
```

Hierarchy: System.Object → System.ComponentModel.Design.ComponentDesigner (System.ComponentModel.Design.IDesigner , System.IDisposable , System.ComponentModel.Design.IDesignerFilter)→ System.Web.UI.Design.HtmlControlDesigner → System.Web.UI.Design.ControlDesigner → CalendarDesigner

CheckBoxDesigner
Class

disposable

System.Web.UI.Design.WebControls (system.design.dll)

This class provides the design-time representation of a System.Web.UI.WebControls.CheckBox control, using an overridden GetDesignTimeHtml() method. If the System.Web.UI.WebControls.CheckBox.Text property is empty, the control's name will be displayed in square brackets.

```
Public Class CheckBoxDesigner : Inherits System.Web.UI.Design.ControlDesigner
' Public Constructors
   Public Sub New()
' Public Instance Methods
   Overrides Public Function GetDesignTimeHtml() As String
End Class
```

Hierarchy: System.Object → System.ComponentModel.Design.ComponentDesigner (System.ComponentModel.Design.IDesigner , System.IDisposable , System.ComponentModel.Design.IDesignerFilter)→ System.Web.UI.Design.HtmlControlDesigner → System.Web.UI.Design.ControlDesigner → CheckBoxDesigner

DataGridColumnCollectionEditor
Class

System.Web.UI.Design.WebControls (system.design.dll)

This class is a System.Drawing.Design.UITypeEditor that provides a graphical interface for configuring the column collection provided in the System.Web.UI.WebControls.DataGrid.Columns property.

```
Public Class DataGridColumnCollectionEditor : Inherits System.Drawing.Design.UITypeEditor
' Public Constructors
   Public Sub New()
' Public Instance Methods
   Overrides Public Function EditValue(ByVal context As System.ComponentModel.ITypeDescriptorContext, _
      ByVal provider As IServiceProvider, ByVal value As Object) As Object
   Overrides Public Function GetEditStyle(ByVal context As System.ComponentModel.ITypeDescriptorContext) _
      As UITypeEditorEditStyle
End Class
```

Hierarchy: System.Object → System.Drawing.Design.UITypeEditor → DataGridColumnCollectionEditor

DataGridComponentEditor
System.Web.UI.Design.WebControls (system.design.dll)

Class

This class provides a custom System.ComponentModel.ComponentEditor used to edit complex property information for the System.Web.UI.WebControls.DataGrid control in a special graphical window with multiple pages. This window, which includes information for configuring columns, paging, format, and borders, can be displayed by choosing "Property Builder" from the context menu.

```
Public Class DataGridComponentEditor : Inherits BaseDataListComponentEditor
' Public Constructors
   Public Sub New()
   Public Sub New(ByVal initialPage As Integer)
' Protected Instance Methods
   Overrides Protected Function GetComponentEditorPages() As Type()
End Class
```

Hierarchy: System.Object → System.ComponentModel.ComponentEditor → System.Windows.Forms.Design.WindowsFormsComponentEditor → BaseDataListComponentEditor → DataGridComponentEditor

DataGridDesigner
System.Web.UI.Design.WebControls (system.design.dll)

Class

disposable

This class provides the design-time representation of a System.Web.UI.WebControls.DataGrid control. A sample table is displayed if no connection is made. If you bind to a data source at design time, the schema is used to create column headings, and the formatting options you have selected are also shown. However, the actual data rows use dummy values (like "abc") generated by the System.Web.UI.Design.DesignTimeData class.

```
Public Class DataGridDesigner : Inherits BaseDataListDesigner
' Public Constructors
   Public Sub New()
' Public Instance Methods
   Overrides Public Function GetDesignTimeHtml() As String
   Overrides Public Function GetTemplateContainerDataItemProperty(ByVal templateName As String) _
      As String
   Overrides Public Function GetTemplateContent(                                        _
      ByVal editingFrame As System.Web.UI.Design.ITemplateEditingFrame, ByVal templateName As String, _
      ByRef allowEditing As Boolean) As String
   Overrides Public Function GetTemplatePropertyParentType(ByVal templateName As String) As Type
   Overrides Public Sub Initialize(ByVal component As System.ComponentModel.IComponent)
   Overridable Public Sub OnColumnsChanged()
   Overrides Public Sub SetTemplateContent(ByVal editingFrame As System.Web.UI.Design.ITemplateEditingFrame _
      , ByVal templateName As String, ByVal templateContent As String)
' Protected Instance Methods
   Overrides Protected Function CreateTemplateEditingFrame(                             _
      ByVal verb As System.Web.UI.Design.TemplateEditingVerb) As ITemplateEditingFrame _
   Overrides Protected Sub Dispose(ByVal disposing As Boolean)
   Overrides Protected Function GetCachedTemplateEditingVerbs() As TemplateEditingVerb()
   Overrides Protected Function GetEmptyDesignTimeHtml() As String
   Overrides Protected Function GetErrorDesignTimeHtml(ByVal e As Exception) As String
```

Overrides Protected Sub **OnTemplateEditingVerbsChanged**()
End Class

Hierarchy: System.Object → System.ComponentModel.Design.ComponentDesigner (
System.ComponentModel.Design.IDesigner , System.IDisposable ,
System.ComponentModel.Design.IDesignerFilter) → System.Web.UI.Design.HtmlControlDesigner →
System.Web.UI.Design.ControlDesigner → System.Web.UI.Design.TemplatedControlDesigner →
BaseDataListDesigner (System.Web.UI.Design.IDataSourceProvider) → DataGridDesigner

DataListComponentEditor — Class

System.Web.UI.Design.WebControls (system.design.dll)

This class provides a custom System.ComponentModel.ComponentEditor used to edit complex
property information for the System.Web.UI.WebControls.DataList in a special graphical window with multiple pages. This window can be displayed by choosing "Property
Builder" from the context menu.

Public Class **DataListComponentEditor** : Inherits BaseDataListComponentEditor
' *Public Constructors*
  Public Sub **New**()
  Public Sub **New**(ByVal initialPage As Integer)
' *Protected Instance Methods*
  Overrides Protected Function **GetComponentEditorPages**() As Type()
End Class

Hierarchy: System.Object → System.ComponentModel.ComponentEditor →
System.Windows.Forms.Design.WindowsFormsComponentEditor → BaseDataListComponentEditor →
DataListComponentEditor

DataListDesigner — Class
disposable

System.Web.UI.Design.WebControls (system.design.dll)

This class provides the design-time representation of a System.Web.UI.WebControls.DataList
control. A message indicating how to configure template options is displayed if no template information is entered.

Public Class **DataListDesigner** : Inherits BaseDataListDesigner
' *Public Constructors*
  Public Sub **New**()
' *Public Instance Properties*
  Overrides Public ReadOnly Property **AllowResize** As Boolean
' *Protected Instance Properties*
  Protected Property **TemplatesExist** As Boolean
' *Public Instance Methods*
  Overrides Public Function **GetDesignTimeHtml**() As String
  Overrides Public Function **GetTemplateContainerDataItemProperty**(ByVal templateName As String) _
    As String
  Overrides Public Function **GetTemplateContent**(—
    ByVal editingFrame As System.Web.UI.Design.ITemplateEditingFrame, ByVal templateName As String, _
    ByRef allowEditing As Boolean) As String
  Overrides Public Sub **Initialize**(ByVal component As System.ComponentModel.IComponent)
  Overrides Public Sub **SetTemplateContent**(ByVal editingFrame As System.Web.UI.Design.ITemplateEditingFrame _
    , ByVal templateName As String, ByVal templateContent As String)
' *Protected Instance Methods*

Overrides Protected Function **CreateTemplateEditingFrame(**
  ByVal verb As System.Web.UI.Design.TemplateEditingVerb) As ITemplateEditingFrame
Overrides Protected Sub **Dispose**(ByVal disposing As Boolean)
Overrides Protected Function **GetCachedTemplateEditingVerbs**() As TemplateEditingVerb()
Overrides Protected Function **GetEmptyDesignTimeHtml**() As String
Overrides Protected Function **GetErrorDesignTimeHtml**(ByVal e As Exception) As String
Overrides Protected Sub **OnTemplateEditingVerbsChanged**()
End Class

Hierarchy: System.Object → System.ComponentModel.Design.ComponentDesigner (
System.ComponentModel.Design.IDesigner , System.IDisposable ,
System.ComponentModel.Design.IDesignerFilter)→ System.Web.UI.Design.HtmlControlDesigner →
System.Web.UI.Design.ControlDesigner → System.Web.UI.Design.TemplatedControlDesigner →
BaseDataListDesigner (System.Web.UI.Design.IDataSourceProvider)→ DataListDesigner

HyperLinkDesigner
Class

System.Web.UI.Design.WebControls (system.design.dll)
disposable

This class provides the design-time representation of a System.Web.UI.WebControls.HyperLink
control, using an overridden GetDesignTimeHtml() method. If the System.Web.UI.WebCon-
trols.HyperLink.Text property is empty, the control's name will be displayed in square
brackets.

Public Class **HyperLinkDesigner** : Inherits System.Web.UI.Design.TextControlDesigner
' *Public Constructors*
  Public Sub **New**()
' *Public Instance Methods*
  Overrides Public Function **GetDesignTimeHtml**() As String
End Class

Hierarchy: System.Object → System.ComponentModel.Design.ComponentDesigner (
System.ComponentModel.Design.IDesigner , System.IDisposable ,
System.ComponentModel.Design.IDesignerFilter)→ System.Web.UI.Design.HtmlControlDesigner →
System.Web.UI.Design.ControlDesigner → System.Web.UI.Design.TextControlDesigner →
HyperLinkDesigner

LabelDesigner
Class

System.Web.UI.Design.WebControls (system.design.dll)
disposable

This class provides the design-time representation of a System.Web.UI.WebControls.Label
control, using an overridden GetDesignTimeHtml() method. If the System.Web.UI.WebCon-
trols.Label.Text property is empty, the control's name will be displayed in square brackets.

Public Class **LabelDesigner** : Inherits System.Web.UI.Design.TextControlDesigner
' *Public Constructors*
  Public Sub **New**()
End Class

Hierarchy: System.Object → System.ComponentModel.Design.ComponentDesigner (
System.ComponentModel.Design.IDesigner , System.IDisposable ,
System.ComponentModel.Design.IDesignerFilter)→ System.Web.UI.Design.HtmlControlDesigner →
System.Web.UI.Design.ControlDesigner → System.Web.UI.Design.TextControlDesigner →
LabelDesigner

LinkButtonDesigner

System.Web.UI.Design.WebControls (system.design.dll)   *disposable*

This class provides the design-time representation of a System.Web.UI.WebControls.LinkButton control, using an overridden GetDesignTimeHtml() method. If the System.Web.UI.WebControls.LinkButton.Text property is empty, the control's name will be displayed in square brackets.

Public Class **LinkButtonDesigner** : Inherits System.Web.UI.Design.TextControlDesigner
' *Public Constructors*
  Public Sub **New**()
End Class

Hierarchy: System.Object → System.ComponentModel.Design.ComponentDesigner (
System.ComponentModel.Design.IDesigner , System.IDisposable ,
System.ComponentModel.Design.IDesignerFilter)→ System.Web.UI.Design.HtmlControlDesigner →
System.Web.UI.Design.ControlDesigner → System.Web.UI.Design.TextControlDesigner →
LinkButtonDesigner

ListControlDataBindingHandler

System.Web.UI.Design.WebControls (system.design.dll)

This class provides a data binding handler that lets you connect controls derived from System.Web.UI.WebControls.ListControl to a data source.

Public Class **ListControlDataBindingHandler** : Inherits System.Web.UI.Design.DataBindingHandler
' *Public Constructors*
  Public Sub **New**()
' *Public Instance Methods*
  Overrides Public Sub **DataBindControl**(ByVal designerHost As System.ComponentModel.Design.IDesignerHost, _
    ByVal control As System.Web.UI.Control)
End Class

Hierarchy: System.Object → System.Web.UI.Design.DataBindingHandler →
ListControlDataBindingHandler

ListControlDesigner

System.Web.UI.Design.WebControls (system.design.dll)   *disposable*

This class provides the design-time representation for several list controls derived from System.Web.UI.WebControls.ListControl. The design-time view displays any items you have added through the ListItemsCollectionEditor, or it may show the text "Unbound" if no data is entered or "Databound" if it is linked to a data source.

Public Class **ListControlDesigner** : Inherits System.Web.UI.Design.ControlDesigner : Implements _
    System.Web.UI.Design.IDataSourceProvider
' *Public Constructors*
  Public Sub **New**()
' *Public Instance Properties*
  Public Property **DataMember** As String
  Public Property **DataSource** As String
  Public Property **DataTextField** As String
  Public Property **DataValueField** As String
' *Public Instance Methods*
  Overrides Public Function **GetDesignTimeHtml**() As String
  Public Function **GetResolvedSelectedDataSource**() As IEnumerable _
    Implements IDataSourceProvider.GetResolvedSelectedDataSource

---

Public Function **GetSelectedDataSource**() As Object Implements IDataSourceProvider.GetSelectedDataSource
Overrides Public Sub **Initialize**(ByVal component As System.ComponentModel.IComponent)
Overrides Public Sub **OnComponentChanged**(ByVal source As Object, _
  ByVal ce As System.ComponentModel.Design.ComponentChangedEventArgs)
Overridable Public Sub **OnDataSourceChanged**()
' *Protected Instance Methods*
Overrides Protected Sub **PreFilterProperties**(ByVal properties As System.Collections.IDictionary)
End Class

Hierarchy: System.Object → System.ComponentModel.Design.ComponentDesigner (
System.ComponentModel.Design.IDesigner , System.IDisposable ,
System.ComponentModel.Design.IDesignerFilter)→ System.Web.UI.Design.HtmlControlDesigner →
System.Web.UI.Design.ControlDesigner → ListControlDesigner (
System.Web.UI.Design.IDataSourceProvider)

ListItemsCollectionEditor
Class

System.Web.UI.Design.WebControls (system.design.dll)

This class is a System.Drawing.Design.UITypeEditor that provides a graphical interface for
adding list items and configuring their properties at design time. It's used to configure
the Items property for controls such as System.Web.UI.WebControls.CheckBoxList,
System.Web.UI.WebControls.RadioButtonList, and System.Web.UI.WebControls.ListBox.

Public Class **ListItemsCollectionEditor** : Inherits System.ComponentModel.Design.CollectionEditor
' *Public Constructors*
Public Sub **New**(ByVal type As Type)
' *Protected Instance Methods*
Overrides Protected Function **CanSelectMultipleInstances**() As Boolean
End Class

Hierarchy: System.Object → System.Drawing.Design.UITypeEditor →
System.ComponentModel.Design.CollectionEditor → ListItemsCollectionEditor

PanelDesigner
Class

System.Web.UI.Design.WebControls (system.design.dll)   *disposable*

This class provides the design-time representation for the System.Web.UI.WebControls.Panel
control. The design-time view corresponds closely with the runtime view, except it
adds a thin border to make the Panel control's size and position clearly visible.

Public Class **PanelDesigner** : Inherits System.Web.UI.Design.ReadWriteControlDesigner
' *Public Constructors*
Public Sub **New**()
' *Protected Instance Methods*
Overrides Protected Sub **MapPropertyToStyle**(ByVal propName As String, ByVal varPropValue As Object)
Overrides Protected Sub **OnBehaviorAttached**()
End Class

Hierarchy: System.Object → System.ComponentModel.Design.ComponentDesigner (
System.ComponentModel.Design.IDesigner , System.IDisposable ,
System.ComponentModel.Design.IDesignerFilter)→ System.Web.UI.Design.HtmlControlDesigner →
System.Web.UI.Design.ControlDesigner → System.Web.UI.Design.ReadWriteControlDesigner →
PanelDesigner

RegexEditorDialog

Class

System.Web.UI.Design.WebControls (system.design.dll)   *marshal by reference, disposable*

This class works in conjunction with the RegexTypeEditor to provide a dialog box for editing regular expressions at design time.

Public Class **RegexEditorDialog** : Inherits System.Windows.Forms.Form
' *Public Constructors*
   Public Sub **New**(ByVal site As System.ComponentModel.ISite)
' *Public Instance Properties*
   Public Property **RegularExpression** As String
' *Protected Instance Methods*
   Protected Sub **cmdHelp_Click**(ByVal sender As Object, ByVal e As EventArgs)
   Protected Sub **cmdOK_Click**(ByVal sender As Object, ByVal e As EventArgs)
   Protected Sub **cmdTestValidate_Click**(ByVal sender As Object, ByVal args As EventArgs)
   Overrides Protected Sub **Dispose**(ByVal disposing As Boolean)
   Protected Sub **lstStandardExpressions_SelectedIndexChanged**(ByVal sender As Object, _
      ByVal e As EventArgs)
   Protected Sub **RegexTypeEditor_Activated**(ByVal sender As Object, ByVal e As EventArgs)
   Protected Sub **txtExpression_TextChanged**(ByVal sender As Object, ByVal e As EventArgs)
End Class

Hierarchy: System.Object → System.MarshalByRefObject → System.ComponentModel.Component
(System.ComponentModel.IComponent , System.IDisposable)→ System.Windows.Forms.Control (
System.Windows.Forms.IOleControl , System.Windows.Forms.IOleObject ,
System.Windows.Forms.IOleInPlaceObject , System.Windows.Forms.IOleInPlaceActiveObject ,
System.Windows.Forms.IOleWindow , System.Windows.Forms.IViewObject ,
System.Windows.Forms.IViewObject2 , System.Windows.Forms.IPersist ,
System.Windows.Forms.IPersistStreamInit , System.Windows.Forms.IPersistPropertyBag ,
System.Windows.Forms.IPersistStorage , System.Windows.Forms.IQuickActivate ,
System.ComponentModel.ISynchronizeInvoke , System.Windows.Forms.IWin32Window)→
System.Windows.Forms.ScrollableControl → System.Windows.Forms.ContainerControl (
System.Windows.Forms.IContainerControl)→ System.Windows.Forms.Form → RegexEditorDialog

RegexTypeEditor

Class

System.Web.UI.Design.WebControls (system.design.dll)

This class is a System.Drawing.Design.UITypeEditor that provides a graphical interface for configuring the ValidationExpression for the System.Web.UI.WebControls.RegularExpressionValidator control. It works in conjunction with the RegexEditorDialog to provide a window that allows you to enter new regular expressions or choose from a list of common options.

Public Class **RegexTypeEditor** : Inherits System.Drawing.Design.UITypeEditor
' *Public Constructors*
   Public Sub **New**()
' *Public Instance Methods*
   Overrides Public Function **EditValue**(ByVal context As System.ComponentModel.ITypeDescriptorContext, _
      ByVal provider As IServiceProvider, ByVal value As Object) As Object
   Overrides Public Function **GetEditStyle**(ByVal context As System.ComponentModel.ITypeDescriptorContext) _
      As UITypeEditorEditStyle
End Class

Hierarchy: System.Object → System.Drawing.Design.UITypeEditor → RegexTypeEditor

RepeaterDesigner

Class

System.Web.UI.Design.WebControls (system.design.dll)   *disposable*

This class provides the design-time representation for the System.Web.UI.WebControls.Repeater control. The design-time view shows headings and other static content, but not data-bound items. If no templates are entered, the control displays the message "Switch to HTML view to edit the control's templates."

```
Public Class RepeaterDesigner : Inherits System.Web.UI.Design.ControlDesigner : Implements _
      System.Web.UI.Design.IDataSourceProvider
' Public Constructors
   Public Sub New()
' Public Instance Properties
   Public Property DataMember As String
   Public Property DataSource As String
' Protected Instance Properties
   Protected Property TemplatesExist As Boolean
' Public Instance Methods
   Overrides Public Function GetDesignTimeHtml() As String
   Public Function GetResolvedSelectedDataSource() As IEnumerable _
      Implements  IDataSourceProvider.GetResolvedSelectedDataSource
   Public Function GetSelectedDataSource() As Object            _
      Implements  IDataSourceProvider.GetSelectedDataSource
   Overrides Public Sub Initialize(ByVal component As System.ComponentModel.IComponent)
   Overrides Public Sub OnComponentChanged(ByVal source As Object,
      ByVal ce As System.ComponentModel.Design.ComponentChangedEventArgs)
   Overridable Public Sub OnDataSourceChanged()
' Protected Instance Methods
   Overrides Protected Sub Dispose(ByVal disposing As Boolean)
   Protected Function GetDesignTimeDataSource(ByVal selectedDataSource As System.Collections.IEnumerable, _
      ByVal minimumRows As Integer) As IEnumerable
   Protected Function GetDesignTimeDataSource(ByVal minimumRows As Integer) As IEnumerable
   Overrides Protected Function GetEmptyDesignTimeHtml() As String
   Overrides Protected Function GetErrorDesignTimeHtml(ByVal e As Exception) As String
   Overrides Protected Sub PreFilterProperties(ByVal properties As System.Collections.IDictionary)
End Class
```

Hierarchy: System.Object → System.ComponentModel.Design.ComponentDesigner (
System.ComponentModel.Design.IDesigner , System.IDisposable ,
System.ComponentModel.Design.IDesignerFilter) → System.Web.UI.Design.HtmlControlDesigner →
System.Web.UI.Design.ControlDesigner → RepeaterDesigner (
System.Web.UI.Design.IDataSourceProvider)

TableCellsCollectionEditor

Class

System.Web.UI.Design.WebControls (system.design.dll)

This class is a System.Drawing.Design.UITypeEditor that provides a graphical interface for adding System.Web.UI.WebControls.TableCell objects to a System.Web.UI.WebControls.TableRow at design time. The same window also allows you to configure System.Web.UI.WebControls.TableCell properties. This designer is accessed through the TableRowsCollectionEditor.

```
Public Class TableCellsCollectionEditor : Inherits System.ComponentModel.Design.CollectionEditor
' Public Constructors
   Public Sub New(ByVal type As Type)
```

```
' Protected Instance Methods
   Overrides Protected Function CanSelectMultipleInstances() As Boolean
   Overrides Protected Function CreateInstance(ByVal itemType As Type) As Object
End Class
```

Hierarchy: System.Object → System.Drawing.Design.UITypeEditor →
System.ComponentModel.Design.CollectionEditor → TableCellsCollectionEditor

TableDesigner
Class

disposable

System.Web.UI.Design.WebControls (system.design.dll)

This class provides the design-time representation of the System.Web.UI.WebControls.Table control. This closely resembles the runtime representation, except when the table is empty (in which case dummy data is used) or if you use code to modify the table programmatically before it is displayed.

```
Public Class TableDesigner : Inherits System.Web.UI.Design.ControlDesigner
' Public Constructors
   Public Sub New()
' Public Instance Methods
   Overrides Public Function GetDesignTimeHtml() As String
   Overrides Public Function GetPersistInnerHtml() As String
End Class
```

Hierarchy: System.Object → System.ComponentModel.Design.ComponentDesigner (
System.ComponentModel.Design.IDesigner , System.IDisposable ,
System.ComponentModel.Design.IDesignerFilter)→ System.Web.UI.Design.HtmlControlDesigner →
System.Web.UI.Design.ControlDesigner → TableDesigner

TableRowsCollectionEditor
Class

System.Web.UI.Design.WebControls (system.design.dll)

This class is a System.Drawing.Design.UITypeEditor that provides a graphical interface for adding System.Web.UI.WebControls.TableRow objects to a System.Web.UI.WebControls.Table at design time. The same window also allows you to configure System.Web.UI.WebControls.TableRow properties.

```
Public Class TableRowsCollectionEditor : Inherits System.ComponentModel.Design.CollectionEditor
' Public Constructors
   Public Sub New(ByVal type As Type)
' Protected Instance Methods
   Overrides Protected Function CanSelectMultipleInstances() As Boolean
   Overrides Protected Function CreateInstance(ByVal itemType As Type) As Object
End Class
```

Hierarchy: System.Object → System.Drawing.Design.UITypeEditor →
System.ComponentModel.Design.CollectionEditor → TableRowsCollectionEditor

XmlDesigner
Class

disposable

System.Web.UI.Design.WebControls (system.design.dll)

This class provides the design-time representation for the System.Web.UI.WebControls.Xml control. The design-time view shows the default message "Use this control to perform XSL transforms" rather than the actual XML content.

```
Public Class XmlDesigner : Inherits System.Web.UI.Design.ControlDesigner
' Public Constructors
   Public Sub New()
' Public Instance Methods
   Overrides Public Function GetDesignTimeHtml() As String
   Overrides Public Sub Initialize(ByVal component As System.ComponentModel.IComponent)
' Protected Instance Methods
   Overrides Protected Sub Dispose(ByVal disposing As Boolean)
   Overrides Protected Function GetEmptyDesignTimeHtml() As String
End Class
```

Hierarchy: System.Object → System.ComponentModel.Design.ComponentDesigner (
System.ComponentModel.Design.IDesigner , System.IDisposable ,
System.ComponentModel.Design.IDesignerFilter)→ System.Web.UI.Design.HtmlControlDesigner →
System.Web.UI.Design.ControlDesigner → XmlDesigner

CHAPTER 37

The System.Web.UI.HtmlControls
Namespace

The System.Web.UI.HtmlControls namespace includes classes for HTML server controls. HTML server controls are ASP.NET controls that raise events on the server and provide a simple object model that allows you to set some basic properties. Unlike web controls, which are found in the System.Web.UI.WebControls namespace, each HTML server control corresponds directly to an HTML element like <textarea> or <input>. Web controls are generally preferred in ASP.NET development because they are abstracted away from the low-level HTML details and they provide a richer object model with many more events, sophisticated data binding, automatic state management, and validation controls. HTML server controls are most often used when upgrading existing ASP pages. A standard HTML element can be converted into an HTML server control by adding the attribute runat="server" in the tag. This makes it extremely simple to convert a static HTML page into a dynamic page that allows controls to be manipulated as objects during postbacks.

All controls in this namespace derive from HtmlControl. This class provides basic functionality, including a name/value collection of attributes and CSS style properties. In addition, controls that require both an opening and closing tag inherit from HtmlContainerControl. This class adds a HtmlContainerControl.InnerText and HtmlContainerControl.InnerHtml property which allow you to access the text contained inside the tag. HTML elements that don't have corresponding classes can be represented by the HtmlGenericControl class. Note that only button and hyperlink controls trigger server postbacks. Many controls provide a ServerChanged event, which won't fire after a control is modified until a postback occurs.

To understand all the available attributes and CSS properties, you may want to refer to an HTML reference. There are many excellent HTML references on the web, or you can refer to O'Reilly's *HTML & XHTML: The Definitive Guide* by Chuck Musciano and Bill Kennedy.

Figure 37-1 shows the types in this namespace.

HtmlAnchor	**Class**
System.Web.UI.HtmlControls (system.web.dll)	*disposable*

This class represents the <A> anchor tag in HTML, which provides a hyperlink. The linked text is contained inside the tag and can be accessed through the InnerHtml

657

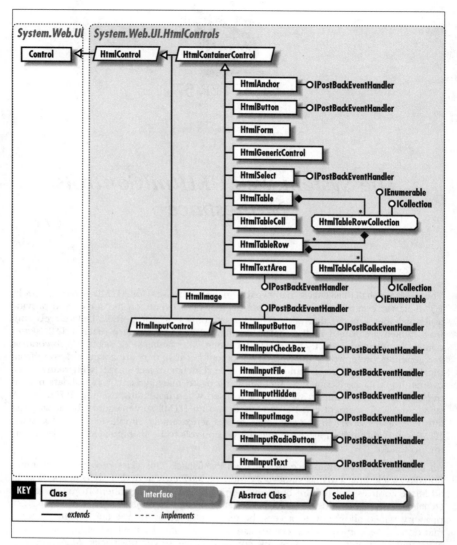

Figure 37-1: The System.Web.UI.HtmlControls namespace

property. You can also programmatically change the linked page (HRef), the target frame (Target), and the window title for the target (Title). Even if the HRef property is not set, you can handle the ServerClick event and use a Response.Redirect statement to load a different page. The HtmlAnchor control also supports data binding to the HRef and Inner-Html properties.

You can use an anchor tag to mark a bookmark in a page, in which case you set the Name property but not the HRef property. In this case, you don't need to include any text inside the tag, as in <a Name="TopicName"/>. To make a link to this bookmark, add #TopicName at the end of the URL requesting this page.

Public Class **HtmlAnchor** : Inherits HtmlContainerControl: Implements System.Web.UI.IPostBackEventHandler
' *Public Constructors*
   Public Sub **New**()
' *Public Instance Properties*
   Public Property **HRef** As String
   Public Property **Name** As String
   Public Property **Target** As String
   Public Property **Title** As String
' *Protected Instance Methods*
   Overrides Protected Sub **OnPreRender**(ByVal e As EventArgs)
   Overridable Protected Sub **OnServerClick**(ByVal e As EventArgs)
   Overrides Protected Sub **RenderAttributes**(ByVal writer As System.Web.UI.HtmlTextWriter)
' *Events*
   Public Event **ServerClick** As EventHandler
End Class

Hierarchy: System.Object → System.Web.UI.Control (System.ComponentModel.IComponent , System.IDisposable , System.Web.UI.IParserAccessor , System.Web.UI.IDataBindingsAccessor)→ HtmlControl (System.Web.UI.IAttributeAccessor)→ HtmlContainerControl → HtmlAnchor (System.Web.UI.IPostBackEventHandler)

HtmlButton

Class

System.Web.UI.HtmlControls (system.web.dll)

disposable

This class represents the HTML 4.0 <button> tag, which is only supported in Internet Explorer 4.0 and later. It differs from other button types, including the standard HtmlInputButton control, because it can be composed from embedded HTML elements like images and other ASP.NET server controls. As with all buttons, it provides a click event that you can handle directly (HtmlInputButton.ServerClick) and a property that lets you disable automatic page validation when a postback is triggered by this control (HtmlInputButton.CausesValidation).

Public Class **HtmlButton** : Inherits HtmlContainerControl: Implements System.Web.UI.IPostBackEventHandler
' *Public Constructors*
   Public Sub **New**()
' *Public Instance Properties*
   Public Property **CausesValidation** As Boolean
' *Protected Instance Methods*
   Overrides Protected Sub **OnPreRender**(ByVal e As EventArgs)
   Overridable Protected Sub **OnServerClick**(ByVal e As EventArgs)
   Overrides Protected Sub **RenderAttributes**(ByVal writer As System.Web.UI.HtmlTextWriter)
' *Events*
   Public Event **ServerClick** As EventHandler
End Class

Hierarchy: System.Object → System.Web.UI.Control (System.ComponentModel.IComponent , System.IDisposable , System.Web.UI.IParserAccessor , System.Web.UI.IDataBindingsAccessor)→ HtmlControl (System.Web.UI.IAttributeAccessor)→ HtmlContainerControl → HtmlButton (System.Web.UI.IPostBackEventHandler)

HtmlContainerControl

MustInherit Class

System.Web.UI.HtmlControls (system.web.dll)

disposable

This abstract class provides functionality for all HTML server controls that require closing tags. For example, an HtmlAnchor control must always be closed (<a>Text</a> and <a/> are valid anchor tags, but <a> alone is not). A HtmlImage control, on the other hand, does not need a closing tag.

Every control that requires a closing tag has the ability to contain text. This information is provided through the InnerText and InnerHtml properties. Both properties retrieve all the content between the opening and closing control tag. The difference is that InnerText automatically encodes and decodes special characters into their corresponding HTML entities. For example, if you set the InnerText property to Hello, the < and > symbols are converted to the HTML equivalents < and >. This instructs the browser to display Hello as plain text. However, if you set the InnerHtml property to Hello, the < and > symbols will be interpreted as HTML markup tags and the word "Hello" will be displayed in bold.

```
Public MustInherit Class HtmlContainerControl : Inherits HtmlControl
' Public Constructors
    Public Sub New()
    Public Sub New(ByVal tag As String)
' Public Instance Properties
    Overridable Public Property InnerHtml As String
    Overridable Public Property InnerText As String
' Protected Instance Methods
    Overrides Protected Function CreateControlCollection() As ControlCollection
    Overrides Protected Sub LoadViewState(ByVal savedState As Object)
    Overrides Protected Sub Render(ByVal writer As System.Web.UI.HtmlTextWriter)
    Overrides Protected Sub RenderAttributes(ByVal writer As System.Web.UI.HtmlTextWriter)
    Overridable Protected Sub RenderEndTag(ByVal writer As System.Web.UI.HtmlTextWriter)
End Class
```

Hierarchy: System.Object → System.Web.UI.Control (System.ComponentModel.IComponent , System.IDisposable , System.Web.UI.IParserAccessor , System.Web.UI.IDataBindingsAccessor) → HtmlControl (System.Web.UI.IAttributeAccessor) → HtmlContainerControl

HtmlControl   MustInherit Class

System.Web.UI.HtmlControls (system.web.dll)   *disposable*

This is the base class for all HTML server controls. It includes basic functionality—like the Disabled property, which you can use to make a control read-only, and the TagName property, which identifies the HTML tag that underlies this control (for example, "div" or "a").

Additionally, you can set and retrieve various other properties through the weakly typed Attributes collection, which contains a name/value collection of all the attributes applied to a tag. You can add a new attribute by assigning to it, as in MyText.Attributes("onblur")="javascript:alert('Focus lost!');". This statement, which adds a client-side JavaScript event through an attribute, is the equivalent of using the tag <input type="text" id="MyText" onblur="javascript:alert('Focus lost!');" runat="server"/>. Some attributes may be provided as properties in the derived class. Another dictionary collection, Style, allows you to specify CSS properties for a tag (as in MyText.Style("width") = "120px").

```
Public MustInherit Class HtmlControl : Inherits System.Web.UI.Control : Implements System.Web.UI.IAttributeAccessor
' Public Constructors
    Public Sub New()
    Public Sub New(ByVal tag As String)
' Public Instance Properties
    Public ReadOnly Property Attributes As AttributeCollection
    Public Property Disabled As Boolean
    Public ReadOnly Property Style As CssStyleCollection
    Overridable Public ReadOnly Property TagName As String
' Protected Instance Properties
```

Overrides Protected Property **ViewStateIgnoresCase** As Boolean
' *Protected Instance Methods*
Overrides Protected Function **CreateControlCollection**() As ControlCollection
Overrides Protected Sub **Render**(ByVal writer As System.Web.UI.HtmlTextWriter)
Overridable Protected Sub **RenderAttributes**(ByVal writer As System.Web.UI.HtmlTextWriter)
Overridable Protected Sub **RenderBeginTag**(ByVal writer As System.Web.UI.HtmlTextWriter)
End Class

Hierarchy: System.Object → System.Web.UI.Control (System.ComponentModel.IComponent , System.IDisposable , System.Web.UI.IParserAccessor , System.Web.UI.IDataBindingsAccessor)→ HtmlControl (System.Web.UI.IAttributeAccessor)

HtmlForm   Class
System.Web.UI.HtmlControls (system.web.dll)   *disposable*

This class represents the HTML <form> tag, which is used as a container for other input controls. All ASP.NET Server Controls that post back to the server must be contained in a HtmlForm tag. The properties of this control shouldn't be changed. The Method property (set to "post") is particularly important. If modified, you may not be able to use the built-in postback and control state management services provided by ASP.NET.

Public Class **HtmlForm** : Inherits HtmlContainerControl
' *Public Constructors*
Public Sub **New**()
' *Public Instance Properties*
Public Property **Enctype** As String
Public Property **Method** As String
Overridable Public Property **Name** As String
Public Property **Target** As String
' *Protected Instance Methods*
Overrides Protected Sub **OnInit**(ByVal e As EventArgs)
Overrides Protected Sub **Render**(ByVal output As System.Web.UI.HtmlTextWriter)
Overrides Protected Sub **RenderAttributes**(ByVal writer As System.Web.UI.HtmlTextWriter)
Overrides Protected Sub **RenderChildren**(ByVal writer As System.Web.UI.HtmlTextWriter)
End Class

Hierarchy: System.Object → System.Web.UI.Control (System.ComponentModel.IComponent , System.IDisposable , System.Web.UI.IParserAccessor , System.Web.UI.IDataBindingsAccessor)→ HtmlControl (System.Web.UI.IAttributeAccessor)→ HtmlContainerControl → HtmlForm

HtmlGenericControl   Class
System.Web.UI.HtmlControls (system.web.dll)   *disposable*

This class is used for HTML elements that are not directly represented by other controls in this namespace (including <span>, <div>, and <body>). The primary use of the HtmlGenericControl is usually to set or modify attributes and styles, using the Attributes and Style properties inherited from HtmlControl. Note that the TagName property can be modified, allowing you to change the tag programmatically before the page is rendered as HTML and sent to the client browser.

Public Class **HtmlGenericControl** : Inherits HtmlContainerControl
' *Public Constructors*
Public Sub **New**()
Public Sub **New**(ByVal tag As String)
' *Public Instance Properties*

Public Property **TagName** As String
End Class

Hierarchy: System.Object → System.Web.UI.Control (System.ComponentModel.IComponent , System.IDisposable , System.Web.UI.IParserAccessor , System.Web.UI.IDataBindingsAccessor)→ HtmlControl (System.Web.UI.IAttributeAccessor)→ HtmlContainerControl → HtmlGenericControl

HtmlImage
Class

System.Web.UI.HtmlControls (system.web.dll)
disposable

This class represents the HTML <img> tag, which is used to display a picture file specified by a URL. You can set various properties for this control, including the image file (Src), and the alignment and size of the picture. The Alt property specifies the alternate text, which will appear in place of the image if it cannot be downloaded, and may be displayed as a tooltip over a successfully downloaded image in uplevel browsers.

Public Class **HtmlImage** : Inherits HtmlControl
' *Public Constructors*
    Public Sub **New**()
' *Public Instance Properties*
    Public Property **Align** As String
    Public Property **Alt** As String
    Public Property **Border** As Integer
    Public Property **Height** As Integer
    Public Property **Src** As String
    Public Property **Width** As Integer
' *Protected Instance Methods*
    Overrides Protected Sub **RenderAttributes**(ByVal writer As System.Web.UI.HtmlTextWriter)
End Class

Hierarchy: System.Object → System.Web.UI.Control (System.ComponentModel.IComponent , System.IDisposable , System.Web.UI.IParserAccessor , System.Web.UI.IDataBindingsAccessor)→ HtmlControl (System.Web.UI.IAttributeAccessor)→ HtmlImage

HtmlInputButton
Class

System.Web.UI.HtmlControls (system.web.dll)
disposable

This class can represent the HTML <input type=button> tag, the <input type=submit> tag, and the <input type=reset> tag. Reset buttons are used to clear input fields on the current form and do not trigger a postback. Submit and input buttons in ASP.NET trigger a postback and provide a ServerClick event that you can use to perform other tasks. Additionally, you can use the CausesValidation property to skip postback page validation when this button is clicked.

Public Class **HtmlInputButton** : Inherits HtmlInputControl : Implements System.Web.UI.IPostBackEventHandler
' *Public Constructors*
    Public Sub **New**()
    Public Sub **New**(ByVal type As String)
' *Public Instance Properties*
    Public Property **CausesValidation** As Boolean
' *Protected Instance Methods*
    Overrides Protected Sub **OnPreRender**(ByVal e As EventArgs)
    Overridable Protected Sub **OnServerClick**(ByVal e As EventArgs)
    Overrides Protected Sub **RenderAttributes**(ByVal writer As System.Web.UI.HtmlTextWriter)

```
' Events
    Public Event ServerClick As EventHandler
End Class
```

Hierarchy: System.Object → System.Web.UI.Control (System.ComponentModel.IComponent ,
System.IDisposable , System.Web.UI.IParserAccessor , System.Web.UI.IDataBindingsAccessor) →
HtmlControl (System.Web.UI.IAttributeAccessor) → HtmlInputControl → HtmlInputButton (
System.Web.UI.IPostBackEventHandler)

HtmlInputCheckBox

Class

System.Web.UI.HtmlControls (system.web.dll)

disposable

This class represents the HTML <input type=checkbox> tag and indicates the user's selection through its Checked property. You can also react to the ServerChange event, which will fire only after a postback is triggered (for example, by clicking a submit button). Note that this control does not have an associated text label.

```
Public Class HtmlInputCheckBox : Inherits HtmlInputControl: Implements System.Web.UI.IPostBackDataHandler
' Public Constructors
    Public Sub New()
' Public Instance Properties
    Public Property Checked As Boolean
' Protected Instance Methods
    Overrides Protected Sub OnPreRender(ByVal e As EventArgs)
    Overridable Protected Sub OnServerChange(ByVal e As EventArgs)
' Events
    Public Event ServerChange As EventHandler
End Class
```

Hierarchy: System.Object → System.Web.UI.Control (System.ComponentModel.IComponent ,
System.IDisposable , System.Web.UI.IParserAccessor , System.Web.UI.IDataBindingsAccessor) →
HtmlControl (System.Web.UI.IAttributeAccessor) → HtmlInputControl → HtmlInputCheckBox (
System.Web.UI.IPostBackDataHandler)

HtmlInputControl

MustInherit Class

System.Web.UI.HtmlControls (system.web.dll)

disposable

This abstract class provides basic functionality for all controls based on the HTML <input> tag. The Value property represents the information entered in the control, and the Type property is a string that identifies the value of the input element's type attribute (for example, a checkbox or text). By default, the Name property is identical to System.Web.UI.Control.UniqueID, although it can be used to group together related HtmlInputRadioButton controls with different identifiers.

```
Public MustInherit Class HtmlInputControl : Inherits HtmlControl
' Public Constructors
    Public Sub New(ByVal type As String)
' Public Instance Properties
    Overridable Public Property Name As String
    Public ReadOnly Property Type As String
    Overridable Public Property Value As String
' Protected Instance Methods
    Overrides Protected Sub RenderAttributes(ByVal writer As System.Web.UI.HtmlTextWriter)
End Class
```

Hierarchy: System.Object → System.Web.UI.Control (System.ComponentModel.IComponent ,
System.IDisposable , System.Web.UI.IParserAccessor , System.Web.UI.IDataBindingsAccessor) →
HtmlControl (System.Web.UI.IAttributeAccessor) → HtmlInputControl

HtmlInputFile
Class

System.Web.UI.HtmlControls (system.web.dll)
disposable

This class represents the HTML <input type=file> tag, which allows the user to upload a binary or text file. This control is rendered as a text box with a paired Browse button. The Browse button opens a standard file selection dialog box. The chosen file is not transmitted until the form is posted to the server (usually through a submit button). You can then add code in the event handler of this button to save or otherwise manipulate the file using the PostedFile property, which provides a System.Web.HttpPostedFile object.

You can use the HtmlInputFile property to specify a comma-separated list of MIME file types that your control will accept. You can also change the maximum path length for the filename (MaxLength) and the width of the file path text box (Size). The HtmlForm.Enctype property of the containing form must be set to "multipart/form-data" to allow file uploads.

```
Public Class HtmlInputFile : Inherits HtmlInputControl : Implements  System.Web.UI.IPostBackDataHandler
' Public Constructors
   Public Sub New()
' Public Instance Properties
   Public Property Accept As String
   Public Property MaxLength As Integer
   Public ReadOnly Property PostedFile As HttpPostedFile
   Public Property Size As Integer
End Class
```

Hierarchy: System.Object → System.Web.UI.Control (System.ComponentModel.IComponent , System.IDisposable , System.Web.UI.IParserAccessor , System.Web.UI.IDataBindingsAccessor)→ HtmlControl (System.Web.UI.IAttributeAccessor)→ HtmlInputControl → HtmlInputFile (System.Web.UI.IPostBackDataHandler)

HtmlInputHidden
Class

System.Web.UI.HtmlControls (system.web.dll)
disposable

This class represents the HTML <input type=hidden> tag, which allows you to store hidden information that will be sent with all postbacks. This technique is commonly used to store information without using cookies or session state. ASP.NET automatically uses a hidden input field to preserve the contents of server controls that have the System.Web.UI.Control.EnableViewState property set to True.

You can also react to the ServerChange event. Because the hidden input field will be changed only through code on the server, this event will fire immediately in response to changes implemented by your code.

```
Public Class HtmlInputHidden : Inherits HtmlInputControl: Implements System.Web.UI.IPostBackDataHandler
' Public Constructors
   Public Sub New()
' Protected Instance Methods
   Overrides Protected Sub OnPreRender(ByVal e As EventArgs)
   Overridable Protected Sub OnServerChange(ByVal e As EventArgs)
' Events
   Public Event ServerChange As EventHandler
End Class
```

Hierarchy: System.Object → System.Web.UI.Control (System.ComponentModel.IComponent , System.IDisposable , System.Web.UI.IParserAccessor , System.Web.UI.IDataBindingsAccessor)→ HtmlControl (System.Web.UI.IAttributeAccessor)→ HtmlInputControl → HtmlInputHidden (System.Web.UI.IPostBackDataHandler)

HtmlInputImage
Class

System.Web.UI.HtmlControls (system.web.dll)
disposable

This class represents the HTML <input type=image> element, which creates a graphical button. Unlike HtmlButton controls, HtmlInputImage controls are supported on all standard browsers. This class includes many of the same properties as HtmlImage, such as settings for alignment. It also includes the alternate text and Src, which specifies the file used for the button image. As with all button controls, it provides a click event you can handle directly (ServerClick) and a property that lets you disable automatic page validation when a postback is triggered by this control (CausesValidation).

```
Public Class HtmlInputImage : Inherits HtmlInputControl: Implements System.Web.UI.IPostBackDataHandler, _
    System.Web.UI.IPostBackEventHandler
' Public Constructors
   Public Sub New()
' Public Instance Properties
   Public Property Align As String
   Public Property Alt As String
   Public Property Border As Integer
   Public Property CausesValidation As Boolean
   Public Property Src As String
' Protected Instance Methods
   Overrides Protected Sub OnPreRender(ByVal e As EventArgs)
   Overridable Protected Sub OnServerClick(ByVal e As System.Web.UI.ImageClickEventArgs)
   Overrides Protected Sub RenderAttributes(ByVal writer As System.Web.UI.HtmlTextWriter)
' Events
   Public Event ServerClick As ImageClickEventHandler
End Class
```

Hierarchy: System.Object → System.Web.UI.Control (System.ComponentModel.IComponent , System.IDisposable , System.Web.UI.IParserAccessor , System.Web.UI.IDataBindingsAccessor) → HtmlControl (System.Web.UI.IAttributeAccessor) → HtmlInputControl → HtmlInputImage (System.Web.UI.IPostBackDataHandler , System.Web.UI.IPostBackEventHandler)

HtmlInputRadioButton
Class

System.Web.UI.HtmlControls (system.web.dll)
disposable

This class represents the HTML <input type=radio> tag. The Checked property indicates whether the radio button is selected. If you set the Name property of more than one radio button to the same value, you form a group that allows only one option to be selected at a time. Note that this control does not have any associated text.

```
Public Class HtmlInputRadioButton : Inherits HtmlInputControl: Implements System.Web.UI.IPostBackDataHandler
' Public Constructors
   Public Sub New()
' Public Instance Properties
   Public Property Checked As Boolean
   Overrides Public Property Name As String
   Overrides Public Property Value As String
' Protected Instance Methods
   Overrides Protected Sub OnPreRender(ByVal e As EventArgs)
   Overridable Protected Sub OnServerChange(ByVal e As EventArgs)
   Overrides Protected Sub RenderAttributes(ByVal writer As System.Web.UI.HtmlTextWriter)
' Events
   Public Event ServerChange As EventHandler
End Class
```

Hierarchy: System.Object → System.Web.UI.Control (System.ComponentModel.IComponent , System.IDisposable , System.Web.UI.IParserAccessor , System.Web.UI.IDataBindingsAccessor) → HtmlControl (System.Web.UI.IAttributeAccessor) → HtmlInputControl → HtmlInputRadioButton (System.Web.UI.IPostBackDataHandler)

HtmlInputText
Class

System.Web.UI.HtmlControls (system.web.dll)
disposable

This class represents the HTML <input type=text> or <input type=password> tag, which allow the user to enter a single line of text. If you use the password type, the user's input will be masked with the "*" character for display purposes.

Text entered in this control is provided in the Value property. You can specify the width of the textbox by using the Size property and the maximum number of allowed characters by using MaxLength. You can also react to the ServerChange event, which will fire only after a postback is triggered (for example, when the user clicks a submit button).

```
Public Class HtmlInputText : Inherits HtmlInputControl: Implements System.Web.UI.IPostBackDataHandler
' Public Constructors
   Public Sub New()
   Public Sub New(ByVal type As String)
' Public Instance Properties
   Public Property MaxLength As Integer
   Public Property Size As Integer
   Overrides Public Property Value As String
' Protected Instance Methods
   Overrides Protected Sub OnPreRender(ByVal e As EventArgs)
   Overridable Protected Sub OnServerChange(ByVal e As EventArgs)
   Overrides Protected Sub RenderAttributes(ByVal writer As System.Web.UI.HtmlTextWriter)
' Events
   Public Event ServerChange As EventHandler
End Class
```

Hierarchy: System.Object → System.Web.UI.Control (System.ComponentModel.IComponent , System.IDisposable , System.Web.UI.IParserAccessor , System.Web.UI.IDataBindingsAccessor) → HtmlControl (System.Web.UI.IAttributeAccessor) → HtmlInputControl → HtmlInputText (System.Web.UI.IPostBackDataHandler)

HtmlSelect
Class

System.Web.UI.HtmlControls (system.web.dll)
disposable

This class represents the HTML <select> tag, which allows the user to choose an option from a drop-down list box. To add an item to the list, use the Add() method of the Items property. The HtmlSelect control also supports data binding to its Items property.

To retrieve the currently selected item, you can use SelectedIndex property to find the ordinal number of the chosen item (-1 if no selection has been made), or the Value property to retrieve the text of the selected item. If you have set Multiple to True, more than one item may be selected and only the first item will be returned by the SelectedIndex and Value properties. Instead, you will have to iterate through the Items collection and check the System.Web.UI.WebControls.ListItem.Selected property for each one.

You can also react to the ServerChange event, which will fire only after a postback is triggered (for example, when the user clicks a submit button).

```
Public Class HtmlSelect : Inherits HtmlContainerControl: Implements System.Web.UI.IPostBackDataHandler
' Public Constructors
   Public Sub New()
```

' *Public Instance Properties*
  Overridable Public Property **DataMember** As String
  Overridable Public Property **DataSource** As Object
  Overridable Public Property **DataTextField** As String
  Overridable Public Property **DataValueField** As String
  Overrides Public Property **InnerHtml** As String
  Overrides Public Property **InnerText** As String
  Public ReadOnly Property **Items** As ListItemCollection
  Public Property **Multiple** As Boolean
  Public Property **Name** As String
  Overridable Public Property **SelectedIndex** As Integer
  Public Property **Size** As Integer
  Public Property **Value** As String
' *Protected Instance Properties*
  Overridable Protected Property **SelectedIndices** As Integer()
' *Protected Instance Methods*
  Overrides Protected Sub **AddParsedSubObject**(ByVal obj As Object)
  Overridable Protected Sub **ClearSelection**()
  Overrides Protected Function **CreateControlCollection**() As ControlCollection
  Overrides Protected Sub **LoadViewState**(ByVal savedState As Object)
  Overrides Protected Sub **OnDataBinding**(ByVal e As EventArgs)
  Overrides Protected Sub **OnPreRender**(ByVal e As EventArgs)
  Overridable Protected Sub **OnServerChange**(ByVal e As EventArgs)
  Overrides Protected Sub **RenderAttributes**(ByVal writer As System.Web.UI.HtmlTextWriter)
  Overrides Protected Sub **RenderChildren**(ByVal writer As System.Web.UI.HtmlTextWriter)
  Overrides Protected Function **SaveViewState**() As Object
  Overridable Protected Sub **Select**(ByVal selectedIndices As Integer())
  Overrides Protected Sub **TrackViewState**()
' *Events*
  Public Event **ServerChange** As EventHandler
End Class

Hierarchy: System.Object → System.Web.UI.Control (System.ComponentModel.IComponent ,
System.IDisposable , System.Web.UI.IParserAccessor , System.Web.UI.IDataBindingsAccessor) →
HtmlControl (System.Web.UI.IAttributeAccessor) → HtmlContainerControl → HtmlSelect (
System.Web.UI.IPostBackDataHandler)

HtmlTable
System.Web.UI.HtmlControls (system.web.dll)

Class

disposable

This class provides a powerful way to access the HTML <table> element. You can also
use it to dynamically generate an HTML table by adding HtmlTableRow objects to the Rows
collection and adding HtmlTableCell objects to each row. Programmatically created tables
must be recreated with every postback.

Most other properties for the HtmlTable class correspond to formatting options, including
the background color (BgColor), alignment (Align), and dimensions (Height and Width).
You can also set values in pixels for the width of the border around the table (Border),
the spacing between cells (CellSpacing), and the spacing between cell borders and con-
tent (CellPadding).

Public Class **HtmlTable** : Inherits HtmlContainerControl
' *Public Constructors*
  Public Sub **New**()
' *Public Instance Properties*
  Public Property **Align** As String

Public Property **BgColor** As String
Public Property **Border** As Integer
Public Property **BorderColor** As String
Public Property **CellPadding** As Integer
Public Property **CellSpacing** As Integer
Public Property **Height** As String
Overrides Public Property **InnerHtml** As String
Overrides Public Property **InnerText** As String
Overridable Public ReadOnly Property **Rows** As HtmlTableRowCollection
Public Property **Width** As String
' Protected Instance Methods
Overrides Protected Function **CreateControlCollection**() As ControlCollection
Overrides Protected Sub **RenderChildren**(ByVal writer As System.Web.UI.HtmlTextWriter)
Overrides Protected Sub **RenderEndTag**(ByVal writer As System.Web.UI.HtmlTextWriter)
End Class

Hierarchy: System.Object → System.Web.UI.Control (System.ComponentModel.IComponent , System.IDisposable , System.Web.UI.IParserAccessor , System.Web.UI.IDataBindingsAccessor) → HtmlControl (System.Web.UI.IAttributeAccessor) → HtmlContainerControl → HtmlTable

HtmlTableCell

Class

System.Web.UI.HtmlControls (system.web.dll)

disposable

This class represents individual <td> (table data) and <th> (table header) elements contained in an HTML table row. The InnerHtml and InnerText properties allow you to access the content stored in an individual cell. Most other properties are used to fine-tune the appearance of a particular cell. You can set NoWrap to configure whether or not the contents in a cell will wrap and RowSpan and ColSpan to specify that a cell should span the specified number of columns or rows.

Public Class **HtmlTableCell** : Inherits HtmlContainerControl
' Public Constructors
Public Sub **New**()
Public Sub **New**(ByVal tagName As String)
' Public Instance Properties
Public Property **Align** As String
Public Property **BgColor** As String
Public Property **BorderColor** As String
Public Property **ColSpan** As Integer
Public Property **Height** As String
Public Property **NoWrap** As Boolean
Public Property **RowSpan** As Integer
Public Property **VAlign** As String
Public Property **Width** As String
' Protected Instance Methods
Overrides Protected Sub **RenderEndTag**(ByVal writer As System.Web.UI.HtmlTextWriter)
End Class

Hierarchy: System.Object → System.Web.UI.Control (System.ComponentModel.IComponent , System.IDisposable , System.Web.UI.IParserAccessor , System.Web.UI.IDataBindingsAccessor) → HtmlControl (System.Web.UI.IAttributeAccessor) → HtmlContainerControl → HtmlTableCell

HtmlTableCellCollection
NotInheritable Class

System.Web.UI.HtmlControls (system.web.dll)

This collection of HtmlTableCell objects is used by the Cells property of the HtmlTableRow class.

Public NotInheritable Class **HtmlTableCellCollection** : Implements ICollection, IEnumerable
' Public Instance Properties
   Public ReadOnly Property **Count** As Integer Implements ICollection.Count
   Public ReadOnly Property **IsReadOnly** As Boolean
   Public ReadOnly Property **IsSynchronized** As Boolean Implements ICollection.IsSynchronized
   Public Default ReadOnly Property **Item** (ByVal index As Integer) As HtmlTableCell
   Public ReadOnly Property **SyncRoot** As Object Implements ICollection.SyncRoot
' Public Instance Methods
   Public Sub **Add**(ByVal cell As HtmlTableCell)
   Public Sub **Clear**()
   Public Sub **CopyTo**(ByVal array As Array, ByVal index As Integer) Implements ICollection.CopyTo
   Public Function **GetEnumerator**() As IEnumerator Implements IEnumerable.GetEnumerator
   Public Sub **Insert**(ByVal index As Integer, ByVal cell As HtmlTableCell)
   Public Sub **Remove**(ByVal cell As HtmlTableCell)
   Public Sub **RemoveAt**(ByVal index As Integer)
End Class

HtmlTableRow
Class

disposable

System.Web.UI.HtmlControls (system.web.dll)

This class represents an individual <tr> table row element in an HTML table. Each table row contains a group of HtmlTableCell objects, which is provided through the Cells property. Most other properties are used for fine-tuning the appearance of a row.

Public Class **HtmlTableRow** : Inherits HtmlContainerControl
' Public Constructors
   Public Sub **New**()
' Public Instance Properties
   Public Property **Align** As String
   Public Property **BgColor** As String
   Public Property **BorderColor** As String
   Overridable Public ReadOnly Property **Cells** As HtmlTableCellCollection
   Public Property **Height** As String
   Overrides Public Property **InnerHtml** As String
   Overrides Public Property **InnerText** As String
   Public Property **VAlign** As String
' Protected Instance Methods
   Overrides Protected Function **CreateControlCollection**() As ControlCollection
   Overrides Protected Sub **RenderChildren**(ByVal writer As System.Web.UI.HtmlTextWriter)
   Overrides Protected Sub **RenderEndTag**(ByVal writer As System.Web.UI.HtmlTextWriter)
End Class

Hierarchy: System.Object → System.Web.UI.Control (System.ComponentModel.IComponent , System.IDisposable , System.Web.UI.IParserAccessor , System.Web.UI.IDataBindingsAccessor)→ HtmlControl (System.Web.UI.IAttributeAccessor)→ HtmlContainerControl → HtmlTableRow

HtmlTableRowCollection

NotInheritable Class

System.Web.UI.HtmlControls (system.web.dll)

This collection of HtmlTableRow objects is used by the Rows property of the HtmlTable class.

Public NotInheritable Class **HtmlTableRowCollection** : Implements ICollection, IEnumerable
' *Public Instance Properties*
    Public ReadOnly Property **Count** As Integer Implements ICollection.Count
    Public ReadOnly Property **IsReadOnly** As Boolean
    Public ReadOnly Property **IsSynchronized** As Boolean Implements ICollection.IsSynchronized
    Public Default ReadOnly Property **Item** (ByVal index As Integer) As HtmlTableRow
    Public ReadOnly Property **SyncRoot** As Object Implements ICollection.SyncRoot
' *Public Instance Methods*
    Public Sub **Add**(ByVal row As HtmlTableRow)
    Public Sub **Clear**()
    Public Sub **CopyTo**(ByVal array As Array, ByVal index As Integer) Implements ICollection.CopyTo
    Public Function **GetEnumerator**() As IEnumerator Implements IEnumerable.GetEnumerator
    Public Sub **Insert**(ByVal index As Integer, ByVal row As HtmlTableRow)
    Public Sub **Remove**(ByVal row As HtmlTableRow)
    Public Sub **RemoveAt**(ByVal index As Integer)
End Class

HtmlTextArea

Class

System.Web.UI.HtmlControls (system.web.dll)

disposable

This class represents the HTML <textarea> tag, which allows the user to enter multiple lines of text. Text entered in this control is provided in the Value property. You can specify the size of the text box by using the Rows property and the Cols property (the character width). Both default to -1 to indicate that a standard size will be used. You can also react to the ServerChange event, which will fire only after a postback is triggered (for example, when a user clicks a submit button).

Public Class **HtmlTextArea** : Inherits HtmlContainerControl : Implements System.Web.UI.IPostBackDataHandler
' *Public Constructors*
    Public Sub **New**()
' *Public Instance Properties*
    Public Property **Cols** As Integer
    Overridable Public Property **Name** As String
    Public Property **Rows** As Integer
    Public Property **Value** As String
' *Protected Instance Methods*
    Overrides Protected Sub **AddParsedSubObject**(ByVal obj As Object)
    Overrides Protected Sub **OnPreRender**(ByVal e As EventArgs)
    Overridable Protected Sub **OnServerChange**(ByVal e As EventArgs)
    Overrides Protected Sub **RenderAttributes**(ByVal writer As System.Web.UI.HtmlTextWriter)
' *Events*
    Public Event **ServerChange** As EventHandler
End Class

Hierarchy: System.Object → System.Web.UI.Control (System.ComponentModel.IComponent , System.IDisposable , System.Web.UI.IParserAccessor , System.Web.UI.IDataBindingsAccessor) → HtmlControl (System.Web.UI.IAttributeAccessor) → HtmlContainerControl → HtmlTextArea (System.Web.UI.IPostBackDataHandler)

CHAPTER 38

The System.Web.UI.WebControls Namespace

The System.Web.UI.WebControls namespace contains types used for web controls. Web controls are ASP.NET's most full-featured controls and range from straightforward elements like Button to sophisticated controls like Calendar, AdRotator, and DataGrid. Web controls are more abstract than HTML controls. Rather than wrapping specific HTML elements, web controls can consist of a combination of HTML elements and vary their user interface depending on the capabilities of the client browser. They also provide a richer set of formatting properties and events. For example, all input controls provide an AutoPostback property that, when set to True, allows your code to react immediately to a Change event (like a checkbox being checked or a new list selection).

This namespace contains the WebControl class, which is the base class for all web controls. Web controls include traditional standards like TextBox, Button, RadioButton, and CheckBox, and more unusual and advanced controls like Calendar, AdRotator, and the list controls CheckBoxList and RadioButtonList.

Some of the most interesting controls in this namespace include those used for data-bound tables. Typically, DataGrid provides the most powerful options, with features for paging, sorting, and automatic selection and editing. You can also use the DataList class for a templated list or the Repeater class for a simple data-bound repeater that allows completely customized layout but has no built-in formatting or support for higher-level features like selection and editing.

Other useful controls in this namespace include the validation controls that derive from BaseValidator. These controls include CompareValidator (which compares data to an expected value), RangeValidator (which ensures that data falls in a specified range), RegularExpressionValidator (which validates data using a regular expression), RequiredFieldValidator (which ensures that data has been entered), and CustomValidator (which allows you to create your own validation routines). Optionally, validation results can be displayed using the ValidationSummary control.

Figure 38-1 shows the controls in this namespace. Figure 38-2 and Figure 38-3 show the remaining types, including delegates and events.

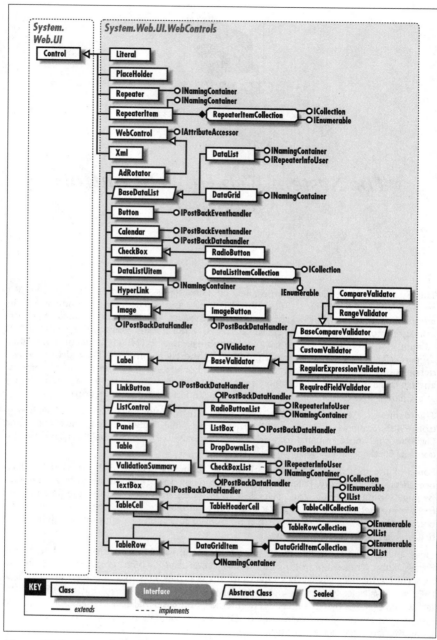

Figure 38-1: Controls in the System.Web.UI.WebControls namespace

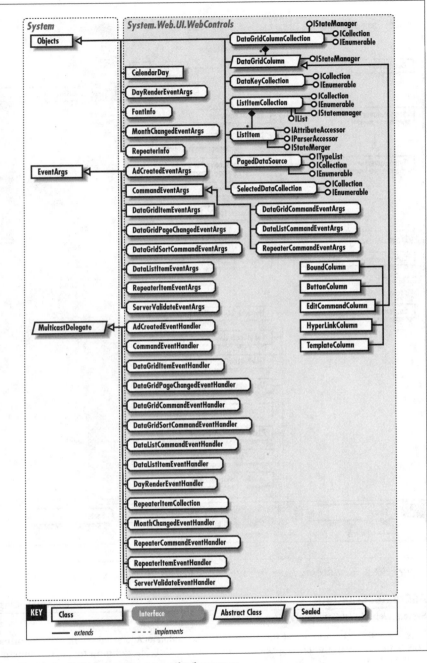

Figure 38-2: Delegates, events, and other types

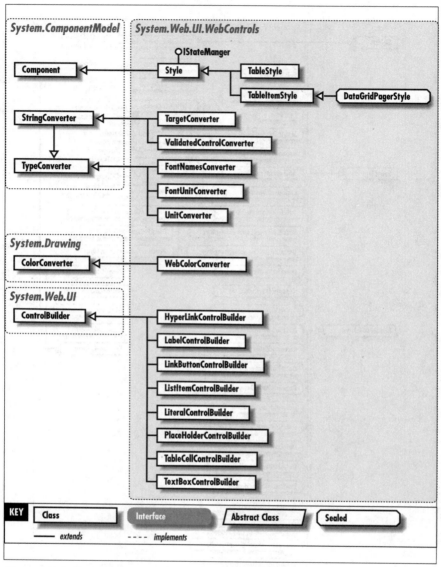

Figure 38-3: Remaining types from the System.Web.UI.WebControls namespace

AdCreatedEventArgs

NotInheritable Class

System.Web.UI.WebControls (system.web.dll)

This class supplies additional information to the AdRotator.AdCreated event. This information is drawn from the corresponding entry in the XML file defining the advertisements for the AdRotator control. In addition, the AdProperties property provides a read-only collection that provides all properties of the current advertisement.

One use of the AdCreatedEventArgs class and AdRotator.AdCreated event is to update a Web Forms page to correspond with the current advertisement. For example, you could use code like this: Sponsor.Text = "Visit our sponsor at" & e.NavigateURL.

```
Public NotInheritable Class AdCreatedEventArgs : Inherits EventArgs
' Public Constructors
    Public Sub New(ByVal adProperties As System.Collections.IDictionary)
' Public Instance Properties
    Public ReadOnly Property AdProperties As IDictionary
    Public Property AlternateText As String
    Public Property ImageUrl As String
    Public Property NavigateUrl As String
End Class
```

Hierarchy   System.Object → System.EventArgs → AdCreatedEventArgs

AdCreatedEventHandler — Delegate

System.Web.UI.WebControls (system.web.dll) — *serializable*

This delegate defines the signature required for the AdRotator.AdCreated event handler.

```
Public Delegate Sub AdCreatedEventHandler(ByVal sender As Object, ByVal e As AdCreatedEventArgs)
```

AdRotator — Class

System.Web.UI.WebControls (system.web.dll) — *disposable*

The AdRotator class allows you to provide one of the hallmarks of the Internet: banner ads. The AdRotator randomly chooses a different graphic to display every time the page is refreshed by reading from a list of entries specified in an XML file (and referenced by the AdvertisementFile property). The XML file specifies details like image URL, the link URL, and an "impressions" value that allows you to weigh an advertisement so that it is displayed more or less frequently than others in the file. If the picture does not fit the size or aspect ratio of the control, it will be stretched, compressed, or otherwise mangled to fit.

The Target property allows you to specify the frame that will be used to display the linked page if the user clicks on a banner ad. You can specify a frame in the current window, or you can use special values like "_blank", "_parent", "_top", or "_self". The KeywordFilter property allows you to specify a subset of advertisements to use for the AdRotator. For example, your site could use a single XML file for all ads, but assign different keywords to different types of ads. Depending on what page the AdRotator is used on, you can decide to use only the group of advertisements that matches the current content.

Clicking on the AdRotator does not fire an event, but automatically transfers the users to the appropriate page. Use the AdCreated event to integrate the current page with the current advertisement. This event provides information in an AdCreatedEventArgs object about the selected ad, which can be modified or used to set corresponding properties on other controls on the current page.

```
Public Class AdRotator : Inherits WebControl
' Public Constructors
    Public Sub New()
' Public Instance Properties
    Public Property AdvertisementFile As String
    Overrides Public ReadOnly Property Font As FontInfo
    Public Property KeywordFilter As String
```

Public Property **Target** As String
' *Protected Instance Methods*
Overrides Protected Function **CreateControlCollection**() As ControlCollection
Overridable Protected Sub **OnAdCreated**(ByVal e As AdCreatedEventArgs)
Overrides Protected Sub **OnPreRender**(ByVal e As EventArgs)
Overrides Protected Sub **Render**(ByVal writer As System.Web.UI.HtmlTextWriter)
' *Events*
Public Event **AdCreated** As AdCreatedEventHandler
End Class

Hierarchy System.Object → System.Web.UI.Control (System.ComponentModel.IComponent ,
System.IDisposable , System.Web.UI.IParserAccessor , System.Web.UI.IDataBindingsAccessor) →
WebControl (System.Web.UI.IAttributeAccessor) → AdRotator

BaseCompareValidator

MustInherit Class

System.Web.UI.WebControls (system.web.dll)   *disposable*

This abstract class provides basic functionality for the CompareValidator and RangeValidator
classes, which perform validation through comparisons. The shared (static) GetFullYear()
method converts a two-digit year (like "98") to a four-digit representation ("1998"),
while CutoffYear sets the maximum four-digit year value that it will allow to be represented in two digits. The shared CanConvert() method determines whether a string can
be converted to a given ValidationDataType, while the Type property sets the Validation-
DataType that the current instance of the control is validating text against.

Public MustInherit Class **BaseCompareValidator** : Inherits BaseValidator
' *Protected Constructors*
Protected Sub **New**()
' *Protected Shared Properties*
Shared Protected Property **CutoffYear** As Integer
' *Public Instance Properties*
Public Property **Type** As ValidationDataType
' *Public Shared Methods*
Public Shared Function **CanConvert**(ByVal text As String, ByVal type As ValidationDataType) As Boolean
' *Protected Shared Methods*
Shared Protected Function **Compare**(ByVal leftText As String, ByVal rightText As String, _
  ByVal op As ValidationCompareOperator, ByVal type As ValidationDataType) As Boolean
Shared Protected Function **Convert**(ByVal text As String, ByVal type As ValidationDataType, ByRef value As Object) _
  As Boolean
Shared Protected Function **GetDateElementOrder**() As String
Shared Protected Function **GetFullYear**(ByVal shortYear As Integer) As Integer
' *Protected Instance Methods*
Overrides Protected Sub **AddAttributesToRender**(ByVal writer As System.Web.UI.HtmlTextWriter)
Overrides Protected Function **DetermineRenderUplevel**() As Boolean
End Class

Hierarchy System.Object → System.Web.UI.Control (System.ComponentModel.IComponent ,
System.IDisposable , System.Web.UI.IParserAccessor , System.Web.UI.IDataBindingsAccessor) →
WebControl (System.Web.UI.IAttributeAccessor) → Label → BaseValidator (System.Web.UI.IValidator
) → BaseCompareValidator

BaseDataList

MustInherit Class

System.Web.UI.WebControls (system.web.dll)   *disposable*

This abstract class provides basic functionality for the DataList and DataGrid web controls. These controls include data binding (through the DataBind() method, properties like DataSource), and simple formatting through various table-specific properties, including CellPadding (the space between content in a cell and the cell borders), CellSpacing (the space between cells), and HorizontalAlign (the position of the table relative to the page or adjacent content).

```
Public MustInherit Class BaseDataList : Inherits WebControl
' Public Constructors
   Public Sub New()
' Public Instance Properties
   Overridable Public Property CellPadding As Integer
   Overridable Public Property CellSpacing As Integer
   Overrides Public ReadOnly Property Controls As ControlCollection
   Overridable Public Property DataKeyField As String
   Public ReadOnly Property DataKeys As DataKeyCollection
   Public Property DataMember As String
   Overridable Public Property DataSource As Object
   Overridable Public Property GridLines As GridLines
   Overridable Public Property HorizontalAlign As HorizontalAlign
' Protected Instance Properties
   Protected Property DataKeysArray As ArrayList
' Public Shared Methods
   Public Shared Function IsBindableType(ByVal type As Type) As Boolean
' Public Instance Methods
   Overrides Public Sub DataBind()
' Protected Instance Methods
   Overrides Protected Sub AddParsedSubObject(ByVal obj As Object)
   Overrides Protected Sub CreateChildControls()
   MustInherit Protected Sub CreateControlHierarchy(ByVal useDataSource As Boolean)
   Overrides Protected Sub OnDataBinding(ByVal e As EventArgs)
   Overridable Protected Sub OnSelectedIndexChanged(ByVal e As EventArgs)
   MustInherit Protected Sub PrepareControlHierarchy()
   Overrides Protected Sub Render(ByVal writer As System.Web.UI.HtmlTextWriter)
' Events
   Public Event SelectedIndexChanged As EventHandler
End Class
```

Hierarchy   System.Object → System.Web.UI.Control (System.ComponentModel.IComponent , System.IDisposable , System.Web.UI.IParserAccessor , System.Web.UI.IDataBindingsAccessor) → WebControl (System.Web.UI.IAttributeAccessor) → BaseDataList

---

BaseValidator

MustInherit Class

System.Web.UI.WebControls (system.web.dll)

disposable

This abstract class is the basis for all validation controls. It supplies a Validate() method, which does not return a value, but updates the IsValid property. When using validation controls on a Web Forms page, you should check the System.Web.UI.Page.IsValid property. This value will be True only if all validation controls on the page have successfully validated their input. The BaseValidator class also provides various other methods that are not used directly when creating a Web Forms page.

The ControlToValidate property specifies the control that a validator will verify. The ErrorMessage property specifies the message that will be displayed in the validation control if validation fails, although this text can be overridden by changing the validation control's Text property. The ErrorMessage will also appear in a page's ValidationSummary control, if present.

By default, ASP.NET will not render any HTML for a control if it is not visible. This means that space will not be allocated for a validation control unless validation fails. The Display property allows you to allocate space for a validation control by specifying ValidatorDisplay.Static, which may be required if your validation control is in a table. You can also set this property to ValidatorDisplay.None to specify that no validation message will be displayed in the control, although one will still be shown in the ValidationSummary control, if used.

```
Public MustInherit Class BaseValidator : Inherits Label : Implements System.Web.UI.IValidator
' Protected Constructors
    Protected Sub New()
' Public Instance Properties
    Public Property ControlToValidate As String
    Public Property Display As ValidatorDisplay
    Public Property EnableClientScript As Boolean
    Overrides Public Property Enabled As Boolean
    Public Property ErrorMessage As String Implements IValidator.ErrorMessage
    Overrides Public Property ForeColor As Color
    Public Property IsValid As Boolean Implements IValidator.IsValid
' Protected Instance Properties
    Protected Property PropertiesValid As Boolean
    Protected Property RenderUplevel As Boolean
' Public Shared Methods
    Public Shared Function GetValidationProperty(ByVal component As Object) As PropertyDescriptor
' Public Instance Methods
    Public Sub Validate()  Implements IValidator.Validate
' Protected Instance Methods
    Overrides Protected Sub AddAttributesToRender(ByVal writer As System.Web.UI.HtmlTextWriter)
    Protected Sub CheckControlValidationProperty(ByVal name As String, ByVal propertyName As String)
    Overridable Protected Function ControlPropertiesValid() As Boolean
    Overridable Protected Function DetermineRenderUplevel() As Boolean
    MustInherit Protected Function EvaluateIsValid() As Boolean
    Protected Function GetControlRenderID(ByVal name As String) As String
    Protected Function GetControlValidationValue(ByVal name As String) As String
    Overrides Protected Sub OnInit(ByVal e As EventArgs)
    Overrides Protected Sub OnPreRender(ByVal e As EventArgs)
    Overrides Protected Sub OnUnload(ByVal e As EventArgs)
    Protected Sub RegisterValidatorCommonScript()
    Overridable Protected Sub RegisterValidatorDeclaration()
    Overrides Protected Sub Render(ByVal writer As System.Web.UI.HtmlTextWriter)
End Class
```

Hierarchy   System.Object → System.Web.UI.Control (System.ComponentModel.IComponent , System.IDisposable , System.Web.UI.IParserAccessor , System.Web.UI.IDataBindingsAccessor) → WebControl (System.Web.UI.IAttributeAccessor) → Label → BaseValidator (System.Web.UI.IValidator)

BorderStyle   Enum

System.Web.UI.WebControls (system.web.dll)   *serializable*

This enumeration is used to set the border style for most web controls. It is used by the WebControl.BorderStyle property.

```
Public Enum BorderStyle
    NotSet = 0
    None = 1
    Dotted = 2
```

Dashed = 3	
Solid = 4	
Double = 5	
Groove = 6	
Ridge = 7	
Inset = 8	
Outset = 9	

End Enum

Hierarchy System.Object → System.ValueType → System.Enum (System.IComparable , System.IFormattable , System.IConvertible) → BorderStyle

BoundColumn

Class

System.Web.UI.WebControls (system.web.dll)

The BoundColumn class represents the default type of column used in a DataGrid control. A BoundColumn is "bound," or linked, to a specific field in a data source. It provides a DataField property that specifies the field used from the data source for the column's content. As with all ASP.NET data binding, the "bind" is in one direction: from the database to the output control.

Public Class **BoundColumn** : Inherits DataGridColumn
' Public Constructors
Public Sub **New**()
' Public Shared Fields
public Shared ReadOnly **thisExpr** As String
' Public Instance Properties
Overridable Public Property **DataField** As String
Overridable Public Property **DataFormatString** As String
Overridable Public Property **ReadOnly** As Boolean
' Public Instance Methods
Overrides Public Sub **Initialize**()
Overrides Public Sub **InitializeCell**(ByVal cell As TableCell, ByVal columnIndex As Integer, _
ByVal itemType As ListItemType)
' Protected Instance Methods
Overridable Protected Function **FormatDataValue**(ByVal dataValue As Object) As String

End Class

Hierarchy System.Object → DataGridColumn (System.Web.UI.IStateManager) → BoundColumn

Button

Class

System.Web.UI.WebControls (system.web.dll)

disposable

This class represents a simple command button (also known as a push button). Button controls always generate a postback when clicked. As with all button-like server controls, you can set the CausesValidation property to determine whether page validation will be performed when the button is clicked, before the button event handling code is executed. Depending on the client browser's support for DHTML, an invalid page may prevent the postback from occurring and the button event handling code from executing if CausesValidation is True.

When clicked, a Button raises a Click event followed by a Command event. The Command event passes extra information about the button in a CommandEventArgs object. This information includes the CommandName and CommandArgument properties of the Button. A typical CommandName identifies the requested action (like "Sort").

```
Public Class Button : Inherits WebControl : Implements System.Web.UI.IPostBackEventHandler
' Public Constructors
   Public Sub New()
' Public Instance Properties
   Public Property CausesValidation As Boolean
   Public Property CommandArgument As String
   Public Property CommandName As String
   Public Property Text As String
' Protected Instance Methods
   Overrides Protected Sub AddAttributesToRender(ByVal writer As System.Web.UI.HtmlTextWriter)
   Overridable Protected Sub OnClick(ByVal e As EventArgs)
   Overridable Protected Sub OnCommand(ByVal e As CommandEventArgs)
   Overrides Protected Sub RenderContents(ByVal writer As System.Web.UI.HtmlTextWriter)
' Events
   Public Event Click As EventHandler
   Public Event Command As CommandEventHandler
End Class
```

Hierarchy   System.Object → System.Web.UI.Control (System.ComponentModel.IComponent ,
System.IDisposable , System.Web.UI.IParserAccessor , System.Web.UI.IDataBindingsAccessor) →
WebControl (System.Web.UI.IAttributeAccessor) → Button (System.Web.UI.IPostBackEventHandler)

ButtonColumn   Class

System.Web.UI.WebControls (system.web.dll)

The ButtonColumn class represents a type of column that can be used in a DataGrid control. This column consists of buttons that raise the DataGrid.ItemCommand event. These buttons can be displayed as graphical push buttons (like Button) or text links, depending on the ButtonType property.

The Text property determines what text is displayed for the button, while the CommandName property specifies a string of additional information that will be sent to the DataGrid.ItemCommand event through the DataGridCommandEventArgs object.

If you set the Text and CommandName properties, all buttons in the column will share the same information. Alternatively, you can set the DataTextField property to use data binding and the DataTextFormatString property to specify formatting rules.

```
Public Class ButtonColumn : Inherits DataGridColumn
' Public Constructors
   Public Sub New()
' Public Instance Properties
   Overridable Public Property ButtonType As ButtonColumnType
   Overridable Public Property CommandName As String
   Overridable Public Property DataTextField As String
   Overridable Public Property DataTextFormatString As String
   Overridable Public Property Text As String
' Public Instance Methods
   Overrides Public Sub Initialize()
   Overrides Public Sub InitializeCell(ByVal cell As TableCell, ByVal columnIndex As Integer, _
      ByVal itemType As ListItemType)
' Protected Instance Methods
   Overridable Protected Function FormatDataTextValue(ByVal dataTextValue As Object) As String
End Class
```

Hierarchy   System.Object → DataGridColumn (System.Web.UI.IStateManager) → ButtonColumn

ButtonColumnType

Enum

System.Web.UI.WebControls (system.web.dll)

serializable

You can use this enumeration to set the ButtonColumn.ButtonType property. Use PushButton to create graphical buttons that look like individual Button controls and LinkButton to create hyperlink-style buttons that look like individual LinkButton controls.

```
Public Enum ButtonColumnType
    LinkButton = 0
    PushButton = 1
End Enum
```

Hierarchy System.Object → System.ValueType → System.Enum (System.IComparable , System.IFormattable , System.IConvertible)→ ButtonColumnType

Calendar

Class

System.Web.UI.WebControls (system.web.dll)

disposable

The class is used for the Calendar control, which displays a single month of the year at a time and allows users to move forward and backward from month to month and select one or more dates. The SelectionMode property determines what type of selections are allowed (day, week, or month). You can also create an event handler for the DayRender event, use it to examine each day in the calendar and decide if you would like to apply special formatting, add additional content in the corresponding table cell, or make the day unselectable.

If only a single day is selected, it will be provided in the SelectedDate property. If you use a SelectionMode that allows the user to select multiple dates, they will be contained in the SelectedDates collection.

The other properties of the calendar are used to customize its appearance, allowing you to hide header and title information, choose styles, and disable month-to-month navigation. Note that if you hide the title portion by setting the ShowTitle property to False, the month navigation controls will also be hidden. You can also respond to a SelectionChanged event that fires when the user chooses a new date and the VisibleMonthChanged event that fires when the user navigates to a different month.

```
Public Class Calendar : Inherits WebControl : Implements  System.Web.UI.IPostBackEventHandler
' Public Constructors
    Public Sub New()
' Public Instance Properties
    Public Property CellPadding As Integer
    Public Property CellSpacing As Integer
    Public ReadOnly Property DayHeaderStyle As TableItemStyle
    Public Property DayNameFormat As DayNameFormat
    Public ReadOnly Property DayStyle As TableItemStyle
    Public Property FirstDayOfWeek As FirstDayOfWeek
    Public Property NextMonthText As String
    Public Property NextPrevFormat As NextPrevFormat
    Public ReadOnly Property NextPrevStyle As TableItemStyle
    Public ReadOnly Property OtherMonthDayStyle As TableItemStyle
    Public Property PrevMonthText As String
    Public Property SelectedDate As Date
    Public ReadOnly Property SelectedDates As SelectedDatesCollection
    Public ReadOnly Property SelectedDayStyle As TableItemStyle
    Public Property SelectionMode As CalendarSelectionMode
```

Public Property **SelectMonthText** As String
Public ReadOnly Property **SelectorStyle** As TableItemStyle
Public Property **SelectWeekText** As String
Public Property **ShowDayHeader** As Boolean
Public Property **ShowGridLines** As Boolean
Public Property **ShowNextPrevMonth** As Boolean
Public Property **ShowTitle** As Boolean
Public Property **TitleFormat** As TitleFormat
Public ReadOnly Property **TitleStyle** As TableItemStyle
Public ReadOnly Property **TodayDayStyle** As TableItemStyle
Public Property **TodaysDate** As Date
Public Property **VisibleDate** As Date
Public ReadOnly Property **WeekendDayStyle** As TableItemStyle
' *Protected Instance Methods*
Overrides Protected Function **CreateControlCollection**() As ControlCollection
Protected Function **HasWeekSelectors**(ByVal selectionMode As CalendarSelectionMode) As Boolean
Overrides Protected Sub **LoadViewState**(ByVal savedState As Object)
Overridable Protected Sub **OnDayRender**(ByVal cell As TableCell, ByVal day As CalendarDay)
Overrides Protected Sub **OnPreRender**(ByVal e As EventArgs)
Overridable Protected Sub **OnSelectionChanged**()
Overridable Protected Sub **OnVisibleMonthChanged**(ByVal newDate As Date, ByVal previousDate As Date)
Overrides Protected Sub **Render**(ByVal writer As System.Web.UI.HtmlTextWriter)
Overrides Protected Function **SaveViewState**() As Object
Overrides Protected Sub **TrackViewState**()
' *Events*
Public Event **DayRender** As DayRenderEventHandler
Public Event **SelectionChanged** As EventHandler
Public Event **VisibleMonthChanged** As MonthChangedEventHandler
End Class

Hierarchy   System.Object → System.Web.UI.Control (System.ComponentModel.IComponent ,
System.IDisposable , System.Web.UI.IParserAccessor , System.Web.UI.IDataBindingsAccessor)→
WebControl (System.Web.UI.IAttributeAccessor)→ Calendar (System.Web.UI.IPostBackEventHandler)

CalendarDay
Class

System.Web.UI.WebControls (system.web.dll)

This class represents a single day in the Calendar control. You can use this class in the
Calendar.DayRender event to programmatically configure specific dates. The Calen-
dar.DayRender event fires once for each day in the Calendar, and it provides the Calendar-
Day object for that day. At this point, you can modify its properties.

For example, you can compare dates against valid date ranges stored in a database and
set the IsSelectable property to False for all dates that you don't want the user to be able
to select. Or you could examine the IsOtherMonth property to verify that the day is in the
currently displayed month and the IsWeekend property to confirm that the day is on a
weekend, and then change the background color of the containing cell to highlight it.
Note, however, that the background color is not a property of the CalendarDay object.
Instead, it is a property of the TableCell object that is also provided to you in the event
through the DayRenderEventArgs class. For more information, refer to the DayRenderEventArgs
object.

Public Class **CalendarDay**
' *Public Constructors*
Public Sub **New**(ByVal date As Date, ByVal isWeekend As Boolean, ByVal isToday As Boolean, _
   ByVal isSelected As Boolean, ByVal isOtherMonth As Boolean, ByVal dayNumberText As String)

' *Public Instance Properties*
  Public ReadOnly Property **Date** As Date
  Public ReadOnly Property **DayNumberText** As String
  Public ReadOnly Property **IsOtherMonth** As Boolean
  Public Property **IsSelectable** As Boolean
  Public ReadOnly Property **IsSelected** As Boolean
  Public ReadOnly Property **IsToday** As Boolean
  Public ReadOnly Property **IsWeekend** As Boolean
End Class

CalendarSelectionMode
Enum

System.Web.UI.WebControls (system.web.dll)
serializable

This enumeration specifies the type of selection that a user can perform with a Calendar control. Day allows the user to select a single day, DayWeek allows the user to select a single day or an entire week, DayWeekMonth allows a specific day, week, or month to be chosen, and None does not allow any kind of date selection. The calendar does not support noncontiguous multiple day selections.

Public Enum **CalendarSelectionMode**
    None = 0
    Day = 1
    DayWeek = 2
    DayWeekMonth = 3
End Enum

Hierarchy   System.Object → System.ValueType → System.Enum (System.IComparable , System.IFormattable , System.IConvertible)→ CalendarSelectionMode

CheckBox
Class

System.Web.UI.WebControls (system.web.dll)
disposable

This class represents a single checkbox that can be selected (True) or left unchecked (False). The CheckBox class also provides a TextAlign property, which specifies whether text will appear on the right or left side of the checkbox. To determine whether a checkbox is selected, examine the Checked property. If you want to use a checkbox with list data, the CheckBoxList control may be more convenient.

Public Class **CheckBox** : Inherits WebControl: Implements System.Web.UI.IPostBackDataHandler
' *Public Constructors*
  Public Sub **New**()
' *Public Instance Properties*
  Overridable Public Property **AutoPostBack** As Boolean
  Overridable Public Property **Checked** As Boolean
  Overridable Public Property **Text** As String
  Overridable Public Property **TextAlign** As TextAlign
' *Protected Instance Methods*
  Overridable Protected Sub **OnCheckedChanged**(ByVal e As EventArgs)
  Overrides Protected Sub **OnPreRender**(ByVal e As EventArgs)
  Overrides Protected Sub **Render**(ByVal writer As System.Web.UI.HtmlTextWriter)
' *Events*
  Public Event **CheckedChanged** As EventHandler
End Class

Hierarchy System.Object → System.Web.UI.Control (System.ComponentModel.IComponent , System.IDisposable , System.Web.UI.IParserAccessor , System.Web.UI.IDataBindingsAccessor) → WebControl (System.Web.UI.IAttributeAccessor) → CheckBox (System.Web.UI.IPostBackDataHandler)

CheckBoxList
System.Web.UI.WebControls (system.web.dll)

Class

disposable

This class represents a list of checkboxes that can be selected in any combination. Though this class is generated out of individual checkboxes, it acts like an integrated list. For example, ASP.NET will add or remove checkbox items as needed when you bind it to a data source. You can use RepeatDirection to specify how checkboxes will be grouped together if RepeatColumns is greater than 1. For example, if you set RepeatDirection to RepeatDirection.Vertical, and RepeatColumns to 2, the first two list items will be displayed in the first columns, the next two will be displayed on the second column, and so on. If you set RepeatDirection to RepeatDirection.Horizontal, your list will still have the same number of rows and columns, but checkbox items will be filled first by column, and then by row.

Individual checkboxes are grouped together automatically in an HTML table, which you can fine-tune with the CellPadding and CellSpacing properties. Alternatively, you can set RepeatLayout to RepeatLayout.Flow to specify that an HTML table should not be used.

Most of the list-specific functionality, such as determining the selected item and reacting to a SelectedIndexChanged event, is provided by the ListControl class, which CheckBoxList inherits from. To determine what items are checked in a checkbox list, iterate through the Items collection and test the ListItem.Selected property of each item in the list.

```
Public Class CheckBoxList : Inherits ListControl: Implements IRepeatInfoUser, System.Web.UI.INamingContainer, _
    System.Web.UI.IPostBackDataHandler
' Public Constructors
    Public Sub New()
' Public Instance Properties
    Overridable Public Property CellPadding As Integer
    Overridable Public Property CellSpacing As Integer
    Overridable Public Property RepeatColumns As Integer
    Overridable Public Property RepeatDirection As RepeatDirection
    Overridable Public Property RepeatLayout As RepeatLayout
    Overridable Public Property TextAlign As TextAlign
' Protected Instance Methods
    Overrides Protected Function CreateControlStyle() As Style
    Overrides Protected Function FindControl(ByVal id As String, ByVal pathOffset As Integer) As Control
    Overrides Protected Sub OnPreRender(ByVal e As EventArgs)
    Overrides Protected Sub Render(ByVal writer As System.Web.UI.HtmlTextWriter)
End Class
```

Hierarchy System.Object → System.Web.UI.Control (System.ComponentModel.IComponent , System.IDisposable , System.Web.UI.IParserAccessor , System.Web.UI.IDataBindingsAccessor) → WebControl (System.Web.UI.IAttributeAccessor) → ListControl → CheckBoxList (IRepeatInfoUser , System.Web.UI.INamingContainer , System.Web.UI.IPostBackDataHandler)

CommandEventArgs
System.Web.UI.WebControls (system.web.dll)

Class

This class is used by the CommandEventHandler to provide extra information to a Command event handler. This information is stored in two properties: CommandName and CommandArgument, which are both strings. These properties are used only by your code, and can thus be used to store any information you need. For example, you might set CommandName to "Sort" and CommandArgument to "Ascending."

```
Public Class CommandEventArgs : Inherits EventArgs
' Public Constructors
    Public Sub New(ByVal e As CommandEventArgs)
    Public Sub New(ByVal commandName As String, ByVal argument As Object)
' Public Instance Properties
    Public ReadOnly Property CommandArgument As Object
    Public ReadOnly Property CommandName As String
End Class
```

Hierarchy   System.Object → System.EventArgs → CommandEventArgs

CommandEventHandler

Delegate

System.Web.UI.WebControls (system.web.dll)

serializable

Many button controls, such as Button, ImageButton, and LinkButton, provide both a Click and a Command event. The Command event allows you to send extra information identifying a command name and command arguments in an instance of CommandEventArgs.

```
Public Delegate Sub CommandEventHandler(ByVal sender As Object, ByVal e As CommandEventArgs)
```

CompareValidator

Class

System.Web.UI.WebControls (system.web.dll)

disposable

This class represents a validation control that compares the input control (ControlToValidate) to a specified value (ValueToCompare) or a value in another control (ControlToCompare). Both values will be converted to the data type specified by Type before they are compared. Note that if you set both ValueToCompare and ControlToCompare, the latter will take precedence.

The Operator property specifies the expression that must be met in order for validation to succeed. In other words, ControlToValidate <Operator> ControlToCompare must be true.

```
Public Class CompareValidator : Inherits BaseCompareValidator
' Public Constructors
    Public Sub New()
' Public Instance Properties
    Public Property ControlToCompare As String
    Public Property Operator As ValidationCompareOperator
    Public Property ValueToCompare As String
' Protected Instance Methods
    Overrides Protected Sub AddAttributesToRender(ByVal writer As System.Web.UI.HtmlTextWriter)
    Overrides Protected Function ControlPropertiesValid() As Boolean
    Overrides Protected Function EvaluateIsValid() As Boolean
End Class
```

Hierarchy   System.Object → System.Web.UI.Control (System.ComponentModel.IComponent , System.IDisposable , System.Web.UI.IParserAccessor , System.Web.UI.IDataBindingsAccessor) → WebControl (System.Web.UI.IAttributeAccessor) → Label → BaseValidator (System.Web.UI.IValidator) → BaseCompareValidator → CompareValidator

CustomValidator

Class

System.Web.UI.WebControls (system.web.dll)

disposable

The CustomValidator control allows you to define your own validation routines. A similar task could be performed by writing manual validation code in the click event for a submit button, but using a CustomValidator allows you to configure client-side validation, create an error message that will be included in the validation summary, and provide a "vote" used for the combined System.Web.UI.Page.IsValid property along with all other validation controls. A CustomValidator can also be reused easily to validate multiple controls.

To provide server-side validation, create an event handler for the ServerValidate event. The string from the input control and the result of the validation is stored in the provided ServerValidateEventArgs object. You can also perform client-side validation, which can improve the responsiveness of your application by reducing the need for round trips to the server. However, because client-side validation will not be performed in some browsers and is easy to circumvent, it should never be used in place of server validation. To use client-side validation, set the ClientValidationFunction to the name of a JavaScript or VBScript function in the *.aspx* code portion of your page (not the code-behind class). This script function should be in a language that the client browser can understand, which means that JavaScript is the best choice if you are supporting non-Microsoft browsers. The function must be in the form function ValidationFunction-Name(source, value), where value is the validated value that. This function should return True or False to indicate whether the validation succeeded. ASP.NET will take care of the code necessary to display the corresponding error message. Note that this is a very bad idea if your function uses "secret" logic to validate a password or key, as this logic will be easily retrievable by the client!

```
Public Class CustomValidator : Inherits BaseValidator
' Public Constructors
    Public Sub New()
' Public Instance Properties
    Public Property ClientValidationFunction As String
' Protected Instance Methods
    Overrides Protected Sub AddAttributesToRender(ByVal writer As System.Web.UI.HtmlTextWriter)
    Overrides Protected Function ControlPropertiesValid() As Boolean
    Overrides Protected Function EvaluateIsValid() As Boolean
    Overridable Protected Function OnServerValidate(ByVal value As String) As Boolean
' Events
    Public Event ServerValidate As ServerValidateEventHandler
End Class
```

Hierarchy   System.Object → System.Web.UI.Control (System.ComponentModel.IComponent , System.IDisposable , System.Web.UI.IParserAccessor , System.Web.UI.IDataBindingsAccessor)→ WebControl (System.Web.UI.IAttributeAccessor)→ Label → BaseValidator (System.Web.UI.IValidator)→ CustomValidator

---

DataGrid   Class

System.Web.UI.WebControls (system.web.dll)   *disposable*

The DataGrid control is, at its simplest, a data-bound list displayed in a table grid structure. It provides a rich set of functionality that makes it the most versatile data-bound control, including support for selection, editing, deleting, paging, and sorting.

Columns can be added to a DataGrid in two ways. First, if the AutoGenerateColumns property is True, a BoundColumn will be created for every column in the data source specified by DataSource. Alternatively, you can define columns by adding nested tags in the *.aspx* file. (If you mix both approaches, the automatically generated columns will always be added last.) Columns can be BoundColumn, ButtonColumn, EditCommandColumn, HyperLinkColumn, or TemplateColumn controls (each of which are described separately in this namespace). The order that the columns appear is determined by the order the column tags are listed in the *.aspx*, and you can manipulate them programmatically through the Columns collection. Note that this collection does not contain automatically generated

---

columns—only ones that have defined templates.

The DataGrid has a number of properties that allow you to control its appearance. You can set TableItemStyle objects for various properties, including footers, headers (used automatically for column titles), and items. (The corresponding DataGrid properties end with the word "Style.") You can also use the ShowHeader and ShowFooter properties to configure whether headers and footers will be displayed.

To allow row selection for DataGrid, set the SelectedItemTemplate to look different than the ItemTemplate. Then add a button column that allows selection (for example, you might use the text "Select") and set the SelectedIndex property to the appropriate row in the ItemCommand event handler. To allow in-place editing, add an EditCommandColumn column and set the EditItemIndex (then rebind to the data source) in the EditCommand event handler. Any properties that are not marked as read-only in the template will be editable through automatically provided text boxes. You can handle the UpdateCommand event to commit the actual change. To disable editing or selection for a DataGrid, set the EditItemIndex or SelectedIndex to -1.

To provide sorting, enable the AllowSorting property and rebind the appropriate sorted data in response to the SortCommand event. Finally, to provide paging, enable the Allow-Paging property and set a number of rows in the PageSize property. When the PageIndex-Changed event is triggered, set the CurrentPageIndex to the appropriate page. Note that automatic paging causes the complete data table to be retrieved, even though only a few rows are being displayed. To optimize performance, you should enable the Allow-CustomPaging property and provide custom data access code in the CurrentPageIndex event handler. When using custom paging, you must also set the VirtualItemCount property to the total number of records to allow the DataGrid to determine the total number of pages needed.

Public Class **DataGrid** : Inherits BaseDataList : Implements System.Web.UI.INamingContainer

' Public Constructors
   Public Sub **New**()

' Public Shared Fields

public const **CancelCommandName** As String	=Cancel
public const **DeleteCommandName** As String	=Delete
public const **EditCommandName** As String	=Edit
public const **NextPageCommandArgument** As String	=Next
public const **PageCommandName** As String	=Page
public const **PrevPageCommandArgument** As String	=Prev
public const **SelectCommandName** As String	=Select
public const **SortCommandName** As String	=Sort
public const **UpdateCommandName** As String	=Update

' Public Instance Properties
   Overridable Public Property **AllowCustomPaging** As Boolean
   Overridable Public Property **AllowPaging** As Boolean
   Overridable Public Property **AllowSorting** As Boolean
   Overridable Public ReadOnly Property **AlternatingItemStyle** As TableItemStyle
   Overridable Public Property **AutoGenerateColumns** As Boolean
   Overridable Public Property **BackImageUrl** As String
   Overridable Public ReadOnly Property **Columns** As DataGridColumnCollection
   Public Property **CurrentPageIndex** As Integer
   Overridable Public Property **EditItemIndex** As Integer
   Overridable Public ReadOnly Property **EditItemStyle** As TableItemStyle
   Overridable Public ReadOnly Property **FooterStyle** As TableItemStyle
   Overridable Public ReadOnly Property **HeaderStyle** As TableItemStyle
   Overridable Public ReadOnly Property **Items** As DataGridItemCollection
   Overridable Public ReadOnly Property **ItemStyle** As TableItemStyle

Public ReadOnly Property **PageCount** As Integer
Overridable Public ReadOnly Property **PagerStyle** As DataGridPagerStyle
Overridable Public Property **PageSize** As Integer
Overridable Public Property **SelectedIndex** As Integer
Overridable Public ReadOnly Property **SelectedItem** As DataGridItem
Overridable Public ReadOnly Property **SelectedItemStyle** As TableItemStyle
Overridable Public Property **ShowFooter** As Boolean
Overridable Public Property **ShowHeader** As Boolean
Overridable Public Property **VirtualItemCount** As Integer
' *Protected Instance Methods*
Overridable Protected Function **CreateColumnSet**(ByVal dataSource As PagedDataSource, _
    ByVal useDataSource As Boolean) As ArrayList
Overrides Protected Sub **CreateControlHierarchy**(ByVal useDataSource As Boolean)
Overrides Protected Function **CreateControlStyle**() As Style
Overridable Protected Function **CreateItem**(ByVal itemIndex As Integer, ByVal dataSourceIndex As Integer, _
    ByVal itemType As ListItemType) As DataGridItem
Overridable Protected Sub **InitializeItem**(ByVal item As DataGridItem, ByVal columns As DataGridColumn())
Overridable Protected Sub **InitializePager**(ByVal item As DataGridItem, ByVal columnSpan As Integer, _
    ByVal pagedDataSource As PagedDataSource)
Overrides Protected Sub **LoadViewState**(ByVal savedState As Object)
Overrides Protected Function **OnBubbleEvent**(ByVal source As Object, ByVal e As EventArgs) As Boolean
Overridable Protected Sub **OnCancelCommand**(ByVal e As DataGridCommandEventArgs)
Overridable Protected Sub **OnDeleteCommand**(ByVal e As DataGridCommandEventArgs)
Overridable Protected Sub **OnEditCommand**(ByVal e As DataGridCommandEventArgs)
Overridable Protected Sub **OnItemCommand**(ByVal e As DataGridCommandEventArgs)
Overridable Protected Sub **OnItemCreated**(ByVal e As DataGridItemEventArgs)
Overridable Protected Sub **OnItemDataBound**(ByVal e As DataGridItemEventArgs)
Overridable Protected Sub **OnPageIndexChanged**(ByVal e As DataGridPageChangedEventArgs)
Overridable Protected Sub **OnSortCommand**(ByVal e As DataGridSortCommandEventArgs)
Overridable Protected Sub **OnUpdateCommand**(ByVal e As DataGridCommandEventArgs)
Overrides Protected Sub **PrepareControlHierarchy**()
Overrides Protected Function **SaveViewState**() As Object
Overrides Protected Sub **TrackViewState**()
' *Events*
Public Event **CancelCommand** As DataGridCommandEventHandler
Public Event **DeleteCommand** As DataGridCommandEventHandler
Public Event **EditCommand** As DataGridCommandEventHandler
Public Event **ItemCommand** As DataGridCommandEventHandler
Public Event **ItemCreated** As DataGridItemEventHandler
Public Event **ItemDataBound** As DataGridItemEventHandler
Public Event **PageIndexChanged** As DataGridPageChangedEventHandler
Public Event **SortCommand** As DataGridSortCommandEventHandler
Public Event **UpdateCommand** As DataGridCommandEventHandler
End Class

Hierarchy System.Object → System.Web.UI.Control (System.ComponentModel.IComponent ,
System.IDisposable , System.Web.UI.IParserAccessor , System.Web.UI.IDataBindingsAccessor)→
WebControl (System.Web.UI.IAttributeAccessor)→ BaseDataList → DataGrid (
System.Web.UI.INamingContainer)

DataGridColumn   **MustInherit Class**

System.Web.UI.WebControls (system.web.dll)

The abstract base class is used for all types of columns that can be added to a DataGrid
control, including BoundColumn, ButtonColumn, HyperLinkColumn, EditCommandColumn, and
TemplateColumn. It includes basic formatting-related properties, including TableItemStyle

---

objects for the header, footer, and items, and an image file to be displayed in the header (HeaderImageUrl). The SortExpression property specifies the field that will be used to order the DataGrid when sorting according to this column.

Public MustInherit Class **DataGridColumn** : Implements System.Web.UI.IStateManager
' *Public Constructors*
  Public Sub **New**()
' *Public Instance Properties*
  Overridable Public ReadOnly Property **FooterStyle** As TableItemStyle
  Overridable Public Property **FooterText** As String
  Overridable Public Property **HeaderImageUrl** As String
  Overridable Public ReadOnly Property **HeaderStyle** As TableItemStyle
  Overridable Public Property **HeaderText** As String
  Overridable Public ReadOnly Property **ItemStyle** As TableItemStyle
  Overridable Public Property **SortExpression** As String
  Public Property **Visible** As Boolean
' *Protected Instance Properties*
  Protected Property **DesignMode** As Boolean
  Protected Property **IsTrackingViewState** As Boolean Implements IStateManager.IsTrackingViewState
  Protected Property **Owner** As DataGrid
  Protected Property **ViewState** As StateBag
' *Public Instance Methods*
  Overridable Public Sub **Initialize**()
  Overridable Public Sub **InitializeCell**(ByVal cell As TableCell, ByVal columnIndex As Integer, _
    ByVal itemType As ListItemType)
  Overrides Public Function **ToString**() As String
' *Protected Instance Methods*
  Overridable Protected Sub **LoadViewState**(ByVal savedState As Object) _
    Implements IStateManager.LoadViewState
  Overridable Protected Sub **OnColumnChanged**()
  Overridable Protected Function **SaveViewState**() As Object Implements IStateManager.SaveViewState
  Overridable Protected Sub **TrackViewState**() Implements IStateManager.TrackViewState
End Class

DataGridColumnCollection   **NotInheritable Class**

System.Web.UI.WebControls (system.web.dll)

This is the collection of DataGridColumn objects in a **DataGrid** control. It is provided through the DataGrid.Columns property. You can use this collection to programmatically add or remove columns, but these changes will not be automatically persisted over postbacks because the DataGrid.Columns property is not stored in view state. This collection will only contain columns that have been added through templates, not automatically generated ones.

Public NotInheritable Class **DataGridColumnCollection** : Implements ICollection, IEnumerable, _
    System.Web.UI.IStateManager
' *Public Constructors*
  Public Sub **New**(ByVal owner As DataGrid, ByVal columns As System.Collections.ArrayList)
' *Public Instance Properties*
  Public ReadOnly Property **Count** As Integer Implements ICollection.Count
  Public ReadOnly Property **IsReadOnly** As Boolean
  Public ReadOnly Property **IsSynchronized** As Boolean Implements ICollection.IsSynchronized
  Public Default ReadOnly Property **Item** (ByVal index As Integer) As DataGridColumn
  Public ReadOnly Property **SyncRoot** As Object Implements ICollection.SyncRoot
' *Public Instance Methods*
  Public Sub **Add**(ByVal column As DataGridColumn)
  Public Sub **AddAt**(ByVal index As Integer, ByVal column As DataGridColumn)

```
    Public Sub Clear()
    Public Sub CopyTo(ByVal array As Array, ByVal index As Integer)  Implements ICollection.CopyTo
    Public Function GetEnumerator() As IEnumerator Implements  IEnumerable.GetEnumerator
    Public Function IndexOf(ByVal column As DataGridColumn) As Integer
    Public Sub Remove(ByVal column As DataGridColumn)
    Public Sub RemoveAt(ByVal index As Integer)
End Class
```

DataGridCommandEventArgs   NotInheritable Class

System.Web.UI.WebControls (system.web.dll)

The DataGridCommandEventArgs class provides more information for the ItemCommand, CancelCommand, DeleteCommand, EditCommand, and UpdateCommand events of the DataGrid control. This information consists of an Item property identifying the affected DataGridItem and a CommandSource property that refers to the button or hyperlink that was clicked. You have to cast this object to an appropriate type to read its properties.

```
Public NotInheritable Class DataGridCommandEventArgs : Inherits CommandEventArgs
' Public Constructors
    Public Sub New(ByVal item As DataGridItem, ByVal commandSource As Object, _
      ByVal originalArgs As CommandEventArgs)
' Public Instance Properties
    Public ReadOnly Property CommandSource As Object
    Public ReadOnly Property Item As DataGridItem
End Class
```

Hierarchy   System.Object → System.EventArgs → CommandEventArgs → DataGridCommandEventArgs

DataGridCommandEventHandler   Delegate

System.Web.UI.WebControls (system.web.dll)   *serializable*

This delegate specifies the parameters for the event handler routine that handles the ItemCommand, CancelCommand, DeleteCommand, EditCommand, and UpdateCommand events of the DataGrid control. This event handler receives additional information about the item that was clicked.

```
Public Delegate Sub DataGridCommandEventHandler(ByVal source As Object, _
    ByVal e As DataGridCommandEventArgs)
```

DataGridItem   Class

System.Web.UI.WebControls (system.web.dll)   *disposable*

This class represents an individual item in the DataGrid control. You can access a DataGridItem through the DataGrid.Items collection or from a DataGrid event handler.

The DataGridItem class inherits most of its properties from System.Web.UI.Control. In addition, it provides a ItemIndex that gives its index in the DataGrid.Items collection, an ItemType property that identifies what type of item this is (a header, footer, alternating row, etc.), and a DataItem property that returns the corresponding data item (such as a System.Data.DataRowView instance).

```
Public Class DataGridItem : Inherits TableRow : Implements System.Web.UI.INamingContainer
' Public Constructors
    Public Sub New(ByVal itemIndex As Integer, ByVal dataSetIndex As Integer, ByVal itemType As ListItemType)
```

' *Public Instance Properties*
   Overridable Public Property **DataItem** As Object
   Overridable Public ReadOnly Property **DataSetIndex** As Integer
   Overridable Public ReadOnly Property **ItemIndex** As Integer
   Overridable Public ReadOnly Property **ItemType** As ListItemType
' *Protected Instance Methods*
   Overrides Protected Function **OnBubbleEvent**(ByVal source As Object, ByVal e As EventArgs) As Boolean
   Overridable Protected Friend Sub **SetItemType**(ByVal itemType As ListItemType)
End Class

Hierarchy   System.Object → System.Web.UI.Control (System.ComponentModel.IComponent , System.IDisposable , System.Web.UI.IParserAccessor , System.Web.UI.IDataBindingsAccessor) → WebControl (System.Web.UI.IAttributeAccessor) → TableRow → DataGridItem (System.Web.UI.INamingContainer)

DataGridItemCollection   Class

System.Web.UI.WebControls (system.web.dll)

This custom collection class contains DataGridItem objects. It is used for the DataGrid.Items property of the DataGrid control.

Public Class **DataGridItemCollection** : Implements ICollection, IEnumerable
' *Public Constructors*
   Public Sub **New**(ByVal items As System.Collections.ArrayList)
' *Public Instance Properties*
   Public ReadOnly Property **Count** As Integer Implements ICollection.Count
   Public ReadOnly Property **IsReadOnly** As Boolean
   Public ReadOnly Property **IsSynchronized** As Boolean Implements ICollection.IsSynchronized
   Public Default ReadOnly Property **Item** (ByVal index As Integer) As DataGridItem
   Public ReadOnly Property **SyncRoot** As Object Implements ICollection.SyncRoot
' *Public Instance Methods*
   Public Sub **CopyTo**(ByVal array As Array, ByVal index As Integer) Implements ICollection.CopyTo
   Public Function **GetEnumerator**() As IEnumerator Implements IEnumerable.GetEnumerator
End Class

DataGridItemEventArgs   Class

System.Web.UI.WebControls (system.web.dll)

This class provides extra information for the DataGrid.ItemCreated and DataGrid.ItemDataBound events, which consists of an Item property with the current DataGridItem object.

Public Class **DataGridItemEventArgs** : Inherits EventArgs
' *Public Constructors*
   Public Sub **New**(ByVal item As DataGridItem)
' *Public Instance Properties*
   Public ReadOnly Property **Item** As DataGridItem
End Class

Hierarchy   System.Object → System.EventArgs → DataGridItemEventArgs

DataGridItemEventHandler   Delegate

System.Web.UI.WebControls (system.web.dll)   *serializable*

This delegate defines the parameter list for methods that handle the DataGrid.ItemCreated and DataGrid.ItemDataBound events. These events provides extra information about the current DataGridItem through the DataGridItemEventArgs class.

Public Delegate Sub **DataGridItemEventHandler**(ByVal sender As Object, ByVal e As DataGridItemEventArgs)

DataGridPageChangedEventArgs
NotInheritable Class

System.Web.UI.WebControls (system.web.dll)

This class provides extra information for the DataGrid.PageIndexChanged event. This information includes the CommandSource, which will always be the DataGridItem that represents the page selection control, and the NewPageIndex, which indicates the selected page (the first page is 0, although it the corresponding link in the DataGrid will be displayed as "1").

Public NotInheritable Class **DataGridPageChangedEventArgs** : Inherits EventArgs
' *Public Constructors*
   Public Sub **New**(ByVal commandSource As Object, ByVal newPageIndex As Integer)
' *Public Instance Properties*
   Public ReadOnly Property **CommandSource** As Object
   Public ReadOnly Property **NewPageIndex** As Integer
End Class

Hierarchy   System.Object → System.EventArgs → DataGridPageChangedEventArgs

DataGridPageChangedEventHandler
Delegate

System.Web.UI.WebControls (system.web.dll)
serializable

This delegate specifies the parameter list that a method must have to handle the DataGrid.PageIndexChanged event. If you are using automatic paging (and have set the DataGrid.AllowPaging property to True, but the DataGrid.AllowCustomPaging property to False), your event handler only needs to set the new DataGrid.CurrentPageIndex (for example, ItemsGrid.CurrentPageIndex = e.NewPageIndex), recreate the data source, and then rebind it.

Public Delegate Sub **DataGridPageChangedEventHandler**(ByVal source As Object, _
   ByVal e As DataGridPageChangedEventArgs)

DataGridPagerStyle
NotInheritable Class

System.Web.UI.WebControls (system.web.dll)
marshal by reference, disposable

This class represents a special style class derived from TableItemStyle that allows you to configure the pager controls for the DataGrid control. It is provided through the DataGrid.PagerStyle property. Pager controls (special links that allow you to see one "page" of data at a time) are displayed in a separate row at the bottom of the table, provided you have enabled the DataGrid.AllowPaging property.

Aside from setting the standard style properties, you can also use the Mode property to configure the type of pager buttons used (multiple numeric or previous/next). If you are using previous/next buttons (PagerMode.NextPrev), you can also set the associated text for the links using the NextPageText and PrevPageText properties (which default to the < and > signs). If you use numeric link buttons (PagerMode.NumericPages), you can also set the maximum number of links that will be displayed at a time through the PageButtonCount property. If there are more pages than specified in this property, a link with ellipses (...) is automatically displayed in the pager row, which allows the user to show the next or previous set of numeric links.

Public NotInheritable Class **DataGridPagerStyle** : Inherits TableItemStyle
' *Public Instance Properties*
   Public Property **Mode** As PagerMode

Public Property **NextPageText** As String
Public Property **PageButtonCount** As Integer
Public Property **Position** As PagerPosition
Public Property **PrevPageText** As String
Public Property **Visible** As Boolean
' *Public Instance Methods*
Overrides Public Sub **CopyFrom**(ByVal s As Style)
Overrides Public Sub **MergeWith**(ByVal s As Style)
Overrides Public Sub **Reset**()
End Class

Hierarchy System.Object → System.MarshalByRefObject → System.ComponentModel.Component
(System.ComponentModel.IComponent , System.IDisposable)→ Style (
System.Web.UI.IStateManager)→ TableItemStyle → DataGridPagerStyle

DataGridSortCommandEventArgs

NotInheritable Class

System.Web.UI.WebControls (system.web.dll)

This class provides extra information for the DataGrid.SortCommand event. This information includes the CommandSource, which will always be the DataGridItem that represents the header row, and the SortExpression, which indicates the column (field) title. If you use a System.Data.DataView for your data source, you can assign this expression to the Sort property.

Public NotInheritable Class **DataGridSortCommandEventArgs** : Inherits EventArgs
' *Public Constructors*
Public Sub **New**(ByVal commandSource As Object, ByVal dce As DataGridCommandEventArgs)
' *Public Instance Properties*
Public ReadOnly Property **CommandSource** As Object
Public ReadOnly Property **SortExpression** As String
End Class

Hierarchy System.Object → System.EventArgs → DataGridSortCommandEventArgs

DataGridSortCommandEventHandler

Delegate
serializable

System.Web.UI.WebControls (system.web.dll)

This delegate specifies the parameter list that a subroutine must have to handle the DataGrid.SortCommand event. This event specifies additional information about the selected column (DataGridSortCommandEventArgs.SortExpression), which you can use to build a new data source. This event handler should then rebind the data source to the DataGrid control to update the display.

Public Delegate Sub **DataGridSortCommandEventHandler**(ByVal source As Object, _
    ByVal e As DataGridSortCommandEventArgs)

DataKeyCollection

NotInheritable Class

System.Web.UI.WebControls (system.web.dll)

The DataKeyCollection class contains a read-only collection of primary field key names as strings. This class is used by the BaseDataList.DataKeys property to faciilitate editing (for example, you can use a unique ID for your key field and use it to build SQL statements when you need to update a record in response to a user edit operation). You must specify the data key you want to use in the BaseDataList.DataKeyField property before you bind the data list.

```
Public NotInheritable Class DataKeyCollection : Implements ICollection, IEnumerable
' Public Constructors
    Public Sub New(ByVal keys As System.Collections.ArrayList)
' Public Instance Properties
    Public ReadOnly Property Count As Integer Implements ICollection.Count
    Public ReadOnly Property IsReadOnly As Boolean
    Public ReadOnly Property IsSynchronized As Boolean Implements ICollection.IsSynchronized
    Public Default ReadOnly Property Item (ByVal index As Integer) As Object
    Public ReadOnly Property SyncRoot As Object Implements ICollection.SyncRoot
' Public Instance Methods
    Public Sub CopyTo(ByVal array As Array, ByVal index As Integer)  Implements ICollection.CopyTo
    Public Function GetEnumerator() As IEnumerator Implements IEnumerable.GetEnumerator
End Class
```

DataList   Class

System.Web.UI.WebControls (system.web.dll)   *disposable*

The DataList control is a databound list that is configured through templates in the *.aspx* file. It does not provide quite the extent of features found in the DataGrid control. It does provide support for automatic selection (by setting the SelectedIndex property) and editing (by setting the EditItemIndex property), but not for automatic paging or sorting. Also, there is no support for default column types or automatically generated rows, so you will always need to specify at least an ItemTemplate. Templates for the DataList are bracketed inside the appropriate template tag (like <ItemTemplate>) and may contain a data binding expression (for example, <%# Container.DataItem("Description") %>). You can also add HTML tags or tags for ASP.NET controls to these templates manually for a customized appearance.

You can use the AlternatingItemTemplate property to allow items to alternate between two styles, the EditItemTemplate to specify how items will appear when they are being edited, and the SelectedItemTemplate to specify how items will appear when they are selected. The HeaderTemplate, FooterTemplate, and SeparatorTemplate allow you to specify layout and content for special rows. The DataList has a number of properties that allow you to control its appearance. You can set TableItemStyle objects for various properties, including footers, headers (used automatically for column titles), and items. (The corresponding DataList properties end with the word "Style.") You can also use the ShowHeader and ShowFooter properties to configure whether headers and footers will be displayed.

```
Public Class DataList : Inherits  BaseDataList: Implements  System.Web.UI.INamingContainer, IRepeatInfoUser
' Public Constructors
    Public Sub New()
' Public Shared Fields
    public const CancelCommandName As String                              =Cancel
    public const DeleteCommandName As String                              =Delete
    public const EditCommandName As String                                  =Edit
    public const SelectCommandName As String                              =Select
    public const UpdateCommandName As String                             =Update
' Public Instance Properties
    Overridable Public ReadOnly Property AlternatingItemStyle As TableItemStyle
    Overridable Public Property AlternatingItemTemplate As ITemplate
    Overridable Public Property EditItemIndex As Integer
    Overridable Public ReadOnly Property EditItemStyle As TableItemStyle
    Overridable Public Property EditItemTemplate As ITemplate
    Overridable Public Property ExtractTemplateRows As Boolean
    Overridable Public ReadOnly Property FooterStyle As TableItemStyle
```

Overridable Public Property **FooterTemplate** As ITemplate
Overrides Public Property **GridLines** As GridLines
Overridable Public ReadOnly Property **HeaderStyle** As TableItemStyle
Overridable Public Property **HeaderTemplate** As ITemplate
Overridable Public ReadOnly Property **Items** As DataListItemCollection
Overridable Public ReadOnly Property **ItemStyle** As TableItemStyle
Overridable Public Property **ItemTemplate** As ITemplate
Overridable Public Property **RepeatColumns** As Integer
Overridable Public Property **RepeatDirection** As RepeatDirection
Overridable Public Property **RepeatLayout** As RepeatLayout
Overridable Public Property **SelectedIndex** As Integer
Overridable Public ReadOnly Property **SelectedItem** As DataListItem
Overridable Public ReadOnly Property **SelectedItemStyle** As TableItemStyle
Overridable Public Property **SelectedItemTemplate** As ITemplate
Overridable Public ReadOnly Property **SeparatorStyle** As TableItemStyle
Overridable Public Property **SeparatorTemplate** As ITemplate
Overridable Public Property **ShowFooter** As Boolean
Overridable Public Property **ShowHeader** As Boolean
' Protected Instance Methods
Overrides Protected Sub **CreateControlHierarchy**(ByVal useDataSource As Boolean)
Overrides Protected Function **CreateControlStyle**() As Style
Overridable Protected Function **CreateItem**(ByVal itemIndex As Integer, ByVal itemType As ListItemType) _
    As DataListItem
Overridable Protected Sub **InitializeItem**(ByVal item As DataListItem)
Overrides Protected Sub **LoadViewState**(ByVal savedState As Object)
Overrides Protected Function **OnBubbleEvent**(ByVal source As Object, ByVal e As EventArgs) As Boolean
Overridable Protected Sub **OnCancelCommand**(ByVal e As DataListCommandEventArgs)
Overridable Protected Sub **OnDeleteCommand**(ByVal e As DataListCommandEventArgs)
Overridable Protected Sub **OnEditCommand**(ByVal e As DataListCommandEventArgs)
Overridable Protected Sub **OnItemCommand**(ByVal e As DataListCommandEventArgs)
Overridable Protected Sub **OnItemCreated**(ByVal e As DataListItemEventArgs)
Overridable Protected Sub **OnItemDataBound**(ByVal e As DataListItemEventArgs)
Overridable Protected Sub **OnUpdateCommand**(ByVal e As DataListCommandEventArgs)
Overrides Protected Sub **PrepareControlHierarchy**()
Overrides Protected Sub **RenderContents**(ByVal writer As System.Web.UI.HtmlTextWriter)
Overrides Protected Function **SaveViewState**() As Object
Overrides Protected Sub **TrackViewState**()
' Events
Public Event **CancelCommand** As DataListCommandEventHandler
Public Event **DeleteCommand** As DataListCommandEventHandler
Public Event **EditCommand** As DataListCommandEventHandler
Public Event **ItemCommand** As DataListCommandEventHandler
Public Event **ItemCreated** As DataListItemEventHandler
Public Event **ItemDataBound** As DataListItemEventHandler
Public Event **UpdateCommand** As DataListCommandEventHandler
End Class

Hierarchy System.Object → System.Web.UI.Control (System.ComponentModel.IComponent ,
System.IDisposable , System.Web.UI.IParserAccessor , System.Web.UI.IDataBindingsAccessor) →
WebControl (System.Web.UI.IAttributeAccessor) → BaseDataList → DataList (
System.Web.UI.INamingContainer , IRepeatInfoUser)

DataListCommandEventArgs   **NotInheritable Class**

System.Web.UI.WebControls (system.web.dll)

The DataListCommandEventArgs class provides more information for the ItemCommand, CancelCommand, DeleteCommand, EditCommand, and UpdateCommand events of the DataList control. This information consists of an Item property identifying the affected DataListItem, and a CommandSource property that refers to the button or hyperlink that was clicked. You will have to cast this object to an appropriate type to read its properties.

Public NotInheritable Class **DataListCommandEventArgs** : Inherits CommandEventArgs
  ' Public Constructors
    Public Sub **New**(ByVal item As DataListItem, ByVal commandSource As Object, _
      ByVal originalArgs As CommandEventArgs)
  ' Public Instance Properties
    Public ReadOnly Property **CommandSource** As Object
    Public ReadOnly Property **Item** As DataListItem
End Class

Hierarchy System.Object → System.EventArgs → CommandEventArgs →
DataListCommandEventArgs

DataListCommandEventHandler

Delegate

System.Web.UI.WebControls (system.web.dll)

serializable

This delegate specifies the parameters for the event handler routine that handles the ItemCommand, CancelCommand, DeleteCommand, EditCommand, and UpdateCommand events of the DataList control. This event handler receives additional information about the item that was clicked.

Public Delegate Sub **DataListCommandEventHandler**(ByVal source As Object, _
  ByVal e As DataListCommandEventArgs)

DataListItem

Class

System.Web.UI.WebControls (system.web.dll)

disposable

This class represents an individual item in the DataList control. You can access it through the DataList.Items collection or from a DataList event.

DataListItem inherits most of its properties from System.Web.UI.Control. In addition, it provides a ItemIndex that gives its index in the DataList.Items collection, a ItemType property that identifies what type of item this is (a header, footer, alternating row, etc.), and a DataItem property that returns the corresponding data item (such as a System.Data.DataRowView instance).

Public Class **DataListItem** : Inherits WebControl : Implements System.Web.UI.INamingContainer
  ' Public Constructors
    Public Sub **New**(ByVal itemIndex As Integer, ByVal itemType As ListItemType)
  ' Public Instance Properties
    Overridable Public Property **DataItem** As Object
    Overridable Public ReadOnly Property **ItemIndex** As Integer
    Overridable Public ReadOnly Property **ItemType** As ListItemType
  ' Public Instance Methods
    Overridable Public Sub **RenderItem**(ByVal writer As System.Web.UI.HtmlTextWriter, ByVal extractRows As Boolean, _
      ByVal tableLayout As Boolean)
  ' Protected Instance Methods
    Overrides Protected Function **CreateControlStyle**() As Style
    Overrides Protected Function **OnBubbleEvent**(ByVal source As Object, ByVal e As EventArgs) As Boolean
    Overridable Protected Friend Sub **SetItemType**(ByVal itemType As ListItemType)
End Class

Hierarchy System.Object → System.Web.UI.Control (System.ComponentModel.IComponent , System.IDisposable , System.Web.UI.IParserAccessor , System.Web.UI.IDataBindingsAccessor)→ WebControl (System.Web.UI.IAttributeAccessor)→ DataListItem (System.Web.UI.INamingContainer)

DataListItemCollection   NotInheritable Class

System.Web.UI.WebControls (system.web.dll)

This custom collection class contains DataListItem objects. It is used for the DataList.Items property of the DataList control.

Public NotInheritable Class **DataListItemCollection** : Implements ICollection, IEnumerable
' *Public Constructors*
  Public Sub **New**(ByVal items As System.Collections.ArrayList)
' *Public Instance Properties*
  Public ReadOnly Property **Count** As Integer Implements ICollection.Count
  Public ReadOnly Property **IsReadOnly** As Boolean
  Public ReadOnly Property **IsSynchronized** As Boolean Implements ICollection.IsSynchronized
  Public Default ReadOnly Property **Item** (ByVal index As Integer) As DataListItem
  Public ReadOnly Property **SyncRoot** As Object Implements ICollection.SyncRoot
' *Public Instance Methods*
  Public Sub **CopyTo**(ByVal array As Array, ByVal index As Integer) Implements ICollection.CopyTo
  Public Function **GetEnumerator**() As IEnumerator Implements IEnumerable.GetEnumerator
End Class

DataListItemEventArgs   NotInheritable Class

System.Web.UI.WebControls (system.web.dll)

This class provides extra information for the DataList.ItemCreated and DataList.ItemDataBound events. This information consists of an Item property that contains the current DataListItem object.

Public NotInheritable Class **DataListItemEventArgs** : Inherits EventArgs
' *Public Constructors*
  Public Sub **New**(ByVal item As DataListItem)
' *Public Instance Properties*
  Public ReadOnly Property **Item** As DataListItem
End Class

Hierarchy System.Object → System.EventArgs → DataListItemEventArgs

DataListItemEventHandler   Delegate

System.Web.UI.WebControls (system.web.dll)   *serializable*

This delegate defines the parameter list for methods that handle the DataList.ItemCreated and DataList.ItemDataBound events. These events provide extra information about the current DataListItem through the DataListItemEventArgs class.

Public Delegate Sub **DataListItemEventHandler**(ByVal sender As Object, ByVal e As DataListItemEventArgs)

DayNameFormat   Enum

System.Web.UI.WebControls (system.web.dll)   *serializable*

This enumeration is used to set the Calendar.DayNameFormat property, which configures how days are displayed at the top of the calendar grid. Days can be displayed in Full (e.g., "Tuesday"), in a Short version ("Tues"), or by using the FirstLetter or FirstTwoLetters ("T" or "Tu").

```
Public Enum DayNameFormat
    Full = 0
    Short = 1
    FirstLetter = 2
    FirstTwoLetters = 3
End Enum
```

Hierarchy System.Object → System.ValueType → System.Enum (System.IComparable , System.IFormattable , System.IConvertible)→ DayNameFormat

DayRenderEventArgs
NotInheritable Class

System.Web.UI.WebControls (system.web.dll)

This object is provided to the DayRenderEventHandler. It identifies the CalendarDay that is about to be added and the TableCell that contains the date, as well as the Day and Cell properties. The Calendar.DayRender event is fired for every currently displayed day. This includes days from the preceding and following month, which are used to fill out the first and last week on the calendar.

```
Public NotInheritable Class DayRenderEventArgs
' Public Constructors
    Public Sub New(ByVal cell As TableCell, ByVal day As CalendarDay)
' Public Instance Properties
    Public ReadOnly Property Cell As TableCell
    Public ReadOnly Property Day As CalendarDay
End Class
```

DayRenderEventHandler
Delegate

System.Web.UI.WebControls (system.web.dll)
serializable

This delegate defines the subroutine used to handle the Calendar.DayRender event. This event fires as each day is added to the currently displayed calendar month and provides additional information about the day in a DayRenderEventArgs object. The properties of this object can be modified to programmatically change the display color for a specific date or to make certain dates unselectable.

```
Public Delegate Sub DayRenderEventHandler(ByVal sender As Object, ByVal e As DayRenderEventArgs)
```

DropDownList
Class

System.Web.UI.WebControls (system.web.dll)
disposable

This class provides a single-selection drop-down list control. Various properties, such as BorderColor, BorderStyle, and BorderWidth, allow you to configure its appearance. To add items programmatically, use the Items collection or use the DataBind() method to bind to a data source (such as a System.Data.DataTable or a System.Array).

Use the SelectedIndex property to determine the selected item or the SelectedItem property, which returns a ListItem object that specifies the associated text.

```
Public Class DropDownList : Inherits ListControl : Implements System.Web.UI.IPostBackDataHandler
' Public Constructors
    Public Sub New()
' Public Instance Properties
    Overrides Public Property BorderColor As Color
    Overrides Public Property BorderStyle As BorderStyle
```

Overrides Public Property **BorderWidth** As Unit
Overrides Public Property **SelectedIndex** As Integer
Overrides Public Property **ToolTip** As String
' *Protected Instance Methods*
Overrides Protected Sub **AddAttributesToRender**(ByVal writer As System.Web.UI.HtmlTextWriter)
Overrides Protected Function **CreateControlCollection**() As ControlCollection
Overrides Protected Sub **RenderContents**(ByVal writer As System.Web.UI.HtmlTextWriter)
End Class

Hierarchy System.Object → System.Web.UI.Control (System.ComponentModel.IComponent , System.IDisposable , System.Web.UI.IParserAccessor , System.Web.UI.IDataBindingsAccessor) → WebControl (System.Web.UI.IAttributeAccessor) → ListControl → DropDownList (System.Web.UI.IPostBackDataHandler)

EditCommandColumn

Class

System.Web.UI.WebControls (system.web.dll)

The EditCommandColumn class is a special type of column used with the DataGrid control. It provides an "Edit" button or link (depending on the ButtonType property) that, when clicked, fires the DataGrid.EditCommand event. This event allows you to initiate editing for a row by using the DataGrid.EditItemIndex property (after which you must rebind to the data source).

While editing is in progress, the EditCommandColumn displays "Cancel" and "Update" buttons instead of an "Edit" button. These will trigger the DataGrid.CancelCommand and DataGrid.UpdateCommand events, respectively. In these events, you can add the code required to commit changes to the data source and cancel editing (by setting DataGrid.EditItemIndex to -1). Rebind to the data source before returning the page.

Note that you must provide values for the CancelText, EditText, and UpdateText properties (like "Cancel", "Edit", and "Update"). Otherwise, the associated command buttons will not appear in the column when editing is underway.

Public Class **EditCommandColumn** : Inherits DataGridColumn
' *Public Constructors*
Public Sub **New**()
' *Public Instance Properties*
Overridable Public Property **ButtonType** As ButtonColumnType
Overridable Public Property **CancelText** As String
Overridable Public Property **EditText** As String
Overridable Public Property **UpdateText** As String
' *Public Instance Methods*
Overrides Public Sub **InitializeCell**(ByVal cell As TableCell, ByVal columnIndex As Integer, _
ByVal itemType As ListItemType)
End Class

Hierarchy System.Object → DataGridColumn (System.Web.UI.IStateManager) → EditCommandColumn

FirstDayOfWeek

Enum

System.Web.UI.WebControls (system.web.dll)

serializable

This enumeration is used by the Calendar.FirstDayOfWeek property to determine how a month is broken up into rows of weeks in the display. If you choose the value Sunday, every row in the calendar display will start on Sunday and end with Saturday. Default instructs ASP.NET to use the current regional settings defined on the web server.

```
Public Enum FirstDayOfWeek
    Sunday = 0
    Monday = 1
    Tuesday = 2
    Wednesday = 3
    Thursday = 4
    Friday = 5
    Saturday = 6
    Default = 7
End Enum
```

Hierarchy System.Object → System.ValueType → System.Enum (System.IComparable , System.IFormattable , System.IConvertible)→ FirstDayOfWeek

FontInfo
NotInheritable Class

System.Web.UI.WebControls (system.web.dll)

This class represents font information and is used in many controls through the WebControl.Font property. This class contains the font properties that are supported in ASP.NET Web Forms and differs slightly from the System.Drawing.Font object used in other types of .NET applications.

```
Public NotInheritable Class FontInfo
' Public Instance Properties
    Public Property Bold As Boolean
    Public Property Italic As Boolean
    Public Property Name As String
    Public Property Names As String()
    Public Property Overline As Boolean
    Public Property Size As FontUnit
    Public Property Strikeout As Boolean
    Public Property Underline As Boolean
' Public Instance Methods
    Public Sub CopyFrom(ByVal f As FontInfo)
    Public Sub MergeWith(ByVal f As FontInfo)
    Public Function ShouldSerializeNames() As Boolean
    Overrides Public Function ToString() As String
End Class
```

FontNamesConverter
Class

System.Web.UI.WebControls (system.web.dll)

The FontNamesConverter class is a type converter that can convert between a font name array and a string that contains a list of font names separated by commas (as often appears in an HTML page). This class is never accessed directly. You can access its functionality through the System.ComponentModel.TypeDescriptor helper class.

```
Public Class FontNamesConverter : Inherits System.ComponentModel.TypeConverter
' Public Constructors
    Public Sub New()
' Public Instance Methods
    Overrides Public Function CanConvertFrom(ByVal context As System.ComponentModel.ITypeDescriptorContext, _
        ByVal sourceType As Type) As Boolean
    Overrides Public Function ConvertFrom(ByVal context As System.ComponentModel.ITypeDescriptorContext, _
        ByVal culture As System.Globalization.CultureInfo, ByVal value As Object) As Object
```

WebControls Namespace

```
Overrides Public Function ConvertTo(ByVal context As System.ComponentModel.ITypeDescriptorContext, _
    ByVal culture As System.Globalization.CultureInfo, ByVal value As Object, ByVal destinationType As Type) _
        As Object
End Class
```

Hierarchy   System.Object → System.ComponentModel.TypeConverter → FontNamesConverter

FontSize
                                                                            Enum
System.Web.UI.WebControls (system.web.dll)   *serializable*

This enumeration is used to set the FontUnit.Type property using one of the font size constants defined by the HTML 4.0 standard.

```
Public Enum FontSize
    NotSet = 0
    AsUnit = 1
    Smaller = 2
    Larger = 3
    XXSmall = 4
    XSmall = 5
    Small = 6
    Medium = 7
    Large = 8
    XLarge = 9
    XXLarge = 10
End Enum
```

Hierarchy   System.Object → System.ValueType → System.Enum (System.IComparable , System.IFormattable , System.IConvertible)→ FontSize

FontUnit
                                                                        Structure
System.Web.UI.WebControls (system.web.dll)

This class represents the size of a font and is used by the FontInfo.Size property. The size of the font can be specified in two ways. You can use the Type property, which uses one of the HTML 4.0 standard font size specifications (which are duplicated as shared read-only fields in this class) or the Unit property, which uses a Unit structure that can specify an exact point size.

```
Public Structure FontUnit
' Public Constructors
    Public Sub New(ByVal type As FontSize)
    Public Sub New(ByVal value As Integer)
    Public Sub New(ByVal value As String)
    Public Sub New(ByVal value As String, ByVal culture As System.Globalization.CultureInfo)
    Public Sub New(ByVal value As Unit)
' Public Shared Fields
    public Shared ReadOnly Empty As FontUnit
    public Shared ReadOnly Large As FontUnit                              =Large
    public Shared ReadOnly Larger As FontUnit                            =Larger
    public Shared ReadOnly Medium As FontUnit                          =Medium
    public Shared ReadOnly Small As FontUnit                             =Small
    public Shared ReadOnly Smaller As FontUnit                         =Smaller
    public Shared ReadOnly XLarge As FontUnit                         =X-Large
```

public Shared ReadOnly **XSmall** As FontUnit	*=X-Small*
public Shared ReadOnly **XXLarge** As FontUnit	*=XX-Large*
public Shared ReadOnly **XXSmall** As FontUnit	*=XX-Small*

' *Public Instance Properties*
Public ReadOnly Property **IsEmpty** As Boolean
Public ReadOnly Property **Type** As FontSize
Public ReadOnly Property **Unit** As Unit
' *Public Shared Methods*
Public Shared Function **Parse**(ByVal s As String) As FontUnit
Public Shared Function **Parse**(ByVal s As String, ByVal culture As System.Globalization.CultureInfo) As FontUnit
Public Shared Function **Point**(ByVal n As Integer) As FontUnit
Public Shared Boolean operator Sub **!=**(ByVal left As FontUnit, ByVal right As FontUnit)
Public Shared Boolean operator Sub **==**(ByVal left As FontUnit, ByVal right As FontUnit)
Public Shared implicit operator Sub **FontUnit**(ByVal n As Integer)
' *Public Instance Methods*
Overrides Public Function **Equals**(ByVal obj As Object) As Boolean
Overrides Public Function **GetHashCode**() As Integer
Overrides Public Function **ToString**() As String
Public Function **ToString**(ByVal culture As System.Globalization.CultureInfo) As String
End Structure

Hierarchy   System.Object → System.ValueType → FontUnit

FontUnitConverter

Class

System.Web.UI.WebControls (system.web.dll)

The FontUnitConverter class is a type converter that can convert between a FontUnit and other basic data types. This class is never accessed directly. You can access its functionality through the System.ComponentModel.TypeDescriptor helper class.

Public Class **FontUnitConverter** : Inherits System.ComponentModel.TypeConverter
' *Public Constructors*
Public Sub **New**()
' *Public Instance Methods*
Overrides Public Function **CanConvertFrom**(ByVal context As System.ComponentModel.ITypeDescriptorContext, _
    ByVal sourceType As Type) As Boolean
Overrides Public Function **ConvertFrom**(ByVal context As System.ComponentModel.ITypeDescriptorContext, _
    ByVal culture As System.Globalization.CultureInfo, ByVal value As Object) As Object
Overrides Public Function **ConvertTo**(ByVal context As System.ComponentModel.ITypeDescriptorContext, _
    ByVal culture As System.Globalization.CultureInfo, ByVal value As Object, ByVal destinationType As Type) _
        As Object
Overrides Public Function **GetStandardValues**(_
    ByVal context As System.ComponentModel.ITypeDescriptorContext) As StandardValuesCollection
Overrides Public Function **GetStandardValuesExclusive**(_
    ByVal context As System.ComponentModel.ITypeDescriptorContext) As Boolean
Overrides Public Function **GetStandardValuesSupported**(_
    ByVal context As System.ComponentModel.ITypeDescriptorContext) As Boolean
End Class

Hierarchy   System.Object → System.ComponentModel.TypeConverter → FontUnitConverter

GridLines

Enum

System.Web.UI.WebControls (system.web.dll)

serializable

This enumeration specifies what grid lines are visible in a table. It is used by the Data-Grid, DataList, and Table classes.

```
Public Enum GridLines
    None = 0
    Horizontal = 1
    Vertical = 2
    Both = 3
End Enum
```

Hierarchy System.Object → System.ValueType → System.Enum (System.IComparable , System.IFormattable , System.IConvertible)→ GridLines

HorizontalAlign
Enum

System.Web.UI.WebControls (system.web.dll)
serializable

This enumeration specifies how contents will be laid out in a container. The classes that use it include DataGrid, Table, and Panel.

```
Public Enum HorizontalAlign
    NotSet = 0
    Left = 1
    Center = 2
    Right = 3
    Justify = 4
End Enum
```

Hierarchy System.Object → System.ValueType → System.Enum (System.IComparable , System.IFormattable , System.IConvertible)→ HorizontalAlign

HyperLink
Class

System.Web.UI.WebControls (system.web.dll)
disposable

This class represents a link to another web page, which is specified by the NavigateUrl property. The control can be displayed as text specified by the Text property or as the image located at ImageUrl. If both properties are set, ImageUrl takes precedence, provided the image file is available, and the Text is used for an image tooltip. The Target property specifies the name of the frame that the linked page will be loaded into. Note that you cannot respond to the link click in code. If you want to provide this type of behavior, use the LinkButton control instead.

The HyperLink control also supports databinding to its Text and NavigateUrl properties.

```
Public Class HyperLink : Inherits WebControl
' Public Constructors
    Public Sub New()
' Public Instance Properties
    Overridable Public Property ImageUrl As String
    Public Property NavigateUrl As String
    Public Property Target As String
    Overridable Public Property Text As String
' Protected Instance Methods
    Overrides Protected Sub AddAttributesToRender(ByVal writer As System.Web.UI.HtmlTextWriter)
    Overrides Protected Sub AddParsedSubObject(ByVal obj As Object)
    Overrides Protected Sub LoadViewState(ByVal savedState As Object)
```

Overrides Protected Sub **RenderContents**(ByVal writer As System.Web.UI.HtmlTextWriter)
End Class

Hierarchy   System.Object → System.Web.UI.Control (System.ComponentModel.IComponent ,
System.IDisposable , System.Web.UI.IParserAccessor , System.Web.UI.IDataBindingsAccessor)→
WebControl (System.Web.UI.IAttributeAccessor)→ HyperLink

HyperLinkColumn

Class

System.Web.UI.WebControls (system.web.dll)

The HyperLinkColumn class represents a column that can be used in a DataGrid control. To
have a column with the same hyperlink in every row, you can set Text (the displayed
anchor text) and NavigateUrl (the link destination). Alternatively, you can bind a data
field to the DataTextField and DataNavigateUrlField properties (which will then take precedence over any set values for the Text and NavigateUrl properties). Typically, this information will be specified by using a data binding expression in a template definition in the
.aspx file.

Additionally, you can set the Target property to indicate the target window or frame
name for the hyperlink. You can also use the DataTextFormatString property to provide a
custom format string to use with the DataTextField property.

Public Class **HyperLinkColumn** : Inherits DataGridColumn
' Public Constructors
   Public Sub **New**()
' Public Instance Properties
   Overridable Public Property **DataNavigateUrlField** As String
   Overridable Public Property **DataNavigateUrlFormatString** As String
   Overridable Public Property **DataTextField** As String
   Overridable Public Property **DataTextFormatString** As String
   Overridable Public Property **NavigateUrl** As String
   Overridable Public Property **Target** As String
   Overridable Public Property **Text** As String
' Public Instance Methods
   Overrides Public Sub **Initialize**()
   Overrides Public Sub **InitializeCell**(ByVal cell As TableCell, ByVal columnIndex As Integer, _
      ByVal itemType As ListItemType)
' Protected Instance Methods
   Overridable Protected Function **FormatDataNavigateUrlValue**(ByVal dataUrlValue As Object) As String
   Overridable Protected Function **FormatDataTextValue**(ByVal dataTextValue As Object) As String
End Class

Hierarchy   System.Object → DataGridColumn (System.Web.UI.IStateManager)→
HyperLinkColumn

HyperLinkControlBuilder

Class

System.Web.UI.WebControls (system.web.dll)

The ASP.NET parser uses this class to generate HTML for any HyperLink controls on a
requested Web Forms page. The AllowWhitespaceLiterals() property is overridden to always
return False. You will not need to use this class directly in application code.

Public Class **HyperLinkControlBuilder** : Inherits System.Web.UI.ControlBuilder
' Public Constructors
   Public Sub **New**()

' Public Instance Methods
　　Overrides Public Function **AllowWhitespaceLiterals**() As Boolean
End Class

Hierarchy　System.Object → System.Web.UI.ControlBuilder → HyperLinkControlBuilder

Image   Class

System.Web.UI.WebControls (system.web.dll)   *disposable*

This class represents an Image control on a Web Forms page, which is used to display
any supported graphic (including *.jpg*, *.bmp*, *.gif*, and *.png* files). To specify the picture
that should appear in this control, set a URL to the file by using the ImageUrl property.
You can specify a string of AlternateText, which will be displayed in browsers that do not
support graphics or if the picture file is not available. You can also set a Font for the
alternate text. Many browsers also show this text as a tooltip when the user positions
the mouse over the image.

An Image control cannot capture mouse clicks. To respond to image click events, use
the ImageButton control instead.

Public Class **Image** : Inherits WebControl
' Public Constructors
　　Public Sub **New**()
' Public Instance Properties
　　Overridable Public Property **AlternateText** As String
　　Overrides Public Property **Enabled** As Boolean
　　Overrides Public ReadOnly Property **Font** As FontInfo
　　Overridable Public Property **ImageAlign** As ImageAlign
　　Overridable Public Property **ImageUrl** As String
' Protected Instance Methods
　　Overrides Protected Sub **AddAttributesToRender**(ByVal writer As System.Web.UI.HtmlTextWriter)
　　Overrides Protected Sub **RenderContents**(ByVal writer As System.Web.UI.HtmlTextWriter)
End Class

Hierarchy　System.Object → System.Web.UI.Control (System.ComponentModel.IComponent ,
System.IDisposable , System.Web.UI.IParserAccessor , System.Web.UI.IDataBindingsAccessor) →
WebControl (System.Web.UI.IAttributeAccessor) → Image

ImageAlign   Enum

System.Web.UI.WebControls (system.web.dll)   *serializable*

This enumeration specifies the alignment used for an Image control. Left and Right specify
an alignment relative to the web page. Text will wrap around an Image control on the
opposite side. Other values are relative to the current text line. For example, Bottom and
Middle align the bottom or middle of an image with the lower edge of a text line. Abs-
Bottom, AbsMiddle, and Top, on the other hand, are relative to the bottom, middle, or top
of the largest element in the same line.

Public Enum **ImageAlign**
　　NotSet = 0
　　Left = 1
　　Right = 2
　　Baseline = 3
　　Top = 4

```
        Middle = 5
        Bottom = 6
        AbsBottom = 7
        AbsMiddle = 8
        TextTop = 9
End Enum
```

Hierarchy   System.Object → System.ValueType → System.Enum (System.IComparable ,
System.IFormattable , System.IConvertible) → ImageAlign

ImageButton   Class

System.Web.UI.WebControls (system.web.dll)   *disposable*

This class extends the Image class to provide an image control that can respond to button clicks. The ImageButton class provides both a Click and a Command event, which will fire when the image is clicked. Use the Command event and the CommandName property to specify additional information that will be provided to the event handler. This technique is sometimes used to allow the same event handler to respond to clicks from multiple ImageButton controls and determine what control fired the event.

By default, clicking an ImageButton control will cause page validation to occur. To change this behavior, set the CausesValidation property to False.

```
Public Class ImageButton : Inherits Image : Implements System.Web.UI.IPostBackDataHandler, _
        System.Web.UI.IPostBackEventHandler
' Public Constructors
    Public Sub New()
' Public Instance Properties
    Public Property CausesValidation As Boolean
    Public Property CommandArgument As String
    Public Property CommandName As String
' Protected Instance Properties
    Overrides Protected Property TagKey As HtmlTextWriterTag
' Protected Instance Methods
    Overrides Protected Sub AddAttributesToRender(ByVal writer As System.Web.UI.HtmlTextWriter)
    Overridable Protected Sub OnClick(ByVal e As System.Web.UI.ImageClickEventArgs)
    Overridable Protected Sub OnCommand(ByVal e As CommandEventArgs)
    Overrides Protected Sub OnPreRender(ByVal e As EventArgs)
' Events
    Public Event Click As ImageClickEventHandler
    Public Event Command As CommandEventHandler
End Class
```

Hierarchy   System.Object → System.Web.UI.Control (System.ComponentModel.IComponent ,
System.IDisposable , System.Web.UI.IParserAccessor , System.Web.UI.IDataBindingsAccessor) →
WebControl (System.Web.UI.IAttributeAccessor) → Image → ImageButton (
System.Web.UI.IPostBackDataHandler , System.Web.UI.IPostBackEventHandler)

IRepeatInfoUser   Interface

System.Web.UI.WebControls (system.web.dll)

This interface specifies the contract for the RepeatInfo class. These requirements include properties that identify whether footer or header information is present (HasFooter and HasHeader) and identify the number of times the chosen control will be repeated (RepeatedItemCount). This interface also requires a method for rendering the chosen control (RenderItem()), which will be used for each repetition.

Public Interface **IRepeatInfoUser**
' *Public Instance Properties*
  Public ReadOnly Property **HasFooter** As Boolean
  Public ReadOnly Property **HasHeader** As Boolean
  Public ReadOnly Property **HasSeparators** As Boolean
  Public ReadOnly Property **RepeatedItemCount** As Integer
' *Public Instance Methods*
  Public Function **GetItemStyle**(ByVal itemType As ListItemType, ByVal repeatIndex As Integer) As Style
  Public Sub **RenderItem**(ByVal itemType As ListItemType, ByVal repeatIndex As Integer, _
  ByVal repeatInfo As RepeatInfo, ByVal writer As System.Web.UI.HtmlTextWriter)
End Interface

Label
Class

System.Web.UI.WebControls (system.web.dll)
disposable

This class represents a Label control, which allows you to place text on a page and modify it in later by using the Text property. You can use HTML tags like <br> and <i> in the text string to format portions of the control.

Public Class **Label** : Inherits WebControl
' *Public Constructors*
  Public Sub **New**()
' *Public Instance Properties*
  Overridable Public Property **Text** As String
' *Protected Instance Methods*
  Overrides Protected Sub **AddParsedSubObject**(ByVal obj As Object)
  Overrides Protected Sub **LoadViewState**(ByVal savedState As Object)
  Overrides Protected Sub **RenderContents**(ByVal writer As System.Web.UI.HtmlTextWriter)
End Class

Hierarchy System.Object → System.Web.UI.Control (System.ComponentModel.IComponent , System.IDisposable , System.Web.UI.IParserAccessor , System.Web.UI.IDataBindingsAccessor) → WebControl (System.Web.UI.IAttributeAccessor) → Label

LabelControlBuilder
Class

System.Web.UI.WebControls (system.web.dll)

The ASP.NET parser uses this class to generate HTML for Label controls on a requested Web Forms page. You don't need to use this class directly in application code.

Public Class **LabelControlBuilder** : Inherits System.Web.UI.ControlBuilder
' *Public Constructors*
  Public Sub **New**()
' *Public Instance Methods*
  Overrides Public Function **AllowWhitespaceLiterals**() As Boolean
End Class

Hierarchy System.Object → System.Web.UI.ControlBuilder → LabelControlBuilder

LinkButton
Class

System.Web.UI.WebControls (system.web.dll)
disposable

This class represents a control that appears like a HyperLink control, but fires a Click and Command event like a Button control would. A good use of this control is to provide a hyperlink that navigates to another web page but allows you to perform some programmatic cleanup (for example, clearing session variables) before you redirect the user.

Like all button controls, the LinkButton class provides a CausesValidation property you can set to prevent page validation from occurring when the control is clicked. It also provides the standard CommandName and CommandArgument properties that allow you to specify additional information that will be sent to a Command event.

```
Public Class LinkButton : Inherits WebControl : Implements System.Web.UI.IPostBackEventHandler
' Public Constructors
    Public Sub New()
' Public Instance Properties
    Public Property CausesValidation As Boolean
    Public Property CommandArgument As String
    Public Property CommandName As String
    Overridable Public Property Text As String
' Protected Instance Methods
    Overrides Protected Sub AddAttributesToRender(ByVal writer As System.Web.UI.HtmlTextWriter)
    Overrides Protected Sub AddParsedSubObject(ByVal obj As Object)
    Overrides Protected Sub LoadViewState(ByVal savedState As Object)
    Overridable Protected Sub OnClick(ByVal e As EventArgs)
    Overridable Protected Sub OnCommand(ByVal e As CommandEventArgs)
    Overrides Protected Sub OnPreRender(ByVal e As EventArgs)
    Overrides Protected Sub RenderContents(ByVal writer As System.Web.UI.HtmlTextWriter)
' Events
    Public Event Click As EventHandler
    Public Event Command As CommandEventHandler
End Class
```

Hierarchy   System.Object → System.Web.UI.Control (System.ComponentModel.IComponent , System.IDisposable , System.Web.UI.IParserAccessor , System.Web.UI.IDataBindingsAccessor) → WebControl (System.Web.UI.IAttributeAccessor) → LinkButton (System.Web.UI.IPostBackEventHandler)

LinkButtonControlBuilder   Class

System.Web.UI.WebControls (system.web.dll)

The ASP.NET parser uses this class to generate HTML for any LinkButton controls on a requested Web Forms page. You will not need to use this class directly in application code.

```
Public Class LinkButtonControlBuilder : Inherits System.Web.UI.ControlBuilder
' Public Constructors
    Public Sub New()
' Public Instance Methods
    Overrides Public Function AllowWhitespaceLiterals() As Boolean
End Class
```

Hierarchy   System.Object → System.Web.UI.ControlBuilder → LinkButtonControlBuilder

ListBox   Class

System.Web.UI.WebControls (system.web.dll)   *disposable*

This class represents a list box control. Use the Rows property to set how many rows you want to be displayed in the control at once (and hence, how much space the list box will occupy). You can also set the SelectionMode property to ListSelectionMode.Multiple if you want a user to be able to select more than one item from the list box at once.

Most of the list-specific functionality, such as determining the selected item and reacting to a SelectedIndexChanged event, is provided by the ListControl class, which ListBox inherits from.

```
Public Class ListBox : Inherits ListControl : Implements System.Web.UI.IPostBackDataHandler
' Public Constructors
   Public Sub New()
' Public Instance Properties
   Overrides Public Property BorderColor As Color
   Overrides Public Property BorderStyle As BorderStyle
   Overrides Public Property BorderWidth As Unit
   Overridable Public Property Rows As Integer
   Overridable Public Property SelectionMode As ListSelectionMode
   Overrides Public Property ToolTip As String
' Protected Instance Methods
   Overrides Protected Sub AddAttributesToRender(ByVal writer As System.Web.UI.HtmlTextWriter)
   Overrides Protected Sub OnPreRender(ByVal e As EventArgs)
   Overrides Protected Sub RenderContents(ByVal writer As System.Web.UI.HtmlTextWriter)
End Class
```

Hierarchy   System.Object → System.Web.UI.Control (System.ComponentModel.IComponent , System.IDisposable , System.Web.UI.IParserAccessor , System.Web.UI.IDataBindingsAccessor) → WebControl (System.Web.UI.IAttributeAccessor) → ListControl → ListBox (System.Web.UI.IPostBackDataHandler)

ListControl

MustInherit Class

System.Web.UI.WebControls (system.web.dll)

disposable

This abstract base class for all list controls includes data-binding functionality (such as DataTextFormatString, which specifies the formatting of bound text), an Items collection, and properties for returning the first selected item (SelectedIndex and SelectedItem).

Note that items in the ListControl class do not correspond to the specific derived control type. For example, a CheckBoxList control returns its selected item as a ListItem, as all list controls do, not as an individual checkbox control.

```
Public MustInherit Class ListControl : Inherits WebControl
' Public Constructors
   Public Sub New()
' Public Instance Properties
   Overridable Public Property AutoPostBack As Boolean
   Overridable Public Property DataMember As String
   Overridable Public Property DataSource As Object
   Overridable Public Property DataTextField As String
   Overridable Public Property DataTextFormatString As String
   Overridable Public Property DataValueField As String
   Overridable Public ReadOnly Property Items As ListItemCollection
   Overridable Public Property SelectedIndex As Integer
   Overridable Public ReadOnly Property SelectedItem As ListItem
' Public Instance Methods
   Overridable Public Sub ClearSelection()
' Protected Instance Methods
   Overrides Protected Sub LoadViewState(ByVal savedState As Object)
   Overrides Protected Sub OnDataBinding(ByVal e As EventArgs)
   Overrides Protected Sub OnPreRender(ByVal e As EventArgs)
   Overridable Protected Sub OnSelectedIndexChanged(ByVal e As EventArgs)
   Overrides Protected Function SaveViewState() As Object
   Overrides Protected Sub TrackViewState()
```

```
' Events
    Public Event SelectedIndexChanged As EventHandler
End Class
```

Hierarchy System.Object → System.Web.UI.Control (System.ComponentModel.IComponent , System.IDisposable , System.Web.UI.IParserAccessor , System.Web.UI.IDataBindingsAccessor)→ WebControl (System.Web.UI.IAttributeAccessor)→ ListControl

ListItem   NotInheritable Class
System.Web.UI.WebControls (system.web.dll)

This class represents an individual item from the list of a ListControl, such as CheckBoxList, DropDownList, RadioButtonList, and ListBox. The Text property returns the text for the list item, the Value property returns the contents of the "hidden" value attribute, and the Selected property indicates whether or not it is currently selected, which is useful for list controls that allow multiple selections.

```
Public NotInheritable Class ListItem : Implements System.Web.UI.IStateManager, System.Web.UI.IParserAccessor, _
        System.Web.UI.IAttributeAccessor
' Public Constructors
    Public Sub New()
    Public Sub New(ByVal text As String)
    Public Sub New(ByVal text As String, ByVal value As String)
' Public Instance Properties
    Public ReadOnly Property Attributes As AttributeCollection
    Public Property Selected As Boolean
    Public Property Text As String
    Public Property Value As String
' Public Shared Methods
    Public Shared Function FromString(ByVal s As String) As ListItem
' Public Instance Methods
    Overrides Public Function Equals(ByVal o As Object) As Boolean
    Overrides Public Function GetHashCode() As Integer
    Overrides Public Function ToString() As String
End Class
```

ListItemCollection   NotInheritable Class
System.Web.UI.WebControls (system.web.dll)

This class contains a collection of ListItem objects, which represents the items in a list control. This collection is used by the ListControl.Items property.

```
Public NotInheritable Class ListItemCollection : Implements IList, ICollection, IEnumerable, _
        System.Web.UI.IStateManager
' Public Constructors
    Public Sub New()
' Public Instance Properties
    Public Property Capacity As Integer
    Public ReadOnly Property Count As Integer Implements ICollection.Count
    Public ReadOnly Property IsReadOnly As Boolean Implements IList.IsReadOnly
    Public ReadOnly Property IsSynchronized As Boolean Implements ICollection.IsSynchronized
    Public Default ReadOnly Property Item (ByVal index As Integer) As ListItem
    Public ReadOnly Property SyncRoot As Object Implements ICollection.SyncRoot
' Public Instance Methods
    Public Sub Add(ByVal item As ListItem)
```

```
Public Sub Add(ByVal item As String)
Public Sub AddRange(ByVal items As ListItem())
Public Sub Clear() Implements IList.Clear
Public Function Contains(ByVal item As ListItem) As Boolean
Public Sub CopyTo(ByVal array As Array, ByVal index As Integer) Implements ICollection.CopyTo
Public Function FindByText(ByVal text As String) As ListItem
Public Function FindByValue(ByVal value As String) As ListItem
Public Function GetEnumerator() As IEnumerator Implements IEnumerable.GetEnumerator
Public Function IndexOf(ByVal item As ListItem) As Integer
Public Sub Insert(ByVal index As Integer, ByVal item As ListItem)
Public Sub Insert(ByVal index As Integer, ByVal item As String)
Public Sub Remove(ByVal item As ListItem)
Public Sub Remove(ByVal item As String)
Public Sub RemoveAt(ByVal index As Integer) Implements IList.RemoveAt
End Class
```

ListItemControlBuilder   Class

System.Web.UI.WebControls (system.web.dll)

The ASP.NET parser uses this class to generate HTML for any ListItem controls on a requested Web Forms page. You will not need to use this class directly in application code.

```
Public Class ListItemControlBuilder : Inherits System.Web.UI.ControlBuilder
' Public Constructors
   Public Sub New()
' Public Instance Methods
   Overrides Public Function AllowWhitespaceLiterals() As Boolean
   Overrides Public Function HtmlDecodeLiterals() As Boolean
End Class
```

Hierarchy   System.Object → System.Web.UI.ControlBuilder → ListItemControlBuilder

ListItemType   Enum

System.Web.UI.WebControls (system.web.dll)   *serializable*

This enumeration specifies the type of item for a row in a DataList, DataGrid, or Repeater control. It is not used for other list controls that derive from ListControl.

Item types include headers and footers, separators, and the controls used to move from one data page to the next (Pager). If an item is currently in edit mode, the value EditItem is returned; if the item is selected, SelectedItem is used. AlternatingItem indicates a alternating item, which will be an even-numbered item (counting is zero-based).

```
Public Enum ListItemType
        Header = 0
        Footer = 1
        Item = 2
        AlternatingItem = 3
        SelectedItem = 4
        EditItem = 5
        Separator = 6
        Pager = 7
End Enum
```

Hierarchy System.Object → System.ValueType → System.Enum (System.IComparable , System.IFormattable , System.IConvertible)→ ListItemType

ListSelectionMode

Enum

serializable

System.Web.UI.WebControls (system.web.dll)

This enumeration specifies whether list controls (which derive from ListControl) allow only one selection at a time or multiple selections.

```
Public Enum ListSelectionMode
    Single = 0
    Multiple = 1
End Enum
```

Hierarchy System.Object → System.ValueType → System.Enum (System.IComparable , System.IFormattable , System.IConvertible)→ ListSelectionMode

Literal

Class

disposable

System.Web.UI.WebControls (system.web.dll)

You can use a Literal control to put plain text on a page (optionally, with embedded HTML markup tags). In this respect, the Literal control is somewhat like the Label control, except it cannot use any special formatting, styles, or fonts.

Do not confuse the Literal control with the System.Web.UI.LiteralControl class. The latter is used by ASP.NET to represent static HTML content found on a web page that will not be made available to your code as a server-side control.

```
Public Class Literal : Inherits System.Web.UI.Control
' Public Constructors
    Public Sub New()
' Public Instance Properties
    Public Property Text As String
' Protected Instance Methods
    Overrides Protected Sub AddParsedSubObject(ByVal obj As Object)
    Overrides Protected Function CreateControlCollection() As ControlCollection
    Overrides Protected Sub Render(ByVal output As System.Web.UI.HtmlTextWriter)
End Class
```

Hierarchy System.Object → System.Web.UI.Control (System.ComponentModel.IComponent , System.IDisposable , System.Web.UI.IParserAccessor , System.Web.UI.IDataBindingsAccessor)→ Literal

LiteralControlBuilder

Class

System.Web.UI.WebControls (system.web.dll)

The ASP.NET parser uses this class to generate HTML for any Literal controls on a requested Web Forms page. You will not need to use this class directly in application code.

```
Public Class LiteralControlBuilder : Inherits System.Web.UI.ControlBuilder
' Public Constructors
    Public Sub New()
' Public Instance Methods
```

Overrides Public Function **AllowWhitespaceLiterals**() As Boolean
Overrides Public Sub **AppendSubBuilder**(ByVal subBuilder As System.Web.UI.ControlBuilder)
End Class

Hierarchy System.Object → System.Web.UI.ControlBuilder → LiteralControlBuilder

MonthChangedEventArgs   NotInheritable Class

System.Web.UI.WebControls (system.web.dll)

This custom System.EventArgs class provides additional information for the Calendar.Visible-
MonthChanged event. The additional information consists of two properties: PreviousDate
and NewDate (which will typically be the first of the newly selected month).

Public NotInheritable Class **MonthChangedEventArgs**
' *Public Constructors*
    Public Sub **New**(ByVal newDate As Date, ByVal previousDate As Date)
' *Public Instance Properties*
    Public ReadOnly Property **NewDate** As Date
    Public ReadOnly Property **PreviousDate** As Date
End Class

MonthChangedEventHandler   Delegate

System.Web.UI.WebControls (system.web.dll)   *serializable*

This delegate specifies the parameter list a subroutine requires to handle the Calen-
dar.VisibleMonthChanged event, which occurs when the user clicks one of the navigation
controls to "page" to another month. This event provides additional information about
the previous and new selected date.

Public Delegate Sub **MonthChangedEventHandler**(ByVal sender As Object, ByVal e As MonthChangedEventArgs)

NextPrevFormat   Enum

System.Web.UI.WebControls (system.web.dll)   *serializable*

This enumeration is used to set the Calendar.NextPrevFormat property. It determines the
appearance of the navigation controls that allow the user to move from month to
month. ShortMonth will display an abbreviated month name on the previous and next
month controls (like "Jan"), with which FullMonth will display the full name of the
month. If you use CustomText, you must set the corresponding Calendar.NextMonthText and
Calendar.PrevMonthText programmatically (typically, in the Calendar.VisibleMonthChanged
event handler).

Public Enum **NextPrevFormat**
    CustomText = 0
    ShortMonth = 1
    FullMonth = 2
End Enum

Hierarchy System.Object → System.ValueType → System.Enum (System.IComparable ,
System.IFormattable , System.IConvertible)→ NextPrevFormat

PagedDataSource   NotInheritable Class

System.Web.UI.WebControls (system.web.dll)

The PagedDataSource class wraps a System.Collections.ICollection data source to implement "paged views" using the best available interface to enumerate over the data. This class uses indexed access if it is available (as in classes derived from System.Array or implementing System.Collections.IList) or the System.Collections.IEnumerable interface if indexed access is not available.

This class is used internally by the DataGrid control to provide its paging abilities. It is not used in your code unless you develop a data bound control that supports paging.

```
Public NotInheritable Class PagedDataSource : Implements ICollection, IEnumerable, _
        System.ComponentModel.ITypedList
' Public Constructors
    Public Sub New()
' Public Instance Properties
    Public Property AllowCustomPaging As Boolean
    Public Property AllowPaging As Boolean
    Public ReadOnly Property Count As Integer Implements ICollection.Count
    Public Property CurrentPageIndex As Integer
    Public Property DataSource As IEnumerable
    Public ReadOnly Property DataSourceCount As Integer
    Public ReadOnly Property FirstIndexInPage As Integer
    Public ReadOnly Property IsCustomPagingEnabled As Boolean
    Public ReadOnly Property IsFirstPage As Boolean
    Public ReadOnly Property IsLastPage As Boolean
    Public ReadOnly Property IsPagingEnabled As Boolean
    Public ReadOnly Property IsReadOnly As Boolean
    Public ReadOnly Property IsSynchronized As Boolean Implements ICollection.IsSynchronized
    Public ReadOnly Property PageCount As Integer
    Public Property PageSize As Integer
    Public ReadOnly Property SyncRoot As Object Implements ICollection.SyncRoot
    Public Property VirtualCount As Integer
' Public Instance Methods
    Public Sub CopyTo(ByVal array As Array, ByVal index As Integer)  Implements  ICollection.CopyTo
    Public Function GetEnumerator() As IEnumerator Implements  IEnumerable.GetEnumerator
    Public Function GetItemProperties(ByVal listAccessors As System.ComponentModel.PropertyDescriptor()) _
        As PropertyDescriptorCollection Implements ITypedList.GetItemProperties
    Public Function GetListName(ByVal listAccessors As System.ComponentModel.PropertyDescriptor()) As String _
        Implements  ITypedList.GetListName
End Class
```

PagerMode

Enum

System.Web.UI.WebControls (system.web.dll)

serializable

This enumeration allows you to configure the type of pager controls used on the Data-Grid control to browse from page to page. Each "page" shows a table with a subset of the data. If you use NextPrev, next/previous buttons will be displayed (which are typically rendered as greater-than and less-than signs). If you use NumericPages, each page will give a number and a series of number links (starting at 1) will be displayed that allow a user to jump to a nonsequential page. Additional pager options, such as the text for next/previous buttons and the number of numeric pages displayed at a time, are available through the properties of the DataGridPagerStyle class.

```
Public Enum PagerMode
    NextPrev = 0
    NumericPages = 1
End Enum
```

Hierarchy System.Object → System.ValueType → System.Enum (System.IComparable , System.IFormattable , System.IConvertible)→ PagerMode

PagerPosition

Enum

System.Web.UI.WebControls (system.web.dll)

serializable

This enumeration specifies the alignment of the pager controls for a DataGrid within the appropriate cell. The pager controls are always placed in the last row after the data and footer.

```
Public Enum PagerPosition
    Bottom = 0
    Top = 1
    TopAndBottom = 2
End Enum
```

Hierarchy System.Object → System.ValueType → System.Enum (System.IComparable , System.IFormattable , System.IConvertible)→ PagerPosition

Panel

Class

System.Web.UI.WebControls (system.web.dll)

disposable

This class represents a Panel control, which acts as a simple container for other web controls. A panel is often used to group related controls, such as RadioButton controls that share the same RadioButton.GroupName. Panels are also used to disable or hide entire groups of controls at once, by setting the Visible or Enabled property of the containing panel. They are also useful for adding dynamically generated controls, as in Panel1.Controls.Add(New LiteralControl("<br>")).

You can set a background image for your panel by specifying a URL for the BackImageUrl property. You can also type text directly into a panel on the design-time surface in Visual Studio.NET. Use the Wrap property to set whether this content is wrapped. If it is not, the Panel is automatically extended to the required width.

```
Public Class Panel : Inherits WebControl
' Public Constructors
    Public Sub New()
' Public Instance Properties
    Overridable Public Property BackImageUrl As String
    Overridable Public Property HorizontalAlign As HorizontalAlign
    Overridable Public Property Wrap As Boolean
' Protected Instance Methods
    Overrides Protected Sub AddAttributesToRender(ByVal writer As System.Web.UI.HtmlTextWriter)
End Class
```

Hierarchy System.Object → System.Web.UI.Control (System.ComponentModel.IComponent , System.IDisposable , System.Web.UI.IParserAccessor , System.Web.UI.IDataBindingsAccessor)→ WebControl (System.Web.UI.IAttributeAccessor)→ Panel

PlaceHolder

Class

System.Web.UI.WebControls (system.web.dll)

disposable

This class represents a "placeholder" control, which is a container used to store controls that may be added to a page dynamically at some point in its processing. Placeholders prevent an HTML page from "collapsing." For example, if you create a text box control and set the TextBox.Visible property to False, no HTML will be rendered for the control. This could cause the layout of the page to change unexpectedly, particularly with tables. Placeholders avert this problem. To add a control to a placeholder, use System.Web.UI.WebControls.PlaceHolder.Controls.Add(). Note that placeholders, unlike most web controls, derive directly from System.Web.UI.Control, not WebControl.

```
Public Class PlaceHolder : Inherits System.Web.UI.Control
' Public Constructors
    Public Sub New()
End Class
```

Hierarchy   System.Object → System.Web.UI.Control (System.ComponentModel.IComponent , System.IDisposable , System.Web.UI.IParserAccessor , System.Web.UI.IDataBindingsAccessor) → PlaceHolder

PlaceHolderControlBuilder   Class

System.Web.UI.WebControls (system.web.dll)

The ASP.NET parser uses this class to generate HTML for any PlaceHolder controls on a requested Web Forms page. You will not need to use this class directly in application code.

```
Public Class PlaceHolderControlBuilder : Inherits System.Web.UI.ControlBuilder
' Public Constructors
    Public Sub New()
' Public Instance Methods
    Overrides Public Function AllowWhitespaceLiterals() As Boolean
End Class
```

Hierarchy   System.Object → System.Web.UI.ControlBuilder → PlaceHolderControlBuilder

RadioButton   Class

System.Web.UI.WebControls (system.web.dll)   *disposable*

This class represents a radio button control that allows a user to select one item from a selection of options. Each option in a group of radio buttons is a distinct RadioButton object, but each control shares the same GroupName. To determine whether a radio button has been selected, examine the Checked property. If you want to use a radio button with list data, the CheckBoxList control may be more convenient.

```
Public Class RadioButton : Inherits CheckBox
' Public Constructors
    Public Sub New()
' Public Instance Properties
    Overridable Public Property GroupName As String
' Protected Instance Methods
    Overrides Protected Sub OnPreRender(ByVal e As EventArgs)
End Class
```

Hierarchy   System.Object → System.Web.UI.Control (System.ComponentModel.IComponent , System.IDisposable , System.Web.UI.IParserAccessor , System.Web.UI.IDataBindingsAccessor) → WebControl (System.Web.UI.IAttributeAccessor) → CheckBox (System.Web.UI.IPostBackDataHandler) → RadioButton

RadioButtonList

Class

System.Web.UI.WebControls (system.web.dll)   *disposable*

This class represents a list of radio buttons that allow only a single selection. Though this class is generated out of individual radio buttons, it acts like an integrated list. For example, ASP.NET will add or remove items as needed when you bind this control to a data source. You can use RepeatDirection to specify how items will be grouped together if RepeatColumns is greater than 1. For example, if you set RepeatDirection to RepeatDirection.Vertical, and RepeatColumns to 2, the first two list items will be displayed in the first columns, the next two will be displayed on the second column, and so on. If you set RepeatDirection to RepeatDirection.Horizontal, your list will still have the same number of rows and columns, but radio button items will be filled first by column, and then by row.

Individual radio buttons are automatically grouped together in an HTML table, which you can fine-tune with the CellPadding and CellSpacing properties. Alternatively, you can set RepeatLayout to RepeatLayout.Flow to specify that an HTML table should not be used.

Most list-specific functionality, such as determining the selected item and reacting to a SelectedIndexChanged event, is provided by the ListControl class, from which RadioButtonList inherits.

```
Public Class RadioButtonList : Inherits ListControl : Implements IRepeatInfoUser, System.Web.UI.INamingContainer, _
      System.Web.UI.IPostBackDataHandler
' Public Constructors
   Public Sub New()
' Public Instance Properties
   Overridable Public Property CellPadding As Integer
   Overridable Public Property CellSpacing As Integer
   Overridable Public Property RepeatColumns As Integer
   Overridable Public Property RepeatDirection As RepeatDirection
   Overridable Public Property RepeatLayout As RepeatLayout
   Overridable Public Property TextAlign As TextAlign
' Protected Instance Methods
   Overrides Protected Function CreateControlStyle() As Style
   Overrides Protected Sub Render(ByVal writer As System.Web.UI.HtmlTextWriter)
End Class
```

Hierarchy System.Object → System.Web.UI.Control (System.ComponentModel.IComponent , System.IDisposable , System.Web.UI.IParserAccessor , System.Web.UI.IDataBindingsAccessor) → WebControl (System.Web.UI.IAttributeAccessor) → ListControl → RadioButtonList (IRepeatInfoUser , System.Web.UI.INamingContainer , System.Web.UI.IPostBackDataHandler)

RangeValidator

Class

System.Web.UI.WebControls (system.web.dll)   *disposable*

This class represents a validation control that tests to make sure the value of the input control (ControlToValidate) is equal to or between the MinimumValue and MaximumValue. All values will be converted to the data type specified by CompareValidator.Type before validation is performed. Valid data types include integer, double, date, currency, and string (which uses an alphabetic character-code based comparison).

Validation automatically succeeds if the input control is empty. To require a value, use the RequiredFieldValidator control in addition to the RangeValidator control.

```
Public Class RangeValidator : Inherits BaseCompareValidator
' Public Constructors
   Public Sub New()
```

```
' Public Instance Properties
   Public Property MaximumValue As String
   Public Property MinimumValue As String
' Protected Instance Methods
   Overrides Protected Sub AddAttributesToRender(ByVal writer As System.Web.UI.HtmlTextWriter)
   Overrides Protected Function ControlPropertiesValid() As Boolean
   Overrides Protected Function EvaluateIsValid() As Boolean
End Class
```

Hierarchy   System.Object → System.Web.UI.Control (System.ComponentModel.IComponent , System.IDisposable , System.Web.UI.IParserAccessor , System.Web.UI.IDataBindingsAccessor)→ WebControl (System.Web.UI.IAttributeAccessor)→ Label → BaseValidator (System.Web.UI.IValidator)→ BaseCompareValidator → RangeValidator

RegularExpressionValidator
Class

System.Web.UI.WebControls (system.web.dll)   *disposable*

The RegularExpressionValidator is a type of validation control that compares an input control against a pattern specified in the ValidationExpression. Regular expression validation is ideally suited for verifying predictable sequences of characters, such as those in social security numbers, email addresses, telephone numbers, and postal codes. Validation will succeed if the input control is empty, unless you also use a RequiredFieldValidator control.

Validation is always performed on the server. If the client browser supports JavaScript, validation will be performed there as well, which can save a roundtrip if errors are present. The regular expression validation performed by the JavaScript code is a subset of the full System.Text.RegularExpressions.Regex syntax.

```
Public Class RegularExpressionValidator : Inherits BaseValidator
' Public Constructors
   Public Sub New()
' Public Instance Properties
   Public Property ValidationExpression As String
' Protected Instance Methods
   Overrides Protected Sub AddAttributesToRender(ByVal writer As System.Web.UI.HtmlTextWriter)
   Overrides Protected Function EvaluateIsValid() As Boolean
End Class
```

Hierarchy   System.Object → System.Web.UI.Control (System.ComponentModel.IComponent , System.IDisposable , System.Web.UI.IParserAccessor , System.Web.UI.IDataBindingsAccessor)→ WebControl (System.Web.UI.IAttributeAccessor)→ Label → BaseValidator (System.Web.UI.IValidator)→ RegularExpressionValidator

RepeatDirection
Enum

System.Web.UI.WebControls (system.web.dll)   *serializable*

This enumeration specifies how items are organized in some list controls. It usually works in conjunction with a RepeatColumns property, which sets the dimensions of the table. For example, if you have a list with twenty elements and you set RepeatColumns to five, you automatically have four rows, regardless of what RepeatDirection you choose.

If RepeatDirection is Vertical, items are filled into columns from left to right, and then row-by-row. If you use Horizontal, the items are filled from top to bottom, and then column-by-column to satisfy the required number of columns.

```
Public Enum RepeatDirection
        Horizontal = 0
        Vertical = 1
End Enum
```

Hierarchy System.Object → System.ValueType → System.Enum (System.IComparable ,
System.IFormattable , System.IConvertible)→ RepeatDirection

Repeater   Class

System.Web.UI.WebControls (system.web.dll)   *disposable*

This class represents a special kind of data-bound list control that can contain repeating
buttons, static text, and other controls. The Repeater control requires more work than a
straightforward DataGrid or DataList control because it contains no built-in styles or layout. Instead, you must create templates for the Repeater using HTML and ASP.NET tags
in the *.aspx* file. Each template is bracketed inside the appropriate template tag (like
<ItemTemplate>). You do not set the corresponding System.Web.UI.ITemplate properties of
this class directly.

Every Repeater control requires an ItemTemplate. Additionally, an AlternatingItemTemplate can
be used to allow items to alternate between two styles. These two templates will be
bound when you use the DataBind() method. The other templates, like HeaderTemplate,
FooterTemplate, and SeparatorTemplate, will not. If the DataSource property is set but no data
is returned, only the HeaderTemplate and FooterTemplate will be rendered. If the DataSource
property is not set (it will be Nothing by default), the control is not rendered at all.

The Repeater control is unique because it allows you enter any HTML content in a template, and even split HTML tags across more than one template. To use a table in your
Repeater control, you should include the begin table tag (<table>) in the HeaderTemplate
and the end table tag (</table>) in the FooterTemplate. You can then use a single table
row tag (<tr>) in the ItemTemplate and multiple table data tags (<td>).

The Repeater has no built-in support for item selection or editing. You can include a
Button control inside an ItemTemplate, although you will have to write its tag manually,
rather than using the Visual Studio.NET designer. When the user clicks this button, a
ItemCommand event will be fired. This event provides additional information about the
selected button and list item.

```
Public Class Repeater : Inherits System.Web.UI.Control : Implements System.Web.UI.INamingContainer
' Public Constructors
    Public Sub New()
' Public Instance Properties
    Overridable Public Property AlternatingItemTemplate As ITemplate
    Overrides Public ReadOnly Property Controls As ControlCollection
    Overridable Public Property DataMember As String
    Overridable Public Property DataSource As Object
    Overridable Public Property FooterTemplate As ITemplate
    Overridable Public Property HeaderTemplate As ITemplate
    Overridable Public ReadOnly Property Items As RepeaterItemCollection
    Overridable Public Property ItemTemplate As ITemplate
    Overridable Public Property SeparatorTemplate As ITemplate
' Public Instance Methods
    Overrides Public Sub DataBind()
' Protected Instance Methods
    Overrides Protected Sub CreateChildControls()
    Overridable Protected Sub CreateControlHierarchy(ByVal useDataSource As Boolean)
```

```
    Overridable Protected Function CreateItem(ByVal itemIndex As Integer, ByVal itemType As ListItemType) _
      As RepeaterItem
    Overridable Protected Sub InitializeItem(ByVal item As RepeaterItem)
    Overrides Protected Function OnBubbleEvent(ByVal sender As Object, ByVal e As EventArgs) As Boolean
    Overrides Protected Sub OnDataBinding(ByVal e As EventArgs)
    Overridable Protected Sub OnItemCommand(ByVal e As RepeaterCommandEventArgs)
    Overridable Protected Sub OnItemCreated(ByVal e As RepeaterItemEventArgs)
    Overridable Protected Sub OnItemDataBound(ByVal e As RepeaterItemEventArgs)
  ' Events
    Public Event ItemCommand As RepeaterCommandEventHandler
    Public Event ItemCreated As RepeaterItemEventHandler
    Public Event ItemDataBound As RepeaterItemEventHandler
End Class
```

Hierarchy   System.Object → System.Web.UI.Control (System.ComponentModel.IComponent , System.IDisposable , System.Web.UI.IParserAccessor , System.Web.UI.IDataBindingsAccessor)→ Repeater (System.Web.UI.INamingContainer)

RepeaterCommandEventArgs
NotInheritable Class

System.Web.UI.WebControls (system.web.dll)

This class provides additional information for the ItemCommand event of the Repeater control, which occurs when a button in an item is clicked. This additional information consists of a Item property, which represents the repeater item where the button is located and a CommandSource property, which refers to the button in the item that fired this event. Before using the CommandSource property, you will have to cast it to the appropriate type (e.g., CType(e.CommandSource, System.Web.UI.WebControls.Button)).

It may seem that the Repeater.ItemCommand event provides more than one way to determine its source. However, these references are not equivalent. The sender parameter indicates the Repeater instance where the event took place, while the Item property specifies the item in the Repeater and the CommandSource property identifies the specific button in the item.

```
Public NotInheritable Class RepeaterCommandEventArgs : Inherits CommandEventArgs
' Public Constructors
  Public Sub New(ByVal item As RepeaterItem, ByVal commandSource As Object, _
    ByVal originalArgs As CommandEventArgs)
' Public Instance Properties
  Public ReadOnly Property CommandSource As Object
  Public ReadOnly Property Item As RepeaterItem
End Class
```

Hierarchy   System.Object → System.EventArgs → CommandEventArgs → RepeaterCommandEventArgs

RepeaterCommandEventHandler
Delegate

System.Web.UI.WebControls (system.web.dll)
serializable

This delegate specifies the parameters for the event handler routine that handles the ItemCommand event of the Repeater control. This event handler receives additional information about the item that was clicked.

```
Public Delegate Sub RepeaterCommandEventHandler(ByVal source As Object, _
  ByVal e As RepeaterCommandEventArgs)
```

RepeaterItem

Class

System.Web.UI.WebControls (system.web.dll)

disposable

This class represents an individual item in the Repeater control. You can access a RepeaterItem through the Repeater.Items collection or from a Repeater event.

RepeaterItem inherits most of its properties from System.Web.UI.Control. In addition, it provides a ItemIndex that gives its index in the Repeater.Items collection, a ItemType property that identifies what type of item this is (a header, footer, alternating row, etc.), and a DataItem property that returns the corresponding data item (such as a System.Data.DataRowView instance).

```
Public Class RepeaterItem : Inherits System.Web.UI.Control : Implements System.Web.UI.INamingContainer
' Public Constructors
   Public Sub New(ByVal itemIndex As Integer, ByVal itemType As ListItemType)
' Public Instance Properties
   Overridable Public Property DataItem As Object
   Overridable Public ReadOnly Property ItemIndex As Integer
   Overridable Public ReadOnly Property ItemType As ListItemType
' Protected Instance Methods
   Overrides Protected Function OnBubbleEvent(ByVal source As Object, ByVal e As EventArgs) As Boolean
End Class
```

Hierarchy System.Object → System.Web.UI.Control (System.ComponentModel.IComponent , System.IDisposable , System.Web.UI.IParserAccessor , System.Web.UI.IDataBindingsAccessor) → RepeaterItem (System.Web.UI.INamingContainer)

RepeaterItemCollection

NotInheritable Class

System.Web.UI.WebControls (system.web.dll)

This custom collection class contains RepeaterItem objects. It is used for the Repeater.Items property of the Repeater control.

```
Public NotInheritable Class RepeaterItemCollection : Implements ICollection, IEnumerable
' Public Constructors
   Public Sub New(ByVal items As System.Collections.ArrayList)
' Public Instance Properties
   Public ReadOnly Property Count As Integer Implements ICollection.Count
   Public ReadOnly Property IsReadOnly As Boolean
   Public ReadOnly Property IsSynchronized As Boolean Implements ICollection.IsSynchronized
   Public Default ReadOnly Property Item (ByVal index As Integer) As RepeaterItem
   Public ReadOnly Property SyncRoot As Object Implements ICollection.SyncRoot
' Public Instance Methods
   Public Sub CopyTo(ByVal array As Array, ByVal index As Integer)  Implements  ICollection.CopyTo
   Public Function GetEnumerator() As IEnumerator Implements  IEnumerable.GetEnumerator
End Class
```

RepeaterItemEventArgs

NotInheritable Class

System.Web.UI.WebControls (system.web.dll)

This class provides additional information for the ItemCreated and ItemDataBound events of the Repeater control. This additional information consists of a Item property, which represents the item that was just added to the Repeater control or bound to the data source.

```
Public NotInheritable Class RepeaterItemEventArgs : Inherits  EventArgs
' Public Constructors
   Public Sub New(ByVal item As RepeaterItem)
```

```
' Public Instance Properties
    Public ReadOnly Property Item As RepeaterItem
End Class
```

Hierarchy   System.Object → System.EventArgs → RepeaterItemEventArgs

RepeaterItemEventHandler   Delegate

System.Web.UI.WebControls (system.web.dll)   *serializable*

This delegate specifies the parameters for the event handler routine that handles the ItemCreated and ItemDataBound events of the Repeater control. This event handler receives additional information about the item that was just created or bound through the RepeaterItemEventArgs class.

```
Public Delegate Sub RepeaterItemEventHandler(ByVal sender As Object, ByVal e As RepeaterItemEventArgs)
```

RepeatInfo   NotInheritable Class

System.Web.UI.WebControls (system.web.dll)

This class includes information about how various list controls, including CheckBoxList, DataList, and RadioButtonList, should repeat their items in a list. It is used primarily by control developers.

```
Public NotInheritable Class RepeatInfo
' Public Constructors
    Public Sub New()
' Public Instance Properties
    Public Property OuterTableImplied As Boolean
    Public Property RepeatColumns As Integer
    Public Property RepeatDirection As RepeatDirection
    Public Property RepeatLayout As RepeatLayout
' Public Instance Methods
    Public Sub RenderRepeater(ByVal writer As System.Web.UI.HtmlTextWriter, ByVal user As IRepeatInfoUser, _
        ByVal controlStyle As Style, ByVal baseControl As WebControl)
End Class
```

RepeatLayout   Enum

System.Web.UI.WebControls (system.web.dll)   *serializable*

This enumeration specifies the layout of items in certain list controls. Table specifies that items are held in separate cells in a table structure, while Flow specifies that no special formatting is used.

```
Public Enum RepeatLayout
    Table = 0
    Flow = 1
End Enum
```

Hierarchy   System.Object → System.ValueType → System.Enum (System.IComparable , System.IFormattable , System.IConvertible)→ RepeatLayout

RequiredFieldValidator

Class

System.Web.UI.WebControls (system.web.dll)

disposable

This class represents a validation control that is used to force user entry in a corresponding input control, like a TextBox. Validation fails if the value in the input control does not differ from the InitialValue property. By default, InitialValue is set to System.String.Empty and validation will succeed as long as some information has been added to the input control.

You can use a combination of different validation controls for a single control. For example, you could use a RequiredFieldValidator to ensure that a value is entered and a RangeValidator to ensure that the value is within a specified data range. This is often required, as validators like RangeValidator will automatically validate a control if it is empty, regardless of the properties you have set.

Public Class **RequiredFieldValidator** : Inherits BaseValidator
' Public Constructors
   Public Sub **New**()
' Public Instance Properties
   Public Property **InitialValue** As String
' Protected Instance Methods
   Overrides Protected Sub **AddAttributesToRender**(ByVal writer As System.Web.UI.HtmlTextWriter)
   Overrides Protected Function **EvaluateIsValid**() As Boolean
End Class

Hierarchy System.Object → System.Web.UI.Control (System.ComponentModel.IComponent , System.IDisposable , System.Web.UI.IParserAccessor , System.Web.UI.IDataBindingsAccessor) → WebControl (System.Web.UI.IAttributeAccessor) → Label → BaseValidator (System.Web.UI.IValidator) → RequiredFieldValidator

SelectedDatesCollection

NotInheritable Class

System.Web.UI.WebControls (system.web.dll)

This class represents a collection of System.DateTime objects. It is used by the Selected-Dates property of the Calendar class to provide all the dates that have been selected.

The Calendar.SelectedDates property is used when the Calendar.SelectionMode property is set to either CalendarSelectionMode.DayWeek or CalendarSelectionMode.DayWeekMonth, both of which allow multiple selections (by week or month). If the Calendar.SelectionMode property is set to CalendarSelectionMode.Day, the Calendar.SelectedDate property should be used to determine the selected date instead.

Public NotInheritable Class **SelectedDatesCollection** : Implements ICollection, IEnumerable
' Public Constructors
   Public Sub **New**(ByVal dateList As System.Collections.ArrayList)
' Public Instance Properties
   Public ReadOnly Property **Count** As Integer Implements ICollection.Count
   Public ReadOnly Property **IsReadOnly** As Boolean
   Public ReadOnly Property **IsSynchronized** As Boolean Implements ICollection.IsSynchronized
   Public Default ReadOnly Property **Item** (ByVal index As Integer) As Date
   Public ReadOnly Property **SyncRoot** As Object Implements ICollection.SyncRoot
' Public Instance Methods
   Public Sub **Add**(ByVal date As Date)
   Public Sub **Clear**()
   Public Function **Contains**(ByVal date As Date) As Boolean
   Public Sub **CopyTo**(ByVal array As Array, ByVal index As Integer) Implements ICollection.CopyTo
   Public Function **GetEnumerator**() As IEnumerator Implements IEnumerable.GetEnumerator

```
   Public Sub Remove(ByVal date As Date)
   Public Sub SelectRange(ByVal fromDate As Date, ByVal toDate As Date)
End Class
```

ServerValidateEventArgs
NotInheritable Class

System.Web.UI.WebControls (system.web.dll)

This derived System.EventArgs class is used for the CustomValidator.ServerValidate event. This class provides a Value property, which specifies the value that needs to be examined, and an IsValid property, which the event handling code sets to indicate whether the value is valid (True) or invalid (False).

```
Public NotInheritable Class ServerValidateEventArgs : Inherits EventArgs
' Public Constructors
   Public Sub New(ByVal value As String, ByVal isValid As Boolean)
' Public Instance Properties
   Public Property IsValid As Boolean
   Public ReadOnly Property Value As String
End Class
```

Hierarchy   System.Object → System.EventArgs → ServerValidateEventArgs

ServerValidateEventHandler
Delegate

System.Web.UI.WebControls (system.web.dll)   *serializable*

This delegate specifies the signature an event handler method must receive the Server-Validate event of the CustomValidator control. This delegate uses a special System.EventArgs object, ServerValidateEventArgs, which passes the value that needs to be validated and allows the event handling code to specify whether validation was successful.

```
Public Delegate Sub ServerValidateEventHandler(ByVal source As Object, ByVal args As ServerValidateEventArgs)
```

Style
Class

System.Web.UI.WebControls (system.web.dll)   *marshal by reference, disposable*

This class represents style attributes that can be applied to a portion of the user interface on a web page. This class is not used by web controls or HTML controls, which allow programmatic access to style attributes through a System.Web.UI.CssStyleCollection object provided through their own Style property. Instead, the Style class is used as a base class for the TableStyle and TableItemStyle classes.

```
Public Class Style : Inherits System.ComponentModel.Component : Implements System.Web.UI.IStateManager
' Public Constructors
   Public Sub New()
   Public Sub New(ByVal bag As System.Web.UI.StateBag)
' Public Instance Properties
   Public Property BackColor As Color
   Public Property BorderColor As Color
   Public Property BorderStyle As BorderStyle
   Public Property BorderWidth As Unit
   Public Property CssClass As String
   Public ReadOnly Property Font As FontInfo
   Public Property ForeColor As Color
   Public Property Height As Unit
   Public Property Width As Unit
```

' *Protected Instance Properties*

Overridable Protected Friend Property **IsEmpty** As Boolean

Protected Property **IsTrackingViewState** As Boolean Implements IStateManager.IsTrackingViewState

Protected Friend Property **ViewState** As StateBag

' *Public Instance Methods*

Public Sub **AddAttributesToRender**(ByVal writer As System.Web.UI.HtmlTextWriter)

Overridable Public Sub **AddAttributesToRender**(ByVal writer As System.Web.UI.HtmlTextWriter, _
ByVal owner As WebControl)

Overridable Public Sub **CopyFrom**(ByVal s As Style)

Overridable Public Sub **MergeWith**(ByVal s As Style)

Overridable Public Sub **Reset**()

Overrides Public Function **ToString**() As String

' *Protected Instance Methods*

Protected Friend Sub **LoadViewState**(ByVal state As Object) Implements IStateManager.LoadViewState

Overridable Protected Friend Function **SaveViewState**() As Object Implements IStateManager.SaveViewState

Overridable Protected Friend Sub **SetBit**(ByVal bit As Integer)

Overridable Protected Friend Sub **TrackViewState**() Implements IStateManager.TrackViewState

End Class

Hierarchy System.Object → System.MarshalByRefObject → System.ComponentModel.Component (System.ComponentModel.IComponent , System.IDisposable)→ Style (System.Web.UI.IStateManager)

Table   Class

System.Web.UI.WebControls (system.web.dll)   *disposable*

This class provides a powerful object model for creating HTML tables. It is similar to, but more abstract than, the System.Web.UI.HtmlControls.HtmlTable class. It also allows ASP.NET to optimize rendering for both down-level and up-level browsers. You can use it to dynamically generate an HTML table by adding TableRow objects to the Rows collection and adding TableCell objects to each row. Note that if you create or modify a table's structure programmatically, these changes will not be preserved across postbacks and you will have to reconstruct them manually; table rows and cells are controls of their own, not properties of Table.

Most other properties for the Table class correspond to formatting options, including a background image (BackImageUrl), alignment (HorizontalAlign), gridlines (GridLines), the spacing between cells (CellSpacing), and the spacing between cell borders and content (CellPadding).

This class is often used by control developers, while the DataGrid and DataList controls are preferred for ASP.NET applications, particularly if data binding is required.

Public Class **Table** : Inherits WebControl

' *Public Constructors*

Public Sub **New**()

' *Public Instance Properties*

Overridable Public Property **BackImageUrl** As String

Overridable Public Property **CellPadding** As Integer

Overridable Public Property **CellSpacing** As Integer

Overridable Public Property **GridLines** As GridLines

Overridable Public Property **HorizontalAlign** As HorizontalAlign

Overridable Public ReadOnly Property **Rows** As TableRowCollection

* *Protected Instance Methods*

Overrides Protected Sub **AddAttributesToRender**(ByVal writer As System.Web.UI.HtmlTextWriter)

Overrides Protected Function **CreateControlCollection**() As ControlCollection

Overrides Protected Function **CreateControlStyle**() As Style
  Overrides Protected Sub **RenderContents**(ByVal writer As System.Web.UI.HtmlTextWriter)
End Class

Hierarchy   System.Object → System.Web.UI.Control (System.ComponentModel.IComponent , System.IDisposable , System.Web.UI.IParserAccessor , System.Web.UI.IDataBindingsAccessor)→ WebControl (System.Web.UI.IAttributeAccessor)→ Table

TableCell
Class

System.Web.UI.WebControls (system.web.dll)
disposable

This class represents individual table cells in a TableRow. The Text property allows you to access the content stored in the cell. Most other properties are used to fine-tune its appearance. You can set Wrap to configure whether or not the contents in a cell will wrap, and RowSpan and ColumnSpan to specify that a cell should span the specified number of columns or rows.

Public Class **TableCell** : Inherits WebControl
' *Public Constructors*
  Public Sub **New**()
' *Public Instance Properties*
  Overridable Public Property **ColumnSpan** As Integer
  Overridable Public Property **HorizontalAlign** As HorizontalAlign
  Overridable Public Property **RowSpan** As Integer
  Overridable Public Property **Text** As String
  Overridable Public Property **VerticalAlign** As VerticalAlign
  Overridable Public Property **Wrap** As Boolean
' *Protected Instance Methods*
  Overrides Protected Sub **AddAttributesToRender**(ByVal writer As System.Web.UI.HtmlTextWriter)
  Overrides Protected Sub **AddParsedSubObject**(ByVal obj As Object)
  Overrides Protected Function **CreateControlStyle**() As Style
  Overrides Protected Sub **RenderContents**(ByVal writer As System.Web.UI.HtmlTextWriter)
End Class

Hierarchy   System.Object → System.Web.UI.Control (System.ComponentModel.IComponent , System.IDisposable , System.Web.UI.IParserAccessor , System.Web.UI.IDataBindingsAccessor)→ WebControl (System.Web.UI.IAttributeAccessor)→ TableCell

TableCellCollection
NotInheritable Class

System.Web.UI.WebControls (system.web.dll)

This collection of TableCell and TableHeaderCell objects is used by the Cells property of the TableRow class.

Public NotInheritable Class **TableCellCollection** : Implements IList, ICollection , IEnumerable
' *Public Instance Properties*
  Public ReadOnly Property **Count** As Integer Implements ICollection.Count
  Public ReadOnly Property **IsReadOnly** As Boolean Implements IList.IsReadOnly
  Public ReadOnly Property **IsSynchronized** As Boolean Implements ICollection.IsSynchronized
  Public Default ReadOnly Property **Item** (ByVal index As Integer) As TableCell
  Public ReadOnly Property **SyncRoot** As Object Implements ICollection.SyncRoot
' *Public Instance Methods*
  Public Function **Add**(ByVal cell As TableCell) As Integer
  Public Sub **AddAt**(ByVal index As Integer, ByVal cell As TableCell)

```
    Public Sub AddRange(ByVal cells As TableCell())
    Public Sub Clear() Implements IList.Clear
    Public Sub CopyTo(ByVal array As Array, ByVal index As Integer) Implements ICollection.CopyTo
    Public Function GetCellIndex(ByVal cell As TableCell) As Integer
    Public Function GetEnumerator() As IEnumerator Implements IEnumerable.GetEnumerator
    Public Sub Remove(ByVal cell As TableCell)
    Public Sub RemoveAt(ByVal index As Integer) Implements IList.RemoveAt
End Class
```

TableCellControlBuilder   Class

System.Web.UI.WebControls (system.web.dll)

The ASP.NET parser uses this class to generate HTML for any TableCell controls on a requested Web Forms page. You will not need to use this class directly in application code.

```
Public Class TableCellControlBuilder : Inherits System.Web.UI.ControlBuilder
' Public Constructors
    Public Sub New()
' Public Instance Methods
    Overrides Public Function AllowWhitespaceLiterals() As Boolean
End Class
```

Hierarchy   System.Object → System.Web.UI.ControlBuilder → TableCellControlBuilder

TableHeaderCell   Class

System.Web.UI.WebControls (system.web.dll)   *disposable*

This class represents individual table header cells in a TableRow. It derives all of its properties from TableCell.

```
Public Class TableHeaderCell : Inherits TableCell
' Public Constructors
    Public Sub New()
End Class
```

Hierarchy   System.Object → System.Web.UI.Control (System.ComponentModel.IComponent , System.IDisposable , System.Web.UI.IParserAccessor , System.Web.UI.IDataBindingsAccessor) → WebControl (System.Web.UI.IAttributeAccessor) → TableCell → TableHeaderCell

TableItemStyle   Class

System.Web.UI.WebControls (system.web.dll)   *marshal by reference, disposable*

This class encapsulates the formatting for a row in a table-based control. It is used to apply formatting to headers, footers, and other items in the DataGrid and Calendar controls. It is not used for the Table control.

```
Public Class TableItemStyle : Inherits Style
' Public Constructors
    Public Sub New()
    Public Sub New(ByVal bag As System.Web.UI.StateBag)
' Public Instance Properties
    Overridable Public Property HorizontalAlign As HorizontalAlign
    Overridable Public Property VerticalAlign As VerticalAlign
    Overridable Public Property Wrap As Boolean
```

' *Public Instance Methods*

Overrides Public Sub **AddAttributesToRender**(ByVal writer As System.Web.UI.HtmlTextWriter, _
ByVal owner As WebControl)

Overrides Public Sub **CopyFrom**(ByVal s As Style)

Overrides Public Sub **MergeWith**(ByVal s As Style)

Overrides Public Sub **Reset**()

End Class

Hierarchy System.Object → System.MarshalByRefObject → System.ComponentModel.Component
(System.ComponentModel.IComponent , System.IDisposable)→ Style (
System.Web.UI.IStateManager)→ TableItemStyle

TableRow
Class

System.Web.UI.WebControls (system.web.dll)
disposable

This class represents an individual row element in a Table control. Each table row contains a group of TableCell objects, which is provided through the Cells property. Most other properties are used for fine-tuning the appearance of a row.

Public Class **TableRow** : Inherits WebControl

' *Public Constructors*

Public Sub **New**()

' *Public Instance Properties*

Overridable Public ReadOnly Property **Cells** As TableCellCollection

Overridable Public Property **HorizontalAlign** As HorizontalAlign

Overridable Public Property **VerticalAlign** As VerticalAlign

' *Protected Instance Methods*

Overrides Protected Function **CreateControlCollection**() As ControlCollection

Overrides Protected Function **CreateControlStyle**() As Style

End Class

Hierarchy System.Object → System.Web.UI.Control (System.ComponentModel.IComponent ,
System.IDisposable , System.Web.UI.IParserAccessor , System.Web.UI.IDataBindingsAccessor)→
WebControl (System.Web.UI.IAttributeAccessor)→ TableRow

TableRowCollection
NotInheritable Class

System.Web.UI.WebControls (system.web.dll)

This collection of TableRow objects is used by the Rows property of the Table class.

Public NotInheritable Class **TableRowCollection** : Implements IList, ICollection, IEnumerable

' *Public Instance Properties*

Public ReadOnly Property **Count** As Integer Implements ICollection.Count

Public ReadOnly Property **IsReadOnly** As Boolean Implements IList.IsReadOnly

Public ReadOnly Property **IsSynchronized** As Boolean Implements ICollection.IsSynchronized

Public Default ReadOnly Property **Item** (ByVal index As Integer) As TableRow

Public ReadOnly Property **SyncRoot** As Object Implements ICollection.SyncRoot

' *Public Instance Methods*

Public Function **Add**(ByVal row As TableRow) As Integer

Public Sub **AddAt**(ByVal index As Integer, ByVal row As TableRow)

Public Sub **AddRange**(ByVal rows As TableRow())

Public Sub **Clear**() Implements IList.Clear

Public Sub **CopyTo**(ByVal array As Array, ByVal index As Integer) Implements ICollection.CopyTo

Public Function **GetEnumerator**() As IEnumerator Implements IEnumerable.GetEnumerator

Public Function **GetRowIndex**(ByVal row As TableRow) As Integer
Public Sub **Remove**(ByVal row As TableRow)
Public Sub **RemoveAt**(ByVal index As Integer) Implements IList.RemoveAt
End Class

TableStyle

Class

System.Web.UI.WebControls (system.web.dll)   *marshal by reference, disposable*

The TableStyle class is primarily used by control developers. It encapsulates some the formatting options that can be applied to an HTML table. These options correspond to properties of the Table class.

Public Class **TableStyle** : Inherits Style
' Public Constructors
  Public Sub **New**()
  Public Sub **New**(ByVal bag As System.Web.UI.StateBag)
' Public Instance Properties
  Overridable Public Property **BackImageUrl** As String
  Overridable Public Property **CellPadding** As Integer
  Overridable Public Property **CellSpacing** As Integer
  Overridable Public Property **GridLines** As GridLines
  Overridable Public Property **HorizontalAlign** As HorizontalAlign
' Public Instance Methods
  Overrides Public Sub **AddAttributesToRender**(ByVal writer As System.Web.UI.HtmlTextWriter, _
    ByVal owner As WebControl)
  Overrides Public Sub **CopyFrom**(ByVal s As Style)
  Overrides Public Sub **MergeWith**(ByVal s As Style)
  Overrides Public Sub **Reset**()
End Class

Hierarchy System.Object → System.MarshalByRefObject → System.ComponentModel.Component
(System.ComponentModel.IComponent , System.IDisposable)→ Style (
System.Web.UI.IStateManager)→ TableStyle

TargetConverter

Class

System.Web.UI.WebControls (system.web.dll)

The TargetConverter class is a type converter that allows conversions between an ordinary string and the "target" string used to specify the target frame or window for a hyperlink, as in AdRotator.Target). This conversion allows the target property to be displayed in the Property Window. This class is never accessed directly. You can access its functionality through the System.ComponentModel.TypeDescriptor helper class.

Public Class **TargetConverter** : Inherits System.ComponentModel.StringConverter
' Public Constructors
  Public Sub **New**()
' Public Instance Methods
  Overrides Public Function **GetStandardValues**(_
    ByVal context As System.ComponentModel.ITypeDescriptorContext) As StandardValuesCollection
  Overrides Public Function **GetStandardValuesExclusive**(_
    ByVal context As System.ComponentModel.ITypeDescriptorContext) As Boolean
  Overrides Public Function **GetStandardValuesSupported**(_
    ByVal context As System.ComponentModel.ITypeDescriptorContext) As Boolean
End Class

Hierarchy System.Object → System.ComponentModel.TypeConverter →
System.ComponentModel.StringConverter → TargetConverter

TemplateColumn
Class

System.Web.UI.WebControls (system.web.dll)

This class represents a type of column that can be added to the DataGrid control. A TemplateColumn allows you to create fully customized output in the DataGrid by using templates. These templates are defined by using the *.aspx* (not the properties of this class), which is similar to the method used by the DataList and Repeater controls. Templates allow you to combine several different fields in a single column and add other HTML elements and ASP.NET controls.

In the TemplateColumn definition in the *.aspx* file, you can define up to four templates: HeaderTemplate, ItemTemplate, EditItemTemplate, and FooterTemplate. Inside these template definitions, you can insert data binding expressions or HTML and ASP.NET elements.

```
Public Class TemplateColumn : Inherits DataGridColumn
' Public Constructors
    Public Sub New()
' Public Instance Properties
    Overridable Public Property EditItemTemplate As ITemplate
    Overridable Public Property FooterTemplate As ITemplate
    Overridable Public Property HeaderTemplate As ITemplate
    Overridable Public Property ItemTemplate As ITemplate
' Public Instance Methods
    Overrides Public Sub InitializeCell(ByVal cell As TableCell, ByVal columnIndex As Integer, _
        ByVal itemType As ListItemType)
End Class
```

Hierarchy System.Object → DataGridColumn (System.Web.UI.IStateManager)→ TemplateColumn

TextAlign
Enum

System.Web.UI.WebControls (system.web.dll)
serializable

This enumeration is used to set the CheckBox.TextAlign and RadioButton.TextAlign properties. This value specifies whether text will be placed to the left or right of the control.

```
Public Enum TextAlign
    Left = 1
    Right = 2
End Enum
```

Hierarchy System.Object → System.ValueType → System.Enum (System.IComparable ,
System.IFormattable , System.IConvertible)→ TextAlign

TextBox
Class

System.Web.UI.WebControls (system.web.dll)
disposable

This class represents the text box web control and provides properties to configure text wrapping, the maximum accepted length, and the size in fixed character widths and row-heights (Columns and Rows). This class also includes a single event, TextChanged, which will fire only when the text box loses focus and a post back is generated.

The text box is abstracted away from any specific HTML element. Depending on your settings, ASP.NET will use the appropriate <input type="text">, <input type="password">, or <textarea> HTML tag.

```
Public Class TextBox : Inherits WebControl : Implements System.Web.UI.IPostBackDataHandler
' Public Constructors
   Public Sub New()
' Public Instance Properties
   Overridable Public Property AutoPostBack As Boolean
   Overridable Public Property Columns As Integer
   Overridable Public Property MaxLength As Integer
   Overridable Public Property ReadOnly As Boolean
   Overridable Public Property Rows As Integer
   Overridable Public Property Text As String
   Overridable Public Property TextMode As TextBoxMode
   Overridable Public Property Wrap As Boolean
' Protected Instance Properties
   Overrides Protected Property TagKey As HtmlTextWriterTag
' Protected Instance Methods
   Overrides Protected Sub AddAttributesToRender(ByVal writer As System.Web.UI.HtmlTextWriter)
   Overrides Protected Sub AddParsedSubObject(ByVal obj As Object)
   Overrides Protected Sub OnPreRender(ByVal e As EventArgs)
   Overridable Protected Sub OnTextChanged(ByVal e As EventArgs)
   Overrides Protected Sub Render(ByVal writer As System.Web.UI.HtmlTextWriter)
' Events
   Public Event TextChanged As EventHandler
End Class
```

Hierarchy System.Object → System.Web.UI.Control (System.ComponentModel.IComponent , System.IDisposable , System.Web.UI.IParserAccessor , System.Web.UI.IDataBindingsAccessor)→ WebControl (System.Web.UI.IAttributeAccessor)→ TextBox (System.Web.UI.IPostBackDataHandler)

TextBoxControlBuilder
Class

System.Web.UI.WebControls (system.web.dll)

The ASP.NET parser uses this class to generate HTML for any TextBox controls on a requested Web Forms page. You will not need to use this class directly in application code.

```
Public Class TextBoxControlBuilder : Inherits System.Web.UI.ControlBuilder
' Public Constructors
   Public Sub New()
' Public Instance Methods
   Overrides Public Function AllowWhitespaceLiterals() As Boolean
   Overrides Public Function HtmlDecodeLiterals() As Boolean
End Class
```

Hierarchy System.Object → System.Web.UI.ControlBuilder → TextBoxControlBuilder

TextBoxMode
Enum

System.Web.UI.WebControls (system.web.dll)
serializable

This enumeration is used for the TextBox.TextMode property. It allows special text box styles, including Password, where all characters will be displayed as asterisks (*) and MultiLine. MultiLine allows text on multiple lines and will automatically wrap text as it is entered (if the TextBox.Wrap property is True).

```
Public Enum TextBoxMode
    SingleLine = 0
    MultiLine = 1
    Password = 2
End Enum
```

Hierarchy System.Object → System.ValueType → System.Enum (System.IComparable , System.IFormattable , System.IConvertible) → TextBoxMode

TitleFormat

Enum

System.Web.UI.WebControls (system.web.dll)

serializable

This enumeration specifies the format used for the title of the Calendar control. Month displays the month but not the year (for example, "September"). MonthYear displays both the month and year (for example, "September 2001").

```
Public Enum TitleFormat
    Month = 0
    MonthYear = 1
End Enum
```

Hierarchy System.Object → System.ValueType → System.Enum (System.IComparable , System.IFormattable , System.IConvertible) → TitleFormat

Unit

Structure

System.Web.UI.WebControls (system.web.dll)

This class is a simple value type used to represent a specific increment of a specific unit of measurement. The Unit class combines a numeric Value property that quantifies the size with a Type property that indicates what scale of measurement is being used. Several shared (static) methods are provided to convert a value of a specific scale to a unit. For example, you can use Percentage() to convert a percentage value to a unit that has the corresponding Type set to UnitType.Percentage.

```
Public Structure Unit
' Public Constructors
    Public Sub New(ByVal value As Double)
    Public Sub New(ByVal value As Double, ByVal type As UnitType)
    Public Sub New(ByVal value As Integer)
    Public Sub New(ByVal value As String)
    Public Sub New(ByVal value As String, ByVal culture As System.Globalization.CultureInfo)
' Public Shared Fields
    public Shared ReadOnly Empty As Unit
' Public Instance Properties
    Public ReadOnly Property IsEmpty As Boolean
    Public ReadOnly Property Type As UnitType
    Public ReadOnly Property Value As Double
' Public Shared Methods
    Public Shared Function Parse(ByVal s As String) As Unit
    Public Shared Function Parse(ByVal s As String, ByVal culture As System.Globalization.CultureInfo) As Unit
    Public Shared Function Percentage(ByVal n As Double) As Unit
    Public Shared Function Pixel(ByVal n As Integer) As Unit
    Public Shared Function Point(ByVal n As Integer) As Unit
    Public Shared Boolean operator Sub !=(ByVal left As Unit, ByVal right As Unit)
```

```
    Public Shared Boolean operator Sub ==(ByVal left As Unit, ByVal right As Unit)
    Public Shared implicit operator Sub Unit(ByVal n As Integer)
' Public Instance Methods
    Overrides Public Function Equals(ByVal obj As Object) As Boolean
    Overrides Public Function GetHashCode() As Integer
    Overrides Public Function ToString() As String
    Public Function ToString(ByVal culture As System.Globalization.CultureInfo) As String
End Structure
```

Hierarchy   System.Object → System.ValueType → Unit

UnitConverter   Class

System.Web.UI.WebControls (system.web.dll)

This class provides the functionality needed to convert a Unit structure to a System.Int32 value. This class is never accessed directly. You can access its functionality through the System.ComponentModel.TypeDescriptor helper class.

```
Public Class UnitConverter : Inherits System.ComponentModel.TypeConverter
' Public Constructors
    Public Sub New()
' Public Instance Methods
    Overrides Public Function CanConvertFrom(ByVal context As System.ComponentModel.ITypeDescriptorContext, _
        ByVal sourceType As Type) As Boolean
    Overrides Public Function ConvertFrom(ByVal context As System.ComponentModel.ITypeDescriptorContext, _
        ByVal culture As System.Globalization.CultureInfo, ByVal value As Object) As Object
    Overrides Public Function ConvertTo(ByVal context As System.ComponentModel.ITypeDescriptorContext, _
        ByVal culture As System.Globalization.CultureInfo, ByVal value As Object, ByVal destinationType As Type) _
        As Object
End Class
```

Hierarchy   System.Object → System.ComponentModel.TypeConverter → UnitConverter

UnitType   Enum

System.Web.UI.WebControls (system.web.dll)   *serializable*

This enumeration is used to support different measurement units, which are used for setting various properties in controls, including WebControl.Height, WebControl.Width, and System.Web.UI.WebControls.WebControl.Font.Size.Unit.

A Point is a unit of measurement that represents 1/72 of an inch. A Pica is equivalent to 12 points. The Percentage value is relative to the parent element. An Em is relative to the height of a parent element's font (so 2 em specifies a font size that is twice as large as that of the parent). An Ex is relative to the height of the lowercase letter "x" of the parent element's font.

```
Public Enum UnitType
    Pixel = 1
    Point = 2
    Pica = 3
    Inch = 4
    Mm = 5
    Cm = 6
    Percentage = 7
```

```
        Em = 8
        Ex = 9
End Enum
```

Hierarchy System.Object → System.ValueType → System.Enum (System.IComparable , System.IFormattable , System.IConvertible)→ UnitType

ValidatedControlConverter

Class

System.Web.UI.WebControls (system.web.dll)

This class is used to provide a list of validatable controls in the property browser. It allows you to set properties like CompareValidator.ControlToValidate at design time.

```
Public Class ValidatedControlConverter : Inherits System.ComponentModel.StringConverter
' Public Constructors
    Public Sub New()
' Public Instance Methods
    Overrides Public Function GetStandardValues(
        ByVal context As System.ComponentModel.ITypeDescriptorContext) As StandardValuesCollection
    Overrides Public Function GetStandardValuesExclusive(
        ByVal context As System.ComponentModel.ITypeDescriptorContext) As Boolean
    Overrides Public Function GetStandardValuesSupported(
        ByVal context As System.ComponentModel.ITypeDescriptorContext) As Boolean
End Class
```

Hierarchy System.Object → System.ComponentModel.TypeConverter → System.ComponentModel.StringConverter → ValidatedControlConverter

ValidationCompareOperator

Enum

System.Web.UI.WebControls (system.web.dll)

serializable

This enumeration specifies the type of comparison that will be performed by a CompareValidator control. The CompareValidator control evaluates the expression ControlToValidate <Operator> ControlToCompare. (You can also substitute CompareValidator.ValueToCompare instead of CompareValidator.ControlToCompare). If the expression evaluates True, the validation result is valid.

```
Public Enum ValidationCompareOperator
        Equal = 0
        NotEqual = 1
        GreaterThan = 2
        GreaterThanEqual = 3
        LessThan = 4
        LessThanEqual = 5
        DataTypeCheck = 6
End Enum
```

Hierarchy System.Object → System.ValueType → System.Enum (System.IComparable , System.IFormattable , System.IConvertible)→ ValidationCompareOperator

ValidationDataType

System.Web.UI.WebControls (system.web.dll)   *serializable*

This enumeration specifies the data type that is used for the CompareValidator and RangeValidator controls.

```
Public Enum ValidationDataType
    String = 0
    Integer = 1
    Double = 2
    Date = 3
    Currency = 4
End Enum
```

Hierarchy   System.Object → System.ValueType → System.Enum (System.IComparable , System.IFormattable , System.IConvertible) → ValidationDataType

ValidationSummary

System.Web.UI.WebControls (system.web.dll)   *disposable*

The ValidationSummary control receives the error text messages from all validation controls on the Web Forms page and presents them in a single paragraph or list. This occurs automatically on post back, provided that the ShowSummary property is set to True. Alternatively (or in addition), you can set the ShowMessageBox property to True to display a message box with the summary when validation errors occur. This message box uses client-side JavaScript and will be provided only if the browser supports it and the EnableClientScript property is set to True. You can also add a title to the summary by using the HeaderText property.

```
Public Class ValidationSummary : Inherits WebControl
' Public Constructors
    Public Sub New()
' Public Instance Properties
    Public Property DisplayMode As ValidationSummaryDisplayMode
    Public Property EnableClientScript As Boolean
    Overrides Public Property ForeColor As Color
    Public Property HeaderText As String
    Public Property ShowMessageBox As Boolean
    Public Property ShowSummary As Boolean
' Protected Instance Methods
    Overrides Protected Sub AddAttributesToRender(ByVal writer As System.Web.UI.HtmlTextWriter)
    Overrides Protected Sub OnPreRender(ByVal e As EventArgs)
    Overrides Protected Sub Render(ByVal writer As System.Web.UI.HtmlTextWriter)
End Class
```

Hierarchy   System.Object → System.Web.UI.Control (System.ComponentModel.IComponent , System.IDisposable , System.Web.UI.IParserAccessor , System.Web.UI.IDataBindingsAccessor) → WebControl (System.Web.UI.IAttributeAccessor) → ValidationSummary

ValidationSummaryDisplayMode

System.Web.UI.WebControls (system.web.dll)   *serializable*

This enumeration specifies the way that a ValidationSummary control will display error messages—either as a combined SingleParagraph, as a List, or as a BulletList.

```
Public Enum ValidationSummaryDisplayMode
    List = 0
    BulletList = 1
    SingleParagraph = 2
End Enum
```

Hierarchy   System.Object → System.ValueType → System.Enum (System.IComparable , System.IFormattable , System.IConvertible) → ValidationSummaryDisplayMode

ValidatorDisplay

Enum

System.Web.UI.WebControls (system.web.dll)

serializable

This enumeration is used to specify how a validation control should display error messages. Static instructs ASP.NET to reserve space on your Web Forms page for a validation control so that the page layout won't change when an error message is displayed. Dynamic specifies that you want to dynamically add the error message to the page. It means that several validation controls can share the same place on the page and that the page layout may change when an error message is displayed (unless you have enclosed the validator in an HTML element that is large enough to accommodate its maximum size).

This enumeration does not affect the display of the error message in a ValidationSummary control.

```
Public Enum ValidatorDisplay
    None = 0
    Static = 1
    Dynamic = 2
End Enum
```

Hierarchy   System.Object → System.ValueType → System.Enum (System.IComparable , System.IFormattable , System.IConvertible) → ValidatorDisplay

VerticalAlign

Enum

System.Web.UI.WebControls (system.web.dll)

serializable

This enumeration allows you to align an object or text along the vertical axis. It is used in TableRow and TableCell controls.

```
Public Enum VerticalAlign
    NotSet = 0
    Top = 1
    Middle = 2
    Bottom = 3
End Enum
```

Hierarchy   System.Object → System.ValueType → System.Enum (System.IComparable , System.IFormattable , System.IConvertible) → VerticalAlign

WebColorConverter **Class**

System.Web.UI.WebControls (system.web.dll)

The WebColorConverter class is a type converter that allows control color properties to be converted from one data type to another. This allows color value to be displayed in the property browser. This class is never accessed directly; you can access its functionality through the System.ComponentModel.TypeDescriptor helper class.

```
Public Class WebColorConverter : Inherits System.Drawing.ColorConverter
' Public Constructors
   Public Sub New()
' Public Instance Methods
   Overrides Public Function ConvertFrom(ByVal context As System.ComponentModel.ITypeDescriptorContext, _
      ByVal culture As System.Globalization.CultureInfo, ByVal value As Object) As Object
   Overrides Public Function ConvertTo(ByVal context As System.ComponentModel.ITypeDescriptorContext, _
      ByVal culture As System.Globalization.CultureInfo, ByVal value As Object, ByVal destinationType As Type) _
         As Object
End Class
```

Hierarchy System.Object → System.ComponentModel.TypeConverter → System.Drawing.ColorConverter → WebColorConverter

WebControl **Class**

System.Web.UI.WebControls (system.web.dll) *disposable*

This class is the base class for all web controls. The WebControl class derives much of its basic functionality from System.Web.UI.Control, including functionality for data binding and using view state. The WebControl class adds additional user-interface specific members for configuring the control's appearance—including a collection of CSS attributes (Style), color options (BackColor and ForeColor), a shortcut key (AccessKey), and various border style, font, and dimension properties. One interesting property that is specific to web controls is CssClass, which sets the Cascading Style Sheet class applied to the control. This is rendered as the class attribute in HTML (for example, <input type=text class="class1" style="ForeColor:red">). Some properties, such as AccessKey, may not be supported on down-level browsers.

All methods and the TagName, TagKey, Attributes, and Style properties are provided for developers to use or override in custom web controls. If you want to create a server control that renders user interface (HTML), you should extend one of the web control classes or inherit directly from WebControl rather than the more basic System.Web.UI.Control class. You should override the RenderContents() method, which provides a System.Web.UI.HtmlTextWriter for generating output. You do not need to manually output style attributes (or the basic HTML tag, if you have supplied it to the base WebControl constructor), as the WebControl class will handle these details automatically. Alternatively, you can override Render() for more fine-grained control. You may also want to implement the interfaces System.Web.UI.IPostBackDataHandler and System.Web.UI.IPostBackEventHandler to allow the control to retrieve postback data and fire events on postback.

```
Public Class WebControl : Inherits System.Web.UI.Control : Implements System.Web.UI.IAttributeAccessor
' Public Constructors
   Public Sub New(ByVal tag As System.Web.UI.HtmlTextWriterTag)
' Protected Constructors
   Protected Sub New()
   Protected Sub New(ByVal tag As String)
' Public Instance Properties
   Overridable Public Property AccessKey As String
```

```
    Public ReadOnly Property Attributes As AttributeCollection
    Overridable Public Property BackColor As Color
    Overridable Public Property BorderColor As Color
    Overridable Public Property BorderStyle As BorderStyle
    Overridable Public Property BorderWidth As Unit
    Public ReadOnly Property ControlStyle As Style
    Public ReadOnly Property ControlStyleCreated As Boolean
    Overridable Public Property CssClass As String
    Overridable Public Property Enabled As Boolean
    Overridable Public ReadOnly Property Font As FontInfo
    Overridable Public Property ForeColor As Color
    Overridable Public Property Height As Unit
    Public ReadOnly Property Style As CssStyleCollection
    Overridable Public Property TabIndex As Short
    Overridable Public Property ToolTip As String
    Overridable Public Property Width As Unit
' Protected Instance Properties
    Overridable Protected Property TagKey As HtmlTextWriterTag
    Overridable Protected Property TagName As String
' Public Instance Methods
    Public Sub ApplyStyle(ByVal s As Style)
    Public Sub CopyBaseAttributes(ByVal controlSrc As WebControl)
    Public Sub MergeStyle(ByVal s As Style)
    Overridable Public Sub RenderBeginTag(ByVal writer As System.Web.UI.HtmlTextWriter)
    Overridable Public Sub RenderEndTag(ByVal writer As System.Web.UI.HtmlTextWriter)
' Protected Instance Methods
    Overridable Protected Sub AddAttributesToRender(ByVal writer As System.Web.UI.HtmlTextWriter)
    Overridable Protected Function CreateControlStyle() As Style
    Overrides Protected Sub LoadViewState(ByVal savedState As Object)
    Overrides Protected Sub Render(ByVal writer As System.Web.UI.HtmlTextWriter)
    Overridable Protected Sub RenderContents(ByVal writer As System.Web.UI.HtmlTextWriter)
    Overrides Protected Function SaveViewState() As Object
    Overrides Protected Sub TrackViewState()
End Class
```

Hierarchy System.Object → System.Web.UI.Control (System.ComponentModel.IComponent , System.IDisposable , System.Web.UI.IParserAccessor , System.Web.UI.IDataBindingsAccessor)→ WebControl (System.Web.UI.IAttributeAccessor)

Xml

Class

System.Web.UI.WebControls (system.web.dll)

disposable

The Xml control is used to display an XML document on your Web Forms page. To specify the XML document, set the Document property to a System.Xml.XmlDocument object, set the DocumentContent property to a string containing XML content, or set the DocumentSource property with a string specifying a filename. If you set more than one property, the most recent one will take effect.

Optionally, you can specify an XSL Transform document, which will format the XML document before it is displayed. To specify an XSL Transform document, set the Transform property to a System.Xml.Xsl.XslTransform object or set the TransformSource property with a string specifying a filename for the XSL file.

```
Public Class Xml : Inherits System.Web.UI.Control
' Public Constructors
    Public Sub New()
```

' *Public Instance Properties*

Public Property **Document** As XmlDocument

Public Property **DocumentContent** As String

Public Property **DocumentSource** As String

Public Property **Transform** As XslTransform

Public Property **TransformArgumentList** As XsltArgumentList

Public Property **TransformSource** As String

' *Protected Instance Methods*

Overrides Protected Sub **AddParsedSubObject**(ByVal obj As Object)

Overrides Protected Sub **Render**(ByVal output As System.Web.UI.HtmlTextWriter)

End Class

Hierarchy   System.Object → System.Web.UI.Control (System.ComponentModel.IComponent , System.IDisposable , System.Web.UI.IParserAccessor , System.Web.UI.IDataBindingsAccessor) → Xml

APPENDIX

Type, Method, Property, Event, and Field Index

Use this index to look up a type or member and see where it is defined. For a type (a class or interface), you can find the enclosing namespace. If you know the name of a member (a method, property, event, or field), you can find all the types that define it.

RegularExpressionValidator, RequiredFieldValidator, Style, Table, TableCell, TableItemStyle, TableStyle, TextBox, ValidationSummary, WebControl

AddCacheItemDependencies(): HttpResponse
AddCacheItemDependency(): HttpResponse
AddError(): HttpContext
AddExtensionWarningComments(): ProtocolImporter
AddFileDependencies(): HttpResponse
AddFileDependency(): HttpResponse
AddHeader(): HttpResponse
AdditionalInformation: DiscoveryClientProtocol
AddOnAcquireRequestStateAsync(): HttpApplication
AddOnAuthenticateRequestAsync(): HttpApplication
AddOnAuthorizeRequestAsync(): HttpApplication
AddOnBeginRequestAsync(): HttpApplication
AddOnEndRequestAsync(): HttpApplication
AddOnPostRequestHandlerExecuteAsync(): HttpApplication
AddOnPreRequestHandlerExecuteAsync(): HttpApplication
AddOnReleaseRequestStateAsync(): HttpApplication
AddOnResolveRequestCacheAsync(): HttpApplication
AddOnUpdateRequestCacheAsync(): HttpApplication
AddParsedSubObject(): BaseDataList, Control, HtmlSelect, HtmlTextArea, HyperLink, IParserAccessor, Label, LinkButton, Literal, TableCell, TextBox, Xml
AddRange(): ListItemCollection, TableCellCollection, TableRowCollection
Address: HtmlTextWriterTag, SoapBinding
AddServiceDescription(): ServiceDescriptionImporter
AddStyleAttribute(): HtmlTextWriter
AddToCache(): WebClientProtocol
AddValidationCallback(): HttpCachePolicy
AdProperties: AdCreatedEventArgs
AdRotator: System.Web.UI.WebControls
AdRotatorDesigner: System.Web.UI.Design.WebControls
AdvertisementFile: AdRotator
AfterDeserialize: SoapMessageStage
AfterSerialize: SoapMessageStage
Age: ProcessInfo
Align: HtmlImage, HtmlInputImage, HtmlTable, HtmlTableCell, HtmlTableRow, HtmlTextWriterAttribute
Alive: ProcessStatus
All: FormsProtectionEnum
AllCaches: HttpCacheRevalidation
AllErrors: HttpContext
AllKeys: HttpApplicationState, HttpCookieCollection, HttpFileCollection, HttpModuleCollection
AllowAutoRedirect: HttpWebClientProtocol
AllowCustomPaging: DataGrid, PagedDataSource
AllowElements: XmlFormatExtensionPointAttribute
AllowPaging: DataGrid, PagedDataSource
AllowResize: ControlDesigner, DataListDesigner, UserControlDesigner

AllowSorting: DataGrid
AllowWhitespaceLiterals(): ControlBuilder, HyperLinkControlBuilder, LabelControlBuilder, LinkButtonControlBuilder, ListItemControlBuilder, LiteralControlBuilder, PlaceHolderControlBuilder, TableCellControlBuilder, TextBoxControlBuilder
Alt: HtmlImage, HtmlInputImage, HtmlTextWriterAttribute
AlternateText: AdCreatedEventArgs, Image
AlternatingItem: ListItemType
AlternatingItemStyle: DataGrid, DataList
AlternatingItemTemplate: DataList, Repeater
Any: OutputCacheLocation
AnyReturnReader: System.Web.Services.Protocols
AOL: HttpBrowserCapabilities
AppDomainAppId: HttpRuntime
AppDomainAppPath: HttpRuntime
AppDomainAppVirtualPath: HttpRuntime
AppDomainFactory: System.Web.Hosting
AppDomainId: HttpRuntime
AppendCacheExtension(): HttpCachePolicy
AppendCookie(): HttpResponse
AppendHeader(): HttpResponse
AppendLiteralString(): ControlBuilder, ObjectTagBuilder
AppendSubBuilder(): ControlBuilder, LiteralControlBuilder, ObjectTagBuilder
AppendToLog(): HttpResponse
Application: HttpApplication, HttpContext, Page, UserControl, WebService
ApplicationHost: System.Web.Hosting
ApplicationInstance: HttpContext
ApplicationPath: HttpRequest
ApplyAppPathModifier(): HttpResponse
ApplyStyle(): WebControl
Area: HtmlTextWriterTag
AspCompatBeginProcessRequest(): Page
AspCompatEndProcessRequest(): Page
AspInstallDirectory: HttpRuntime
AsUnit: FontSize
Async: LogicalMethodTypes
AsyncCallbackParameter: LogicalMethodInfo
AsyncResultParameter: LogicalMethodInfo
AsyncState: WebClientAsyncResult
AsyncStateParameter: LogicalMethodInfo
AsyncWaitHandle: WebClientAsyncResult
Attachments: MailMessage
Attribute: PersistenceMode, PersistenceModeAttribute
AttributeCollection: System.Web.UI
Attributes: HtmlControl, ListItem, UserControl, WebControl
Authenticate: DefaultAuthenticationModule, FormsAuthenticationModule, PassportAuthenticationModule, WindowsAuthenticationModule
Authenticate(): FormsAuthentication
AuthenticateRequest: HttpApplication

AuthenticationMode: System.Web.Configuration
AuthenticationType: FormsIdentity, PassportIdentity
AuthorizeRequest: HttpApplication
AuthUrl(): PassportIdentity
AuthUrl2(): PassportIdentity
AutoGenerateColumns: DataGrid
AutoPostBack: CheckBox, ListControl, TextBox

B

B: HtmlTextWriterTag
BackColor: Style, WebControl
Background: HtmlTextWriterAttribute
BackgroundColor: HtmlTextWriterStyle
BackgroundImage: HtmlTextWriterStyle
BackgroundSounds: HttpBrowserCapabilities
BackImageUrl: DataGrid, Panel, Table, TableStyle
Bare: SoapParameterStyle
Base: HtmlTextWriterTag
Base64: MailEncoding
BaseCompareValidator: System.Web.UI.WebControls
BaseDataList: System.Web.UI.WebControls
BaseDataListComponentEditor: System.Web.UI.Design.WebControls
BaseDataListDesigner: System.Web.UI.Design.WebControls
Basefont: HtmlTextWriterTag
Baseline: ImageAlign
BaseParser: System.Web.UI
BasePartialCachingControl: System.Web.UI
BaseValidator: System.Web.UI.WebControls
BaseValidatorDesigner: System.Web.UI.Design.WebControls
Bcc: MailMessage
Bdo: HtmlTextWriterTag
BeforeDeserialize: SoapMessageStage
BeforeDoneWithSession: HttpContext
BeforeSerialize: SoapMessageStage
BeginClass(): ProtocolImporter, ProtocolReflector, SoapProtocolImporter
BeginEventHandler: System.Web
BeginInvoke(): AdCreatedEventHandler, BeginEventHandler, BuildMethod, BuildTemplateMethod, CacheItemRemovedCallback, CommandEventHandler, DataGridCommandEventHandler, DataGridItemEventHandler, DataGridPageChangedEventHandler, DataGridSortCommandEventHandler, DataListCommandEventHandler, DataListItemEventHandler, DayRenderEventHandler, DefaultAuthenticationEventHandler, EndEventHandler, EndOfSendNotification, FormsAuthenticationEventHandler, HttpCacheValidateHandler, HttpSimpleClientProtocol, ImageClickEventHandler, LogicalMethodInfo, MonthChangedEventHandler,
PassportAuthenticationEventHandler, RenderMethod, RepeaterCommandEventHandler, RepeaterItemEventHandler, ServerValidateEventHandler, SoapHttpClientProtocol, WindowsAuthenticationEventHandler
BeginMethodInfo: LogicalMethodInfo
BeginNamespace(): ProtocolImporter, SoapProtocolImporter
BeginProcessRequest(): IHttpAsyncHandler
BeginRequest: HttpApplication
Behavior: HtmlControlDesigner
BelowNormal: CacheItemPriority
Beta: HttpBrowserCapabilities
Bgcolor: HtmlTextWriterAttribute
BgColor: HtmlTable, HtmlTableCell, HtmlTableRow
Bgsound: HtmlTextWriterTag
Big: HtmlTextWriterTag
BinaryIssuer: HttpClientCertificate
BinaryRead(): HttpRequest
BinaryWrite(): HttpResponse
Binding: OperationBinding, Port, ProtocolImporter, ProtocolReflector, SoapBinding, SoapDocumentMethodAttribute, SoapRpcMethodAttribute, System.Web.Services.Description
BindingCollection: System.Web.Services.Description
BindingContainer: Control
Bindings: ServiceDescription
BinDirectory: HttpRuntime
Blockquote: HtmlTextWriterTag
Body: HtmlTextWriterTag, MailMessage
BodyEncoding: MailMessage
BodyFormat: MailMessage
Bold: FontInfo
Border: HtmlImage, HtmlInputImage, HtmlTable, HtmlTextWriterAttribute
BorderCollapse: HtmlTextWriterStyle
Bordercolor: HtmlTextWriterAttribute
BorderColor: DropDownList, HtmlTable, HtmlTableCell, HtmlTableRow, HtmlTextWriterStyle, ListBox, Style, WebControl
BorderStyle: DropDownList, HtmlTextWriterStyle, ListBox, Style, System.Web.UI.WebControls, WebControl
BorderWidth: DropDownList, HtmlTextWriterStyle, ListBox, Style, WebControl
Both: GridLines
Bottom: ImageAlign, PagerPosition, VerticalAlign
BoundColumn: System.Web.UI.WebControls
Br: HtmlTextWriterTag
Browser: HttpBrowserCapabilities, HttpRequest
Buffer: HttpResponse
BufferOutput: HttpResponse
BufferResponse: WebMethodAttribute
BuildCachedControl(): StaticPartialCachingControl
BuildColor(): ColorBuilder, IWebFormsBuilderUIService
BuilderType: ControlBuilderAttribute

BuildMethod: System.Web.UI
BuildProfileTree(): Control
BuildTemplateMethod: System.Web.UI
BuildUrl(): IWebFormsBuilderUIService, UrlBuilder
BulletList: ValidationSummaryDisplayMode
Button: HtmlTextWriterTag, System.Web.UI.WebControls
ButtonColumn: System.Web.UI.WebControls
ButtonColumnType: System.Web.UI.WebControls
ButtonDesigner: System.Web.UI.Design.WebControls
ButtonType: ButtonColumn, EditCommandColumn

C

Cache: HttpContext, HttpResponse, HttpRuntime, Page, System.Web.Caching, UserControl
CacheControl: HttpResponse
CachedControl: PartialCachingControl
CacheDependency: System.Web.Caching
CacheDuration: WebMethodAttribute
CacheItemPriority: System.Web.Caching
CacheItemRemovedCallback: System.Web.Caching
CacheItemRemovedReason: System.Web.Caching
Calendar: System.Web.UI.WebControls
CalendarAutoFormatDialog: System.Web.UI.Design.WebControls
CalendarDataBindingHandler: System.Web.UI.Design
CalendarDay: System.Web.UI.WebControls
CalendarDesigner: System.Web.UI.Design.WebControls
CalendarSelectionMode: System.Web.UI.WebControls
CancelCommand: DataGrid, DataList
CancelCommandName: DataGrid, DataList
CancelText: EditCommandColumn
CanConvert(): BaseCompareValidator
CanConvertFrom(): DataFieldConverter, DataMember-Converter, DataSourceConverter, FontNamesConverter, FontUnitConverter, UnitConverter
CanEnterTemplateMode: TemplatedControlDesigner
CanRead(): DiscoveryDocument, ServiceDescription
CanSelectMultipleInstances(): ListItemsCollectionEditor, TableCellsCollectionEditor, TableRowsCollectionEditor
Capacity: ListItemCollection
Caption: HtmlTextWriterTag
Capture: MatchAttribute, MimeTextMatch
CausesValidation: Button, HtmlButton, HtmlInputButton, HtmlInputImage, ImageButton, LinkButton
Cc: MailMessage
CDF: HttpBrowserCapabilities
Cell: DayRenderEventArgs
Cellpadding: HtmlTextWriterAttribute
CellPadding: BaseDataList, Calendar, CheckBoxList, HtmlTable, RadioButtonList, Table, TableStyle
Cells: HtmlTableRow, TableRow
Cellspacing: HtmlTextWriterAttribute
CellSpacing: BaseDataList, Calendar, CheckBoxList,

HtmlTable, RadioButtonList, Table, TableStyle
Center: HorizontalAlign, HtmlTextWriterTag
CertEncoding: HttpClientCertificate
Certificate: HttpClientCertificate
ChainStream(): SoapExtension
Changed: CacheDependency
Charset: HttpResponse
CheckBox: System.Web.UI.WebControls
CheckBoxDesigner: System.Web.UI.Design.WebControls
CheckBoxList: System.Web.UI.WebControls
CheckControlValidationProperty(): BaseValidator
Checked: CheckBox, HtmlInputCheckBox, HtmlInputRadioButton, HtmlTextWriterAttribute
CheckedChanged: CheckBox
ChildrenAsProperties: ParseChildrenAttribute
Cite: HtmlTextWriterTag
Class: HtmlTextWriterAttribute
ClassName: ProtocolImporter
ClassNames: ProtocolImporter
Clear: FormsAuthPasswordFormat
Clear(): AttributeCollection, ControlCollection, CssStyleCollection, DataBindingCollection, DataGridColumnCollection, HtmlTableCellCollection, HtmlTableRowCollection, HttpApplicationState, HttpCookieCollection, HttpResponse, HttpSessionState, ListItemCollection, SelectedDatesCollection, StateBag, TableCellCollection, TableRowCollection
ClearChildViewState(): Control
ClearContent(): HttpResponse
ClearError(): HttpContext, HttpServerUtility
ClearHeaders(): HttpResponse
ClearSelection(): HtmlSelect, ListControl
Click: Button, ImageButton, LinkButton
Client: OutputCacheLocation, ServiceDescriptionImportStyle, SoapClientMessage
ClientCertificate: HttpRequest
ClientCertificates: HttpWebClientProtocol
ClientFaultCode: SoapException
ClientID: Control
ClientProtocol: DiscoveryReference
ClientTarget: Page
ClientValidationFunction: CustomValidator
Close(): HtmlTextWriter, HttpResponse, HttpRuntime, HttpWriter, ITemplateEditingFrame
CloseConnection(): HttpWorkerRequest
CloseControl(): ControlBuilder
ClrInstallDirectory: HttpRuntime
ClrVersion: HttpBrowserCapabilities
Cm: UnitType
cmdHelp_Click(): RegexEditorDialog
cmdOK_Click(): RegexEditorDialog
cmdTestValidate_Click(): RegexEditorDialog
Code: HtmlTextWriterTag, SoapException
CodegenDir: HttpRuntime

CodeNamespace: ProtocolImporter
CodePage: HttpSessionState
CodeTypeDeclaration: ProtocolImporter
Col: HtmlTextWriterTag
Colgroup: HtmlTextWriterTag
Color: HtmlTextWriterStyle
ColorBuilder: System.Web.UI.Design
Cols: HtmlTextArea, HtmlTextWriterAttribute
Colspan: HtmlTextWriterAttribute
ColSpan: HtmlTableCell
Columns: DataGrid, TextBox
ColumnSpan: TableCell
Command: Button, ImageButton, LinkButton
CommandArgument: Button, CommandEventArgs, Image-
  Button, LinkButton
CommandEventArgs: System.Web.UI.WebControls
CommandEventHandler: System.Web.UI.WebControls
CommandName: Button, ButtonColumn, CommandEven-
  tArgs, ImageButton, LinkButton
CommandSource: DataGridCommandEventArgs, Data-
  GridPageChangedEventArgs, DataGridSortCommandE-
  ventArgs, DataListCommandEventArgs,
  RepeaterCommandEventArgs
CommitTransaction: TemplateControl
Compare(): BaseCompareValidator
CompareValidator: System.Web.UI.WebControls
CompiledTemplateBuilder: System.Web.UI
CompileIntoType(): PageParser, TemplateParser
CompletedSynchronously: WebClientAsyncResult
CompleteRequest(): HttpApplication
Compress(): PassportIdentity
ConcreteSchemas: ProtocolImporter
ConnectionGroupName: WebClientProtocol
Construct(): TemplateControl
ConstructorNeedsTagAttribute: System.Web.UI
ContainerType: TemplateContainerAttribute
Contains(): BindingCollection, ControlCollection, Discov-
  eryClientDocumentCollection, DiscoveryClientRefer-
  enceCollection, DiscoveryClientResultCollection,
  DiscoveryExceptionDictionary, DiscoveryReferenceCol-
  lection, FaultBindingCollection, ImportCollection, Lis-
  tItemCollection, MessageCollection,
  MessagePartCollection, MimePartCollection, Mime-
  TextMatchCollection, OperationBindingCollection,
  OperationCollection, OperationFaultCollection, Oper-
  ationMessageCollection, PortCollection, PortTypeCol-
  lection, SelectedDatesCollection, ServiceCollection,
  ServiceDescriptionCollection, ServiceDescriptionFor-
  matExtensionCollection, SoapHeaderCollection, Val-
  idatorCollection
ContentEncoding: HttpRequest, HttpResponse
ContentLength: HttpPostedFile, HttpRequest
Contents: HttpApplicationState, HttpSessionState
ContentType: HttpPostedFile, HttpRequest,

HttpResponse, SoapMessage
Context: DefaultAuthenticationEventArgs, FormsAuthenti-
  cationEventArgs, HttpApplication, PassportAuthenti-
  cationEventArgs, WebService,
  WindowsAuthenticationEventArgs
Contract: ContractReference
ContractReference: System.Web.Services.Discovery
ContractSearchPattern: System.Web.Services.Discovery
Control: System.Web.UI
ControlBuilder: System.Web.UI
ControlBuilderAttribute: System.Web.UI
ControlCollection: System.Web.UI
ControlDesigner: System.Web.UI.Design
ControlParser: System.Web.UI.Design
ControlPersister: System.Web.UI.Design
ControlPropertiesValid(): BaseValidator, CompareValida-
  tor, CustomValidator, RangeValidator
Controls: BaseDataList, Control, Repeater
ControlStyle: ITemplateEditingFrame, WebControl
ControlStyleCreated: WebControl
ControlToCompare: CompareValidator
ControlToValidate: BaseValidator
ControlType: ControlBuilder
Convert(): BaseCompareValidator
ConvertFrom(): DataFieldConverter, DataMemberCon-
  verter, DataSourceConverter, FontNamesConverter,
  FontUnitConverter, UnitConverter, WebColorConverter
ConvertTo(): DataBindingCollectionConverter, Font-
  NamesConverter, FontUnitConverter, UnitConverter,
  WebColorConverter
ConvertValue(): ObjectConverter
Cookie: HttpClientCertificate
CookieContainer: HttpWebClientProtocol
CookiePath: FormsAuthenticationTicket
Cookies: HttpBrowserCapabilities, HttpRequest, HttpRe-
  sponse
CopyBaseAttributes(): WebControl
CopyFrom(): DataGridPagerStyle, FontInfo, Style, TableIt-
  emStyle, TableStyle
CopyTo(): BindingCollection, ControlCollection, DataBind-
  ingCollection, DataGridColumnCollection, Data-
  GridItemCollection, DataKeyCollection,
  DataListItemCollection, FaultBindingCollection,
  HtmlTableCellCollection, HtmlTableRowCollection,
  HttpCookieCollection, HttpFileCollection, HttpMod-
  uleCollection, HttpSessionState, HttpStaticOb-
  jectsCollection, ImportCollection, ListItemCollection,
  MessageCollection, MessagePartCollection,
  MimePartCollection, MimeTextMatchCollection, Oper-
  ationBindingCollection, OperationCollection, Opera-
  tionFaultCollection, OperationMessageCollection,
  PagedDataSource, PortCollection, PortTypeCollection,
  RepeaterItemCollection, SelectedDatesCollection,
  ServiceCollection, ServiceDescriptionCollection,

ServiceDescriptionFormatExtensionCollection, Soap-HeaderCollection, TableCellCollection, TableRowCollection, ValidatorCollection

Count: AttributeCollection, Cache, ControlCollection, CssStyleCollection, DataBindingCollection, DataGridColumnCollection, DataGridItemCollection, DataKeyCollection, DataListItemCollection, HtmlTableCellCollection, HtmlTableRowCollection, HttpApplicationState, HttpSessionState, HttpStaticObjectsCollection, ListItemCollection, PagedDataSource, RepeaterItemCollection, SelectedDatesCollection, StateBag, TableCellCollection, TableRowCollection, ValidatorCollection

Crawler: HttpBrowserCapabilities

Create(): AppDomainFactory, IAppDomainFactory, LogicalMethodInfo

CreateApplicationHost(): ApplicationHost

CreateBuilderFromType(): ControlBuilder

CreateChildControls(): BaseDataList, Control, Repeater

CreateColumnSet(): DataGrid

CreateComponentsCore(): WebControlToolboxItem

CreateControlCollection(): AdRotator, Calendar, Control, DataBoundLiteralControl, DesignerDataBoundLiteralControl, DropDownList, HtmlContainerControl, HtmlControl, HtmlSelect, HtmlTable, HtmlTableRow, Literal, LiteralControl, Table, TableRow

CreateControlHierarchy(): BaseDataList, DataGrid, DataList, Repeater

CreateControlStyle(): CheckBoxList, DataGrid, DataList, DataListItem, RadioButtonList, Table, TableCell, TableRow, WebControl

CreateDiscardableUndoUnit(): IWebFormsDocumentService

CreateDummyDataTable(): DesignTimeData

CreateFrame(): ITemplateEditingService, TemplateEditingService

CreateFromLastError(): HttpException

CreateHtmlTextWriter(): Page

CreateInstance(): MimeFormatter, TableCellsCollectionEditor, TableRowsCollectionEditor

CreateItem(): DataGrid, DataList, Repeater

CreateObject(): HttpServerUtility

CreateObjectFromClsid(): HttpServerUtility

CreatePlaceHolderDesignTimeHtml(): ControlDesigner

CreateResourceBasedLiteralControl(): TemplateControl

CreateSampleDataTable(): DesignTimeData

CreateTemplateEditingFrame(): DataGridDesigner, DataListDesigner, TemplatedControlDesigner

Credentials: WebClientProtocol

CryptIsValid(): PassportIdentity

CryptPutHost(): PassportIdentity

CryptPutSite(): PassportIdentity

CssClass: Style, WebControl

CssStyle: AttributeCollection

CssStyleCollection: System.Web.UI

Currency: ValidationDataType

Current: HttpContext

CurrentExecutionFilePath: HttpRequest

CurrentPageIndex: DataGrid, PagedDataSource

CustomAttributeProvider: LogicalMethodInfo

CustomText: NextPrevFormat

CustomValidator: System.Web.UI.WebControls

D

Dashed: BorderStyle

Data: ToolboxDataAttribute

DataBind(): BaseDataList, Control, Repeater

DataBindControl(): CalendarDataBindingHandler, DataBindingHandler, HyperLinkDataBindingHandler, ListControlDataBindingHandler, TextDataBindingHandler

DataBinder: System.Web.UI

DataBinding: Control, System.Web.UI

DataBindingCollection: System.Web.UI

DataBindingCollectionConverter: System.Web.UI.Design

DataBindingCollectionEditor: System.Web.UI.Design

DataBindingHandler: DesignTimeData, DesignTimeParseData, System.Web.UI.Design

DataBindingHandlerAttribute: System.Web.UI

DataBindings: HtmlControlDesigner, IDataBindingsAccessor

DataBindingValueUIHandler: System.Web.UI.Design

DataBoundLiteralControl: System.Web.UI

DataField: BoundColumn

DataFieldConverter: System.Web.UI.Design

DataFormatString: BoundColumn

DataGrid: System.Web.UI.WebControls

DataGridColumn: System.Web.UI.WebControls

DataGridColumnCollection: System.Web.UI.WebControls

DataGridColumnCollectionEditor: System.Web.UI.Design.WebControls

DataGridCommandEventArgs: System.Web.UI.WebControls

DataGridCommandEventHandler: System.Web.UI.WebControls

DataGridComponentEditor: System.Web.UI.Design.WebControls

DataGridDesigner: System.Web.UI.Design.WebControls

DataGridItem: System.Web.UI.WebControls

DataGridItemCollection: System.Web.UI.WebControls

DataGridItemEventArgs: System.Web.UI.WebControls

DataGridItemEventHandler: System.Web.UI.WebControls

DataGridPageChangedEventArgs: System.Web.UI.WebControls

DataGridPageChangedEventHandler: System.Web.UI.WebControls

DataGridPagerStyle: System.Web.UI.WebControls

DataGridSortCommandEventArgs: System.Web.UI.Web-
Controls
DataGridSortCommandEventHandler: Sys-
tem.Web.UI.WebControls
DataItem: DataGridItem, DataListItem, RepeaterItem
DataKeyCollection: System.Web.UI.WebControls
DataKeyField: BaseDataList, BaseDataListDesigner
DataKeys: BaseDataList
DataList: System.Web.UI.WebControls
DataListCommandEventArgs: System.Web.UI.WebCon-
trols
DataListCommandEventHandler: System.Web.UI.Web-
Controls
DataListComponentEditor: System.Web.UI.Design.Web-
Controls
DataListDesigner: System.Web.UI.Design.WebControls
DataListItem: System.Web.UI.WebControls
DataListItemCollection: System.Web.UI.WebControls
DataListItemEventArgs: System.Web.UI.WebControls
DataListItemEventHandler: System.Web.UI.WebControls
DataMember: BaseDataList, BaseDataListDesigner,
HtmlSelect, ListControl, ListControlDesigner,
Repeater, RepeaterDesigner
DataMemberConverter: System.Web.UI.Design
DataNavigateUrlField: HyperLinkColumn
DataNavigateUrlFormatString: HyperLinkColumn
DataSetIndex: DataGridItem
DataSource: BaseDataList, BaseDataListDesigner, HtmlS-
elect, ListControl, ListControlDesigner, PagedData-
Source, Repeater, RepeaterDesigner
DataSourceConverter: System.Web.UI.Design
DataSourceCount: PagedDataSource
DataTextField: ButtonColumn, HtmlSelect, HyperLinkCol-
umn, ListControl, ListControlDesigner
DataTextFormatString: ButtonColumn, HyperLinkColumn,
ListControl
DataTypeCheck: ValidationCompareOperator
DataValueField: HtmlSelect, ListControl, ListControlDe-
signer
Date: CalendarDay, ValidationDataType
Day: CalendarSelectionMode, DayRenderEventArgs
DayHeaderStyle: Calendar
DayNameFormat: Calendar, System.Web.UI.WebControls
DayNumberText: CalendarDay
DayRender: Calendar
DayRenderEventArgs: System.Web.UI.WebControls
DayRenderEventHandler: System.Web.UI.WebControls
DayStyle: Calendar
DayWeek: CalendarSelectionMode
DayWeekMonth: CalendarSelectionMode
Dd: HtmlTextWriterTag
DeadlockSuspected: ProcessShutdownReason
DeclaringType: LogicalMethodInfo
Decompress(): PassportIdentity

Decrypt(): FormsAuthentication, PassportIdentity
Default: CacheItemPriority, ControlBuilderAttribute,
DataBindingHandlerAttribute, FirstDayOfWeek, Par-
seChildrenAttribute, PersistChildrenAttribute, Persis-
tenceModeAttribute, SoapBindingStyle,
SoapBindingUse, SoapParameterStyle, Toolbox-
DataAttribute, TraceMode
DefaultAuthentication: HttpApplication
DefaultAuthenticationEventArgs: System.Web.Security
DefaultAuthenticationEventHandler: System.Web.Secu-
rity
DefaultAuthenticationModule: System.Web.Security
DefaultFilename: ContractReference, DiscoveryDocumen-
tReference, DiscoveryReference, SchemaReference
DefaultNamespace: ProtocolReflector, WebServiceAt-
tribute
DefaultProperty: ParseChildrenAttribute
DefaultTabString: HtmlTextWriter
Del: HtmlTextWriterTag
DeleteCommand: DataGrid, DataList
DeleteCommandName: DataGrid, DataList
Dependency: BasePartialCachingControl
DependencyChanged: CacheItemRemovedReason
Description: WebMethodAttribute, WebServiceAttribute
Deserialize(): LosFormatter, WebControlToolboxItem
Designer: IHtmlControlDesignerBehavior
DesignerDataBoundLiteralControl: System.Web.UI
DesignerHost: DesignTimeParseData
DesignerInitialize(): Page, UserControl
DesignTimeData: System.Web.UI.Design
DesignTimeElement: IHtmlControlDesignerBehavior
DesignTimeElementView: IControlDesignerBehavior
DesignTimeHtml: IControlDesignerBehavior
DesignTimeHtmlRequiresLoadComplete: BaseDataList-
Designer, ControlDesigner
DesignTimeParseData: System.Web.UI
DesignTimeTemplateParser: System.Web.UI
Detail: SoapException
DetailElementName: SoapException
DeterminePostBackMode(): Page
DetermineRenderUplevel(): BaseCompareValidator,
BaseValidator
Dfn: HtmlTextWriterTag
DidUnderstand: SoapHeader
Dir: HtmlTextWriterTag
Direction: SoapHeaderAttribute
Disabled: HtmlControl, HtmlTextWriterAttribute
DiscardUndoUnit(): IWebFormsDocumentService
Discover(): DiscoveryClientProtocol, SoapHttpClientProto-
col
DiscoverAny(): DiscoveryClientProtocol
DiscoveryClientDocumentCollection: System.Web.Ser-
vices.Discovery
DiscoveryClientProtocol: System.Web.Services.Discovery

DiscoveryClientReferenceCollection: System.Web.Services.Discovery

DiscoveryClientResult: System.Web.Services.Discovery

DiscoveryClientResultCollection: System.Web.Services.Discovery

DiscoveryClientResultsFile: System.Web.Services.Discovery

DiscoveryDocument: System.Web.Services.Discovery

DiscoveryDocumentLinksPattern: System.Web.Services.Discovery

DiscoveryDocumentReference: System.Web.Services.Discovery

DiscoveryDocumentSearchPattern: System.Web.Services.Discovery

DiscoveryExceptionDictionary: System.Web.Services.Discovery

DiscoveryReference: System.Web.Services.Discovery

DiscoveryReferenceCollection: System.Web.Services.Discovery

DiscoveryRequestHandler: System.Web.Services.Discovery

DiscoverySearchPattern: System.Web.Services.Discovery

Display: BaseValidator

DisplayMode: ValidationSummary

Dispose(): BaseDataListDesigner, BasePartialCachingControl, CacheDependency, Control, DataGridDesigner, DataListDesigner, DefaultAuthenticationModule, FileAuthorizationModule, FormsAuthenticationModule, HtmlControlDesigner, HttpApplication, IHttpModule, PassportAuthenticationModule, RegexEditorDialog, RepeaterDesigner, SessionStateModule, TemplateEditingService, TemplateEditingVerb, UrlAuthorizationModule, WindowsAuthenticationModule, XmlDesigner

Disposed: Control, HttpApplication

Div: HtmlTextWriterTag

Dl: HtmlTextWriterTag

DocRef: ContractReference

Document: DiscoveryDocumentReference, SoapBindingStyle, Xml

DocumentableItem: System.Web.Services.Description

Documentation: DocumentableItem

DocumentContent: Xml

Documents: DiscoveryClientProtocol

DocumentSource: Xml

DocumentUrl: DesignTimeParseData, IWebFormsDocumentService

DoDelayLoadActions(): CalendarAutoFormatDialog

DoGCCollect(): IISAPIRuntime, ISAPIRuntime

Domain: HttpCookie

Dotted: BorderStyle

Double: BorderStyle, ValidationDataType

DoubleQuoteChar: HtmlTextWriter

Download(): DiscoveryClientProtocol

Downstream: OutputCacheLocation

DropDownList: System.Web.UI.WebControls

Dt: HtmlTextWriterTag

Duration: PartialCachingAttribute

Dynamic: ValidatorDisplay

DynamicDiscoveryDocument: System.Web.Services.Discovery

E

EcmaScriptVersion: HttpBrowserCapabilities

EditCommand: DataGrid, DataList

EditCommandColumn: System.Web.UI.WebControls

EditCommandName: DataGrid, DataList

EditComponent(): BaseDataListComponentEditor

EditItem: ListItemType

EditItemIndex: DataGrid, DataList

EditItemStyle: DataGrid, DataList

EditItemTemplate: DataList, TemplateColumn

EditText: EditCommandColumn

EditValue(): DataBindingCollectionEditor, DataGridColumnCollectionEditor, RegexTypeEditor, UrlEditor, XmlFileEditor

Element: MessagePart, SoapUnknownHeader

ElementName: XmlFormatExtensionAttribute

Em: HtmlTextWriterTag, UnitType

Embed: HtmlTextWriterTag

Empty: FontUnit, Unit

EmptyControlCollection: System.Web.UI

EnableClientScript: BaseValidator, ValidationSummary

Enabled: BaseValidator, Image, WebControl

EnableSession: WebMethodAttribute

EnableUndo(): IWebFormsDocumentService

EnableViewState: Control, Page

Encode(): UrlEncodedParameterWriter

EncodeAttributeValue(): HtmlTextWriter

Encoded: SoapBindingUse

EncodedInnerDefaultProperty: PersistenceMode, PersistenceModeAttribute

EncodedMustUnderstand: SoapHeader

EncodeUrl(): HtmlTextWriter

Encoding: HtmlTextWriter, HttpWriter, MailAttachment, SoapBodyBinding, SoapFaultBinding, SoapHeaderBinding, SoapHeaderFaultBinding

Encrypt(): FormsAuthentication, PassportIdentity

Encryption: FormsProtectionEnum

Enctype: HtmlForm

End: SessionStateModule

End(): HttpResponse

EndClass(): ProtocolImporter, ProtocolReflector, SoapProtocolImporter

EndEventHandler: System.Web

EndInvoke(): AdCreatedEventHandler, BeginEventHandler, BuildMethod, BuildTemplateMethod,

CacheItemRemovedCallback, CommandEventHandler,
DataGridCommandEventHandler, DataGridItemEven-
tHandler, DataGridPageChangedEventHandler, Data-
GridSortCommandEventHandler,
DataListCommandEventHandler, DataListItemEven-
tHandler, DayRenderEventHandler, DefaultAuthentica-
tionEventHandler, EndEventHandler,
EndOfSendNotification, FormsAuthenticationEven-
tHandler, HttpCacheValidateHandler, HttpSimple-
ClientProtocol, ImageClickEventHandler,
LogicalMethodInfo, MonthChangedEventHandler,
PassportAuthenticationEventHandler, RenderMethod,
RepeaterCommandEventHandler, RepeaterItemEven-
tHandler, ServerValidateEventHandler, SoapHttp-
ClientProtocol, WindowsAuthenticationEventHandler

EndMethodInfo: LogicalMethodInfo
EndNamespace(): ProtocolImporter, SoapProtocol-
Importer
EndOfRequest(): HttpWorkerRequest, SimpleWorkerRe-
quest
EndOfSendNotification: System.Web
EndProcessRequest(): IHttpAsyncHandler
EndRequest: HttpApplication
EndTagLeftChars: HtmlTextWriter
EnsureChildControls(): Control
EnsureInStage(): SoapClientMessage, SoapMessage,
SoapServerMessage
EnsureOutStage(): SoapClientMessage, SoapMessage,
SoapServerMessage
EnsureStage(): SoapMessage
EnterTemplateMode(): TemplatedControlDesigner
EnumFromString(): PropertyConverter
EnumToString(): PropertyConverter
Equal: ValidationCompareOperator
Equals(): ControlBuilderAttribute, DataBinding, FontUnit,
ListItem, ParseChildrenAttribute, PersistChildrenAt-
tribute, PersistenceModeAttribute, ToolboxDataAt-
tribute, Unit
EqualsChar: HtmlTextWriter
EqualsDoubleQuoteString: HtmlTextWriter
Error: HttpApplication, HttpContext, PassportIdentity,
TemplateControl
ErrorMessage: BaseValidator, IValidator
ErrorPage: Page
Errors: DiscoveryClientProtocol
Eval(): DataBinder
EvaluateIsValid(): BaseValidator, CompareValidator, Cus-
tomValidator, RangeValidator, RegularExpressionVal-
idator, RequiredFieldValidator
Ex: UnitType
Exception: SoapMessage
ExcludePathInfo: System.Web.Services.Discovery
ExcludePaths: DynamicDiscoveryDocument
Execute(): HttpServerUtility

ExitTemplateMode(): TemplatedControlDesigner
Expiration: FormsAuthenticationTicket
Expired: CacheItemRemovedReason, FormsAuthentica-
tionTicket
Expires: HttpCookie, HttpResponse
ExpiresAbsolute: HttpResponse
Expression: DataBinding
ExtensionPoints: XmlFormatExtensionAttribute
Extensions: Binding, FaultBinding, InputBinding, Mes-
sageBinding, MimePart, OperationBinding, Output-
Binding, Port, Service, ServiceDescription, Types
ExtensionType: SoapExtensionAttribute
ExtractTemplateRows: DataList

F

FaultBinding: System.Web.Services.Description
FaultBindingCollection: System.Web.Services.Description
Faults: Operation, OperationBinding
Fieldset: HtmlTextWriterTag
FileAuthorizationModule: System.Web.Security
Filename: DiscoveryClientResult, MailAttachment
FileName: HttpParseException, HttpPostedFile
FilenameFromUrl(): DiscoveryReference
FilePath: HttpRequest
Files: HttpRequest
Filter: HttpRequest, HttpResponse
FilterAttributes(): HtmlTextWriter
Finalize(): PassportIdentity, TemplateEditingService, Tem-
plateEditingVerb
Find(): ServiceDescriptionFormatExtensionCollection
FindAll(): ServiceDescriptionFormatExtensionCollection
FindByText(): ListItemCollection
FindByValue(): ListItemCollection
FindControl(): CheckBoxList, Control
FindPartByName(): Message
FindPartsByName(): Message
First: Pair, Triplet
FirstDayOfWeek: Calendar, System.Web.UI.WebControls
FirstIndexInPage: PagedDataSource
FirstLetter: DayNameFormat
FirstTwoLetters: DayNameFormat
Flags: HttpClientCertificate
Flow: OperationMessageCollection, RepeatLayout
Flush(): HtmlTextWriter, HttpResponse, HttpWriter
FlushResponse(): HttpWorkerRequest, SimpleWorkerRe-
quest
Font: AdRotator, HtmlTextWriterTag, Image, Style, Web-
Control
FontFamily: HtmlTextWriterStyle
FontInfo: System.Web.UI.WebControls
FontNamesConverter: System.Web.UI.WebControls
FontSize: HtmlTextWriterStyle, System.Web.UI.WebCon-
trols

ValidatedControlConverter

GetStandardValuesSupported(): DataFieldConverter, DataMemberConverter, DataSourceConverter, FontUnitConverter, TargetConverter, ValidatedControlConverter

GetStatusDescription(): HttpWorkerRequest

GetStyleAttribute(): IHtmlControlDesignerBehavior

GetStyleKey(): HtmlTextWriter

GetStyleName(): HtmlTextWriter

GetTagKey(): HtmlTextWriter

GetTagName(): Html32TextWriter, HtmlTextWriter

GetTagPrefix(): IWebFormReferenceManager

GetTemplateContainerDataItemProperty(): DataGridDesigner, DataListDesigner, TemplatedControlDesigner

GetTemplateContainerDataSource(): BaseDataListDesigner, TemplatedControlDesigner

GetTemplateContent(): DataGridDesigner, DataListDesigner, TemplatedControlDesigner

GetTemplateEditingVerbs(): TemplatedControlDesigner

GetTemplateFromText(): TemplatedControlDesigner

GetTemplatePropertyParentType(): DataGridDesigner, TemplatedControlDesigner

GetTextFromTemplate(): TemplatedControlDesigner

GetToolAttributeValue(): WebControlToolboxItem

GetToolHtml(): WebControlToolboxItem

GetToolType(): WebControlToolboxItem

GetTypeHashCode(): Page

GetUnknownRequestHeader(): HttpWorkerRequest

GetUnknownRequestHeaders(): HttpWorkerRequest

GetUriPath(): HttpWorkerRequest, SimpleWorkerRequest

GetUrlContextID(): HttpWorkerRequest

GetUserToken(): HttpWorkerRequest, SimpleWorkerRequest

GetValidationProperty(): BaseValidator

GetVaryByCustomString(): HttpApplication

GetVirtualPathToken(): HttpWorkerRequest

GetWebRequest(): HttpGetClientProtocol, HttpPostClientProtocol, HttpWebClientProtocol, SoapHttpClientProtocol, WebClientProtocol

GetWebResponse(): HttpWebClientProtocol, WebClientProtocol

GreaterThan: ValidationCompareOperator

GreaterThanEqual: ValidationCompareOperator

GridLines: BaseDataList, DataList, System.Web.UI.WebControls, Table, TableStyle

Groove: BorderStyle

Group: MatchAttribute, MimeTextMatch

GroupName: RadioButton

H

H1: HtmlTextWriterTag

H2: HtmlTextWriterTag

H3: HtmlTextWriterTag

H4: HtmlTextWriterTag

H5: HtmlTextWriterTag

H6: HtmlTextWriterTag

Handled: ServiceDescriptionFormatExtension

Handler: HttpContext

HandlerTypeName: DataBindingHandlerAttribute

HasAspCode: ControlBuilder

HasBody(): ControlBuilder

HasChanged: CacheDependency

HasControls(): Control

HasDataBindings: IDataBindingsAccessor

HasEntityBody(): HttpWorkerRequest

HasFlag(): PassportIdentity

HasFooter: IRepeatInfoUser

HasHeader: IRepeatInfoUser

HashPasswordForStoringInConfigFile(): FormsAuthentication

HasKeys: HttpCookie

HasProfile(): PassportIdentity

HasSavedPassword: PassportIdentity

HasSeparators: IRepeatInfoUser

HasTicket: PassportIdentity

HasWeekSelectors(): Calendar

HaveConsent(): PassportIdentity

Head: HtmlTextWriterTag

Header: ListItemType

HeaderAccept: HttpWorkerRequest

HeaderAcceptCharset: HttpWorkerRequest

HeaderAcceptEncoding: HttpWorkerRequest

HeaderAcceptLanguage: HttpWorkerRequest

HeaderAcceptRanges: HttpWorkerRequest

HeaderAge: HttpWorkerRequest

HeaderAllow: HttpWorkerRequest

HeaderAuthorization: HttpWorkerRequest

HeaderCacheControl: HttpWorkerRequest

HeaderConnection: HttpWorkerRequest

HeaderContentEncoding: HttpWorkerRequest

HeaderContentLanguage: HttpWorkerRequest

HeaderContentLength: HttpWorkerRequest

HeaderContentLocation: HttpWorkerRequest

HeaderContentMd5: HttpWorkerRequest

HeaderContentRange: HttpWorkerRequest

HeaderContentType: HttpWorkerRequest

HeaderCookie: HttpWorkerRequest

HeaderDate: HttpWorkerRequest

HeaderEtag: HttpWorkerRequest

HeaderExpect: HttpWorkerRequest

HeaderExpires: HttpWorkerRequest

HeaderFrom: HttpWorkerRequest

HeaderHost: HttpWorkerRequest

HeaderIfMatch: HttpWorkerRequest
HeaderIfModifiedSince: HttpWorkerRequest
HeaderIfNoneMatch: HttpWorkerRequest
HeaderIfRange: HttpWorkerRequest
HeaderIfUnmodifiedSince: HttpWorkerRequest
HeaderImageUrl: DataGridColumn
HeaderKeepAlive: HttpWorkerRequest
HeaderLastModified: HttpWorkerRequest
HeaderLocation: HttpWorkerRequest
HeaderMaxForwards: HttpWorkerRequest
HeaderMessages: ProtocolReflector
HeaderPragma: HttpWorkerRequest
HeaderProxyAuthenticate: HttpWorkerRequest
HeaderProxyAuthorization: HttpWorkerRequest
HeaderRange: HttpWorkerRequest
HeaderReferer: HttpWorkerRequest
HeaderRetryAfter: HttpWorkerRequest
Headers: HttpRequest, MailMessage, SoapMessage
HeaderServer: HttpWorkerRequest
HeaderSetCookie: HttpWorkerRequest
HeadersSent(): HttpWorkerRequest
HeaderStyle: DataGrid, DataGridColumn, DataList
HeaderTe: HttpWorkerRequest
HeaderTemplate: DataList, Repeater, TemplateColumn
HeaderText: DataGridColumn, ValidationSummary
HeaderTrailer: HttpWorkerRequest
HeaderTransferEncoding: HttpWorkerRequest
HeaderUpgrade: HttpWorkerRequest
HeaderUserAgent: HttpWorkerRequest
HeaderVary: HttpWorkerRequest
HeaderVia: HttpWorkerRequest
HeaderWarning: HttpWorkerRequest
HeaderWwwAuthenticate: HttpWorkerRequest
Height: HtmlImage, HtmlTable, HtmlTableCell,
  HtmlTableRow, HtmlTextWriterAttribute, HtmlTextWriterStyle, Style, WebControl
HexPUID: PassportIdentity
High: CacheItemPriority, MailPriority
Horizontal: GridLines, RepeatDirection
HorizontalAlign: BaseDataList, Panel, System.Web.UI.WebControls, Table, TableCell, TableItemStyle, TableRow, TableStyle
Hr: HtmlTextWriterTag
Href: HtmlTextWriterAttribute
HRef: HtmlAnchor
Html: HtmlTextWriterTag, MailFormat
Html32TextWriter: System.Web.UI
HtmlAnchor: System.Web.UI.HtmlControls
HtmlAttributeEncode(): HttpUtility
HtmlButton: System.Web.UI.HtmlControls
HtmlContainerControl: System.Web.UI.HtmlControls
HtmlControl: System.Web.UI.HtmlControls
HtmlControlDesigner: System.Web.UI.Design
HtmlDecode(): HttpServerUtility, HttpUtility

HtmlDecodeLiterals(): ControlBuilder, ListItemControlBuilder, TextBoxControlBuilder
HtmlEncode(): HttpServerUtility, HttpUtility
HtmlForm: System.Web.UI.HtmlControls
HtmlFormParameterReader: System.Web.Services.Protocols
HtmlFormParameterWriter: System.Web.Services.Protocols
HtmlGenericControl: System.Web.UI.HtmlControls
HtmlImage: System.Web.UI.HtmlControls
HtmlInputButton: System.Web.UI.HtmlControls
HtmlInputCheckBox: System.Web.UI.HtmlControls
HtmlInputControl: System.Web.UI.HtmlControls
HtmlInputFile: System.Web.UI.HtmlControls
HtmlInputHidden: System.Web.UI.HtmlControls
HtmlInputImage: System.Web.UI.HtmlControls
HtmlInputRadioButton: System.Web.UI.HtmlControls
HtmlInputText: System.Web.UI.HtmlControls
HtmlIntrinsicControlDesigner: System.Web.UI.Design
HtmlSelect: System.Web.UI.HtmlControls
HtmlTable: System.Web.UI.HtmlControls
HtmlTableCell: System.Web.UI.HtmlControls
HtmlTableCellCollection: System.Web.UI.HtmlControls
HtmlTableRow: System.Web.UI.HtmlControls
HtmlTableRowCollection: System.Web.UI.HtmlControls
HtmlTextArea: System.Web.UI.HtmlControls
HtmlTextWriter: System.Web.UI
HtmlTextWriterAttribute: System.Web.UI
HtmlTextWriterStyle: System.Web.UI
HtmlTextWriterTag: System.Web.UI
HttpAddressBinding: System.Web.Services.Description
HttpApplication: System.Web
HttpApplicationState: System.Web
HttpBinding: System.Web.Services.Description
HttpBrowserCapabilities: System.Web
HttpCacheability: System.Web
HttpCachePolicy: System.Web
HttpCacheRevalidation: System.Web
HttpCacheValidateHandler: System.Web
HttpCacheVaryByHeaders: System.Web
HttpCacheVaryByParams: System.Web
HttpCapabilitiesBase: System.Web.Configuration
HttpClientCertificate: System.Web
HttpCompileException: System.Web
HttpConfigurationContext: System.Web.Configuration
HttpContext: System.Web
HttpCookie: System.Web
HttpCookieCollection: System.Web
HttpException: System.Web
HttpFileCollection: System.Web
HttpGetClientProtocol: System.Web.Services.Protocols
HttpMethod: HttpRequest
HttpMethodAttribute: System.Web.Services.Protocols
HttpModuleCollection: System.Web

HttpOperationBinding: System.Web.Services.Description
HttpParseException: System.Web
HttpPostClientProtocol: System.Web.Services.Protocols
HttpPostedFile: System.Web
HttpRequest: System.Web
HttpResponse: System.Web
HttpRuntime: System.Web
HttpServerUtility: System.Web
HttpSessionState: System.Web.SessionState
HttpSimpleClientProtocol: System.Web.Services.Protocols
HttpStaticObjectsCollection: System.Web
HttpTransport: SoapBinding
HttpUnhandledException: System.Web
HttpUrlEncodedBinding: System.Web.Services.Description
HttpUrlReplacementBinding: System.Web.Services.Description
HttpUtility: System.Web
HttpValidationStatus: System.Web
HttpWebClientProtocol: System.Web.Services.Protocols
HttpWorkerRequest: System.Web
HttpWriter: System.Web
HyperLink: System.Web.UI.WebControls
HyperLinkColumn: System.Web.UI.WebControls
HyperLinkControlBuilder: System.Web.UI.WebControls
HyperLinkDataBindingHandler: System.Web.UI.Design
HyperLinkDesigner: System.Web.UI.Design.WebControls

I

I: HtmlTextWriterTag
IAppDomainFactory: System.Web.Hosting
IAttributeAccessor: System.Web.UI
IControlDesignerBehavior: System.Web.UI.Design
Id: HtmlTextWriterAttribute
ID: Control, ControlBuilder, ControlDesigner, Page
IDataBindingsAccessor: System.Web.UI
IDataSourceProvider: System.Web.UI.Design
Identity: PassportAuthenticationEventArgs, WindowsAuthenticationEventArgs
IdleTimeout: ProcessShutdownReason
Iframe: HtmlTextWriterTag
IgnoreCase: MatchAttribute, MimeTextMatch
IgnoreParams: HttpCacheVaryByParams
IgnoreThisRequest: HttpValidationStatus
IHtmlControlDesignerBehavior: System.Web.UI.Design
IHttpAsyncHandler: System.Web
IHttpHandler: System.Web
IHttpHandlerFactory: System.Web
IHttpModule: System.Web
IISAPIRuntime: System.Web.Hosting
Image: System.Web.UI.WebControls
ImageAlign: Image, System.Web.UI.WebControls

ImageButton: System.Web.UI.WebControls
ImageClickEventArgs: System.Web.UI
ImageClickEventHandler: System.Web.UI
ImageUrl: AdCreatedEventArgs, HyperLink, Image
ImageUrlEditor: System.Web.UI.Design
Img: HtmlTextWriterTag
Import: System.Web.Services.Description
Import(): ServiceDescriptionImporter
ImportClass(): SoapTransportImporter
ImportCollection: System.Web.Services.Description
ImportContext: SoapExtensionImporter, SoapTransportImporter
ImportMethod(): SoapExtensionImporter
Imports: ServiceDescription
In: SoapHeaderDirection
INamingContainer: System.Web.UI
Inch: UnitType
Indent: HtmlTextWriter
Index: TemplateEditingVerb
IndexOf(): BindingCollection, ControlCollection, DataGridColumnCollection, FaultBindingCollection, ImportCollection, ListItemCollection, MessageCollection, MessagePartCollection, MimePartCollection, MimeTextMatchCollection, OperationBindingCollection, OperationCollection, OperationFaultCollection, OperationMessageCollection, PortCollection, PortTypeCollection, ServiceCollection, ServiceDescriptionCollection, ServiceDescriptionFormatExtensionCollection, SoapHeaderCollection
Init: Control
Init(): ControlBuilder, DefaultAuthenticationModule, FileAuthorizationModule, FormsAuthenticationModule, HttpApplication, HttpCapabilitiesBase, IHttpModule, ObjectTagBuilder, PassportAuthenticationModule, SessionStateModule, TemplateBuilder, UrlAuthorizationModule, WindowsAuthenticationModule
InitialHeight: ITemplateEditingFrame
Initialize(): AnyReturnReader, BaseDataListDesigner, BoundColumn, ButtonColumn, CalendarDesigner, ControlDesigner, DataGridColumn, DataGridDesigner, DataListDesigner, FormsAuthentication, HyperLinkColumn, ListControlDesigner, MimeFormatter, NopReturnReader, RepeaterDesigner, SoapExtension, TextControlDesigner, TextReturnReader, UrlEncodedParameterWriter, ValueCollectionParameterReader, WebControlToolboxItem, XmlDesigner, XmlReturnReader
InitializeAsUserControl(): UserControl
InitializeCell(): BoundColumn, ButtonColumn, DataGridColumn, EditCommandColumn, HyperLinkColumn, TemplateColumn
InitializeItem(): DataGrid, DataList, Repeater
InitializePager(): DataGrid
InitializeRequest(): HtmlFormParameterWriter,

MimeParameterWriter

InitialValue: RequiredFieldValidator

InitialWidth: ITemplateEditingFrame

InitOutputCache(): Page

InnerDefaultProperty: PersistenceMode, Persistence-ModeAttribute

InnerHtml: HtmlContainerControl, HtmlSelect, HtmlTable, HtmlTableRow

InnerProperty: PersistenceMode, PersistenceModeAt-tribute

InnerText: HtmlContainerControl, HtmlSelect, HtmlTable, HtmlTableRow, IUserControlDesignerAccessor

InnerWriter: HtmlTextWriter

InOut: SoapHeaderDirection

InParameters: LogicalMethodInfo

InProc: SessionStateMode

Input: HtmlTextWriterTag, OperationBinding, Operation-MessageCollection

InputBinding: System.Web.Services.Description

InputMessage: ProtocolImporter, ProtocolReflector

InputStream: HttpPostedFile, HttpRequest

Ins: HtmlTextWriterTag

Insert(): BindingCollection, Cache, FaultBindingCollec-tion, HtmlTableCellCollection, HtmlTableRowCollec-tion, ImportCollection, ListItemCollection, MessageCollection, MessagePartCollection, MimePartCollection, MimeTextMatchCollection, Oper-ationBindingCollection, OperationCollection, Opera-tionFaultCollection, OperationMessageCollection, PortCollection, PortTypeCollection, ServiceCollection, ServiceDescriptionCollection, ServiceDescriptionFor-matExtensionCollection, SoapHeaderCollection

Inset: BorderStyle

InstantiateIn(): CompiledTemplateBuilder, ITemplate, TemplateBuilder

Integer: ValidationDataType

InTemplateMode: TemplatedControlDesigner

Invalid: HttpValidationStatus

Invoke(): AdCreatedEventHandler, BeginEventHandler, BuildMethod, BuildTemplateMethod, CacheItemRe-movedCallback, CommandEventHandler, DataGrid-CommandEventHandler, DataGridItemEventHandler, DataGridPageChangedEventHandler, DataGridSort-CommandEventHandler, DataListCommandEven-tHandler, DataListItemEventHandler, DayRenderEventHandler, DefaultAuthenticationEven-tHandler, EndEventHandler, EndOfSendNotification, FormsAuthenticationEventHandler, HttpCacheVali-dateHandler, HttpSimpleClientProtocol, ImageClick-EventHandler, LogicalMethodInfo, MonthChangedEventHandler, PassportAuthentication-EventHandler, RenderMethod, RepeaterCommandE-ventHandler, RepeaterItemEventHandler, ServerValidateEventHandler, SoapHttpClientProtocol,

WindowsAuthenticationEventHandler

IParserAccessor: System.Web.UI

IPostBackDataHandler: System.Web.UI

IPostBackEventHandler: System.Web.UI

IReadOnlySessionState: System.Web.SessionState

IRepeatInfoUser: System.Web.UI.WebControls

IRequiresSessionState: System.Web.SessionState

ISAPIRuntime: System.Web.Hosting

IsAsync: LogicalMethodInfo

IsAttributeDefined(): HtmlTextWriter

IsAuthenticated: FormsIdentity, HttpRequest, Pass-portIdentity

IsBeginMethod(): LogicalMethodInfo

IsBindableType(): BaseDataList

IsBindingSupported(): ProtocolImporter, SoapProtocol-Importer

IsBoundBy(): Operation

IsClientConnected: HttpResponse

IsClientConnected(): HttpWorkerRequest

IsClientScriptBlockRegistered(): Page

IsCompleted: WebClientAsyncResult

IsCookieless: HttpSessionState

IsCustomErrorEnabled: HttpContext

IsCustomPagingEnabled: PagedDataSource

IsDebuggingEnabled: HttpContext

IsDefaultAttribute(): ControlBuilderAttribute, ParseChil-drenAttribute, PersistChildrenAttribute, Persistence-ModeAttribute, ToolboxDataAttribute

IsDirty: ControlDesigner, StateItem

IsEmpty: FontUnit, Unit

IsEnabled: TraceContext

IsEndMethod(): LogicalMethodInfo

IsEntireEntityBodyIsPreloaded(): HttpWorkerRequest

IsFirstPage: PagedDataSource

IsHandled(): ServiceDescriptionFormatExtensionCollec-tion

IsIndex: HtmlTextWriterTag

IsItemDirty(): StateBag

IsLastPage: PagedDataSource

IsLiteralContent(): Control

IsLoading: IWebFormsDocumentService

IsNewSession: HttpSessionState

IsOnUNCShare: HttpRuntime

IsOperationFlowSupported(): ProtocolImporter, SoapPro-tocolImporter

IsOtherMonth: CalendarDay

IsPagingEnabled: PagedDataSource

IsPersistent: FormsAuthenticationTicket

IsPostBack: Page, UserControl

IsPresent: HttpClientCertificate

IsPropertyBound(): ControlDesigner

IsReadOnly: ControlCollection, DataBindingCollection, DataGridColumnCollection, DataGridItemCollection, DataKeyCollection, DataListItemCollection,

HtmlTableCellCollection, HtmlTableRowCollection, HttpSessionState, HttpStaticObjectsCollection, ListItemCollection, PagedDataSource, RepeaterItemCollection, SelectedDatesCollection, TableCellCollection, TableRowCollection, ValidatorCollection

IsRequired(): ServiceDescriptionFormatExtensionCollection

IsReusable: DiscoveryRequestHandler, IHttpHandler, Page

IsSecure(): HttpWorkerRequest

IsSecureConnection: HttpRequest

IsSelectable: CalendarDay

IsSelected: CalendarDay

IsStartupScriptRegistered(): Page

IsStyleAttributeDefined(): HtmlTextWriter

IssueDate: FormsAuthenticationTicket

Issuer: HttpClientCertificate

IsSupported(): ValueCollectionParameterReader

IsSupportedTransport(): SoapTransportImporter

IsSynchronized: ControlCollection, DataBindingCollection, DataGridColumnCollection, DataGridItemCollection, DataKeyCollection, DataListItemCollection, HtmlTableCellCollection, HtmlTableRowCollection, HttpSessionState, HttpStaticObjectsCollection, ListItemCollection, PagedDataSource, RepeaterItemCollection, SelectedDatesCollection, TableCellCollection, TableRowCollection, ValidatorCollection

IStateManager: System.Web.UI

IStateRuntime: System.Web.SessionState

IsToday: CalendarDay

IsTrackingViewState: IStateManager

IsValid: BaseValidator, HttpClientCertificate, IValidator, Page, ServerValidateEventArgs

IsVoid: LogicalMethodInfo

IsWeekend: CalendarDay

Italic: FontInfo

Item: AttributeCollection, BindingCollection, Cache, ControlCollection, CssStyleCollection, DataBindingCollection, DataGridColumnCollection, DataGridCommandEventArgs, DataGridItemCollection, DataGridItemEventArgs, DataKeyCollection, DataListCommandEventArgs, DataListItemCollection, DataListItemEventArgs, DiscoveryClientDocumentCollection, DiscoveryClientReferenceCollection, DiscoveryClientResultCollection, DiscoveryExceptionDictionary, DiscoveryReferenceCollection, FaultBindingCollection, HtmlTableCellCollection, HtmlTableRowCollection, HttpApplicationState, HttpCacheVaryByHeaders, HttpCacheVaryByParams, HttpCapabilitiesBase, HttpCookie, HttpCookieCollection, HttpFileCollection, HttpModuleCollection, HttpRequest, HttpSessionState, HttpStaticObjectsCollection, ImportCollection, ListItemCollection, ListItemType, MessageCollection, MessagePartCollection, MimePartCollection,

MimeTextMatchCollection, OperationBindingCollection, OperationCollection, OperationFaultCollection, OperationMessageCollection, PassportIdentity, PortCollection, PortTypeCollection, RepeaterCommandEventArgs, RepeaterItemCollection, RepeaterItemEventArgs, SelectedDatesCollection, ServiceCollection, ServiceDescriptionCollection, ServiceDescriptionFormatExtensionCollection, SoapHeaderCollection, StateBag, TableCellCollection, TableRowCollection, ValidatorCollection

ItemCommand: DataGrid, DataList, Repeater

ItemCreated: DataGrid, DataList, Repeater

ItemDataBound: DataGrid, DataList, Repeater

ItemIndex: DataGridItem, DataListItem, RepeaterItem

ITemplate: System.Web.UI

ITemplateEditingFrame: System.Web.UI.Design

ITemplateEditingService: System.Web.UI.Design

Items: DataGrid, DataList, HtmlSelect, HttpContext, ListControl, Repeater

ItemStyle: DataGrid, DataGridColumn, DataList

ItemTemplate: DataList, Repeater, TemplateColumn

ItemType: DataGridItem, DataListItem, RepeaterItem

IUserControlDesignerAccessor: System.Web.UI

IValidator: System.Web.UI

IWebFormReferenceManager: System.Web.UI.Design

IWebFormsBuilderUIService: System.Web.UI.Design

IWebFormsDocumentService: System.Web.UI.Design

J

JavaApplets: HttpBrowserCapabilities

JavaScript: HttpBrowserCapabilities

Justify: HorizontalAlign

K

Kbd: HtmlTextWriterTag

Keys: AttributeCollection, CssStyleCollection, DiscoveryClientDocumentCollection, DiscoveryClientReferenceCollection, DiscoveryExceptionDictionary, HttpSessionState, StateBag

KeySize: HttpClientCertificate

KeywordFilter: AdRotator

L

Label: HtmlTextWriterTag, System.Web.UI.WebControls

LabelControlBuilder: System.Web.UI.WebControls

LabelDesigner: System.Web.UI.Design.WebControls

Large: FontSize, FontUnit

Larger: FontSize, FontUnit

LCID: HttpSessionState

Left: HorizontalAlign, ImageAlign, TextAlign

Legend: HtmlTextWriterTag

Methods: ProtocolReflector
Middle: ImageAlign, VerticalAlign
MimeContentBinding: System.Web.Services.Description
MimeFormatter: System.Web.Services.Protocols
MimeMultipartRelatedBinding: System.Web.Services.Description
MimeParameterReader: System.Web.Services.Protocols
MimeParameterWriter: System.Web.Services.Protocols
MimePart: System.Web.Services.Description
MimePartCollection: System.Web.Services.Description
MimeReturnReader: System.Web.Services.Protocols
MimeTextBinding: System.Web.Services.Description
MimeTextMatch: System.Web.Services.Description
MimeTextMatchCollection: System.Web.Services.Description
MimeXmlBinding: System.Web.Services.Description
MinimumValue: RangeValidator
MinorVersion: HttpBrowserCapabilities
Mm: UnitType
Mode: DataGridPagerStyle, HttpSessionState, PersistenceModeAttribute
Modules: HttpApplication
Monday: FirstDayOfWeek
Month: TitleFormat
MonthChangedEventArgs: System.Web.UI.WebControls
MonthChangedEventHandler: System.Web.UI.WebControls
MonthYear: TitleFormat
MSDomVersion: HttpBrowserCapabilities
MultiLine: TextBoxMode
Multiple: HtmlSelect, HtmlTextWriterAttribute, ListSelectionMode
MustUnderstand: SoapHeader
MustUnderstandFaultCode: SoapException

N

Name: Binding, FontInfo, FormsAuthenticationTicket, FormsIdentity, HtmlAnchor, HtmlForm, HtmlInputControl, HtmlInputRadioButton, HtmlSelect, HtmlTextArea, HtmlTextWriterAttribute, HttpCookie, ITemplateEditingFrame, LogicalMethodInfo, Message, MessageBinding, MessagePart, MimeTextMatch, Operation, OperationBinding, OperationMessage, PassportIdentity, Port, PortType, Service, ServiceDescription, ValidationPropertyAttribute, WebServiceAttribute, WebServiceBindingAttribute
Names: FontInfo
Namespace: ContractReference, DiscoveryDocument, DynamicDiscoveryDocument, HttpBinding, Import, MimeContentBinding, MimeTextBinding, SchemaReference, ServiceDescription, SoapBinding, SoapBodyBinding, SoapFaultBinding, SoapHeaderBinding, SoapHeaderFaultBinding, WebServiceAttribute, WebServiceBindingAttribute, XmlFormatExtensionAttribute, XmlFormatExtensionPrefixAttribute
NamespaceName: TagPrefixAttribute
NamingContainer: Control
NamingContainerType: ControlBuilder
NavigateUrl: AdCreatedEventArgs, HyperLink, HyperLinkColumn
NeedsTag: ConstructorNeedsTagAttribute
NeedsTagInnerText(): ControlBuilder, TemplateBuilder, UserControlControlBuilder
NewDate: MonthChangedEventArgs
NewLine: HtmlTextWriter
NewPageIndex: DataGridPageChangedEventArgs
NextMonthText: Calendar
NextPageCommandArgument: DataGrid
NextPageText: DataGridPagerStyle
NextPrev: PagerMode
NextPrevFormat: Calendar, System.Web.UI.WebControls
NextPrevStyle: Calendar
No: PersistChildrenAttribute
NoAbsolute: UrlBuilderOptions
NoAbsoluteExpiration: Cache
Nobr: HtmlTextWriterTag
NoCache: HttpCacheability
NoCodeGenerated: ServiceDescriptionImportWarnings
Noframes: HtmlTextWriterTag
NoMethodsGenerated: ServiceDescriptionImportWarnings
None: AuthenticationMode, BorderStyle, CalendarSelectionMode, FormsProtectionEnum, GridLines, HttpCacheRevalidation, OperationFlow, OutputCacheLocation, ProcessShutdownReason, UrlBuilderOptions, ValidatorDisplay
NopReturnReader: System.Web.Services.Protocols
Normal: CacheItemPriority, MailPriority
Noscript: HtmlTextWriterTag
NoSlidingExpiration: Cache
NotEqual: ValidationCompareOperator
Notification: OperationFlow
NotRemovable: CacheItemPriority
NotSet: BorderStyle, FontSize, HorizontalAlign, ImageAlign, VerticalAlign
Nowrap: HtmlTextWriterAttribute
NoWrap: HtmlTableCell
NumericPages: PagerMode

O

Object: HtmlTextWriterTag
ObjectConverter: System.Web.UI
ObjectFromString(): PropertyConverter
ObjectTagBuilder: System.Web.UI
Off: SessionStateMode
Ol: HtmlTextWriterTag

OnAbortTransaction(): TemplateControl

OnActivated(): CalendarAutoFormatDialog

OnAdCreated(): AdRotator

OnAppendToParentBuilder(): ControlBuilder

OnAttributeRender(): HtmlTextWriter

OnAutoFormat(): BaseDataListDesigner, CalendarDesigner

OnBehaviorAttached(): ControlDesigner, HtmlControlDesigner, PanelDesigner, ReadWriteControlDesigner,
TemplatedControlDesigner

OnBehaviorDetaching(): HtmlControlDesigner

OnBindingsCollectionChanged(): ControlDesigner, Html-
ControlDesigner

OnBubbleEvent(): Control, DataGrid, DataGridItem,
DataList, DataListItem, Repeater, RepeaterItem

OnCancelCommand(): DataGrid, DataList

Onchange: HtmlTextWriterAttribute

OnCheckedChanged(): CheckBox

OnClear(): ServiceDescriptionBaseCollection

Onclick: HtmlTextWriterAttribute

OnClick(): Button, ImageButton, LinkButton

OnColumnChanged(): DataGridColumn

OnColumnsChanged(): DataGridDesigner

OnCommand(): Button, ImageButton, LinkButton

OnCommitTransaction(): TemplateControl

OnComponentChanged(): BaseDataListDesigner, ControlDesigner, ListControlDesigner, ReadWriteControlD-
esigner, RepeaterDesigner, TemplatedControlDesigner

OnControlResize(): ControlDesigner

OnDataBinding(): BaseDataList, Control, HtmlSelect,
ListControl, Repeater

OnDataSourceChanged(): ListControlDesigner, Repeater-
Designer

OnDayRender(): Calendar

OnDeleteCommand(): DataGrid, DataList

OnEditCommand(): DataGrid, DataList

OnError(): TemplateControl

OneWay: OperationFlow, SoapClientMessage, SoapDocumentMethodAttribute, SoapMessage, SoapRpcMethodAttribute, SoapServerMessage

OnGetUIValueItem(): DataBindingValueUIHandler

OnInit(): BasePartialCachingControl, BaseValidator, Control, HtmlForm, UserControl

OnInsert(): OperationMessageCollection

OnInsertComplete(): ServiceDescriptionBaseCollection

OnItemCommand(): DataGrid, DataList, Repeater

OnItemCreated(): DataGrid, DataList, Repeater

OnItemDataBound(): DataGrid, DataList, Repeater

OnLoad(): Control

OnOKClicked(): CalendarAutoFormatDialog

OnPageIndexChanged(): DataGrid

OnPreRender(): AdRotator, BaseValidator, Calendar,
CheckBox, CheckBoxList, Control, HtmlAnchor, Html-
Button, HtmlInputButton, HtmlInputCheckBox,

HtmlInputHidden, HtmlInputImage, HtmlInputRa-
dioButton, HtmlInputText, HtmlSelect, HtmlTextArea,
ImageButton, LinkButton, ListBox, ListControl,
RadioButton, TextBox, ValidationSummary

OnPropertyBuilder(): BaseDataListDesigner

OnRemove(): ServiceDescriptionBaseCollection

OnSelChangedScheme(): CalendarAutoFormatDialog

OnSelectedIndexChanged(): BaseDataList, ListControl

OnSelectionChanged(): Calendar

OnServerChange(): HtmlInputCheckBox, HtmlInputHidden, HtmlInputRadioButton, HtmlInputText, HtmlSelect, HtmlTextArea

OnServerClick(): HtmlAnchor, HtmlButton, HtmlInputButton, HtmlInputImage

OnServerValidate(): CustomValidator

OnSet(): OperationMessageCollection, ServiceDescriptionBaseCollection

OnSetParent(): HtmlControlDesigner, TemplatedControlD-
esigner

OnSortCommand(): DataGrid

OnStyleAttributeRender(): Html32TextWriter, HtmlTextWriter

OnTagRender(): Html32TextWriter, HtmlTextWriter

OnTemplateEditingVerbsChanged(): BaseDataListDesigner, DataGridDesigner, DataListDesigner

OnTemplateModeChanged(): IControlDesignerBehavior,
TemplatedControlDesigner

OnTextChanged(): TextBox

OnUnload(): BaseValidator, Control

OnUpdateCommand(): DataGrid, DataList

OnValidate(): OperationMessageCollection, ServiceDescriptionFormatExtensionCollection

OnVisibleMonthChanged(): Calendar

Open(): ITemplateEditingFrame

Operation: OperationMessage, ProtocolImporter, ProtocolReflector, System.Web.Services.Description

OperationBinding: MessageBinding, ProtocolImporter,
ProtocolReflector, System.Web.Services.Description

OperationBindingCollection: System.Web.Ser-
vices.Description

OperationBindingSyntaxException(): ProtocolImporter

OperationCollection: System.Web.Services.Description

OperationFault: System.Web.Services.Description

OperationFaultCollection: System.Web.Services.Descrip-
tion

OperationFlow: System.Web.Services.Description

OperationInput: System.Web.Services.Description

OperationMessage: System.Web.Services.Description

OperationMessageCollection: System.Web.Ser-
vices.Description

OperationOutput: System.Web.Services.Description

Operations: Binding, PortType

OperationSyntaxException(): ProtocolImporter

Operator: CompareValidator

Option: HtmlTextWriterTag
OptionalExtensionsIgnored: ServiceDescriptionImport-Warnings
OtherMonthDayStyle: Calendar
Out: SoapHeaderDirection
OuterTableImplied: RepeatInfo
OutParameters: LogicalMethodInfo
Output: HttpResponse, OperationBinding, OperationMessageCollection
OutputBinding: System.Web.Services.Description
OutputCacheLocation: System.Web.UI
OutputMessage: ProtocolImporter, ProtocolReflector
OutputStream: HttpResponse, HttpWriter
OutputTabs(): HtmlTextWriter
Outset: BorderStyle
Overline: FontInfo

P

P: HtmlTextWriterTag
Page: Control, System.Web.UI
PageButtonCount: DataGridPagerStyle
PageCommandName: DataGrid
PageCount: DataGrid, PagedDataSource
PagedDataSource: System.Web.UI.WebControls
PageIndexChanged: DataGrid
PageParser: System.Web.UI
Pager: ListItemType
PagerMode: System.Web.UI.WebControls
PagerPosition: System.Web.UI.WebControls
PagerStyle: DataGrid
PageSize: DataGrid, PagedDataSource
Pair: System.Web.UI
Panel: System.Web.UI.WebControls
PanelDesigner: System.Web.UI.Design.WebControls
Param: HtmlTextWriterTag
ParameterFormatter: HttpMethodAttribute
ParameterOrder: Operation
ParameterOrderString: Operation
Parameters: LogicalMethodInfo
ParameterStyle: SoapDocumentMethodAttribute, SoapDocumentServiceAttribute
Params: HttpRequest
Parent: Control, ServiceDescriptionFormatExtension
Parse(): FontUnit, Unit
ParseChildrenAttribute: System.Web.UI
ParseControl(): ControlParser, DesignTimeTemplateParser, TemplateControl
ParseTemplate(): ControlParser, DesignTimeTemplateParser
ParseText: DesignTimeParseData
Part: MimeContentBinding, MimeXmlBinding, SoapHeaderBinding, SoapHeaderFaultBinding
PartialCachingAttribute: System.Web.UI

PartialCachingControl: System.Web.UI
Parts: Message, MimeMultipartRelatedBinding, SoapBodyBinding
PartsString: SoapBodyBinding
Passport: AuthenticationMode
PassportAuthenticationEventArgs: System.Web.Security
PassportAuthenticationEventHandler: System.Web.Security
PassportAuthenticationModule: System.Web.Security
PassportIdentity: System.Web.Security
Password: TextBoxMode
Path: ExcludePathInfo, HttpCookie, HttpRequest
PathInfo: HttpRequest
Pattern: ContractSearchPattern, DiscoveryDocumentLinksPattern, DiscoveryDocumentSearchPattern, DiscoverySearchPattern, MatchAttribute, MimeTextMatch, XmlSchemaSearchPattern
PatternMatcher: System.Web.Services.Protocols
PeakMemoryUsed: ProcessInfo
Percentage: UnitType
Percentage(): Unit
Persist: PersistChildrenAttribute
PersistChildrenAttribute: System.Web.UI
PersistControl(): ControlPersister
PersistenceMode: System.Web.UI
PersistenceModeAttribute: System.Web.UI
PersistInnerProperties(): ControlPersister
PhysicalApplicationPath: HttpRequest
PhysicalPath: HttpRequest
Pica: UnitType
Pics(): HttpResponse
PingFailed: ProcessShutdownReason
Pixel: UnitType
Pixel(): Unit
PlaceHolder: System.Web.UI.WebControls
PlaceHolderControlBuilder: System.Web.UI.WebControls
Platform: HttpBrowserCapabilities
Point: UnitType
Point(): FontUnit, Unit
PopEndTag(): HtmlTextWriter
Port: ProtocolImporter, ProtocolReflector, System.Web.Services.Description
PortCollection: System.Web.Services.Description
Ports: Service
PortType: Operation, ProtocolImporter, ProtocolReflector, System.Web.Services.Description
PortTypeCollection: System.Web.Services.Description
PortTypes: ServiceDescription
Position: DataGridPagerStyle
PostedFile: HtmlInputFile
postEventArgumentID: Page
postEventSourceID: Page
PostRequestHandlerExecute: HttpApplication
Pre: HtmlTextWriterTag

PreAuthenticate: WebClientProtocol
PreFilterEvents(): HtmlControlDesigner
PreFilterProperties(): BaseDataListDesigner, ControlDesigner, HtmlControlDesigner, ListControlDesigner, RepeaterDesigner, TemplatedControlDesigner
Prefix: XmlFormatExtensionPrefixAttribute
PrepareControlHierarchy(): BaseDataList, DataGrid, DataList
PreRender: Control
PreRequestHandlerExecute: HttpApplication
PreSendRequestContent: HttpApplication
PreSendRequestHeaders: HttpApplication
PreviousDate: MonthChangedEventArgs
PrevMonthText: Calendar
PrevPageCommandArgument: DataGrid
PrevPageText: DataGridPagerStyle
Priority: MailMessage, SoapExtensionAttribute
Private: HttpCacheability
ProcessID: ProcessInfo
ProcessInfo: System.Web
ProcessMessage(): SoapExtension
ProcessModelInfo: System.Web
ProcessRequest(): DiscoveryRequestHandler, HttpRuntime, IHttpHandler, IISAPIRuntime, ISAPIRuntime, IStateRuntime, Page, StateRuntime
ProcessShutdownReason: System.Web
ProcessStatus: System.Web
PropertyConverter: System.Web.UI
PropertyName: DataBinding
PropertyType: DataBinding
ProtocolImporter: System.Web.Services.Description
ProtocolName: ProtocolImporter, ProtocolReflector, ServiceDescriptionImporter, SoapProtocolImporter
ProtocolReflector: System.Web.Services.Description
Proxy: HttpWebClientProtocol
ProxyCaches: HttpCacheRevalidation
Public: HttpCacheability
PublicKey: HttpClientCertificate
PushButton: ButtonColumnType
PushEndTag(): HtmlTextWriter

Q

Q: HtmlTextWriterTag
QueryString: HttpRequest

R

RadioButton: System.Web.UI.WebControls
RadioButtonList: System.Web.UI.WebControls
RaiseBubbleEvent(): Control
RaisePostBackEvent(): IPostBackEventHandler, Page
RaisePostDataChangedEvent(): IPostBackDataHandler
RaiseResizeEvent(): ControlDesigner

RangeValidator: System.Web.UI.WebControls
RawUrl: HttpRequest
Read(): AnyReturnReader, DiscoveryDocument, HtmlFormParameterReader, MimeParameterReader, MimeReturnReader, NopReturnReader, ServiceDescription, TextReturnReader, UrlParameterReader, ValueCollectionParameterReader, XmlReturnReader
ReadAll(): DiscoveryClientProtocol
ReadDocument(): ContractReference, DiscoveryDocumentReference, DiscoveryReference, SchemaReference
ReadEntityBody(): HttpWorkerRequest
ReadOnly: BoundColumn, ControlDesigner, HtmlTextWriterAttribute, TextBox
ReadStringResource(): TemplateControl
ReadWriteControlDesigner: System.Web.UI.Design
ReasonCachePolicy: HttpWorkerRequest
ReasonCacheSecurity: HttpWorkerRequest
ReasonClientDisconnect: HttpWorkerRequest
ReasonDefault: HttpWorkerRequest
ReasonFileHandleCacheMiss: HttpWorkerRequest
ReasonResponseCacheMiss: HttpWorkerRequest
Redirect(): HttpResponse
RedirectFromLoginPage(): FormsAuthentication
Ref: ContractReference, DiscoveryDocumentReference, SchemaReference
References: DiscoveryClientProtocol, DiscoveryDocument
ReferenceTypeName: DiscoveryClientResult
Reflect(): ServiceDescriptionReflector
ReflectionContext: SoapExtensionReflector
ReflectionImporter: ProtocolReflector
ReflectMethod(): ProtocolReflector, SoapExtensionReflector
ReflectMethodBinding(): ProtocolReflector
RegexEditorDialog: System.Web.UI.Design.WebControls
RegexTypeEditor: System.Web.UI.Design.WebControls
RegexTypeEditor_Activated(): RegexEditorDialog
RegisterArrayDeclaration(): Page
RegisterAttribute(): HtmlTextWriter
RegisterClientScriptBlock(): Page
RegisterHiddenField(): Page
RegisterOnSubmitStatement(): Page
RegisterRequiresPostBack(): Page
RegisterRequiresRaiseEvent(): Page
RegisterStartupScript(): Page
RegisterStyle(): HtmlTextWriter
RegisterTag(): HtmlTextWriter
RegisterValidatorCommonScript(): BaseValidator
RegisterValidatorDeclaration(): BaseValidator
RegisterViewStateHandler(): Page
RegularExpression: RegexEditorDialog
RegularExpressionValidator: System.Web.UI.WebControls
ReleaseHandler(): IHttpHandlerFactory, WebServiceHandlerFactory

ReleaseRequestState: HttpApplication

Remove(): AttributeCollection, BindingCollection, Cache, ControlCollection, CssStyleCollection, DataBindingCollection, DataGridColumnCollection, DiscoveryClientDocumentCollection, DiscoveryClientReferenceCollection, DiscoveryClientResultCollection, DiscoveryExceptionDictionary, DiscoveryReferenceCollection, FaultBindingCollection, HtmlTableCellCollection, HtmlTableRowCollection, HttpApplicationState, HttpCookieCollection, HttpSessionState, ImportCollection, ListItemCollection, MessageCollection, MessagePartCollection, MimePartCollection, MimeTextMatchCollection, OperationBindingCollection, OperationCollection, OperationFaultCollection, OperationMessageCollection, PortCollection, PortTypeCollection, SelectedDatesCollection, ServiceCollection, ServiceDescriptionCollection, ServiceDescriptionFormatExtensionCollection, SoapHeaderCollection, StateBag, TableCellCollection, TableRowCollection, ValidatorCollection

RemoveAll(): HttpApplicationState, HttpSessionState

RemoveAt(): ControlCollection, DataGridColumnCollection, HtmlTableCellCollection, HtmlTableRowCollection, HttpApplicationState, HttpSessionState, ListItemCollection, TableCellCollection, TableRowCollection

RemoveAttribute(): IHtmlControlDesignerBehavior

Removed: CacheItemRemovedReason

RemovedBindings: DataBindingCollection

RemoveOutputCacheItem(): HttpResponse

RemoveStyleAttribute(): IHtmlControlDesignerBehavior

Render(): AdRotator, AttributeCollection, BaseDataList, BasePartialCachingControl, BaseValidator, Calendar, CheckBox, CheckBoxList, Control, DataBoundLiteralControl, DesignerDataBoundLiteralControl, HtmlContainerControl, HtmlControl, HtmlForm, Literal, LiteralControl, RadioButtonList, TextBox, ValidationSummary, WebControl, Xml

RenderAfterContent(): Html32TextWriter, HtmlTextWriter

RenderAfterTag(): Html32TextWriter, HtmlTextWriter

RenderAttributes(): HtmlAnchor, HtmlButton, HtmlContainerControl, HtmlControl, HtmlForm, HtmlImage, HtmlInputButton, HtmlInputControl, HtmlInputImage, HtmlInputRadioButton, HtmlInputText, HtmlSelect, HtmlTextArea

RenderBeforeContent(): Html32TextWriter, HtmlTextWriter

RenderBeforeTag(): Html32TextWriter, HtmlTextWriter

RenderBeginTag(): Html32TextWriter, HtmlControl, HtmlTextWriter, WebControl

RenderChildren(): Control, HtmlForm, HtmlSelect, HtmlTable, HtmlTableRow

RenderContents(): Button, DataList, DropDownList, HyperLink, Image, Label, LinkButton, ListBox, Table, TableCell, WebControl

RenderControl(): Control

RenderEndTag(): Html32TextWriter, HtmlContainerControl, HtmlTable, HtmlTableCell, HtmlTableRow, HtmlTextWriter, WebControl

RenderItem(): DataListItem, IRepeatInfoUser

RenderMethod: System.Web.UI

RenderRepeater(): RepeatInfo

RenewTicketIfOld(): FormsAuthentication

RepeatColumns: CheckBoxList, DataList, RadioButtonList, RepeatInfo

RepeatDirection: CheckBoxList, DataList, RadioButtonList, RepeatInfo, System.Web.UI.WebControls

RepeatedItemCount: IRepeatInfoUser

Repeater: System.Web.UI.WebControls

RepeaterCommandEventArgs: System.Web.UI.WebControls

RepeaterCommandEventHandler: System.Web.UI.WebControls

RepeaterDesigner: System.Web.UI.Design.WebControls

RepeaterItem: System.Web.UI.WebControls

RepeaterItemCollection: System.Web.UI.WebControls

RepeaterItemEventArgs: System.Web.UI.WebControls

RepeaterItemEventHandler: System.Web.UI.WebControls

RepeatInfo: System.Web.UI.WebControls

RepeatLayout: CheckBoxList, DataList, RadioButtonList, RepeatInfo, System.Web.UI.WebControls

Repeats: MimeTextMatch

RepeatsString: MimeTextMatch

Request: HttpApplication, HttpContext, Page, UserControl

RequestCount: ProcessInfo

RequestElement: SoapServiceRoutingStyle

RequestElementName: SoapDocumentMethodAttribute, SoapRpcMethodAttribute

RequestEncoding: MimeParameterWriter, UrlEncodedParameterWriter, WebClientProtocol

RequestHeaderMaximum: HttpWorkerRequest

RequestNamespace: SoapDocumentMethodAttribute, SoapRpcMethodAttribute

RequestQueueLimit: ProcessShutdownReason

RequestResponse: OperationFlow

RequestsLimit: ProcessShutdownReason

RequestType: HttpRequest

Required: ServiceDescriptionFormatExtension, SoapHeaderAttribute

RequiredExtensionsIgnored: ServiceDescriptionImportWarnings

RequiredFieldValidator: System.Web.UI.WebControls

Reset(): DataGridPagerStyle, Style, TableItemStyle, TableStyle

Resize(): ITemplateEditingFrame

Resolve(): DiscoveryReference

ResolveAll(): DiscoveryClientProtocol, DiscoveryDocumentReference

ResolveOneLevel(): DiscoveryClientProtocol
ResolveRequestCache: HttpApplication
ResolveUrl(): Control
Response: HttpApplication, HttpContext, Page, UserControl
ResponseElementName: SoapDocumentMethodAttribute, SoapRpcMethodAttribute
ResponseHeaderMaximum: HttpWorkerRequest
ResponseNamespace: SoapDocumentMethodAttribute, SoapRpcMethodAttribute
Results: DiscoveryClientResultsFile, HttpCompileException
RetrievalUrl: ServiceDescription
ReturnFormatter: HttpMethodAttribute
ReturnType: LogicalMethodInfo
ReturnTypeCustomAttributeProvider: LogicalMethodInfo
RewritePath(): HttpContext
Ridge: BorderStyle
Right: HorizontalAlign, ImageAlign, TextAlign
RootBuilder: System.Web.UI
RoutingStyle: SoapDocumentServiceAttribute, SoapRpcServiceAttribute
Rows: HtmlTable, HtmlTextArea, HtmlTextWriterAttribute, ListBox, Table, TextBox
Rowspan: HtmlTextWriterAttribute
RowSpan: HtmlTableCell, TableCell
Rpc: SoapBindingStyle
Rt: HtmlTextWriterTag
Ruby: HtmlTextWriterTag
Rules: HtmlTextWriterAttribute

S

S: HtmlTextWriterTag
Samp: HtmlTextWriterTag
Saturday: FirstDayOfWeek
Save(): ITemplateEditingFrame
SaveActiveTemplateEditingFrame(): TemplatedControlDesigner
SaveAs(): HttpPostedFile, HttpRequest
SaveComponent(): CalendarAutoFormatDialog
SavePageStateToPersistenceMedium(): Page
SaveViewState(): Calendar, Control, DataBoundLiteralControl, DataGrid, DataGridColumn, DataList, DesignerDataBoundLiteralControl, HtmlSelect, IStateManager, ListControl, UserControl, WebControl
Schema: SchemaReference
SchemaExporter: ProtocolReflector
SchemaReference: System.Web.Services.Discovery
Schemas: ProtocolImporter, ProtocolReflector, ServiceDescriptionImporter, ServiceDescriptionReflector, Types
Script: HtmlTextWriterTag
ScriptTimeout: HttpServerUtility

Second: Pair, Triplet
SecretKeySize: HttpClientCertificate
Secure: HttpCookie
Select: HtmlTextWriterTag
Select(): HtmlSelect
SelectCommandName: DataGrid, DataList
Selected: HtmlTextWriterAttribute, ListItem
SelectedDate: Calendar
SelectedDates: Calendar
SelectedDatesCollection: System.Web.UI.WebControls
SelectedDayStyle: Calendar
SelectedIndex: DataGrid, DataList, DropDownList, HtmlSelect, ListControl
SelectedIndexChanged: BaseDataList, ListControl
SelectedItem: DataGrid, DataList, ListControl, ListItemType
SelectedItemStyle: DataGrid, DataList
SelectedItemTemplate: DataList
SelectionChanged: Calendar
SelectionMode: Calendar, ListBox
SelectMonthText: Calendar
SelectorStyle: Calendar
SelectRange(): SelectedDatesCollection
SelectWeekText: Calendar
SelfClosingChars: HtmlTextWriter
SelfClosingTagEnd: HtmlTextWriter
SemicolonChar: HtmlTextWriter
Send(): SmtpMail
SendCalculatedContentLength(): HttpWorkerRequest
SendKnownResponseHeader(): HttpWorkerRequest, SimpleWorkerRequest
SendResponseFromFile(): HttpWorkerRequest, SimpleWorkerRequest
SendResponseFromMemory(): HttpWorkerRequest, SimpleWorkerRequest
SendStatus(): HttpWorkerRequest, SimpleWorkerRequest
SendUnknownResponseHeader(): HttpWorkerRequest, SimpleWorkerRequest
Separator: ListItemType
SeparatorStyle: DataList
SeparatorTemplate: DataList, Repeater
Serialize(): LosFormatter, WebControlToolboxItem
Serializer: ServiceDescription
SerialNumber: HttpClientCertificate
Server: HttpApplication, HttpCacheability, HttpContext, OutputCacheLocation, Page, ServiceDescriptionImportStyle, SoapServerMessage, UserControl, WebService
ServerChange: HtmlInputCheckBox, HtmlInputHidden, HtmlInputRadioButton, HtmlInputText, HtmlSelect, HtmlTextArea
ServerClick: HtmlAnchor, HtmlButton, HtmlInputButton, HtmlInputImage
ServerFaultCode: SoapException

ServerIssuer: HttpClientCertificate
ServerSubject: HttpClientCertificate
ServerValidate: CustomValidator
ServerValidateEventArgs: System.Web.UI.WebControls
ServerValidateEventHandler: System.Web.UI.WebControls
ServerVariables: HttpRequest
Service: Port, ProtocolImporter, ProtocolReflector, System.Web.Services.Description
ServiceCollection: System.Web.Services.Description
ServiceDescription: Binding, Import, Message, PortType, ProtocolReflector, Service, System.Web.Services.Description
ServiceDescriptionBaseCollection: System.Web.Services.Description
ServiceDescriptionCollection: System.Web.Services.Description
ServiceDescriptionFormatExtension: System.Web.Services.Description
ServiceDescriptionFormatExtensionCollection: System.Web.Services.Description
ServiceDescriptionImporter: System.Web.Services.Description
ServiceDescriptionImportStyle: System.Web.Services.Description
ServiceDescriptionImportWarnings: System.Web.Services.Description
ServiceDescriptionReflector: System.Web.Services.Description
ServiceDescriptions: ProtocolImporter, ProtocolReflector, ServiceDescription, ServiceDescriptionImporter, ServiceDescriptionReflector
Services: ServiceDescription
ServiceType: ProtocolReflector
ServiceUrl: ProtocolReflector
Session: HttpApplication, HttpContext, Page, UserControl, WebService
SessionID: HttpSessionState
SessionStateMode: System.Web.SessionState
SessionStateModule: System.Web.SessionState
Set(): HttpApplicationState, HttpCookieCollection
SetAll(): ProcessInfo
SetAttribute(): IAttributeAccessor, IHtmlControlDesignerBehavior
SetAuthCookie(): FormsAuthentication
SetCacheability(): HttpCachePolicy
SetCookie(): HttpResponse
SetDataBoundString(): DataBoundLiteralControl
SetEndOfSendNotification(): HttpWorkerRequest
SetETag(): HttpCachePolicy
SetETagFromFileDependencies(): HttpCachePolicy
SetExpires(): HttpCachePolicy
SetItemDirty(): StateBag
SetLastModified(): HttpCachePolicy
SetLastModifiedFromFileDependencies():

HttpCachePolicy
SetMaxAge(): HttpCachePolicy
SetNoServerCaching(): HttpCachePolicy
SetNoStore(): HttpCachePolicy
SetNoTransforms(): HttpCachePolicy
SetOption(): PassportIdentity
SetParent(): BindingCollection, FaultBindingCollection, ImportCollection, MessageCollection, MessagePartCollection, OperationBindingCollection, OperationCollection, OperationFaultCollection, OperationMessageCollection, PortCollection, PortTypeCollection, ServiceCollection, ServiceDescriptionBaseCollection, ServiceDescriptionFormatExtensionCollection
SetProxyMaxAge(): HttpCachePolicy
SetRenderMethodDelegate(): Control
SetRevalidation(): HttpCachePolicy
SetSlidingExpiration(): HttpCachePolicy
SetStaticString(): DataBoundLiteralControl
SetStringResourcePointer(): TemplateControl
SetStyleAttribute(): IHtmlControlDesignerBehavior
SetTagInnerText(): ControlBuilder, TemplateBuilder, UserControlControlBuilder
SetTemplateContent(): DataGridDesigner, DataListDesigner, TemplatedControlDesigner
SetValidUntilExpires(): HttpCachePolicy
SetVaryByCustom(): HttpCachePolicy
SHA1: FormsAuthPasswordFormat
Short: DayNameFormat
ShortMonth: NextPrevFormat
ShouldCodeSerialize: HtmlControlDesigner, UserControlDesigner
ShouldSerializeNames(): FontInfo
ShowDayHeader: Calendar
ShowFooter: DataGrid, DataList
ShowGridLines: Calendar
ShowHeader: DataGrid, DataList
ShowMessageBox: ValidationSummary
ShowNextPrevMonth: Calendar
ShowSummary: ValidationSummary
ShowTitle: Calendar
ShutDown: ProcessStatus
ShutdownReason: ProcessInfo
ShuttingDown: ProcessStatus
SignOut(): FormsAuthentication, PassportIdentity
SimpleWebHandlerParser: System.Web.UI
SimpleWorkerRequest: System.Web.Hosting
Single: ListSelectionMode
SingleLine: TextBoxMode
SingleParagraph: ValidationSummaryDisplayMode
SingleQuoteChar: HtmlTextWriter
Site: Control, HttpApplication
Size: FontInfo, HtmlInputFile, HtmlInputText, HtmlSelect, HtmlTextWriterAttribute

T

HtmlInputControl, HtmlTextWriterAttribute, Http-
BrowserCapabilities, MessagePart, MimeContentBinding, MimeTextMatch, Unit
Types: ServiceDescription, System.Web.Services.Descrip-
tion

U

U: HtmlTextWriterTag
Ui: HtmlTextWriterTag
Underline: FontInfo
Underused: CacheItemRemovedReason
Unexpected: ProcessShutdownReason
UniqueID: Control
Unit: FontUnit, System.Web.UI.WebControls
UnitConverter: System.Web.UI.WebControls
UnitType: System.Web.UI.WebControls
Unknown: HtmlTextWriterTag
Unload: Control
UnLock(): HttpApplicationState
UnsupportedBindingsIgnored: ServiceDescriptionImport-
Warnings
UnsupportedBindingWarning(): ProtocolImporter
UnsupportedOperationBindingWarning(): Protocol-
Importer
UnsupportedOperationsIgnored: ServiceDescriptionIm-
portWarnings
UnsupportedOperationWarning(): ProtocolImporter
UpdateCommand: DataGrid, DataList
UpdateCommandName: DataGrid, DataList
UpdateControlName(): ITemplateEditingFrame
UpdateDesignTimeHtml(): ControlDesigner, Templated-
ControlDesigner
UpdateRequestCache: HttpApplication
UpdateSelection(): IWebFormsDocumentService
UpdateText: EditCommandColumn
Url: ContractReference, DiscoveryClientResult, Discovery-
DocumentReference, DiscoveryReference, HttpRe-
quest, SchemaReference, SoapClientMessage,
SoapMessage, SoapServerMessage, WebClientProto-
col
UrlAuthorizationModule: System.Web.Security
UrlBuilder: System.Web.UI.Design
UrlBuilderOptions: System.Web.UI.Design
UrlContentBase: MailMessage
UrlContentLocation: MailMessage
UrlDecode(): HttpServerUtility, HttpUtility
UrlDecodeToBytes(): HttpUtility
UrlEditor: System.Web.UI.Design
UrlEncode(): HttpServerUtility, HttpUtility
UrlEncodedParameterWriter: System.Web.Services.Pro-
tocols
UrlEncodeToBytes(): HttpUtility
UrlEncodeUnicode(): HttpUtility

UrlEncodeUnicodeToBytes(): HttpUtility
UrlParameterReader: System.Web.Services.Protocols
UrlParameterWriter: System.Web.Services.Protocols
UrlPathEncode(): HttpServerUtility
UrlReferrer: HttpRequest
Use: SoapBodyBinding, SoapDocumentMethodAttribute,
SoapDocumentServiceAttribute, SoapFaultBinding,
SoapHeaderBinding, SoapHeaderFaultBinding
User: FormsAuthenticationEventArgs, HttpApplication,
HttpContext, Page, PassportAuthenticationEventArgs,
WebService, WindowsAuthenticationEventArgs
UserAgent: HttpCacheVaryByHeaders, HttpRequest, Http-
WebClientProtocol
UserCharSet: HttpCacheVaryByHeaders
UserControl: System.Web.UI
UserControlControlBuilder: System.Web.UI
UserControlDesigner: System.Web.UI.Design
UserData: FormsAuthenticationTicket
UserHostAddress: HttpRequest
UserHostName: HttpRequest
UserLanguage: HttpCacheVaryByHeaders
UserLanguages: HttpRequest
UsesWriteRequest: HtmlFormParameterWriter, MimePa-
rameterWriter
UUEncode: MailEncoding

V

Valid: HttpValidationStatus
Validate(): BaseValidator, IValidator, Page
ValidatedControlConverter: System.Web.UI.WebControls
Validation: FormsProtectionEnum
ValidationCompareOperator: System.Web.UI.WebControls
ValidationDataType: System.Web.UI.WebControls
ValidationExpression: RegularExpressionValidator
ValidationPropertyAttribute: System.Web.UI
ValidationSummary: System.Web.UI.WebControls
ValidationSummaryDisplayMode: System.Web.UI.Web-
Controls
ValidatorCollection: System.Web.UI
ValidatorDisplay: System.Web.UI.WebControls
Validators: Page
ValidFrom: HttpClientCertificate
ValidUntil: HttpClientCertificate
Valign: HtmlTextWriterAttribute
VAlign: HtmlTableCell, HtmlTableRow
Value: HtmlInputControl, HtmlInputRadioButton, HtmlIn-
putText, HtmlSelect, HtmlTextArea, HtmlTextWriterAt-
tribute, HttpCookie, ListItem,
ServerValidateEventArgs, StateItem, Unit
value__: AuthenticationMode, BorderStyle, ButtonColum-
nType, CacheItemPriority, CacheItemRemovedReason,
CalendarSelectionMode, DayNameFormat, FirstDay-
OfWeek, FontSize, FormsAuthPasswordFormat,

FormsProtectionEnum, GridLines, HorizontalAlign, HtmlTextWriterAttribute, HtmlTextWriterStyle, HtmlTextWriterTag, HttpCacheability, HttpCacheRevalidation, HttpValidationStatus, ImageAlign, ListItemType, ListSelectionMode, LogicalMethodTypes, MailEncoding, MailFormat, MailPriority, NextPrevFormat, OperationFlow, OutputCacheLocation, PagerMode, PagerPosition, PersistenceMode, ProcessShutdownReason, ProcessStatus, RepeatDirection, RepeatLayout, ServiceDescriptionImportStyle, ServiceDescriptionImportWarnings, SessionStateMode, SoapBindingStyle, SoapBindingUse, SoapHeaderDirection, SoapMessageStage, SoapParameterStyle, SoapServiceRoutingStyle, TextAlign, TextBoxMode, TitleFormat, TraceMode, UnitType, UrlBuilderOptions, ValidationCompareOperator, ValidationDataType, ValidationSummaryDisplayMode, ValidatorDisplay, VerticalAlign

ValueCollectionParameterReader: System.Web.Services.Protocols

Values: DiscoveryClientDocumentCollection, DiscoveryClientReferenceCollection, DiscoveryExceptionDictionary, HttpCookie, StateBag

ValueToCompare: CompareValidator

Var: HtmlTextWriterTag

VaryByControls: PartialCachingAttribute

VaryByCustom: PartialCachingAttribute

VaryByHeaders: HttpCachePolicy

VaryByParams: HttpCachePolicy, PartialCachingAttribute

VaryByUnspecifiedParameters(): HttpCacheVaryByHeaders

VBScript: HttpBrowserCapabilities

Verb: HttpBinding, ITemplateEditingFrame

Verbs: BaseDataListDesigner, CalendarDesigner

VerifyRenderingInServerForm(): Page

Version: FormsAuthenticationTicket, HttpBrowserCapabilities

VersionMismatchFaultCode: SoapException

Vertical: GridLines, RepeatDirection

VerticalAlign: System.Web.UI.WebControls, TableCell, TableItemStyle, TableRow

VirtualCount: PagedDataSource

VirtualItemCount: DataGrid

VirtualPath: HttpConfigurationContext

Visible: Control, DataGridColumn, DataGridPagerStyle, Page

VisibleDate: Calendar

VisibleMonthChanged: Calendar

W

W3CDomVersion: HttpBrowserCapabilities

Warn(): TraceContext

Warnings: ProtocolImporter

Wbr: HtmlTextWriterTag

WebClientAsyncResult: System.Web.Services.Protocols

WebClientProtocol: System.Web.Services.Protocols

WebColorConverter: System.Web.UI.WebControls

WebControl: System.Web.UI.WebControls

WebControlToolboxItem: System.Web.UI.Design

WebMethodAttribute: System.Web.Services

WebService: System.Web.Services

WebServiceAttribute: System.Web.Services

WebServiceBindingAttribute: System.Web.Services

WebServiceHandlerFactory: System.Web.Services.Protocols

WebServiceParser: System.Web.UI

Wednesday: FirstDayOfWeek

WeekendDayStyle: Calendar

Width: HtmlImage, HtmlTable, HtmlTableCell, HtmlTextWriterAttribute, HtmlTextWriterStyle, Style, WebControl

Win16: HttpBrowserCapabilities

Win32: HttpBrowserCapabilities

Windows: AuthenticationMode

WindowsAuthenticationEventArgs: System.Web.Security

WindowsAuthenticationEventHandler: System.Web.Security

WindowsAuthenticationModule: System.Web.Security

Wrap: HtmlTextWriterAttribute, Panel, TableCell, TableItemStyle, TextBox

Wrapped: SoapParameterStyle

Write(): DiscoveryDocument, DynamicDiscoveryDocument, HtmlTextWriter, HttpResponse, HttpWriter, ServiceDescription, TraceContext

WriteAll(): DiscoveryClientProtocol

WriteAttribute(): HtmlTextWriter

WriteBeginTag(): HtmlTextWriter

WriteBytes(): HttpWriter

WriteDocument(): ContractReference, DiscoveryDocumentReference, DiscoveryReference, SchemaReference

WriteEndTag(): HtmlTextWriter

WriteFile(): HttpResponse

WriteFullBeginTag(): HtmlTextWriter

WriteLine(): HtmlTextWriter, HttpWriter

WriteLineNoTabs(): HtmlTextWriter

WriteRequest(): HtmlFormParameterWriter, MimeParameterWriter

WriteString(): HttpWriter

WriteStyleAttribute(): HtmlTextWriter

WriteUTF8ResourceString(): TemplateControl

X

X: ImageClickEventArgs

XLarge: FontSize, FontUnit

Xml: HtmlTextWriterTag, System.Web.UI.WebControls

XmlDesigner: System.Web.UI.Design.WebControls

XmlExporter: SoapProtocolImporter
XmlFileEditor: System.Web.UI.Design
XmlFormatExtensionAttribute: System.Web.Services.Configuration
XmlFormatExtensionPointAttribute: System.Web.Services.Configuration
XmlFormatExtensionPrefixAttribute: System.Web.Services.Configuration
XmlImporter: SoapProtocolImporter
XmlReturnReader: System.Web.Services.Protocols
XmlSchemaSearchPattern: System.Web.Services.Discovery
XmlUrlEditor: System.Web.UI.Design
XslUrlEditor: System.Web.UI.Design
XSmall: FontSize, FontUnit
XXLarge: FontSize, FontUnit
XXSmall: FontSize, FontUnit

Y

Y: ImageClickEventArgs
Yes: PersistChildrenAttribute

Index

We'd like to hear your suggestions for improving our indexes. Send email to *index@oreilly.com*.

About the Authors

G. Andrew Duthie is the founder and Principal of Graymad Enterprises, Inc., providing training and consulting in Microsoft Web development technologies. In addition to his work on O'Reilly books, Andrew is a frequent speaker at industry conferences, including the DevConnections family of conferences, VSLive!, Software Development, and Microsoft's DeveloperDays. He has also written articles on ASP.NET for *SQL Server Magazine* and *MSDN Magazine*. When not writing, speaking, or consulting, Andrew enjoys relaxing with his wife, Jennifer, reading science fiction and fantasy novels, and smoking his meershaum pipe. You can reach Andrew by email at *andrew@graymad.com*.

Matthew MacDonald is an author, educator, and MCSD developer. He's a regular contributor to programming journals such as *Inside Visual Basic* and *C# Today*. He is the author of several books about .NET programming, including *The Book of VB.NET* (No Starch Press). Matthew is coauthor of O'Reilly's *Programming .NET Web Services* and a contributor to *C# in a Nutshell*.

Colophon

Our look is the result of reader comments, our own experimentation, and feedback from distribution channels. Distinctive covers complement our distinctive approach to technical topics, breathing personality and life into potentially dry subjects.

The animal on the cover of *ASP.NET in a Nutshell* is a stingray. The stingray is a flat, rectangular fish with no dorsal or anal fins that lives in shallow coastal areas around the world. It hides itself in the sandy or silty sea bottom while feeding on fish, crustaceans, and mollusks. The stingray is best known for its long tail, which holds a serrated spine near the tail base. When threatened, this spine injects a powerful, and often fatal, venom into its victim. The venom contains proteins that can slow an animal's respiration rate to dangerous levels. Humans are often surprised to learn, however, that the animal is normally gentle and nonaggressive.

Contrary to popular belief, stingrays usually sting humans only when stepped on by unsuspecting swimmers. When threatened in this manner, the animal reflexively whips its tail back to defend itself. This defense is effective against most animals, except for its main predator, the shark.

Populations living near stingrays have valued the animal for centuries—particularly in Polynesia, Malaysia, Central America, and Coastal Africa, where the stingray's spine was used to create spears, knives, and other tools. More recently, the stingray has become a popular tourist attraction; the stingray has been a major source of tourist income over the past decade in some island resorts in the Carribbean. Resorts in the Cayman Islands have taken special measures to educate humans about the stingray. Some resorts in this area even advertise beaches where tourists can swim and play with the animal.

Ann Schirmer was the production editor and copyeditor for *ASP.NET in a Nutshell*. Claire Cloutier, Jane Ellin, and Colleen Gorman provided quality control. Phil Dangler provided production assistance. Joe Wizda wrote the index.

Emma Colby designed the cover of this book. The cover image is a 19th-century engraving from the Dover Pictorial Archive. Emma Colby produced the cover layout with QuarkXPress 4.1 using Adobe's ITC Garamond font.

David Futato designed the interior layout based on a series design by Nancy Priest. The Intrinsic Class Reference was created by translating DocBook XML source into a set of *gtroff* macros using a Perl filter developed at O'Reilly by Norman Walsh. Steve Talbott designed and wrote the underlying macro set on the basis of the GNU *gtroff* -gs macros; Lenny Muellner adapted them to XML and implemented the book design. The GNU *gtroff* text formatter Version 1.11.1 was used to generate Post-Script output. The rest of the book was converted into FrameMaker 5.5.6 with a format conversion tool created by Erik Ray, Jason McIntosh, Neil Walls, and Mike Sierra that uses Perl and XML technologies. The text and heading fonts are ITC Garamond Light and Garamond Book. The illustrations that appear in the book were produced by Robert Romano and Jessamyn Read using Macromedia Free-Hand 9 and Adobe Photoshop 6. This colophon was written by Ann Schirmer.

More Titles from O'Reilly

Microsoft .NET Programming

VB.NET Language in a Nutshell, 2nd Edition

By Steven Roman, Ron Petrusha &
Paul Lomax
2nd Edition May 2002
682 pages, ISBN 0-596-00308-0

The documentation that comes with
VB typically provides only the bare
details for each language element; left
out is the valuable inside information
that a programmer really needs to
know in order to solve programming
problems or to use a particular language element effectively. *VB .NET Language in a Nutshell*, 2nd Edition documents the undocumented and presents the kind of wisdom
that comes from the authors' many years of experience
with the language. Bonus CD ingegrates the book's reference section with Visual Studio .NET.

Programming C#, 2nd Edition

By Jesse Liberty
2nd Edition February 2002
650 pages, ISBN 0-596-00309-9

The first part of *Programming C#*,
2nd Edition introduces C# fundamentals, then goes on to explain the development of desktop and Internet
applications, including Windows
Forms, ADO.NET, ASP.NET (including
Web Forms), and Web Services. Next, this book gets to the
heart of the .NET Framework, focusing on attributes and
reflection, remoting, threads and synchronization, streams,
and finally, it illustrates how to interoperate with COM objects.

Programming Visual Basic .NET

By Dave Grudgeiger
1st Edition December 2001
460 pages, ISBN 0-596-00093-6

Starting with a sample application and
a high-level map, *Programming Visual Basic .NET* will give you an idea of
where the various parts of .NET fit
with VB .NET. Ensuing chapters break
down and present the language, the
common language runtime, Windows Forms, ASP.NET and
Web Forms, Web Services, and ADO.NET. The book then
moves into topics on developing transactional applications, internationalization, security, and debugging.

Programming ASP.NET

By Jesse Liberty & Dan Hurwitz
1st Edition February 2002
960 pages, ISBN 0-596-00171-1

Programming ASP.NET is aimed at
experienced programmers and web
developers, who have the desire to
quickly create ASP.NET applications.
Rudimentary topics such as language
syntax, datatypes, and program con-
trol are treated concisely so greater attention can be
devoted to applications development. By design, this book
features many short examples, rather than a single,
unmanageably large application, in order to show the
widest range of constructs, both valid and invalid.

C# in a Nutshell

By Peter Drayton & Ben Albahari
1st Edition March 2002
856 pages, ISBN 0-596-00181-9

C# is likely to become one of the most
widely used languages for building
.NET applications. *C# in a Nutshell*
contains a concise introduction to the
language and its syntax, plus brief
tutorials used to accomplish common
programming tasks. It also includes
O'Reilly's classic-style, quick-reference material for all the
types and members in core .NET namespaces, including
System, System.Text, System.IO, and System.Collections.

Microsoft .NET Programming

.NET Framework Essentials, 2nd Edition

By Thuan L. Thai, Hoang Lam
2nd Edition February 2002
320 pages, 0-596-00302-1

.NET Framework Essentials, 2nd Edition is a concise and technical overview of the Microsoft .NET Framework. Covered here are all of the most important topics—from the underlying Common Language Runtime (CLR) to its specialized packages for ASP.NET, Web Forms, Windows Forms, XML and data access (ADO.NET). The authors survey each of the major .NET languages, including Visual Basic .NET, C# and Managed C++.

C# Essentials, 2nd Edition

By Brad Merrill, Peter Drayton &
Ben Albahari
2nd Edition January 2002
216 pages, 0-596-00315-3

Concise but thorough, this second edition of *C# Essentials* introduces the Microsoft C# programming language, including the Microsoft .NET Common Language Runtime (CLR) and .NET Framework Class Libraries (FCL) that support it. This book's compact format and terse presentation of key concepts serve as a roadmap to the online documentation included with the Microsoft .NET Framework SDK; the many examples provide much-needed context.

COM and .NET Component Services

By Juval Löwy
1st Edition September 2001
384 pages, 0-596-00103-7

COM & .NET Component Services provides both traditional COM programmers and new .NET component developers with the information they need to begin developing applications that take full advantage of COM+ services. This book focuses on COM+ services, including support for transactions, queued components, events, concurrency management, and security.

VB.NET Framework Class Library in a Nutshell

By Budi Kurniawan
1st Edition May 2002 (est.)
640 pages (est.), ISBN 0-596-00257-2

With both a fast-paced tutorial and a reference, *VB.NET Framework Class Library in a Nutshell* meets the needs of two primary audiences: programmers who want a quick introduction to using the FCL, and those who want a comprehensive reference to the FCL in book form. This book is a sequel to *VB.NET Language in a Nutshell* in that it covers the classes in the .NET framework using VB syntax. It's a hardworking manual that belongs on every VB developer's bookshelf.

How to stay in touch with O'Reilly

1. Visit our award-winning web site

http://www.oreilly.com/

★ "Top 100 Sites on the Web"—PC Magazine
★ CIO Magazine's Web Business 50 Awards

Our web site contains a library of comprehensive
product information (including book excerpts
and tables of contents), downloadable software,
background articles, interviews with technology
leaders, links to relevant sites, book cover art,
and more. File us in your bookmarks or favorites!

2. Join our email mailing lists

Sign up to get email announcements of new
books and conferences, special offers, and
O'Reilly Network technology newsletters at:

http://www.elists.oreilly.com

It's easy to customize your free elists subscription
so you'll get exactly the O'Reilly news you want.

3. Get examples from our books

To find example files for a book, go to:

http://www.oreilly.com/catalog

select the book, and follow the "Examples" link.

4. Work with us

Check out our web site for current employment
opportunites:

http://jobs.oreilly.com/

5. Register your book

Register your book at:

http://register.oreilly.com

6. Contact us

O'Reilly & Associates, Inc.
1005 Gravenstein Hwy North
Sebastopol, CA 95472 USA
TEL: 707-827-7000 or 800-998-9938
       (6am to 5pm PST)
FAX: 707-829-0104

order@oreilly.com
For answers to problems regarding your
order or our products. To place a book
order online visit:

http://www.oreilly.com/order_new/

catalog@oreilly.com
To request a copy of our latest catalog.

booktech@oreilly.com
For book content technical questions or
corrections.

proposals@oreilly.com
To submit new book proposals to our editors
and product managers.

international@oreilly.com
For information about our international
distributors or translation queries. For a list
of our distributors outside of North America
check out:

http://international.oreilly.com/distributors.html

O'REILLY®